SAMUEL BRONFMAN

Samuel Bronfman, 1951.

Samuel Bronfman

The Life and Times of Seagram's Mr. Sam

Michael R. Marrus

Brandeis University Press

Published by University Press of New England

Hanover and London

Published in Canada in 1991 by Penguin Books Canada Ltd.,
10 Alcorn Avenue, Toronto, Ontario, Canada M4V 3B2

University Press of New England publishes books under its own imprint and is the
publisher for Brandeis University Press, Brown University Press, Clark University
Press, University of Connecticut, Dartmouth College, Middlebury College Press,
University of New Hampshire, University of Rhode Island, Tufts University, University of Vermont, and Wesleyan University Press.

BRANDEIS UNIVERSITY PRESS
Published by University Press of New England, Hanover, NH 03755

Printed in the United States of America

∞

Library of Congress Cataloging in Publication Data

Marrus, Michael Robert.
  [Mr. Sam]
Samuel Bronfman: the life and times of Seagram's Mr. Sam / Michael R. Marrus.
  p. cm.
Originally published: Mr. Sam. Toronto, Ont. : Penguin Books Canada, c1991.
Includes bibliographical references.
ISBN 0-87451-571-8 (alk. paper)
  1. Bronfman, Samuel, 1891-1971. 2. Businessmen -- Canada -- Biography. 3.
Whiskey industry -- Canada -- History.   I. Title.
HD9395.C22B766   1992
338.7'66352'092 -- dc20
  [B]   91-31775   CIP

For Carol Randi Marrus

By the Same Author

THE POLITICS OF ASSIMILATION: The
French Jewish Community at the Time of the
Dreyfus Affair

VICHY FRANCE AND THE JEWS (with
Robert O. Paxton)
National Jewish Book Award (1982)

THE UNWANTED: European Refugees in
the Twentieth Century
Present Tense Literary Award (1985)

THE HOLOCAUST IN HISTORY
Wallace K. Ferguson Award (1988)
Joseph Tanenbaum Prize (1989)

Contents

SAMUEL BRONFMAN

Preface

SAM BRONFMAN HAS become a mythic figure in Canadian life — even more so in the twenty years after his death than during his long and eventful career. And increasingly, the myth bears less and less relationship to the life itself. It is as if Canadians have found in the creator of the mighty Seagram whisky* empire a board on which to pin their sometimes contradictory feelings about business, power, wealth and perhaps even ethnic politics as well.

Why does Sam Bronfman loom so large? Part of the explanation lies in our attraction to the colourful folklore of prohibition, and the seductive myth that anyone who became so rich and so successful in the whisky trade must have been up to no good. Sam came of age and began his fledgling liquor business just as the stern temperance movement was clamping down restrictions in Canada and the United States. Myth-makers would prefer to have Sam Bronfman in the thick of the rum running, driver of getaway cars racing across the American border in the dead of night, or the organizer of armies of bootleggers who operated south of the Canadian border. In fact, Sam and his brothers kept basically within the framework of Canadian law, nestled comfortably in the loopholes of provincial and federal regulations as they supplied American bootleggers

---

* Canadian or Scotch whisky is spelled without an "e"; American or Irish whiskey is spelled with an "e."

11

from coast to coast, and competed furiously against others in a similar line of work—the most prominent of which was the Hudson's Bay Company, which for a time was the leader in the field.

So why is it Sam, rather than other whisky men of the period—Harry Hatch or Sir Albert Gooderham are possibilities—whose life has been chosen for fanciful embroidery? Why has Sam Bronfman attracted some of Canada's most gifted writers of fiction and nonfiction—James Gray, Peter Newman and Mordecai Richler—when others have not? A second explanation is our continuing interest in ethnic origins in this country of immigrants. Looked at in this way, Sam's is a Canadian tale of rags to riches. Son of a labouring Jewish pioneer from Czarist Russia, he built a gigantic, worldwide company, renowned for the quality of its products and its business acumen. The story of Sam's rise to fame and fortune from a hard life on the Canadian prairies is inherently dramatic and yet touches a familiar nerve in a broad spectrum of the population. And what followed his first successes has even further, almost universal appeal. For even after he prospered, when his family's struggles in Brandon and Winnipeg were left far behind, and when he was established in Montreal as a powerful industrialist, Sam remained an outsider as a Jew, and felt the cold exclusion of a society that barred his entry into the establishment of the day.

Part of Sam's story, as almost everyone knows, was his failure to achieve the recognition he felt he deserved. To the extent that few of us receive *all* that we want by way of acceptance, honours or acclaim, there is something in Sam's response to his disappointments that most people recognize in themselves. His frustrations when beating against a closed, hidebound, prejudiced society—feelings that sometimes burst forth in his famous explosions of rage—are emotions that many of us feel when our desires or ambitions are thwarted and when we suffer the injustice of it all. Sam, on such occasions, would not take it lying down—and there may be something in his protests against outrageous fortune, and outrageous individuals, which each one of us feels at one time or another, even if we do not have his arsenal of profane language or a captive audience of employees or associates to hear us out.

In part, Sam's sense of himself as an outsider was shared by most Canadian Jews — newly arrived, for the most part, and not only excluded from the social and political rewards of their society, but also widely despised and discriminated against as well. Sam identified closely with his fellow Jews, and like most of them he comported himself in a subdued fashion in dealing with officialdom — in stark contrast with official spokesmen for Jews and other minorities in our own time. As a Jewish leader, Sam helped define ethnic politics when people scarcely knew such a thing existed. In 1939, when he was elected president of the Canadian Jewish Congress, he became head of a tiny, ragtag, fractious community, just about to face the trials of the Jewish refugee crisis, the Second World War, and the Nazi Holocaust. This was the darkest moment in the history of modern Jewry, when the doors of immigration slammed shut at home and murder roamed freely abroad. In the agony that followed and during the subsequent birth of the State of Israel, it was Sam Bronfman who heard the cries of pain, who responded to the appeals for financial aid to the fledgling Jewish state, and who helped bring into being a remarkably successful network of Jewish public institutions in Canada. For some thirty years, as Canadian Jewry came of age, he was the foremost Jew in the country, putting his stamp on a community that has become one of the most successfully integrated pieces of the Canadian mosaic.

A third reason for our fascination has to do with our odd attitudes to material success, and particularly success in Sam Bronfman's line of work, the manufacture and the sale of whisky. People in general, and perhaps Canadians even more so, tend to be censorious about three essential aspects of his life — money, ambition and liquor. Indeed, the most widely read work on the Bronfmans, *Bronfman Dynasty*, by Peter C. Newman, excites our inclination to dislike all three. Our reactions to the first two are most easily acknowledged. Wealthy, aspiring individuals are not widely loved in our society, at least not genuinely and not in public expression. Although we are endlessly curious about the rich and famous, we do not overflow with good will when it comes to understanding or attributing motives to them. Some say that these attitudes flow from jealousy; we wish ourselves to be rich and famous, and since most of us cannot, the simplest recourse is to despise the few who are. But it seems at least as likely that contempt for the monied and ambitious flows from some of the gentler instincts of our society: aware, as we cannot help being, of the stunted and frustrated lot of so many people around us, not to mention the world outside, we vicariously join ourselves with the unfortunate by disliking those whose material success is the most evident. Are Canadians even more disposed than others to suspect the rich and disdain the ambitious among us? I think the answer is yes, and the reason why probably has something to do with Canadians' views of themselves. We are frequently told that Canadian society is less competitive, less cruel, less rapacious than other societies. True or not, this is certainly our image of ourselves, a flattering self-definition capable of reducing the stature of any who appear in an opposite guise.

Add to these tendencies the basis of Sam's fortune, liquor, and one has a formidable set of negative associations. Note that this is an important industry. As writer Hugh MacLennan once observed, "apart from the CPR and the mining and forest industries, from the earliest beginnings of British North America the most successful and permanent businesses were brewing and distilling."[1] But these were not businesses like all the others. Public condemnation of alcohol consumption is older than Canada itself, and reached a crescendo of popular enthusiasm in the early part of Sam's career, when he turned his family whisky business into a formidable economic force. To be sure, most Canadians today would scarcely approve the strident appeals of the Woman's Christian Temperance Union, the tireless harangue against the "demon rum," or the battery of laws and regulations that stood in the way of even private consumption of beer, wine and alcohol. Relatively few remember the halcyon days of the "noble experiment" in the United States, when prohibition put close to half a million Americans into prison at one time or another for violations of the Volstead Act, and where the criminalization of drink drove millions to illegality, sickened countless numbers with poisonous concoctions, unloosed legions of gangsters to prey upon society, and eventually disgusted an entire country with the hypocrisy and damage it had wrought.

Nevertheless, the moral force of the campaign against drink remains with us still — despite all the other social ills to which we have become too easily accustomed. Many Canadian cities still have a Temperance Street, often appropriately now in a shabby, run-down, neglected part of town, testimony to the continuing presence of the good old cause, as our battered century nears its end. Despite our commitment to individual choice, despite our discomfort with the hectoring, proselytizing, intolerant, class-ridden, and sometimes nativist assumptions associated with the war on drink, its moral case retains a small but tenacious presence in our national psyche.

Canadians are bound to be struck by another part of Sam's story at this moment of deep uncertainty about our nation's future. Although his whisky empire became a gigantic American enterprise, and although for decades he commuted to New York for most of the working week, Sam never left Canada and never abandoned his enthusiastic identification with the country in which his career began. By contemporary standards, his patriotism appears almost quaint, and his yearning for recognition at home — the most famous instance being his quest for a seat in the Canadian Senate — excessive to the point of absurdity. Yet to Sam, Canada mattered, and his affection for his country was both genuine and deeply felt. At a time when patriotism is increasingly on the defensive, we cannot help but remark about Sam's unvarnished love of country and perhaps appreciate something of the way things used to be.

There is an economic side of Sam's love of country that reflects ironically on some of our contemporary debates over free trade. Seagram's huge whisky empire, as we shall see, rose spectacularly by taking advantage of the huge American market after the repeal of U.S. Prohibition in 1933. From that point, Sam's business, and his profits, grew by leaps and bounds. Indeed, he was so successful that his American competitors denounced the Canadian interloper as imposing unfair, "alien competition," and lobbied in Washington for protection against what they claimed was an aggressive "foreign takeover" of an American industry.

Entering the newly opened United States market in the 1930s
with millions of gallons of aging whisky stored in Canada, Sam
undoubtedly had an advantage over his American counterparts at
the time of repeal. But he also had raw talent, which like other
Canadians from time to time, he knew how to use abroad. Beating
the biggest and the most powerful in the United States at their
own game, Sam revealed a marketing genius that took the breath
away from his Madison Avenue advertising agents. In a business
environment where critics suggested that corners were always
being cut, Sam was a fanatic for quality and took the most
extraordinary care to see that his products were always "the
best." The buying public, for the most part, agreed that they
were, and sought them out.

Finally, Sam Bronfman's complex and many-sided character is
its own source of fascination. Like so many who are the stuff of
legend, Sam appears to us larger than life, and also full of
paradox. Sam was a died-in-the-wool Victorian in his personal
habits, his family relations and his social attitudes. The society
and the style he most appreciated were those he first met when he
visited England and Scotland in the 1920s, when he learned about
Scotch whisky from the masters of the trade. And yet he was
obsessed with the future, was endlessly curious, constantly
probing how things were done, to see if there was a better way.
He did not seem, on the surface at least, to be introspective. He
left no diaries, no self-reflecting letters, nothing to suggest he
suffered from doubt or uncertainty about fundamental values. At
the same time, he was deeply emotional, carried away at times by
gusts of anger or episodes in which he seemed pathetically
vulnerable. His feelings, associates felt, were on the surface,
where everyone could see.

People unhesitatingly viewed Sam Bronfman as a force to be
reckoned with. Deeply admired, both by intimates and those with
whom he had no personal contact, he was also widely feared. He
was portly and diminutive, often photographed with a quizzical,
gentle expression of professorial inquiry, but he was known for
explosive bursts of rage, extravagant profanity, crushing
denunciations and withering disapproval. To some who knew
him, Sam will forever be a forthright, curious, warm and even
playful visionary; but to others he was a volcanic authoritarian,

coarse and iron-willed, who brooked not the slightest deviation from directions he defined.

Sam Bronfman lived his life, as he once put it, "at the head table." A shy person, uncomfortable with publicity, he nevertheless found himself frequently in the public eye, facing any number of interpretations of his motives, ambitions and his actions. He is not an easy person to assess, and writers have had difficulty getting him right. Much depends on vantage point. And much also results from the failure of most people to get the full measure of the man in his widely disparate activities as husband, father, family leader, head of the Seagram whisky empire, Jewish community chief and public figure. It is almost as if Sam were too diverse and complex, too big a character to encompass fully. The few writers who have tried have fallen short, I think. I am struck by how Mordecai Richler, in his recent *roman à clef* about the Bronfman family, *Solomon Gursky Was Here*, uses two characters (Bernard and Solomon), and not one, to represent Mr Sam. I acknowledge that this is my interpretation; let me venture that this is at least as credible as Richler's own contention that his book is not about the Bronfmans at all!

My own approach is to set Sam in his historical context, in a way impossible for contemporaries for whom his powerful personality was either too near or too far, and for whom the society in which he lived was too close for an objective view. I am wary of what Joyce Carol Oates has recently called "pathography" —with its emphasis on the faults of the subject, rather than his contribution to society; and I hope I have shunned the opposite pitfall, an undeserved, uncritical admiration. Between these two poles, there are many courses that can be steered. In the end I think my view is right, but I cannot insist: in what follows I hope there is enough so that readers can decide for themselves.

■

MY INVOLVEMENT IN this project began in the spring of 1987 in a conversation with Charles Bronfman in Montreal. Two years later I agreed to write the book, supported by the Seagram Company and under terms which kept the project's sponsors at a congenial arm's length. From those early discussions to the present, there has been complete agreement on one essential point: I was to have complete independence in the research and writing of the book, and take full responsibility for any interpretations and judgements about my subject. As I wrote, members of the family and other knowledgeable readers made written suggestions and comments, relayed to me through an astute and diplomatic authority on American business history, Carl Brauer. I have found this process extraordinarily helpful, and I want to record my sincere gratitude to those who have participated in it: Charles Bronfman, Edgar Bronfman, Phyllis Lambert, Irving Abella, Mel Griffin and Fritz Stern. Special thanks are also due to the following who read all or part of the work, who discussed it with me, and provided useful criticisms and suggestions: Anne Gross, Sol Kanee, Randi Marrus, David Rome, Beverley Slopen, Harold Troper and Gerald Tulchinsky.

I am grateful for having had access to Samuel Bronfman's private papers, and being able to tap the voluminous documentation in the Seagram archives as well. An unpublished manuscript by the late Terence Robertson was of use in the writing of several chapters. From beginning to end, I have relied upon substantial help—from members of the Bronfman family, whom I have interviewed; from contemporaries and associates of Sam Bronfman whom I have drawn upon for their recollections and opinions; from a previous researcher John Scott, with his incomparable knowledge of the material discussed here; and from dozens of Canadian historians who have helped educate me to the culture and society in which Sam lived.

I have interviewed many of Sam's contemporaries, and have also drawn upon transcripts of taped interviews made to assist Saidye Bronfman in the preparation of two volumes of memoirs, published privately in 1982 and 1986. Opinions about Sam, I have found, are strongly felt and I have spent much time listening to sometimes discordant voices speaking about him. My thanks to the following, whose words and opinions I have tried to treat with respect, whether I agreed with them or not: Monroe Abbey, Jacob Brin, Charles Bronfman, Edgar Bronfman, Marjorie Bronfman, Saidye Bronfman, Richard Cohen, Joan Comay,

Walter Goelkel, Harvey Golden, Mel Griffin, Avraham Harman, Sol Kanee, Ben Kayfetz, Victor Koby, Leo Kolber, Teddy Kollek, Lilianne Lagadec, Phyllis Lambert, Ben Lappin, Chaim Lewin, Stanley Lewis, Roy Martin, Abe Mayman, Max Melamet, Alex Mogelon, Shimon Peres, John Pringle, David Rome, Alan Rose, Robert Ruppel, Robert Sabloff, Mark Shinbane, Herb Siblin, Pearl Silver, Ivan Straker, Claire Taylor, Noah Torno and David Weiss.

Venturing into sometimes poorly charted historical territory, I found my way with the help of some excellent guides, and of the many who assisted me I want particularly to thank Pierre Anctil, Abraham Arnold, Carl Berger, William Berman, Michael Bliss, Craig Brown, John Courtney, Davis Dyer, Adam Fuerstenberg, Alain Goldschläger, Roger Hall, Elaine Hochman, Robert Magocsi, Jack McClelland, Erna Paris, Paul Rutherford, Franz Shulze, Arthur Silver, Gerald Slan, Stephen Speisman, Sylvia Van Kirk, Miriam Waddington, Harold Waller, Ron Weir, Larry Zolf and Ron Zweig. For facilitating my research at various points my thanks to Nehama Chalom, Herbert Pankratz, Janice Rosen, Theresa Rowat, Sallyann Sack, Gidon Saguy, Lawrence Tapper, Michael Tavis, Bonnie Trebogov, Stephen Velychenko, George Viragh and especially Richard White. I am grateful to Joe Conforti, Herbert Greenstein, Michael Levine and Robert Rabinovitch who helped steer the project in a direction that an independent-minded author found comfortable. My special thanks as well to Mary Adachi, Lori Ledingham and Cynthia Good for their excellent editorial work in the final stages of the book.

This project would never have started, and once started would never have been completed, without the sage advice and assistance of my friend and literary agent, Beverley Slopen. I simply cannot thank her enough. And for everything else, one more time, I am deeply grateful to my wife, Carol Randi Marrus.

M.R.M.
Toronto, May 1991

CHAPTER I

Growing Up on the Prairies

THE BRONFMANS' EUROPEAN background was, for all Sam's life, a closed book. Consistently, he claimed to have been born in Brandon, Manitoba, on March 4, 1891. The family came, it was said, from somewhere in "southern Russia," seeking refuge, as did so many other Jews, from pogroms and the cruel conscription of Jewish youth into the Czarist army. Sam's parents, Mindel and Ekiel Bronfman, whom he revered, migrated with their three young children—Abe, Harry and Laura. They also came, as family lore had it, with a Hebrew religious teacher, or *melamed*—a sign of the parents' piety and commitment to Jewish education for their youngsters.

Beyond this, Sam and his brothers offered only scraps, despite the countless testimonial dinners and speeches that referred to their immigrant background and their family's fresh start in Canada. Unlike some Jewish immigrants, there were no sentimental memoirs of East European Jewish life; and neither was there a visceral antipathy to the Russian Empire as a place where Jews had suffered for generations. For Sam, in particular, the focus was on Canadian roots. The "Old Country," in his parlance, meant England and Scotland—usually referring to the home of Scotch whisky.

Family members knew the real story about his birthplace, although they provided little information. Harry Bronfman, the second eldest, who was almost three years old when the family

21

came to Canada, dictated a memoir in 1937 about their life almost fifty years before—one of the very few sources we have on the family's early years in Canada. Necessarily shaky on details, Harry nevertheless undercut his brother's claim to be a native son of Manitoba: their mother gave birth to Samuel, he said, "on the way over from Europe."[1] Sam's widow, Saidye, told an interviewer that her husband was six weeks old when the family reached North America. Sam's naturalization certificate, issued in January 1937, gave his birthdate as February 27, 1889, as did his last passport; his marriage certificate of 1922, however, had his birthdate as 1891, and his birthplace as Winnipeg. Late in life, erratic on this subject as on some others, Sam himself did allude to being born in the Russian Empire, referring in 1961 to "a small town" in the province of Bessarabia. But Brandon remained his birthplace for all public purposes, and he never dwelt upon his family's life before their emigration.

Sam's reluctance to dwell upon his family's European background fits a well-defined pattern among Jewish immigrants at the turn of the century. Like so many others who rose from poverty to make their fortune in the New World, he preferred not to look back. Patriotism was one obvious motive. Sam did not go so far as film mogul and contemporary Louis Mayer, also an immigrant from Eastern Europe, who designated his birthday as the fourth of July, in joyous tribute to his adopted home in the United States. But Sam's enthusiastic Canadianism, which he liked to stress, appeared far better against a backdrop of Brandon in its pioneering heyday than some obscure village in Russia. Another reason was political, and linked to antisemitism. "Russia," after the First World War, was the home of Bolshevism, sometimes thought of as "Jewish Bolshevism," and the less contact one had with *that*, the better. Undoubtedly Sam also felt his true place and date of birth were details too insignificant to worry about. Given that he and his siblings may not have known their real birthdates according to the Christian calendar in any case, and given that the eldest, Abe, was only seven when the family arrived, Sam was prepared to fib, just a little.

Sam's father Ekiel Bronfman, or Yechiel as he was called in Yiddish, may well have contributed his own obfuscation of the family's past in the wrenching upheaval involved in travelling to Canada. For according to what Sam's children remember hearing in their youth, the family's name in Russia may not indeed have been Bronfman at all, but rather something else—possibly Weizmann. This change of name, if it indeed occurred, would also not have been unusual. Many Jews used precisely such a stratagem to outwit the Czarist bureaucracy in their desperate quest for exit permits and in their efforts to evade the dreaded military service. Here too, the surviving documentation provides little help. The Canadian birth registration of Sam's sister Rose in 1898 has Yechiel signing an English-language form with an X, and states the family name as "Braufman"; it similarly appears on the birth registration of Sam's younger brother Allan in 1895, and on a Brandon municipal registry at the turn of the century. Later, in 1904, Sam's mother Mindel signed her name on a legal document, in Yiddish, in a firm hand, unmistakably "Bronfman."

■

IN ALL LIKELIHOOD the "southern Russia" to which Sam referred in 1961 was indeed Bessarabia, a substantial province in the southwestern part of the Empire, on the border with Rumania. According to Sam's childhood friend from Winnipeg, Mark Shinbane, and other close associates who knew the family well, the Bronfmans came from the Bessarabian town of Soroki, together with several other Jewish families who left for Western Canada at precisely the same time.[2] Sam's naturalization certificate mentioned Bessarabia as his birthplace, and several accounts of his father's origins in Czarist Russia also referred to that province. And his Yiddish speech, notes one authority, had a distinctly Bessarabian accent.[3]

Between the river Dniester on the east and Pruth on the west, and extending south to the Danube delta and the Black Sea, Bessarabia was tossed back and forth by the powerful rulers of the territories north of the Black Sea. From the thirteenth to the fifteenth century control was exercised by the Mongol invaders of Europe who incorporated it within their state known as the Golden Horde. After the decline of the latter the Ottoman Turks emerged pre-eminent, ruling until the time of Napoleon. Then the Ottomans yielded it to the Russians in 1812, who lost a substantial portion to the emerging Rumanian state between 1856 and 1878. Yechiel Moshe Bronfman, Sam's father, who was born in the province in 1851, may thus have grown up under Rumanian authority. As a result of the Treaty of Berlin in 1878, the formerly Rumanian parts of the province returned to Russian control, and remained there until 1918. Between the world wars it reverted once again to Rumania. It is now within the U.S.S.R. as Moldava, officially the Moldavian Soviet Socialist Republic, seething with opposition to rule from Moscow as this book is being written.

Bessarabia was a very old centre of Jewish settlement, where Jews had benefited from Czarist settlement policies relaxing restrictions on Jewish cultivation of land. Part of what was known as the Pale of Settlement, the western borderlands of the Empire between the Baltic and the Black Sea where Jews were allowed to live, the province was disputed territory, which the Czars sought to bind to the core of the empire. Many Jews had come to Bessarabia from elsewhere in the Empire during the reign of Nicholas I (1825–1855), who promised them exemption from military conscription if they would move to the province, and presumably assist the extension of Czarist control. Jews from neighbouring provinces continued to flock to the region when it was ruled by his successor, Czar Alexander II (1855–1881). Numbering nearly 20,000 in 1847, the Bessarabian Jewish population grew to about 180,000 in 1889, some 11 percent of the entire population when the Bronfman family emigrated. In Bessarabian cities at the end of the nineteenth century their proportion of the entire population was as high as 37 percent, outnumbering not only the Moldavians, but also the Ukrainians and the Russians as well. In Kishinev, the provincial capital, there were more than 50,000 Jews in 1897, about a fifth of the city's total.[4]

Compared to those in other parts of the Empire, the Jews of Bessarabia prospered. Government surveys showed that most earned their living from trade, commerce and handicrafts. The region was famous for its Jewish agricultural colonies, some seventeen of which had been founded in the first part of the nineteenth century, and still thrived at the beginning of the 1880s.

Conditions took a turn for the worse, however, immediately following the assassination of Alexander II in 1881 and the passage of the so-called May Laws the next year. These supposedly "temporary laws" were an official, calculated response to anti-Jewish riots in the southern part of the empire that followed the Czar's assassination; as it turned out, they were the beginning of a long-term assault upon the Jewish minority under Czarist rule. The new laws obliged Jews to abandon village settlements and move to larger towns, placed new obstacles in the way of acquisition of property, and crippled much of Jewish commercial activity. Throughout the empire they prompted a new round of official harassment, economic restrictions and attendant hardships. If anything, conditions worsened more quickly in the southwest than elsewhere. The government drove Jews out of a strip of territory along its western border, forcing many impoverished victims into overcrowded cities.[5] In addition, the government closed down the previously successful Bessarabian Jewish settlements.

Aftershocks of the May Laws were certainly felt in Soroki, where the Bronfman family probably lived. Originally a thriving community on the river Dniester, and a centre of the tobacco trade, Soroki was a medium-sized market town and regional administrative centre. It was also intensely Jewish — local Jews constituted considerably more than half of the city's population at the end of the nineteenth century. Many Jewish immigrants had come to the Soroki area from Lithuania, Ukraine and White Russia around the time of Nicholas I, taking advantage of liberal settlement policies. This was when several Jewish agricultural colonies were founded in the area. In 1864, 4,135 Jews were registered in the town. Their numbers reached 8,783 in 1897, as a result of expulsions from border areas and nearby villages.[6] The town was an attractive place, one of the most beautifully situated in all of Russia according to one well-travelled visitor at the turn of the century. Set on the river bank, warmed by the southern sun, it rose along the side of a mountain slope in "picturesque indentations."[7] Many of the local Jews had been engaged in agricultural pursuits in the surrounding countryside — the growing of tobacco, grapes and various other fruits, and the production of wine or spirits, using the local produce. Hard times came to Soroki in the 1880s and 1890s, not only due to an agricultural downturn, but also because the building of railway bridges across the Dniester substantially undercut the town's role as a trading place along the waterway. For local Jews, the May Laws posed additional difficulties — expulsions from the land, police harassment, and also the imposition of a government liquor monopoly, which ruined the traditional livelihood of distilling and innkeeping.

There were no pogroms in Soroki, although one of the worst of the outbreaks against Jews, with a heavy toll of victims, did occur in 1882 in the town of Balta, some 100 kilometres away.[8] But the real problem, after the first round of attacks, was the grinding poverty and the administrative harassment that increasingly made life miserable for the Jewish inhabitants. Some of the evidence comes from an unlikely source, Prince Serge Dmitriv-evich Urussov, scion of an old Russian family, who became governor of the province in 1903 and wrote a remarkable description of Bessarabian Jewish life at the time. Jammed into their urban refuge, Urussov noted, the Jewish artisans were in a particularly hopeless situation: "The observer is struck by the number of Jewish signs in Bessarabian towns. The houses along second-rate and even back streets are occupied in unbroken succession by stores, big and small, shops of watch-makers, shoe-makers, locksmiths, tinsmiths, tailors, carpenters, and so on. All these workers are huddled together in nooks and lanes amid shocking poverty. They toil hard for a living so scanty that a rusty herring and a slice of onion is considered the tip-top of luxury and prosperity."[9]

The governor found that the Jews were under constant assault by a notoriously corrupt police force, ever-rising barriers to public education and a dizzying array of new taxes. Most dreaded of all, he reported, was the reimposed military conscription, which involved the seizure of Jewish boys aged twelve to eighteen, packing them off to the army for as long as twenty-five years. Terrorized Jewish communities sought to evade such service, prompting in response the introduction of new, punitive military measures to accompany the battery of restrictions in the

May Laws. These regulations cancelled previous exemptions, imposed disproportionately heavy service upon Jews, blocked their military advancement, and provided mechanisms to punish Jewish families when their offspring failed to answer the military call.[10]

There are only scraps of evidence placing the Bronfman family in this troubled Bessarabian setting. Local records reveal that in the mid-nineteenth century, when Yechiel was born, a family named Bronfman lived in the village of Atak, also on the Dniester, not far from Soroki. In 1854 Moshe Anchel Yankelovich Bronfman, still living as a serf in Atak, ran away from the estate where he lived with his seven sons. Among these, one Shmuel (Samuel) Bronfman was then only fourteen. There is no sign of Yechiel Moshe Bronfman, however, and his family may not have had any relationship to these Bronfmans of Atak. However, several other Bronfmans appear in archival documents from the Soroki region in the 1880s — executing a will, hiring workmen and selling land — but Yechiel Moshe and his wife Mindel are nowhere to be found. Mindel Bronfman's family was probably named Elman and a family by that name does appear in other Soroki notarial records. One of these, Yankel Elman, was a tobacco grower in the region and sold his holdings to another Elman family member in 1884.[11]

Harry Bronfman described his parents as having been "well to do" before their emigration, and said that they operated "a large tobacco plantation" before their departure. Tobacco was certainly grown in the Soroki region at the time, and many Jews in the region earned their living this way. But as with so many other Jewish pursuits, tobacco farming turned sour in the years after Alexander II. Economic pressures and administrative restrictions forced many Jews to abandon their farms. Many Jews left the Soroki area at this time for precisely such reasons. Yechiel came to Canada with tobacco seed, and so it may be that Harry accurately and fully presented the family's circumstances and the economic context of their emigration.

In a 1966 interview Sam himself suggested a slight variation — that his father "owned a grist mill, and supplemented its earnings by raising tobacco."[12] On the surface this may seem like a minor discrepancy, which it certainly was as an explanation of the family's economic standing, but it opens an interesting and quite different line of speculation, namely that even in the old country, decades before they launched their Canadian whisky business, the Bronfmans may have been involved in the liquor trade.

Bronf-man, as Yiddish speakers know, means "whisky man," suggesting a remarkable early family association with alcoholic drink—either distilling or innkeeping, both of which were traditional Jewish occupations throughout the Pale of Settlement and the province of Bessarabia in particular. Reference to a grist mill further enhances this possibility, for distilling was frequently undertaken in conjunction with the grinding of grain, utilizing some of the product of milling for this purpose. Unfortunately, direct evidence of the family's early involvement in distilling does not exist. But there are some intriguing possibilities.

Jewish contemporaries would certainly have identified a "bronf-man" as someone who made or sold whisky, for family names often designated occupational or other characteristics of those who held them. Patronymics in the Czarist Empire were of recent date for Jews, most having adopted them by 1818, and the rest being obliged to do so in 1845. Therefore, even if Yechiel did not himself distill spirits, his family may well have done so before him. (I am supposing, for the moment, that the family name was indeed Bronfman, and not Weizmann or something else.) Yechiel's tobacco growing might also point to the whisky trade. Jews who leased land from noblemen to raise tobacco often obtained as well permission to run a tavern or produce wine or spirits on the estate.[13] Jews were heavily involved in all of these pursuits throughout the Soroki region and elsewhere in the empire during this time. As we have already noted, Jewish involvement in the whisky trade suffered from the imposition of government monopolies in the 1880s. Jewish sale of liquor became an increasingly sensitive issue in the period of pogroms and intensified anti-Jewish feeling. Jews were blamed for promoting drunkenness among the peasantry, poisoning the Russian masses and corrupting society. Even some Jewish writers, like the historian Simon Dubnow for example, condemned the trade and by implication sanctioned the collapse of one traditional Jewish livelihood.[14] Few people bothered to defend the Jewish whisky men and their prospects were dim indeed at the end of the 1880s. And so if the Bronfmans had indeed been in the liquor trade at some point, it is quite likely that they had abandoned or were abandoning it by the time the family left the Old World. This might well have been one reason for their emigration.

While the Bronfman family may have suffered just prior to their departure, certain details suggest that Harry was right when he referred to them as relatively prosperous when they set out for Canada. It was certainly unusual for a couple to bring their own Hebrew teacher — together with his wife and two children, as Harry indicated. Harry also mentioned a manservant and a maid — exceptionally rare if true, and possibly confused in his mind with the *melamed* and his wife. Yet even if the family had some independent means, their uprooting must have been one of high adventure, full of risks, perils and uncertainties. The couple was not young by old-country standards: Yechiel was thirty-seven when they left, and his wife Mindel was thirty. Their children were very young and there were no sons or daughters of working age to assist the family in the difficult period that was to follow. Assuming they left in February, as Harry says, Abe was seven, Harry was two years and ten months, and Laura was then an infant of thirteen months. Until 1925 Sam designated his birthdate as February 27 and it may indeed have been as an infant, known by the Yiddish diminutive Zundal ("Sonny"), that Sam Bronfman came with this small party to Canada.

The Bronfmans embarked upon their voyage with the great tide of Jewish migration that brought about 2.5 million Jews from Eastern Europe to the West between the 1880s and the First World War. They came at the very beginning of that great movement of humanity, before anything save the most rickety structures were set in place to assist the immigrants, and before patterns of settlement had clearly established themselves. Detailed information on their destination was scarce, and much of that was distorted. For Yechiel, Mindel and their four children, together with those who accompanied them, Canada was practically another planet.

Why did the family choose British North America? The

simplest reason may be that they knew countrymen who were heading in the same direction. One of these, Alexander Klenman (sometimes spelled Kleiman), reached the Northwest Territories in 1888, scouting out the area for a small party of Bessarabian Jews who awaited word in Montreal. Another was Leib Pelenovsky, also from Soroki, and probably like Yechiel a tobbaco grower. As with the elder Bronfman, he too came to the wastelands of the Northwest Territories with precious packets of tobacco seedlings.[15]

Canada was not completely unknown to these immigrants, despite what may seem their lack of preparation for the hardships of the prairies. Several years before their departure an immigration handbook on Manitoba circulated among Jews in the Pale of Settlement, translated into Yiddish from a version in German. The Hebrew journal *Ha-Melitz* carried accounts of life in Winnipeg in the early 1880s, admittedly not the most inviting of descriptions ("this desert of Winnipeg" went one heartrending report in 1882; "they have sent us to a wilderness in order that we sell ourselves as slaves and domestics"), although spirits brightened in a subsequent issue.[16]

Beyond this, there were the attractions of the Canadian government settlement policy, offering pioneers a "quarter-section," or 160 acres of land, plus the benefits of a free life in a British Dominion. "Dissatisfied with the prospect of government regulation which existed [in Russia]," wrote Harry in 1937, using his own industrialist's idiom, rather than Yechiel's, the family wanted "to establish themselves under the British flag where they felt freedom and equality were open to all who wished to avail themselves of that government which is known as British fair play." There may even have been more romantic inspirations. Vladimir Grossmann was an immigrant from Eastern Europe who came much later, in 1920, and like the Bronfmans went first to a Jewish farm colony on the prairies. According to him, Canada was widely admired in some parts of Eastern Europe, at least by 1900 or so:

From my earliest youth I had dreams of Canada. Nor was I the only dreamer; a whole generation was dream-lorn about it. The Saint Lawrence and the prairies of Western Canada were pictured at the beginning of the century as the veritable gateway to Paradise. The sun that made the waters of the Gulf shimmer as one approached Quebec, shone in some heavenly way and the air that one breathed on the colourful giant mountains was unlike the air in any other part of the world. These millions of men, free and untrammelled, were meant to settle on the distant and vast steppes of Alberta, Manitoba and Saskatchewan. They seemed to beckon and say: Come hither! Come to the happy, golden land![17]

The Bronfmans first made their way to the teeming port of Odessa, on the Black Sea, from which they embarked for the New World. With them on the ship was another Bessarabian Jew, Abe Cristall, who remembered a few details of the journey, many years later. Son of another tobacco grower on the Dniester, and probably also from Soroki, Cristall seems to have travelled alone, eventually to settle in Edmonton, where he became a successful hotel owner and Jewish community leader. About twenty-two years old when he left, he travelled in steerage: "the best spot on the ship," Cristall told his biographer, "that is, it was the best spot in the ship to tell whether the engines were running properly." Cristall claimed that the Bronfmans were with him in these crowded, uncomfortable quarters, together with so many others. He used to help the family, he later recalled, "by taking their six-week-old baby son, Sam, for 'fresh air' walks on the deck."[18]

Steerage passengers descended into dark dormitories for their overseas crossing as one Jewish contemporary, Harris Rubin, described in a vivid memoir. On the *British Queen*, Rubin's ship, steerage reeked with a "dreadful, salty, suffocating smell," and voyagers slept fitfully in shallow wooden boxes. "In a little while our entire stateroom was filled with sick and 'nurses,' " Rubin continued. "There was a running to the sailors for water and to the doctor for help and medicine. Instead of water and medicine we received a bawling out for having disturbed their sleep." Passing via England, which Sam once claimed was the route his family took to North America, steamships took between ten and fourteen days to traverse the Atlantic. Below decks conditions varied from one vessel to the next, but the hardships were remarkably similar: seasickness, unsanitary conditions, poorly prepared food, lack of privacy, and noise: "the clattering of the dishes, the groans and wailing of the men, women and children, the bad effects of nausea," which "could drive anyone insane," according to another emigrant.[19] For parents accompanied by four small children, two of them infants, the trip must have been a nightmare.

As the voyage neared its end it is unlikely that the couple dwelt, as did the young Vladimir Grossmann, upon the sun shimmering on the waters of the Gulf of St Lawrence or the majestic mountains near Quebec. More likely, they were preoccupied with children, food and shelter. Their port of arrival was Montreal, to which most Russian Jewish immigrants came at the end of the 1880s and where a party of Bessarabian Jews was already preparing to continue west, to the Canadian prairies. The largest port in Canada, and with the largest concentration of Jews in the country at the time, Montreal had a tiny Jewish élite who supported colonization schemes to settle Jewish refugees and other immigrants in the barren wilderness west of Manitoba. Up to that time, local Jews had provided rudimentary support for immigrants in transit. By the end of the 1880s, however, their charitable impulses were sorely tested.

Embarrassed at the constant stream of indigent newcomers to their community, the well-established Montreal Jewish leaders felt overwhelmed, and hard pressed to provide even short-term assistance. Most of this task was undertaken by the Young Men's Hebrew Benevolent Society, an organization dating back to the 1860s. Its records suggest that the second half of the 1880s was a particularly difficult time. Montreal Jews even attempted to stem the tide of emigration in London, where the Canadian High Commissioner had been encouraging Jewish settlement in Canada, or to pass some of the burden of support on to their English co-religionists. Another possibility, which certainly occurred to the Montreal authorities, was to speed the immigrants on their way west.[20]

■

THE BRONFMANS WASTED little time in eastern Canada, and

probably headed directly for Winnipeg, to which the Canadian authorities paid transportation costs. Other Jewish immigrants, as we have already seen, had come this way just a few years before. The earlier party consisted of 350 Russian Jews who landed in the city in 1882, most ending up in rough accommodations in sheds on the banks of the Assiniboine, where they were the object of great curiosity and some unease. Winnipeg's entire Jewish population numbered not more than thirty families at the time, and the newly arrived indigents found themselves thrown upon the mercy of the City Council and local church leaders. Only after great hardships were the immigrants finally settled, with one group of twenty-seven pioneers founding the first Jewish agricultural colony on the prairies, near Moosomin, in the Northwest Territories, just across the Manitoba border in what is now eastern Saskatchewan.[21]

Unknown to the Bronfmans, authorities in Ottawa, London and Montreal were at that very moment preoccupied with Jewish immigration to Canada, and were eager to prevent the sort of mismanagement that accompanied these first waves of Jewish immigration. Sensitive to the plight of Jews in flight from Czarist persecution, many sympathetic onlookers in London and Canadian High Commissioner Sir Alexander Galt sought Dominion government encouragement for agricultural colonies of Jews similar to those being established at the time by Mennonites or a group of Scottish tenant farmers. The goal, Galt wrote to the minister of interior in Ottawa about the Jews in 1884, was to test "the suitability of these people for agriculture."[22]

Already in 1888 the first test seemed a failure. The Moosomin settlers, gathered in a colony they hopefully named "New Jerusalem," had run into bad luck, the effects of which were complicated by their own inexperience. After three years of crop failures, physical hardship and mounting debt, the little Jewish outpost collapsed. From London, Galt signalled his impatience with the Jews, suggesting that these "vagabonds" had reverted "to their natural avocation of peddling." At the same moment, however, another party of Jews, this one with some agricultural experience, prepared to try their hand nearby, about twenty miles from Moosomin, in the Wapella district, just a few hours walk from the nearby CPR railway station. This was the colony to which Yechiel Bronfman and his tiny brood made their way, and where Samuel Bronfman spent his first few years in Canada.[23]

The leading figures of the Wapella colony were Alexander Klenman, also from Bessarabia, and John Heppner, who had been dispatched from London by the Jewish philanthropist and railway promoter Herman Landau, an enthusiast for Jewish agricultural colonies. The intrepid Klenman, aged fifty-seven, investigated the Wapella area the year before, burrowing underground like a prairie gopher to spend the winter in Wapella while awaiting the arrival of the rest of the party from Montreal. In 1889 the colonists began to arrive. Edel Brotman, who had studied to become a rabbi in Galicia, was among the first; he became the spiritual leader of the little settlement, as well as farming his own quarter-section. Solomon Barish was another. He was Klenman's son-in-law, and suffered from tuberculosis. On the advice of a doctor, Barish went to Chicago during Klenman's first winter in Wapella, studied to become a *shoichet*, or ritual slaughterer, and thus was able to provide a much-needed service for the little community. More than twenty families, in all, came by 1892. These were the Bronfmans' earliest Canadian contacts, some of whom remained close to the family for many years to come. They were a hardy lot, as the handful of faded photographs of the pioneering Jewish settlers suggest — heavily bearded, thick-set men, grim-looking women in long dresses, rough-hewn, hard-working agriculturalists whom we now know to have been desperately anxious not only to prosper in the New World, but to prove to the Alexander Galts and everyone else, including themselves, that Jews could succeed as agriculturalists on the new land allotted to them.[24]

Both at Moosomin and Wapella, the Jewish colonists proclaimed communal as well as individual objectives. Quite apart from their desire to scrape a living from the Canadian prairies, these pioneers saw collective Jewish agricultural life as a value in itself, participating in an idealistic current that swept East European Jewry in the early 1880s, and that is sometimes associated with the movement known as *Am Olam*, the Eternal People. For its adherents, and for many others moved by Tolstoian schemes that circulated through the Czarist Empire at the time, Jewish society was to be "normalized" in the soil of the New World. Jewish agricultural colonies and farm cooperatives, they hoped, would build a healthy new Jewish social structure, quite different from the traditional world of tradesmen and middlemen in Eastern Europe. Eventually, these rugged visionaries founded more than a dozen agricultural colonies in the Canadian west at the end of the nineteenth and beginning of the twentieth centuries.[25]

Eight miles from the Wapella railway station, more than two hundred miles west of Winnipeg, the world undoubtedly looked different. Most of the land had not yet been cleared, and the roads were hardly more than dirt tracks. Families reached their allotments by oxcart, passing through the cluster of buildings by the railway station on their way to their land. The Pelenovsky daughters remembered Wapella at the time as consisting of the Queen's Hotel, a general store, a blacksmith shop and a few houses. That was all. And Wapella, moreover, hardly grew. Seventeen years later, in 1906, a legendary Jewish character reached Wapella as a sixteen-year-old juvenile delinquent from the East End of London. Moishe "Two-Gun" Cohen, as he was known, later famous for his fabulous exploits with the Nationalists in China, and who eventually crossed paths with Sam Bronfman, remembered the entire township as having but a few hundred people, a handful of wooden buildings, dirty streets and three or four grain elevators. This was his uninviting, first stop in Canada.[26]

Solomon Jacobson, who came to the Wapella colony in 1888 with the very first settlers, described the scene: "The mosquitos were terrible. Nobody claimed any taxes and there were no roads. But there were plenty of wolves and bears, which troubled us. The land in the neighbourhood was covered with scrub and trees 18 in. in diameter. The land was stony and there were lots of pea vine and flowers." Jacobson came to his land in 1888 with minimal capital—a team of oxen, one cow, one calf, three sections of harrows and a plough. He had no cooking utensils. "I broke up two and a half acres of land and cleared five acres of bush and built a shack, but I lost my summer's work for I failed to make legal entry for that quarter section and somebody else came along and claimed the land."[27]

While clearing the land, the pioneers often worked for those who were already established and built their own first homes — rough dwellings of logs, with roofs covered with sod. "We cut down poplar trees for logs and chinked the cracks with mud," reported one of the earliest settlers. "We'd make plaster out of a mixture of the clay, straw and manure from the cattle. And we mixed it with our feet. . . ." Winters were the greatest trial, and figured importantly in all of the pioneers' memoirs. "The winter was very cold," recounted Harry Jacobson, "and we had no sleighs and no warm clothing. We drove about half clothed in wagons until the snow stopped all travel. There was very little money for no work could be obtained in the winter. So we lived very economic." Once properly sheltered, the most enterprising settlers ventured forth in the freezing weather to sell what they could in nearby Wapella or Moosomin. Brothers Ben and Sam Barish told how a few of the farmers would load their wagons during the day. "After supper they would set out and travel all night, because they couldn't afford to lose a day's work. They would carry along bundles of hay to feed the oxen and some bread, or potatoes, in their pockets, for themselves. During the winter it would be 30 degrees below zero or maybe colder. They would stop to build a fire on the trail to warm up and to bake the potatoes. Arriving in Moosomin in the morning, they would have plenty of daylight to sell or trade the wood, and be home the next night."[28]

Moosomin, a veritable metropolis by comparison, was the nearest commercial centre. One of the leading social centres there was R.D. McNaughton's store, owned by the father of World War II Canadian commander General Andrew McNaughton, born in Moosomin two years before the Bronfmans arrived. Photographs of McNaughton's show it to be a substantial stone structure, built in the mid-1880s and literally jammed from floor to ceiling with goods. Moosomin's own Queen's Hotel, dating from 1882, seems much smaller, a two-storey frame structure with a second-storey balcony. The town also boasted a distinguished brick church, reputed to be one of the finest west of Winnipeg. To the Wapella colonists, this was civilization. The round trip from Wapella to Moosomin took one day using horses, and two nights and a day with oxen.[29]

One of the people passing through Moosomin and other towns in the vicinity just as the Bronfmans were settling into their new homestead was Newton Wesley Rowell, a senior law student and Methodist lay preacher. By remarkable coincidence more than thirty-five years later, he would interrogate the Bronfman brothers on their whisky business before a Royal Commission investigating smuggling and other infractions of the law. Rowell went west in 1890 to check on some legal accounts, but he had plenty of time to explore the small towns and villages of southwestern Manitoba. Untroubled by the hardships of the Jewish pioneers in Wapella, Rowell worried rather about the weak hold that Christian civilization had on the vast Canadian prairies. On meeting one genial fellow traveller in Brandon, Rowell was chagrined to be asked whether he would spend a sabbath driving or hunting. "I told him that it had not been my custom to do this kind of work on Sunday. He admitted I was right but said that out west they got into a different way of living. This gentleman was as decent a fellow as you would care to meet and most obliging, but such is life."[30]

Harry Bronfman recounted how Yechiel bought oxen and a cow, built a house, and cleared land for planting "a crop of wheat or coarse grains." (Apparently the settlers realized early on that there was no future in tobacco.) At this point Yechiel had spent most of the cash that he had brought with him, and given the rest away to assist his fellow pioneers. Then came disaster: their crops were ruined. The problem seems to have been excessively dry summer weather, combined with a killing frost in late summer or early autumn. For nearly the entire decade of 1881 to 1891 settlers suffered from similar conditions. Eighteen-eighty-nine, by all accounts, was a particularly devastating year. Western farmers had not yet heard of the hardy, fast-ripening wheat strains that could survive the short northern season, and it is hardly surprising that new immigrants like Yechiel failed to produce a marketable harvest.[31] Harry recalled the family's disappointment. "The first crop of wheat froze, and consequently that winter was spent going into the bush, cutting logs, loading them onto a sleigh and drawing them twenty miles with a yoke of

oxen so that when they were sold there probably would be . . .
money to buy a sack of flour, a few evaporated apples, dried
prunes and probably some tea and sugar to bring back to his
family so that body and soul could be kept together."

More than a year passed while Yechiel, aged thirty-nine,
struggled against the elements. Then came a drastic decision:
Yechiel decided to go to Brandon, hoping to earn some cash.
Mindel and the children remained behind, alone in their sod
house. This was the most difficult time in their Wapella
experience and Mindel Bronfman's greatest trial. Harry, for
whom this may have been one of his first memories, described the
great difficulties his mother had providing for the four children.
One memory was especially vivid: Mindel's heroic effort to build
a bake oven such as she had remembered at home in the old
country. As Harry recalled, his mother laboriously hauled the
stones herself, using a strong apron tied about her waist.
Painstakingly, she then attempted to construct the oven, using a
wooden frame. Unfortunately, the stones kept collapsing.

> She built this oven three times, but because she had no
> knowledge of how to build an arch, and did not realize it was
> necessary to let the arch dry long enough so that it would stand
> up after a fire had been put in it, she proceeded to put a fire in
> the oven which would burn the wooden stays that had been
> erected inside for holding up such a thing, allowing the oven to
> fall. At the fourth attempt she learned it was best to let the
> structure stand long enough so that it would dry of its own
> accord sufficiently to have strength enough to hold its own
> arch after the wood had been burned out. This was done and
> the result was an oven capable of baking bread, cooking and
> so on. . . .

Meanwhile, Yechiel had his own troubles in Brandon, and for a
time he had no money to send. When the provisions he left
behind ran out, Mindel must have been desperate. As Harry
wrote, "there was nothing left but potatoes in the house. She
proceeded to bake and cook potatoes in the various forms
possible to feed his children, and kept the secret of distress from
her neighbours." This lasted for some six weeks, until cash

finally arrived. After four months of this arrangement, Yechiel finally returned, and decided to take the family with him to Brandon. The Bronfmans' homesteading days were over.

Yechiel returned to Wapella in the spring of 1892 to celebrate Passover, and then began the move. He traded his oxen for a team of horses, which could be hitched to a farmer's wagon. Then, he loaded all their belongings on it and, with their cow, set out for Brandon.

■

"NOBODY WHO SAW Brandon in its infancy ever forgot the spectacle," wrote one long-standing resident of the city who was witness to its creation.[32] Brandon emerged almost literally overnight in May 1881, when a CPR agent, seemingly lining his own pocket, obtained title to some squatter's land which happened to be on the route of the new transcontinental railway then driving its way westwards to the prairies and beyond. That summer, tents dotted the hillside overlooking the Assiniboine River, in what was soon to be the centre of a new city. The encampment rang with the sound of hammers as the construction of frame buildings proceeded apace. A story is told of a labourer who made his way to the site at that time, specifically to what the surveyors referred to as the corner of Tenth and Rosser Streets. Where, he asked, was Brandon? "Right here," was the curt reply.[33]

Nine years later, when the Bronfman family moved to Brandon, they came to a booming Manitoba city, growing faster than anyone could calculate. Celebrating the town's tenth anniversary in 1890, local boosters pointed to "magnificent buildings, excellent streets and five thousand enterprising people." (In fact, Dominion enumerators counted only 3,780 people, prompting the locals to exaggerate just a bit, correcting what they saw as an irksome underestimation.) The census takers also noted 380 horses, 232 cows, and some sheep and hogs. Proud municipal leaders drew attention to one hundred and fifty electric streetlights, lit for the first time just three years before, and the Calvary Congregational Church, Manitoba's first place of worship lit by electricity. Other amenities included two-inch plank sidewalks, eight feet wide on the main streets. Although the latter were unpaved, the gutters and drains were of cobblestones, so that the ladies "could walk on clean, solid roads one half hour after a thunderstorm," as the chivalrous city fathers put it. Brandon, moreover, was linked to the wider Canadian world. A daily wire service to Toronto flashed the city's market quotations to the east, and in 1891 a newly inaugurated fast train to Winnipeg, 130 miles away, took three hours, instead of the previous five hours and fifteen minutes. Appropriately, one of the largest buildings begun in Brandon was the Land Titles Office. Unfortunately, its forty-ton arched roof collapsed in 1890, when supports were removed without proper authorization.[34]

Upon reaching Brandon, Yechiel installed his family in a long, cheap workmen's tenement near the CPR railway tracks, known as the Brandon House, at the corner of Sixth Street and Pacific Avenue. One of his first tasks was to find better accommodation. Harry, who as a successful businessman could remember with stunning accuracy the amount of money spent upon insignificant commodities many years before, recalled that Yechiel had earlier paid twelve dollars for a lean-to near the railway. This is where he had lived while the family remained in Wapella. Now, in a land sale that broke up an estate on the southern edge of town, Yechiel purchased a lot in a new suburb, and simply moved his little shack to the more desirable location. Apparently the *melamed* and his wife were still with the family, for they crop up in Harry's memoir as he described the Bronfmans' move to their first real Brandon home, in a neighbourhood that was called the Johnstone Estate. Mindel was pregnant at the time, giving birth to a baby girl, Jean, in April 1892.

Throughout, Yechiel toiled furiously. While the family was still in Wapella he had worked at a local sawmill, known as Christie Mills, one of the major enterprises in town. At the mill he noted the waste slabs and blocks that accumulated when the logs were cut into planks. Yechiel realized that this discarded wood could be sold to households as cooking fuel; he bought it from Christie Mills at seventy-five cents a wagonload, and sold it for a dollar seventy-five, making a tidy profit. The family's team of horses and wagon were immediately pressed into service. The Bronfmans were now in the fuel business.

At the same time, Yechiel worked on his own to construct a proper home on the Johnstone Estate, weatherproofing the exterior, building a fence, planting a vegetable garden — still homesteading, in effect, but in an urban landscape rather than the wilderness of Wapella. He also built a small stable for his horses and the cow. By the end of their first summer in Brandon, according to Harry, both the Bronfmans' and their teacher's houses had real doors and windows — a major improvement — sufficient to provide shelter for the winter.

Winter brought new problems, however, because the sawmill ceased to function and Yechiel was left without merchandise. Taking advantage of the season, he began a new venture — the frozen-fish business. The idea was to travel by sleigh over sixty miles east to Westbourne, at the southern end of Lake Manitoba, and buy frozen fish which he would market in towns and villages in southern Manitoba. For several years the frozen-fish business did well, and became the family's regular winter occupation. Harry, not yet in his teens, sold some of the fish in Brandon, and with the proceeds managed to acquire a second wagon and another team of horses. He then accompanied his father to Westbourne and doubled the Bronfmans' inventory.

One trip stood out particularly in his mind, and must have been a frightening experience for the boy-entrepreneur. It began on a wintry day, when Yechiel reached Westbourne with Harry, only to find that storms had delayed the arrival of the fish. Yechiel then decided to go sixty miles farther, directly to the fishermen, setting off on Thursday evening. After driving all day Friday, the father faced a trial of conscience as the sun began to set. Up to that point his son had remained faithful to Jewish religious tradition, and had never driven on the sabbath. Yechiel felt unable now to force the boy to break the sabbath laws. He therefore decided to leave Harry with a local farmer while he took another man to fetch the fish. Harry described what happened next:

There was a snowstorm during Saturday and because I was too young to realize that travelling an additional thirty-five miles, loading the fish and returning these thirty-five miles would take at least three days I began to get uneasy when Sunday night came and he had not yet returned. The farmer's family with whom he left me endeavoured to console and assure me that he would return, but I will never forget the long, tedious hours of anxiety which I spent during the day and night until my father arrived with the two loads of fish.

Harry and his father then struggled through another snowstorm, wandering through a swamp, with Yechiel leading the way and his son guiding his sleigh in the tracks. Finally they reached Westbourne, fed and rested their horses, and made their way back to Brandon.

As a result of his enterprise, Yechiel managed to meet the needs of his family, although they still teetered on the edge of poverty. The family remained in the fuel and the fish business for some years, adding to it some hauling of gravel and occasional contracting work associated with Brandon's construction boom. A few documents from the time note Yechiel's occupation as "labourer." Jean's Brandon birth registration of April 16, 1892 listed her father as a "teamster," in the "livery" business. His wife, Mindel, the document went on, was a "housewife," aged thirty-three. One day in May 1892, no doubt a memorable occasion, Yechiel travelled to Winnipeg and became a naturalized Canadian citizen. On the document his name appeared as "Eichel" — one of several renderings used at the time, eventually becoming Anglicized as Ekiel.

The Bronfmans lived for eight years in the house that grew from Yechiel's original lean-to by the CPR railway tracks. About 1900, Ekiel moved his family to more spacious accommodations, closer to the schools his children now attended. And all the while, the family continued to expand. In rapid succession, Mindel gave birth to Jean, Bessie (Bea), Allan and Rebecca (Rose) — eight children, in all, ten mouths to feed, not counting the *melamed* and his family who by this point may have been on their own. According to Harry, his father paid $1,000 for their new home, a two-storey, solid brick house at 550 Eleventh Street, between Victoria and McTavish Avenue. Ekiel put down $200 for the house, as Harry remembered. "When mother announced that she had the $200 to make the first payment my eyes almost popped out of my head. I had never in my life heard of so much money."

The family lived in this house for the rest of their time in Brandon, until 1906. According to one account, it included a barn in the back yard, where Ekiel kept the horses. Ekiel soon expanded the house by adding a kitchen and a small granary, to store oats. Eventually, signs of gentility also made their appearance, for Allan, born in 1895, recalled burgundy red plush furniture in the parlour, which the children could only rarely enter.[35]

Sam recorded little of his childhood in Brandon, except to reiterate how painfully he experienced the poverty in which his family lived. He worried that his parents might fail to make their payments on the family home. With his brothers Abe and Harry, and his sister Laura, he attended what was known as the West Ward school, one of only two in town, probably beginning in September 1895, when he was six years old. Sam later recalled the shame of appearing before his classmates in torn clothes — a humiliation he recounted to his own children for the rest of his life. Occasionally, the Bronfman boys were jeered by their classmates, who knew enough about their family name to call them "whisky man."[36] After the move to Eleventh Street Sam attended the new Brandon public school, situated on the corner of Sixth Street and Louise Avenue. Around this time Abe and Harry went to work to contribute to the family's slender income. Sam remained in school with the rest of the children, however, working at odd jobs after classes and in his spare time. At age ten, Harry remembered, he spent his holidays helping with the family's fuel deliveries.

In their exposure to Brandon's schools and to its civic culture, Ekiel's children experienced with particular intensity the prairie patriotism at the turn of the century. In all likelihood this dimension of Sam's childhood left a profound mark upon him, evident later in life whenever he came within sight or sound of royalty or the trappings of the British Empire in its heyday. Brandon at the turn of the century, one could hardly fail to note, was a chip off the block of Empire — celebrated deliriously with Queen Victoria's Diamond Jubilee in 1897, when young Sam was probably in the second grade. That June, the boom city reverberated with festivity—flags flying from both public buildings and private homes, a service of great solemnity in Saint Matthew's Church, a parade, including the 90th Regimental Band and municipal fire-fighters in full regalia and a political rally for the local citizenry sponsored by the Liberal Association. Two years later, war came to Brandon—or rather, more directly, to South Africa, where the Boers rose in revolt against the British. People went wild. When Pretoria fell in 1900 fire bells pealed, and fireworks blazed. "From almost every Rosser Avenue window, flags flew, streamers stretched across the streets and private residences were gaily decorated. Citizens on horseback, fire brigade members, 'with polished engines, bright uniforms and prancing steeds,' the Citizens' Band, Brandon Infantry Company, school cadets, collegiate students, public school children and benevolent association representatives bearing lodge emblems paraded along Princess and Rosser Avenues before returning to the starting point, City Hall Square, where Mayor McDiarmid delivered a balcony oration."[37]

In public schools, only recently established as secular institutions, the trumpets of Empire constantly sounded. Teachers sought to blend the diverse cultures represented among the students into a homogeneous, enthusiastic British citizenship. Classrooms were adorned with world maps of Empire in Mercator projection, with the points of British civilization coloured pink. Textbooks celebrated the superiority of British ways and the beneficence of British rule. As historian Gerald Friesen notes: "Students memorized the classic verses and songs of British imperialism such as *We'll Never Let the Old Flag Fall, Children of the Empire, Union Jack, Rule Britannia,* and *England, My England.* Their history classes were built around an appreciation of British history and parliamentary government."[38]

The Empire notwithstanding, the Bronfmans maintained strong links to Judaism and to the community of their fellow Jews. The census of 1891 listed twenty-two Jews in town, hardly a conspicuous minority and not one that was growing quickly in the early years. So far as one can tell, there was no significant hostility towards them. Several years before, in 1887, members of the Wapella Liberal Conservative Association had protested against the Jews, grumbling that the land should go to "wealthy

Englishmen" who had money to spend, unlike the poor Jewish settlers, who allegedly contributed nothing to the local economy. Unless something was done, the protesters ominously declared, "it would fare hard with the Jews." The protest, however, seems to have gone nowhere. Occasionally, there were rumblings about "Jew pedlars" in Manitoba, and a tendency to lump Jews together with other unpopular East European immigrants, such as the Ukrainians or "Galicians." But on the whole, the Jews felt secure.[39]

Ekiel Bronfman became one of the leaders of the tiny Brandon Jewish community. Sam remembered him as charitable, sending money overseas to help the Jews of Eastern Europe at the turn of the century, and especially at the time of the Kishinev pogrom of 1903; Sam also recalled a *pischka*, or collection box for the poor, on the wall of their home. In 1892, when the family first arrived, the city lacked a proper *minyan*, a quorum of ten men for prayers, even on the High Holy Days. At the Jewish New Year, the Bronfmans therefore took the train to Winnipeg, leaving their animals in the care of a neighbour. Ekiel maintained his contacts with the Winnipeg Jews, and soon became active in their new congregation, Rosh Pina, an offshoot of the city's first synagogue. The "minuts" of the Rosh Pina founders, quaintly inscribed in a mixture of Yiddish and English known as "Henglish," show Ekiel Bronfman as a moving force among the elders and a man of the world — drawing upon his experience as a handyman-builder and advising on the financing of the new institution. "Ess iz gemooft und gessekent az ah shul sol gelbildet veren," went the text. "Reb Yechiel Bronfman git ah siggeshun az ah kommittee sol appointed veren un ah plan oistsuarbeiten. Oich bei ah kontrakter oder a muggitch kompany ess tzu farmuggitchen. Dan zol men bei dee poblik hilf foderren." ("It was moved and seconded that a synagogue be built. Reb Yechiel Bronfman makes the suggestion that a committee be appointed and that a plan be worked out. Furthermore, that it be mortgaged with either the contractor or a mortgage company. Then the public should be approached for assistance.")[40]

Back in Brandon, several years later, a site for the town's first synagogue was acquired on the Johnstone Estate where the Bronfmans lived, and in 1903, at Victoria Avenue and Thirteenth

Street, ex-mayor McDiarmid laid the cornerstone of a new building, to house the Children of Israel congregation. Ekiel seems to have been instrumental in building this synagogue, and served as its president for many years.[41]

Mindel was revered by her children and praised for her sacrificial devotion to their welfare. Harry recounted how she "sat up many nights mending and re-making clothes from one child for another, doing housework and seeing to it that the children went decently dressed to school." A traditional Jewish household, the Bronfmans stretched their resources in the interests of their children. Among Harry's earliest memories was how Ekiel took the boys for new clothes, shoes and hats before Passover and Rosh Hashana, the Jewish New Year, and Mindel did the same for the girls.

After a few years of the fish and the fuel business, with their income supplemented by peddling, road building and other jobs, Ekiel and his sons accumulated a little capital and were ready for more ambitious ventures. For a time they entered the horse trade, for which Brandon was one of the most important centres in the west, including Montana and North Dakota. Some called it, indeed, the Horse Capital of Canada. Trotter and Trotter, the town's aptly named firm that led the field, estimated in the early twentieth century that they had brought over three million dollars' worth of horses into the district. Brandon's October horse fair was a major event, jamming hotels with customers and bringing buyers and sellers from far and wide.[42]

Ekiel and his sons travelled about the surrounding country-side, attempting to get a foothold in this most difficult and precarious commerce. They helped round up wild horses on the prairies and sold some of them for cartage teams at auctions back in Brandon. This required breaking the wild horses by hitching them to teams with others already trained — something the father and his sons apparently managed to do. Harry learned to toss a lariat and rope a horse, and saw himself for a time as a bronco buster. The trade also required, as veteran horseman Beecham Trotter described in his memoirs, an exquisite feel for business negotiation. "The livery stable was a school in horse sense," Trotter wrote, "a graduator in the study of human nature, and, it can modestly be said, an academy for statesmanship."[43]

Sam, too young to take an active part, nevertheless had distinct recollections of the trade, which could hardly have failed to capture the imagination of a boy of ten or eleven. This may have been the future Seagram president's first whiff of a business deal. Many years later, in what was possibly an apocryphal tale, he told interviewers how he sat on the corral behind Brandon's Langham Hotel, an alert and astute youngster carefully watching his father sweating in the hot sun, giving his pitch to one farmer after another. Whenever a sale was completed, buyer and seller would repair to the hotel for a drink. At the end of one day, Sam claimed, he solemnly told Ekiel: "The bar makes more profits than we do, Father. Instead of selling horses we should be selling the drinks." "You may be right," Ekiel is supposed to have said, "perhaps we should."[44]

While having achieved a measure of security, Ekiel seems to have sought a greater degree of success for his sons. For all his efforts, he remained a labourer. Now over fifty, his hope seems to have been that his sons might do better. But how? Abe, the eldest, was apprenticed to a cigar manufacturer in town, and quickly learned the trade. After a time, cigar-making took Abe to Winnipeg, where he fell in with some card-playing colleagues — "city slickers" from the Main Street poolrooms, according to writer James Gray — much to his parents' distress.[45] Harry, meanwhile, made his own probes into the fish business and other enterprises. Some time after Abe's return from the clutches of the Winnipeg cigar-makers, Ekiel and Mindel encouraged their two eldest sons to go into business together. This seems to have been the origin of the family's next venture, which was to take them first to Winnipeg to test the waters, and then throughout southern Manitoba and Saskatchewan where they were to achieve some notoriety. The idea was to scrape together what little money they had, to buy a hotel.

■

In 1903, ABE and Harry took their first plunge into the hotel business in Emerson, Manitoba, a town situated on the American border, on an important railway link south to Minneapolis. While this was a bold step in building the Bronfman family fortunes, the move into the hotel business was hardly as ambitious as it might be today. Hotels at the time were often flimsy, frame structures, more akin to large rooming houses and sometimes lacking even elementary comforts such as electricity or indoor plumbing. These establishments were sometimes owned by mortgage companies that had foreclosed on previous owners, and could sometimes be picked up at bargain prices. Friendly entrepreneurs, notably those who would stock the bars, naturally had an interest in keeping the hotels going. In the case of Emerson, Harry obtained part of the money to buy the hotel from the local "liquor interests" — George Veely, a liquor store owner, and Patrick Shea, a brewer in town. The rest came from the family — some $3,200, as Harry later recalled.[46] Ekiel mortgaged his house on Eleventh Street and his teams of horses, risking the family's entire fortune, the product of fifteen years' labour, on this new venture. Only eighteen, Harry and his brother Abe, then twenty-two, thus became the proud proprietors of the Anglo-American Hotel. Men of property now, both brothers were married that year: Abe to Sophie Rasminsky, who was born in Rochester, New York, and whose brother David was the father of a future Governor of the Bank of Canada; and Harry to Anna Gallaman, a Winnipeg girl who was born in Kiev, and who came from a very Orthodox Jewish family.

In short order the brothers did well, and after six months Harry was able to return to Brandon with the money Ekiel had lent them. "On my arrival home I informed Mother and Father that I had the money with me so that we could redeem our house and horses, and the following morning we proceeded to the Hooper Bank informing Hooper that we were ready to pay the mortgage. I passed the money over to my father, who, in turn, counted it out at the teller's desk, and as he was counting this money I noticed tears running down his cheeks. I asked father why he was crying, and he said this time it was for the joy of knowing that God was kind enough to us — we had not failed and the roof we had over our heads was ours again."[47]

After a year or so, Abe and Harry quarrelled and the older brother was sent back to Brandon. Reading between the lines of Harry's account and subsequent interviews given by Sam, one gathers that the trouble was Abe's weakness for card playing and gambling—habits picked up among the cigar-makers of Winnipeg. But both parents and brother were ready to forgive and decided to set Abe up in his own hotel, closely supervised by Ekiel and with its operations monitored from afar by his younger brother. Harry found a fair-sized hotel for Abe in Yorkton, Saskatchewan, called the Balmoral, which was to play an important role in the Bronfmans' subsequent whisky business. Built in 1897, the Balmoral was a solid, three-storey brick structure at the upper end of the hotel market; passengers alighting from the railway, even in the early days, would be met by a special horse-drawn bus that would drop them off at the front door.[48] Harry remembered the family paying $22,000 for the enterprise, with a down payment of $13,000.

Abe took over the operation of the Balmoral, and Sam, then about fifteen, accompanied him, for a time, as bellboy and all-purpose assistant. Harry, meanwhile, returned to Winnipeg, moved in with his wife's family, and invested the family's capital in a small apartment block with stores on the ground floor, at the corner of Isabel Avenue and Pacific Avenue, across from the Midland railway yards.

In the summer of 1906, Ekiel, Mindel and their children moved to Winnipeg to join Harry and assist him in the management of the new properties. Father and mother moved into the building, serving as rental agents and caretakers for the other apartments and the stores—no easy task, according to Harry, for the property was not in the best of neighbourhoods, and the tenants "not of the highest type." The family's finances were still in a precarious state at this point, and everything depended on keeping the building fully rented. Nevertheless, things seem to have worked out satisfactorily. Thereafter, Winnipeg became home to the Bronfman family, even while the brothers moved from one hotel and one venture to another in southern Manitoba and Saskatchewan. Until his marriage in 1922, Sam thought of Winnipeg as home.

The English poet Rupert Brooke, who came to Winnipeg in 1913, liked the place. He found it "a little more American than the other Canadian cities, but not unpleasantly so. The streets are wider, and full of a bustle which keeps clear of hustle. The people have something of the free swing of Americans, without the bumptiousness; a tempered democracy, a mitigated independence of bearing. The manners of Winnipeg, of the West, impress the stranger as better than those of the East, more friendly, more hearty, more certain to achieve graciousness, if not grace. . . ."[49] Less attuned, perhaps, to Brooke's aesthetic priorities, the Bronfmans must nevertheless have found Winnipeg a thriving metropolis, even after the phenomenal development they had witnessed in Brandon.

The Bronfmans arrived just at the beginning of the "great boom," the most important upswing in the history of the province so far, and a similarly dramatic growth of the provincial capital. Winnipeg's population more than tripled between 1901 and 1911, when the numbers reached 142,000. New office buildings sprouted in the centre of town, where one of the attractions was a lavish T. Eaton Co. department store, completed in 1905. Electric streetcars clattered down the paved expanse of Portage Avenue, which had not long before been a dirt trail on the way west to Edmonton. Construction sites were everywhere, and the city's first "skyscrapers" — eventually to reach an unheard-of fourteen storeys in 1910 with the McArthur building — rose from the city's business centre. That district hummed with the success of prairie agriculture, the source of much of Winnipeg's and the province's prosperity after 1896. Winnipeg was "the strategic centre of the Canadian grain trade," where the most important decisions were made; it was also the main railway centre of Western Canada and a vital communication link between East and West. "The growing stream of new settlers and merchandise was funnelled out to the West through Winnipeg, and, flowing in the opposite direction, a swelling tide of grain and cattle converged from the plains to the city, for onward shipment over the trunk railway lines eastwards."[50]

Winnipeg was also, in contrast with Brandon, a remarkably diverse, cosmopolitan city — "an international bazaar," as one historian puts it, describing the scene at the busy CPR station, downtown: "the noise of thousands of voices and a dozen tongues circled the high marble pillars and drifted out into the street, there to mingle with the sounds of construction, delivery wagons, perambulatory vendors, and labour recruiters."[51] The Jews, numbering about 7,000, contributed substantially to this local colour, with a community known for both its vigour and its variety. Every kind of Jew was represented — from the Orthodox to Reform (admittedly weak) to the secular, from the Socialist to the Zionist. There were Jewish sports associations, Yiddish theatrical productions, a Jewish political club and Jewish schools, the latter of every ideological stripe. In 1904, a Jewish alderman, Moses Finkelstein, was elected to the city council. With practically every dimension of Jewish life represented in some way, Winnipeg became known as "the Jerusalem of the West."[52] After all their efforts to maintain a Jewish existence in Wapella and in Brandon, Ekiel and Mindel Bronfman could hardly have been disappointed with this aspect of their new home. And with six children still to be married — four daughters and two sons — the existence of a large, prosperous Jewish community was a distinct asset.

As the Bronfman sons spread their wings in their hotel operations in southern Manitoba and Saskatchewan, the family nevertheless maintained its unity, with the parental home as headquarters of all family enterprises and a constant source of advice and assistance. Money, so far as one can tell, went into a single pool. About this time Sam dropped out of school to work in the family's establishments. Rose Epstein, a Winnipeg native with a well-to-do background, was slightly younger than Sam; when she was ten years old, she recalled later in life, she spied him through the window of one of his family's hotels one day and made fun of his long white apron, coming almost to his ankles.[53] Although the brothers had occasional spats, they continued to work together as a unit. James Gray interviewed old-timers who remembered the Bronfmans in Winnipeg at the time and reported the impression that the eight Bronfman children even looked alike, despite a significant spread in their ages.

Mindel and Ekiel's household was a busy place, with father and sons constantly coming and going. Harry and Abe returned to Winnipeg from time to time. Ekiel himself kept his hand in the management of the hotels, bailing Abe out of difficulties and helping to finance new operations. Together with his younger brother Allan, soon to enter law school at the University of Manitoba, Sam remained at home, although he travelled periodically to help out Harry or Abe. Visitors turned up as well.

One of these was Barney Aaron, a pious, scholarly young man with some rabbinical training who lived in Lipton, one of the Jewish agricultural colonies, and whose family had known the Bronfmans in Brandon. Shortly after the move to Winnipeg Aaron became engaged to Sam's sister Laura, when both were only nineteen, although they did not marry for another five years.

Gradually, the family's standard of living improved. Ekiel moved twice more — first to 514 Alexander Avenue, "in an old, but well-maintained working-class district," according to Gray; and then to a moderate-sized, frame house at 60 Lily Street, which remained the family home until Mindel and Ekiel died, after the First World War."[54]

Of all the Bronfmans' ventures in this period, the Balmoral Hotel in Yorkton seems to have been the most successful. Harry joined his brother Abe to help him run the place, and eventually took over its management on his own. An establishment of fifty or sixty rooms, the Balmoral was renovated, improved and upgraded. Then in his late teens, Sam visited from Winnipeg to take a hand at the desk, checking people in. Bit by bit, his involvement expanded: he learned some accounting and kept the books for a time; and after some coaching from the cook, he bought the groceries for the hotel, retaining a life-long expertise on cuts of meat. Sam also learned a passable game of pool — sufficient to beat his sons regularly at the table some forty years later. He played the game, he later claimed, as a way of keeping an eye on the customers, who could be a pretty rough lot.[55]

From the Balmoral's profits, the brothers gradually acquired several more hotels. They first sought a "situation" for the scholarly Barney Aaron, their prospective brother-in-law who was without a livelihood. Ekiel and Harry set Aaron up in the Royal Hotel in Yorkton, a rudimentary frame structure on Front Street (rooms cost $1.00 a day in 1905, with "special attention given to commercial travellers," according to an advertisement) only a few blocks from the Balmoral, where he could remain under Harry's careful supervision.[56] Then there was Abe. Although he had blotted his copybook in Yorkton, the eldest son was given another chance in Port Arthur, on the shores of Lake

Superior, when the family took over a resort hotel known as the Mariaggi.

Sam went along with Abe, but before long the two had a falling out — "a terrible quarrel," according to Harry, whose sympathies were not surprisingly with his younger brother, given his own previous troubles with Abe. Ekiel, Mindel and Harry then had an emergency conference in Winnipeg, and decided it was time to set Sam up on his own. Harry looked over the terrain, and settled upon the Bell Hotel in Winnipeg, at the corner of Main Street and Henry Street and a short walk from the family home on Lily Street. According to Harry's memory bank, the price was $200,000, with a $16,000 down payment — a great strain on the family's resources, but one that they could manage, given the modest success they had achieved. Sam was overjoyed. The year was 1912, and he was twenty-three.[57]

It was almost certainly upon taking over the Bell that Sam began to understate his age by two years, claiming ever after that this happened when he was twenty-one. He adopted a Canadian birthplace, Brandon, to go with his amended year of birth, now set as 1891. One can only speculate on the reason why he did so, while noting that among Jewish immigrants from the Pale of Settlement declaring a later (or an earlier) birthdate was not uncommon. Prior to emigration, this seems to have been a defensive strategy for dealing with the Czarist bureaucracy, particularly when under the menace of military conscription. In Canada, the practice continued, to suit any number of purposes. In 1911, the year before Sam acquired the Bell, his older sister Laura understated her age by three years on the marriage certificate when she married Barney Aaron. This put her birth in Canada, in 1891 — although she *did* acknowledge having been born in Russia. In her case she may have simply wanted to appear younger than her husband, who was twenty-four at the time.

As for Sam, a likely reason for his altering the circumstances of his birth was his desire to certify Canadian origins when dealing with Canadian officialdom. Certainly this *became* advantageous after the Bolshevik Revolution of 1917, even if it was not particularly salient in 1912. Finally, Sam's extremely youthful appearance may have had something to do with the matter. Like everyone who knew him then, Harry describes Sam as boyish looking, "with a very young face." Lopping two years off his age might also have been a way of coping with that embarrassing fact while remaining within the age of majority. But however motivated, Sam's new "Canadian" birthdate stuck, for most of his life.

Speaking to the writer Terence Robertson, Sam, in his last years, dwelt upon his early time in the hotels as indicative of the aggressive, entrepreneur-in-the-making — competing furiously with his brothers, quickly mastering financial difficulties, building up his income to a phenomenal $30,000 a year, and making himself into "one of the most eligible bachelors in Winnipeg."[58] In his memoir Harry certainly acknowledged, albeit somewhat grudgingly, "the efficient and business-like manner with which [Sam] carried on his business." But apron strings still bound the future industrialist closely. When he was not in synagogue, Ekiel spent most of his time at the Bell, keeping a watchful eye. Sam shared a bedroom in the hotel with his younger brother Allan, an elegant youth who became the pride of the family when he attended law school at the University of Manitoba. Both brothers took most of their meals at home — only three blocks away — at their mother's insistence. When Mindel became frail (she died in 1918), Harry returned home from Yorkton on the weekends, so most of the family would be together and the men could plot their business strategies together. Sam would indeed emerge from this closely knit family environment, but his rise to pre-eminence was undoubtedly slower, less dramatic and more painstaking than subsequent claims have had it.

CHAPTER II

Bootlegging in the West

By 1912 THE Bronfmans appeared headed for success in the innkeeping trade, with four hotels in three provinces—two in Yorkton, one in Winnipeg and one in Port Arthur. Despite their quarrels, the brothers managed their establishments as part of a collective enterprise, presided over by their father, Ekiel. After an apprenticeship served with Harry and Abe, Sam became a full-fledged contributor when he took over the Bell in Winnipeg, which seems to have been the most profitable of the lot. Although the records of the hotels have been lost, indications are that they generated a healthy income, mainly through the bars, which attracted travellers and locals alike. Unexpectedly, however, the climate changed, not long after Sam acquired the Bell. Wheat prices fell drastically, and fewer hopeful migrants took the trains and roads to the west. At the same time, temperance forces mounted a nation-wide campaign against drink, challenging the family's new livelihood. And then in the summer of 1914 Canada went to war, bringing what was the family's greatest challenge to date—and, as Sam saw it, their greatest opportunity.

■

IN THE YEARS before the First World War the Bronfmans' family enterprise did remarkably well. Harry pressed for expansion, acquiring several more hotels throughout Saskatchewan—in the small towns of Sheho, Leslie, Wynyard and Saltcoats. Versatile and ambitious, Harry also bought land, a livery stable, a garage, and eventually took over a Saskatchewan-wide dealership of Gray-Dort automobiles, fine touring cars manufactured in Chatham, Ontario. Harry managed all of this without ruffling too many feathers. To several people who remembered him from those years, the second-eldest Bronfman brother was mild and easy-going — quite different from Sam, who even then was known for his intensity, explosive temper and remarkable profanity. Widely liked, Harry even thought briefly of running for mayor of Yorkton, until he ran up against the formidable Levi Beck, a rich farmer and one of the most important town notables. Beck, who was also one of Yorkton's leading temperance activists, was reportedly enraged at the very thought of a Jew becoming mayor. Harry decided not to try.[1]

At home in Winnipeg, Sam also showed signs of restlessness. On the advice of a friend, Otto Silverberg, he went briefly into the fur business, one of Winnipeg's key industries, turning a $50,000 profit, he later claimed, on a single deal.[2] But for the most part, Sam concentrated on the Bell, in the city's central core, not far from the CPR railway station and just a short walk from the spanking new Royal Alexandra. The Bell still exists today, its seedy neighbourhood now part of Winnipeg's skid row and its once tasteful interior scarred by countless renovations undertaken on the cheap. A large square brick building, its battered façade has undergone too many face lifts to be recognizable as the establishment of which Sam was so proud in 1912. The Bell seems to have been one of the better grade of hotels at the time, boasting a barber shop and a billiard parlour, and obviously benefiting from Sam's ministrations. Claiming to have been far more interested in improvements than either Abe or Harry, he devoted considerable effort to cleaning up the lobby and redecorating the bar. Sam toned down the harsh lighting, and replaced worn tables and upholstery to create a more pleasant atmosphere. He also dressed the waiters in smart uniforms, lifting the Bell considerably above some of the dives that had given Main Street its unsavoury reputation.[3]

Only Abe, at the Mariaggi, was having trouble. A large, four-storey frame building, still remembered for its splendour by citizens of what is today Thunder Bay, the Mariaggi was named after a Corsican restaurateur and former street musician who ran it as a quality tourist hotel.[4] Not long after Abe took over, the Mariaggi slipped into debt. Apparently Abe was gambling with his guests and at one point had even lost the furniture in a poker game. Ekiel sent Harry and Sam to Port Arthur to bail him out in 1913, and the brothers managed to refinance the operation and set it back on its feet. As with Abe's previous peccadilloes family loyalties prevailed, confidence in Abe was officially restored, and he continued to soldier on.[5]

Despite all their efforts, however, the success of this thriving little empire depended heavily upon one part, and, as it turned out, a highly vulnerable part of the family's establishments — the bars. For although there were plenty of customers, the nature of the hotel business at the time was that profits could only come if customers bought drinks. This was the essential fact of innkeeping life that witnesses repeatedly stressed before the Royal Commission on the Liquor Traffic in Canada in 1894, and had not changed in the two decades that followed. Hotel owners mainly lost money with the meals and accommodation they provided, but amply made it up in the sale of beer and whisky.[6] Clearly, therefore, the Bell's own bar deserved the attention that Sam lavished upon it.

Hotel bars before the First World War were not for the faint of heart; but neither were they all the dens of iniquity that have sometimes been portrayed. Temperance advocates broadcast descriptions of the most sleazy and decrepit among them, when in fact there was a rich variety, ranging in Winnipeg from the most run-down establishments on Main Street to the splendid facilities at the Fort Garry Hotel, which opened in 1913. Often the single public recreational centre in small western towns, and among the very few in large cities as well, these bars were actually at the upper end of the gathering places for males. At the lower end were sometimes fly-by-night saloons, "wholesale boozeries," dimly lit, smoke-filled, grimy little rooms, their sawdust-covered floors stinking of tobacco juice, cigar butts and assorted filth. Whisky in such places was plentiful, poisonous, and, mercifully at times, cut with wine or water. In 1895 the royal commissioners were staggered to hear what people in such places actually drank. But they also heard amply from hotelkeepers protesting their good name as businessmen. The latter pointed their fingers at other licencees, or those with no licences at all.

Whatever their claims to gentility, however, hotels had a difficult time shaking their poor image among respectable people in small and large western communities. In 1908, Harry and Abe ran into trouble with a group of citizens in Yorkton when they had to renew their liquor licence for the Balmoral. Appealing to the provincial authorities, more than a dozen petitioners alleged that the Bronfman brothers were not fit to be granted a licence because of previous liquor violations and because of illicit gambling at the hotel. (The chief complainant was a lady of uncertain reputation named Lottie Ball, who pointed a finger directly at Abe.) In the end the Bronfmans somehow straightened the matter out, mollifying at least some of the petitioners.[7] Abe, as we have already seen, was sent back to Winnipeg and Harry worked hard to upgrade the Balmoral's image. *Henderson's Yorkton Directory* for 1913 noted that twenty of its seventy rooms had private baths and telephones and its claim to be the "headquarters for commercial men." Eventually the hotel became known for its kitchen and Sunday evening dinners: "Harry," local high-livers acknowledged, "always set a good table."

Sam probably needed a thicker skin at the Bell, for Winnipeg was a much larger place, its sins more sinful and its moral shortcomings much more exposed to rebuke.[8] J.S. Woodsworth, the future leader of the socialist CCF, was one of the most articulate and devoted censors of Winnipeg's transgressions during this period. Then a Methodist minister and critic of industrial society, Woodsworth cast an eagle eye over Winnipeg's downtown core in his book on social conditions in 1910, with a map of the "social centres" of the downtown area that included the Bell, together with so many other traps for the innocent. Woodsworth made clear that the problem was not only hotels (marked with and without pool rooms) and their bars, but also pool halls, "picture theatres" and "disorderly houses" — a discreet reference to brothels.[9] Years later, at the United States Senate Kefauver Committee hearings in 1951, a small-time gangster accused the Bronfman hotels of having been in fact a string of whorehouses. Although no evidence was ever presented, the suggestion was too good to ignore, and it has slipped into legend. Sam's supposed response, when confronted with the story near the end of his life, was good-natured enough: "If they were, they were the best in the West."[10] Quality, as we shall see, was close to his heart.

Run-of-the-mill prudery was one thing, and the Bronfmans, like many westerners then and now, confidently addressed the tastes of ordinary people rather than the socially pretentious. But it was quite another thing to withstand the evangelical fervour that swept much of Canada, including the West, in the years before the First World War, and which had as one of its most important objectives a war upon drink.

Fired by the movement within Protestant churches known as the "social gospel," Canadian clerics and lay people alike mounted an inspired assault upon the ills of society, beginning in the last two decades of the nineteenth century. Outraged by signs that the world was not right, that urbanization brought with it materialism, corruption, social dislocation and economic distress, these religious idealists combined a practical bent for reform with the zeal of the righteous for setting moral examples. Their goal, quite simply, was to purify the world and to prepare the Kingdom of God on earth. As historian Ramsay Cook has observed, this special brand of reform upset the traditional Christian focus, making "society rather than the individual . . . the object of salvation."[11] Social gospellers cast a critical searchlight on society, lighting up its dark corners and pushing tirelessly for social change. Typical concerns were carrying the message of God to the poor, public observance of the sabbath, improving conditions of the labouring masses, and, of course, putting an end, once and for all, to the "demon rum." By the First World War this tide of social gospel had come to dominate Canadian Protestantism and ran headlong against, among so many other things, the Bronfman family business.

No one, of course, knew exactly what the Kingdom of God would be like. But one thing was certain for all of those who championed it with so much activism and devotion: in the Kingdom of God there would be no alcohol. And so while there was always plenty to do in the relentless war against sin, eliminating drink became a common denominator among the Christian campaigners to set the world right. That is the principal reason why the "temperance" lobby became so powerful from the end of the nineteenth century to the 1920s, mobilizing what has probably been the most potent mass movement in Canadian history. Champions of the social gospel breathed fire into the organizations set up in the second half of the nineteenth century to address the problem of drink—the Woman's Christian Temperance Union (WCTU), launched in Canada in 1874, and the Dominion Alliance for the Total Suppression of the Liquor Traffic, constituted in 1876 as a federation of hundreds of groups all working for the same end.

The movement to control or eliminate drink originally prompted the federal parliament to pass a Canada Temperance Act in 1878, giving local governments the authority to ban the retail sales of alcohol, but only after popular votes. Taking advantage of this new opportunity, the prohibitionists campaigned for bans throughout the country, often quite successfully. All the while, they kept up the pressure on Ottawa to do more at the national level, hammering away at the issue, particularly during the 1896 election. When Sir Wilfrid Laurier and the Liberals emerged victorious that year, the government agreed to consult Canadians on the matter, nationwide, in 1898. That plebiscite showed the extraordinary strength of the temperance movement across Canada—but also its limitations. Anti-drink forces won every province except Quebec and defeated their opponents—but only by a narrow margin—a majority of 13,687 out of more than half a million votes cast. As was quickly observed, the turnout was low, with less than half of the electorate taking the trouble to vote. Even more important, Quebec remained decisively "wet," as did Catholics elsewhere, posing with stark clarity the government's dilemma: to heed the will of the voters, in this case to ban the sale of alcohol, meant offending a very significant part of the population; to continue with the existing regime meant rejecting a dynamic, highly popular call for change. Daunted by the costs of imposing prohibition, Laurier took the line of least resistance: he left things alone. His reason, he explained politely to the head of the

Dominion Alliance, was that an insufficient proportion of the people had supported the temperance cause.

Deeply disappointed, the anti-drink forces deployed in the various provinces determinedly carried on their struggle. Periodically encouraged by victories on this level, they sharpened their swords for the final battle, readying themselves to overthrow evil and enthrone the righteous. In the interim, there could be no resting, no compromise, no acquiescence in halfway measures. "The only proper attitude of Christians towards the unholy traffic," said a leading Methodist spokesman in 1913, "is one of relentless hostility, and all members of the Methodist Church who possess the elective franchise are urged to use their influence to assure the nomination of municipal and parliamentary candidates known to favour and support prohibition and to use their votes as a solemn trust to elect such candidates."[12]

This was precisely the arena in which the Bronfmans first ran up against the mighty forces of prohibition. Like all licencees, the family wanted to be on the right side of the party in power, particularly when the winds of temperance were beginning to blow. Parties in power were understandably more sensitive than their opposition to the practical difficulties of prohibition and were therefore reluctant to yield to those who wanted to ban the bars. They also enjoyed the patronage that came their way as licencing authorities — another reason to keep the status quo. For these reasons, ruling parties became the family's natural protectors.

In Saskatchewan, where the Liberals were firmly ensconced, Harry was one of their strongest supporters in Yorkton; he did not forget his embarrassing experience of 1908, and knew where his liquor licences came from. In Manitoba, on the other hand, where the powerful Conservative apparatus controlled by Rodmond P. Roblin held sway from 1900 to 1915, Samuel Bronfman became a Tory stalwart. This connection with the Manitoba Conservatives is ironic considering Sam's subsequent support for the Liberals both federally and in Quebec, and in view of the rough treatment the Bronfmans received after the Tories came to power in Ottawa in 1930. But in his calculation, then and later in his career, ideology counted far less than practical results—a fact of life on which he was becoming an expert.

In 1914, therefore, Sam lent the services of the Bell to Roblin's Tory machine. Known as a pompous and arrogant leader, Roblin had helped to fight off temperance forces at the turn of the century; and as a result, the Dominion Alliance and other prohibitionist activists hounded his government for the rest of its days. Sensing an opportunity, Roblin's opponents, the Manitoba Liberals, hoisted the temperance banner — together with a rather unpleasant strain of nativism, which certainly did not endear them to Manitoba's Jews. For Sam Bronfman the choice was clear. During the summer, as Europe slid into war, the provincial voters prepared to go to the polls to decide whether Roblin's government would remain in place against a coalition of temperance, feminist and nativist campaigners. Sam did what he could for the premier, registering dozens of potential Tory voters at his hotel as the rules of the day permitted. Even for the time, however, those rules were stretched, and the opposition cried foul.

As the Liberal *Free Press* charged on July 2, hundreds of fraudulent voters were added to the electoral rolls as a result of bogus naturalizations. According to the paper, the person responsible was Roblin's Winnipeg campaign organizer, Michael J. Johnstone, who just happened to be the chief liquor licence inspector for the Province of Manitoba. It was alleged that Johnstone had drawn hotel and night-club owners — among them Samuel Bronfman — into the practice of illegally registering voters. Together with others, the proprietor of the Bell was hauled before a Court of Revision and required to give evidence so that the fraudulently registered could be kept from the polls. Tight-lipped, Sam offered whatever excuses he could when case after case was presented and his names were struck off the lists. For two days he sweated out the process of inquiry—a highly unpleasant encounter that he endured stoically.[13] Later that month, Roblin's Conservatives squeaked past the Liberals in a narrow electoral victory, only to fall from power the next year, soaked in scandal. For Sam, the experience unquestionably left a very bad taste.

No sooner was this electoral episode off the front pages in

Winnipeg, however, than a much more serious challenge to the Bronfmans' hotels appeared. Across Canada, the outbreak of war energized the temperance movement and drew thousands of citizens to support a campaign to "banish the bars." Temperance, its advocates now insisted, was the cause of patriotism itself, and accusations against drink rained down in a torrent: huge sums were wasted annually, they claimed, on the "liquor traffic" instead of being spent on the war effort; alcohol drained the energies of Canadian manhood; it lowered the productive capacity of the nation and reduced the fighting trim of the troops. The *Banish-the-Bar Crusader* even suggested that drinking places "are meeting places for our Empire's enemies and breeding-places for sedition," "centres for spies and plotters against the country's peace." Quite apart from all their other sins, those who sold whisky were now deemed un-British and disloyal. Speaking in Regina, the General Superintendent of the Methodist Church pulled out all the stops. "The dealings of the liquor trade were the dealings of unpatriotic acts of the men behind the trade," he declared. "[T]he liquor traffic was killing off men by the thousands when the country demanded the best of its sons and when every living person was an asset." Put even more bluntly, as the *Western Prairie* did on one occasion, the liquor interests were in league with the Kaiser.[14]

Having come so far from Ekiel's frozen-fish business, the Bronfman brothers worried now about the vulnerability of their livelihood. Already in 1913, Harry noted in his memoir, the western hotels were in difficulty. The end of the great western boom had come — the collapse of real-estate values, the rise of freight rates and a precipitous fall of farm prices. As a result, fewer travellers rode the railways and stayed at the Bronfmans' hotels. Even more seriously, waves of temperance lapped at the edges of the family's little chain — which now extended into Alberta, thanks to Harry's expansion. One province after another now succumbed to prohibition, with Saskatchewan the first to be engulfed. In the summer of 1915, the province closed its bars and replaced them with government liquor stores; the next year a plebiscite gave the government the authority to close even these. Ontario, Manitoba and Alberta went the same way in 1916, followed by British Columbia the next year. Quebec alone remained wet.

Some time that year, Sam met his older brother Harry in Winnipeg for a council of war; something obviously needed to be done if the family enterprise were to remain afloat. Indications are that Sam was at least Harry's equal at this point, with Abe having relinquished any claim to leadership. Harry bubbled with ideas, but their scope was relatively modest. Mainly, he wanted to concentrate on the automobile business, selling stylish Gray-Dorts, as well as Nashes, Reos, Cadillacs and Oldsmobiles to Saskatchewan farmers. He also speculated, for a time, in real estate. Then a new prospect came along in the person of Philip Brotman, whose family had pioneered at Wapella at the same time as the Bronfmans, and whose father Edel had been the rabbi of the settlement. In 1915 Edel ran a liquor store in Winnipeg. His son invented a "medicated wine" that tasted fine to Harry and seemed likely to catch on in an increasingly parched Saskatchewan. Harry and brother-in-law Barney Aaron went into business with Brotman, and for a time sold all the medicated wine he could produce, operating cheerfully within the law. Difficulties accumulated, however. The partners found impurities in their product, and spent much time filtering and clarifying their concoctions. Before long the Saskatchewan government cast a critical eye on their operation, and closed it down by banning the "medication" that gave the drink its punch.

■

FOR A TIME, Sam continued to run the Bell as a "temperance hotel," but its profits soon disappeared. His good friend Mark Shinbane recalled running into him on Main Street in Winnipeg just as prohibition in Manitoba was imposed in 1916. Winnipeg was about to become bone dry. "Shin," said Sam, "I've got to earn a living. The hotel's not worth a damn."[15] Meanwhile, Harry seemed content to stay with the hotels and his other enterprises, hoping for better times. Sam remembered giving his brother an ultimatum: "You can run flop houses or piddle about in land deals if you want. I'm going east to get into the liquor business."[16]

This idea involved an ingenious leap into the interprovincial liquor trade, a stratagem effectively permitted by Canadian law. For although the provinces had the right to restrict the sale of liquor *within* their boundaries, and had effectively done so, the importation, manufacture and the selling of liquor from one province to another fell within federal jurisdiction. And the authorities in Ottawa, despite being challenged to do so, were slow to move against the liquor business. So the way was clear to sell from province to province, under the cover of federal law.

To acquire stock, Sam went off to Montreal where the major importers and wholesale operations were located and where provincial laws set no restrictions on the sale of liquor. According to Harry, the family treasury was almost bare at that point — he mentions a figure of $15,000 — although Sam later claimed there was more than six times as much money in reserve. But whoever was right, the plunge into this new business was obviously a considerable gamble, given the great scale of operation that Sam contemplated and the uncertain legal prospects in 1916 for selling liquor in Canada.

Sam, who had never been east before, arrived in Montreal with one of his employees from the Bell, a bilingual coachman named Bob Ramsay who went along to negotiate in French. Sam headed directly to one of his few contacts, the large wine and liquor importing firm of Boivin, Wilson & Co., with whom he had dealt as owner of the Bell. This brought him into the orbit of the company's proprietor, Senator Joseph Marcelin Wilson, a prominent businessman of mixed French-Canadian and Scottish parentage, a director of the Bank of Hochelaga and president of the Melcher's Distillery Company of Berthierville — a man, in short, loaded with connections. Through Boivin, Wilson and with the help of one of their associates, the distinguished French-Canadian lawyer Aimé Geoffrion, Sam obtained the licence he needed to import spirits, sell to other provinces and to run a retail operation in Montreal. In short order he opened the Bonaventure Liquor Store Company, downtown, at 563 James Street, in premises formerly occupied by a jewellery shop. From his new storefront, Sam could sell to customers coming in from the street; at the back, where there was a substantial warehouse, liquor could be piled high to the ceiling, and then sent across the country by rail, from the CNR depot a few blocks away.

Using the mails, Sam adapted a marketing format that was extremely important in small towns and isolated settlements such as the Bronfmans had known in Manitoba and Saskatchewan. Westerners, says historian John Thompson, were familiar with "national mail order houses, which sold everything from yard goods to lumber."[17] Patterned on the giant Sears, Roebuck in the United States or the Hudson's Bay Company in Canada, mail-order companies dispatched catalogues far and wide, stored their goods in warehouses conveniently situated for their markets, and reaped the advantages of a very low overhead. Cash arrived before the merchandise was shipped, and so relatively little capital outlay was required.

While an ingenious way around prohibitionist laws, Sam's use of mail-order distribution for whisky was not original, and had been widely used to circumvent prohibition in the United States in the nineteenth century when state and local laws closed down retail outlets. Express companies slashed their rates for large dealers, one of the most important of which was the Hayner Distillery Company of Dayton, Ohio. According to one estimate, some twenty million gallons of liquor reached American consumers through the post in 1911.[18] In Canada, Sam followed in the liquor marketing tracks of the Hudson's Bay Company, even down to the latter's price schedule. But while Hudson's Bay had a huge line of goods and a large corporation to mobilize, Sam enjoyed the advantages of specialization, not to mention an almost unlimited reservoir of his own energy ready to be pumped into the business.

As soon as he set himself up in Montreal, Sam activated his family back in Winnipeg and deployed his brothers in a Napoleonic display of leadership and delegation of authority. Barney Aaron arrived in Montreal, and took over the warehouse at the back of the Bonaventure Liquor Store. Sam then organized warehouse operations in Ontario and Saskatchewan to supply markets in neighbouring provinces. His brother Abe, at loose ends since the Mariaggi bar went dry, was stationed in Kenora,

Ontario, near the Manitoba border and the best export point to
reach the Winnipeg market. Early in the spring of 1916, Sam
found a Kenora hotel that remained wet under local option and
where the liquor licence permitted the importation and storage of
whisky sent from Montreal. In order to buy the hotel, Sam had to
outbid the local mayor, who also wanted it for export purposes.
Rather than wait for the return of the owner, who was away at a
lumber camp in the Lake of the Woods area, Sam went directly to
see him, travelling for six days by dogsled, with a guide. "I was
cold, uncomfortable, and hungry for six of the longest days of my
life," he told Terence Robertson. The guide, it seems, relied on
hunting to feed the two of them. "We ate deer meat every day.
Then, when I got to the camp and made the deal with the owner
of the hotel, I could hardly face the return trip. All that
son-of-a-bitch could shoot was deer. He never even found a
rabbit, a bird or even a bear."[19]

With Abe in Kenora, gateway to the rich markets of Manitoba,
Sam also drew upon Harry in Yorkton, whose Balmoral Hotel
became the relay point for distribution on the prairies.
Thereafter, while the bars closed across much of Canada, the
brothers cheerfully dispatched liquor westwards. Sam busied
himself with mailing lists, catalogues and the running of the
warehouses, travelling constantly to supervise the operation. He
later estimated that he was on trains for all but one hundred days
during the first year. All the merchandise was prepaid by
certified cheque or money order, and his main problem was
getting enough whisky to meet a burgeoning demand. Thanks to
his success in doing so, mainly by buying wholesale lots of
whisky from Canadian and Scotch distillers, the family business
organized itself on a continental scale.[20]

Many years later, when running a giant corporation, Sam liked
to stress two key dimensions of his business that were an echo of
his time as a mail-order salesman. The first was packaging — a
critical concern at the Bonaventure Liquor Store, to ensure that
bottles of Dewar's, Black and White or local rye would reach
their customers without breaking. The second was consumer
trust — an element essential to mail-order houses, where
customers sent money with their orders, confident that the goods
would arrive by return post. Because of attention to these and

other details, and because the demand was so great, business boomed — despite competition from the well-established Hudson's Bay Company, from Boivin, Wilson in some places, and from major Canadian distillers such as Seagram, Corby and Hiram Walker.

Unhappily for the fledgling Bronfman enterprise, however, the federal government of Sir Robert Borden moved to close the mail-order loophole by tightening restrictions at the end of 1917 and the beginning of 1918, and making it illegal to import liquor into Canada and to dispatch it across provincial boundaries. As of April 1, 1918 when the ban on interprovincial shipments became effective, the mail-order business closed down. Later, the government went even further, stopping the manufacture and sale of liquor until one year after the war's end.

Undaunted by Dominion-wide prohibition, Sam discovered a loophole in the legislation. According to what he learned at Boivin, Wilson, it was perfectly legal in Saskatchewan for druggists to import large quantities of liquor to sell "for medicinal purposes." Sam immediately picked up the phone and called Harry. His purpose, as Sam later enjoyed telling it, was to give his older brother his marching orders: "Harry, I'm leaving for Winnipeg tonight. Meet me there. We're going to open up again." And so they did. Within twenty-four hours, according to his memoir, Harry had a wholesale druggist's licence in hand and was preparing to ship whisky to druggists throughout Saskatchewan. Still based in Yorkton, he set up the Canada Drug Pure Company — a thinly disguided liquor outlet that soon pumped more whisky into retail drugstores than any other wholesaler in Saskatchewan. Armed with a provincial licence to sell "patent medicines, druggist sundries," and the like, the Bronfmans then obtained permission from the federal government to open a bonded warehouse in Yorkton and to store whisky shipped from the east. Now a pharmaceutical entrepreneur, Sam continued to run ahead of the tide of prohibition.

These were exciting times for Sam Bronfman, not yet out of his twenties, unmarried, still dining regularly at his parents' table and still living with his younger brother Allan, when he was in Winnipeg at least. For much of the year he was on the road, the one brother who surveyed the whole of the family business and coordinated its several parts. Business, it seems, was Sam's sole preoccupation, save for a brief interruption after the implementation of military conscription in Canada in 1917, when both he and Allan had to report for military duty. Both escaped active service due to flat feet, but according to Harry they underwent training nevertheless — terrified that their frail mother should see them in uniform and learn that they had been mobilized. Mindel, apparently, was unwell, and her health declined rapidly towards the end of the war. She died in November 1918, carried away by the dreadful influenza epidemic that cut such a wide swath across Europe and North America.

The family gathered in Winnipeg for the traditional *shiva*, the week-long period of mourning for the next of kin. During their time together the brothers and sisters resolved to maintain their family's unity which they were told was their mother's last wish. This had been a common theme since the pioneering days in Wapella in 1889. In 1918, however, their solidarity was expressed against a background of growing affluence and not the desperate poverty of their homesteading on the prairies. Thanks largely to Sam, the family was already financially secure, and Sam a rich man. One cannot be certain just how rich, for there are no surviving records of the mail-order operation, and in any event, the proceeds went not to individuals but to the common family coffer — "the Bronfman interests," as Sam put it. Sam's recollection at the end of his life, admittedly hazy, was that he began the mail-order operation with $100,000 in 1916 and wound up with about $500,000 in April 1918 — an enormous success if true, and a substantial war chest with which to make the next move.[21]

FOR A PERIOD of one year after the end of the war, wartime restrictions were in force, and Canada was supposed to be free of alcohol. In fact, however, this was the beginning of a Canadian bonanza in the marketing of "medicinal spirits" — the only booze that could legally be sold. Saskatchewan led the way, with the Bronfman brothers assuming a commanding position in that province. Other entrepreneurs sprang up elsewhere and doctors eagerly lent a hand by supplying prescriptions. In Ontario, wrote Stephen Leacock, to get a bottle of liquor one had merely "to go to a drugstore . . . and lean up against the counter and make a gurgling sound like apoplexy. One often sees these apoplexy cases lined up four deep." In British Columbia, just after the war, one doctor issued 4,100 prescriptions a month and four others signed more than 1,000 each.[22] Regulations differed across the country, but in Saskatchewan, for example, not only could medicinal alcohol be purchased by prescription, but potions with considerable alcoholic content could be bought over the counter. Alongside bottles of familiar brands for prescription only, wonderful remedies now appeared on drugstore shelves: Liver and Kidney Cure, Dandy Bracer, Zig Zag, Rock-a-Bye Cough Cure, and—one of the most fearsome of the lot, according to government inspectors—a "blood purifier" known as Ayers Saspirilla.

Hoping to make Canada permanently bone dry, prohibitionists were understandably affronted by such abuses and mounted a campaign to extend the ban on alcohol sales beyond the end of restrictions set for 1919. Temperance activists marched, petitioned, pledged and prayed. In mid-1919 the legislation they sponsored seemed at the point of passage, despite the province of Quebec's reluctance to join the bandwagon. But it was not to be. In June, responding to pressure from French Canadians, the Senate defeated a temperance bill, and the parliamentarians then agreed to submit the matter to provincial referenda—a course that had been pursued before, and which tended heavily to support the prohibitionists. However, votes were not to be taken until the soldiers returned home and were integrated into society—postponing balloting on the prairies, for example, until October 1920. In the interim, the restrictions were off, and booze flowed again. Across the country whisky dealers now strove frenetically to sell as much as possible before the electorate rang down the curtain on liquor sales.[23]

In short order, the Bronfmans came back to mail-order sales, with a volume even greater than before. It was a golden opportunity, Sam later recalled. "We were back in business. But I made up my mind that this time we would operate right across

Canada."[24] Barney Aaron took up his position in Montreal, now seconded by Abe. Harry stayed in Yorkton, where the family operated a warehouse for their drug business near the Balmoral Hotel. Sam opened new warehouses in Alberta and British Columbia, staffing them with friends and relatives. In Vancouver, operations were handled by Moe Brotman, brother of the inventor of the medicated wine, and a Bronfman brother-in-law Harry Druxerman, married to sister Bea. Druxerman's brother Frank and his sons went to the Edmonton outlet. Sam took charge of purchases, as he later explained to a Royal Commission in 1927, buying huge quantitites of liquor — some from Boivin, Wilson, some from the American companies eagerly unloading supplies on the eve of U.S. Prohibition, and some from Britain. As in the first round of mail-order sales, he raced about the country distributing circulars, stocking warehouses, overseeing the shipments from one province to another. In response to a question posed in 1927, Sam made it clear that he was the one in charge: "I knew more about the liquor bsuiness than Mr Harry Bronfman. In 1920 Mr Harry Bronfman spent more time looking after the City Garage than the liquor business."[25]

Harry, of course, told the story differently. He claimed to have been instrumental in the financing of the business, originally through his Yorkton credit at the Bank of British North America. When the latter was taken over by the Bank of Montreal, Harry said, he went directly to the head office in Montreal and obtained a credit line of $300,000 from president Sir Frederick Williams Taylor — marking him as one of the bank's most favoured customers.[26] Moreover, the drug company Harry oversaw in Yorkton proved to be strategically important for the importation of spirits from the United States, for the Americans permitted exports only for "non-beverage" purposes. In two years no less than 300,000 gallons of liquor flowed from the United States into the warehouse of the Canada Pure Drug Company as medicine, later to be blended, bottled and fed into a Canada-wide sales operation.[27]

The Bronfmans' business was certainly not made to last. Sam knew that it was a temporary, highly fragile enterprise, built on constantly shifting legal sands. Speed was essential. Scotch, gin, brandy and rum arrived in Montreal by the shipload and in a few days was unpacked and sent off westwards by rail. Operating now on a continental scale, Sam spawned some sixteen companies across Canada, all but two of which, the Bonaventure Liquor Store and Canada Pure Drugs in Yorkton, he did not even bother to incorporate. Nor did he trouble himself with income tax — a technicality, he later acknowledged, finally resolved by his lawyers in 1921 when the family settled on a figure of about $200,000 including interest, for the period since 1917.[28]

As before, Sam's mail-order model and principal competitor was the Hudson's Bay Company. In the whisky trade, he obviously felt that he was their peer — despite the fact that he had been a mere hotel owner, one of the "small fry" as he put it himself, just a few years before. Sam and Harry picked up the agency for Dewar's Scotch from the Hudson's Bay Company, and contended that the Bronfmans matched the larger firm in quality goods. Sam loved to tell the story of how he was approached by an executive from the Hudson's Bay wanting urgently to buy two thousand cases of Dewar's, and offering to pay above the normal price if necessary, because they had miscalculated and badly needed the goods to fill an order. Sam's reply was chivalrous, and staked out his claim to be treated seriously by the marketing giant: "I don't want your money. Just let me have the same amount back as soon as you can." His point was that it would be foolish to capitalize on his momentary advantage. With his eye to the long run, as so often, Sam wanted a relationship of trust with "the mighty Hudson's Bay Company," as he called them, and, remarkably, he achieved just this.[29]

When it came to interprovincial trading, the Hudson's Bay Company helped clear the legal ground, testing several aspects of the mail-order business in the courts, and securing the right to proceed. The commerce in medicinal spirits was quite another matter, and involved massive, and usually winked-at misrepresentation on the part of everyone involved — licencing authorities, wholesalers, druggists, doctors and patients. What led to more serious breaches of the law, however, and what gave the entire process of selling liquor in this period the aura of "bootlegging" was a parallel traffic that sprang up alongside the mail-order and pharmaceutical trade, associated in particular with the "export houses" on the prairie provinces. These warehouse outlets caused relatively few difficulties when the selling was from province to province, but things threatened to get out of hand when business turned to the United States, where a huge market opened up with the advent of American prohibition, in 1919.

Remarkably, the start of the second round of the mail-order whisky business in Canada coincided with the ratification of the Eighteenth Amendment to the United States Constitution in January 1919, and the banning of the manufacturing, selling, importing or transporting of "intoxicating liquors" within the United States. In fact, much of the United States had already been dry for some time. Temperance campaigners had been active in that country as in Canada, and were successful, beginning in 1907, in laying down a blanket of restrictions through state and local laws. In 1917 Washington imposed heavy wartime restrictions on alcoholic beverages, and these continued in force during the campaign for ratification of the Eighteenth Amendment. The Volstead Act, designed to enforce prohibition, was passed in October 1919, thus ensuring a smooth transition from one restrictive regime to the next.

As a result, the Canadians selling whisky north of the U.S. border found that many of their customers were Americans. Ready to meet the demand from the United States, the Bronfmans had stored huge supplies of Scotch, rye and gin, plus considerable quantities of pure alcohol in their headquarters in Yorkton. Much of this went through the mails to Canadian customers, but with the beginning of American Prohibition an increasing proportion travelled south, with bootleggers from the U.S. Indeed, the relay points for legitimate interprovincial trade — essentially warehouses in small towns near the provincial borders where whisky was stocked and sold to neighbouring provinces — quickly specialized in the American trade. These "export houses," as they were known, sprouted like mushrooms on the prairies, particularly in Saskatchewan, which became the most important link in the Bronfmans' whisky chain. From the Canadian standpoint, this trade was entirely legal, and was closely monitored by provincial governments, which taxed it through licence fees. What was not legal, however, and what worried the provincial authorities in charge was the constant leakage of liquor to local bootleggers and "blind piggers" who ran an illicit trade alongside that permitted by law. And further, although sale to the Americans was within the law, customers south of the border were generally a rough lot — sometimes small-scale gangsters in fact. As the liquor trade became more important, the stakes became higher and more than a few of the bottleggers extended their lawbreaking into Canada. The result was an occasional shootout, clashes between rival gangs, bank robberies and other breaches of the peace that shocked western opinion and obliged the authorities to crack down.

The key to understanding all this illegal activity was that law enforcement was slack. This was, of course, a feature of prohibition generally — governments had neither the heart, nor the resources, nor the will to keep people away from the whisky they wanted. As columnist Walter Lippmann ruefully observed, "Americans desire to do so many things which they also desire to prohibit."[30] Prohibition politics and administration were greased with abundant hypocrisy, and this in turn encouraged the illicit sale of drink. Political leaders who publicly supported the laws privately stocked their own cellars. In Washington, Congress starved the federal enforcement agencies responsible for eliminating the traffic in alcohol; on the state and local levels conditions varied so widely that the booze had no difficulty finding a way to flow to where it was wanted. Indeed, enforcement proved to be such a colossal headache that the only result of the "noble experiment," in the view of many, was to bring the law into contempt. As a disappointed Clinton Howard of the United Committee for Prohibition Enforcement summed it up in 1925, "prohibition has been enforced half-heartedly at best and with definite intention that it be broken at worst; the law has not been enforced beyond the point where, in the opinion of the enforcers, it would hurt the party in power by enforcing it."[31]

One result of the failure to enforce fully American Prohibition was that Canada became the principal source of supply for drinkers south of the border. From the Maritimes to British Columbia, liquor poured into the United States, by land, sea and air. By the end of 1920, according to a liquor inspector in

Saskatchewan, whisky outlets in that province were handling about 28,000 cases a month — 95 percent of it going to the United States.[32] Official statistics on the value of Canadian liquor exports to the United States, noting only that portion of the trade that kept within Canadian law, registered $3,081,000 in 1922, and soared out of sight thereafter.[33] The American authorities, increasingly angry at the flagrant breach of their laws, protested vigorously to Ottawa and began an acrimonious debate that was concluded only with the end of Prohibition in 1933.

In this vast movement south, a highly competitive trade on the Canadian side, the Bronfmans found themselves particularly well situated in Saskatchewan. Through his drug firm, Harry had accumulated a vast stock in Yorkton. Then, as business picked up, Sam opened subsidiaries in small towns near the American border, in Gainsborough, Estevan, Carievale, Oxbow, Carnduff and Bienfait. Other entrepreneurs did likewise, and eventually some sixty-nine export houses dotted the landscape — "the scandal of Saskatchewan" as the local prohibitionists said. Of the twenty or so houses along the American border, the Bronfmans owned about half. Most of the rest were controlled by two Regina-based associates, Meyer Chechik and Harry Rabino- vitch, operating within the framework of the Prairie Drug Company and the Regina Wine and Spirit & Co. The Hudson's Bay Company and Boivin, Wilson Company of Montreal also had export houses in Regina and Saskatoon, and, in the early days at least, did a heavy volume of business.[34]

To temperance activists, these export houses were a "reproach to civilization," their owners "anarchists," and their customers the scum of the earth. The most common problem was bad cheques — amounting to over $100,000 in losses in the last three months of 1920 alone, according to an inspector from the Saskatchewan Liquor Commission. One of the largest, the same source reported, cost the Bronfmans' house in Bienfait $9,500.[35] Violence, however, was a much greater threat to the general public. "The most desperate men are engaged in the business," reported the *Presbyterian Witness* in 1921. "Rifles can be seen in some instances sticking out of the cars. Airplanes have also come north and have loaded up with liquor and returned."[36] The inhabitants of sleepy western towns could hardly have appreciated the implantation of virtual fortresses, bristling with defences against the very criminal elements they attracted: the export houses barred their windows, padlocked all the doors, stationed armed guards at the entrances, and equipped themselves with burglar alarms. Even so there was trouble occasionally, and periodic visits from the police. Raids from hijackers who attacked liquor convoys occurred; gunfights sometimes resulted, with defenders barring themselves in the houses for their own protection.

American rum runners perfected their techniques and pioneered in the use of automobiles for smuggling purposes. The bootleggers who loaded up at the export houses preferred specially outfitted touring cars with lots of room — Studebakers were one favourite, but Hudsons, Chryslers or any large sedan would do. Rum runners removed the rear seats, and souped up the motors. Sometimes called "whisky sixes" because of their powerful six-cylinder engines, the rum runners' vehicles were equipped with spotlights to blind the eyes of pursuers by night, and thirty-foot chains to raise huge clouds of dust along dirt roads, assisting the cars to escape capture. For most, the Canadian side of the border was the quietest. The real trouble came once the cars entered the United States, sometimes to find enforcement agents waiting in ambush. An even greater danger came from hijackers who would make off with the money on the outward journey, or the whisky on the return trip. For all the difficulties, the trips were extremely lucrative. Once into the United States, prairie rum runners drove as far as Kansas or Colorado with their hauls of booze; closer at hand, huge markets beckoned in Chicago, St Paul, Minneapolis or Omaha. According to historian Daniel Boorstin, the use of these automobiles stampled out a new colloquial vocabulary — "getaway car," or "taking someone for a ride" — linking the automobile to a pervasive, motorized criminality associated with the Prohibition era.[37]

Until they were closed by Saskatchewan law in 1922, the export houses reaped handsome profits by selling to the Americans. The Bronfman brothers — largely Harry, with Sam exercising control from afar — dominated the trade in that province, along with the Chechik-Rabinovitch group. The

family installed trusted friends and relatives in their Saskatchewan branches: Monte Rosebourne in Bienfait, Harry's brother-
in-law Dave Gallaman in Estevan, Max Heppner, whom the
family knew from the Wapella days, in Gainsborough. Paul
Matoff, the husband of the Bronfmans' sister Jean, had a hand in
several export houses, and found himself in Bienfait—fatally, it
turned out—in the autumn of 1922.

To understand how this commerce worked in detail, one must
take care not to overstress the more flamboyant aspects of the
trade. Admittedly, the criminal element lent an aura of glamour
and notoriety to liquor sales, and gave ample ammunition to the
still-frustrated temperance campaigners. So did the presence of
so many Jews in the trade, a point hardly overlooked by those for
whom the sale of whisky was a moral abomination and an assault
upon Christian society. Yet most of the commerce was routine,
closely monitored by the Saskatchewan liquor authorities, and in
their eyes above board. As such it left a trail of paper—utterly
routine correspondence, penned without the slightest apprehen-
sion that some of the traffic might be illegal.

The Saskatchewan Temperance Act required export houses to
submit *daily* returns on a special form E 110, listing the name and
address of each purchaser, together with the kind and quantity of
liquor purchased. Similar reports had to be sent weekly—
duplicating much of the paper work. So far as the Saskatchewan
Liquor Commission was concerned, the family's export houses
discharged their obligations reliably, and historian Erhard Pinno,
citing one inspector, notes that the Bronfmans were "most
businesslike in their operation and very anxious to keep within
the letter of the law."[38] Several months' worth of reports for the
Bronfmans' export house in Bienfait have survived for 1920 and
1921 and help bring down to earth some of the more extravagant
suppositions about the export trade and the secretive commerce
associated with them. Only ten miles from the American border,
Bienfait (pronounced "Bean-fate" by the locals) became one of
the principal outlets for American rum runners coming into
Canada from neighbouring North Dakota. Originally a mail-
order outlet for Alberta, Manitoba and even Ontario, the Bienfait
house was by 1921 catering almost exclusively to the American

rum runners from border towns such as Crosby, Portal, Larson and Bowbells.

Liquor was sold by the case — as many as two dozen could be carried away by car, but usually the shipments involved much less — by gallon jugs or by the bottle. Stock sheets show a wide range of brands — Corby, Seagram, Canadian Club, Booth's Dry Gin, together with no-name products at the lower end of the scale. Each day the Bronfmans' Yorkton Distributing Company, Bienfait Branch enumerated for the provincial authorities in Regina the precise amount of liquor, pure alcohol or beer carried away by the American visitors. Each report was methodically acknowledged by mail from the Chief Inspector's office of the Saskatchewan Liquor Commission. Periodically, inspectors from the Liquor Commission in Regina showed up. Writing from Oxbow in December 1920, a genial Inspector R. Forsyte pronounced Bienfait to be "one of the best houses I have inspected," and offered particular commendation for the manager, Monte Rosebourne. Occasionally one gathers, the inspectors went away from Bienfait with a few complimentary bottles of Scotch or rye as a sign of good will. Other documentation suggest that while the Bienfait export house more than earned its keep, it hardly reaped the spectacular profits that have sometimes been alleged. An accounting for a period of just over six months in the first half of 1922 shows that on gross sales of $63,778.15 there was a profit of $14,271.02, or 22 percent, after deducting the cost of the liquor itself and such expenses as wages of $3,176.05, shipping $954.34, rent of $825.00, telephone of $326.10 and a $1,000 licence fee.[39]

It is possible that the Bronfmans, or at least Sam, tried to keep relations with important American bootleggers at arm's length. Long afterwards, Sam claimed he warned Harry to steer clear of criminal elements. Sam himself cultivated the American market through an agent, a former Winnipeg bartender named Harry Sokol whose job was to line up customers south of the border, and to convince them of the advantages of dealing with the Bronfman family enterprise. Sokol, a nondrinking bachelor and reputed ladies' man who was living in the Royal Alexandra Hotel at the time, apparently worked with a St Paul, Minnesota, bootlegger named Fred Lundquist, who in turn had links with the tough liquor men of Minneapolis and Chicago. Part of the inducement Sokol offered, it seems, was a guarantee to the Americans that while on the Canadian side of the border the Bronfmans would assist them if they got into trouble with the police.[40] As we shall see, these arrangements eventually backfired, bringing the entire Bronfman operation into the public eye and causing Harry, in particular, considerable difficulty with the law.

■

LOOKING BACK, ONE can see how the Bronfmans' border trade, particularly in Saskatchewan, was heading for trouble. For one thing, the provincial authorities came under heavy pressure from temperance groups to limit the liquor traffic, restrict the operation of the export houses or put them out of business altogether. Indeed, the entire liquor trade seemed to be coming to a dead end, with provincial votes scheduled on the liquor question. The likelihood was that some form of prohibition, perhaps on the order of the tight wartime restrictions, would soon come into place. All expectations were that interprovincial sales and exports to the United States would soon cease — prompting everyone to work furiously for as long as the commerce lasted and not worry too much about details. Finally, some law enforcement agents grew bitter at the whisky trade; for them it was a short-term anomaly that slipped through legal loopholes and made some people fabulously rich, while others stood by and watched.

One of the persistent problems the brothers faced as they shipped their liquor across the American border was supply: Sam seems to have been selling whisky through the mails and the export houses as fast as it could be obtained in Montreal. To increase supply, and to put yet another notch on his gun as someone who "knew more about the liquor business than Mr Harry," Sam took an audacious step: he decided to blend his own stock. Yorkton was the obvious place to do so, since as we have seen, the Canada Pure Drug company was in a position to import vast quantities of neutral spirits from the United States, supposedly to be made into medicine — something the Bronfmans were permitted to do under their provincial and federal charters.

Blending, moreover, offered the family an extraordinary business opportunity. By mixing large quantities of relatively inexpensive over-proof neutral spirits with distilled water and a relatively small amount of over-proof whisky, plus a dash of colouring and flavouring, a small quantity of expertly distilled whisky could be made to go a long way. In very crude outline, this is what blenders and wholesalers in England and Scotland normally did, but in the case of the Bronfman brothers, completely inexperienced, without proper equipment, and with no time to age the blend in barrels, the project almost led to disaster.

For their very first batch Sam and Harry mixed 100 gallons of rye whisky, 318 gallons of raw alcohol and 382 gallons of water, to make 800 gallons of "whisky." Unfortunately, when the ingredients were all poured into brand-new redwood tanks, the result was ghastly — a dirty-bluish liquid instead of the expected warm, caramel-coloured spirit. Something had gone terribly wrong, and in the Bronfmans' view the problem was the wooden tanks. The details came out months later, when the family sued the Winnipeg company from which they had purchased the allegedly faulty equipment.[41]

Before the Court of King's Bench in Yorkton, the supply company's lawyers tried to undermine Sam's authority as a blender, pointing out that he had no technical experience and had never worked for a large blending firm. On the witness stand, Sam stubbornly stood his ground. His experience, he insisted, derived "from my own business." As for Harry, Sam replied somewhat airily: "he has blended whisky all his life and met with general success." To bolster his claim, Sam argued that the family had lost considerable money on this batch, not to mention what they had paid for the poor-quality equipment. Nevertheless, as he boldly explained, they salvaged what they could: "I tried to work it off in every 100 gallons of the regular blends 10 gallons of this discoloured liquor." Sam claimed to have given instructions to his blenders "all over Canada" (he certainly exaggerated here) to maintain an acceptable coloration, making it clear that "the blends that I make up is what they go by." He then went on to give a little lesson in his newly learned blender's trade: "You take two or three classes of liquor, take the dearer and cheaper blends to bring down the cost of the liquor. You bring it down that way by mixing. If you have got a lot of customers who want to buy a lot of cheaper liquor you blend the higher grade of liquor with the lower grade spirit." Sam claimed to have cut his losses to about fifty cents a gallon, through careful blending and diluting of the dirty-blue batch.

In the end, not only did the family fail to carry the day against the Blenders' and Bottlers' Supply Company, they also suffered from the extensive publicity given to the trial by the anti-whisky *Winnipeg Tribune* and the sport that was made ever since of the Seagram magnate's first blending efforts. But one should remember that the Bronfmans, and not the supply company, wanted to go to court. At the time, no one suggested that their Yorkton operation was illegal, and the reason the matter came to trial in the first place was that the brothers were convinced they were in the right. In 1927 the Royal Commission on Customs and Excise returned to the case, charging the brothers with illegally compounding whisky—a mixing of extraneous spirits, such as rum with brandy or gin with whisky, a practice frowned upon in the trade. Sam's reply was that he had blended, not compounded—"we would do what every mail or liquor house or wholesale liquor house has done as long as Canada has been in the liquor trade to my knowledge, make up blends of their own . . ."[42]

For much of the market in the early 1920s standardized products, modern bottling techniques and efficient quality control were things of the future.[43] Given the brothers' inexperience with the blender's art, therefore, it is hardly surprising that they ran into trouble. And given as well the poor quality whisky that many customers normally drank, discolouration may have been the least of problems periodically encountered. Still, what happened with the "blue" whisky was probably not the Bronfmans' fault at all, and there is no indication that their liquor was substandard. According to Mel Griffin, a former Seagram production manager, such discolouring as they experienced is not uncommon, and was likely caused by the presence of a tiny piece of metal in the brand-new wooden vats in which the whisky was prepared. Old hands in the field, which the Bronfmans decidedly were not at this point, knew how to rectify matters almost immediately by adding a small quantity of cow's milk, then agitating and filtering the whisky.[44] Nevertheless, to many readers of the *Winnipeg Tribune*, not kindly disposed to the "liquor interests" in the first place, the story of the "bad batch" probably suggested that the Bronfmans were producing poisonous mixtures, for exorbitant profits.

Seventy years later, it is impossible to compute accurately just how much money the brothers earned from the blending part of their business. Calculations have been made ever since the *Tribune* tried its hand in 1922, and the results have varied enormously. In the bad-batch case, Harry testified that his costs amounted to $5.25 a gallon, but this did not include bottling, packaging and marketing, plus overhead for the production and storage facilities. On the basis of an output of 20,000 gallons a month (and using somewhat shaky arithmetic), the *Tribune* calculated a gross revenue of $500,000 a month and a cost of $109,000—for a profit of $391,000 a month. (The profit, correctly calculated, should have been $395,000.) Since the paper grossly understated costs, this figure could probably be cut in half, but for obvious reasons we will never know for sure.[45]

Much easier to grasp, however, is what lay behind the whole move into blending—Sam's boundless drive and his unshakeable belief that, in a furiously competitive trade, he could outproduce and outsell anyone in the field. For this, it is clear, is what led the brothers into blending in the first place. As writer James Gray points out, Sam and Harry "probably knew as much about chemistry as they knew about chiropractic or choreography."[46] Nevertheless, they boldly undertook to produce their own whisky, made substantial investments in equipment, and imported huge quantities of alcohol from Illinois and Ontario distillers. And despite their misstep, they soon were bottling their own liquor, in vast quantities.

Sam and Harry were undoubtedly sincere when they cried foul at the press campaign against them, and Sam's subsequent obsession with quality, which became legendary in his Seagram whisky empire, may well have begun at this point, if it did not exist before, stung by the indignity of having his products challenged in the public press. Certainly the brothers must have regretted mightily going to court with their equipment supplier. Thereafter, the brothers had to be on their guard constantly to see that their liquor passed muster, and some evidence suggests that they were successful. One former customer from Calgary, a Jewish retailer named Jack Diamond, noted that he seldom had a complaint about the Bronfmans' brands: "we did a lot of business with Sam Bronfman, who was the one we dealt with. We could get their brands for fifty cents or a dollar a case less than the Hudson's Bay or the Montreal wholesalers would charge. We thought it was every bit as good but then, as you know, Jews have never cultivated a taste for whisky so we had to rely on what our customers told us."[47]

The brothers were soon putting their own blends on the market as fast as labels arrived from a supplier in Montreal. Sam later recalled some of his first brands — "Prince of Wales," "Old Highland Scotch," "Superior Rye," or "Parker's Irish Whisky." Sam dreamed up the names and the company printed the labels. Soon he found an even better source of supply with Bulman Brothers from Winnipeg who provided their own "stock" labels — "Special Vat Old Highland Scotch," "Gold Label Special Blend Scotch Whisky," "Melrose Special Reserve," "Old Private Stock" and so on. All of these were "fictitious" — not only in the sense of not being established brands but in the extravagant claims of Scottish ancestry as well.

Still, it is unlikely that contemporaries took such claims seriously. Indeed, for many of the Bronfmans' western customers established brands were themselves an unnecessary frill — certainly nothing one would be willing to pay for. Most Canadian customers were used to buying whatever was offered, and many indeed preferred to mix their own drinks, just as people rolled their own cigarettes, buying two- or five-gallon tins of alcohol that could then be diluted with water and flavoured as they liked. American bootleggers sometimes had more refined tastes, but they too carried away substantial quantities of straight alcohol to be made into whisky south of the border.

Some of the boldness of the Bronfmans' operation may be explained by Sam's feeling that his entire operation was living on borrowed time. Opinion ran increasingly against the "liquor interests," even among those who opposed all-out prohibition. Many so-called "wets" did not favour a completely open system at all, but rather the reverse, in the form of government control. This "moderationist" view, which ultimately prevailed in Canada, was almost as threatening to the Bronfmans' business at the time as outright prohibition. When the referendum finally occurred in October 1920, a substantial majority of the voters supported the "drys," although the force of their victory was weakened once again by a low turnout. After this referendum and similar votes elsewhere, Ottawa announced it would end the shipping of liquor from province to province in early 1921. This doomed the mail-order business, and while it still permitted the export houses to operate, they could continue only so long as their existing supplies of liquor lasted. The noose began to tighten.

In response to these developments Sam and Harry tapped a rich vein of trouble when they entered into a partnership with Meyer Chechik, Harry Rabinovitch and Zasu Natanson—three flamboyant characters with a talent for complicated business transactions that teetered on the edge of legality. Sam and Harry's objective seems to have been that they should pool resources with their chief competitors in the Saskatchewan export trade, divide the rapidly shrinking market between them, and, as the export houses began to close, keep their operations afloat for as long as they could. Fine in theory, the partnership soon foundered on the sharp personalities of the individuals involved.

Sam and Harry were somewhat feisty, as we have seen, but they were the very essence of diplomacy in comparison with their new associates, who displayed an unending appetite for quarrelling with everyone, including each other. Harry Rabinovitch was wanted by the police in Minneapolis for having jumped $15,000 bail on charges relating to the death of a trucker in a liquor hijacking case. Natanson was a Regina junk dealer who ran one of their branch operations, the Regina Wine and Spirit Company. Chechik, who turned out to be the most quarrelsome of the lot, was a former Winnipeg wine merchant and one-time chicken wholesaler, highly sensitive to his own lack of polish and education.[48] From Sam's point of view, the partnership was not ideal. "We should never have gotten mixed up with those people," he later said, claiming that the relationship was Harry's idea, and not his own. "They were slick operators, too smart for their own good. But I didn't think the grass could stay green much longer, so if this crowd were willing to ship our stuff south as well as their own I couldn't complain." They had only, Sam figured, about six months left.[49]

In mid-1921 the partners set up shop in the Craftsman Building in Regina, at the corner of McIntyre Street and Sixth Avenue, constituting themselves as the Dominion Distributors. Establishing the partnership took some doing, for there were endless complications involved in pooling their stocks when liquor was not supposed to be sold at all within provincial boundaries. To get around this difficulty, each group maintained title to their own liquor; Dominion Distributors would control export sales, and the partners would divide the profits. From the start, however, the partners had difficulty determining how much each party brought to the arrangement. Everyone submitted claims and counterclaims, and each side disputed the bookkeeping of the other. Then too, problems arose over the quality of some of the liquor that Chechik and Rabinovitch fed into the pool; Harry complained that much of this was "poor stuff," needing to be reblended and rebottled before it could be sold. To solve all of these problems required time, energy and money. Meanwhile, business on the United States border continued at its frenetic pace.

The storms at Dominion Distributors continued to rage until the partnership was dissolved at the end of 1922 — at which point the parties were hardly on speaking terms. Throughout the course of the arrangement Chechik continued to live in Winnipeg and travelled extensively in Europe, supposedly on business. He complained constantly that his former partners, based in Regina, or his present partners, or both, were trying to cheat him of the profits of the business. Innocent of bookkeeping, Chechik was mystified by the accounting system the business used. "I didn't know much about books," he told lawyers for the other partners when questioned in 1923. "If a man will explain to me I will understand it, otherwise I am no good at books."[50] Most of his time was spent quarrelling with Rabinovitch and Natanson; later, however, he argued that Harry Bronfman had been behind all the difficulty, stirring up his original partners against him. At a certain point it was agreed that the Bronfmans would buy out their unhappy partner (something that would have required an heroic legal effort, given the laws in force), but since Chechik was embroiled in lawsuits against Natanson and Rabinovitch, the Bronfmans' lawyer, A.J. Andrews, K.C., advised them to wait until these actions were settled. And so the relationship festered.

Sam seems to have been content to let Harry run the operation—a thankless task given the personalities involved. In Harry's view, Chechik and Rabinovitch were "entirely useless to meet any contingency that arose and [were] of no assistance to the business whatever." To his own lawyers, Harry complained about the suffering his partners caused him:

> They merely sat around the office figuring out how to get all they could for everything they put into the partnership and how to give the Bronfmans as little as possible for what they put in, and generally scrutinizing everything with a view of destructive criticism, at the same time carefully going over everything and informing themselves as to all the details of the business and watching carefully their interests in the settlements. Chechik's main objective throughout was to get advances of monies from time to time in anticipation of receipts so much so that the Bronfmans had on two occasions in addition to holding their cheques until monies came in, to loan the partnership $25,000 once and $20,000 another time in order to be able to carry on. Chechik and Rabinovitch always obtained and cashed their cheques first.[51]

In October 1921, in one of his lightning visits to Regina, Chechik became suspicious of his original partners, and hired private detectives to investigate. He concluded that Rabinovitch and Natanson had been cheating him—and the government—by secretly removing liquor from bond and hiding the liquor behind a secret partition in their warehouse.

Details about this affair became clouded over the years, with Chechik's account shifting, and also differing notably from the other participants. By 1927, when he testified before a Royal Commission, Chechik was placing the principal blame for wrongdoing on the Bronfmans, and charged Sam with bullying him into keeping quiet about the theft lest the authorities get wind of more extensive illegality; at the time, however, his main grudge seems to have been against his original partners and his inclination was to call upon the Bronfmans as mediators, with a view to putting the partnership back in working order. Harry maintained that he "was continually kept on the jump smoothing over various difficulties that arose from time to time."

Sam himself made no record of his involvement, leaving Harry to represent the family's position in subsequent legal actions and hearings before the Royal Commission. During much of 1921 and 1922, as we shall see, Sam was on the road, closing the mail-order side of the business, moving stock from one place to another, and preparing to wind down the export operation. He was also deeply in love: his courtship of Saidye Rosner in Winnipeg began the same time that the troubles with Meyer Chechik reached a crisis. Harry, living now in Regina, found himself therefore on the firing line.

Harry also bore the burden of a clash with a resentful, impecunious customs official, Cyril Knowles, whose detestation of the Bronfmans blossomed in 1921 and continued to flower for at least a decade thereafter. Slight, pale and thin-faced, Cyril Knowles had been diligently working as an employee of the Department of Customs and Excise while rum runners were making fortunes on the Canadian prairies. Having briefly served as a foot soldier in the Conservative Party, he had risen laboriously through the ranks of the Customs Department to become assistant preventative officer in the Port of Winnipeg in 1919. (His younger brother Vernon, a newspaperman, had done better, and was managing editor of the *Winnipeg Tribune* — in a position to do the Bronfmans a bad turn, as we have already seen.) Then a law student, Sam's friend Mark Shinbane occasionally went trout fishing with Cyril Knowles about that time, and recalled him as "a peculiar fellow [who] had a very suspicious mind against all and any people who dealt in drugs or whisky." A bitter, unhappy, uncommunicative individual, Knowles was married to an Eskimo woman who spoke very little English: "she was a decent but a simple kind of person," Shinbane went on, "and Cyril was very rough with her. I couldn't help in this small cabin overhear what was going on. I had a small cot there and I could hear high words."[52]

As James Gray observes, Knowles was not the sort of civil servant who would have been satisfied pushing papers in Winnipeg.[53] Obstinate and aggressive in his pursuit of customs violators, Knowles picked up information from some of his informers about rum runners who frequented some of the Bronfmans' border houses in Saskatchewan. One day in December 1920, accompanied by Constable Allan Piper of the RCMP, Knowles pounced upon some of the American visitors who had stocked up at the Gainsborough outlet and were on their way back to the United States. Surprised at being arrested and doubtless believing that they were legally in the clear, the rum runners invoked the name of Harry Bronfman, whom they expected could straighten out the entire matter. Knowles followed their suggestion that he visit Harry, and later claimed that Bronfman had offered him a bribe — a figure of $3,000 was mentioned — which he promptly refused.[54]

Harry's version was different. What happened, he later claimed, was that the customs officer had grossly overstepped his authority and improperly seized the liquor and cash in the cars. Harry admitted only to losing his temper and raging at Knowles: "You are no man at all. . . . If you will take off your badge and come outside with me as man to man, if you will stand up to me for ten minutes I will give you twice as much money."[55]

Knowles stuck to his story about a bribe, claiming that he immediately reported it to Ottawa, but found officials there curiously unresponsive. Indeed, Knowles began to suspect that Harry had somehow gotten the ear of his superiors, who blocked payment to him of the bounties that customs officers normally received when they seized illegally transported whisky. Undaunted, however, the zealous customs inspector remained on the Bronfmans' track, seeking some infraction by the export houses and keeping a careful watch on their customers as well, hoping to catch them violating Canadian law. Continuing his pursuit of illegal liquor, he may have been behind a raid on one of the family's export houses in Moose Jaw, run by

Harry's brother-in-law David Gallaman and an associate, Sam Tadman.

Knowles must have believed revenge was near one evening in January 1922, when he raided Dominion Distributors in the Craftsman Building in Regina, suspecting that the company was compounding and bottling whisky in violation of the Customs and Excise Act. Rummaging through the warehouse, Knowles uncovered what he believed to be incriminating evidence — whisky-making equipment, labels from Bulman Brothers, plus materials allegedly used to make counterfeit U.S. revenue stamps. Knowles returned to the warehouse the next day, and, according to one of the employees present, he spent several hours smashing casks and breaking open cases. Even more concrete evidence of lawbreaking came to light at Zasu Natanson's junk dealership, leading to Natanson's arrest.

A few days later, Chechik, Rabinovitch, Harry and Sam met at Harry's house to deal with the emergency. In Harry's words, "the most important thing . . . was to get Knowles away from Regina and after some long distance telephoning and expense [Harry mentioned the sum of $2,000] the Bronfmans arranged this."[56] Sure enough, Knowles was recalled to Ottawa shortly thereafter.

The Bronfmans had evidently pulled some strings — possibly with the help of Sam's influential friends at Boivin, Wilson in Montreal. Sam then mobilized his younger brother Allan to go with him to Ottawa to see the minister, the Hon. Jacques Bureau — a Liberal politician friendly to the liquor interests and a notoriously unscrupulous character, later implicated in what was perhaps the worst customs scandal in Canadian history. Unabashed, Sam and his brother made their case. In Allan's words, "I simply related the facts of what had happened at the Craftsman Building to the minister. We complained that Inspector Knowles had behaved rather badly by showing complete lack of respect for private property. Though we didn't specifically ask disciplinary action be taken, it was probably implicit in our complaint."[57]

Did cash or favours change hands? Knowles believed so, but no conclusive evidence has ever come to light. What is certain is that Knowles was crushed. In 1927 he told the Royal

Commission of how he waited outside the minister's office in the corridor for about two hours while Sam and Allan made their complaints. When he was finally called on the carpet, he received a brutal message: he had exceeded his authority, and was to be recalled immediately. For a time, very short as it turned out, the heat was off the Bronfmans' whisky enterprise.

■

NEARLY ALWAYS ON the road during the last phase of interprovincial trading, the thirty-three-year-old Sam maintained a residence in Winnipeg, keeping in touch with the far-flung family sales network by telephone and telegraph. For Sam, as for his brothers and sisters, Winnipeg was still home. Nevertheless, things changed dramatically after Mindel's death in 1918. Ekiel retreated from his sons' businesses, and became increasingly involved in Jewish community affairs, loans to poor Jewish immigrants, and the construction of a Jewish orphanage in 1919. He became ill that year, and went with his sons to the Mayo Clinic in Rochester, Minnesota, for treatment. But to no avail. Ekiel died at the end of December, on the last day of Chanuka, as Harry remembered — exactly thirteen months after Mindel passed away. Sister Rose, for a time, maintained the family home on Lily Street, but eventually it was sold, and the money donated to the Talmud Torah school in Winnipeg. Sam, Allan and Rose then moved into the opulent Fort Garry Hotel, where they lived until mid-1922.

Sam's relationship with Harry was sometimes difficult, but the bond between the two was strong. "Hello Opposition," Harry began one good-natured letter to Sam from Winnipeg, which perhaps sums up the older brother's view of the increasingly domineering member of the family. Sam responded via Saidye Rosner, who, as we shall see, had become his fiancée: "Thank Harry for his letter, and tell him to make the best of his time while the opposition is away. But no doubt he is doing his best making hay while the sun shines. Pretty easy sailing just now eh?"

Sam's closest associate at the time was his brother Allan, twenty-five years old and a member of the prominent Winnipeg law firm of Andrews, Andrews, Burbidge and Bastedo. To the extent one can tell, Sam's politics continued to be Conservative: his lawyer was the senior partner in Allan's firm, A.J. (Alf) Andrews, a one-time mayor of Winnipeg and a friend of Tory chieftain Arthur Meighen, then a leading member of Sir Robert Borden's Unionist government. During the Winnipeg general strike of 1919 Andrews was a key man in a "Citizens Committee of One Thousand," an influential group opposed to the strikers. Taking a hard line, Andrews nevertheless restrained some of the more extreme anti-strike activists — including Meighen himself, then acting minister of justice in Ottawa. Together with his wife, Andrews attended Sam's wedding in 1922, and their correspondence from a few years later, when Sam had moved to Montreal, shows warmth and mutual respect. And it was Alf Andrews, as we shall see, who sat by Sam's elbow during the Royal Commission on Customs and Excise hearings in 1927. To Sam, a young businessman hungry for political support, Andrews was a valued contact.

Besides his business, Sam had few interests. Family loyalties came first, as the brothers and sisters reminded each other in their occasional correspondence. A university student in Winnipeg at the end of 1918, Sam's sister Rose sent him a few photographs of their mother who had died several weeks before. Rose noted that each morning while he was on the road Sam was saying *kaddish*, the mourner's prayer. She wrote to thank him for having sent her a sealskin coat, but also to commune about the loss of their mother, for the wound was deep. "Should you face any matter that may cause you reason for reflection — think of Mother, study her photograph, and think of her sincerely, think of how she would advise you; of her teachings and love for you, what she would want you to do, and feel sure you will not go amiss. For she always taught us the right ways, her life was devoted to us and the least we can do to repay her utter unselfishness is to honour her memory in every way possible and above all to follow in the path she pointed out for us . . . all I know she would wish is that we should keep together and love each other and think of helping each other."[58]

Ekiel's death in 1919 brought the brothers and sisters to the family home on Lily Street for one last time. The children, according to Harry, "never realized how great the loss would be until we were actually confronted with this grave condition." Having just finished the prescribed year of *kaddish* for their mother, they then carried on with another year of prayers for their father. Bronfman lore had it that "keeping the family together" had been Ekiel's last wish, as it had been Mindel's. Later, Sam recounted a further refinement for his own family, which he repeated for *Fortune* magazine nearly half a century later, according to which Ekiel had designated Sam, though only the third eldest, to look after them all and to become, in effect, the head of the family.[59]

The Bronfman brothers' involvement in Jewish community affairs began at the time of Ekiel's death and was one way of carrying out their parents' wishes. Allan took on Ekiel's work with the Jewish orphanage, becoming its president in 1921. In the spring of that year, the Zionist leader Chaim Weizmann travelled through Canada and the United States to drum up support for the Jewish colonization of Palestine. Most who heard this message at the time understood it as a philanthropic exercise, and among them were certainly Sam and Allan. Sam later claimed to have met Weizmann in Montreal and to have travelled on the train with him all the way to Winnipeg, having extensive discussions of Zionist affairs. The story may have become embellished over the years; still, Weizmann did stay in the Fort Garry Hotel and the two may indeed have met. Nearly twenty years later the brothers reminded Weizmann of their earlier encounter, when they telegraphed their congratulations to the Zionist elder statesman as first president of the recently declared State of Israel.[60]

Sam belonged to the local lodge of the B'nai B'rith, a Jewish fraternal order, and made a point of attending at least the social side of its North American convention held at the Fort Garry Hotel in Winnipeg in January 1922. His main interest at that meeting, however, was not the business to be discussed by the B'nai B'rith delegates from across Canada and the United States. For weeks he had been looking forward to the convention supper dance because of his date — Saidye Rosner, a girl whom he had known for years, but who increasingly occupied his thoughts at the end of 1921.

Six years younger than Sam, Saidye Rosner came from a warm, closely knit Jewish family from Plum Coulee, a small farming community about sixty miles from Winnipeg. Her father, Samuel Rosner, like the Bronfmans from Bessarabia, had immigrated to Canada at the age of eighteen, and had established himself in Plum Coulee about the time the Bronfmans began homesteading at Wapella. After a stint at peddling, and a job in a *matzah* factory where he lost part of a finger, Samuel Rosner opened a general store with his nephew Abe Brownstone, known as "Ab," and simultaneously bought land from some Mennonite refugees. Mainly as a result of Samuel's land purchases, the family acquired considerable local standing. Saidye remembered her father as a "gentleman farmer" who owned a number of properties in the vicinity and had the respect of the local agriculturalists. He was mayor of the town for a time, and, like many Jews, an enthusiastic supporter of the pro-immigration Liberal Party.

Saidye's first memories were of Plum Coulee where she was born in 1896, and the boisterous, open house for Jewish visitors that was her home. The second of four daughters, she grew up in a household that seems to have been perpetually full of people — her sisters Frances, Monica (Buster) and Freda, friends, a servant or two, Jewish travellers on their way west who stopped in for a meal or several nights, plus a famous visiting rabbi who stayed for weeks on end and to whom Saidye herself had to carry specially prepared kosher meals because he would not accept them from a Gentile maid. The family was more affluent than most in town: "The Rosners lived like none of the rest of us," reported Pearl Silver, a childhood friend. "Mrs Rosner really had a great deal of class about her and their table was beautifully set at all times."[61] The family were among the first in their small community of about six hundred people to acquire the appurtenances of modern society. Saidye remembered the coming of a bathtub: "It was installed in the kitchen next to the stove. The tub was not only an appliance, it was also a kitchen decoration. . . . Soon bathing became a family ritual. Each of us would use the tub, adding warmer water to it from the great big kettles set on the coal and wood stoves in the kitchen."[62] A cultivated family by Plum Coulee standards, the Rosners gave their daughters piano lessons and worried about their educational prospects in the local two-room schoolhouse.

This was probably the immediate reason for the family's move to Winnipeg about 1908 — two years after the introduction of the tub, and about the same time as the Bronfmans arrived from Brandon. Frances, their eldest daughter, was already boarding at Winnipeg's Havergal College at the time, and when Saidye's turn for high school came, the Rosners set up their home in Winnipeg while Samuel commuted from Plum Coulee for several years. Another reason for the move must have been the parents' concerns about finding Jewish husbands for their four daughters. Samuel Rosner seems to have been the leader of the tiny group of Jews in Plum Coulee, and was extensively involved in Jewish affairs. Intermittently observant, he led prayers and blew the *shofar* at the community services during the High Holy Days, and in 1919 was a delegate to the first meeting of the Canadian Jewish Congress. He was also, Saidye remembered, "an ardent Zionist." From a Jewish point of view Plum Coulee clearly had limitations: the Rosner girls received a rudimentary Hebrew education from Reb Ratner, the town's *shoichet* or ritual slaughterer, but hated every minute of it: for want of organized Jewish classes, they also attended the local Presbyterian Sunday School — learning a few hymns, bits of the Old Testament, and participating in Christmas plays. It is hardly surprising that Samuel and his wife, broadminded though they were, felt drawn to the far richer Jewish world of Winnipeg. And by 1908, having become reasonably wealthy, the Rosners moved with ease. The family installed itself in the comfortable suburb of Fort Rouge; Saidye remembered her father driving about with a chauffeur and her mother's careful attention to interior decoration.[63]

Sam first saw Saidye in Winnipeg in 1913, when he escorted her older sister Frances to the grand opening of the Fort Garry Hotel. But there was no direct contact between the two until a cold spring afternoon in 1921, according to Saidye's vivid recollection, when Sam caught sight of her on the street. Saidye had just returned from a winter holiday with her parents in Santa Monica, where she had bought "a beautiful brown wool cape, with a smaller shoulder cape trimmed with red fox. I put on my new cape and went for a walk on Portage Avenue. Sam and his brother Allan were out driving — Allan was at the wheel — and as I was crossing the street they nearly ran me over. Later I learned that my future husband asked Allan, 'Who is that attractive girl?' 'That's Saidye Rosner,' Allan told him, and I guess he made up his mind then and there to follow up his curiosity."[64]

But "following up" in affairs of the heart took time in 1921 in the Bronfman and Rosner milieu, and meant conforming to the highly circumscribed rituals of a society utterly innocent by our own standards. Indeed, the next encounter was not until several months later, on *Yom Kippur*, at the Shaarey Tzedec synagogue in downtown Winnipeg. Sam spied Saidye Rosner sitting beside her aunt, Bea Shragge, in the front row of the women's section in the balcony. During a break in the services about 4:00 P.M. he went for a walk with her — something that the two of them did for years thereafter to commemorate the beginning of their "Holy Courtship," as Sam would jokingly put it. Sam was smitten. A few weeks later he telegraphed Saidye from Vancouver, inviting her to the B'nai B'rith dance. "Something was cooking," Saidye knew. "Sam didn't think he could dance very well . . . and he never liked to do anything he didn't do well."[65]

Saidye was a playful, spirited young woman — "the devil in the family" as she described herself — popular, fun-loving and fond of parties. Twenty-six years old in 1922, she had recently completed two years at the University of Manitoba and was working as a typist for the Red Rose Tea Company in Winnipeg. Sam Bronfman, reserved and gentle as a suitor, who had a car and a chauffeur when in town and who raced across the country keeping his liquor business on an even keel, appeared "much older" than her contemporaries (he was thirty-three) and a man of the world. Responding to his telegram, an eager Saidye began with an ironic reference to etiquette: "According to Mr Hoyle it is not considered good form for a young lady to answer a gentleman's letter too promptly. . . . I thank you very kindly. I should be delighted to be escorted by you. . . . We have had ideal weather. That's an inducement to hurry back . . . with kindest regards."

The B'nai B'rith dance, one gathers, was a success, for a month later, on Saint Valentine's Day, the couple became engaged. Sam sent Saidye two dozen American Beauty roses, she remembered:

"They were so lovely that my mother couldn't bear to throw them away. She made them into a delicious rose petal jam." Telegrams went immediately to family and friends announcing the engagement, and the wedding was set for June. But with the Bronfman family's liquor business then winding up and new government regulations being imposed, Sam was urgently needed at his export houses. Within a few days he began a trip to the west coast that lasted about a month. Writing almost daily, he showered Saidye Rosner with letters, telegrams and also telephone calls to her home at 116 Wilmot Place. Heading west with Allan, who had just become engaged himself to Lucy Bilsky from Ottawa, Sam stayed at Harry's house in Regina on February 21. "My own sweet darling," he began his letter that night. "Gee, but it was good to hear your sweet voice last evening. Shush — it is now one in the morning. The people have retired and I am downstairs in the living room writing to and picturing my sweet 'Baby-Face' before me."

"Oh how I love you," Sam wrote a few days later, explaining that he thought of Saidye constantly — even while working through mounds of business correspondence. "All the time while reading I could see you before me. And I feel that you are part of me." Both young people were heavily preoccupied with their families. "I know myself how happy my parents would be, and I even feel somehow that they know and are happy because of this Union," said Sam. Saidye responded by sending her love to Harry, Harry's wife, and Harry's mother-in-law and sister Rose who were also in Regina. Sam invariably scrawled his greetings to Saidye's mother, father and sisters — particularly Freda ("Babical"), the youngest, to whom he added special messages of endearment. The Rosners' residence, his letters make clear, was already his second home. He paid tribute to Saidye's mother, calling attention to her unselfish devotion to the children and commending Saidye's parents as models they should follow: "that is the blessing of our Jewish people — that they have real mothers. And though as a class Jewish parents are admirable, your parents my dear are everything that could be wished for. I pray that they will be spared to us for many many years to come and if we have the good sense (and I know we have) to emulate them, we will have cause to be proud of ourselves." But Saidye

not fronting for his employer, Sir Mortimer Davis. A prominent member of the Upper Canadian establishment, Gooderham stoutly opposed the latter both because he was a Jew and a Montrealer.[38]

Sam faced Hatch as a direct challenger in 1926, when the Tory electoral success in Ontario opened new horizons for distillers. Distillery stocks shot upward on the Montreal and Toronto stock exchanges at the end of that year, in anticipation of a new liquor regime in Ontario. As they climbed, news reached Sam that Hatch had purchased the giant Ontario-based Hiram Walker distillery for $14 million, in what was the biggest Canadian business deal of the year. Hiram Walker, a huge modern plant located directly across the river from Detroit and strategically located for the export trade, was a definite plum, and it was now in enemy hands. Sam could not have been pleased.[39]

During 1927, as we shall see, Sam became heavily preoccupied with exports, as well as a nasty investigation by the Royal Commission on Customs and Excise before which the Bronfmans had to appear on several gruelling occasions. Meyer Chechik hounded Sam and Harry from Winnipeg with ever-angrier contentions about their long-dead partnership, and occasionally showed up in Montreal with fresh demands. And on January 24, in the midst of concluding the partnership with the DCL, Sam and Saidye's second child was born, and named Phyllis (in Yiddish, Fradel Beila), after her maternal great-grandmother. "Our hearts are filled with joy even though it is not a boy," wired Sam's mother-in-law from Winnipeg. "Sam told me he didn't care if it is another girl so long as she is like Mindel in all ways," Mrs Rosner wrote to her daughter. "Tell the little darling baby to start growing quickly and come to see her Bubby [grandmother] like Mindel did." If Sam was disappointed, he left no trace. A week after the baby's birth he left a card for Saidye: "Today is our little Darling's first Birthday — one week old. May she grow up to be a great Pride to her Dear Mumsie and Daddy. And love her oldest sister. And may we always be happy. Sam."

Meanwhile, despite the waning of prohibition in Ontario, conditions at the old Seagram distillery continued to deteriorate.

Under intense pressure, Sam nevertheless found time to explore the possibility of acquiring the plant, working closely with William Cleland, DCL's representative in Canada. Sam obviously liked the traditional aura of the Waterloo distillery, which reflected, in his mind, the company's outstanding pedigree. Even more important, Seagram had potential. Its name was still good in the whisky trade, despite the problems of the past decade. Its annual capacity, in 1927, was a relatively modest 400,000 gallons, compared to 3,000,000 at the LaSalle plant, but there was ample warehouse storage space and, most important, something that really counted in the whisky trade, inventory — close to 1,400,000 gallons of whisky aging in barrels.[40]

To consummate the deal, the Bronfmans and their partners created a new holding company, Distillers Corporation-Seagrams Limited (DC-SL), with a capital of $1,500,000, to acquire both the Distillers Corporation and the Seagram company. The Bronfmans and DCL together took 75 percent of the shares, divided equally between them, and the Seagram shareholders took the remainder. Shares in the new DC-SL were offered to Seagram's shareholders on a share-for-share basis; and as the market boomed, these and other investors from the general public flocked to the company. William Ross presided over the new board from across the Atlantic but Sam, as the sole vice-president, effectively took command, seconded by Allan. DCL's Canadian representative William Cleland, who had learned the ropes at the Clydesdale Distillery in Scotland before coming to Canada in 1907, and who described himself as a Conservative and a Presbyterian, took over the Waterloo plant, while Sam remained in charge at LaSalle. Sam, Allan and Harry all drew the same salary — $25,000 a year, as of August 1928, a very substantial sum at the time.[41]

Curiously, the Bronfmans were not sufficiently well known at the time for the press to have played up their role in the new order. The headline in the *Financial Post* announcing the deal on February 3 declared "Britons Secure Control at Waterloo" — a play upon the Napoleonic record, in which the family was not even mentioned. A week later the *Post* remained similarly misinformed, declaring that Seagram had been "taken over by the Distillers Corporation, Limited, of Scotland."

With an eye to the future, Sam and Cleland coordinated their production and began a vigorous expansion and an upgrading of old equipment. Waterloo concentrated on rye whisky, while LaSalle turned out bourbon, rye, Scotch-type whisky and gin. Within a year they had raised the annual output of both plants to nearly 4,000,000 gallons and enhanced their bottling capacity as well, so that the combined output was 3,500 cases daily. Storage capacity climbed to 11 million gallons.[42] In the first annual shareholders meeting at the Mount Royal Hotel in October 1929, presided over by Sam in William Ross's absence, DC-SL announced net earnings of over $2.5 million—an excellent beginning, even if still trailing Hiram Walker which had just over $4 million. "Great British-Canadian Company Presents Strong Statement," proclaimed a headline in the *Financial Post*, just five days before the crash of the stock market on Wall Street.[43] Both companies, the paper pointed out, had just completed a round of new investment that would take some time to be reflected in earnings, and a bright future seemed in store. For the first time, Sam and Allan's pictures appeared in the *Financial Post*, beneath those of Ross and Cleland; unfortunately, the paper got it wrong, transposing the names of the two Bronfman brothers.

■

EVEN AS IT eroded in Canada, prohibition remained in force in the United States, presenting a remarkable opportunity for Canadian entrepreneurs — and not excluding those who managed the nation's affairs in Ottawa. For businessmen, the possibilities were obvious. "Canadian distilleries have arisen manfully to the task and have striven to satiate the thirst of the great republic to the south," wrote one journalist in 1925. "Four hundred percent more whisky is being manufactured legally in distilleries now than before the adoption of prohibition in the United States."[44] For the Canadian government, American prohibition meant a much-appreciated boost to foreign trade, and Canadian officials treated whisky exports accordingly. Canadian customs officials collected duty regularly on "intoxicating liquors" destined for south of the border and regulated the rum-running commerce just as any other. A national revenue circular of 1929, for example, signed by George Taylor, Commissioner of Excise, designated seventeen docks for customs excise officers in the Windsor area "for the acceptance of entry and clearance of such goods for export."[45] Taylor and his colleagues in Ottawa had not the slightest doubt that the boats leaving those docks took their cargoes to Detroit.

Wonderfully situated to take advantage of a huge market, Sam and other Canadian distillers sold to middlemen throughout Ontario, Quebec and the Maritimes. From there, liquor entered the American market thanks to the work of a colourful fraternity of rum runners who sent their merchandise by every conveyance imaginable. Most went by boat, via the Great Lakes and the Atlantic waters of the United States. But automobiles, airplanes, carts, bicycles — everything was used. Enterprising rum runners in the Maritimes, to take one case, packed whisky into hollowed-out logs, and hauled them by sled across the international frontier. Hundreds of thousands of bottles, it was estimated, went by this means alone.[46]

By the mid-1920s cash from these sales began to pour into the Bronfman family coffers. "This was when we started to make our real money," Sam told Terence Robertson. "We were late starters in the two most lucrative markets — on the high seas and across the Detroit River. The big whisky makers of Europe and Canadian distillers had been in it from the very beginning, in 1920. We had relied mostly on mail order business in Canada itself and what came out of the border trade in Saskatchewan was insignificant by comparison. At this point we joined the major leagues in the United States market."[47]

Mindful of the great costs and difficulty involved in stopping this traffic, the American authorities made only half-hearted efforts to enforce the law against the importation of spirits. Postwar presidents Warren Harding and Calvin Coolidge were not much interested. On the state level commitment to rooting out drink varied considerably, but after the first few years of prohibition the energy devoted to it began to drain away. And once bootleggers got their feet in some doors, there was less incentive to mount a guard elsewhere. "By 1926," according to one computation, "state legislatures in the United States were appropriating annually a total of only $698,855 for prohibition enforcement, an amount estimated as approximately one-eighth of that which the same governments were spending to police their laws for the control of fish and game. Some states were spending nothing at all."[48] One of these was New York, a huge market for whisky, which was particularly half-hearted in its commitment to prohibition, given the opposition to the Volstead Act of Alfred E. Smith, governor in 1919-20 and again in 1923-28. Rum running there became a major industry, and much of the liquor brought into New York leaked outside the state and found its way across the eastern part of the country.

From the start of prohibition, the American authorities saw that without Canadian cooperation it would be practically impossible to stop the illegal importation of liquor. Washington repeatedly tried to enlist help to the north and finally, with a Canadian-American Convention in June 1924, a first step was taken: each government promised to send the other information about vessels thought to be carrying illegal goods into the other country. In practice, however, the Convention did not work — mainly because the Dominion government refused the American requests to forbid clearances of vessels bringing whisky to American coasts. The Americans did not give up, however, and bombarded their neighbours with evidence of the flow of alcohol across the border. It was reported in the summer of 1927, for example, that more than 90 percent of the value of liquor exported from Canada travelled illegally to the United States. Canadians knew that there was no law against the export of alcoholic beverages from Canada and believed it was up to the Americans to enforce their own laws. A headline in the *Ottawa Journal* put it succinctly: "U.S. Enforcement, Like Charity, Should Begin at Home."[49] While some Canadians disagreed with this view, Prime Minister William Lyon Mackenzie King stuck to it, doing his best to avoid giving in to the Americans. In the Canadian Department of External Affairs, operating increasingly independently of British interests with its under-secretary O.D. Skelton, young officials like Hume Wrong, Hugh Keenleyside, Lester Pearson and Vincent Massey cut their diplomatic teeth on the issue of liquor smuggling, working out the means to defend their country against American pressures on the issue. Whisky, practically speaking, was extremely important in the achievement of full Canadian sovereignty.

Already in 1924 Canadian exports of alcoholic beverages were rocketing upwards—from $3.1 million in 1922 to approximately $10 million two years later. And these were *official* statistics: no one thought to disguise such sales to the United States, because no one questioned the legality of the trade in Canada. In their report to DCL in 1926, before the Bronfmans' LaSalle distillery was selling any whisky, top executives Ross and Herd noted that Gooderham and Worts sent between 7,000 and 8,000 cases per month through the port of Windsor. In the previous year, Hiram Walker had exported 100,000 cases, "mainly to Cuba"—in reality to the United States, simply bypassing the stated destination of Havana. All Canadian distillers profited from exports to the United States, and the distilling industry (along with brewing, of course) benefited enormously from the increased volume. Whisky stocks remained firm in a fluctuating market, tending even to rise; meanwhile production costs dropped and prices climbed by as much as 300 percent.[50]

From the Canadian government's standpoint, these exports were extremely advantageous because of the tax revenues they generated. One report for 1928, for example, suggested that "approximately one-eighth of all Dominion and all Provincial revenue was derived from the trade in alcoholic beverages," and that federal and provincial shares amounted together to more than $72 million.[51] In 1930 the Montreal *Gazette* reported that stopping clearances for the U.S. would cost over $750,000 annually in lost sales taxes alone, leaving aside the huge sacrifice of business—not only that of the distillers, but also railways, printing trades, glass and bottle makers, advertising firms and so on. By 1930 whisky exports were estimated to generate an annual revenue of $23 million directly, plus several million dollars for local manufacturers and suppliers. Such trades feared mightily any interruption of liquor sales. The Quebec Retail Lumber Dealers' Association, for example, makers of wooden cases, begged Ottawa not to stop clearances, fearing their business would be ruined; they charge that such a move would require a $5 million expenditure on enforcement and an additional tax burden upon Canadians of $2.80 per person.[52]

Like the Canadian government, distillers made no bones about liquor exports to the United States. The Bronfmans' Scottish partners were in the trade from the beginning, and when they bothered to justify such shipments, which was seldom enough, they could even wrap themselves in a Scottish flag: "As the United States are asking for Scotch whisky," one Scottish trade periodical declared, "surely it is better for them to get the genuine goods than the filthy spirit provided in Germany." Appearing before a British Royal Commission in 1930, Sir Alexander Walker said exactly what the Bronfmans would say about their whisky destined for the United States: "Some goods may be ordered by a . . . Belgian, a Frenchman, or otherwise, for consignment. He pays for the goods and he gives a consignment to St. Pierre or Miquelon. We get paid from them probably in this country in cash. The question of destination does not interest us as long as we do not have the goods entering an agency area."[53]

Similarly Sam, reflecting on shipments to American bootleggers, indicated that while he had no doubts about the real destination, he did not look too closely at the ultimate delivery: "Of course we knew where it went," he told an interviewer for *Fortune*, "but we had no legal proof. And I never went on the other side of the border to count the empty Seagrams bottles."[54] How much of his business were these "exports"? The proportion became larger at the end of the 1920s, when prohibition was breaking down completely and American demand soared. Sam sometimes referred to exports as constituting about half of his business in this period, but in a rare, frank letter to his chief competitor Harry Hatch in 1932, the last year of prohibition, Sam was more concrete, and suggested an even higher fraction. The domestic market, he said, was normally about 500,000 cases or 750,000 proof gallons annually. Export markets even under depressed circumstances, on the other hand, amounted to over 800,000 cases, or 1.7 million proof gallons, and of these, Sam claimed, DC-SL supplied well over 60 percent.[55]

During the last phase of whisky sales to American bootleggers on the prairies, Barney Aaron and Abe engaged in similar trading on a smaller scale in New Brunswick, operating out of Saint John.

Beginning with carloads sent overland, Abe and his brother-in-law soon graduated to higher volume cargoes dispatched by schooner from the ports of Saint John and Halifax. First under the name of the Canadian Distributing Company, then Atlantic Importing, and then Atlas Shipping in 1926, the eastern branch of the Bronfman family business kept the liquor flowing. When the volume increased, some buyers placed their orders in Montreal, where the family's Distillers Corporation and then Distillers Corporation-Seagrams Limited maintained large quantities of British brands and was also beginning to stock their own Canadian production. Nominally in charge of eastern exports in Montreal as well, Abe operated out of the Distillers Corporation offices on St James Street together with his three brothers while Barney Aaron remained on the front lines in New Brunswick, providing the essential paperwork for merchandise that was eventually smuggled into the United States. As commander-in-chief, Sam looked to the orders from England and Scotland that kept the warehouses full, oversaw sales, and regulated production in the LaSalle and Waterloo plants.

Exports from the east were released from bond in Saint John and Halifax and sold to rum runners who delivered the whisky to what was known as "Rum Row" on the eastern seaboard of the United States, from Boston to Atlantic City.[56] To escape Canadian excise taxes and to avoid troubles with Canadian officials who were supposed to stop shipments declared for the United States, the Bronfmans and other exporters adopted a simple strategy: when cargoes were released to the American rum-running customers, the documentation declared the destination to be somewhere else—usually Havana, Cuba, but sometimes Bermuda, the Bahamas, British Honduras (now known as Belize) and increasingly, at the end of the 1920s, the French islands of St Pierre and Miquelon. In practice the whisky ended up along Rum Row as intended, but in order to meet the Canadian requirements and to obtain release of the bond guarantees that exporters had to supply, the Bronfman companies and their customers participated in a charade that really fooled no one. With the help of well-paid agents in the various official destinations they obtained "landing certificates" attesting that the liquor had duly arrived in Cuba, the Bahamas or wherever. Thus satisfied, the Canadian Customs authorities kept the paperwork moving.

When he was called before the Royal Commission on Customs and Excise in 1926, the intellectually minded Barney Aaron had trouble denying that there was something fishy about the destinations of the cargoes of whisky. "Are you under the impression that these cargoes went to Havana and Honduras and other points?" he was asked. Aaron replied: "I am under the impression that at the time of shipping that is where they told me they were taking them to." Did Aaron believe that the destination of the cargoes was really the American coast?

A: I had doubts, but I could not prove it.

Q: I am not asking you what you proved, but what you believed.

A: When I say "I believe there is a God above us" I believe it. When, however, you ask, "Do you believe this?" I cannot say, because that belief has not impressed itself on my mind, and I could not say so to the same extent. Now, what do you mean?

Q: I want to know your own conviction.

A: That is a true conviction? I cannot say except from what I actually see, or if I know the facts. I have to take a man's story as he tells it, and make the best of it.

Aaron protested that he himself never chartered vessels, and that his responsibility ended when the whisky was on board the ship and the merchandise was paid for. "Were they Canadian or American purchasers?" Aaron answered: "They may have been Americans living in the United States or they may have been Americans living in Canada, or vice versa. As a rule they would say: 'Why should you be so inquisitive? Here is my name and here is my money.' That was their answer to me. They looked to be good business fellows, and they paid for their undertakings, and would say: 'That is all you are interested in.' "[57]

Rum running on the eastern seaboard had distinct advantages over smuggling on the Great Lakes, as a recent book on the latter makes clear. Whisky shipped from Halifax or Saint John was nearly as cheap, and did not have to travel several hundred miles by road to reach customers in major centres like Boston or New York. "To deliver booze to these markets via the lakes involved extra costs for trucks, drivers, and maintenance. There were also extra risks. Three hundred miles of trucking provided many opportunities for hijackers."[58] Although the American authorities were never able to stop the smuggling on the Great Lakes, they made a genuine effort to do so—in marked contrast to the energy expended elsewhere. In the mid-1920s the Coast Guard deployed a little fleet of seventy-five-foot cutters, known as "six-bitters," together with smaller picket boats to stop rum runners entering American waters. Armed with small cannons and machine guns, these vessels played hide-and-seek with their quarry until 1925 when, as C.W. Hunt says, the battle began to shift in the government's favour.

Despite such disadvantages, however, Bronfman whisky was carried by rum-running vessels plying the Great Lakes, especially the narrow waters of the Detroit River opposite Windsor, Ontario, not far from the Seagram plant at Waterloo. For the most part oriented towards ocean-going transport because of their headquarters in Montreal, the Bronfmans nevertheless found themselves drawn to the Great Lakes activity once they had purchased the Seagram distillery. The future Canadian auditor general, Maxwell Henderson, then a young accountant at the Seagram plant, recalled how the export system worked from Waterloo. Every day Allan or Harry Bronfman would telephone orders from Montreal to the general manager, Daniel Alger. To send the liquor on its way, Alger would then scurry about making all kinds of arrangements and finally speed off into the night in a fast car to complete the deal. "Extreme care was exercised not to commit anything beyond the absolute minimum to paper while always ensuring that the transactions were strictly legal," Henderson noted in his memoirs.[59] Another Seagram employee, Roy Martin, remembered calling the customers ahead of time "to make sure that they had the money on deposit before we let the goods go." Every morning he had to fill out government export forms (called B-13) in triplicate— even for the smallest orders, which amounted to as few as three cases, sent across to Detroit by rowboat. The meticulous Martin signed his name to B-13 forms so often, he claimed, that sixty years later his signature was still a terrible scrawl.[60]

As the water-borne export trade grew in importance, Sam gradually became involved—even though his main interest remained the distillery at LaSalle. Given his eldest brother's erratic track record, Sam was obviously reluctant to leave so important a branch of the family's business under Abe's exclusive direction, and, in any case, his competitive urges must have tempted him to engage his main Canadian rival, Harry Hatch, whose position on the Great Lakes was so strong.

Sam sensed that it was pointless to challenge Hatch directly on the Great Lakes, for the "King of Canadian Distillers," as the *Toronto Daily Star* referred to him after the Hiram Walker purchase, was overwhelmingly dominant there. Harry and Herb Hatch had spent much effort organizing a fleet of smugglers at the eastern end of Lake Ontario referred to as "Hatch's Navy," and by the mid-1920s they effectively controlled Great Lakes liquor traffic. Sam thought it best to look east. Leaving the B-13s and the Great Lakes traffic to others, Sam managed to obtain rights from the government of Nova Scotia to bring British whisky into that province for purposes of export in 1926; writer Terence Robertson suggested that Sam had "powerful contacts" in other provincial capitals as well, and used these energetically to clear the path for exports on the Atlantic coast. One friend with links to Ottawa was Albercis Gélinas—a Montreal millionaire close to Minister of Customs Jacques Bureau. Gélinas, who was a guest at Sam's wedding, is said to have been the guarantor on many of the bonds taken out by Abe for shipments to Cuba.[61]

In 1927, Sam's interests suddenly shifted to the craggy islands of St Pierre and Miquelon, only fifteen miles off the coast of Newfoundland. With an ice-free port, the bleak and rocky islands had the advantage of being under the French flag, perfectly situated for seafaring adventurers who ventured beyond the pounding surf, and for businessmen, who gathered at Parisian-style cafés near the central port of the principal island, St Pierre. For some years Canadian whisky sellers had been doing business on the French Islands, selling to American traders who would relay their merchandise to Rum Row. As with shipments supposedly going to Havana, merchandise sent first to French territory was exempt from Canadian duty—thus lowering the price. Quickly, the idea of using the nearby French territory caught on. During 1923, beginning what was known locally as *le temps de la fraude*, 500,000 cases of liquor were unloaded on the docks of this sleepy little fishing community, and more than a thousand vessels entered its port. One of the first to run liquor out of St Pierre was a legendary figure, Captain Bill McCoy, known for his honest trading in forbidden drink: all his customers, it is said, knew his whisky as "the real McCoy" — originating that designation as a seal of authenticity. Soon the liquor unloaded amounted to ten gallons a week for every man, woman and child in the islands. Warehouses sprang up all over the islands; lumber-poor, the local inhabitants built entire structures out of discarded liquor cases—including one particularly handsome cottage, known as "Cutty Sark Villa." By the mid-1920s all the major Canadian distillers opened agencies on the islands, cutting out the middlemen and selling directly to customers from the United States.[62]

Going to the islands was a move that bore Sam's signature because of its boldness and remarkable prescience—putting Distillers Corporation in a position to outfox all of their competitors a few years later. For remarkably, the Bronfmans' move to St Pierre occurred just as law enforcement began to have a real effect on Great Lakes rum running, cutting down substantially the amount of liquor entering the United States by this route. Under pressure from the Americans, the Canadian government began to make life complicated for Canadian exporters in Windsor, reducing the number of export docks allotted to them. More important, American law enforcement on the Great Lakes finally began to have some effect. According to one calculation, the number of whisky cases crossing the Detroit River each month declined from 150,000 during the summer and autumn of 1928 to fewer than 50,000 by September 1929.[63] This meant, of course, big trouble for Hiram Walker-Gooderham and Worts, with its flagship plant at Walkerville so close to Detroit and with almost all of its rum-running eggs in the Great Lakes basket.

Then, in 1930, came a major shock. Battered by pressure from the Americans and from parts of the public fed up with bootleggers, Prime Minister Mackenzie King blocked clearances of liquor cargoes that everyone knew were bound directly for the United States. Much of the Great Lakes traffic thereby came to an end, leaving only the French islands as a base for Canadian exports.

Sam's mechanism for doing business on the islands was his family's Atlas Shipping Company, which entered into partnership with local interests in St Pierre under a new structure at the end of 1927, the Northern Export Company. Managed by Monte Rosebourne, who once ran the family's ill-fated export house in Bienfait, Northern Export began to feed huge quantities of liquor into the American market, drawing on three sources — Distillers Corporation-Seagrams Limited in Montreal, DCL in Edinburgh, and various European exporters of wines, liquors, brandies and champagnes. To skirt all restrictions and payments of Canadian duty the company completed its trading outside Canada — while negotiating the deals on Canadian soil, usually in Montreal. Within months, Northern Export became the biggest seller on the islands; at its height, says the historian of *le temps de la fraude*, the company had seventy employees in the office and warehouses and a huge volume of telegram traffic back and forth to Montreal. The Bronfmans maintained a weekly insurance policy on the warehoused stocks at St Pierre, with a coverage of between $1 million and $1.5 million during several years.[64] To avoid snooping by competitors — not to mention the U.S. Coast Guard — correspondence was often in secret code. According to the RCMP and U.S. enforcement agents, Abe Bronfman even set up his own radio station for such signals in 1931.[65] Dozens of vessels came and went from the harbour of St Pierre, often crewed by fishermen from Lunenburg, Nova Scotia. Pierre Andrieux lists many of the little ships' names, about which stories could doubtless be told — *Connoisseur, Accuracy, May and June, Radio I, Pronto,* and one vessel, possibly christened by a Bronfman company agent or associate, *Mazel Tov.*[66]

Several years later, when it launched an unsuccessful prosecution of the Bronfmans, the RCMP claimed that in addition to the American trade, the family maintained an agency in St John's, Newfoundland, a subsidiary of Atlas Shipping, for the purpose of selling to Canadian bootleggers, who then

smuggled whisky into Canada.[67] While admitting that the
overwhelming proportion of the family's business was with
the United States, the Mounties nevertheless seized upon the
Canadian trade, for it alone was in breach of Canadian law. From
Newfoundland, according to the government's case, the Bronfmans helped to bring vast quantities of liquor illegally into
Canada, defrauding the authorities of up to $5 million in customs
and excise duties. But although the evidence of widespread rum
running into Canada was unchallengeable, and although there
was strong indication that Abe, at least, knew where some of the
whisky sold in St John's was headed, the prosecutors failed to
prove their case. Eastern Trading Company, as the St John's
agency was called, did import vast quantities of liquor from
overseas, and was, as Sam's accountants, Price Waterhouse,
argued, a legitimate part of the family's business. Once the
Bronfmans' customers bought the liquor, the judge who heard
the Mounties' case made clear, it was they and not the Bronfmans
who were responsible for any breaches of the law.

Since the records of Atlas Shipping were suspiciously
destroyed around the end of prohibition, just about the time the
RCMP began their prosecution, the government had to guess at
the volume of traffic on the eastern seaboard. For the year 1930,
they estimated, the business transacted through Atlas Shipping
Company amounted to about $8 million — with much of the
proceeds received in cash. Between 1928 and 1930, they
contended, the company received no less than $1,367,505 in cash
alone — including 828 thousand-dollar bills, 331 five-hundred-
dollar bills, and 2,627 hundred-dollar bills.[68] More systematic
estimates are really guesswork. One gets a sense of the scale of the
traffic by looking at the performance of Distillers-Seagrams,
given that more than half of the whisky sold by DC-SL went
abroad, and most of this went through the warehouses of
Northern Export on St Pierre. DC-SL's overall earnings from
spirits amounted to $2,448,000 in 1929, compared to $3,918,000
for Hiram Walker; but in the next year, when the Canadian
government outlawed clearances via the Great Lakes, Hiram
Walker fell to $2,357,000 while Distillers-Seagrams climbed to
$3,641,000.[69] The difference was due to DC-SL's commanding
position on St Pierre, and the continuing demand from the

United States. Not for the last time, Sam seems to have gotten it right.

■

"CANADA IS BECOMING rapidly alcoholized," wrote one American clergyman in 1929, sounding the alarm. In every province, he noted, sales were increasing. Per capita consumption was going up. The country had become a "bootlegger's paradise." Quoting the Bureau of Statistics, he noted that in the previous year "one-eighth of all Dominion and all Provincial revenue was derived from the trade in alcoholic beverages" — and as a result, politicians were being corrupted.[70] There was plenty to condemn if one shared this frame of mind, and as the Bronfman family came into the limelight during the 1920s as one of the major forces in Canadian whisky, they had increasingly to contend with the unpopularity, in important quarters, of the liquor trade.

A powerful if subdued temperance sentiment was probably the strongest element in the continued condemnation of the "liquor interests" that reflected on the Bronfman family. This is certainly what moved the Hon. E.C. Drury, former premier of Ontario, to complain in a public speech that government control under the Liquor Control Board of Ontario would produce the worst: "we shall see the debauching of womanhood. The barroom was bad, vile, degrading. The drinking in the home strikes deeper into the very vitals of the nation."

But another element with which the Bronfmans had to contend was antisemitism. For there is no doubt that the DCL visitors from Edinburgh who came to Canada in 1927 observed accurately that "the Jews . . . are not generally regarded with favour in Canada," and distilling was hardly exempt from the general antipathy. The Scots would certainly have noted the same in the United States, where Jews were extremely prominent in the whisky industry before prohibition and emerged once again as soon as it was lifted. When the prestigious *Fortune* magazine profiled the major American whisky manufacturers in 1934, for example, it snidely grouped "four gentlemen of the faith" for discussion — Weiskopf, Schwarzhaupt, Rosenstiel and

Klein. *Fortune* slipped a tasteless, antisemitic aside into its description of another liquor entrepreneur, declared to be "an anomaly: he was a prodigal Jew."[71]

It is impossible to tell how Sam responded to the anti-Jewish jibes that certainly came his way, for he was not one to call attention to them. But neither was he one to let slights go by. One associate suggested that Sam's burning dislike of Harry Hatch may have stemmed from the day that Hatch branded him "that Jew boy from Montreal" — although the story is not corroborated.[72] According to Mark Shinbane, Sam, with his massive ego, "could not imagine that anyone could hold anything against him." Proud and feisty, Sam liked to choose the grounds on which he would strike back, and he did not like to do so defending himself as a Jew.

Nor did he have much to say at the time about the "people of disrepute" who came into the industry, not least because a few of them were trading heavily in DC-SL's whisky. Sam, it has been said, had links with American gangsters during the rum-running era, and within the galaxy of U.S. crime two of the most brilliant figures have been mentioned — Meyer Lansky and Frank Costello. But the story rests far more on fantasy than fact.

About Lansky there appears to be no evidence at all beyond Lansky's vague claims of a connection that would trivialize his own violence-ridden achievements in the criminal fraternity. An unrepentant Lansky in Israel near the end of his life, claiming to be a refugee from an unjust American prosecution, complained to writer Uri Dan: "I admit quite frankly that I made a fortune in bootlegging. . . . The most important people in the country — respectable businessmen, politicians, senators, congressmen — they all bought illegal booze from me or from other men in the business. There are big companies today that had their beginnings in running illegal liquor into the country. What about Sam Bronfman who ran it from Canada across Lake Erie, which we called the Jewish lake?" More recently, Lansky's widow has claimed that her husband has been unfairly singled out, for the highly respected Sam Bronfman was also deeply involved in bootlegging; further, she suggested that Sam and her husband had a long-term partnership in the liquor business. But neither

Lansky offered a shred of evidence for this contention, and it is highly doubtful if any exists.[73]

The tie with the notorious racketeer Frank Costello rests on nothing more than the latter's semi-coherent testimony at the U.S. Senate Kefauver Committee hearings on organized crime in the United States in 1951.[74] On February 15 an extremely nervous Costello told the senators in his raspy voice that he knew Sam from the prohibition days and that he "might have bought some liquor from him." Before the television cameras and blinding lights a few weeks later, he went over the same ground once more:

> Q: Did you ever buy liquor from Sam Bronfman?
> A: I personally, no.
> Q: Well, who did?
> A: Well, whoever I done business with.
> Q: Well, did you have an arrangement with Sam Bronfman whereby he would ship liquor to the United States?
> A: No.

Asked to clarify his previous contentions about Sam, the best Costello would do was the following: "what I meant is if I bought liquor from him, that means I met him in the United States and bought it from him in the United States. . . . I come to the conclusion that I never bought it from him in Canada . . . I bought it in New York . . . either from Bronfman or independent people . . . I want to make it specifically on the record that I bought in New York, whether it was Bronfman or anyone else, and if Bronfman shipped it to anyone else, I bought it from someone else."[75] On Costello, as with Lansky, there is little more than that. Kefauver's investigators certainly perked up at the mention of the Canadian millionaire Sam Bronfman, but they never uncovered more than Costello's vague ramblings and never even inquired about the possible contact with Lansky. As a result, Sam himself was never called to the stand.[76]

On the other hand, there is more to be said about some less distinguished underworld characters, as Sam later acknowledged ruefully—and in the case of one acquaintance, James "Niggy"

Rutkin, Sam came mightily to regret he ever set eyes upon the man. Rutkin was a middle-echelon racketeer from New Jersey who challenged Sam and others to a lengthy legal duel in the late 1940s and early 1950s, as we shall see. His associate during the prohibition era was one of Sam's most important American customers, a bootlegger named Joseph Reinfeld—a jovial, avuncular Jewish immigrant from Poland who before the advent of prohibition ran a saloon in a tough, predominantly Italian neighbourhood of Newark. In 1923, even before Sam had moved to Montreal, Reinfeld went into the whisky business on the island of St Pierre, and a few years later became heavily involved in smuggling. Reinfeld operated what he later referred to as a "high seas business," importing liquor along Rum Row and selling at least part of the merchandise through his own bar, which he maintained in Newark. In subsequent legal testimony Reinfeld explained how Rutkin "muscled in" on Reinfeld's consortium, and how a group of criminals, including Abner "Longy" Zwillman, also became part of the combine.[77]

According to a former U.S. Treasury Department agent in 1951, Reinfeld's syndicate eventually carved out a major part of the U.S. bootleg market during prohibition, earning as much as $50 million in all. Waxey Gordon and Dutch Schultz and other major figures "were pikers compared to this mob," the witness maintained.[78] Within the partnership Reinfeld's main job was to make the purchases, and this brought him into contact with Sam, beginning in 1927. Drawing on lengthy interviews, Terence Robertson contended that "Reinfeld was one of Sam's best customers. He took delivery of Sam's goods at St Pierre and had them shipped down to 'Rum Row' where his 'clients' ran them ashore in fleets of motor boats. He had been in the industry for longer than Sam and to some extent it was on his advice . . . that Sam began to build up inventory."[79] Sam always thought of Reinfeld as a respectable dealer, forced by prohibition to deal with some unsavoury criminal elements whom he in fact despised. However, dealing with Reinfeld put Sam himself in touch with some genuine gangsters.

One of these was Abner Zwillman, an enterprising crook who killed himself in his mock-Tudor mansion in West Orange, New Jersey, in 1959, at age fifty-five. A six-foot-two-inch son of a chicken pedlar, "Longy," as he was known, drove trucks for Reinfeld's syndicate and fended off hijackers until his talent in the "business" side of bootlegging earned him a promotion. Known for his skill in political payoffs, the precocious and well-manicured Zwillman eventually obtained an important part of the action. Rising rapidly through the ranks, he achieved particular notoriety because of a torrid affair with film idol Jean Harlow and his close friendship with Meyer Lansky and "Lucky" Luciano. After Dutch Schultz was shot dead in a Newark restaurant in 1935, the FBI referred to Zwillman as New Jersey's "Public Enemy Number One."[80] Longy's biographer claimed that Reinfeld once introduced the rising star of New Jersey crime to Sam Bronfman, who commented on how respectable he appeared, given his reputation. Reinfeld's brother Abe noted that when he saw him in Montreal, Sam "kept telling me how well-behaved Longy is, how studious-looking. You'd never guess he was a *shtarker* [a Yiddish word for strong-arm man], Sam tells me. Also had a head on his shoulders, Sam said."[81]

A few other accounts of Sam's association with prohibition-era criminals follow this pattern: a link is imputed through a rumoured meeting or indirect contact, without anything more substantial on the relationship. And as with the Kefauver investigations, the trail quickly turns cold. A reasonable conclusion is that, given the great volume of Bronfman whisky destined for the United States in the late 1920s and early 1930s, criminal elements dealt with it as much as anyone else. It is hardly surprising that the Bronfman name was known by the likes of Meyer Lansky, Frank Costello or Lucky Luciano, without any relationship having existed. Sam's association with Joe Reinfeld may have brought him into occasional contact with some high-ranking American bootleggers, including perhaps Longy Zwillman, but the connection does not seem to have gone further than that. Sam's only regular link to this world was Joe Reinfeld, so far as can be ascertained.

The fact that so many of these characters were of Jewish background, however — not only Lansky, Schultz and Zwillman, but also Arnold Rothstein, Louis Rothkopf, Irving "Waxey Gordon" Wexler, Benjamin "Bugsy" Siegal, Charles "King"

Solomon, to name only a few — invites some comment, for it relates to the environment in which Sam worked. That Jews had their share of urban crime ought to surprise no one, for in an enterprising immigrant community hungry for success it was inevitable that some would be drawn to such high-risk, high-profit enterprises for which the capital consisted mainly of brains, daring and ingenuity. Rabbi Arthur Hertzberg adds another explanation, related to the grim past of many Jewish immigrants: "The law had always been the enemy of the Jews; to circumvent it was often the only way to survive, and, therefore, to outfox authority was a praiseworthy act."[82]

Beyond this, however, the particular concentration of Jews in the bootleg whisky trade is striking, and may derive in part from a rich East European Jewish tradition of selling liquor and evading liquor laws, especially in Polish territory that came under Czarist rule. "From the sixteenth to the nineteenth centuries," observes Chaim Bermant, "when many Jews acted as lessees of Polish landowners, they often established breweries and distilleries to increase their revenues . . . and other Jews, though not direct lessees, became tavern keepers. When Poland was dismembered in the latter years of the eighteenth century, about fifteen percent of Jews in the towns and about eighty-five percent of those in the country were engaged in the manufacture, distribution or sale of alcoholic beverages."[83] A related reason for the heavy proportion of Jews was simple continuation of the heavy Jewish involvement in the wholesale and retail liquor trade from the days before prohibition. Joe Reinfeld, in Sam's account, went into bootlegging reluctantly, simply in order to stay in business after the passage of the Volstead Act. Finally, historian Albert Fried suggests that the Jewish liquor rings had to be particularly tough: "Jewish communities, being negligible consumers of alcohol, furnished them with no huge market of their own. To capture their main chance Jewish gangsters had to secure a foothold elsewhere, in gentile neighborhoods. Their task, as we can imagine, was especially difficult and their accomplishments were especially notable."[84]

However understood, the extensive involvement of Jews was one of the facts of life in the bootleg liquor trade that Sam encountered, and quite likely smoothed the way for his subsequent conquest of so much of the American market. Sam seems to have struck up a genuine friendship with Joe Reinfeld, whom he never condemned in later days, even though it might have been politic to do so. So without having been involved with hard-core American criminals as some have contended, Sam had an easy familiarity with at least part of this world of the *shtarkers* south of the border. During prohibition he had little or nothing to do with them himself, but neither did he shrink from contact when so many "went straight," after the repeal of prohibition. Many ended up as his distributors after 1933, and their loyalty and affection for Sam was intense, based to some extent on personal rapport, and a feeling of kinship that overlooked former breaches of the law.

On the much more law-abiding Canadian side of the frontier Sam's most regular contact with the world of lawbreaking was probably his former partner Meyer Chechik, whose enterprise veered towards extortion in the late 1920s, with his target none other than Sam Bronfman himself — a venture that turned out to be Chechik's major mistake.

Ever since their partnership ended in 1922, Meyer Chechik had been pursuing, albeit intermittently, various legal courses against his former partners for redress of what he considered wrongs that were done to him during their stormy business relationship. Meanwhile, as the Bronfmans rose to new heights, Chechik's fortunes sank. In 1924 the Saskatchewan Court of Appeal blocked one important avenue of litigation against his previous associates. Shortly after, Chechik drifted on the financial rocks when the government of New Brunswick seized over a million dollars' worth of his whisky for non-payment of taxes, while Ottawa went after him for additional tax payments going back to his Saskatchewan liquor operations.[85] Desperate for cash, Chechik negotiated various terms of settlement with the Bronfmans during 1925.

But no sooner did Chechik come within reach of an agreement than he demanded more — in a blackmailing pattern that Sam was to encounter several times in his life. During the autumn of 1925, when Sam was still heavily preoccupied with the LaSalle plant, he spent several weeks in Winnipeg going over the books and negotiating with Chechik's attorney, C.H. Locke, K.C. As Sam made clear, he considered the "moral tone" of the agreement "more important" than the "actual terms"; he refused to be bullied, and worked out a settlement that did not accept Chechik's shifting accusations of wrongdoing. Sam's lawyer, Alf Andrews, was impressed: "I must hand it to Sam as a settler," he wrote to Allan on November 12. "The best thing about the whole thing is that Locke told us that he was perfectly satisfied that all of the transactions between the boys and Chechik had been honest and straightforward. . . . Locke has a very high opinion of Sam's fairness and honesty." But the deal proved increasingly fragile as time passed.

Early in January, as the final details were being settled in Winnipeg, Sam received a call from Chechik, who was in Montreal and wanted to see him immediately at the Windsor Hotel. The next day Sam went to Chechik's room and chatted amiably, until the conversation took a sharply different tack. "The settlement made in Winnipeg is a lawyer's settlement," said Chechik, "that's alright, I will sign whatever papers they ask me to sign, but as between us, I have three points which must be settled." Chechik then produced a paper enumerating three new claims, totalling $75,000. "If you don't want to discuss settlement on these points, I must do anything I can to get what I can," Chechik went on, "you can think this over and if you don't consider these points don't blame me for what I do." Sam explained later, in a handwritten note to Andrews: "I was so dumbfounded by the audacity of the rat that I just looked at him and wondered how it was possible for anyone to be so low."

A week later Chechik met Sam again, urging him to "consider his claims privately and not bother the lawyers." Sam broke off the meeting. Furious, he sent an account to Andrews. "I told Locke on many occasions that this rat owed us plenty of money and that my coming to Winnipeg was not so much to get anything as to prove to Locke . . . my good name, and if I wanted to go into real figures I could present a pretty bill against the skunk." Chechik kept up the pressure, "telephoning about ten times a day both at the office and at the house," Sam told Andrews at the end of January.

There the matter remained: Chechik went ahead with the negotiated settlement at the beginning of 1926, pocketed some

$89,000, but conducted a kind of guerilla warfare against the Bronfmans for years afterwards, demanding the books of the partnership and claiming that, despite a release signed in 1926, certain issues remained outstanding. Eventually, as Chechik's fortunes continued to decline, his capacity to cause trouble drained away. Chechik, according to writer Peter Newman, "spent the last few years of his life at Montreal's Mount Royal Hotel, across Peel Street from the Seagram headquarters, constantly telephoning any Bronfman who would take his calls, and appearing at their offices. 'They don't like it that I'm here,' he wrote to his son in one of his last letters before he died in his hotel room of a heart attack on March 4, 1947."[86]

Just when the dispute with Meyer Chechik was reaching its sordid dénouement, dark clouds appeared on the horizon in the form of a wide-ranging scandal in the Federal Customs Department — triggered by one of the most deplorable accounts of bribery, corruption and embezzlement the Canadian House of Commons has ever heard. At its origins, the scandal had little to do with whisky. Rather, businessmen realized that the boats and trucks carying booze south of the border often returned to Canada filled with tobacco and other consumer products, which entered the Canadian market duty free. Canadian government officials, it was alleged, colluded with this traffic and refused to do anything about it. In parliament, the first blast was sounded in February 1926 by Harry H. Stevens, a maverick Conservative M.P. from British Columbia. Originally driven by a desire on the part of Canadian manufacturers for protection against unfair American competition, the charges eventually turned in a different direction, concentrating on the whisky trade and the Department of Customs. And on the firing line, even though he had left his post and been retired to the Senate, was someone who had gone to bat for Sam in the past, former customs minister Jacques Bureau.

Stevens's revelations pushed the beleaguered minority government of Mackenzie King to launch a full-dress parliamentary enquiry and then a Royal Commission on Customs and Excise, with a mandate to look into the widespread liquor smuggling, tax evasion and high-level wrongdoing. It was probably at this first sign of trouble, with the parliamentary enquiry, that the Bronfmans deliberately destroyed the books of several defunct exporting companies — almost certainly with a view to shielding their early operations from inquisitorial eyes.[87] The family prepared to weather the storm.

Prime Minister King, eager to restore the public confidence in his battered Liberal Party, turned to a party stalwart from Ontario to act as the royal commission's chief counsel, a man of deep Methodist conviction and unimpeachable rectitude — Newton Wesley Rowell. King could hardly have done better if he wanted to appear before the public as someone determined to clean house in matters relating to drink. For Rowell, whom we have glimpsed before as a law student travelling through Manitoba in 1889 lamenting the desecration of the sabbath, was also a lay preacher and a determined teetotaller, much of whose early political career had been dedicated "to blot out the curse of the liquor traffic," as he once announced from the hustings. Rowell's detestation of alcohol was a religious conviction, with whisky seen as the instrument of Satan himself. "You have on the one hand organized Christianity, and on the other hand the organized liquor interests," Rowell announced in an electoral campaign in 1914 as leader of the Liberals and author of the slogan "ban-the-bar."[88] Howard Ferguson, one of Rowell's more cynical Tory opponents, responded condescendingly to such enthusiasms: "I feel sorry for him. . . . He was brought from the pure atmosphere of the Layman's Missionary Movement and plunged into the slimy pool of Liberal politics."[89]

Only slightly more mellow twelve yars later, Rowell was a fastidious, hard-working, voluble moralist, who until 1926 had never seen a play on a stage. He "didn't smoke, didn't drink, didn't drink tea or coffee, he only drank water," according to Mark Shinbane. "I remember him as a goody-goody, very strait-laced," said one of Sam's employees.[90] Assured by the prime minister that he would be protected from fellow Liberals when the muck started to fly, Rowell determined to get to the bottom of the lawbreaking on the part of the "liquor interests." Hearings began in December 1926. Combing the country from west to east, the Royal Commission heard testimony in fourteen cities from Victoria to Saint John, audited no fewer than two hundred and seven companies, and issued ten interim reports before its final assessment.

As the commission got under way Sam was distracted by the purchase of the Seagram company and his jousting with Harry Hatch. But trouble appeared in February when a still-bitter Cyril Knowles testified in Winnipeg, accusing Harry of having attempted to bribe him. For weeks things did not go well. During its western sittings the commission aggressively investigated the export houses, spending a good deal of time on the Bronfmans' Saskatchewan operations. Summing up his findings in a letter to Mackenzie King on March 27, Rowell told the prime minister about the Bronfmans' dominance, together with the "Chechik-Rabinovitch group," of the liquor exports from that province and of the virtual "reign of terror" that they caused along the American border. For King, then particularly eager to smooth relations with Washington, this could not have been good to read.[91]

Sam, Allan and the family lawyers devoted considerable time to the hearings, preparing their testimony and plotting their strategy. They appeared supremely confident, even when communicating among themselves. "I am satisfied that we can knock Rowell and his evidence into a cocked hat," Allan wrote to Alf Andrews on April 8. "I think we must take all this very cooly but it is wise to quietly prepare evidence in case we find it necessary to use the material." Allan believed the family could deal easily with the bribery charge by discrediting the testimony of Knowles and his associates. Even more important, Allan told Andrews on May 7, the audit went well: "the Customs Auditors went through our distillery books and found everything absolutely clean. They asked if they could look at our Brintcan books stating frankly that they wanted to see if any improper payments had been made or if any political contributions had been made out of Brintcan [instead of from the Distillery business]. We told them they were at liberty to see anything they wanted and they went through them and found everything absolutely satisfactory."

Preparing his own testimony, Sam remained cool, even while having to fend off a pestering Meyer Chechik, who showed up awkwardly at the Windsor Hotel in Montreal. "Friend Chechik has been having social intercourse with me during recent weeks and I have not even bothered to write you about it," Sam told Andrews on June 15. Chechik, it seems, was still after a "settlement." "I paid no attention to these blackmailing bluffs," Sam continued, "for it was quite obvious that he was trying to take advantage of the situation, thinking that I was nervous about the Commission.... He is only seeking some way of getting some money...."

Following Barney Aaron and Harry, Sam appeared on the witness stand in Halifax in July, and then in Ottawa in September. Calm and collected, he made it clear that he did not want to talk about liquor exports, which were the work of sales companies, run by others. "I am the Managing Director of Distillers Corporation Limited. That is the business I look after."[92] And in fact, the questioning turned mainly on the mail-order and interprovincial whisky trade, subjects on which Sam proved unyielding. He, and not Harry, had been in charge, he insisted. He was the one who "instructed how the liquor should be blended," following processes, he told Rowell, commonly employed in the Old Country.[93] He gave the commissioners a brief lecture on the difference between blending and compounding and the practice of whisky making in Scotland. On "fictitious labels," he told the commissioners that these were widely used in Scotland. "You can get a bottler in the Old Country to make you up a label and make the blend of Scotch whiskey at whatever price you are willing to pay, and they will put you on a stock label over there just exactly as the liquor houses in Canada.... [T]he practice existed in Canada long before I was in the liquor business," he went on, "and anything I learned of the liquor business I learned in Canada."[94] Questioned about other matters — the "dirty-blue" batch of whisky, the family's failure to pay income taxes for four years before a general settlement in 1921, and the meeting in Jacques Bureau's office in Ottawa regarding Cyril Knowles, Sam proved to be an equally tough and unshakeable witness.

Throughout the hearings Sam maintained a relationship of sporting rivalry with Rowell and was not above a salacious jibe at the chief counsel's expense, according to a story told by Mark

Shinbane. Apparently Rowell asked Sam if he could see how whisky was made and Sam obliged, taking the former head of the Methodist Church Commission to see the vats with their bubbling, fermenting brew of grain mash. His visitor must have been the first "uplifter" to visit a Bronfman distillery, and Sam was ready to make the most of it. Rowell found the stench unbearable. "It's horrible," he said. "No wonder people should not drink this horrible stuff." At which point Sam leaned over to the chief counsel and replied: "Rowell, do you know how babies are born? It stinks too!"[95]

For a time it looked as if the Royal Commission might come down hard on the Bronfmans — even to the point of recommending criminal prosecutions — and it certainly would have done so if Rowell had had his way. But several of the commissioners believed the chief counsel had strayed beyond his evidence, and in the end they decided accordingly. Interim reports primarily blamed the customs officials for the contraventions of excise laws and other irregularities. Most important, in Sam's eyes, was the clean bill of health given to Distillers Corporation, apart from a minor technicality — an issue that was, indeed, before the courts. This contrasted sharply with Sam's competitors — Gooderham and Worts, Wiser's, Hiram Walker, Seagram (under pre-Bronfman ownership), and United Distillers — none of whom came out so well. The latter were all accused of various infractions of the law, most involving the smuggling of liquor into the United States, and also the making of large, undocumented political payoffs.[96]

One in the long list of recommendations issued by the Royal Commission did prove to be dangerous, however: the commissioners believed Cyril Knowles's story about attempted bribery and urged that Harry Bronfman be prosecuted. Unexpectedly, this particular recommendation became a major issue in Saskatchewan politics in 1929, one of the most turbulent election years in provincial history. During the campaign, tales about the nefarious exploits of Harry Bronfman provided convenient ammunition in the hands of opponents of "Jimmy" Gardiner, premier of the province and the manager of the once-powerful Liberal machine that ruled in Regina. Throughout the entire

year, Saskatchewan politics were in turmoil, churned up by
Protestant anger against Catholics, French Canadians and
immigrants—a break from the usual discontents about grain
marketing, freight rates and the like. In an effort to bring the
Liberals down, Saskatchewan Tories made common cause with a
variety of hate-inspired malcontents, including a new force on
the provincial scene, an import from the United States—the
Ku Klux Klan.[97]

Practically all of these antagonists of the Liberals found reason
to go after Harry—the ideal scapegoat, as James Gray notes: "He
was rich, he was a Liberal, but most of all he was a 'bootlegger'
and a Jew."[98] Harry's name first came up in the Arm River
provincial by-election of October 1928, when the Conservatives
pointedly raised the question: "Why had the government not
prosecuted the notorious bootlegger, Harry Bronfman?" Shaken
by a near-defeat of the Liberals in Arm River, Gardiner's
attorney general, T.C. Davis, promised to pursue the case. On the
other side, the Conservatives helped fund the Klan, which called
for a defence of the English language, racial purity and
opposition to the Jews. Their slogan encompassed an entire
spectrum of bigotry and hostility that rose to the surface—"One
Flag, One Language, One School, One Race, One Religion."
And in practically all of their campaigning and rallies the call
became deafening: "Why has the government not prosecuted
Harry Bronfman?"

In the raucous provincial electoral contest that ensued, the
Conservative *Regina Star*, financed by federal Tory leader R.B.
Bennett, was among the backers of the Klan and leader of the
mob that called for Harry's scalp. For days on end the paper
printed small boxed editorials, just under the paper's masthead,
demanding that "Harry Bronfman, wealthy Regina bootlegger"
be brought to justice. Practically every single day in May the
articles appeared below an appropriate headline: "Above the
Law," "Afraid to Act," "Time to Clean House," "What Is
the Answer?" "Justice Still Dumb," "A Ghastly Mockery" and
so on. Each day the editorial reminded the readers in a fixed
opening sentence that time was passing: "It is now 7 months and
14 days since Attorney General T.C. Davis pledged his word in
the Town Hall of Craik to the Arm River electors, that the

prosecution of Harry Bronfman, wealthy Regina bootlegger — as recommended by the Royal Commission on Customs Scandals [*sic*] — would be 'carried through to the end.' " "Under Gardiner machine rule," the paper declared, "while the machine rules the people, the bootlegger rules the machine."[99]

When Jimmy Gardiner went down to defeat in June, it was only a matter of time before the prosecution began. The family's ordeal, for such it was, began in November — embarrassingly for the Bronfmans, just after a DCL group from Edinburgh, headed by Ross and Herd, appeared in Montreal for a Distillers Corporation directors meeting. Harry was accused not only of bribing customs inspector Knowles in 1920, but also of tampering with witnesses in a 1922 liquor charge levelled against his brother-in-law David Gallaman.

Preliminary legal manoeuvres involved even more embarrassment; seeking dismissal of the charges using *habeas corpus* proceedings, Harry's lawyers needed to have him in an Ottawa jail while they appealed to Mr Justice Lyman Duff of the Supreme Court of Canada. Taken from Regina to Ottawa by the Mounties, Harry then languished in prison for several weeks. The distinguished jurist Duff, between bouts of heavy drinking, ruled against Harry, setting a trial in Estevan the following March on the bribery charge.[100]

Leading Harry's defence team was a celebrated Calgary criminal lawyer Alex McGillivary, K.C., a former high-ranking member of the Saskatchewan Conservative Party, well-known also for his weakness for the bottle. "I loved Alex, but he loved drink too much," remembered Sam's friend, Mark Shinbane, who also joined the team and helped line up witnesses. From Montreal, Sam and Allan joined the fray, with Sam's lawyer Laz Phillips passing along suggestions. Allan even contacted the famed San Francisco attorney and prairie spellbinder Aaron Sapiro, a former rabbinical student turned crusader for agricultural marketing cooperatives, and a man renowned for his speeches throughout the Canadian and American west. "I am with you completely," Sapiro wrote to Allan on January 23, promising to intervene with the new provincial government — possibly moved by the strong undercurrent of antisemitism that appeared to be behind the prosecution.

In his closing address in Estevan on the bribery charge, McGillivary presented Knowles as a man "possessed of a mania 'to get Bronfman' at all costs" and to destroy Harry's reputation. McGillivary also referred to the unmistakable antisemitic dimensions of the campaign against Harry. "I have a partner who is a Jew and I am proud of him," McGillivary told the jury. "Has the day come when race and prejudices are to play a part in our courts? Surely the day has not come in this fair western country when passion and prejudices will send some poor devil to incarceration because of some political hate."[101] The jury apparently agreed, for after deliberating four hours it announced its decision: Harry was acquitted.

The witness-tampering trial, which opened in Regina in September, was on a much grander scale and drew considerable public attention because of Harry's glittering legal talent and because of the high political visibility of the Crown's case. The *Manitoba Free Press* billed it as "one of the biggest legal battles ever known in the courts of Saskatchewan." As the case was being prepared, Sam went to Winnipeg to be close at hand and to join in the plotting of strategy. Saidye wrote to him at the Fort Garry Hotel on August 26: "I only hope that very soon all will be over and we shall be able to enjoy the fruits of your toil, endeavors and ambitions." After speaking with Sam on the telephone Saidye told him on August 30: "You sounded quite cheerful but I know how deep there is that awful fear of what is about to take place. School opens Wednesday, Mindel is so excited. Imagine having a daughter going to school." Two days later she wrote again: "I know when everything is over, please God, what a source of satisfaction and pleasure it will be to you to know that your efforts were rewarded, especially for your own brother."

As the lawyers plotted, tensions increased. Sam was at the breaking point, blowing up at Mark Shinbane inexplicably one day, raving about "blood-sucking lawyers." Sam was so violent, his friend recalled, that Shinbane quit the case on the spot. Three days later, a contrite Sam appeared in his friend's office — in a pattern that repeated itself often in his life. "Look Shin," he said, "I owe you an apology. I shouldn't have said it, you didn't deserve it. . . . I don't want you to leave the case."[102] In Montreal, Saidye knew what a toll the affair was taking. On

September 3, she reported to Sam on little Mindel's first day of school, but also expressed her concern: "I do hope that when this horrible mess is over you will have a chance to relax." "I am with you in spirit my darling every hour of this horrible ordeal," she told him on the 9th. "I know what courage it takes to face it all but darling justice must be meted out and Harry must get it." Near the end of his three weeks she wrote again: "I know only too well what a horrible ordeal you are going through . . . was glad to hear that so far everything looks favourable."

Sam, it seems, was not merely a spectator at the Fort Garry Hotel. In his own account, at least, it was his idea to investigate one of the Crown's key witnesses, William Denton, with the result that his suspicions were confirmed: Denton was "as complete a scalawag as Prohibition had produced, in Saskatchewan or anywhere else," as James Gray puts it, a notorious liar whose testimony could go to the highest bidder.[103] In an extraordinary coup, Sam and the defence team decided to lay a trap for Denton, drawing him to a meeting in a Regina hotel room with a friendly agent who pretended to bribe him to change his story. Harry's lawyers concealed a court reporter in the room when Denton accepted the offer, utterly exploding the prosecution's case when a transcript of the meeting was later presented in court. As a result, Harry was acquitted. It took the jury ten minutes to decide.

Enormously relieved, Sam and Harry returned to Montreal. Evidently, the relationship between the two had suffered. For although deeply loyal to his brother, Sam was also mortified by the specter of a Bronfman in the dock and charges against the family constantly in the press. It is impossible to say what Sam really thought of the accusations against Harry—Saidye's reference to "justice must be meted out" suggests the possibility that he might even have believed him guilty. While it is obvious that his main goal was to win an acquittal, it seems likely that Sam blamed Harry in part at least for what had happened. Unfairly, perhaps, but entirely characteristically, Sam did not let such things pass. Returning to work, Harry did not join Sam and Allan in the new headquarters on Peel Street in Montreal, but took up his tasks instead at LaSalle—"carrying out as best I could the wishes and desires that came from the head office," as he put it in his memoir. Harry never became a director of Distillers Corporation-Seagrams, and after seven more years, during which there were additional strains in his relationship with Sam, he went into an early retirement, disgruntled and unhappy about how he had been treated.[104]

■

BY MID-1930 the Depression was beginning to eat away at the Bronfmans' whisky empire. Alcohol securities fell with all the others. In both Canada and the United States, as belts tightened, less liquor was consumed. Prices plummeted and Canadian taxes on whisky increased. Meanwhile, provincial, federal and U.S. government enforcement of liquor laws tightened, with a measure of success reported in the war against smugglers. In March, having long resisted American pressure, Mackenzie King took steps to ban clearances of vessels loaded with whisky bound for the United States, making it plain in his House of Commons speech that he was acting for moral reasons, if necessary in defiance of public opinion. An immediate result, the *Financial Post* estimated, was that Canada would lose about $20 million a year in excise taxes.

Following the ban on clearances, competition among distillers intensified and prices tumbled, with all companies trying to boost exports and find a way to St Pierre and Miquelon—the main legal outlet for liquor bound for the United States.[105] From Washington, the Canadian *chargé d'affaires*, Hume Wrong, noted with alarm the heavier traffic of Canadian ships carrying liquor to and from the French islands, some of them guided by secret high-seas radio stations that directed them to smaller, faster boats that ran past the U.S. Coast Guard on their way to Rum Row.[106]

Sam's exports could not easily be challenged, Seagram having built up the strongest position of any company on St Pierre and Miquelon. But although its share of the market more than held its own, profits of Distillers Corporation-Seagrams declined along with other companies—from $3.8 million in 1930 to $2.7 million in 1931 and $1.5 million in 1932. Weathering the storm, the company decided not to pay dividends to its shareholders but to

reinvest instead. Sam was, for once, in a defensive posture. Even at home things looked grim. Following elections in July 1930, R.B. Bennett's Conservatives ousted the Liberals from power in Ottawa, which was another blow to Sam, who had long since supported the Liberal Party. Sam had reason to believe, owing to the Tories' machinations in Saskatchewan, that the new prime minister had a particular grudge against his family.

Sam's analysis was that the Canadian industry as a whole was over-capitalized, had too great a producing capacity with stocks far in excess of sales requirements. With annual sales of just 2.5 million gallons a year, Canadian distillers were by this time carrying an expensive inventory of over 40 million gallons — a staggering sixteen-year supply, aging in barrels. One result was a disastrous price war in the export field, and the prospect of "unrestricted and suicidal competition in the domestic market" as well.[107] In an effort to address the crisis, Sam got together with his major competitors at the beginning of 1931 to conclude a pooling agreement, through a new company, Dominion Factors Ltd. Put simply, the five major distillers hoped to divide the shrinking market among them, based on what they determined to be the market share of each company at the time. Sam was the obvious leader, by virtue of the strength of DC-SL. Distillers Corporation took 38.2 percent of the shares, Hiram Walker 26.7 percent, Canadian Industrial Alcohol 18.7 percent, the British Columbia Distillery 9.675 percent, and United Distillers 6.725 percent. The parties agreed, or thought they agreed, that their export sales would be handled exclusively by Dominion Factors, although the pool excluded Scotch-type whisky and gin manufactured or blended in Canada. To head the new company, the shareholders elected the decorous Lord Shaughnessy of the Canadian Industrial Alcohol Company, son of the builder of the CPR. Sam was vice-president.[108]

In pressing for a pooling arrangement, Sam almost certainly had in mind a Canadian equivalent of his British mentor, the Distillers Company Limited. His own DC-SL would be *primus inter pares* in a coalition of the leading figures of the whisky trade determined to put order into the business. For a very short time the prospects seemed promising, and prices rose along the Atlantic coast. But from the start the participants squabbled over which sales fell within the quotas and which did not; Sam challenged what he felt were the excessively high prices the pool imposed, suggesting that this was unfair to his customers. Even worse, after several challenges of the pool's legality, Sam began receiving opinions that the pool contravened the law because it suggested a direct intention to export liquor to the United States — something explicitly forbidden by Mackenzie King's Export Act of 1930.

Seeking a solution, Sam and Allan travelled to England in the summer of 1931 together with Harry Hatch and the other representatives of the Big Five for a high-level conference of British and Canadian distillers. From Montreal, Harry regularly cabled his brothers at the Carlton Hotel about the operation of the pool, which was showing signs of strain. From time to time he also sent messages about the families, including news on Sam's four children — Mindel and Phyllis, ages six and four; Edgar, born in 1929 and now two years old; and the baby, Charles, who had arrived just a few weeks before Sam set sail. Meeting at Kinnaird House in London, the participants considered the possibility of a grand Canadian merger, as Sam preferred — only to see the discussions shatter on legal difficulties and the participants' inability to agree upon the relative importance of their own business. Despite Thomas Herd's warnings of future price-cutting that would affect the industry worldwide, the talks collapsed.[109]

During the discussions in London the possibility first arose of a merger between Hiram Walker and Distillers Corporation — an option that neither Sam nor Hatch relished, but towards which each felt drawn because of the ruinous price war and the prospects of a further shrinking market. For about a year conditions remained the same. In the spring of 1932 Sam and Saidye travelled to Europe on the *Empress of Australia* on a business trip to Britain followed by, as Sam put it, "a little jaunt around Europe by way of celebrating our tenth wedding anniversary." Writing to Sam from Montreal, Allan relayed news regularly, suggesting that great changes were in the offing in the liquor industry: Hiram Walker, which had suffered mightily from its weak position after clearances were stopped, was still selling whisky in Detroit and routing it through St

Pierre. Meanwhile, the "noble experiment" was being seriously challenged in the United States and rumours circulated that prohibition might be repealed.

Merger discussions were in the air once again in the summer of 1932, with Thomas Herd and Harry Hatch feeling each other out on the prospects for a union of Walkers and the British conglomerate. Sam was kept abreast of all these communications and he urged his British colleagues not to accept Hatch's terms. Full of confidence, Sam telegraphed Herd on October 18, raising the possibility of "favourable change" in the United States. In that event, he went on, "our superiority [of] products and well known brands would ensure far greater returns [to] our company. You may take Walkers earnings [in the] past year [as] nil, Distillers as $1 million." As rumours began to circulate about the merger of two Canadian giants, Walkers and Distillers Corporation, discussions between Sam and Harry Hatch opened in the autumn of 1932.

Writing to Hatch on November 16, Sam noted that while the fixed assets of Walkers and DC-SL were roughly the same, his company's overall sales were almost three times as great as Walkers', due to Sam's overwhelming superiority in exports. By Sam's calculation his firm was responsible for 60 percent of the entire Canadian overseas trade. Given the instability in both domestic and foreign sales, Sam raised the question of whether the two firms should not "by mutual concession and good will regulate the situation for the benefit of all." Two weeks later Hatch replied, disputing Sam's evaluation of Walkers. As he saw it, the end of prohibition "is already in sight," and when it was over Sam's advantages would largely disappear. Considerably before repeal, therefore, the seeds of a new round of rivalry were sown.

From Edinburgh, Thomas Herd suggested that Sam break off negotiations and instead approach the smaller companies first, still pursuing the goal of a big Canadian combine. Desultory exchanges in this vein continued, until finally, a few months later, the prospect of repeal stared everyone in the face. Suddenly, everything looked different, and Sam's attention turned to meet the new opportunities. Distillery stock prices soared, and talk of mergers became a thing of the past.[110]

CHAPTER IV

The Empire Grows

"I BUILD BRICK on brick," Sam liked to say. Ten years after the first foundations were laid in Montreal, Sam could look with pride at the edifice he had constructed. After a decade, the Bronfman name carried weight in Canadian industry. By 1933 Sam and his British partners had conquered some 40 percent of the Canadian whisky market and the family's Brintcan holding company listed assets amounting to $5,568,147 — $2.2 million in Distillers Corporation-Seagrams Limited shares, $1.7 million in investments in various companies, over $1 million in real estate and properties, and more than $500,000 in loans, mortgages and miscellaneous holdings.[1]

These achievements turned Distillers Corporation-Seagrams into a global force, running neck and neck with Harry Hatch's Hiram Walker-Gooderham and Worts. As the *Financial Post* noted in mid-January 1930, "the claim that the company operates the largest distillery in the world is not an idle one."[2] Carefully nurtured by Sam himself, the LaSalle and Waterloo plants meshed entirely different processes — distilling, blending, aging and bottling — all of which received a great boost, thanks to British capital and technology. DC-SL may have been considered by some the second Canadian distiller, given Hatch's slight edge in inventory, but we have seen Sam's confident dismissal of his rival's standing. Seagram had much more of the kind of whiskies sought in the American market, Sam told his rival Hatch in November 1932, and its volume of trade was almost three times that of Hiram Walker. With a much stronger trading position at the time of repeal, Sam was already, in his own mind, number one.[3]

◼

SAM'S VIEWS ON the style of life appropriate to this pre-eminence were happily contradictory—and never troubled him for a moment. On the one hand, he took little interest in luxury goods and had no time for interior decoration, automobiles, resort vacations and the like. But on the other hand, he wanted to surround himself with quality, and took considerable trouble to communicate this fact to the outside world. Sam would have agreed with film producer Adolph Zukor, who once justified his own prodigious material consumption by saying: "I have always believed that if a man surrounds himself with good things, he sets a standard in his own eyes as well as those of others." Uninterested in money for what it could buy, Sam never carried any cash, and "it was almost impossible to get him to spend it," especially on himself, according to his son Edgar. But money was nevertheless important. "You were somebody if you had money," Edgar now explains Sam's view, "and if you had a lot of money you were more of a somebody."

Parsimonious about small things, likely the imprint of his family's struggle with poverty in Brandon and Winnipeg, Sam was famous for turning off the lights in his office and complaining about minor extravagances. There was a time when Edgar used to get his hair cut every week—"so that I wouldn't look like I just had a haircut," he told an interviewer. "I only get my hair done every three or four weeks," Sam told his son, with a twinkle in his eye. (Sam had little hair by then.) "What do you do with the money you save?" Edgar asked. "I give it to you, of course," was Sam's cheery reply. "That's how I can afford it."[4] As one close associate remembered, Sam used to carry a spare pair of socks in his briefcase in case the streets were wet and he wanted a change. Upon seeing this "I made no comment," wrote Max Melamet, "but thought to myself that all he had to do was to press a button, and half a dozen secretaries would have been available to do for him whatever shopping he required."[5]

Sam's nightmare was being poor, as his daughter Phyllis recalls. "In early life poverty was an overriding shame. At fifty my father would shudder when talking about going to school with holes in his pants — he did not want his children to be subject to such ignominy." Sam's sister Laura once lived in a mansion and, in his eyes, cut corners by moving chairs from the dining room to the living room. Sam found this way of living repellent and told his family so.[6]

"I don't care how many dresses you buy, but buy good ones," Sam admonished his wife when they were first married. And so it was with his home. Sam did not want to be troubled by details, but he also spared no expense to preserve his family from material hardship. Living on Comte Street, Saidye recalled, the family had a cook, two maids and two nurses, one for each daughter. So far as money was concerned, Sam made clear to his wife, "what's mine is yours." There was no question of separate bank accounts. "At almost any time during our marriage I could have signed my name on cheques for millions of dollars if I had wanted to do so," Saidye declared.[7]

In the summer of 1928, after about four years in relatively small rented accommodations, Sam bought a very large house at 15 Belvedere Road, in Westmount, high on the slopes of Mount Royal. Named "Oaklands" for the stately trees that grow thick on the property, the brick house was in very poor repair, but sat in the midst of a magnificent, heavily wooded lot in what was then a pleasant, relatively recent suburb — though by no means, however, the first choice of Montreal's anglophone élite, running second to a posh district called the Golden Square Mile. Sam's original intention was to tear down the crumbling structure and build two new houses, one for Allan and one for himself. But in the end he and Saidye decided to remodel the old home, advised by its original architect Robert Findley. This process took about two years and involved a substantial reordering of rooms and some addition to the 1905 structure.

Meanwhile, Allan purchased an adjoining property, and eventually the two brothers had the house in between torn down to build a bicycle path for their children, and, much later, a

swimming pool. During this time, Charles recalls, a neighbourhood friend, Benny Parsons, now a senior partner with the
Clarkson Tetrault law firm, would walk daringly on the steel
beams of the old house, to the admiration of the Bronfman
boys.[8]

When it came to furnishing the mansion, Sam took no direct
part, but his injunction to Saidye was the same as with her
clothing: "Buy the best."[9] Saidye energetically took up the
challenge. In keeping with the customs of the day among affluent
Montrealers, all the furniture was specially manufactured, using
drawings of antique designs; throughout the large house
everything had to be chosen—draperies, carpets, panelling.
Saidye later engaged George Haycock, a famous Montreal
decorator, selecting pieces with care and making periodic trips to
New York to purchase works of art. The result, she later recalled,
was in the fashion of the 1930s, "very dark and heavy," and was
later redone as fashion turned to genuine antique pieces.

As with the making of whisky, the Old Country was the model
in putting together the Bronfmans' new home, drawing on the
magnificent houses and hotels the couple visited in Britain and
Europe. For Saidye, these visits were a revelation. She first
accompanied her husband in his travels overseas in 1929 when
she was pregnant with Edgar, and from the beginning of
February to the end of March they were abroad—spending time
with Thomas Herd and his wife in Glasgow and Edinburgh, then
visiting London for a month to see the DCL people, taking a day
at Epsom Downs, and finally a vacation in Cannes. "I had never
been overseas," she wrote. "We sailed on one of the Allen Line
ships from Halifax to Greenock. . . . I had about eight or nine
evening gowns, all made especially for me, because in those days
you couldn't buy maternity clothes."[10]

Typically, while Sam was preoccupied with business talk and
was practically oblivious to his physical surroundings, Saidye
noted every detail of the houses they visited—to the point of
taking notes after dinner parties, describing the menu, the order
of service and so on. She made careful observations of
furnishings, entertainment and social customs. "I was particularly interested and learned a great deal from the way in which
people with different lifestyles and ideas decorated their houses."

More than a half century later, she remembered particulars — the practice of "elevenses," or tea at eleven o'clock, for society ladies in Edinburgh; the races at Ascot, where the Bronfmans occupied the DCL company box; their luxurious suite in the Carlton Hotel in London with windows facing the Thames, equipped, remarkably, with its own telephone; and the glittering spectacle of the casino at Cannes, when Saidye was stunned at the jewellery worn by other women and, although wrapped in a floor-length white ermine cape, she felt in comparison "like Little Orphan Annie."[11]

By the early 1930s, Sam was well known in the British liquor industry, and the couple lived regally when travelling abroad. "We met many people in British leadership circles," Saidye wrote of their visit to Europe in 1932. "We had to bring two steamer trunks of evening dress because we were invited to a different party every night of the week."[12] While travelling on the Continent that summer, there was one business acquaintance whose reception and lifestyle they reflected upon afterward with some attention — Joachim von Ribbentrop, introduced to Sam by his wine-merchant friend Franz Sichel. Ribbentrop, who became Hitler's foreign minister and was eventually hanged at Nuremberg, had spent about four years in Canada as a champagne salesman, and had joined the Nazi Party only a few weeks before meeting Sam and Saidye Bronfman from Montreal. Particularly in retrospect, they felt shaken by the encounter. Years later, Sam told Jewish audiences of his premonitions regarding Nazism, and of how he questioned the newly registered Hitler supporter about Nazi policies towards Jews. Ribbentrop's answer, according to Sam, was dismissive: "I can assure you that nothing will happen to the Jews when we take over. This is all politics. Everything will be fine. In fact, some wealthy Jews secretly supported us and we will remember that."[13]

When the renovation of Oaklands was finally completed, the Bronfmans occupied a house with twenty rooms and engaged as many as eight servants. Harry and Abe bought houses nearby, and so all four brothers lived within a few blocks of each other. With four young children, and close relatives next door, Sam and Saidye's home was a lively place, not unlike what each had known in their childhood. Having grown up in small towns and in

Winnipeg, both came from large families that entertained often, and both had lived in affluence for some time before their marriage. As a result, the couple adapted easily to family life in an atmosphere of solid, quiet luxury—even if not the imperial splendour that has sometimes been attributed to them.

As well as a home, Oaklands became a meeting place for both business and community purposes—once again a reflection of Sam and Saidye's childhood experience in the West, in an age before public facilities were commonly available. When in Montreal, Sam would often confer with business associates in the small mahogany-panelled library on Saturday or Sunday mornings; he held larger meetings, usually Jewish community gatherings, in a large basement room where the children otherwise used to play. Later Sam dubbed the latter "the sweatshop," the place where he would raise money for various Jewish causes, subjecting his guests to the fund-raiser's relentless pressure. Saidye organized countless luncheons, dinners and receptions at Oaklands—sometimes a formidable logistical challenge, for which she developed a particular flair. Lilianne Lagadec, daughter of the family's chauffeur, had vivid recollections of those parties, and how they looked from her family's apartment over the garage: the butler Jensen "ran the inside," and her father, Eugène Bourdeau, "looked after the outside." "He would get several people to park the cars, my Dad, and he'd stay at the door and receive everyone, because he knew everyone, open the door for them and all that. And the cars were taken and being parked. A real system. Almost something like you see in the movies."[14]

Although boisterous with the playing of children, the coming and going of family and other visitors, the Bronfmans' home was governed by an old-world formality, with the tone set in part by the servants. Bourdeau the chauffeur, himself of the old school, dressed in a dark navy uniform, with a double-breasted jacket, britches and boots. With his singleminded sense of duty, his daughter remembered, he would ignore her and her mother rather than stop for them when he was driving up the steep hill on the way to 15 Belvedere Road. For a time before the outbreak of war in 1939 the Bronfmans owned two automobiles—a Rolls-Royce and a Packard. Bourdeau would drive all the children to school—although Sam insisted that this not be in the Rolls. Bourdeau not only looked after the Bronfmans' cars, he would also buy them, since Sam himself was completely uninterested in doing so. When it came time to replace the family's automobile, dealers would bring their stock to the house and park their cars on display all around the circular driveway.

Jensen, the butler, also set an Old Country tone from the moment he greeted people, with a quizzical smile, when he opened the door. A Danish engineer who worked for the family until 1953, Jensen was handsome, reserved and dignified—as befit the Danish Royal Guard, of which he was a veteran. Sometimes the children teased him, trying to break his austere mien, but Jensen kept a straight face, as Phyllis later recalled: "the sentinel watching us—often quite disapprovingly—while standing behind the Master's chair."[15] The children's friends were vaguely frightened of Jensen, being unused to dealing with anyone in his role. More generally, according to Phyllis, Oaklands was just too formal for friends to visit; from a child's point of view, "our house was a most forbidding place."[16]

While neither stiff nor uncommunicative, Sam observed a certain formality about his home. Immaculately dressed, usually in dark suits, he never ate without his jacket, and wanted his sons to do the same. Photographs of Sam in relaxed circumstances— whether lounging around the house, in the country at Ste Marguerite, or even, once, on a camel in Egypt—practically always show him with a necktie and a well-pressed, buttoned suit. Keen on decorum, Sam was too nervous to hold his children when they were babies, fearing he might drop them. When they were older, the children regularly joined their parents for a traditional sabbath dinner on Friday night and again for a Sunday lunch; the only meals they took together as a family, these were formal affairs, with the boys at Sam's end of the table and the girls at Saidye's, and with all four youngsters dressed in their best clothes.

"There was a constant dichotomy between our Jewish upbringing and the life of the upper class," Phyllis recalls, identifying "a style that probably came from British royalty." "We had Danish, Canadian, French nurses and governesses, who meted out cod liver oil and some form of punishment every day (mostly spankings), Milk of Magnesia once a week, and insisted on a bland diet and keeping neat and clean and doing our homework."[17] The youngsters received some Jewish training, on the margins of their childhood — Sunday school, private tutoring in Hebrew, and the family-centred Jewish festivities a few times a year. Much more prominent were the obligations of a patrician childhood — piano lessons, horseback-riding lessons, ceremonial meals and so on — a regimen that Phyllis and Edgar, at least, seem to have found increasingly restrictive. Edgar remembered his nurse asking him, on the occasion of his *bar mitzvah*, what he wanted as a present. "I want you to leave," was his succinct reply.[18]

Family photographs, especially the formal poses, show the children as the very models of young English aristocracy: immaculately dressed and groomed, the girls appear with huge hair bows and long taffeta dresses with lace cuffs and collars, and the boys with peaked caps, suits with short pants and stiff collars. High Holy Day dinners and the Passover seder were memorable as a time for dressing up — a coming together of Jewish tradition and the ways of the upper-class Protestant élite of the day. But the Bronfmans did not mix easily with Jews or non-Jews outside their family and a small Jewish circle in Westmount. Indeed, Phyllis recalls how confining was the Bronfmans' social life — limited largely to family and to business associates in the early years, and explained not only by social circumstances but also by Sam's periodic absence, as we shall see, commuting regularly to New York. Within the Jewish community in the 1930s, one should add, the Bronfmans stood apart as a result of their wealth and prominence — to the point that the Bronfman children were stared at as they entered and left synagogue, and people commented on the absence of Jewish children at formal dances given at the family home.[19]

One of the hazards of being very rich and prominent in the early 1930s was kidnapping, which had a vogue in the Depression era and which from time to time has haunted the Bronfman family ever since. Everyone became conscious of this nightmarish possibility in the spring of 1932, when kidnappers seized the baby of Charles Lindbergh, the internationally revered aviator who several years before had flown solo across the Atlantic. Sam and Saidye were en route to Europe on the *Empress of Australia* when the Lindbergh baby was found murdered in May, and the couple was jittery. "Children lovely, everybody well," Allan cabled to them on the 17th, sensing their fears.

Although he did not know it at the time, Sam himself had a brush with kidnappers in 1931, the year after the family moved to Belvedere Road, when Edgar was just two years old and Charles was not yet born. That year a group of Detroit and Chicago gangsters on the hunt for Canadian millionaires targeted both the London, Ontario brewer John Labatt and Sam Bronfman. Since Labatt was ill and apparently unavailable, two carloads of crooks, armed to the teeth with submachine guns and assorted weapons, went after Sam in Montreal, and might even have succeeded in taking him if they had approached the task more professionally. The night before the planned "snatch," however, the gang participated in a boisterous party in the Mount Royal Hotel and matters got out of hand: posing as a plainclothes police officer one of their number forced his attentions upon a lady in an adjoining room; before the evening was over he was arrested and charged with impersonating an officer. Fearing their colleague would reveal the intended kidnapping, the rest of the gangsters immediately left town and abandoned their plans. All this came to light after the same crooks abducted John Labatt in 1934, and then were caught and tried for this crime the next year.[20]

Sam and Saidye remained fearful of kidnapping during the 1930s, and took what precautions they could. Sam had a high security fence built around the houses on Belvedere Road and attempted, when his children were young at least, to keep them out of the public limelight. For the children in particular, their parents' precautions became a further confining element of life at Oaklands. Still, Montreal was a relatively safe city, as Sam realized, and this was certainly a consideration when he decided to remain there after the end of prohibition and commute to New York rather than uproot his family.

About the same time that the workers began renovating Oaklands, Sam created the perfect expression of his own imperial style with the building of a new Distillers Corporation headquarters at 1430 Peel Street—a miniature copy of a sixteenth-century castle, modelled, in Sam's view, on the castles of Scotland he so much admired. Kitsch though it may appear today, with its battlements, turrets and spiked portcullis, the Seagram headquarters must have seemed like a bit of home to the Scotsmen from DCL who attended the first meeting when the building opened in the spring of 1929. For among the Scotch whisky makers, Scottish kitsch was a respected motif. The visitors from the Old Country likely attended the Wembley Empire Exhibit in 1924, for example, and if they had done so they could not have missed the "Palace of Industry," where some forty Scotch whisky firms displayed their products in a specially constructed model of a fifteenth-century baronial castle, over the portcullis of which was the motto "Alba Gu Brath," or "Scotland Forever"—the battle cry of the Gordon Highlanders at Waterloo, hopelessly outnumbered as they charged and scattered their enemy.[21]

As with the construction of the LaSalle plant, Sam pored over the plans of this building and lavished attention on the smallest details. His idea was to plant the company's headquarters in the centre of Montreal, choosing a spot immediately opposite the huge new Mount Royal Hotel, the talk of the town in 1929 and an obvious attraction for an affluent travelling public. "I told the architect I wanted to build a baronial castle," Sam explained. The architect, David Jerome Spence, who also designed the Sacred Heart Convent in Montreal and McGill University's Strathcona Hall, toiled over the drawings with Sam, who proved a hard man to please. Priority was given to the building's appearance from the street, and only when that was decided did Sam yield to Harry and the architect who designed the interior together. The result, says one unfriendly critic, is "the worst of Tudor and Gothic with early Disneyland."[22] Sam was and remained immensely proud of the building, however. "Did you notice the Scottish thistles?" he asked an interviewer about the façade many years later.

Sam's sense of his standing in his industry required an almost constant validation from the community at large, a confirmation that his company and its achievements were respected and appreciated. In November 1932, DC-SL's annual report for the first time carried a crest "By appointment to his Excellency the Governor General of Canada," signifying, as the report explained, that "Seagram's Famous Rye Whiskies have received the signal honour of having been selected for use in the residence of His Excellency Lord Bessborough." (Similar affirmations, it might be noted, were commonly used in the Scottish whisky industry, and this form might have been one more thing Sam picked up during his visits to Britain.) Immensely proud of such endorsements, Sam also worked hard to establish his firm and his family as community benefactors, and in so doing ran circles around the staid anglophone business élite of Montreal.

One of the great Montreal events of 1930, for example, was the visit of the giant British dirigible R-100, sent across the Atlantic to demonstrate the viability of trans-oceanic flights that would link the Commonwealth. (Unfortunately, the effort collapsed catastrophically later that year when a sister ship R-101 crashed to the ground in France.) Wishing the intrepid crew and passengers godspeed as the refuelled R-100 left Montreal, heading back to England, were none other than Sam and Allan Bronfman, who hosted a luncheon for the visitors at the Mount Royal Hotel. After a hearty meal of English lamb chops, the officers and crew sailed away with a rendition of Tennyson's "Locksley Hall" on their souvenir menus:

For I lept into the future as far as human eye could see,
Saw the Vision of the world and all the wonders that would be;
Saw the heavens filled with commerce, argosies of magic sails,
Pilots of the purple twilight, dropping down with costly bales.

"Sam Bronfman, who acted as chairman, expressed the feeling of enthusiasm which the visit of the R-100 aroused in the breasts of all Canadians," said the report in the *Montreal Star*.[23]

In the early 1930s, Sam and Allan conceived a brilliant series of promotional events that set new standards in the field, winning hearts in the Montreal sports community. Such were the Seagram-sponsored marathon snowshoe races between Montreal and Quebec City, with prize money of over $10,000 in cash — "a typically Canadian sport which had, previously, been allowed to drift into discard," as the *Montreal Herald* noted appreciatively.

Other events included the Seagram Belt for the featherweight boxing championship of the universe, swimming marathons, foot races and a Seagram Gold Cup golf tournament at the General Brock Hotel links in Niagara Falls — in all a whopping $200,000 outlay by "the Bronfman brothers," according to the calculations of *Le Petit Journal*.[24]

In the Jewish community too, the Bronfmans began to stand out. From the time they arrived in Montreal the family donated large sums to Jewish causes, but they played no leadership role for several years. Allan and Abe took the first steps, launching an appeal for a Jewish hospital in the beginning of 1927, and carrying on a massive fund-raising exercise until the building was finally completed in 1934. According to several accounts, Allan "was sort of designated by the family" in 1929 to lead the hospital campaign — to which the Bronfmans all made prodigious contributions. Sam remained more or less in the background, taking on the job of public relations for which he was showing a remarkable aptitude. But he was a continuous presence. "Every bit of literature was submitted to Sam for approval," said Sam Cohen, who later became hospital administrator.

With Sam Jacobs, Liberal member of parliament from Montreal and senior statesman of Canadian Jewry, Sam was elected joint chairman of the Jewish Immigrant Aid Society in 1931, deepening his involvement. He became prominent in the Federation of Jewish Philanthropies of Montreal at the same time and took over its presidency three years later — putting him at the forefront of Jewish public life in the most important city for Canadian Jewry. All this, as we shall see, occurred during a difficult, stressful period — the wrangling over the distillers' marketing pool, the ending of prohibition in the United States, and, in 1935, a damaging criminal investigation of the Bronfman family by the RCMP.

■

DID SAM FORESEE the end of prohibition in the United States? Many signs pointed in that direction, and in an industry so heavily dependent on exports to the U.S., every one of them was keenly watched in Montreal. Under the presidency of Herbert

Hoover, evidence accumulated that the enforcement of liquor laws was a shambles, increasingly discredited by American public opinion. Press magnate William Randolph Hearst, previously a stalwart supporter of the drys, deserted the cause in 1929, contending that the Volstead Act actually discouraged temperance by creating a criminal subculture that thrived on drink. The American Bar Association agreed, joining the bandwagon for repeal the same year. A public-opinion poll by the *Literary Digest* in 1930 suggested that about 30 percent of Americans wanted modification of the Eighteenth Amendment, 30 percent wanted no change, and 40 percent favoured outright repeal.[25] State authorities, meanwhile, short of funds, hungered after the tax revenues that would be theirs when beer, wine and liquor flowed again.

Repeal became a particularly vexing issue in American political life when the economic depression prompted calls for social and economic change. This is one reason why Herbert Hoover's high-level investigation of prohibition enforcement — the Wickersham Commission — so dissatisfied people when it opposed any modification of the Volstead Act in 1931. Walter Lippmann expressed the widespread disappointment with the findings: "What was done was to evade a direct and explicit official confession that federal prohibition is a hopeless failure."

Politicians were more sensitive to the straws in the wind — and notably Franklin Delano Roosevelt, the Democratic candidate who carefully eased himself into the anti-prohibition camp. To tumultuous applause in their Chicago convention hall the following year, the Democrats called the repeal, and the Republicans, previously supporters of the status quo, now backed modification. "Prohibition," H.L. Mencken wrote triumphantly, "has suddenly fallen over like a house of cards."[26]

After Roosevelt's victory in the presidential elections of November 1932, Congress began the elaborate process to bury the Volstead Act by passing a new constitutional amendment. Both the House and Senate passed resolutions calling for repeal, after which conventions in the various states assembled to vote on the issue. It took two hundred and eighty-eight days to secure the thirty-six states needed to overturn prohibition — a considerably shorter time for repeal, it was pointed out, than to pass the original Eighteenth Amendment fourteen years before.

Years after, Sam maintained that he had long predicted the end of prohibition — able to see the woods because he was not too close to the trees, as one journalist argued.[27] Sam seems indeed to have had such a long view, but the trees did matter at the time, and Sam was mightily concerned about them. Travelling in Europe with Saidye as the political world shifted decisively away from prohibition, Sam received bulletins on this subject every few days from Allan. "I have been devouring whatever I could lay my hands on in connection with the American situation," Allan wrote to Sam at the Carlton Hotel in London, on June 22, 1932, passing along some *New York Times* articles on the struggle against the Volstead Act. A week later Allan reported on a conversation with Lew Rosenstiel, a veteran American distiller who dropped in on the Democratic National Convention in Chicago to assess prospects for repeal. "He states with more definiteness than ever that unquestionably the change is coming." "This letter should clear up the doubt which you raised when I was talking to you at Geneva," Allan went on, "and if there is really going to be a change, then we should not delay our plans both as regards agencies generally and as regards arrangements with the DCL for the United States."[28]

Still, it was not clear that with repeal Canadian liquor would be able to enter the United States freely. In a letter of November 16 to Harry Hatch, Sam exuded caution: "it is too optimistic to hope for favourable governmental action in the United States on spirits for a considerable length of time," he wrote, reminding Hatch how cumbersome and slow legislative action on such matters was — perhaps with the intent of lulling his competitor into a partnership on his conditions. But Sam worried about the short term, in particular about the uncertainties associated with the end of prohibition. Canadian distillers seemed to be on the verge of a destructive price war that might undercut any advantages repeal provided. "No one knows the conditions which will govern this export market," Sam told his rival, "but I think you and I are agreed that for a certain length of time there will be a heavy demand after which there will be practically none. It is during this period that we should be in a position to sell to the best advantage, and to explore what opportunities for future activity the situation presents."

In June 1933, DCL sent a secretive, high-level team headed by managing director Thomas Herd to New York to test the American waters. Through the summer, as rumours of mergers swirled and their stocks suddenly soared, Canadian distillers tried to position themselves for repeal. Herd came to Montreal for talks with the Bronfmans, but nothing concrete emerged. American interests deluged the Scots with offers to sell in the United States, and in characteristic style the Scots listened, but made no decision.[29] Sam's impatience mounted. Finally, in September, he and Allan, accompanied by their lawyer Aimé Geoffrion, travelled to Edinburgh to bring matters to a head, hoping to enter the American market in strength with the help of their partners, DCL.

Writing to Saidye from London on the Jewish New Year, Rosh Hashana, Sam was in a reflective mood. "Happy New Year, my own Darling baby-face," he began. "Sitting in the synagogue yesterday and today, I was picturing the Shaar Hashomayim [their synagogue in Montreal]. Our pew where the men sit and looking to the left picturing my own precious baby-face with our two little girlies, praying for a happy, healthy and prosperous New Year . . . darling much as we miss each other being apart in these high holidays, we have much to be thankful for, each sharing the grand and glorious love we have for each other and this sharing with our sweet and wonderful daughters and sons. God bless them all."

Sharing his apprehensions, Sam told his wife about the prospective meeting in four days with a committee of the DCL board. Those to whom he had spoken already "are going out of their way to be more than nice to us. . . . However, we shall soon see how nice they act when it comes down to see how fair they want to be when we get to grips over the deal. In any case we shall do the best we can. Although I can't see how they can ever give us enough for the damage they are causing us in all these months and months of delay."

Although the talks in Edinburgh were amicable enough, Sam found his own interests clashing with his Scottish partners on several key points. First was the question of how to respond to the opportunities in the United States. As the Scots saw it, repeal created a high demand for matured stocks of whisky, desperately needed by American companies; DCL wanted to sell to American producers quantities of bourbon and rye aging in the warehouses of Distillers Corporation-Seagrams. Sam flatly rejected this idea. He wanted to market his own whisky in the United States and was seeking an American partner to help him do so. When such a partner appeared in the form of the Schenley company, headed by Lew Rosenstiel, Sam favoured an arrangement, while the Scots resisted it vigorously.

Second, the Old Country representatives of DCL declared their principal commitments to Scotch whisky and gin, and did not want to market other liquor in the United States as they would have to, if they remained in partnership with the Bronfmans. As the Scots were well aware, Sam had a major investment in ryes and bourbons particularly suitable for the American market. In order to avoid conflict of interest, the Scots concluded, they would be best off in the American market on their own.

Finally, there was the question of the supposed poor reputation of the Bronfmans in the United States and the Scots' determination "to see nothing is done which would reflect against the DCL."[30] Many years later, Sir Ronald Cumming of DCL stressed this aspect of the decision in conversation with Terence Robertson. "The real reason [for the break]," he said, "was that Sam's brothers, Abe and Harry, seemed to be accident prone. They had not by all accounts behaved as discreetly as would have been wise during prohibition and we felt that continued association with the Bronfmans might prove embarrassing in future marketing in the United States. We knew that the American government was not entirely happy with the amount of liquor shipped into the United States and we felt that the reputation of our brands had to be protected at all costs. What made it so distasteful for us was that without exception we were all terribly fond of Sam and Allan. We hated to think that they should in any way suffer for the indiscretion of others in the Canadian liquor industry."[31]

One should not exaggerate the importance of this third factor, however, as some have done. After a careful examination of the

Scottish side of the discussions, the historian of DCL concludes that such concerns influenced "the manner in which the split took place, but not the substance." In the final analysis DCL preferred to do business in the United States on their own terms, marketing their own whisky and making their own strategic decisions.[32] However, although the partnership was dissolved, DCL by no means broke completely with their Canadian partners. DC-SL and the Bronfmans continued to market DCL whiskies and gins in Canada and did so with "the active interest and most friendly cooperation of our Old Country friends," as Sam told the shareholders meeting in January 1934. There was no question of cutting those ties with DCL.[33]

After protracted discussions, Sam concluded an agreement in December to buy out the Scots' 562,833 shares of DC-SL. The price was $3,376,998 — $1 million in cash and the balance in thirty months, at 5 percent interest. "We parted the best of friends," Sam commented later — and with a new and extremely profitable agreement, he might have added, for the marketing of DCL's secondary brands of Scotch and gin in Canada.

Sam remembered DCL board chairman William Ross laying down the law on one point when they discussed their future together: "We will not under any circumstances be associated with Mr Rosenstiel." This was obviously a serious warning, because Ross tended to see himself as the moral and ethical guardian of the Scotch whisky industry. Sam, it will be recalled, had been seeking precisely such an association with Rosenstiel in order to dominate the American market, and seems to have been genuinely surprised when the Scots dug in their heels. Soon after, Sam himself broke with Rosenstiel, beginning a life-long rivalry that reached epic proportions.

To outsiders unacquainted with what lay behind the quarrel, the two titans of the liquor industry appeared remarkably alike. Both self-made men of Jewish background, Sam and Lew Rosenstiel were tough, autocratic visionaries who had built their businesses from the ground up. Neither had a modest view of his own achievements. Theodore H. White's novel, *The View from the Fortieth Floor* (1960), has a leading character Lou Bronstein, creator of the gigantic Bruno Liquors empire, apparently modelled upon both Sam and Rosenstiel. In a revealing scene, Bronstein tongue-lashes his sons with a speech that either of the two rivals might in reality have uttered: "A business is something living, something you put together with your belly and your heart. It isn't something you put together just with money and brains you hire. Brains like you I can hire anywhere. Business is when you want something to be alive because you had a dream about it. We were a Triple-A credit rating before you pissers were able to button your own pants."[34]

Two years younger than Sam, Lew Rosenstiel, or LSR as he was sometimes known, was a brilliant and impulsive workaholic who began his career in whisky and somehow managed to stay with the trade, and out of jail, throughout the prohibition era. A descendant on his mother's side of the first colonial governor of Virginia, Rosenstiel betrayed nothing of his genteel heritage: loud, excitable, opinionated and with a volcanic temper, he may also have been, in Stephen Birmingham's phrase, "a certifiable sociopath."[35] A tyrant in his own company, Rosenstiel once had all of his executives' telephones tapped to find out if they were conspiring against him; nipping a conspiracy in the bud, he once spread a rumour that he had died, in order to test the reactions of his company's officers to the news. One of his salesmen pictured Rosenstiel as "a very attractive personality, literally vibrating with ideas." From his office in the Empire State Building in New York, sitting at his desk in shirtsleeves and with an eyeshade low on his forehead, he sent out waves of energy that seemed, in the mind of that employee, to make the entire skyscraper shake.[36]

Together with his partner Sidney Hellman, Rosenstiel made a fortune in medicinal alcohol during prohibition, a highly risky but above-board business that enabled him to plough his profits into whisky stocks while awaiting the repeal that he long predicted. Rosenstiel and Hellman, according to a *Fortune* article in 1936, "came near to being the biggest lawful whiskey men of the dry years, averaging gross sales of $4,000,000 a year."[37] It is possible, however, that Rosenstiel was not *entirely* above-board, and that word to this effect even reached the boardroom of DCL, accounting for William Ross's veto in 1933. Rummaging through the records of the New York State Joint Legislative Committee on Crime of the late 1960s, Hank Messick discovered secret testimony by Rosenstiel's estranged fourth wife about her husband's extensive involvement in bootlegging during prohibition. Indicted for illegal liquor trading in 1929, Rosenstiel somehow escaped prosecution; federal agents remained certain, however, that he was part of a bootlegging consortium with notorious gangsters like Meyer Lansky, Joe Fusco and Frank Costello, and was thought to have bought liquor in Canada and sold it in the United States. Messick implied that Rosenstiel, a well-known friend of FBI director J. Edgar Hoover and a militant anti-Communist, may have wriggled off the hook because of his right-wing connections — the real mystery being the role of the FBI chief himself.[38]

There is no evidence that Rosenstiel bought whisky from the Bronfmans as part of a bootleg consortium. However, at the end of the 1920s he was very much interested in a common venture with them, speculating on the likelihood that the American market would reopen one day and richly reward those who had plenty of whisky in stock. For similar reasons, Sam joined with Rosenstiel when the latter's Schenley distillery, a major producer of medicinal spirits, was seeking capital for expansion. Sinking $585,000 in the venture in 1929, Sam acquired about 20 percent of the Schenley company as a result of some complex trading, and struck up a friendship with Rosenstiel at the same time — playing gin rummy with him, as Rosenstiel recalled years later, at half a cent a point. Rosenstiel came frequently to Montreal in the last days of prohibition, visited Sam and Saidye, and had many discussions about the future of the industry. Sam, it seems clear, wanted to get involved on the American side of the border, and saw Rosenstiel as his vehicle. Both looked down the road to the likelihood of repeal; both were eager to build up their whisky holdings, and both expanded their stocks when few dared to do so.

Before repeal, Sam seems to have been genuinely interested in Rosenstiel's proposal that the two strike out together in the American market, and the idea still appealed to him when he entered discussions with the DCL board in September 1933. But Rosenstiel was impatient and Sam cautious; as Lew raised the pressure, Sam became nervous. The breaking point came when he visited the Schenley plant in Pennsylvania and found, to his horror, that one of their brands, Golden Wedding, was being bottled "hot off the still" — without so much as twenty-four hours aging in barrels. Sam thought the practice abominable and the liquor undrinkable. Meeting Rosenstiel in New York a few days later he told him the deal was off.

"What the hell," was supposed to have been Rosenstiel's justification, "the people are going to want whisky . . . they'll guzzle it down too fast to taste it. I'm out to make money, not cultivate the public taste." Sam's reply was blistering: "I told him what I thought of his 'hot' whisky and added that a man who does that sort of thing is not for me. I told him from the outside his distillery was a piece of junk and that on the inside it was even worse."[39]

From that point the rivalry grew, with Sam using "Rosen-schlemiel," as he called him, as a foil for his self-image as the Scottish-trained craftsman against a Philistine among whisky makers. Merely a mention of his hated rival threatened to detonate in Sam an overpowering rage. "He takes the low road and I take the high road," Sam told an interviewer in 1966. Priding himself as a producer who stood for quality above all else, Sam heaped contempt upon anything Schenley produced. "I have no respect or admiration for the man," Sam insisted many years later.

Without Schenley and without the DCL, taking on the American market must have seemed like a daunting prospect, even for someone like Sam, not normally given to self-doubt or uncertainty. Temperamentally, however, he could hardly sit back. In the end, he explained, quoting a favourite passage from the poet Tennyson, one has to decide: "a person makes a decision of what is a good thing to do. 'Grasp the skirts of happy chance.' Chances always come. Do you grasp or do you not?"[40] Sam decided to grasp.

At the time of repeal, Saidye recalled, she and her husband had a long discussion in the library of their house on Belvedere Road. With his business turning increasingly towards the United States, Sam found himself spending most of his time in New York. Saidye offered to join him with the children, but Sam was resolutely opposed — for reasons that reflect, at least in part, his innate conservatism. Kidnapping, he felt, was a serious threat and a much more dangerous prospect in New York than in Montreal. Apartment living with the children was out of the question, and the alternative, buying a house outside New York City in Westchester County or Long Island, was impossible because Saidye "would know no one." Sam was reluctant as well to uproot his wife from their families in Montreal, and from her growing involvement in Montreal Jewish communal affairs. On a scale little practised in the 1930s, therefore, Sam decided to commute.[41]

Sam did so for the next five years, living most weekdays in New York, leaving Manhattan on the Friday-night train and arriving in Montreal on Saturday morning after a twelve-hour journey. He still maintained a punishing pace in 1939, when he was spending between a third and a quarter of his time in New York.[42] Saidye described his rhythm: "After a good breakfast at home on Saturday, he would have a snooze, then lunch with me and the children. It was the only time he had to spend with us. In the afternoons and evenings there would be business meetings and get-togethers with decision makers of the many community organizations in which he was deeply involved. Sundays were more of the same. On Sunday evening he boarded the train back to New York, and for another long week he was gone. We missed him terribly."[43]

With Saidye's help, Sam set himself up in a series of fashionable hotels in New York—first the Pierre, then the Sherry-Netherland, and finally the St Regis, on 55th Street just off Fifth Avenue, in a suite on the sixteenth floor that he kept for over thirty years and where he was close to Allan, who lived at the Ambassador Hotel on Park Avenue. The apartment was comfortable but hardly palatial. Served by a cook who lived in the maid's room, it included a huge, oak-panelled living room, a dining room, a narrow library, and three bedrooms, one of which had two bathrooms and a dressing room. Seagram paid the bills, amounting in 1935 to $12,500 a year.

Saidye visited regularly to help her husband who adjusted, with difficulty, to the new order of things. In the winter of 1934, as Saidye recalled, she spent several weeks with him in the Sherry-Netherland when he became deathly ill and was unable to return to Montreal. Felled by the flu, Sam took to his bed while his wife hired a nurse to look after the patient—who on at least one occasion started off for the office with a temperature of 104 degrees. The kitchens of the Sherry-Netherland proved unhelpful in this crisis, when they dispatched to the sickroom some excessively lumpy cream of wheat. "I'd never cooked before," Saidye wrote in a memoir (they had been married for ten years), but she nevertheless did so then, making "simple things like eggs, chicken soup and applesauce."[44] Apparently, Sam's illness nearly cost him an important deal, as he was bedridden for many days. Ever after, his doctor Abe Mayman recalls, Sam was nervous about catching cold, fearful that he might similarly be out of action when there was important business to be done.[45]

■

AMERICANS, IT IS commonly believed, drank about as much alcohol under prohibition as before, the only difference being that the whisky trade was criminalized. But this is quite wrong: in fact, the per capita annual intake of alcohol declined drastically over the fourteen years in which the Eighteenth Amendment was in force—from about 2.4 gallons per adult in 1915 to 0.9 gallons at the end of the "noble experiment." While the American public consumed about 147 million gallons of tax-paid spirits in 1915, they drank only about 35 million gallons the year after repeal. "The decline in consumption is almost too staggering to be believed," observed *Fortune* in 1934, when legal drinking resumed, pointing out the possibility that researchers might have missed the considerable quantities of bootleg liquor still being drunk immediately after repeal. Still, *Fortune* found the evidence generally persuasive: "the Demon Rum has not run amuck," it concluded, as signs indicated a drastic falling off of drinking and much continued abstention even after liquor sales resumed. "Repeal . . . has done the best thing its backers promised for it: it has sobered us up."[46]

One must keep this in mind in order to appreciate how adventurous was Sam's plunge into the American market at the end of 1933. At the time, no one knew what the prospects were. No one knew how much Americans would drink, or what they would drink. No one could be sure, moreover, that the temperance forces were permanently vanquished—something that seems so obvious to us now. And no one knew anything about the ground rules that Washington or the various states would impose.

Plenty of old whisky hands were on the scene with advice—Lew Rosenstiel, of course, being one of the noisiest and most prominent. But the industry was stacked with "dead wood" in 1933, full of old-timers whose practical experience dated back to the days before the First World War. No one really knew the modern ropes, and there were no guides to a field that was being created overnight. Being a Canadian in this new environment did not make things any easier for Sam, as his wife later reported: "Sam worked long hours under terrific pressure. At first he had a hard time adjusting to doing business in the United States. He said that business was more competitive than in Canada, and because he was Canadian, his competitors tried to use government lobbies and all kinds of things to keep him out."[47] Working closely with Sam and Allan in the 1930s, one employee admired their adjustment: "They were backed by ample capital (which they had earned themselves), but they admitted that they didn't know it all and wanted to get at the facts. Up to this time, their experience had been, for the most part, in Canada—so, every day was a great adventure in which they learned something about the market in the United States."[48]

Like all strategists on unfamiliar terrain, Sam fell back upon training and experience. What America needed, in his view, was blended, rather than what was commonly referred to as "straight" whisky, championing the preferences of his Scottish mentors and predicting for the United States market what had succeeded so well for his company in Canada. Blended whisky, as we saw in the previous chapter, was made by marrying straight whisky with relatively flavourless grain neutral spirits, in a manner pioneered by the distillers of Scotland with the advent of patent stills in the nineteenth century. Compared to straights, blended whiskies were generally "lighter," that is to say had fewer impurities or congeners in the final product; a good blender was also able to maintain, it was argued, a greater degree of uniformity from one batch to the next by altering the proportions of different ingredients.

Throughout his professional life, Sam declared his unshake-able belief in the qualitative superiority of blends over straights—a faith that he articulated with almost religious devotion. Blending was the only way, he believed, to maintain the quality and the consistency of his products. "I am a confirmed blender," Sam told a sales meeting at the Waldorf Astoria in 1954. "I learnt many years ago, by observation at the distillery, that you can make the same whisky from the same grain, using the same yeast and the same distiller, but your whisky will vary from day to day."[49] Blending was intended to compensate for such variations. In his description of the process Sam was like an artist, evoking the mystical processes of creativity:

I am convinced that there is only one way of making whisky and that is to make a lot of different kinds of whisky, observe the whiskies grow—whisky grows like life—and to make these whiskies compatible with each other is the blender's job. He is the same as the man who puts various paints on the pallet and paints a beautiful picture. So is the man who takes varying degrees and percentages of whiskies, studies them, gets to know them, gets to know how they develop, blends them together, and that is what you get in Seagram's whiskies, compatibility with quality, and the uniformity that you would get in no other method of manufacture.

"Whiskies are like people," he would say, with the force of his imagery compensating for his broken syntax:

People are all born equal, but they don't develop equally. The same applies to a product, and particularly whisky. It is much the same that you find in a family of two, six, or eight children. They come from the same father and mother, and some are tall, some short, some fat, and some lean.... Therefore ... if the whisky is too sweet, you add a little of the drier whisky; and if one has become too light, you add a heavier whisky. It was one way of proving that year after year, and month after month, you can only get uniformity by one way and that is by blending.

Quite apart from the uniformity of the product and the ability to maintain quality, Sam also claimed to have discerned his customers' preferences for the "lighter" whiskies that came from the blending process. For Sam, this consumer choice was part of a great historical trend. Prior to blending, he lectured his employees, heavier malt whiskies were the order of the day — and whisky was "a pretty crude form of beverage alcohol." All this changed, however, when the Scottish whisky makers discovered blending:

> As time went on they found that people began to eat lighter foods, and smoke lighter tobacco. The machine age had come along. Steam developed in England to a point where machinery took over many tasks previously done by hand. People weren't quite so rough and tough, and they wanted life to be lighter and easier. You know, today people don't want heavy cloth in their suits; they want everything light and easy. They don't want stiff collars any more. The girls wear their blouses low; they want fresh air.

At the end of prohibition, American distillers pointed in a quite different direction — away from blends. To authentic champions of straights, like the Kentucky bourbon king, Julian "Pappy" Van Winkle, blends were "compounds," and their manufacturers mere "chemists." Although blends were popular before 1919, under the Eighteenth Amendment straight whiskey was the only kind that could be legally produced in the United States (for medicinal purposes, of course), and straight rye or bourbon was taken to be an American tradition. American distillers entered the market after repeal with little experience in blending, and many were positively disposed against it. Rosenstiel's Schenley company produced both straights and blends, but tilted heavily towards straights — its unblended Old Quaker brand becoming, in the years immediately following repeal, one of America's top sellers. Banking on blends, therefore, was in many ways a long shot, seen by one contemporary writer as the Bronfmans' "outstanding gamble."[50]

Looking back from the vantage point of 1948, *Fortune* thought that Sam's preferences at repeal had been brilliantly vindicated.

"Bronfman came down from Canada knowing exactly what he was after, and taught the American companies a severe lesson in merchandising firewater in the modern manner, like a food product. He initiated, and consistently led, the post-prohibition trend to blends that now encompasses the whisky market. Mildness and uniformity of taste were his formula, following the standard estimate of the American taste developed in the 1920s by merchandisers of ham and cheese and cigarettes."[51]

Along with blends, Sam needed inventory to supply the huge American market and to sustain competition with the others in the field. When the starting gun was fired at the end of 1933, *Fortune* outlined the worldwide stocks of whisky, staking out the relative strengths of the various contenders: the British led the field, with 170 million gallons, representing slightly more than 70 percent of the total, nearly all of it Scotch and mostly controlled by DCL; there were 41 million gallons in Canada, both rye and bourbon and just over 20 percent of the total, with Hiram Walker's 14.5 million gallons putting it just slightly ahead of Distillers Corporation-Seagrams with 13.5 million gallons; and finally there were 21 million gallons, or 8.8 percent held by American firms, half of which was owned by National Distillers and 25 percent by Rosenstiel's Schenley company.[52]

The race to build inventory started even before repeal, as we have seen, and for a time drove Sam and Rosenstiel together. Suddenly, everyone wanted American whiskey—much more valuable now that Washington imposed a five dollars a gallon import duty on all stocks brought into the country. Harry Hatch was not idle, and with his popular Canadian Club brand he had a strong card to play when seeking partners south of the border. Hatch worked out a cooperative arrangement with National Distilleries, the largest American player, and sunk a fortune into a huge new plant in Peoria, Illinois—worth $13 million, it was said, and dubbed the largest distillery in the world.[53] The Bronfmans too were on the lookout for stocks, either American pre-prohibition whiskey or liquor distilled in the United States by special government permit after 1929. For the most part this was to be had through the purchase of existing plants, often decaying and nearly worthless in themselves but with their warehouses full of extremely precious, aging whiskey.

Sam, as all his close lieutenants attested, developed a virtual mania for inventory, his every instinct calling for more whisky to be purchased or produced and put away in barrels.[54] "Inventory wins them all," was one of his favourite remarks. Sam's post-repeal buying spree began in November 1933 when he picked up the 147-year-old Rossville Union Distilleries in Lawrenceburg, Indiana. In exchange for 172,623 shares of DC-SL stock, valued at about $3.8 million, DC-SL received $2.4 million in cash, Rossville's plant at Lawrenceburg and, most important, approximately 400,000 gallons of whiskey. At breakneck speed Sam set Harry to work to modernize the operation, pouring in huge sums of money thanks to a generous line of credit from Bankers Trust of New York.[55] At the same time, Sam formed an American subsidiary of DC-SL, Joseph E. Seagram & Sons, Inc., to run the new facility. Just a few months later, DC-SL paid just over 70,000 shares of Seagram stock for the Calvert distillery in Relay, Maryland; and in another year the company started construction of an ultra-modern plant in Louisville, Kentucky.[56]

Sam's purchase of the Calvert company in the spring of 1934 illustrates his priorities as well as his business style. Throughout the negotiations, he dealt with an old friend, Emil Schwarzhaupt, described by *Fortune* as "one of the most experienced whiskey traders in the U.S." Schwartzhaupt's evaluation of Sam was succinct: "One of the smartest men I ever did business with," he said. Knowing the desperate hunt for inventory, Schwarzhaupt prepared himself for long, tough bargaining sessions. "I intended to trade Calvert over a table for the stiffest price I could get out of him. But he threw it all back to me and said, 'You set the price and whatever it is, it's a deal.'" As *Fortune* described it in 1948, "Schwarzhaupt did all the figuring, and, having nobody to trade against, set the price some distance below what he would have liked to trade up to. Bronfman told his people to accept without question and Schwarzhaupt to this day is genially rueful about it."[57]

Sam also looked farther afield, to the Old Country, in an effort "to become a truly great international distilling company," as he later put it. Through his friend Jimmy Barclay, he heard that the Robert Brown Company of Glasgow was coming on the market and he moved boldly, as he often did when a unique opportunity came his way. Wanting to prevent Brown's use of certain British and American trademarks in the name of "Crown" (a brand name that Sam had just taken), and eager to acquire Brown's stock of aged Scotch whisky, Sam managed to buy the firm in 1935. "With this company as our base," Sam later reminisced, "we began immediately to lay down stocks of select Scotch whiskies for maturing" — a strategy that served him well years later, when despite a worldwide shortage of Scotch he was able to draw upon long-aged, quality whiskies for his famous Chivas brand.[58]

Seagram brought to the post-repeal United States a commitment to what Sam called "a totally integrated operation" — a sharp break with the American past, when whisky making had traditionally involved a cluster of small firms that required close coordination. "The Canadian distillers and the large Scottish distillers generally attended to all phases of production," Sam explained, "distilling, maturing, blending, quality control and bottling, and also to marketing. I was determined that as American distillers we would follow the same procedure."[59] As it soon became apparent, the large, integrated units that Sam preferred were the only structures able to survive in the highly competitive, costly struggle to carve out part of the American market. Sam's contempt for excessively "young" whiskies such as Rosenstiel produced, and his eventual practice of aging the neutral spirits before blending, one might add, did not make things easy for him in this regard. Commitment to producing whisky for sale four or more years down the road tied up a vast amount of capital and required careful educated guesses about market conditions much further in the future than businessmen of the time were used to making. That is another reason why, to many, Sam's plunge into the American market was such a gamble.

For most of 1934, when his competitors were selling furiously in the United States, Sam bided his time. "I let the parade go by the first year," he said, explaining how his new plants, although quickly in production, did not put whisky on the market as early as others. Sam shipped already-aged whiskies from his Canadian plants to Lawrenceburg and to Relay for blending with neutral spirits produced in the American distilleries. Part of Sam's blending credo was to age the neutral spirits before beginning this process, so that the newly produced distillate would have "at least some development in wood." "I insisted on this delay," Sam later explained, "even though some shareholders called on me to protest that we were doing nothing while other distillers were busy marketing and making lots of money. This was true. During this period other U.S. distillers were enjoying a bonanza in sales. No matter, I waited. Quality in the bottle, and our reputation for quality, were much more important to me than immediate profits."[60]

Within a year after repeal Sam's gamble paid off with a spectacular American success — the Crown brands, whose rise to the top became "one of the sensations of the industry," as *Fortune* put it, and one of the great achievements of the American whisky business. Up to that point Sam had limited himself to the relatively high-priced V.O. and eighty-three whiskies, carefully building up American distribution channels with these élite brands but holding back while other companies hurtled into U.S. sales.

Then, in the middle of June 1934, Seagram announced its medium-priced Five Crown and Seven Crown — light, quality-blend Canadian-style whiskies — with the object of selling from coast to coast. To launch the Crowns, Sam's sales director Frank Schwengel assembled his team of 175 distributors in the opulent ballroom of the Waldorf Astoria Hotel in New York. "What the hell are you doing with all those people?" Sam asked his marketing chief. "What we were doing," Schwengel replied, "was telling the industry what Sam had decided — and a revolutionary set of decisions it was: We were going to go with two blended whiskeys, and we were going to make them into the first national brands in history."[61] Immediately, Seagram's marketing engines roared to life with the slogan, "Say Seagram's and Be Sure"; company distributors fanned out across the country to do battle on behalf of the new product.

Sales rocketed upward — 10,000 cases in the first month, even more the next, and several hundred thousand cases by the end of the year, by which point Five Crown and Seven Crown became the undisputed leaders in volume of all brands on the American market.[62] In 1935 sales reached an unheard-of million cases.

Newspapers across the country carried an ad entitled "Thanks a Million," registering this stunning coup to the buying public: "You have made the Seagram Crown Whiskies Number One in America." For the next six years the Crown brands led the American field, hovering at about 1.3 million cases annually. With this breakthrough, the Seagram name became known throughout the United States. Sam's judgement was triumphantly vindicated.

One of Sam's vital roles in the success of the Crown brands was to have chosen the talented builder of the Seagram sales network, General Frank Schwengel. Three years older than Sam, Schwengel joined the First Illinois Cavalry at age eighteen, about the time the Bronfmans first settled in Winnipeg. Serving in various military posts and glittering with medals from First World War service, Schwengel worked in the marketing and advertising field during the 1920s and early 1930s. One day at the end of 1933 he strolled into Sam's office in the Chrysler Building in New York seeking the Seagram account — a dapper, distinguished-looking man of medium height, with slightly greying hair. Sam, who prided himself on his ability to size up characters, decided on the spot to hire the salesman, obviously drawn to his crisp, no-nonsense military style.

Taken aback, Schwengel appeared the next day to ask Sam if he were serious. "I told him I had never been more serious," Sam replied, setting him up immediately as vice-president and director of sales. Schwengel provided a superb counterpoint to Sam's excitable temperament — "a spokesman of impeccable judgment," as Sam put it, "a man whose presence inspired confidence and respect." Mobilizing a far-flung sales force, Schwengel appreciated the diversity of interests in the burgeoning Seagram empire; it was he who formulated a company motto that Sam loved to repeat: "A fair profit to the wholesaler, a fair profit to the retailer, and a fair price to the consumer."[63]

So great had been the demand for Five and Seven Crown whiskies, Sam told a shareholders meeting of DC-SL in July 1935, that in April, only ten months after their introduction, the Seagram plant in Lawrenceburg celebrated the shipment of the forty millionth bottle. Sam also announced a new string to the company bow—another American subsidiary, to be headed by one of the legendary personalities of the whiskey trade, Julius Kessler.

Seventy-eight years old at the time, Julius Kessler was a Jewish immigrant-entrepreneur who had lived through the entire history of the modern liquor industry in the United States, and was described in 1936 as someone "who had sold more whiskey than any man living."[64] Born in Budapest, he worked as a journalist in Omaha and Denver before discovering his lifetime vocation as a liquor salesman. Kessler eventually rose to the top of what was known as the Whiskey Trust, a marketing pool of more than forty distillers, becoming the most important name in American liquor sales before prohibition. A kind of senior statesman of the American whiskey business, he was exiled in Budapest during the dry years, returning only with repeal. Sam's friend William Wachtel described him as "the handsomest man in the industry; gray curly hair in abundance, a beautiful handlebar mustache, a handsome likeness to Franz Joseph, emperor of Austria."[65] Exuding old-world charm, and of aristocratic bearing, Kessler projected precisely the kind of image Sam wanted for his liquor business.

"Everything about him was the finest money could buy," Wachtel later wrote. There was only one problem: Kessler was broke; upon his return to the United States, he found that during his absence his secretary's boyfriend had absconded with his fortune. Kessler, then, needed a job. For a time, Lew Rosenstiel toyed with the idea of using his name for one of the Schenley brands on a royalty basis. Sam went one step further. He named his new subsidiary the Julius Kessler Distilling Company, placing the old man, whom Sam described as "looking for new fields to conquer," in charge. One of Sam's employees remembered the boss looking over his shoulder as he designed the label for the new "Kessler's Special" bottle saying, "Make the name 'Kessler' bigger—bigger."[66] Thanks to Sam, the dean of the American whiskey trade now enjoyed a substantial salary of $25,000 a year, a limousine and a chauffeur—and was working for Sam Bronfman. He was no mere figurehead, for Kessler quickly achieved a volume of over a million cases; in 1940, when he died, the Kessler brand was the best seller in its category in the United States.

Not surprisingly, Kessler became a fervent admirer of his benefactor. William Wachtel met him regularly in New York, and the two of them talked shop together. At one time Wachtel, who was one of Sam's closest associates, was considering jumping ship and working for Rosenstiel, the hated rival. Asked for his advice about the offer, Kessler replied to his friend "Wilhelm" (as he always referred to him): "You must make your own decision. But since I know LSR and Sam so well, I have only this to say: If you want to be a millionaire, work for Lew; if you want to be happy, work for Sam."

Selling brands like Kessler's to the American public just after prohibition was like exploring the surface of the moon: no one had been there before and procedures had to be invented from scratch. Not only were there no "national" brands in the United States in 1933, there was practically no "brand identity" — the set of associations carried by particular products and that prompt people to choose one over another. Working for the Schenley company just after repeal, Philip Kelly surveyed and found that the American public had no idea what the differences were between blends and straights, why whisky was aged, or what prices were appropriate. "Merchandising leadership," Kelly concluded, "was wide open."[67]

Sam entered this marketing jungle with a particular goal in mind — to establish whisky drinking as a modern, socially responsible activity and an accoutrement of the good life. Just when, as we shall see, the Canadian law enforcement authorities launched a wide-ranging prosecution of Sam and his brothers, forcefully reminding him of the poor associations many people still had with liquor, he determined to transform popular perceptions of his product and, ultimately, of himself.

Part of the legacy of prohibition was that many Americans continued to see the production and consumption of alcohol as anti-social — associated with sleazy environments, disreputable individuals and even criminality. Yet against this trend, another current moved in precisely the opposite direction. Widespread disregard of the Volstead Act among the more affluent during the

1920s undercut some of the stigma against alcohol, turning liquor into an article of conspicuous consumption and a symbol of status. Extending from rebellious intellectuals to more staid members of the middle-class who eventually supported the New Deal, opponents of prohibition often saw themselves as part of a wider process of social change, casting aside much that was hidebound and traditional in American life. To those who had championed such a course, drinking had connotations of liberation and self-fulfilment. During prohibition, "the defiant rebel with his pocket flask had become an almost irresistible symbol of dignity, courage, manhood, and liberation from hypocrisy and pigheaded repression—a symbol which could elevate drinking into a sacrament of true individualism."[68] Films of the years after repeal showed characters like Humphrey Bogart, cigarette and glass in hand, projecting a sophisticated, adult lifestyle, admirable for its courage and independence.

Sam Bronfman fit neatly into this historical framework, supplying a reassuring social context for a once-marginal product. Practically everything about Seagram's advertising in the period immediately following repeal was designed to reassure. Here is a sample advertisement, from 1934:

> From the oldest stocks in Canada . . . Distillers Corporation-Seagrams Limited own and have in storage more than 15 million gallons of fine aged whiskies. Behind it stands the reputation of these world famous distilleries and the guardianship of the Canadian government . . . distilled, matured and bottled under the strict supervision of the Canadian government.

Unhappy with the image of whisky being gulped by poor people in grimy bars, Sam wanted to portray it "being sipped in the quiet dignity of a London men's club by cultured gentlemen."[69] The exclusion of women, in this case, was deliberate, part of the cultural baggage of the day and one of the guarantees of social stability. Society in the 1930s was only barely able to countenance women drinking at all; immoderation on their part, always a danger, was awful to contemplate. As Sam himself recalled, the inspiration for one of his most successful advertising campaigns came to him in 1934 when having lunch across the street from the Chrysler Building at the bar of the Commodore Hotel in Manhattan. Sam was horrified to see women "bellying up to the bar," unable to hold their liquor. Tipsy drinkers were bad enough, he felt, but tipsy *women* drinkers were, in his own word, "disgusting." Sam's goal was to project the opposite — respectability, responsibility and success, attributes that were best protected within the sphere of male sociability.[70]

The rest of the liquor industry saw the virtue of this approach, generally adopting themes Sam originated or defined on his own. Until 1958, the Distilled Spirits Institute, an industry watchdog in the United States, banned women from liquor advertising in its code of ethics, and even in that year, when women were finally permitted in whisky ads, they could not be shown actually *drinking.*

In 1938, a leading advertising periodical, *National Ad-Views,* presented Seagram's U.S. subsidiary with its "Socrates' High Award," according it first place among advertisers in all fields of industry. In the view of the experts, Seagram astutely beamed its sales messages to the upper end of the drinking scale: "This company . . . recognizes that confidence is the dominant influence in liquor buying; toward this end Seagram's tailors its advertising campaigns to stress the acceptance of its products by discriminating drinkers," the journal noted. "It does this by placing Seagram's whiskies against a background of quality, and selling each brand by impression. Few distillers adhere as faithfully as does Seagram's to definite campaign themes, thereby building maximum recognition value for newspaper advertising."[71]

"We realized from the very beginning that the industry must build itself on a class basis," Sam once told a meeting of his salesmen, and there is no clearer demonstration of what he meant by "class," and no more characteristic demonstration of how he would communicate this to the public than Seagram's brilliant "moderation" campaign that began in October 1934. With an ad entitled "We who make whiskey say: 'Drink Moderately,' " the series was launched to considerable fanfare with an article in the *New York Times.* A spokesman for Seagram announced that his company was determined to win the respect of the American public: "Whisky is definitely a luxury and can never take the place of bread and meat," he explained. "We do not want to see a single dollar that should be spent for the necessities of life used for buying liquor." Working with the Blackman Agency at the time, Sam claimed to have proposed the moderation theme himself, to be met by disbelief. He curtly assured the man in charge of the account that he was deadly serious. "If you don't have that ad on my [desk] the next time I'm in New York," he said, "I am going to get another agency." When the ad finally did appear, he thought it perfect. "I didn't change a word," he recalled.[72]

The original "moderation" ad was a brilliant marriage of the themes of responsible consumption and gracious living, both of which were to be associated with the Seagram company.[73] Whisky before repeal, the text implied, was a raw, harsh, inexpensive product that was often consumed unwisely, in excess. Seagram whisky, in contrast, "properly distilled and then brought to full mellowness, full wholesomeness by aging," was "in the tradition of fine living." And this was where moderation came in. "The real enjoyment which whiskey can add to the pleasures of gracious living is possible only to the man who drinks good, aged whiskey and drinks moderately." "We feel sure that you will agree with us," the ad concluded:

> that the desirable way of life is thoughtful, informed by experience, guided by common sense. Realizing this, we feel sure that you will prefer moderation in the enjoyment of the finest to the empty satisfaction that follows upon profusion of the second rate.

"As one of America's leading distillers," declared a Seagram advertisement in February 1938, "we recognize a definite social responsibility. The very existence of legalized liquor in this country depends upon the civilized manner in which it is consumed."[74] First appearing on the anniversary of repeal, Seagram's "moderation" series pursued Sam's mandate thereafter, year after year, with annual variations on the theme. In 1937 the ads announced "Drinking and Driving Do Not Mix," inviting readers "to join us in the crusade for safer, saner driving." On Father's Day, in 1938, fathers were told that they were heroes to their sons: "Nothing is quite so disillusioning to the clear eyes of a youngster as the sight of a man—his own father—who has used liquor unwisely." Other themes involved hunters ("Alcohol and Gunpowder Do Not Mix"), alcoholics ("Some People Should Not Drink") and so on. Continuing into the 1960s, the series also took up sensitive issues ("How much should you drink?"), New Year's Eve warnings ("No thanks. I've had enough" or "How to keep the life of the party alive") and one particularly memorable slogan: "One for the road . . . be sure it's coffee."

Sam devoted much attention to these and other advertisements, demanding that all copy and layout be submitted to him. Robert Sabloff, who joined the Seagram organization in Montreal in the 1950s as a lowly assistant advertising manager, quickly learned one of the rules of the company: "no advertising got published unless the boss okayed it."[75] But like practically everyone else who worked with Sam on such publicity, Sabloff found that Sam had an unerring eye. As Rex Vickers, head of the firm that ran Seagram's Canadian advertising put it, "It's a question whether he's a better distiller or advertiser. If he weren't in distilling I'm sure he'd make just as much money in advertising."[76]

Can Sam's advertising preferences be understood as a simple craving for respectability, part of his personal struggle against "feelings of social and professional inferiority," as one writer puts it?[77] The "moderation" campaign can be seen in this vein, as can his weakness for monarchical or aristocratic themes in presenting his products. There is no doubt that Sam loved the slogans for V.O., for example — "Honoured the World Over," or "Known by the Company It Keeps" — and these were similar in theme to his Calvert company's "Men of Distinction" series, associating prominent Americans with his products. However, such messages should also be seen in the context of the mid- and late-1930s when they were conceived, conditioned both by Depression and by prohibition. Like so much of popular culture in the economically bleak 1930s, such advertising appealed to visions of the good life drawn from fantasies of wealth, luxury and success. Sam Bronfman was hardly alone in communicating such fantasies, and there is little doubt that, as advertising, they worked extraordinarily well — as they were intended to do.

As well, Sam took unusual pride in his marketing abilities, sometimes referring to himself as "Salesman Sam." "Marketing," he once told an interviewer, "is the problem in all business. If you don't sell you don't have anything to make."[78] "The highest cost of selling is not selling," was another of his dicta. But he always stressed that everything depended on the quality of what he had to sell: "a good product, available to the buyer when he wants it at the price which makes sense to him, is the key to commercial success."[79] One of his great ambitions as a young man, Sam once said, was "to create something so fine and so superior that the consumer would come into distributing outlets and say 'Give me some of *that*.' " When that happens, he felt, the man "has paid you an enormous compliment."[80] Sam's interest in advertising was a salesman's interest, based on pride in what he sold and his enthusiastic commitment to selling.

Moreover, there are strong indications that in his advertising, as in so much of his business, Sam was heavily indebted to his British mentors, especially the Scottish distillers of DCL whom he first visited in the mid-1920s, ten years before launching his famous advertising campaigns. Advertising, indeed, was one of the great innovations of the Edinburgh distillers who made up the Distillers Company Limited. John Haig & Sons, for example, plastered much of Britain with their slogan "Don't be vague — ask for Haig," at one time sailing a yacht up and down the south coast of England in holiday season with the message emblazoned on its sails. As in the United States in the 1930s, British distillers in the decade before were extremely concerned to establish their role as responsible, public-spirited industrialists, which is why DCL took care to appoint Field Marshal Earl Haig, hero of the First World War, to their board in 1922 — despite his distance from his family's firm. Like Sam, the British whisky makers' association made strenuous efforts to appear on the side of "true temperance," against "the inordinate consumption of alcohol for the sheer delight of intoxication," as DCL board member Sir Alexander Walker put it.[81] They too, in short, championed moderation, respectability and status — and needed no sense of social and professional inferiority to prompt them to do so.

With the messages of moderation and social distinction ringing in their ears, Seagram's army of distributors, commanded by General Schwengel, deployed throughout the United States to place their product on retail-store shelves. Here too Seagram was fast off the mark, unashamedly mobilizing many former bootleggers who, in greatly different circumstances, had learned all the essential tricks of the trade. Philip Kelly, who got to know many of them when he worked as a salesman in Wachtel's Calvert company, noted that many of these grizzled veterans of the whisky business "had shaky reputations with the Alcohol Tax Unit and with the government — but never with the public or the trade."[82] Often fearful that their bootlegging pasts would catch up with them, they clung loyally to the Seagram organization as a badge of respectability; surviving in a highly competitive environment in the mid 1930s, many became wealthy as a result of their distributorships, which were sometimes passed on to a second generation. In 1973 *Forbes* magazine made the remarkable observation that the majority of Seagram's 476 distributors had been with the company since repeal, forty years before. One of these veteran salesmen underscored the principal reason why: the huge success of 7 Crown, in a league with Gillette razor blades or Coca-Cola as one of the most dependably profitable products in American industry.

Sam loved to meet with his sales force and deliver pep talks about the early days in the industry. Sam reminisced in 1951,

At the beginning of this business, nobody knew whether the retailer was going to be in business for a day, a week or a month, or get rich quick. Your dads had to sift out which ones had the dough to pay for it, which ones to trust and which not. They bought small buildings and in no time the buildings were too small and they, in turn, as I remember, many of them used not only to be the bookkeeper, the salesman, but the shipper and they drove trucks delivering some of the orders in rush times. There was no such thing as price maintenance in those days. You were in a market where you were meeting tough competition. There was no stability, and in those early days there was no fair trade. Prices were being cut at random and the distributor, instead of making his profit . . . was working for practically nothing.

Delivering these talks with genuine enthusiasm, Sam inspired deep loyalty among his listeners. The key, at least in Kelly's view, was the highly aggressive spirit that Sam helped inspire: "the philosophy of the parent Seagram Company was: do your staff work well behind the line, and when you attack, attack vigorously, and never give up until you win. Go all out—don't keep your foot on first base, ready to retreat in case you fail." Kelly remembered how lively the Seagram organization was; when he left for Seton Porter's cold and dignified National Distillers, one of Sam's major American competitors, he felt it was like going from a department store to a bank.

■

IN MID-SEPTEMBER 1934, Sam received disturbing news from Montreal, from his friend and legal adviser, Laz Phillips. According to what Laz had learned, the RCMP was preparing to bring charges against Sam, his brothers and Barney Aaron, together with dozens of others, for illegal activities in their prohibition "export" trade: specifically, the prosecution alleged that the Bronfmans had conspired to defraud the Canadian government of $5 million in customs duties on liquor that was smuggled back into Canada. Sam's reaction, as he described it to Terence Robertson, was first shock, then amazement, and then outrage: "I've never heard such damned hogwash in all my life," he told Laz. But damage was already being done.

In Montreal and in New York Sam's bankers got wind of the Mounties' investigation just as Seagram was preparing to launch its Crown brands. The trouble clearly could not have come at a worse time. Financial circles in Toronto published damaging rumours of impending legal fireworks, and the market for DC-SL stocks declined as a result.[83] To his horror, Sam learned that the RCMP was rummaging through the Seagram offices on Peel Street. He sputtered with anger on the telephone to his friend Mark Shinbane. "Shin, do you know what? Those sons of bitches, the Mounted Police, are coming into our offices . . . every goddamn day and they're combing through everything. What right have they got, these bastards, to do that? . . . They just come in, the bastards, they come in the morning, they come back in the afternoon, they're here all the goddamned time."[84]

The Bronfman camp suspected that the ultimate source of the prosecution was none other than the prime minister himself, R.B. Bennett. Laz Phillips originally suggested to Sam that the Tory leader was seeking to punish the prominent Liberal industrialist, and as the rumours of impending action swirled about Ottawa and Montreal Sam's friends appealed to the prime minister and his minister of justice, Hugh Guthrie, hoping to limit the damage. A. Jackson Dodds, for example, Joint General Manager of the Bank of Montreal, passed along a memorandum warning that Canadian prosecution might encourage the American government to follow suit: this would drag the other Canadian distillers through American courts and would badly injure Canadian trade. Aimé Geoffrion, Sam's distinguished Montreal counsel, telegraphed the prime minister on December 8, suggesting that the whole thing "must be the result of a terrible misunderstanding." Horrified to hear of the impending arrests, Allan Bronfman's sister-in-law Lillian Freiman, a prominent Conservative and the best-known Jewish woman in Canada, wrote to Bennett about "subjecting this whole family to attack." The matter, she wrote, "is vitally close to me from a personal and a Jewish standpoint." Bennett responded the same day, noting that her letter "does credit to you personally and as a representative of your people." On the other hand, Bennett reminded her that he could not interfere with the course of justice. Sam's lawyers visited the prime minister on December 12, underscoring the seriousness of the situation, but the best they came away with was an assurance that the charges involved the Bronfmans personally, and not their company. It was precious little comfort, in view of the potential damage the charges would have.[85]

There is no indication, however, that the prime minister was overly concerned. A wealthy, somewhat uncommunicative bachelor, self-centred, nearly friendless and difficult to approach, Bennett was known for his formality, appearing regularly in pre-First World War morning coat and striped trousers. A champion of the Empire, he was also a strict observer of the sabbath, uninterested in sports or the arts, and obsessed with his work. Having been brought up in a Bible-reading Methodist home, the Tory leader was deeply opposed, on the public platform at least, to all aspects of the liquor trade. His friend Lord Beaverbrook remembered how, as a young man, Bennett honed his oratory at temperance meetings, "where he would speak for an hour or more with fire and fury." Having made a fortune in Alberta businesses before the First World War, Bennett developed a deep opposition to the whisky culture of the west; during the election of 1921, in which he was roundly defeated, he is supposed to have antagonized westerners by a reply to a question he had been asked in the east: "What was the West thinking?" "The West is not thinking," Bennett said, "the West is drinking."[86]

It is highly unlikely that Bennett prompted the investigation, and while there were well-founded suspicions of an antisemitic element in the decision to go after Sam and not other distillers, no one ever forged a link to the prime minister himself. But the assumption remained. Writing to the prime minister on December 18, 1934 Aimé Geoffrion did not hesitate to raise the antisemitic climate of the case — underscored by a shrieking headline in the ultra-nationalist newspaper Le Patriote (with two swastikas on its masthead) — "LES JUIFS BRONFMAN S'ENFUIENT!" (Those Jews the Bronfmans flee) that appeared at the end of November. The publicity surrounding the case against the family, "together with their nationality," Geoffrion wrote, made it impossible for them to get a fair trial from a jury. Geoffrion wanted to see the matter before a judge in a federal court — the course that was ultimately taken. It is not known how Bennett responded, and for obvious reasons he sought to distance himself from the case. On thin political ice at the end of 1934 and preparing to launch his "New Deal" for Canada, it is unlikely that the prime minister had time in any event to pursue a vendetta against the Liberal and Jewish whisky man.

Sam's Toronto lawyer, Peter White, K.C., may have been closer to the mark when he looked to the RCMP for the origins of the prosecution. "My information is that the Mounties are still sore over the defeat of their plans in connection with your brother in the west and are still on the trail," he wrote to Sam in New York. In fact, the Mounties began their investigation of the Bronfmans at the end of 1933, as part of an extensive inquiry into smuggling of liquor into Quebec.[87] There is no doubt that the RCMP was flexing its muscles at the time, going through a major period of growth and reform pushed through by a Bennett appointee, Major General James Howden MacBrien. A veteran of the South African constabulary, MacBrien rose through the ranks of the Canadian Army to become Chief of Staff of Overseas Forces at the end of the First World War. Named RCMP commissioner in 1931, he raised standards throughout the force, injected a badly needed dose of professionalism and declared his independence from political manipulation in law enforcement at the federal level. In the wake of the Stevens Inquiry and the Royal Commission of 1927, MacBrien directed particular attention to criminal activity in customs and excise.[88]

Under MacBrien the Mounties aggressively tracked down smugglers who continued, even after repeal, to carry liquor into the United States to avoid customs duties. Thanks to his vigour the RCMP had just broken up a major rum-running ring when the Bronfman prosecution was announced. But there was always a feeling within the force that the "higher-ups" were escaping the net. The Bronfmans were certainly "higher up," but so were others, such as Harry Hatch or Colonel Albert Gooderham of Gooderham and Worts. The Mounties' confidential correspondence was generally free of antisemitism. However, in this letter by the RCMP Quebec chief, Superintendent Frederick Mead, to one of the principal investigators in the case, Major Mark Vernon, the guard dropped:

> I do know ... that money has been paid over to Harry Bronfman in Montreal by Quebec bootleggers for alcohol smuggled into Canada and all this stuff will come out, as our good French Canadian citizens are not going to break rock in our Government Hotel and allow these jews [*sic*] to sit pretty and make a few more millions.[89]

It hardly escaped notice when the King's New Year's Day

Honours List was published in January 1935 that Albert Gooderham, yachtsman and automobile collector of distinction, long associated with the Royal Grenadiers of Toronto, became a knight commander of St Michael and St George, while Samuel Bronfman and his brothers found themselves awaiting trial. "One man is knighted, the other is indicted," the Jewish M.P. Sam Jacobs quipped at the time. If antisemitism did lurk behind the decision to go after the Bronfmans, and Jewish community leaders had little doubt about it, then it likely came from the RCMP itself, a ferociously anti-Communist milieu in which there was plenty of dislike of potential subversives, foreigners and Jews.

At the same time, the Mounties undoubtedly believed they had a strong case, issuing warrants for the arrest of sixty-one persons in five provinces, all of them Canadians. According to the police investigators, the Bronfmans had been behind a vast conspiracy during U.S. prohibition to defraud the governments of Canada and Quebec of taxes on the sale of whisky in Canada, amounting to at least $5 million. The focus was clearly on Sam and his brothers, the others arrested being minor participants or "lesser fry," as the *Gazette* put it, mostly from the Maritimes.[90] The indictment claimed that a great deal of whisky bound for the American market was in fact re-routed into Canada, smuggled on to Canadian shores and sold illegally, without payment of the Canadian taxes. Four of the five charges against the accused involved this offence; in the fifth charge, as if an afterthought, they were accused of smuggling liquor into the United States.

Moving quickly through the crowd of reporters hungry for stories about the sensational indictment, Sam and his brothers, together with Barney Aaron, turned themselves in at RCMP headquarters in Montreal on Monday, December 17. Sam and Allan appeared at 9:00 A.M. with Aimé Geoffrion, and were formally served by RCMP Inspector Detective F.W. Zaneth, in charge of the case. Harry and Abe arrived a half-hour later with Barney Aaron, and gave themselves up to Corporal Scrogg. All were formally arrested, photographed and fingerprinted. Around eleven o'clock the accused were bundled into RCMP cars and taken to court for arraignment. Leaving the building later that morning on bail amounting to $100,000 each, the Bronfman brothers were again besieged by photographers and reporters; Harry tried to cover his face, but, as the *Gazette* reported, "he desisted at the request of his brother, Sam."[91]

On January 11 a preliminary hearing began in the Court of King's Bench in Montreal before Mr Justice Jules Desmarais. Referred to in the press as the "huge liquor conspiracy" and "the biggest case in the history of the RCMP," the benches were jammed, and proceedings had to be moved to a larger courtroom than usual to accommodate the fifty-nine accused, twelve attorneys, witnesses, police, reporters and spectators. Ominous, for the Bronfmans, was the presence of a U.S. customs officer sent to monitor the testimony, presumably with the idea that criminal indictments might be issued in the United States.

Acting for the accused was a glittering array of legal talent headed by the leading Bronfman lawyers Aimé Geoffrion, Laz Phillips and Lucien Gendron. To the Montreal public, Geoffrion was unquestionably the star. Sixty-two years old in 1934, he came from a leading French-Canadian family that had made its mark in federal politics as well as on the bench; his father had been a minister in the Laurier Cabinet and his maternal grandfather a federal minister of justice and later Chief Justice of the Court of Appeal in Montreal. Referred to when he died in 1946 as "the unchallenged leader of the legal profession in Canada," Geoffrion was acclaimed already in the 1930s as one of the greatest constitutional lawyers the country had ever seen. He was a familiar figure at the Privy Council in London where he argued dozens of cases, was long associated with McGill University as a professor of civil law, and was a director of the Canadian Pacific Railway.

Sam's friend Laz Phillips, then only thirty-seven, also sat at Sam's side; nephew of Hirsch Cohen, one of the country's most distinguished rabbis, Laz was a brilliant legal strategist and the perfect complement to the more experienced Geoffrion, whose skills lay rather in the cut and thrust of legal debate. Other attorneys included Joseph Cohen, Philippe Brais, Lionel Forsythe and Lionel Sperber—twelve lawyers in all for the entire group of defendants, enough legal talent, according to Shinbane, to constitute "a minor bar convention." Sharing the prosecution were Jean Penverne, soon to run unsuccessfully as a

Tory candidate in the federal riding of Outrement, and James Crankshaw—no mean figures in the Quebec bar themselves, and fresh from a victory in a related $1.7 million liquor-smuggling case a few months before.

Tension filled the air as arguments got under way in the crowded courtroom. The Bronfman brothers "looked tired and distinctly worried," according to a reporter on the scene, who noted that there were top executives from the Peel Street offices of Seagram in the audience to give what moral support they could.[92] Sam obviously hated every minute, and as his friend Sol Kanee astutely observes, the courtroom was a special torture: it was the one place Sam knew he was not in control.[93] Preliminary sparring centred on the Bronfmans, addressing the all-important fifth charge, smuggling liquor into the United States through Atlas Shipping Company. Leaving aside the detailed issue of whether the Bronfmans and Atlas Shipping were themselves involved in carrying whisky to Rum Row—a charge the family stoutly denied—Geoffrion got to the heart of the matter of U.S. rum running: "I have never discovered a statute which makes it illegal in Canada to smuggle into the United States." Or as he put it the next day: "I cannot see how the Crown can argue that conspiracy to commit a crime in the United States is a crime in Canada. . . . It would be fantastic if it were suggested that Quebec had to start administering the revenue laws of the United States."[94]

A full-dress debate on the subject flared on the 15th, when the Bronfman attorneys dramatically went on the offensive. What law, they demanded, were their clients accused of breaking if liquor was smuggled into the United States? Would Canadian customs officials, who collected nine dollars a gallon on whisky bound for the American market, be indicted as co-accused? Joseph Cohen asked whether the Crown believed it a crime to export textbooks on evolution to Tennessee, "since Mr Darwin is barred in that great and glorious state." As the defence saw it, if the Crown's contention were accepted, not only would all Canadian distilleries be equally culpable, so would all those connected with the purchase from them and all those associated with the movement of the goods, such as the banks, railway companies and their employees—not to mention Canadian customs officials who processed the documents on clearance and collected duties. At the end of the day, and after hearings that had lasted only four days, Justice Desmarais adjourned the court to decide upon the matter.[95]

Desmarais reappeared on February 4, sinking like a stone the prosecution's charges about smuggling into the United States: the Crown, he ruled, "did not show an indictable offense in Canada which could be the subject of criminal conspiracy." At least one reporter felt a "sigh of relief" among the defendants and their counsel, for with the dangerous charge of smuggling into the United States thrown out, the rest of the Crown's case began to appear shaky.[96] Obviously heartened, the defence lawyers sought to thin out the formidable array of evidence prosecutors lugged to the courtroom with them. Essentially, the Crown attempted to establish links between well-known bootleggers and the Bronfmans, particularly Abe, who had dealt with some rather shady characters in Saint John. The Crown Attorney put a series of witnesses on the stand—mainly rough-hewn, seafaring men, obviously out of place in a Montreal courtroom. For the most part, however, Penverne tried to prove his case with elaborate calculations based on the financial records of the Bronfmans' trading companies—a rather dreary exercise, which at times tested the patience of Justice Desmarais.

Unwilling to leave the entire direction of the case to Laz and Aimé Geoffrion, and possibly bored himself with the proceedings, Sam summoned Mark Shinbane from Winnipeg, hoping that his friend, who had once been a counsel for the RCMP in Manitoba, could cast some light on the prosecution's strategy.[97] Although he undoubtedly knew that this complicated case was best left in the hands of the professionals, Sam was temperamentally incapable of letting the "prima donnas," as he referred to his lawyers, run the whole show. On his own, Sam begged his friend to go to the island of St Pierre—apparently to try to find out why Sam was being charged, "and not all the other boys." "Snoop around and find out what this is all about," Sam said. "I know you speak a pretty fair French." Sam also told Shinbane to send messages back to Montreal in secret code, fearing a phone tap by the RCMP. It is highly unlikely that Shinbane's two-week adventure—which he remembered vividly because he became

horribly ill on the island, the effects of which were complicated
on the way back by an overdose of Jamaica rum — had any effect
whatever on the outcome. (In recompense, Sam and Allan set
Shinbane up like a prince with a suite in the Royal Victoria
Hospital when he staggered back to Montreal.) Only a few traces
of this bizarre expedition remain — mainly outgoing telegrams in
the files of the Seagram Company. A typical one of these, with an
attached translation requesting information about warehousing
procedures on the island, began as follows.

SRLKJ RABHC DELZS FYGRO HITYJ KLJEM NLHOY PWPKQ
RSLWT EKUVD WKXRL YHNZB JATBC ONDHY EFSKG HWOIJ
KHLJM BHNOX PKQSW RSUTV KUZVW ABXYK ZAUVB KWCDF

Whether Shinbane's mission and these cryptic messages helped
the defence on some minor points may be disputed; what seems
more certain, however, is that he was able to divert some of Sam's
formidable energies into a tangential intrigue — keeping him off
the backs of his hard-pressed lawyers.

As the proceedings dragged on into March, the Crown focused
on the Bronfman brothers and three employees, consigning the
cases against the other defendants to provincial jurisdictions.
Charging that the family had destroyed key records bearing on
the case during the preceding summer, RCMP officers combed
through Peel Street yet again. The Mounties needed vital
documents that were mysteriously missing, the prosecutors
said — leaving Penverne open to suggestions that his case against
the Bronfmans had been weak to begin with.

Other signs suggested that by this point the Crown's case was
beginning to crumble. Interrupting Penverne's account of how
liquor had been smuggled into Canada without payment of duty,
Justice Desmarais asked what turned out to be the vital question:
"Is it proved, and where is it proved, that the Bronfman brothers
knew that this liquor was being sold for unlawful shipment into
Canada?" And again: "Are you not taking it for granted that they
knew about certain operations, merely because they got profits
from those operations?"[98] Summing up the defence arguments on
April 11, Aimé Geoffrion declared that if his clients were guilty,
"then every distillery director in the country is guilty of

infraction of the law" — or, as the *Montreal Daily Star* put it in its headline: "If Bronfmans Guilty — All Liquor Heads Are." The Bronfmans did not dispute that some of their liquor might have been smuggled into Canada, but they stoutly denied that they were part of a conspiracy to do so or that they were responsible for what bootleggers might have done with the whisky they bought. In any event, given the millions they were making feeding the huge American market at the time, the more than occasional diversion of liquor to Canadian shores by the four brothers did not seem like a plausible or worthwhile venture.

When the arguments were completed, Justice Desmarais delivered his decision to a packed courtroom on April 11, dismissing all charges against the Bronfmans and their employees.[99] In his view there was no prima facie proof of conspiracy. At the heart of the case, it was clear, was the responsibility of distillers and whisky importers in the rum running that had been rampant in the Maritime provinces, Newfoundland and the French islands during prohibition. Selling to rum runners, as Justice Desmarais made clear, was not against Canadian law. "It is well known," he said, "that at that time, and previously, a great number of Canadian distilleries organized themselves to sell outside of Canada as many of their products as they could. This mode of action certainly contains no illegality as far as Canada is concerned." The Bronfmans' export companies, which figured so heavily in the Crown's case, were not illegal; nor were the brothers obliged to ascertain the ultimate destination of the liquor they sold. "After taking delivery of the whisky, the buyer could dispose of his purchase as seemed to him best. The accused Bronfman had no further interest in those liquors, nor control over their destination." The Crown had failed to link the brothers to smuggling into Canada and consequently the entire edifice built by the prosecution collapsed.

Clearly relieved, Sam acted nonchalant. "I've got work to do," he claimed, years later, to have told Laz Phillips, setting off for New York the next day. In reality, Sam was probably much more deeply scarred by these events than he allowed. He was candid about one thing, however: he saw plenty of work to do at the time.[100]

■

SAM HAD EVERY reason to believe that with the failure of the prosecution's case in 1935 he had established the blamelessness of his family's business operations during the rum-running years. Unfortunately, there were no indications that the American government saw matters this way. To the contrary, Washington was unhappy.

Reminded by the RCMP's case of how Canadians had flouted U.S. law during prohibition, the Americans received another unpleasant message on January 5, 1935: arbitrators issued their decision in the related case of a Canadian schooner, *I'm Alone*, and found against the United States government. Six years before, this tiny ship, of Canadian registry, was challenged in the Gulf of Mexico by United States Coast Guard cutters on the hunt for rum runners. The ship tried to escape, and after an extended chase the Americans opened fire with a small cannon, sinking the vessel. During the clash, a sailor was drowned. Protests came immediately from the Canadian side. In the clamour that followed, the *I'm Alone*'s experienced skipper, a Newfoundlander named John Randell, insisted that his ship was outside the U.S. two-hundred-mile limit — and that the Americans had no right to challenge his vessel, let alone fire upon her. Over the next six years the Canadian and American authorities wrangled over the case, with Ottawa seeking to establish that Washington had been in the wrong. Finally, as a result of the arbitration, the Americans had to concede: they made a formal apology, paid the Canadian government $25,000, plus additional compensation to the captain, the crew and the widow of the man who was drowned.

What the papers did not say, but what the Americans knew well, was that the whisky that had gone to the bottom of the Gulf of Mexico had come from the Bronfmans. Indeed, so far as the Americans were concerned, the family had helped to keep the embarrassing affair alive after the ship went down, being in cahoots with the ship's former owner, Montreal businessman George Herne. Herne continually pressed for compensation through his lawyer, Sam's friend Laz Phillips — and the Americans noted the connection. The United States consular representatives in Montreal kept a watch on this problem, reading about new machinations by Herne in the Toronto scandal sheet *Hush*, on April 21, 1934. A few months later, when the consulate first heard rumours of the RCMP prosecution of the Bronfman brothers, the consul general recommended that the U.S. Immigration Service investigate the legality of the continued presence of Sam and his brothers in New York — warning, however, that the Bronfmans "will probably be in a position to exert local pressure to prevent their deportation to Canada and to prevent prosecutions in the United States of themselves and their American associates."[101] Clearly there was plenty of trouble afoot.

For related reasons there had been concerns in the U.S. Department of Justice about the Bronfmans, particularly Sam, going back at least to 1931. Officials there had been looking into the involvement of Canadians in the American bootleg trade and had targeted the family for further investigation. The famed Aaron Sapiro, the prairie-cooperative spellbinder whom the Bronfmans had briefly employed during Harry's trials in Saskatchewan, kept an eye on the matter for the family in Washington, did what lobbying he could on their behalf, and advised Laz Phillips on how to approach the Americans.[102]

Justice Department officials even went so far as to prepare an indictment against Sam for bootlegging in March 1933; Sapiro's intervention helped quash it — at least according to his own interpretation of what happened. Writing to Laz Phillips in August, Sapiro confirmed that "the Department of Justice had dismissed the indictment against Sam Bronfman on the application of a mutual friend in New York City" and following up a few days later, Sapiro submitted a bill for a hefty $12,500 — "a very small fee to pay for what was achieved in the recommendation of dismissal." Justifying his charges, Sapiro reminded Laz of what an achievement it was to have stopped the prosecution, for "Sam Bronfman was the one particular person that the Federal Government would rather have than all the others put together."[103]

Repeal might have been expected to have dissipated the cloud under which Canadian distillers operated in the United States. Many, indeed, predicted a windfall, with millions of gallons of aged Canadian liquor pouring freely across the border. Writing from Washington on the very eve of repeal, R.B. Bennett's influential brother-in-law William Herridge anticipated the possible sale in the United States of "virtually the entire surplus stocks of whisky held by Canadian distillers."[104] These expectations never materialized, however. Having boldly opened the door to the production and sale of alcohol, the Roosevelt Administration suddenly balked when it came to new trading ground rules for the Canadians.

To appreciate Washington's reluctance to embrace free trade in whisky, one must recall the circumstances of the American market in 1933 and 1934. Almost everyone, it soon turned out, had exaggerated the demand for alcohol by the United States public. Many Americans had simply lost the drinking habit during prohibition, and many others were simply too hard hit by the Depression to purchase liquor. Bootleg whisky still existed in vast quantities, driving down demand for legitimate products, and salesmen reported consumer resistance to high prices and poor quality — particularly resented now that prohibition had been officially struck down. Given these disappointing market conditions, American producers called for barriers against Canadian imports, along with reduced taxes on liquor sold in the United States to wipe out bootleg sales.

Taking into account all the various interests involved, Washington raised excise taxes levied on imported whisky to a very considerable five dollars a gallon. Canadian whisky still entered the United States to be blended with spirits produced in U.S. plants, but the importation was expensive and this contributed to the many other hazards of entering the American market. Sam had good reason to suspect that his American competitors — or at least one of them, Lew Rosenstiel — were doing their best to make it more difficult for him to operate in the United States. Rosenstiel, for his part, developed a lifelong hatred for Sam from this point — "unscrupulous, alien competition," as he typically referred to Seagram and its proprietor.[105]

The feud between the two giants of the American whiskey industry escalated from this time and was suspected by many in the industry to have been behind a new headache that Sam had to face in 1934—menacing moves against his company and other Canadian distillers by the Department of the Treasury, pressed by the powerful Secretary, Henry Morgenthau, Jr.[106]

Treasury, as one might imagine, was not the distillers' favourite department. Associated by most Americans with printing banknotes and with the management of the money supply, whisky people looked upon it as a determined, bureaucratic obstacle to doing business — "a reliquary of Antique Laws, Regulations, and Interpretations into which [distillers] pay 720 million dollars a year for security," as one of Sam's men put it.[107] Canadian whisky people had yet another reason to dislike the department in the wake of prohibition; Morgenthau himself, a Roosevelt loyalist known for his earnestness and intellectual rigidity, was a virtual crusader against "the bootlegger" — a generic term he used to describe all those who participated in the illegalities of prohibition. Unlike most, who were willing to let bygones be bygones once the Eighteenth Amendment was no more, Morgenthau could not abide that, as he put it himself, "a whole generation grew up, taking it for granted they could break the law and no one would punish them."[108] There may also have been another bias at work, with the aristocratic and Jewish assimilationist Morgenthau looking askance at the nouveaux riches "Jewish bootleggers," the Bronfmans, north of the border. And so quite apart from the vigorous pursuit of post-repeal lawbreakers, wiping out the remaining bootleggers and closing down illicit exports from neighbouring territories, something more had to be done, he believed, to set things right.

That something turned out to be a massive claim against the Canadian distillers who had previously sold their whisky through American bootleggers during the entire prohibition era. Huge sums were owing to the American government in taxes not paid by these companies, Morgenthau argued; and if they wanted to continue doing business in the United States, they would have to pay. To prepare the ground, he commissioned a full-scale report on the whisky industry in 1934 by Samuel Klaus, who took a particularly jaundiced view of Canadian distillers. The latter were living off the avails of huge profits once earned by rum running, he contended; and behind them, it was alleged, lay the sinister hand of the British DCL with nearly unlimited supplies of capital and whisky. The tone of the report could only have satisfied those American companies for whom the Canadian presence in the American market was an illegitimate presumption. And it could only mean new problems for Sam Bronfman whose Seagram company, the report observed, "is the first in Canada in stocks as in sales."

CHAPTER V

Turning New Leaves

DESPITE TREMENDOUS GROWTH and the careful nurturing of a creditable image for his business, Sam had difficulty polishing his tarnished reputation of the prohibition years. A story is told of Sam's youngest child, Charles, innocently enquiring at one family dinner, "Daddy, what's a bootlegger?" Sam dropped the carving knife and fired off one of his crushing replies: "Don't you ever say that word again!" Charles had clearly touched a raw nerve. For as the Canadian and American governments set their new course for the whisky trade, Sam chafed over the indignities he had suffered in the past. Indeed, his appetite for respectability grew with his standing within the industry.

Cautious in dealing with the Canadian authorities after his collision with the RCMP in 1935, Sam was scrupulously accurate when applying for naturalized citizenship documents two years later. Based on a prior naturalization of "Eichel Bronfman" in the County Court of Winnipeg, on May 18, 1892, he declared his birthplace to have been Bessarabia, Rumania, and his birthdate February 27, 1889. Publicly, however, Sam continued to present himself as Brandon-born, giving the year of his birth as 1891 and his birthdate March 4, the same as that of his daughter Mindel. Like many Jews from the Czarist Empire Sam probably did not know his true birthdate according to either the Christian or the Hebrew calendars, and for some reason he wanted the same birthday as his first-born child, named after his mother in 1925.

Sam's naturalization papers also included a brief description: five feet six inches tall, blue eyes, fair hair and complexion. Now in his late forties, with thinning hair, Sam remained remarkably youthful looking, round-faced with his left eyebrow occasionally arched in a quizzical expression, and with his somewhat plump physique accentuated by the square-shaped, double-breasted suits of the era.

■

"SAM, YOU KNOW something," Mark Shinbane once declared. "You're a millionaire and, Sam, between you and me, I live better than you do, because you don't in many ways live, you just exist for business." Shinbane may have been one of the few people who could get away with such a remark to Sam Bronfman, and even he drew the wrath of the head of Seagrams for having said what people who knew Sam intimately appreciated only too well. The exchange took place, according to Shinbane, because Sam could not understand why his friend would not leave Winnipeg and join him in the Peel Street offices in Montreal. When Shin said no for family reasons, Sam was stupefied, and reacted with his characteristically purple prose. "You know you son of a bitch, you're the first goddamn person who has never asked anything from me. And all these other sons of bitches, I made them rich beyond their dreams of avarice, and that included Laz too. Why? Are you a damn fool, or crazy?"[1]

A journalist preparing an article on Sam in 1937 claimed that he worked fifteen hours a day—almost certainly an underestimate. Indeed, those who knew him well had difficulty identifying a time when Sam was *not* working. Throughout most of the 1930s, as we have seen, he commuted regularly between New York and Montreal, with only the weekends to spend with his wife and children. And even those weekends were heavily booked with meetings—conferences with business associates and, increasingly in the 1930s, Jewish community matters. Coming home late one evening, Sam quipped brightly to Leo Kolber: "Saidye doesn't understand, I've got to make a living!"[2] Around the house, his family remembered Sam as literally sprouting ideas: he used to write little notes to himself on scraps of paper that he stuffed into his pockets at irregular moments — a walking loose-leaf notebook, Saidye once said.

After interrupting this rhythm of commuting during the war years, Sam continued to commute into the 1950s, spending at least a few days a week in New York during most of the year. Commuting meant travel by train, of course, and even when commercial air travel between the two cities became common Sam preferred the train for a long time. Unequivocal on large matters, Sam often put off to the last moment the decision on whether or not to leave for New York. He had a standing reservation on the Delaware and Hudson to Manhattan on every night except Friday and Saturday, to be taken or not as the situation warranted. At Peel Street, an office manager named Jimmy Ingham had the unenviable task of attending to the reservations on a continuing basis. Both his wife and children recalled how difficult this arrangement was, particularly when the family was young. "I was pleased at what he was achieving," Saidye told Terence Robertson, "but not particularly happy at having to be father as well as mother to the children." "Business was one of his children — his first child," was Edgar's succinct assessment.[3]

As a result of his protracted absences, Sam was largely unfamiliar with the children's routines, and received periodic briefings from his wife on how the household operated. "Lunch period is over," Saidye wrote to him on September 7, 1933. "It is quite an institution now in our house. The boys take their lunch at 12, Phyllis takes hers at 12:45, since her school is out at 12:30 and Mindel has hers at 1:15. . . . This afternoon we go first to see Dr Goldbloom. Mindel is complaining of a pain in her knee, then to the milliner's to try the girls' hats on and then we are having a special treat — tea downtown. So you see darling I am having rather a busy time. But how proud I feel to take my daughters with me." Frequently absent, Sam nevertheless fretted about his children's welfare. Having posted this letter about Mindel's sore knee, Saidye realized she had committed a gaffe, and immediately sent another bulletin: "I realized after I had written to you about it how foolish it was of me, especially knowing your temperament. . . . There is just a slight strain of a ligament. . . . We are now off to Eaton's for a treat." "I had quite a thrill

watching Mindel. I took her to her first music lesson today,"
Saidye wrote a few days later. "Edgar came into my room this
morning and said, 'Isn't Daddy home yet?' His face fell when I
told him it would be quite a long time yet before Daddy would be
home."

Unhappy with Sam's commuting, Saidye responded stoically,
deferring to her husband's priorities. "Sleeping alone is not so
hot," she wrote to him at the Fort Garry Hotel in Winnipeg in
August 1930. "Have had to take my medicine each night since
you left. What is this power you have over me?" Supervised and
cared for by a series of nurses and governesses, the children
remember their mother as the one stable element in their
lives — "the rock," as Charles puts it. Often short-tempered
when he was back at home, Sam could be a forbidding person,
particularly fearsome during one of his explosions of anger.
Wrapped up in his own world, Sam was utterly oblivious to the
effect these eruptions had, particularly on his children. As Phyllis
recalls, "I remember saying to him when I was about 14 or 15
how petrified I was of him and he said, 'Me, your father?' He
could not understand how he could terrify people. He just
couldn't."[4]

Whether physically present or not, and most of the time he was
not, Sam totally dominated his household and ruled as a
Victorian autocrat. His idea of family was unqualifiedly
patriarchal: he was the lord and master, Saidye was his devoted
helpmate, his sons were to take over the business, and his
daughters were to be refined and marriageable. Sex was taboo.
The children followed a well-defined regimen, with the accent on
proper behaviour and respect for their parents. When his
attention focused on his children, Sam imposed strict requirements and expected to be obeyed. Many years after, Minda
remembered being banished from the family table in tears when
she once appeared wearing lipstick at a meal.

As with his employees, Sam was sparing of compliments in
dealing with his children. "Compliments almost didn't exist. . . .
You were expected to do well," Edgar commented, somewhat
ruefully in his case, given his poor grades in college that
constantly had to be explained away, and given Sam's conviction

that his children all had to be as talented as he was. "I never got credit for being me," Edgar went on, "it was just that you were Sam's son." "Blood counts," was one of Sam's favourite expressions, meaning that if his children did well in any particular area, "you are good because you are my son . . . not because you are you." Since Sam anticipated that his sons would take over the empire, not his daughters, these paternal expectations weighed particularly heavily on them. On one occasion Charles thought that he had been the smartest person involved in a particular company matter. When he told his father, Sam looked up from his game of solitaire and snapped: "I should hope so!"[5]

"As a child I . . . hated the sometimes strutting declarations of self-satisfaction," Phyllis comments, "but I knew that he would listen seriously to a serious problem."[6] Despite his tyrannical behaviour, Sam prescribed an ideal of a loving family, and somehow communicated this along the mysterious channels with which children receive messages from their parents. Despite his iron exterior, he loved his family deeply, and in retrospect, at least, they realized it. When Minda went to Smith College in 1943 she told her parents about how her own family contrasted with those of her classmates. "Boy, you certainly learn a lot about life at college," she wrote in a revealing passage.

> I have always loved you and my family (immediate!) but seeing the wrecked family lives of so many people around here I appreciate you very much and realize as I never could otherwise what a priceless gift I have in you all. There are an awful lot of very nice girls here but because of an unhappy home life or because of parents who do not fulfill their roles, they have such a twisted sense of proportion . . . they don't have that sense of security and self-confidence which comes from the knowledge that one's parents and family are a very happy contented unit in a perfect little world of their own.

At their Friday night dinners together, when the meal was over, the children were expected to recite poetry or to make little speeches about the family — usually in praise of their parents. These were awkward exercises — Phyllis, the rebel of the four youngsters, remembers refusing to partake — but Sam insisted on the ritual and the verse-making, at least, became a family tradition, to be considerably upgraded when Sam hired one of Canada's foremost poets, Abraham Klein, as his speech-writer. For years, however, the verses were handmade. Holidaying as a family in the summer of 1936, the children presented a diary to Saidye, inscribed from all four, but probably written by Minda:

An orchid is deemed a most precious flower
And you Mum and Dad become so by the hour
You have such talent for making good blends
And we are the recipients of those dividends
So thank you for picking each other we say
May great happiness like yours be ours one day

The four B-Brats

On Father's Day, some time in the mid-1940s, the children presented Sam with a gift, together with this poem by Charles:

Today is the day
When all children pay
A tribute to their pappy
I for one
Your son of a gun
Would like to give you Pappy
A small presentation
That won't cause a sensation
But which I hope makes you happy
And my brother and sisters
Are not going to give you blisters
But we are giving you a sweater
Which on a cold, wintry day
That certainly isn't like May
Is going to make you feel better
Happy Father's Day, Dad

Charles

To protect themselves against Sam's stern regimen, Edgar reflected, the children developed a common bond — one that is certainly evident today. "We had to take care of each other because of this violent temper, this ogre," is how Edgar puts it. Certainly the children benefited from their mother's interventions — soothing her husband when he was on edge, calming him down, providing the support that he withheld. But they also saw an affectionate side of their father — his devotion to Saidye above all, but also the depth of his commitment to his family, the strength of his family loyalties and the intensity of his feelings about them. Distant though he certainly was, Sam was a constant presence.

Preoccupied with business and community affairs, Sam nevertheless revelled in domesticity, and felt most comfortable at home. Visitors knew the house on Belvedere Road as *"balebatisch"* — a Yiddish word signifying graciousness, and implying abundant hospitality. Saidye presided over this domestic order, organizing community meetings, luncheons and receptions — imitating some of the service observed at houses they had visited as a couple in England, Scotland and the Continent. So long as her parents were alive, Saidye kept a fully kosher kitchen, and while this order eventually lapsed, vestiges remained, in the manner of so many North American Jews — separate dishes for Passover, no ham or bacon, and so on. Sam and Saidye maintained a traditional, though not strictly observant Jewish home — with some ritual blessings on Friday night, an annual breaking of the fast dinner on Yom Kippur, and family seders on Passover, which Sam would run good-humouredly. As befit a captain of industry, at the seders Sam bargained attentively with his children for the *afikomen* — a piece of *matzah* crucial for the ritual meal and which is traditionally hidden, then found by the youngsters and replaced after they are rewarded. He attended synagogue on the High Holy Days of Rosh Hashana and Yom Kippur and occasionally on other holidays, and to observe his parents' *Yahrzeit*, the anniversary of their deaths.[7]

In social circumstances outside his home Sam was prone to feel ill at ease, restless and impatient. He was notoriously so on holidays, as we shall see. Uninterested in sports, he tried on various occasions to play golf, which was much in vogue among his peers in Montreal. Sam became a member of the Elm Ridge, the Jewish golf club in Dorval, about fifteen minutes from downtown Montreal. But he proved hopeless at the game, becoming furious at himself when he performed badly. One day, after struggling through two or three holes, Sam's caddy blurted out the truth: "Sir, you're a terrible golfer." Sam turned to the boy, and said evenly: "Young man, you will never in your life be closer to death than you are at this moment."[8] Skiing, similarly, was impossible. At Ste Marguerite, in the Laurentians during the war, Sam tried to coast down small hills. But immediately, he became distracted by the mechanical problem of downhill skiing — that it only works downhill. (A side problem was that he found it physically impossible to climb even the small inclines.) There had to be a way, Sam thought, to ski down a hill and have sufficient momentum at the bottom to coast to the top of the next; since he could not achieve this suspension of the law of gravity, he lost interest in the activity altogether.

Essentially a shy person, with very few friends, Sam relied almost entirely upon Saidye for the couple's social life. Few people besides his wife knew how anxious he was in an unfamiliar social situation. "When he knew few of the people present," Saidye says now, "I always went first."[9] Together with the wives of a few often like-minded husbands, Saidye organized a Saturday night set that would regularly get together — including Laz and Rosalie Phillips, Alvin and Hannah (Hank) Walker, Jack and Ethel Klein, Ben and Saidye Marks, and a few others. Sam and Saidye felt comfortable with this group, although the Bronfmans were, at least as one participant remembered, "a little more formal" than some of the others. What set them apart, however, was not so much their wealth, for they were all well off — "it didn't matter if you were very, very, very rich or just comfortably rich," as Ethel Klein put it — but also Sam's and sometimes Saidye's frequent absence from Montreal. "My father did not 'live' anywhere," Phyllis observes, emphasizing his relative social isolation. "He was always between New York and Montreal."

Most of all, Sam enjoyed the social occasions associated with his business, the get-togethers that became a hallmark of the

Seagram organization — and where his social pre-eminence was assured. With their corny hymns in praise of the company or the boss, these events were part of the corporate culture of the 1930s. They were also highly emotional experiences for Sam, celebrations of Seagram's success and the corporate community he had built. Even at home he liked to sing the company songs celebrating Seagram or Calvert.[10] Family members recall one rousing song in particular about Seagram sales "climbing and climbing," ever upward:

Our Seven Crown's booming
Our V.O.'s zooming,
Other brands have fallen away.

Oh, there's fun and there's glory in selling this line.
Everyone's saying that Seagram is fine.

Forever and ever, let's all sing together,
Seagram is a grand old name.

As with the little world of Oaklands, and later with the Jewish community, at company parties Sam was the father — honoured, respected and loved — and in the end it was father, perhaps with the memory of his own beloved father, Ekiel, that he wanted most to be.

■

"THE PEOPLE WHO make the most money out of liquor are the governments," Sam liked to say, reminding everyone who would listen about the great sums he paid in taxes and the tremendous public benefits that resulted. From time to time, at social events in Ottawa, he would refer to David Sim, deputy minister of revenue, as "my senior partner." Canadians were particular beneficiaries of his company, Laz Phillips told the Canadian government in 1936, for "while 90% of our sales were in the United States, 50% of the taxes were paid and remained in Canada."[11] After the unpleasant experience of the 1935 prosecution Sam's emissaries reported from Ottawa that the

Bennett government was increasingly sympathetic, and seemed to be seeing Sam's point. But given the importance of the U.S. market, the future of the whisky trade hung on the hopes for lower American duties and a better trade relationship with Washington. Would the Canadian government help?

Worried about rising American trade barriers, Canadian whisky men increasingly looked to Ottawa for assistance, seeking to ease the way for Canadian liquor to enter the United States. As the two countries engaged in preliminary discussions, a serious obstacle appeared in the shape of Secretary of the Treasury Henry Morgenthau, Jr. The moralistic Morgenthau, as we have seen, bore a grudge against the Canadian whisky interests and felt that they should have been punished for having taken advantage of American prohibition. To achieve this, officials in his office were preparing unspecified claims against the Canadians, holding them responsible for the nonpayment of taxes by bootleggers during the prohibition era. For the Canadian authorities this was obviously a delicate matter, and there could be no official policy on it. But there was unofficial involvement, which possibly made matters worse for the Canadian distillers.

On August 23, 1935, the Canadian minister in Washington, William Herridge, R.B. Bennett's brother-in-law, telephoned the Secretary of the Treasury — a call that was transcribed in Morgenthau's office by his secretary Henrietta Klotz, as was his practice.[12] Herridge, an influential Conservative policymaker keen on expanding trade with the United States, worried that difficulties over whisky might obstruct the negotiations towards lower tariffs he was urging upon the prime minister. Ostensibly, Herridge called about a proposed Liquor Revenue Bill then before Congress, but in more general terms he was hoping to improve the climate by signalling official Canadian sympathy with Morgenthau's position. Herridge insisted that the Bronfmans and the other distillers were eager for a settlement with the Americans on claims outstanding from the prohibition period. His conversation, with its transparent effort to ingratiate himself to the hard-headed Secretary, might even have whetted Morganthau's appetite in his vendetta against the Canadian distillers in general, and the Bronfmans in particular:

Herridge: Good morning. How are you?

Morgenthau: Fine.

Herridge: Hope you had a good holiday.

Morgenthau: I don't know when.

Herridge: Oh, you mean to say you haven't been away?

Morgenthau: No, no.

Herridge: Oh, gosh. Do you mind me speaking to you personally about something?

Morgenthau: Go right ahead.

Herridge: It's about that bill. I don't know whether you've gone over it yourself. It's your revenue — Liquor Revenue Bill. . . . Now, last week — I'm just saying this privately because I won't want to be improper, but last week the Bronson [sic] people, that is the seat of that big crowd . . . asked me if I'd see if they couldn't get next to a Treasury solicitor, try to settle something, clean it up. They're doing well, you know. They just don't want to be suspect. Now, the other people, I know, have been told to do the same thing, so that's the whole picnic. . . .

Morgenthau: I see.

Herridge: I said, if I were in your shoes I'd get busy and get this damn thing cleaned up. I said, the Treasury's well disposed toward my government and we shouldn't have any difficulty.

Morgenthau: That's right.

Herridge: . . . Well, they've been coming backwards and forwards and gradually getting their nerve up and I think they've had some bum advice. They've been told, you're not to disclose a hand. I said, that's all damn nonsense, you go down there and ask to see one of the Treasury lawyers and you'll find them perfectly fair and talk business; see where you're getting on then . . . [Laz] Phillips came to see me last week and said, would you mind getting me an entrée down there. . . . Now, as soon as they move — the Walker people have been very reluctant, but they will have to move, too. You see, they can't take a chance of these fellows getting a prior settlement to them. And that's your whole works.

Herridge reiterated that the key Canadian players in any

prospective negotiations were the "Bronsons" and the Hiram Walker company. And without even knowing the nature or the amount of the Treasury Department claim, he insisted that the Bronfmans would settle: "the Bronsons are anxious; they've been phoning you this week to know that they can come down and what I can fix up. . . . They want to settle, they just don't want to peddle [sic] over this. They want to do business in a nice friendly way." It seems quite likely that the Canadian minister in Washington weakened the bargaining position of the Bronfman representatives by this conversation and, if so, he opened the door to punitive Treasury Department claims. By the end of the year, in any event, Treasury indicated they sought an astronomical hundred million dollars or more. Morgenthau seems to have been encouraged.

While these discussions were under way, a Canadian election campaign began, in which the possibility of freer trade with the Americans became a popular issue — seen by many Canadians as a way of addressing severe unemployment and economic stagnation. Coached in part by Herridge, Bennett supported a trade agreement with the United States. With his unerring sense of the politically advantageous, Mackenzie King and the opposition Liberals also backed free trade, and indeed managed to appear to the voters as being more capable than Bennett of achieving such an arrangement with Washington. In the end Bennett went down to a crushing defeat, punished by the voters for his failure to solve the problems of the Depression and for his implausible, sudden shift to the left shortly before the election.

Following King's victory the new government took up their predecessors' uncompleted negotiations and successfully concluded trade negotiations at the end of 1935. Canadian distillers rejoiced. "Canada's surplus whisky, aged in wood since 1931 or even earlier, will now have a market," the *Financial Post* predicted.[13] And so it did. But if they had looked closely at the discussions, whisky traders north of the border might have seen continued reason for worry. For at the very end of the negotiations with the Americans, Morgenthau almost torpedoed the complicated deal on the grounds that a few of the Canadian beneficiaries — Seagram, Hiram Walker and the rest — still had not addressed Treasury's claims against them.[14] The zealous Secretary withdrew his objections at the last moment, Hume Wrong cabled from the Canadian embassy in Washington, but the matter was far from over.

Indeed, the embassy saw real trouble ahead for Sam. Canadian diplomats believed that Morgenthau "is particularly intent on forcing the issue with respect to Consolidated Distillers-Seagrams [*sic*]," and Hume Wrong gave particular evidence from Washington that the Secretary of the Treasury was serious: "Special Agents have recently been sent to West Indian ports in order to try to link this firm with the ownership of smuggling vessels," he wrote on November 18.[15] Moreover, this action was not just the result of Morgenthau's personal animus. Behind him, O. D. Skelton of External Affairs speculated, were the American distilling interests, seeking protection for their products.[16] The diplomats' gloomy assessments seemed justified at the beginning of 1936. As the duties on Canadian whisky entering the United States were lowered, from five dollars to two dollars and fifty cents a gallon, pressure from Morgenthau's men mounted. With their claims still not specified, Treasury Department officials threatened to embargo Canadian imports of whisky to the United States in the absence of satisfactory assurances that the distillers would settle. Hume Wrong reported that the Treasury people "were obstinate to the point of perversity" and that Morgenthau's personal antipathy to the whisky interests was probably the reason.

Secretary of State Cordell Hull, however, now weighed in on the other side. A Wilsonian idealist, believing strongly in low tariffs and international cooperation, Hull feared that Morgenthau's dislike of Canadian whisky men might injure the trade deal with Ottawa and relations north of the border. State Department advisers told him, moreover, that the Treasury claims "were legally very dubious."[17] After talking to Hull, Roosevelt himself intervened, bringing about a series of discussions between the Canadian distillers and the Treasury Department. Laz Phillips and Sam Jacobs represented the Seagram company. Morgenthau refused to take part himself, having "grave objections to sitting down and compromising with important criminals. . . . It was necessary to regard the Canadian distillers as gangsters and mobsters," he claimed, despite the fact that "within the last few years they have become immensely wealthy and have turned respectable."[18]

Eventually the Americans got down to specifics, claiming over $53,000,000 from the Canadian distillers — based upon unpaid customs, excise and income taxes on their whisky that was illegally brought into the United States during prohibition. Of this, Seagram's bill amounted to $25,183,292.53, Hiram Walker's just over $19 million, and the other companies' much less — just over $9 million. On their side, the Canadian distillers denied any wrongdoing, while seeing the necessity of having to deal with the American government. Max Henderson, who helped prepare Seagram's case, recalled "American briefs containing various specific charges citing names, dates, and precise particulars of violations but never any of a size or volume to justify the colossal sum they were demanding from the Canadians."[19]

Offers and counter-offers were exchanged through the spring of 1936. In May, at the end of a fixed period of negotiation, the distillers were ready to pay $3 million, and the State Department, which participated on the U.S. side, agreed. Treasury held out for $6 million. Worried about a possible breakdown of Canadian-American relations and unhappy with Morgenthau's interference in what he considered a matter of foreign policy, Cordell Hull went to see Roosevelt to break the log-jam. "What do you think our claims are really worth?" the president asked. "Frankly," Hull replied, "they're probably worth nothing legally." Thereupon, as Hull described in his memoirs, Roosevelt telephoned Morgenthau:

"Henry," he said, "Cordell Hull is in my office about the whisky claims against Canada. I'd like to have you do a little figuring with me. Can you put a piece of paper and a pencil before you? All set?

"Now put down on the left side of the paper what you say the claims are worth. That's $6,000,000. Now opposite that, on the right side of the paper, put down what Cordell has settled for. That's $3,000,000.

"Now under your own figure I want you to put down a figure I'm going to give you. This is my own estimate of what the claims are worth. Are you ready? All right, put down zero. Now draw a line below your figure and mine, and add them together. What do you get? $6,000,000. O.K., now that is the sum total of what you and I think the claims are worth. Now take the average. Since there are two of us, divide by 2. What do you get? $3,000,000.

"Well that balances exactly with what Cordell settled for. How about settling for that?"

There was a moment of silence. Then the president laughed and hung up. He turned to me.

"It's O.K.," he said.[20]

Sam was greatly relieved. Convinced that his American competitors, probably Rosenstiel, had been behind the Treasury claims, he considered the payments as a licence to do business in the United States. He knew, moreover, that there was no time to waste: if Canadian whisky had been kept out of the American market for just a few years his competitors' products would have had time to age and he would have lost the edge on his competition. The deal, therefore, was welcome. Seagram agreed to pay half of the $3 million, Walker a million, and the smaller distillers the rest. Although left with the highest bill, Sam was undoubtedly pleased at the unspoken distinction the settlement accorded to his company: in the eyes of the lawyers on all sides Seagram's weight was three times as great as its nearest Canadian competitor. And as a sign of a brighter future, the Americans agreed to lower import duties on aged whisky coming into the United States from five to two dollars and fifty cents a gallon.[21]

■

"SON, IF YOU'VE gotta spend the money," Sam told Bob Sabloff, one of his advertising men, "go first class."[22] Sam's admonition was hardly restricted to advertising, and indeed extended to every nook and cranny of his business. "First class" in Sam's mind meant quality, and a concern for quality was meant to govern every phase of his operation, from distilling to blending, aging, packaging, advertising and sales. "He was a fiend for quality," Edgar contends, insisting that his father, who was reluctant to spend money in principle, would lavish fortunes to upgrade his equipment or improve his techniques. And he would spurn short-cuts in the interests of higher profits, insisting that no control of quality could be relaxed, that no exception be permitted, and no concession made for short-term gains.

Quality, says Mel Griffin, a production specialist who worked with Sam for twenty-five years, "appeared to me . . . the goal in everything he did. It was more important than mere profit."[23] Quality began in the production process, which Sam had studied intensively in Scotland during the 1920s and which he prided himself on having mastered, down to the most minute detail. Like all distillers, for example, Sam developed special strains of yeast, the most important component of the fermentation process. "Yeasts are the workhorses of the distilling industry," Sam used to say, and as one writer noted, awed by the no less than 240 strains in the yeast room of the Seagram company and the elaborate procedures to prevent their contamination, "officers of other distilling companies testify to the consuming interest Mr Bronfman had in quality control aspects of the Seagram operation."[24]

Sam put a special emphasis on blending, which was at the heart of his philosophy of whisky-making. "Distilling is a science; blending is an art," he said, in a quotation that was affixed to the back cover of a handsome, expensively published volume he commissioned in 1970. A company press release in 1937 noted that the president, Samuel Bronfman, "is also the company's official and final taster. Every vat of liquor produced in any of the company's plants, either in the United States or Canada, is first sampled by him before being placed on the market. If he does not happen to be in Louisville, Lawrenceburg or Maryland when a new vat is turned out, samples are sent to him."[25] Charles remembers seeing his father regularly in the blending lab, concentrating intently on the glasses before him, adding a little of this, a little of that, in a constant effort to improve his blends.[26]

And as even the experts agreed, Sam's tasting abilities matched the very best. Roy Martin, chief blender at the Waterloo plant in 1933 who eventually took charge of blending at all the Canadian distilleries, believed that Sam had "very sensitive, delicate taste buds" and a remarkable ability to recognize differences among whiskies. Perhaps even more important, Sam knew unerringly "that what he liked, the general public liked," and what the public wanted, he claimed, was quality.[27]

"Taste, to him, was a wonderful thing," comments Noah Torno, a friend and associate in the postwar years.[28] Claiming that there was a philosophic foundation to his ideas on the subject, Sam argued that survival was mankind's first need, and that people had to eat in order to survive. Taste, therefore, was essential, a thought that led to a question immediately on coming to work: "What are we gonna have for lunch?" Torno and others remember Sam's close attention to lunch at the office, with his preference for boiled beef or delicately steamed fish, with boiled potatoes on the side—almost tasteless to the uninitiated, but which Sam clearly relished. "If you didn't have any money and you had to start all over again, what would you do?" Torno asked him one day. "I'd open a restaurant," Sam immediately replied. "I'd serve what I like and I'm sure everybody else will like it."[29]

"The best whisky has not yet been made," Sam liked to repeat to his production people, urging them constantly to improve, to upgrade their operations and set higher standards for themselves. Former plant manager Walter Goelkel remembers Sam's inspection tours, in which local people felt terrorized lest anything be out of place or a speck of dirt appear on the equipment. Sam's personal involvement in just about everything associated with his plants astounded his employees, and extended to seemingly irrelevant details—all in the interests of raising the standards of his production. He insisted, for example, that the employees in his bottling plant at LaSalle wear white at a time when this was not generally done in industry, arguing that "if they work in a distillery that is clean, it is a better class of people working there," and "if they're clean, they'll do cleaner work." Roy Martin certainly shared this mania for improvement: "I'd never put a new formula into effect unless it tasted in my opinion as good or better than the previous one, because if you start compromising, well . . . you'll go downhill. That's a slippery path." "We were continually making our whiskies better," he continued, "it's a hell of a responsibility."[30]

Tireless in his pursuit of quality, Sam seems to have been genuinely driven to test his own capacities, as if to reassure himself, constantly, that he could live up to his Seagram mottoes "Canada's Finest," "Honoured the World Over," "Make Finer Whiskies, Make Them Taste Better." Driven in part by his own insecurities, Sam cared greatly about the *appearance* of his products, as well as their taste. Seagram's packaging, he proudly told shareholders in 1935, was "amongst the most dignified and attractive on the market."[31] "He just adored doing packages," Charles says today. Sam personally selected bottles and labels for hundreds of whiskies. "Not a detail escaped his eye," William Wachtel observed. "On important items he would sometimes ponder for weeks before giving final approval. These delays frequently frustrated the staff but to no avail; the final package had to be just right according to his ideas and standards before a final O.K. was given."[32] In his Peel Street office on Saturday mornings, for example, Sam used to spend hours with Frank Laflèche of the Dominion Glass Company, pondering the different types of glass to be used for his Crown Royal bottles.[33] Packaging had to be not only the right design, it also had to be of the highest quality. Mel Griffin noted how this extended even to cheaper brands. Labels were die-cut and embossed; bottles were specific to each brand, with no standardization; labels and cartons were multi-coloured and heavy; special attention was lavished on élite brands like V.O. and Crown Royal, using the most expensive graphics and materials.[34]

At the plant level, quality-control experts prowled the bottling lines on the lookout for imperfections — a tiny spot on a label, for example, or a label off-centre by as little as a thirty-second of an inch or so. Seagram's quality-control department, under the management of Dr E.H. Scofield, dispatched inspectors to Seagram facilities like commissars, responsible only to central authority and completely outside the plant manager's chain of command. "They had absolute authority," says Walter Goelkel. And the moment they spied anything wrong with the bottles, the problem had immediately to be set right. Concerns with costs were thrown to the winds as bottles were removed from cases and sometimes simply discarded. "We were spending money like mad," Goelkel remembers. "Some months we'd have twenty-five thousand dollars of glass that we just threw away."[35]

Quality, in Sam's mind, was intertwined with prestige. "The selling power of prestige has always been and continues to be the basic idea behind all of your Company's advertising," he told shareholders in 1938.

> Every Seagram advertisement is designed primarily to accomplish one thing—to sell Seagram's—and not just whiskey—to sell the fundamental principles of the House of Seagram, the craftsmanship, the traditions, the experience, the quality and the prestige that have made Seagram whiskies famous since 1857. But prestige cannot be acquired quickly. It cannot be bought. It cannot be claimed. It must be earned by the slow process of winning respect and goodwill through fine products and consistently fine advertising. Men want to feel a confidence in the quality of the brand of liquor they drink. They want to feel proud to serve their guests a brand that enjoys the highest prestige.[36]

Sam hungered for quality in part because it was associated in his mind with the tried and true, the venerable Old Country of England and Scotland, the well-established traditional society of which he wanted to be a part. He craved the status and gentility associated with "the best," just as he abhorred the disabilities that went with the poverty of his childhood and youth. Beyond this, he also sensed that millions of North Americans had similar aspirations; in the depths of the Depression, ordinary people would also respond to the appeals of quality. As Roy Martin suggested, Sam knew instinctively that customers would choose and be willing to pay, and even pay a little more, for "the best."

As with the castle on Peel Street, Sam loved images that evoked, in his mind, the English and Scottish past. He lavished attention on the Seagram crest, with winged horses framing a shield and its motto "Integrity, Craftsmanship and Tradition."

Sam had a special weakness for coats of arms, which adorned the bottles of many of his products. (Later, when he became president of the Canadian Jewish Congress, Sam oversaw the preparation of several crests for that organization, but with none did he have the flair or impact as on his whisky bottles.) Sam also commissioned historical investigations of the distilleries he bought in Scotland, both to satisfy his own curiosity, and also to inspire the presentation of the whiskies they produced, by establishing accurate pedigrees.

Sam's marketing of the Crown brands in the U.S. may have been the first important test of his belief that quality would sell, and it was a stunning success. Deliberately, it will be recalled, he "let the parade go by" in the first year after repeal, letting his competitors get the jump on Seagram with brands of inexpensive, relatively young whiskies. Then, in April 1935, a headline in the *Financial Post* registered the astonishing shift in American tastes created, in large measure, by the launching of Seagram's Five and Seven Crown brands: "BETTER WHISKY IS NOW SOUGHT BY U.S.A. WETS: CANADIAN DISTILLERY STOCKS GO UP AS TASTES SWING TO MATURED STOCKS."[37] At the end of his career, Sam looked back upon this achievement as one of his greatest — a triumphant vindication of his marketing instincts.

In Canada, Robert Sabloff felt Sam's beliefs were confirmed in the distortions he discovered in consumer surveys about brand preference in the 1950s. In these polls, the overwhelming majority of people surveyed declared that they drank Seagram's super premium brand, Crown Royal, as opposed to the inexpensive King's Plate. But in fact, the poll was utterly unreliable on this point: "We knew from sales that they really drank King's Plate," Sabloff observes.[38] Even if they could not afford Crown Royal, Sam's customers wanted to be associated with prestige products, and prestige was one of the important things Sam sold, and sold brilliantly, with his emphasis on quality. Coming into his own as an industrialist and marketer during the Depression, Sam sensed intuitively his customers' attraction to images of luxury and ease. The care and attention he lavished on his products, springing authentically from his own temperament and constituting a kind of personal religion, had a genuine popular appeal.

Sam's advertising strategy was the very opposite from that taken in 1935 by his rival Lew Rosenstiel with the latter's highly successful Old Quaker brand — a young, inexpensive straight whiskey that was launched with an advertising theme: "You don't have to be rich to enjoy rich whiskey!" In buying Sam's whiskey, customers were supposed to *feel* rich, partaking of one of the finer things of life. "Treat whiskey as a luxury," said the famous Seagram moderation advertisement of 1934. "A pint of good, aged whiskey will bring you more enjoyment, more satisfaction, than a quart of whiskey of dubious quality."

In May 1936 Sam found in William Wachtel a perfect associate to communicate his message to the consuming public. Forty-four years old when he met Sam Bronfman, and with a pencil-thin moustache that made him look like Adolphe Menjou, Wachtel was the sales manager of a large biscuit company in Kansas City, with many years of experience in advertising and a reputation for ability and integrity. Although he "took a drink every evening before dinner," as he explained when first approached by Seagram, he had also voted for the Eighteenth Amendment and was therefore an unlikely candidate to work in the whisky trade. However, he agreed to hear Sam out. Ushered into his office in the Chrysler building, he found before him a "human dynamo" who unabashedly declared his business priority — to achieve respectability. "We need a man of high moral standards who will add to the stature of an industry that has been much maligned and misunderstood," Wachtel remembered Sam as saying. This has happened, Sam continued,

> because of a futile and impractical and unrealistic law that plagued the people, all because an organized small but vociferous minority scared some politicians into passing a law that could not be and was not enforced. On the contrary it created a stink of corruption of enforcement officials and even judges and permitted an enormous crime syndicate to thwart all laws, endanger life and limb with their "Murder In-corporated" and ruthless disregard for authority. Four years

have passed since the repeal of the Eighteenth Amendment and
it is now necessary to build a new and honorable image of a
legal business catering to the wants and desires of millions of
our best citizens.

"Who could fail to be flattered by such a challenge?" Wachtel
reflected. Having expressed interest, he soon discovered that
Sam was serious about the need for someone of personal probity:
he learned that a private agency was investigating his character,
family life and financial standing. Whereupon Wachtel decided
to investigate the Bronfmans. Both reports having proven
successful, Sam offered Wachtel a job, and he accepted.[39]

The offer, as Wachtel tells it, revealed something important
about Sam's management style. Sam looked at him, he
recollected, "with those steely blue eyes that seemed to look into
your very soul" and presented him with an alternative—to head
the Seagram or the Calvert sales organization. Wachtel chose
Calvert, precisely because it was in trouble at the time: "If I take
the Seagram job and do well, it will be assumed it was due to its
momentum. On the other hand, if I make a success of Calvert,
you'll have to admit that I am pretty good." Wachtel later learned
that the Seagram job had *already* been filled, and Sam's offer was
a ruse—an example of the canny way "the Boss," as he called
him, tested people and got the measure of them. Thereafter the
two worked well together, and became close personal friends.

Having placed Wachtel at the helm, Sam told him to run
Calvert as if he owned it, and to compete with the U.S. Seagram
company as with anyone else in the field—adopting a
competitive organizational model that he preferred for the rest of
his career. Possibly with the British DCL example in mind, in
which White Horse, Haig & Haig, Black & White, Johnnie
Walker and Sanderson's Vat 69 maintained a separate existence
and competed with each other under the DCL rubric, Sam
believed that the Calvert sales competition "straightened out the
Seagram organization and got them off their fanny." And so it
did, with a series of advertising campaigns on Sam's well-worn
theme—quality. Wachtel began by laying down the law to his
staff: "I expect you will conduct yourselves with decorum in
public. Good manners, moderation in drinking, conducting

yourselves as gentlemen . . . all are imperative if we are to build the proper image for the industry as well as for Calvert. Any Calvert employee who gets drunk in a public place will be dismissed from our service."[40] Next, he schooled his salesmen in the production side of the industry, and sent them into the field as missionaries (in the company they were actually called "missionary men") carrying the message about blends — what he called "the Blend Story," upon which salesmen could be called to discourse, at the drop of a hat. "No longer were our men going into stores to pass the time of day, or to talk about baseball or the championship prize fight," Wachtel declared. "Now they were seriously devoting their conversation to the quality of the product in a technical and convincing manner."[41]

On Sam's theories of whisky making, Wachtel became one of the empire's most stirring orators. He warmed up audiences from Congressional committees to salesmen's conventions, convincing them all of his own sincerity and his company's prowess. He appeared on the trade lecture circuit addressing such themes as: "Can You Drink and Still Be a Gentleman?" or "Be Proud of Your Industry So Your Industry May Be Proud of You." "To hear Bill Wachtel tell the story of Calvert and its blended whiskey, you would think that you were listening to a prohibitionist," Philip Kelly recalled. "He was not only vehement in his protestations against the evils of heavy strong liquor but he sold the virtues of blended whiskey with the religious zeal of an Apostle Paul."[42]

Calvert once had a false start with a slogan "Clear Heads Call for Calvert" — a claim that sounded alarm bells in Washington because it seemed to imply that heads would remain clear no matter how much Calvert they drank. Sol Kanee remembers accompanying Sam to a meeting with "the bigwig of a bigwig agency" who presented the slogan, hoping the boss would like it. Sam ran the ad, but wanted no trouble with the government on the matter, and when the protests came, the series was immediately stopped.[43] Wachtel's most celebrated advertising campaign responded perfectly to Sam's aspirations for his products — the "Man of Distinction" series, which featured prominent Americans who announced to the world their preference for Lord Calvert whiskey, then the most expensive blend on the U.S. market. At first, professional models were used, but before long genuinely prominent persons appeared, highball glass of Lord Calvert in hand—beginning with Hollywood director John Cromwell and extending to Ralph Bellamy and other actors. After a discreet solicitation, a flood of volunteers pressed forward for the privilege of having their picture published, in full colour, from coast to coast. (There were two other emoluments—a thousand dollars to a charity chosen by the "man of distinction," and a case of Lord Calvert with the photograph on the back label of each bottle.) Stars from the entertainment industry came naturally enough, but financiers and industrialists lined up as well. Sales of Lord Calvert, meanwhile, climbed steeply—from practically nothing to almost a million cases in three or four years.[44]

Sam liked the "Man of Distinction" ads when they began, but after a while he tired of them, claiming that the series sold suits of clothes and not whisky. He may well have concluded that glamour was crowding out his central concern, what went into the bottles, and probably felt uncomfortable when the phrase "Men of Distinction" slipped into the vocabulary of the age via newspaper columnists, script writers and even a play in New York. Sam liked publicity, but only when it reinforced his objectives; he became nervous when it took on a life of its own or diverted attention from his own objectives.

Sam's insistence on quality set him on a collision course with his older brother Harry who since his Regina prosecution had been confined to the construction of distilleries, warehouses and the installation of equipment. Harry's last great project, which occasioned his break with the company, was the building of a brand new plant in Louisville, Kentucky, the traditional home of American whiskey making. Planned at the end of 1935, the plant was intended to produce bourbon for the American market. But Sam had much more in mind than that. He intended the new facility to be "the showpiece of the industry," as he told Terence Robertson, and after visiting the site he presented Harry with a drawing that looked like "a cloistered university set in placid countryside, and surrounded by oaks and elms in full foliage." As Robertson had Sam saying, this was not so much a distillery as an academy: "A seat of learning, a laboratory. People will come to it from all over the world to study the art of making and blending whiskies. Research, Harry. The industry needs more of it. . . . We can't stand still, Harry. We have to progress, be in advance of progress." Apparently, Harry stood slack-jawed at hearing this visionary outburst, while Sam returned to the papers on his desk. Looking up a moment later, Sam saw Harry still standing there, absorbing his younger brother's message. "God damn it, Harry," Sam said, "what the hell are you waiting for?"[45]

Harry's 1937 memoir makes it clear that relations between the two brothers became particularly strained with the construction of the Louisville plant. In his account, Harry presented himself as overwhelmed with technical problems — not only at Louisville, but in the Lawrenceburg, Indiana distillery and the Calvert distillery in Relay, Maryland — while Sam and Allan were preoccupied with sales and lavished money (far too much money, Harry implied) on advertising. Then only fifty-one, the older brother clearly resented being shut out of decision-making at the top and bypassed along the chain of command; he also saw himself as the victim of a vicious plot against him by the Calvert management. However, as his memoir suggests, he submitted — as indeed Allan would, many years later when he found himself in a position of humiliating subordination. For among the four brothers there was by this point no question who was boss, and neither Harry nor Allan dared to challenge Sam's position.

The crisis broke in 1937 when Sam hired Frederick Willkie as vice-president in charge of all production in the United States. Brother of Wendell Willkie who was to run against Roosevelt for president in 1940, Willkie was a creative inventor who had formerly worked for Harry Hatch at the huge Hiram Walker plant in Peoria, and had unusually broad production, scientific and technical experience. Upon arriving in Louisville, Willkie immediately ordered the plant shut down, "dry as a bone," for nearly three months. The trouble — of which no written account exists — seems to have been Harry's unorthodox decision to line the large, concrete fermenting tanks with green tiles — attractive, two-colour tiles, between and behind which bacteria could grow and render all the equipment unserviceable.[46] Identified by Willkie as highly unprofessional, Harry's work at Louisville became a grave embarrassment, not to be discussed openly in order to preserve the façade of family loyalty: years later Sam attributed Harry's departure to fatigue, while Harry himself dwelt upon the intrigues against him and attributed the shutdown to the unusually high price of wheat. Neither brother, publicly at least, would point a finger at the other.

Harry was ill at the time, as he explained in a 1939 memorandum: "The change from the tremendous job I had to relaxation showed me that my health had been undermined, and for a long time it was hard for me to pull myself together."[47] He was even told at one point that he had a brain tumour, his daughter-in-law Marjorie Bronfman recalls, and he was treated by the famous McGill University neurosurgeon Wilder Penfield.[48] According to Harry, the brothers then quarrelled bitterly over their shares in the family business. Sam and Allan demanded a revision of the agreement made in 1922, when the Bronfmans had established their shares in their common enterprise. Harry contended that he was browbeaten, especially by his younger brother Sam, whom he described as "the emotional one of the family." Sam, he went on, "claimed that all the things that had been done towards the success of the company were instigated by him, and the total success of the family was due to his ingenuity." Laz Phillips, Harry felt, colluded with the other brothers to reduce his share and to ease him, and eventually his sons, out of an active role in the business, even while posing as the "family lawyer" supposed to advise them all. In the end the brothers agreed upon a new division of their shares in the company: Sam received 40 percent, Harry 22, Allan 19, Abe 14 and Barney Aaron 5. "Allan has definitely turned to work with Sam," Harry lamented, "and between themselves they have endeavoured in every way to show a domineering control in the affairs of the company."

Meanwhile, Willkie was giving the huge Seagram operation a distinctly scientific cast, light years away from the primitive concoctions of Harry's Yorkton period and the first moves to large-scale production in which Harry had played an important part. "I am engaging you to take full charge of our production and giving you a free hand in research," Sam told his new production boss, launching a programme that would have a profound effect on the entire whisky-making process.[49] Willkie was not overly impressed with the scientific level of the post-Repeal whisky business — a "Rip Van Winkle" technology, as he described it, having been asleep during the entire period of prohibition. To improve matters, he had his scientists vigorously challenge old routines. "Change was the order of the day," as he put it. "Traditions were swept away like autumn leaves in a November wind, their nostalgic colors flowing out from the frosty nip of science."[50] Remarkably, given his own romantic affinity for traditions and his veneration of craftsmanship, Sam backed this new course with enthusiasm.

Within a short time Seagram sponsored in-house courses, with promotion and pay increases following successfully passed examinations; the company also sponsored employees' study at universities and correspondence schools. For a time, Sam got along famously with Willkie. Known for his concerns with quality, Seagram's new research chief certainly shared the boss's priorities. "He was a guy who believed in not cutting any corners and doing everything right," one of the company's top production men recalls. "First-class equipment, first-class material, making a first-class product."[51] Sam warmed to the idea of having Ph.D.s on the payroll — something that was relatively inexpensive during the Depression; and the company certainly benefited from the development of new processes — such as Willkie's new system for "cooking" the grain mixture evenly, without variations in temperature. Far-sighted enough to invest heavily in scientific development, Sam also found, with Willkie, that science provided yet another mark of good corporate citizenship. "At one time to be associated with the whiskey industry was a challenge to self-respect," Willkie wrote, in a passage that might have come from one of Sam's own inspirational messages to his employees. "At one time no reputable university would entertain its problems. Now [in 1944] these things have passed with the cloud of ignorance that canopied the old regime. Today from India, China, South America, Puerto Rico, and Mexico come engineers, chemists, and sociologists to the distilling plants of the United States to study and take back with them the new processes of democracy."[52]

Visiting Willkie's headquarters a few years after its establishment, a reporter for *Fortune* found an atmosphere of a university — "Ph.D.s studiously operating mash tubs and fermenters with automatic controls, holding classes for foreign students, and conducting psychology tests on the intricacies of taste."[53] Not merely a centre of learning, *Fortune* noted that Willkie's laboratories had become a scientific champion of blends over straights — striking out, from the heart of bourbon whiskey country, against the old-time champions of straights "in frock coats and string ties." Seagram men challenged vexatious regulations of Washington's Alcohol Tax Unit armed with scientific evidence, and presented learned disputations against the claims of straight whisky for regulatory advantages. Willkie was particularly proud of the quality control he helped bring into the production field — with science so much more reliable than the "prejudice and . . . indisposition of the expert." Quality, in his hands, was to become precisely measurable, notably with the introduction of spectroscopy in determining the characteristics of various whiskies. Surveying the impact of science upon industry he illustrated the high standards applied to packaging with a photograph of four crisply uniformed technicians scrutinizing bottles of Calvert Special, on the lookout for any defects. This was, he wrote, one of the "ethical responsibilities" of the industrial manager to the consumer.[54] All of this was very much what Sam appreciated.

But some time after the end of the war Sam's top scientist fell out of favour and the novelty of his scientific research wore off. One reason was that Willkie liked to publish papers on his scientists' discoveries, such as the new cooker, for example, while Sam felt that such ideas belonged to the company alone. To his horror, Sam learned that Willkie conferred periodically with Seagram's competitors, even giving them advice on how to improve their operations. (Willkie's idea was that Seagram should share its discoveries with others in the industry to prevent them from stagnating, for if Seagram went too far out in front it would eventually lose its competitive edge.) Sam also objected to Willkie's practice of rotating his highly trained personnel through different departments, to the point that there were too many generalists and too few technical experts. Never completely won over by the researchers, Sam referred to them as "long-haired, short-brained fellows" and even sneered, at meetings, when referring to scientists and engineers. In the final analysis what he respected most in the whisky industry was craftsmanship, and he developed a healthy distrust for work that he deemed "too scientific."[55]

■

IN MAY 1970, when Sam's true age was eighty-one, the governing council of the World Jewish Congress met in Montreal and dined at the Bronfman home. Congress official Max Melamet remembered that the atmosphere was a little stiff at the outset, and he and some others decided to break the ice with communal singing: "Before long the whole atmosphere was different. Nobody enjoyed the singing and the camaraderie more than Sam. He rose in his seat, with a glass of wine in his hand, and began to sing Yiddish songs that he must have learned from his father as a young child. His face was ruddy, his eyes sparkled, and it was obvious that he was having a helluva time."[56] Towards the end of his life, Sam's dining room could indeed resound with Yiddish songs. But in the mid-1930s, when his family was young and business a consuming preoccupation, Sam did not move in social circles where Yiddish songs were heard. Between one time and the other, lies a major portion of Canadian Jewish history, part and parcel of Sam's own life as well.

Montreal's Jewish community grew from some 7,000 at the turn of the century to 58,000 in 1931, when Jews represented 5.8 percent of the city's population. During these three decades Jews remained distinct from both the French majority that, through the Catholic Church, set the tone for much of the society, and the Anglo-Protestant minority, whose powerful socio-economic élite controlled most of the business and financial life of the metropolis and dominated a large Irish-Catholic population at the lower end of the social scale. After these dominant groups, Jews were the leading ethnic community in the city and maintained, to a quite remarkable degree, an independent communal identity. Geographically concentrated in a few neighbourhoods, they found their place in a society clearly segmented along national-religious lines — much more so than other centres in North America but strongly reminiscent, in this respect, of Eastern Europe where most of them were born. More than a third came from Russia and Poland, settling in Canada about a generation later than the massive wave of other East European Jews who reached the United States. Almost all had come from a Yiddish-speaking environment. Strikingly, more than 99 percent of Montreal Jews listed Yiddish as their native tongue in the census of 1931, although almost all of these spoke English as well. About a third, moreover, could speak French.[57]

Writing in 1944, novelist Gwethalyn Graham felt that all three groups — French, English and Jews — suffered from an inferiority complex: "the French because they are a minority in Canada, the English because they are a minority in Quebec, and the Jews because they are a minority everywhere."[58] Such feelings almost certainly entered into the makeup of personalities like Marc Reiser and Erica Drake — the Jewish-Protestant couple whose trials are at the centre of Graham's novel *Earth and High Heaven.* But the insecurity of which she wrote was not close to the surface, at least, of the principal Jewish spokesmen of the time — the community establishment towards which the Bronfmans gravitated when they first established themselves in Montreal.

To the contrary, Montreal's leading Jewish citizens constituted a highly self-conscious and proud élite, assured not only of their own place in Montreal society but convinced of their superior position vis-à-vis their fellow Jews by virtue of their culture, affluence and relatively long establishment in the society. These were the Jews who had established the first synagogues in Canada, who had founded the first Jewish institutions in the country, and had proven their loyalty to the British Empire. "Comfortably installed on the slopes of Mount Royal," as Pierre Anctil describes them, "anglicized and reassured by nearly a century of equal political rights," these Jews faced the occasional challenge to their Jewish standing with equanimity.[59] Within Jewish Montreal at the time, as Anctil notes, there were "two solitudes" of Jewish life — the so-called *uptowners* of the Mount Royal neighbourhoods, affluent, confident and well-established; and the masses of *downtowners* — mainly immigrants, living along the Main (St Lawrence Boulevard), closer to the heart of the city, economically less secure and far more assertive of their traditional Jewish culture.

By their substantial fortune alone the Bronfmans were associated with the Jewish patriciate by other Jews, for whom such wealth among their co-religionists in Canada was a source of awe and respect. Sam and Saidye lived with much of the Jewish élite in the affluent suburb of Westmount, and, through Allan, were related by marriage to some of the most prominent Jews in the country. Their Westmount synagogue was the Conservative Shaar Hashomayim, founded in 1846 as the Congregation of English, German, Polish and Lithuanian Jews of Montreal, and an offshoot of the oldest congregation in Canada. Distinctly oriented to the Anglo-Jewish élite in Canada at the time, with its services modelled on the Bayswater Synagogue of London, the Shaar accented the "dignity and decorum" of its ritual, in contrast with the noisy, unruly immigrant houses of prayer. In 1922 the Shaar occupied an imposing new building on Côte St Antoine, seating 1,800 worshippers and declared to be the largest synagogue in Canada.

Sam met many uptown Jews at the aristocratic Montefiore Club, the gathering place for the Montreal Jewish establishment founded in 1880 as the "Montefiore Social and Dramatic Club" and patterned on the haunts of English gentlemen in London. As a confirmed anglophile, Sam would have had difficulty resisting this establishment, which indeed became the centre of much of his Jewish communal activity. Describing the club in the mid-1920s, historian Arthur Hart noted that the entrance hall was the "gem" of the entire building: "On entering it one feels completely at ease. The whole interior is furnished in the Dutch style, with heavily beamed ceilings, great fireplaces, which reach to the ceiling, polished floors, and leaded windows. It is twenty feet square, is panelled eight feet high, and has a lofty mantel. Opening off this are the lounging room, cafe, writing room, cloak rooms and broad staircase leading to the first floor. The lounging room and the cafe are further examples of good taste and judgment in selection of their decoration. The walls are panelled in a plain, heavily woven fabric, which forms an excellent background for pictures. The furniture, electric fixtures, which are of pewter, and Donegal rugs, are especially designed to suit these rooms."[60]

Concerned as they obviously were to emulate the lifestyle of the Anglo-Protestant élite, the uptown Jews were at the same time deeply involved in Jewish philanthropy and community service. The Montefiore Club, indeed, spent much of its time raising money for indigent Jews in its early days, and it was wealthy uptown Jews who founded the earliest welfare institutions in the city — such as the Baron de Hirsch Institute, for example, or the most important of all, the Federation of Jewish Philanthropies of Montreal, which brought together several different charities in 1916. In its first year the Federation collected over $123,000 for its various organizations, an extraordinary sum at the time, and fund-raising was approaching $200,000 within a decade. Firmly in the hands of the Jewish establishment, the Federation prided itself on its high standards of public relief and the range of its services: "No needy person was turned away," declared David Kirsch, president of its executive committee in 1924. "No homeless child was deprived of the home that it was our duty to provide. No tubercular fighting the white plague was refused aid. . . . Throughout the whole organization we are better equipped for our work than ever before."[61]

Because of the highly segmented quality of Montreal society, uptown Jews were more disposed than their counterparts elsewhere to participate in Jewish community life and to become involved in Jewish charitable causes — giving a special twist to Montreal Jewish life not found elsewhere in North America. "Social prestige comes from being a *macher* [leader] in the Jewish community," observed one analyst in 1950, "not from patronizing the Art Gallery or contributing to the McGill Alumni Fund or to the Montreal General Hospital, where the honors follow the substantial donations of railroad and brewery magnates and those of other Big Business captains. Jewish campaign chairmen and their wives may not want to invite the door-to-door canvassers for Federation to their homes, newly 'done' by an interior decorator, but their *koved* [honour] comes from their prominence in the United Israel Appeal and similar charitable endeavors, and they know it."[62] New to Montreal in the mid-1920s and from a quite different Jewish milieu, Sam had none of the uptowners' sense of ease as a kind of Jewish aristocracy, or their feelings of *noblesse oblige* in relating to their fellow Jews. But he heartily assumed an obligation of service, based on an ingrained sense of loyalty, something that was true of his siblings as well. Sam had a curt dismissal of multi-millionaire Sir Mortimer Davis, for example, who despite his charitable donations was not known for his involvement in Jewish affairs. "Mr No-Good Jew," was how he referred to him, according to Mark Shinbane.[63]

Although outsiders to the tightly knit group of Westmount Jews when they first settled in Montreal, Sam and Saidye gravitated naturally to this Jewish world. For although Sam mixed easily with non-Jews in his business, and when exasperated with his co-religionists could issue pungent denunciations that could fill the armoury of a fervent antisemite, he felt most comfortable among Jews. His social life, however limited, was very substantially among the wealthy, well-established Jewish élite.
     Among these, Laz Phillips was the very model of a Jewish aristocrat, and someone to whom Sam was powerfully attracted. "For most of three decades," Peter Newman notes, "Lazarus Phillips served as the Bronfmans' visible face and public voice. He was their chief go-between. He had the manners and the contacts, the social acceptability and political prestige to which the brothers could only aspire."[64] A McGill University graduate of the class of 1918, Laz was the law partner of Sam Jacobs, the Liberal M.P. from Montreal's Cartier riding. Closely associated with the Liberal Party, Laz opened numerous doors for Sam in Ottawa; Sam came to depend heavily upon Laz's connections and funnelled his own donations to the Liberals through his influential lawyer, thereby increasing the latter's standing with the party hierarchy.
     Laz was linked to some of the leading Jews of Montreal, among whom his standing was like one of the upper nobility. On his mother's side he was part of the Cohen family, and his uncles

included Hirsch Cohen, a leading Orthodox rabbi, and Lazarus Cohen, a founder of the Montreal Jewish community and a pillar of the Shaar Hashomayim, who lived in a mansion in Westmount before the turn of the century. Laz's cousin, the wealthy clothier Lyon Cohen (son of Lazarus Cohen), has been called "the undisputed leader of uptown Jewry"; active in a wide range of Jewish activities, he was a well-respected Liberal, president of the Montefiore Club and the first president of the Canadian Jewish Congress.[65] And finally, Laz was married to a beautiful South African woman, Rosalie Idelson, whose accent seemed to many Jews in Montreal to be itself a sign of rare Jewish gentility.

Sam deeply admired the social world of these Jewish patricians and respected their standing in Montreal society. When the distinguished-looking Horace Cohen, son of Lyon Cohen, came to visit, Phyllis recollects, "there was an aura of someone to be treated with deference because of a social order represented, as well as some sense that this was a good catch."[66] Poorer Jews, and the East European Jewish immigrants who flocked to Montreal during the 1920s, were entirely outside the Bronfmans' social circuit, and Sam sometimes felt uncomfortable in his encounters with them. "Loud talking, gesturing with hands when speaking" were habits he found embarrassing, Phyllis recalls. "Awful, just awful," he would say, seeing immigrant Jews relaxing on their front porches when driving with his children through a Jewish neighbourhood on the way to the family's country home in Ste Marguerite. It was "awful, just awful for our people" to behave that way. "Gradually he took on the role of a judgmental paterfamilias responsible not only for his own immediate family and wider family group," Phyllis observes, ". . . he was also concerned about these outward signs for 'our Jewish people.' "[67]

Although he was hardly what one would call an observant Jew, Sam believed in religious tradition, which Phyllis says, "was essentially a social sense of decorum and continuity."[68] For years, Saidye attested, he would doze through the services at the Shaar, although he gratefully appreciated the honour of being called up to the Torah for the blessings during the High Holy Days.[69] Like many Jews, he had an undogmatic but visceral antipathy to some non-kosher foods. Charles remembers having breakfast with his brother and Sam one time in Boca Raton, Florida, when the two boys ordered bacon and eggs. "He let us eat it, and I give him credit for that," Charles recalled, "but he said that's the last time you eat pork or bacon in front of me . . . I just can't stand it."[70] Opposed to pork, Sam happily ate forbidden seafoods outside his home — shrimp, scallops, lobster and so on. The reason, he said, was simple: "My mother always told me meat from the pig was forbidden. But since we lived 3,000 miles from the ocean, she had never heard of seafood and never told me not to eat it."[71] On other matters too, Sam's Jewishness was undogmatic. During the war, when the Bronfmans spent winter holidays in the Laurentians, the children wanted to have a Christmas tree: Sam and Saidye said no, but offered them a compromise; they could take in branches from fir trees and decorate the branches with lights — a small sign of Christmas perhaps, but not enough to worry about.

Sam did not like being lectured to, and prominent rabbis, therefore, risked Sam's wrath if they even seemed, however obliquely, to be doing so. A good example is Sam's extreme displeasure in the mid-1930s with Maurice Eisendrath, then rabbi of Holy Blossom Temple in Toronto. Eisendrath was not the most modest of rabbinical personalities, and having come to Toronto in 1924 as a haughty twenty-seven-year-old seminary graduate he clashed with Jews in that city on two volatile issues — religion and politics. During his Toronto debut he flouted tradition by appearing bareheaded in his pulpit on the High Holy Days, which was bad enough; even worse, he opposed the Zionist aspirations of much of the community leadership during the Arab massacre of Jews in Hebron and Jerusalem in 1929. Clearly this widely popular young firebrand, whose Sunday morning sermons at his Bond Street synagogue attracted Jews and non-Jews alike, did not shrink from challenging the high and mighty.

In November 1934, when rumours of the RCMP investigation of the Bronfmans on bootlegging charges swirled about, Eisendrath ventured into the Jewish press with a few editorials that infuriated Sam. Appearing in the *Canadian Jewish Review*, where he was a contributing editor, these columns never mentioned the Bronfmans by name, but Sam was sure they targeted him. Under the headline " 'Industrial Tyrants' Are Scored by Rabbi," repeating the theme of a sermon he had just delivered, Eisendrath defended the anti-smuggling parliamentarian Harry Stevens, the man whose charges of corruption led to the Royal Commission on Customs and Excise of 1927. Stevens was a maverick Conservative who was then under attack, said Eisendrath, because of "his conviction that the working people of Canada were being victimized by greedy industrialists." A sharp critic himself of business leaders, Eisendrath told his readers that their anger "should be vented against those few grim reapers at home who in their avarice and greed would plunge our nation into . . . class strife."[72] In the next issue, commenting on the Ontario liquor laws, the young rabbi quoted J.B. Priestley: "both cheap movies and strong drink are but an escape from the ugliness and sordidness in the dark bog of greedy industrialism."[73]

While these were hardly serious assaults, and framed, in any case, within articles that had nothing directly to do with whisky or the Bronfmans, Sam took offence at these words during a moment of extreme vulnerability. "In the greatest crisis in his life," Canadian Jewish Congress activist H.M. Caiserman paraphrased Sam in a letter to Eisendrath, "you knifed him."[74] Three years after the rabbi's statements Sam still smouldered over the slight, and when Caiserman came to see him about a Congress matter he flew into a towering rage over the Eisendrath affair—linked with the Congress in Sam's mind because of Eisendrath's previous involvement with that body. "In my whole experience," a shaken Caiserman reflected, "this discussion was one of the most violent that I had ever witnessed or participated in." Since coming to Montreal, Sam thundered, "he had done his utmost to do the right thing in every respect." Congress leaders, for their part, ought to have stood up for him when he had been attacked. Sam felt betrayed, he told the Congress administrator, threatening dire consequences if amends were not made. "Mr Bronfman made a confidential statement in the greatest agitation," Caiserman reported, "that he is seriously thinking of completely withdrawing his support of Jewish causes and dedicating his philanthropy in such channels that will spare him a continuous crucifixion."[75]

"The greatest crisis of his life," as Sam pointed out, erupted when he had already achieved some prominence as a Jewish community leader. His first involvement stemmed from the end of the 1920s, when Montreal Jews launched a campaign to build the Jewish General Hospital in that city and Sam, Allan and Abe became heavily involved. The community needed the hospital, its leaders felt, to provide more sympathetic treatment for Jewish patients and posts for Jewish doctors, who had great difficulty getting appointments at the city's other institutions — an important dimension of the antisemitism in Quebec society during this period. In the campaign's early days it was Allan, not Sam, who took the most prominent role, helping to form a hospital committee in 1927 and co-chairing a mammoth $800,000 fund-raising effort together with Michael Hirsch that began in 1929. But in the views of several participants, Sam remained in control of the family's communal strategy — assigning his younger brother, as it were, to the figurehead job, while he took charge of what he considered the all-important task of publicity. In 1929, at least, Sam's Jewish profile was still low. Moreover, then and for a long time thereafter the family's charitable donations were very much a corporate affair — the $75,000 that the Bronfmans donated at the start of the campaign, and that put them in the very front rank of hospital supporters, coming from "the Bronfman interests and B. Aaron," as the family fortune was then called.[76]

While Allan's community work was largely limited to the Jewish Hospital, Sam took on one Jewish portfolio after another, coming more and more into the public eye. In 1929 he became an officer of the businessmen's council of the Federation of Jewish Philanthropies, and two years later, as we have seen, he and Sam Jacobs took over the chairmanship of the important Jewish Immigrant Aid Society (JIAS), the most active Jewish communal organization in this period.[77] Saidye's first important community involvement began at the same time with the Young Women's Hebrew Association in 1929. At its annual meeting at the Montefiore Club in June 1934 Sam was elected president of the Federation — a post he held until 1950, when he became honorary president of its successor organization, the Allied Jewish Community Services.

These positions were almost exclusively concerned with fund-raising—an uphill task in the early 1930s, when the Depression drained much of the prosperity of the Montreal Jewish population along with that of other Canadians. By 1932 hard times were being felt: with unemployment affecting as much as one-third of Montreal's population, Federation fund-raisers found themselves $63,000 short of their $330,000 target at the year's end. Sam and Saidye sat at the head table of the campaign's closing banquet at the Mount Royal Hotel on December 12. To meet the emergency, the leaders made the extraordinary move to extend the campaign for a week and the audience cheered when Saidye, who headed the women's division, indicated her support. Sam, in what might have been his first speech to a large community gathering, offered a similarly well-received, edifying message: "The test of character was shown when an organization admitted defeat but refused to accept a decision in that light," he was reported as saying.[78]

Sam's deepening involvement in Jewish community affairs accompanied an important change in the Jewish community's structure—towards a much greater involvement of downtown Jews in its affairs. Hitherto, uptown Jews dispensed philanthropy as a mark of Jewish solidarity; but they practically monopolized decision-making and kept the downtown Jews at arm's length. Now, their monopoly was undermined. The basic reason was that fund-raising on the scale that was necessary for the Jewish Hospital and the widespread distress among indigent Jews required far more extensive participation than before: no longer could a small group of uptowners support the expanded needs of the entire Jewish community on their own. At the launching of the hospital campaign, therefore, the familiar faces of the Jewish establishment were present—Peter Bercovitch and Joseph Cohen, members of the Quebec Legislative Assembly, Liberal Party stalwart and community leader Marcus Sperber, Lyon Cohen, Sam Jacobs, and others; but when fund-raising actually began the organizers reached out to the less affluent downtown Jews and the immigrants, or "greeners," as they were known. Outside the circle of Westmount Jewry there were close to sixty immigrant cultural associations, loan associations, fraternal organizations and the like. Attuned to such groups because of their own humble origins, the Bronfman brothers knew how to address them on their own terms. Sam and Allan actually visited these associations and spoke Yiddish with their membership, appealing to them to join the communal endeavour. This was hardly in the manner of the uptown Jewish élite, and for the Jewish community of Montreal it was a sign of the Bronfman style that was to come.[79]

Sam added the United Palestine Appeal to his list in March 1936, when he was named its Honorary Dominion Chairman at a well-attended meeting at the Mount Royal Hotel. But his commitment to Jewish settlement in Palestine, as with many other Westmount Jews and as with many gentile supporters for that matter, was to Palestine as a refuge and a haven for persecuted Jews, rather than as a focus for Jewish national revival. To Sam, support for Jews in Palestine was not only compatible with his patriotism, it complemented it. "Those of us who live in a free country like Canada," he told a United Palestine Appeal banquet in April 1938, "should express [our] gratitude by making it possible for other Jews to find freedom and security in Palestine."[80] Sam and Allan, it will be recalled, had met the Zionist leader Chaim Weizmann in 1921 during his Canadian tour, and the brothers donated several thousand dollars to Weizmann's educational projects in the succeeding period. There is only one Bronfman letter in the Weizmann papers, dated March 18, 1927 — Allan's request for the Zionist leader's advice on shares in Commercial Solvents Corporation, the firm that held the licence to Weizmann's chemical patents.[81] Sam, who probably knew better than to trouble the World Zionist Organization president for stock-market advice, was also politically astute enough to ignore the nationalist element in Zionist mobilization — as did the overwhelming majority of Canadian Jews at the time. He was now a Jewish community leader, sought after not only for his personal support but also for his ability to mount successful fund-raising campaigns. And that depended upon a feel for the political sensibilities of the Jewish masses, something that Sam Bronfman, remarkably, appeared to have.

■

SAM'S JEWISH FOCUS at the beginning of the 1930s was exclusively on Montreal, the leading Jewish city in the Dominion as well as the centre of his business operations. Beyond Montreal, indeed, there was little to command his attention. Jewish socialism, a powerful, internationally oriented movement among immigrant Jews, had no appeal for a capitalist like Sam; and Zionism, while it did engage his interest briefly as we have seen, did so only in a philanthropic sense, completely ignoring the movement's Jewish national dimension. The Canadian Jewish Congress also had little appeal. Originally founded in 1919, the Congress lapsed into inactivity, but sputtered to life once again after a meeting in the King Edward Hotel in Toronto in January 1934, thanks to the devoted attention of Hannaniah Meir Caiserman, its general secretary. But the Congress had as yet little standing among Canadian Jews, and Sam was not attracted to its seemingly unproductive political preoccupations. It was a "useless organization," he believed, "which was doing Canadian Jewry more harm than good."[82]

Laz Phillips's partner Sam Jacobs was elected president of the Congress at the 1934 meeting and in his address to the delegates he sounded a bland if optimistic note: "We desire to create a permanent all-Canadian Jewish organization which we trust will grow and develop, having for its object the study of all inner problems of Jewish life in this great Dominion. We know that the vast majority of the population of Canada is opposed to racial discrimination of all kinds, and we have ample evidence of this from the public utterances of all the leaders of public opinion throughout this fair land."[83]

As it turned out, Jacobs was much too optimistic. With political nerves set on edge by the Depression, ugly manifestations of antisemitism surfaced across Canada, assuming sometimes menacing forms. Even more than in the preceding period hotel-keepers barred the doors to Jewish guests; employers refused Jewish applicants for jobs; universities and professions imposed quotas or refused Jews altogether; street gangs battled Jews in Toronto, Winnipeg, Vancouver and elsewhere. In Quebec the nationalist right, with the support of the

Catholic hierarchy, stigmatized Jews as outsiders, modernists, secularists, capitalists, Communists — and worse. A genuinely fascist rabble, for a time, occupied part of the French-Canadian socio-political landscape, and a hate campaign against Jews sounded as part of its ideological message. The Congress, headed by an admired but ailing parliamentarian, was hardly up to the task before it. "Jacobs was too busy in Parliament to spend much time on Congress activities," historian Irving Abella notes, and while "tough, passionate and committed, Caiserman was a hopeless administrator. The uptown community in Montreal would still have little to do with an organization it felt was too far left, too Zionist and too much the mouthpiece of the immigrant community. The Congress was shunned by the Reform community, who denounced the organization for its 'militant Zionism.' "[84] In truth, none of these ideological opponents need have worried about the Congress. "A puny little organization," was the harsh observation of one of its future leaders, Michael Garber, "without leadership or programme."[85]

"It is inconceivable that the Canadian Government should stand passively by and fail to lift its voice against these assaults upon humanity, or to utter its condemnation of the violation of the fundamental principles of human rights." These were the words of Sam Jacobs, heading a Congress delegation in a meeting with Prime Minister R.B. Bennett in August 1935. In his eloquent statement, Jacobs called upon the government to denounce the assaults upon German Jewry by the Nazi regime — without, however, offering any specific proposals for action. The prime minister listened, and seemed responsive. "Mr Bennett left no room for doubt as to where his sympathies lie," an appreciative editorial in the widely read *Canadian Jewish Chronicle* observed after the meeting, "and the delegation left with the feeling that our stricken brethren in Germany are not short of friends and sympathizers in the non-Jewish world."[86]

So began a pattern that was all too common in the crisis years of the late 1930s and the Second World War: Jewish delegations, moved by the suffering of Jews overseas, and wounded occasionally by antisemitic outbursts at home, approached the seat of power to communicate their distress and to appeal for government response. In Ottawa, while sympathy was not always absent, the will to action was; other considerations were regularly more pressing; hostile opinion had to be balanced against calls for action on behalf of persecuted Jews; bureaucratic delays and engrained habits of mind took their toll; and the Jews came away with practically nothing.

These things are coldly clear to us now. But from the standpoint of Congress petitioners in the mid-1930s, attending upon a prime minister whose sympathies they had reason to doubt from the start, their cause seemed much more fragile and the government's reaction much less indefensible than they appear to us. We tend to see their efforts as feeble, and doomed from the start to frustration; they did not always think they had such a strong card to play, and they were frequently gratified when they received the crumbs that they did.

Canadian Jews also took a certain level of anti-Jewish hostility for granted in the society in which they lived, and while there were important exceptions, most of them were too preoccupied with their own communities and their own trials to devote much attention to it. Thus as the tide of antisemitism rose dramatically in Canada, and far more dangerously in Europe, Canadian Jews did not immediately flock to the banners of the Canadian Jewish Congress, the one national organization claiming to speak on behalf of the Jewish cause nationwide. Indeed, the petitioners who went to see R.B. Bennett in the summer of 1935 knew well how weak their position was, even within their own community. Not only were the Jews sharply divided between immigrants and well-established Jews, Zionists and non-Zionists, capitalists and socialists, religious and secularists, assimilationists and tradition-alists, they also failed to sustain the Congress, the one organization that claimed to speak for Judaism in all of its diversity. And Canadian Jews continued to withhold support, even as the news from abroad became more and more alarming.

Rumanian-born H.M. Caiserman, a devoted student of Yiddish literature who had worked as a tailor in the sweatshops along Montreal's St Lawrence Boulevard, struggled to keep the Congress afloat after its 1934 reconstitution, operating practi-cally without a budget. Caiserman barely managed to pay his secretary a salary of eight dollars a week, scrounged passes from the railway companies to travel across the country and went unpaid himself sometimes for weeks at a time. Six months after his election, Sam Jacobs sponsored a $225,000 campaign for the relief of European Jewry, declaring that "Canadian Jews will meet the challenge." Canadian Jews' response was insignificant — a mere $36,000, as Caiserman lamented: "They answered the appeal with pennies, with doled-out pennies."[87] This disappointment highlighted the principal weakness of the Congress as a representative body of Canadian Jewry — its failure to win the support of the wealthiest segment of the community, who preferred to donate their time and money to philanthropic as opposed to Jewish political institutions. Unlike American Jews, whose wealthy élite had founded activist organizations like the American Jewish Committee in 1905 to protect the rights of Jews, and the Joint Distribution Committee in 1914 for overseas relief for victims of war and persecution, their Canadian counterparts steered clear of politically tinged movements, were leery of public advocacy of Jewish causes, and shied away from direct contact with the Jewish masses.

For nearly five years after the reconstitution of the Congress, Caiserman toiled practically alone as the organization's only staff person, with just nominal support from the president. In his early sixties, Jacobs was tired and discouraged. He felt uncomfortable among Congress supporters, heavily made up of Labour Zionists with whom he had little affinity. Jacobs was also critical of his colleague Caiserman, whom he felt lacked tact and diplomacy for work outside a highly circumscribed Jewish community. As early as January 1936 Jacobs seriously thought of stepping down from his post; he was also ill, inattentive to his post, and in just over two years he was dead.[88]

Caiserman struggled on until 1938, when the Congress faced its nadir, practically overwhelmed by a series of extraordinary trials. First, the circumstances of European Jewry worsened catastrophically in the wake of Hitler's absorption of Austria in March and the crisis over Czechoslovakia in September. In Germany the climate deteriorated, culminating in the nationwide pogrom of *Kristallnacht* in November. More than ever before, Jewish refugees pounded on the gates of western countries, seeking desperately to escape the Nazi tyranny. Second, the efforts of Jewish representatives—led by the three parliamentarians Jacobs, A.A. Heaps and Sam Factor—to petition the government for the admission of refugees were consistently rebuffed, discrediting the quiet diplomacy of the fledgling national leadership of Canadian Jewry. Among the Jews, mutual recrimination grew louder. Some contested the ability of Caiserman or the Jewish parliamentarians to speak for Jewish interests; Westerners, particularly Heaps, blamed Congress leaders (Caiserman, in effect) for poor organization and the failure to mobilize Jewish supporters; Ontario leaders felt those from Montreal were too weak. Frustration, anger and shame seeped into Jewish politics, to the growing consternation of those like Caiserman who sought a clear, confident Jewish voice. Third, the death of Sam Jacobs in August created a void that could not adequately, it seemed, be filled. His passing, declared an editorial in the *Canadian Jewish Chronicle*, "leaves Canada without a top-ranking Jewish personality who is not identified in the mind of the Jewish public with one specific movement."[89]

Through his leadership of the Jewish Immigrant Aid Society, Sam was already involved in Congress activities, for following the rise of Nazism the two organizations agreed to work together in approaching the government on refugee-related matters. Together with Sam Jacobs in 1936, Sam signed an appeal on behalf of German-Jewish refugees to Minister of Immigration Thomas Crerar—his first public statement on behalf of Canadian Jewry, as historian David Rome points out.[90] Sam's involvement deepened with a JIAS-initiated programme to settle Central European Jewish refugees, assisted by the colonization departments of the Canadian railways.

Then, in what seemed to be the Congress's darkest hour, Caiserman approached Sam with a highly emotional appeal— virtually the only kind of appeal Caiserman knew how to make. Visiting him in the autumn of 1938, two months after Jacobs's death, the Congress official apparently managed to persuade the busy industrialist to support the national organization in a moment of grave crisis.[91] In November Sam joined a Congress-sponsored refugee committee, along with his brother Abe, Laz Phillips, Benjamin Robinson, Monroe Abbey, Sidney

Pierce, Louis Fitch and Marcus Sperber. Shortly thereafter he accompanied a delegation sent to Prime Minister King, once again to beg for the admission to Canada of Jewish refugees — in vain, as it turned out. After several meetings in Toronto and Montreal, Congress leaders established a nationwide body, the Canadian Jewish Committee for Refugees, and on January 4, 1939, Sam agreed to become its chairman.[92]

Jewish political lines were buzzing the third week of January 1939, when delegates from across Canada assembled at the Royal York Hotel in Toronto for the Fourth National Assembly of the Canadian Jewish Congress. With war clouds gathering and their European brethren being turned away from places of refuge, Congress activists knew that leadership was the crying need of the moment. The kingmakers, it turned out, were the Labour Zionists, whose Poale Zion movement had consistently championed the broadest possible framework for collective Jewish organization in Canada. With their extensive links to their European counterparts and their deep involvement in the Yiddish cultural world and Eastern Europe, the Labour Zionists probably had a sharper sense of crisis than any other group on the Canadian Jewish scene.

Among the most prominent Labour Zionist leaders was the forty-eight-year-old Moshe Dickstein, a successful insurance broker who was a veteran of the movement in his native Poland and had been in Canada since 1912. Well-known within the circle of Montreal Yiddishists, Dickstein was a sophisticated intellectual, one of the founders of the Yiddish-language *Volks Shule* or Jewish People's School in Montreal, and a lifelong supporter of the Poale Zion. In November, as part of the preparation for the Congress meeting in Toronto, Dickstein took the floor at a Labour Zionist meeting on St Lawrence Boulevard to make a remarkable suggestion: Sam Bronfman should become president of the Canadian Jewish Congress.

Famous for his wealth and his whisky, Sam had virtually no standing among the Poale Zion stalwarts; to the extent he was appreciated in Jewish circles, it was for his refugee work, his donations to Jewish causes, and possibly his efforts on behalf of the Jewish Hospital. None of those in the largely immigrant audience knew Sam personally, and the world of Westmount

Jewry was almost as far from their experience as Buckingham
Palace. David Rome, who had only recently moved to Montreal,
happened to be at that meeting and recorded the first
reaction—shock and dismay. Bronfman was not a top figure
among the Montreal Jewish patriciate and was not known as an
ardent supporter of the Canadian Jewish Congress. He was not a
Zionist and had no broad leadership experience within the Jewish
world. He was innocent of ideology—difficult for many of those
present even to imagine, given that ideology was the lifeblood of
the Labour Zionist movement. His only claim to fame, among
those assembled at the meeting, was as a millionaire industrialist—hardly a commendable point for the socialist ideologies of
the Poale Zion.[93]

Dickstein made a case, however, that Sam Bronfman could be
the statesman Canadian Jews so badly needed. He was
strong-willed and dynamic. He could get things done. He could
help mobilize the wealthy Jews who had hitherto remained aloof
from Congress affairs—and from the fund-raising that was the
lifeline of the organization. Essentially, Dickstein looked to the
future, and believed that Bronfman could rise to the formidable
challenge. It was a hunch, and he sought the support of the
meeting to sound out Bronfman himself.

Dickstein was able to persuade those present because of his
own special qualities: "the man had a magic about him," Rome
remembered, "he could convince you."[94] Dickstein succeeded,
and apparently managed to convince Sam as well, for the
candidate agreed to stand. After much discussion and no little
anguish, the Labour Zionists agreed: they would go to Toronto
with their unlikely nominee, Samuel Bronfman.

In January, in Toronto, Dickstein's proposal captured the
imagination of the delegates, beginning with the other Poale Zion
activists, but extending to more established figures—Archie
Bennett and J. Irving Oelbaum of Toronto, Lavy Becker and
Monroe Abbey of Montreal, and others. Sam received
encouragement from two leading Congress figures, Michael
Garber and Benjamin Robinson, who also supported the Labour
Zionists' nominee. That Sam was a complete outsider may have
even helped his candidacy at this point; each faction preferred

him to someone from a rival camp, and no one feared that with his victory one of the groups would dominate all the others.

At the last moment Sam became suspicious that someone might be trying to clip the new president's wings, before they had even been fastened on his shoulders. Sol Kanee, then practising law in his home town of Melville, Saskatchewan, and who later became one of Sam's closest friends, found himself in the key position of chairman of the nominating committee with the task of nominating Sam Bronfman. Surprised at being offered this unexpected task, Kanee realized the limitations of his own mandate: "Somebody said, 'here's this schnook lawyer from a jerkwater town in Saskatchewan, so there'll be no difficulty with him, make him the chairman.' "[95] Doing what he thought was expected of him, Kanee began by receiving a nomination for an *honorary* president of the Congress—intended to be Zionist veteran A.J. Freiman of Ottawa. Immediately, there was trouble. Escorted out of the meeting by Monroe Abbey, who had spotted the difficulty, Kanee was taken to see Sam Bronfman himself. "So there was this little fellow," Kanee recalled, "and I said to him, 'Where's the problem? So you're going to be president, what have you got against Archie Freiman?' He said, 'I didn't ask for this position. I agreed to take it under one condition, that there be no superimposed authority over me.' I said, 'Since when is an honorary president a superimposed authority?' He said, 'Anyway, I'm not going to discuss it. No honorary president.' I said, 'All right, any objection to honorary vice-presidents?' He said, 'No.' "

Kanee then returned to the meeting. Sensitive to the slight Freiman and the Zionists had suffered when the initial nomination had to be withdrawn, Kanee decided that the committee should fill only one post as honorary vice-president and that Freiman would be the only one to hold that position. To his chagrin, Kanee was pulled out of the chair a second time to see the prospective presidential nominee. "How stupid can you get?" Sam blustered. "I agreed to honorary vice-president*s*, not *the* honorary vice-president!" At this, Kanee was fed up. "I went back and said, 'I don't know how you people operate here, but where I come from we do things a little differently. And since I'm used to doing things a little differently, obviously I can't continue as chairman.' And I walked out. And he was elected, and that was that."

After this shaky beginning, the electoral formalities were completed on Monday evening, January 23, and the process ended on a much more elevated note, when Sam rose to the podium to address the expectant audience. "There comes a time in a man's life when he feels somewhat embarrassed," Sam began. "I am so greatly honoured by the Jews of Canada." Notably, he said not a word about Nazism, the crisis facing European Jewry, Canadian immigration policy, or the failure of Jews hitherto to support the Canadian Jewish Congress. All of those subjects had been discussed, resolutions on them passed, and the mood of crisis had been underscored for the wider community by the guest speaker, Jan Masaryk, the former Czechoslovak ambassador to England. Instead, Sam made two points that would become the hallmark of his stewardship. First, Jews had to be patriotic; second, Jews had to speak as one.

"If I might define the aims and objects of this Congress," Sam told the delegates, "I would say that they are to make our people a better people. . . . I am glad that we are living in the British Empire where we can discuss our problems openly, and if we have any differences of opinion or criticism we can bring it out without fear. We call a spade a spade, and when we do I would like to feel that any time any of us criticises one another, it is for the object of improving our position, and the position of Jewry." Sam then made the classic case for Jewish identification with the nation in which they all lived. He continued,

Canada is a senior sister in the British Commonwealth of Nations. We have, by and large, a good section of the whole community who are, or were originally from England, Ireland and Scotland. We as Jews, have a chance to build up a full position of citizenship and equality which is a privilege belonging to the citizens of the British Empire. It is the responsibility of Congress to see that the Jews are good citizens in their respective communities across Canada, and so to conduct themselves that they will gain the respect of their fellow citizens — the non-Jewish citizens. We have got to be just that much better to gain this respect.

Unity was Sam's second theme, and his model for all of Canadian Jewry in this regard was the community of Montreal. Unity, he implied, under the guidance of a leadership such as existed in Montreal, produced a public-spirited Jewish community and warm appreciation from non-Jewish society. One would never have guessed from Sam's speech that the Montreal landscape was periodically disturbed by antisemitism, that fascist gangs occasionally marched through the streets chanting anti-Jewish slogans, or that opinion ran strongly against the admission of Jewish refugees. "In Montreal we have a good feeling within the Jewish community and with the other sections of the community at large. This good feeling has been built up over a period of years and, to a large extent, by the citizens of the community in Montreal going out of their way to make themselves friendly with other sections of the community." Sam praised the uptown Jews, though not by name, for their "fine leadership" and for having achieved this "nice relationship."

Sam ended by admonishing those present to join in a common Jewish cause. "We know that in all our communities we have differences of opinion. We must agree to sink those localised dissatisfactions [*sic*] into one great body of Jewish thinking.... Unity is and must be the watchword of the Canadian Jewish Congress."

Beneath this rhetoric one can detect Sam's deep dissatisfaction with the Jewish community he was about to lead. He was unhappy with its ideological differences, which he did not understand and in which he had little interest; he was impatient with the divisions — geographic, administrative and personal — that he first encountered over refugee policy; and he deplored the lack of public spirit among many Jews, turned inward with their problems to the neglect of the wider world, particularly the Canadian reality with its rich British heritage. His call for unity, therefore, was not a mere platitude; it sprang from his understanding of the Jewish problem in the Canada he knew. There was also an apologetic tone — common enough in the Jewish culture of the 1930s, particularly among the assimilated élite with whom he had been largely associated — and which did not go unnoticed or unappreciated in the community at large. Distributed as a press release, Sam's remarks were praised by the

Montreal Daily Star, for example, which saw in them "a great deal of sound common sense." "Public men lose no opportunity of calling for unity, harmony and self-respect," said the *Star*, "but they do not always, as Mr Bronfman did, emphasize as a pre-requisite to this desirable state the necessity of each section doing its utmost to merit the respect of the other sections of the Dominion."[96] More practically, the *Canadian Jewish Chronicle* said that the Bronfman name "should serve to bring into Congress activity those elements which, for one reason or another, have held themselves, like expensive ostriches, blind and aloof from the major Jewish problems of the time."[97]

There were several ways to interpret Sam's words, which lacked the luminous clarity of the speeches that the poet A.M. Klein crafted for him on subsequent occasions. But on the essential point Sam was clear enough: the Canadian Jewish Congress had found a leader who intended change, who would respect the diversity of a heavily immigrant community but who in the end would not be bound by the Jews he was supposed to lead.

Mindel Bronfman, Sam's
mother, c. 1914.

Sam's father, Ekiel Bronfman,
c. 1914.

Sam, age about thirty.

Marriage of Saidye Rosner and Samuel
Bronfman, 20 June 1922.

Saidye and Sam after their weddin

The family house before the renovations, c. 1929.

Sam with Edgar (left) and Charles (right), 1936.

Sam becomes President of
the Canadian Jewish
Congress. Toronto,
January 1939.

Edgar's bar mitzvah, 1942. From left, Charles, Saidye, Sam, Phyllis, Minda and Edgar.

Allan, Harry and Sam with Julius Kessler (seated) c. 1945.

Saul Hayes, 1938.

Laz Phillips, c. 1940.

Edgar, Sam and Charles, 1947.

Sam's honorary degree at the
Université de Montréal, 1948.
Congratulations from the
Archbishop of Montréal,
Joseph Charbonneau.

Sam and General Frank Schwengel, Waldorf Astoria, New York 1944.

Monroe Abbey, Saul H
and A.M. Klein celebra
the publication of *The
Second Scroll*, 1951.

Sam and Saidye before Coronation of
Queen Elizabeth II, London 1953.

Opening celebration at the Seagram building in New York, 1957. Left to righ
Alain de Gunzburg, Charles Bronfman, Ludwig Mies van der Rohe, Genera
Schwengel, Phyllis Lambert, Philip Johnson, Sam and Edgar Bronfman.

Sam (right) and Vic Fischel (left), kneeling with barrel between them, and other members of the Seagram Family Achievement Association in 1952. Edgar is just behind Sam.

Ben-Gurion and Sam at the opening of the Bronfman Biblical Museum in Israel, 1962.

Saidye and Samuel Bronfman on his
75th birthday, 4 March 1966.

CHAPTER VI

War Years

NEXT TO THE outbreak of war in September, the biggest Canadian news story of 1939 was the visit of Their Royal Highnesses King George VI and Queen Elizabeth in the late spring, the first time a reigning British monarch had ever come to North America. Landing at Quebec City, where hushed crowds greeted the king and queen with "awed reverence," according to the *New York Times*, the royal couple and their entourage began their stately tour—across French Canada to Ontario and the Prairies, then to Vancouver and a swing through the United States, finishing with the Maritimes and Newfoundland. Rapturous throngs from every corner of the Dominion broadcast their enthusiasm—even the French Canadian nationalist premier Maurice Duplessis, who assured Their Majesties of the "sentiments of joy, respect, loyalty and affection of the entire Province of Quebec." In Winnipeg, the five-year-old Larry Zolf, whose father was a gutsy exemplar of Jewish socialism, was appropriately dressed for the occasion:

My father, devout Jewish nationalist and fanatical monarchist, had outfitted me in full Union Jack regalia. Instead of a skullcap I wore a Union Jack beanie; instead of a prayer shawl, a Union Jack shirt; instead of a *kapota* (the traditional long grey coat of Orthodox Jews) my torso and legs flaunted an exquisite Union Jack-decorated set of short pants. And as I

267

watched my father desperately and in vain trying to break through the police cordon to thank Their Majesties personally for providing him with a sanctuary and home in Canada, I was neither embarrassed nor surprised. I knew my father was doing right, and I was proud of him.[1]

Opponent of Mr Zolf senior on Jewish issues and every other political question, Sam Bronfman agreed with him wholeheartedly, as did virtually all Canadian Jews, on the British monarchs. Sam's own patriotic utterances were spontaneously felt, and came naturally to someone who had attended public school in the heyday of British imperial splendour and who deeply admired the business associates from whom he had learned so much in the Old Country. "We join in paying homage to Their Gracious Majesties whose crowns are a symbol of the democracy, freedom, tolerance and justice to the whole world," Sam told a Jewish audience during the royal visit, speaking in his official capacity as head of the Canadian Jewish Congress.[2] Crowns certainly were on Sam's mind that spring: his Five and Seven Crown whiskies were doing extremely well; the Seagram offices were decked out with crown displays for the regal visit; and to mark that occasion the company announced its latest brand, Crown Royal — the expensive premium rye whisky that remains one of Seagram's great sales successes. Once again, though in this case in the long run, Sam's extraordinary business sense paid off: his own and the public's sincere feelings, his insistence on quality, and his craftsman's care for detail all combined to produce a rare marketing coup.

Sam had taken the first steps after the phenomenal success of Five and Seven Crown in the mid-1930s; at the time he had planned a "super crown," in a crown-shaped bottle, but had never gone forward with the idea. In 1939, to salute Their Majesties, Sam reintroduced the bottle and had a special blend prepared, personally supervising every step of the process — right down to the regal purple bags in which the bottles were eventually sold, a Canadian institution in themselves. For permission to present Crown Royal to the king and queen before it was authorized for sale on the Canadian market, Seagram persuaded the Quebec and Ontario Liquor Commissions to stock a mere one hundred cases of the unknown blend and then bought up the entire stock itself. Thereafter, as Their Majesties train travelled to the west coast from Montreal, it went with an ample supply of liquor — ten cases of Crown Royal — the entire exercise being "a terrific lesson about whisky," Sam later boasted.[3]

Characteristically, Sam introduced the new blend very slowly in Canada, and it was not sold in the United States until 1962. The reason was, as Sam explained in a promotional film made in the early sixties, that Crown Royal was intended, as befit the royal visit, to be "the top premium brand of our company's products." The problem, as so often with premium blends, was inventory — it took years to accumulate enough to blend for regular marketing on an international scale. Once again, Sam's signature — the long view, an obsession with quality, driven by his own tastes and sentiments.

■

SAM'S ELECTION AS president of the Canadian Jewish Congress came at a moment of crisis, caused by the desperate plight of Jews in Europe. In the beginning of 1939, tens of thousands of refugees frantically sought to leave the European way-stations in which they were trapped, often without papers, without visas, and without the right to remain where they were; tens of thousands more sought desperately to escape — not only from Nazi Germany and the expanded German Reich, but also from East European countries where governments and sometimes people turned harshly against the Jews. "Shall All Come In?" asked an editorial in the London *Daily Express* in response to the pleadings of Austrian Jews. In one country after the next the authorities worked out how to say no.[4]

"Despite all sentiments of humanity," said Canadian Secretary of State Fernand Rinfret in January, "so long as Canada has an unemployment problem there will be no 'open door' for political refugees here." And to give the policy teeth, the government in Ottawa actually raised the capital floor required for admission from a hefty $5,000 to an exorbitant $15,000.[5] Most Canadians seemed to agree, but some, at least, did not. Across the country, many newspaper editorials sounded a humanitarian note, and influential voices were raised in favour of admitting Jewish refugees. A non-denominational Canadian National Committee on Refugees and Victims of Political Persecution, headed by Senator Cairine Wilson, called urgently for a more liberal immigration policy. But there was wide recognition that, as the *Financial Post* put it, "the present opportunity is not likely to be repeated." "We must act and act quickly," wrote a sympathetic Professor George Wrong of the University of Toronto. "Our own fibre will be improved if we face and overcome the difficulties."[6]

In their anger and frustration, some Jewish activists lashed out at their own leaders and what appeared to some to be an unacceptably low-keyed approach. "Particularly in Toronto," wrote historians Irving Abella and Harold Troper, "The abject failure of the Congress's tactics was the subject of attack by trade unions, *landsmannschaften* and other Yiddish-speaking groups."[7] Among such organizations the feeling was widespread that established Jewish leaders had not done enough to press the government to change its policies. New to office, Sam's response was to ignore the opposition of the Jewish activists and to proclaim the loyalty of Canadian Jews, attempting by a statesmanlike posture to bring all Jewish groups under the Congress and his own personal authority. Like other leaders, he became absorbed in the tasks he felt could actually be accomplished. Unfortunately, the critics had little concrete to suggest themselves, beyond invoking the Jewish "masses" and threatening some undefined assault upon those in power in Ottawa.

Statesmanship brought Sam into some unusual company. Returning to Montreal after his election in January 1939, he learned that former prime minister R.B. Bennett, whom Sam always suspected had directed his prosecution by the RCMP just a few years before, was staying at the Mount Royal Hotel, across the street from the Seagram Building, preparing to leave Canada to live in England. Sam wrote to him now, "to pay respects to one who gave his talents and devoted a lifetime in the interests of his country."[8] Sam made it clear that the rancour of the past was forgotten and the priority now was to put Canadianism first. A few weeks later, Sam jumped at an offer from the abrasive and

independent-minded Charlotte Whitton, the future mayor of
Ottawa, to join the board of the Canadian Welfare Council, an
advisory group concerned with social problems. Whitton, a
conservative maverick, was a former associate of R.B. Bennett
and someone who had opposed the admission of large numbers of
Jewish refugees to Canada. But in his correspondence, at least,
Sam never raised the issue with her. Like most Canadians, he
accented national unity as the nation slid into war.

As a member of the Canadian Welfare Council Sam took tea at
the home of Thérèse Casgrain, a former champion of women's
suffrage, wife of a prominent Liberal politician and herself a
future leader of the Quebec CCF. Courted now in such quarters,
Sam doubtless reflected on how far he had come: not only was he
introduced to a stratum of gentile society where Jews had never
tread, he also entered the salons of some, like Charlotte Whitton
herself, whose formative political years had been spent in a
temperance milieu, where the Bronfman name was the object of
abuse.[9]

In the spring and summer of 1939, as war loomed and the
plight of European Jewry became more desperate, Sam appeared
several times on public platforms, attempting to fashion a
common Jewish response. The most immediate problem was the
competition among fund-raisers within the Jewish community,
each with his own strategy for assisting persecuted Jews overseas.
Complicating matters, representatives of the New York-based
Joint Distribution Committee, an organization with worldwide
responsibilities, appeared in Montreal hoping to raise money in
Canada, providing a formidable challenge to Canadian appeals.
In response to this disarray, Sam called for a common effort — a
"Jewish community chest," in the phrase of the time — a political
goal that took him several years to accomplish.

August found Sam in Calgary where he addressed the Western
Division of the Canadian Jewish Congress and where he
stumbled badly, for once, following his own instincts rather than
the political signals coming from his widely divergent constitu-
encies. In his first speech to a major Jewish gathering outside
Montreal and Toronto, Sam sounded a particularly patriotic note
while ignoring the burning Jewish concerns of the hour.
"Canadian Jews," he told the eighty assembled delegates, "are, or

should be, first of all, Canadians. . . ." The problem was that they had allowed "petty jealousies and bickerings to affect [their] outlook as Canadians," and while he conceded that Jews had a right "to consider our problems solely as Jews" he urged them now to do otherwise: "by considering ourselves first as Canadians, and as such, guiding ourselves and our affairs, we shall not only meet one of the first requisites of good citizenship, but, what is equally important, we shall increase our prestige in the eyes of that larger body of citizens of Canada." To an audience which included many Zionists, outraged by the highly restrictive White Paper on Palestine just issued in May, Sam commended the policies of the mother country: "If you draw up a list of countries and nations which deal fairly with all the different groups within their realm, the name of the British Empire would head the list." "I am profoundly thankful that Britannia rules the waves," he concluded. "May she long continue to hold her sway, to be mistress of the seas, a bulwark against intolerance and the practice of inhumanities."[10] He issued no protest against restrictive Canadian immigration policies, was silent on the Jewish claims in Palestine, and glossed over the Nazis' persecution of the Jews.

No sooner had Sam finished his speech than protests filled the hall — not against Sam himself, at least according to the published reports, but certainly against the opinions he had voiced. "I am bitterly disappointed with the attitude of the government to refugees," complained Winnipeg socialist M.P. A.A. Heaps, much more in tune with the delegates' mood of frustration and anger. "Many doors are closed to industrialists and wealthy refugees who would need no financial assistance. There is no labour problem here, but one of humanity, and there is no heart nor head to the attitude of the government," he told his audience. Saskatoon lawyer J.M. Goldenberg expressed another view that could not have pleased Sam Bronfman — that the Congress had to pay more attention to its deep regional divisions. The direction of Jewish affairs should not be left to the will of an individual, he insisted pointedly, its "strength must lie in the strength of the branches of Congress."[11] Zionist opinion was angrier still. "This Congress protests the policy of the White Paper on Palestine of May, 1939, as being not only contrary to the spirit and letter of the Balfour declaration but also as detrimental to the interests of Great Britain," went one of the conference resolutions. The delegates denounced British restrictions on Jewish immigration to Palestine as a breach of faith with the Jewish people and the "greatest blow" to Jewish aspirations.

Sam's conciliatory approach towards Great Britain and his accent on Canadian patriotism won high praise from the anglophone press of Montreal. An editorial in the *Star* entitled, "A Jew Speaks for Canada," lauded his "eloquent tribute to British liberty and to the freedom which is enjoyed by the Jewish people under the British flag." The *Gazette* had similar sentiments: "Mr Bronfman has said what too many people in these days are inclined to take for granted." Other minority groups in Canada and in other parts of the Empire should take heed, the paper noted, adding how fitting it was that these words "should come from an influential member of one of the great minority groups."[12] Jewish leaders, on the other hand, were horrified. Those who had battled in vain for the admission of Jewish refugees and those who felt British Palestine policy was a callous betrayal found Sam's remarks insensitive at best. Particularly among the Congress old guard, the Poale Zion activists like Moshe Dickstein who had backed Sam for president some months before, there was disappointment and dismay.[13]

Interestingly, no one felt confident enough to challenge Sam directly. In an editorial, likely written by A.M. Klein, the *Canadian Jewish Chronicle* even supported Sam's approach, and while stressing how keen had been the Jews' disappointment with British Palestine policy, the paper insisted that Jewish protests had been "a loyal opposition."[14] Privately, however, Jewish leaders told their president how unhappy they were with what he had said. According to David Rome, who joined the Congress staff to handle publicity about this time, Sam's response was positive. Sam realized he had blundered, and one of the first things he did was to get rid of his Seagram-provided public-relations man who had drafted his Calgary speech.[15] Sam understood how out of touch he was with much of Jewish opinion—particularly that of the Zionists with whom he had never been close—despite the fact that he was the nominal head of the United Palestine Appeal in Canada.

By the time war broke out a month later, Sam had become a more articulate spokesman for Canadian Jewry. Jewish opinion had shifted by then—towards the fervent patriotism that Sam personally felt and to which he had tried to give voice in Calgary. As important, by the autumn of 1939 Sam was receiving effective advice. One of the lessons of Sam's Calgary speech was that he could not function alone as president of the Canadian Jewish Congress. Thereafter, he worked closely with two outstanding appointees—Saul Hayes and A.M. Klein, completely different personalities, each of whom, in his own way, contributed decisively to Sam's Jewish leadership.

Abraham Moses Klein, who became one of Canada's greatest poets, first crossed paths with Sam Bronfman in the late 1920s, when he was a student at McGill University and had a summer job as a "spieler," or tour guide, on a Montreal sightseeing bus—a job arranged for him, coincidentally enough, by his older friend and fellow student Saul Hayes.[16] Spielers—the word comes from the Yiddish—provided a stream of patter for the tourists, mainly Americans, who flocked to Montreal during the summer months. The posts were packed with Jewish talent, including Hayes and the future CCF leader, David Lewis. According to Klein's biographer he was in much demand as a spieler, and was eventually hired to shepherd visitors to the newly constructed Seagram distillery at Ville LaSalle, outside Montreal. Seagram set up a special bureau for these tours—the brainchild of Vic Fischel, one of Sam's earliest Montreal employees. The plant was noteworthy for its state-of-the-art equipment, but mainly it was a curiosity as a distillery for American tourists, coming from a country still locked in prohibition. Klein's skill as a spieler was so great, apparently, that he eventually had a short audience with the head of the company, Sam Bronfman himself.[17]

It is doubtful if Sam met Klein much, if at all, during the 1930s, when both were active in Jewish causes. Sam, the millionaire industrialist, raised funds for the Jewish General Hospital and other philanthropic activities, and moved in the highest circles of Westmount Jewry; Klein, who had become a lawyer and was deeply interested in poetry, was part of

Montreal's Yiddish-speaking intelligentsia and made his political home in the intensely ideological world of Zionism, as educational director of the Canadian Zionist Organization and editor of its monthly, *The Canadian Zionist*. After a short, unhappy period practising law in the northern Quebec town of Rouyn, Klein returned to Montreal in 1938 and took over the editorship of the *Canadian Jewish Chronicle*—the most widely read English-language Jewish weekly in Canada, put out by Hirsch Wolofsky's Eagle Publishing Company.

Klein's first editorial in the *Chronicle* appeared in November 1938, immediately after the outbreak of *Kristallnacht*, the riotous assault on Jews throughout Germany by Nazi storm troopers, and his prescient column gave eloquent voice to the horror and revulsion felt by Canadian Jews:

There is a lunatic abroad in Europe; and the world had better give heed. . . . A conquering nation does not treat its prisoners of war with that ruthlessness with which the German Reich has treated its Jewish citizens. Decency is exiled from that land; honour has been expelled from it; civilization has been placed in a ghetto. If ever there was a case of violent insanity which merited segregation, it is the case of the German leaders, mad with Hitlerics; if ever there was source of pestilence which deserved quarantine, it is that of the German pirate ship of state.[18]

Continuing as editor until his retirement in 1955, Klein poured his creative energies into weekly editorials and articles, addressing the most important events of twentieth-century Jewish history, in a style marked by his uncommon poetic sensibility. Klein peppered his prose with literary references, drawing upon an extraordinary familiarity with both ancient and modern texts. "Probably never in Canadian journalism was English poetry invoked so freely and so naturally in comment on current political issues," David Rome observes.[19] "In his empathetic sensitivity to the events of those years," says Usher Caplan, "Klein spoke personally for a nation, thereby revealing the complete range of his own emotions—his fears, his pain and despair, his quixotic outrage in the face of injustice, his sardonic wittiness, even his sometimes ghoulish attraction to the humorous side of tragedy, and his rare moments of jubilation."[20]

Twenty years Klein's senior, Sam first noticed the younger man's Jewish journalism early in 1939, when he took over the Canadian Jewish Congress. Shortly after, he invited Klein to work for him as a speech-writer, secretary, public-relations consultant and adviser on Jewish affairs. Klein, who had difficulty earning a living as a lawyer — a profession he disliked — readily agreed, continuing some legal work, however, along with some public speaking and his editorial tasks. He probably devoted about half of his time to Sam, and received, in 1948 at least, what was a substantial half-time salary — three thousand dollars, plus a thousand in expenses, all paid by the Seagram company.[21] In addition to Jewish matters, his principal focus, Klein did other writing for Sam — including DC-SL annual reports, birthday and anniversary greetings Sam sent to friends and family members, and even, in all likelihood, some highly personal correspondence, such as a long letter to his son Charles on the occasion of his *bar mitzvah*. Characteristically, Sam would spend much time on such compositions, going over the ideas carefully with Klein; the thoughts and the feelings in these cases were undoubtedly Sam's, but the expression bore the unmistakable literary signature of one of the great poets of the day.[22]

Given Klein's subsequent fame as a poet and his tragic emotional collapse in the late-1950s, some critics have decried the link between the men as ruinous for the poet's creative sensibility, and ultimately for his mental stability as well.[23] The relationship between the mercurial, rough-hewn industrialist and the troubled, gentle poet was certainly problematic, and Sam could, at times, be brutally unaware of the damaging effects it had on Klein. Nevertheless, the usually gruff millionaire deeply respected his fragile assistant, whom he considered far more a friend than an employee. Although Sam could treat his friends badly, and was utterly self-absorbed, he had a special admiration for Klein — one of the few people, apart from Saidye, to be spared his occasional explosive outbursts and brutal language. For Sam, Klein represented an intellectual world for which he had little patience or inclination, but to which as an enquiring, thoughtful person, he was powerfully attracted.

Language, indeed, was one of the things that drew Sam to Klein in the first place. Never having completed high school, Sam impressed some who knew him superficially as crude and unpolished. However, he put great energy into self-education, much of it centring on literature. "When I would use an expression that he liked," Mark Shinbane remembered, "he would say write it out." Shinbane heard the great industrialist recite lines of poetry. "Sam could spill it," he testified. "He wouldn't do well at a meeting of the Institute for International Affairs," and his limitations must have been a source of continuing frustration, but for a person without formal education or a scholarly temperament his literary interests were considerable.[24] Sam was constantly reading, Saidye remembered. "Besides the business papers he brought home every evening, he enjoyed good books — not novels, but biographies, history and poetry. He liked the stirring words of Longfellow, Browning, Wordsworth and Sir Walter Scott, and he could quote reams of poetry by heart." "He read to me in bed," she recalled, "his favourite poem was Tennyson's *In Memoriam*. It's a very long poem [and] he'd fall asleep easily, the book would drop down on the floor and he'd be asleep."[25]

Unlike many high-powered businessmen, Sam had a genuine respect for "people who were learned," as he would call them — a category he ranked, according to Shinbane, together with "industrialists who had made the top grade" as the persons most worthy of respect. To Sam, Abe Klein certainly fit that mould. "What a pleasure it has been for me to learn to know intimately a man of such depth of thought, intellect and character as I have found [in] you," Sam wrote to him in 1941.[26] Sam's appreciation, one should note, was not for a literary celebrity. In 1938 Klein's fame as a poet was still in the future and while he was already acclaimed, this was largely within literary circles. In this case the tycoon genuinely admired the poet, and more than that, Klein "elicited an unusual gentleness and consideration" from a normally feisty and quick-tempered Sam, as Adam Fuerstenberg observes.[27]

Sam's reliance upon Klein for his public utterances had its humorous side, as Saul Hayes once recalled. In one of his speeches on the war situation the poet prepared a passage that referred to "the myrmidons of Hitler." "Sam, you are going to say this in a speech?" Hayes protested. "When someone asks, 'what the hell are myrmidons?' what are you going to say?" Sam for once, was off balance: "Why are you telling me that?" "I'm telling you very simply," Hayes replied, "that if you want someone to help you, and there is no sin in that, and that person knows how you speak, you don't talk about myrmidons."[28]

Suave and diplomatic, in contrast with the reclusive, scholarly Klein, Saul Hayes helped steer Sam through the sometimes treacherous political waters of Jewish community affairs for his entire career as head of the Congress. Hayes was three years older than Klein and had also attended McGill, where he received a law degree in 1932. His first direct contact with the famous industrialist was in the mid-1930s, when Sam became president of the Federation of Jewish Philanthropies and Hayes, then practising law, became the leading spirit in the development of a Jewish Vocational Service and Guidance Bureau for Montreal.[29] Jewish refugees from Nazism, however, were the young lawyer's most important concern in the late 1930s, and the force that led him to a career as a Jewish civil servant.

Sam brought Saul Hayes into the centre of Congress's refugee work in early 1939, when he hired him to be executive director of the newly formed Canadian Jewish Committee for Refugees. Hayes, Sam sensed, had the skills to negotiate with non-Jewish interests, and to represent the Jewish cause with force and dignity. As opposed to Caiserman, "a man who dealt with problems by bursting into tears," as David Rome puts it, Saul Hayes had no trouble commanding and holding attention. "Agile and well-connected" was how Ben Lappin, one of his associates, remembered him, "and above all poised." Hayes was tall and debonair, an impressive figure who projected the air of mastery, competence, and savoir-faire that Sam so deeply admired. People saw a glamour about him, Lappin reflected — prompting someone to dub Hayes "the Anthony Eden of Canadian Jewry."[30] Over the next two years, Hayes's responsibilities were broadened, until in 1942 Sam made him Congress's executive director. He was yet another example of Sam's knack, in both his business and commual activities, for the brilliant appointment.

Sam and Saul Hayes formed an extraordinary team. One was the smooth professional, the consummate diplomat widely respected for his style and his knowledge of the Canadian scene; the other a crusty man of affairs who, along with his admiration for uptown Jewry, had an affinity for ordinary Jews — not so much their politics as their deepest aspirations to succeed and to be respected by their fellow Canadians. Hayes, it has been said, got along better with the people he lobbied than those on whose behalf he lobbied; Sam, on the other hand, could not completely separate himself from the immigrant Jews, even when he did not share their social environment or their political or ideological outlook. Despite occasional harsh words — usually precipitated by one of Sam's explosions — the relationship was marked by trust and loyalty. "They had a fundamentally deep regard and affection for one another," said Alan Rose, Hayes's friend and eventual successor as Congress executive director. "They almost worked as one person."[31]

■

WAR CAME TO Canada on September 10, 1939, a week after Great Britain issued its own declaration against Nazi Germany. There was never any doubt about what Canada would do. It was unthinkable, most English Canadians felt, to stand aside when the mother country went to war; far more than concerns for Poland, or for democracy, and certainly for the Jews, it was loyalty to the Empire that moved Parliament, the prime minister and the vast majority of the population.

Immediately after war was declared, Sam issued a message to Canadian Jews on the occasion of the Jewish New Year. His thoughts were unqualifiedly patriotic and contained no reference to the refugee crisis or the agony of Jews in Europe: "The gravest danger which faces us today, and one which we must avoid, is that of despair. As sons of the Eternal People, we must regard our plight from a long-range viewpoint: and so regarding it, recognize faith in God, Custodian of Israel, as the Scriptures say — 'Who sleeps not, neither does he drowse.' Particularly should we recognize and appreciate the significance of the fact that great numbers of our people reside under the protection of the British flag, and that the Empire itself is the staunchest bulwark of all liberal principles which are so vital to us. . . ."[32]

Conscious of their weak position in Canadian society, and attentive to the hostility towards Jews that lurked beneath the surface everywhere, Jewish leaders knew that war would test their community and would put them in the public eye. For Sam, as he had stated in his inaugural speech to the Canadian Jewish Congress a few months before, the primary task was to bring the sometimes discordant groups making up Canadian Jewry under a single framework. War, by accenting the vulnerability of Canadian Jews, made this task more urgent than ever. "This quest for unity," said Saul Hayes, "was, one might say, his organizational coat-of-arms, since in season, out of season, one speech or another speech, in discussion with groups at every opportunity, he hammered home the point that he wished to make of Canadian Jewry a unified Jewry."

Meeting with Congress leaders, Sam made it clear that his model of decision-making was consensual: full discussion could precede decisions, if necessary, but once a decision was reached there could be no deviation. He liked to make the analogy with cabinet government: "the Canadian Jewish Cabinet must go to the public, be it the government, the media, be it to the non-Jewish world, with one point of view and not disparate attitudes and views on a particular subject matter."[33] Unity, in Sam's view, was a virtue in itself, a commitment to practical work and a sign of good citizenship. "In a country such as this composed of several constituent elements there must be a definite relationship between the component parts," he told an audience in Toronto. "Jews as all sections of a machine must work in unison if the machine is to operate efficiently. So must the elements in a country co-operate in order to obtain the maximum of efficient effort. We have our share of that responsibility."[34]

Sam showed the way in October 1939 by calling into being the United Jewish Refugees and War Relief Agencies Campaign (UJRA), operating in conjunction with the Joint Distribution

Committee and bringing under one Congress roof a variety of previously independent refugee assistance organizations. Working with his brother Abe, in whose name meetings were first called in Montreal, Sam assumed the office of national president and, on the recommendation of Laz Phillips, secured Saul Hayes's appointment as executive director of the new body, effectively assuring Congress control.[35] Even the mighty Joint, with its global responsibilities, was humbled in the end, accepting the supremacy of the Canadian Jewish Congress.

The outbreak of war spurred Sam's quest for unity. In October 1939 he issued a "Message to the Jews of Canada," a solemn recitation of Canadian Jewry's support for the war effort. Congress, he reported, had established four national committees — "a *Patriotic Efforts Committee* to aid in Red Cross work, in patriotic fund-raising, and kindred purposes; a *Committee of Coordination of Labour and Industry*, to mobilize the industrial and labour resources of Canadian Jewry in such a manner as best to serve the Government; and a *Committee of Information and Public Relations* for the purpose of keeping Canadian Jewry in touch with the daily duties incumbent in time of war, and maintaining a united *esprit de corps* with fellow-citizens." These three committees together constituted a *National Emergency Committee* under Sam's presidency.

Leaving these bodies to do their work, Sam made a flurry of speeches across the country, rallying Canadian Jews to the colours. At the Montefiore Club Sam announced the formation of military recruitment centres from coast to coast, "in close contact with the Ministry of National Defence at Ottawa." He publicly pledged his support for war bonds, to "build a Maginot Line on the economic front against Nazi barbarism." In Toronto, at a Jewish rally at the Victory Theatre, he denounced "the menace of the double-headed monster that has arisen against civilization." In Saint John, he told the Maritimes Section of Congress that "Britain was the last great fortress of our freedom in the world." Sam's photograph appeared regularly in the Jewish and the general press — breaking ground for a new synagogue, meeting dignitaries and to signal his public addresses. Carefully crafted by Abe Klein, Sam's pronouncements were released on the eve of the Jewish New Year; others were distributed as posters in the format of war bulletins.[36]

Preparing publicity for Sam, still relatively unknown as a Jewish leader, was an uphill task. Ben Lappin, who joined the Congress Central Region in Toronto at the time and who was editor of the English-language section of the *Hebrew Journal*, recalled receiving a telephone call one day from David Rome in Montreal advising him that Sam Bronfman was coming to town and should be given the full publicity treatment. Lappin asked Rome for background information, and was told to use the library of the *Toronto Daily Star*, one of the city's major newspapers. But when Lappin looked up Bronfman at the *Star*, he was horrified. The file was full of stories on prohibition, rum running and the RCMP prosecution of 1935. "I said, Jesus, how am I ever going to give this guy publicity?" Word was already out on Spadina Avenue that this Bronfman was "a bootlegger, a gangster, Al Capone's partner, and so on."[37] Since they could hardly avoid the problem, the Congress staff prepared a short biography some time in 1941 that made the appropriate emphases, including reference to Sam's family background as "a religious orthodox one and inspired by a sense of right and wrong"; "his sense of fair play is an outstanding characteristic"; "ethical teachings of early environment reflected in daily business activities"; "outstanding characteristic: in business, personal and communal activities — SINCERITY OF PURPOSE."[38]

After some months, Saul Hayes and David Rome decided that the publicity was becoming excessive. Sam, Hayes recollected, "was a man of consummate ambition, with an inordinate quest for publicity. He wanted to be known throughout the country." Sam had hired a public-relations man, Bill Lawrence, to present the Congress president to the public, and the Congress professionals felt he had mishandled the task. "There was too much of Bronfman," Hayes went on, "in the *Gazette*, Bronfman — in the *Star*, Bronfman — in the *Canadian Jewish Review*, Bronfman — in the *Congress Bulletin*, Bronfman. Bronfman in a score of newspapers. Rome and I decided that we would be doing Mr Bronfman a favour if we were to tone down on it."

As Hayes recalled in a roughly drafted memoir, Sam took the advice badly. "Mr Bronfman was furious. He blew up. He called me into his office and he denounced me." But Hayes was unyielding.

I said to him, "this job is not worth abuse. One of my reasons for taking it was not to enjoy any abuse, and . . . I did not intend to take it. I was making a living in law. This is only a leave of absence. I see nothing immoral if I go back to a job which is waiting for me. My name is still on the letterhead — which it was. My name is still painted on the door of the office — which it was. I can easily go back at a moment's notice" . . . I said to him, "You know what you can do with this job?"

As often in such situations when his critics stood their ground, Sam heard his antagonist out even through his anger; indeed, having vented his wrath he seems to have felt it easier to accept criticism rather than reject it; and in this case, as in others, Sam was astute enough to draw back. "From that time," Hayes noted, "I never had a quarrel with him." And the personal publicity does seem to have been toned down.[39]

Sam not only saw Hayes's point on how the Congress president should be presented, he came to appreciate his associate's diplomatic touch in strengthening the authority of the Congress. Temperamentally impatient, Sam was persuaded that he had to go more slowly towards unity than he would have wished. "I have been unable to bring about complete nationalization in all our departments," he wrote to Archie Bennett of Toronto in July 1941. "However, I have always worked to that end, trying to establish nationalization wherever possible until our final goal will be achieved, probably at the next convention, by making certain changes in personnel."[40] As time passed, Hayes noted, Sam built up trust among his constituents, who gradually came to share his vision of a Jewish community unified under a central organization.

Meanwhile, wartime presented its own strong case for unity, a widely felt need for a single body to mobilize Canadian Jews. More than ever before, Jews across Canada felt they needed an advocate. In September 1940, the *Winnipeg Free Press* alluded to one reason—wartime gossip that "the Jews won't join up." "That is a lie," the paper said. "The first man to join up from the staff of this newspaper last fall was a Jew, and nobody who knows the Jews of Winnipeg . . . doubts that the Jews are playing their full part."[41] But was the *Free Press* right? The very suggestion that Jews might not be flocking to the colours was a source of great embarrassment for Jews, and Sam worried deeply about it.[42] Obviously, only a national Jewish body could address this delicate issue. Congress, as we have seen, launched a War Efforts Committee to stimulate and accelerate the rate of enlistments. Sam's brother Allan, who with him had been briefly in uniform during the First World War, joined the reserves and headed a recruiting drive in Montreal. Sam spent a good deal of time, when travelling across the country, making sure that enlistments were up. Congress painstakingly kept track of voluntary Jewish recruits, together with data on casualties, Jews taken prisoner and Jews decorated for wartime service—all in an effort to refute charges of Jewish pusillanimity.

Ben Lappin recalled being given the thankless task of knocking on doors of relatives of men missing in action to ask, "Are you Jewish?" When the war was over, Congress published the results of the survey in two dignified volumes. On the bottom line, as Abe Klein noted, was "a gloriously eloquent statistic: 9.6% of the Canadian Jewish population had served with the Army, Navy, and Air Force—a percentage one-tenth greater than the national average."[43]

Sam's high visibility as a Jewish leader had one very attractive side for Canadian Jews: at a time when many Jews felt uneasy in their own society, his wealth and standing as a powerful industrialist enabled him to communicate, as few other Jews could, his own and his community's patriotic aspirations. Wartime, indeed, provided Sam with his first positive taste of public recognition and Canadian Jewry with a nationally acknowledged contributor to the war effort. Answering a national appeal to buy war bonds in January 1940, for example, Sam immediately put himself and his brothers down for $500,000—a huge sum at the time—and Distillers Corporation-Seagrams Limited subscribed another $250,000.[44] Sam had other war-related work that came to him as head of Seagram:

membership on Canada's War Alcohol Production Board, where he sat together with Harry Hatch; and the Canadian War Production Board, which advised Ottawa on wartime production priorities.

Sam particularly enjoyed sitting on the War Technical and Scientific Development Committee (WTSDC), a government body established in 1940 to administer funds donated privately to the National Research Council (NRC) to further the war effort. The committee was formed to raise money for the NRC, an ailing Crown corporation that vastly expanded its activities during the Second World War. James Duncan, deputy minister of defence for air, originally approached the head of Eaton's department store, John David Eaton, and Sir Edward Beattie of the CPR, each of whom contributed $250,000. Sam matched their donation (noted in Board documents as having come from "Samuel Bronfman and brothers") and as a result took a seat on the top-secret WTSDC committee. Sam, along with Eaton, Beattie's representative R.E. Stavert and six government appointees, took a special oath of secrecy and allegiance, and became privy to some of the top Allied scientific secrets of the war — including chemical weaponry, radar, sonar, and some research that pointed towards the atomic bomb.[45]

In 1942, Sam actually donated a ship — HMCS *Montreal II*, a small, submarine-chasing training vessel, presented to the navy by Sam and Joseph Simard, president of Marine Industries Limited. Before a large crowd at the Royal St Lawrence Yacht Club of Dorval, not a normal haunt of Montreal Jews, Saidye broke the traditional bottle of champagne across the prow of the new ship while a beaming Sam looked on — nattily attired for the occasion and photographed with the minister of the navy, an admiral, and assorted naval brass. "Mrs Bronfman conducted the service of blessing," said the report in the *Montreal Herald*, and she was later presented with a silver tray with a commemorative inscription by the vessel's commanding officer.[46] The Bronfman name was also associated with the Canadian Aid to Russia Fund, a very popular patriotic effort at the time, although Allan was the principal figure in this effort, not Sam. The fund was launched in January 1943, with a huge rally in the Montreal Forum chaired by Allan and featuring Eleanor Roosevelt — once a confirmed supporter of prohibition — as the star attraction. To convince the American president's wife to speak, Allan enlisted his and Sam's friend Joseph E. Davies, a well-connected Washington lawyer who had been ambassador to the U.S.S.R. in 1937–38, special adviser to Cordell Hull and was then chairman of Franklin Delano Roosevelt's War Relief Control Board. Davies unhesitatingly recommended to Mrs Roosevelt that she attend: "I have known the Bronfman brothers for years," he telegraphed to her. "They are high-minded philanthropic great and fine men. I can commend them to you without reservation."[47] Mrs Roosevelt's visit went well, and the cash for Russia flowed. The Bronfmans (together with Sam's brother-in-law Barney Aaron) were among the top donors, with a gift of $10,000, along with J.W. McConnell of the *Montreal Star*, Molson's brewery, the CPR, the Bank of Montreal and a handful of others.[48]

Saidye's work for the Red Cross Society complemented Sam's own involvement in the war effort, and added to the family's stature in the Jewish community. At the beginning of the war, the Honourable Margaret Shaughnessy, a leading personality in the world of the Red Cross, visited a group of Jewish women at the Montefiore Club to request the formation of a special "Jewish section." One of those present remembers an objection to this idea, on the grounds that Jews should not be separated from other Red Cross workers; Shaughnessy's reply was that a distinctly Jewish group would be more effective in supporting the cause. It is not clear whether there were less reputable reasons for Shaughnessy's suggestion, but it may well be that she was right when it came to productivity: with Saidye as president, the Montreal Jewish Branch of the Quebec Provincial Division of the Canadian Red Cross Society immediately registered hundreds of volunteers at the Montefiore Club to knit, sew bandages and prepare packages for men overseas. Eventually, some 7,000 women became involved and their output was prodigious. Working furiously, under Saidye's energetic and virtually full-time direction, the Montreal Branch kept track of its productivity with Stakhanovian precision: after a year's operation Saidye announced that "33,526 articles had been completed for the Red Cross by the Jewish women of Montreal"; in 1941, she reported the ladies had knitted 10,219 garments for the army, navy, women's auxiliary and civilians, from 3,081 pounds of wool.[49]

With Saidye working at the Red Cross five days a week, and with Sam's war-related work for the Congress taking up a good deal of his time, the global conflict made its mark on the Bronfman household on Belvedere Road. In June 1944, Sam mentioned this in a handwritten *bar mitzvah* letter to his thirteen-year-old son. Charles's *bar mitzvah* festivities were tinged with sadness because of the "wicked men who have sought to destroy our civilization," his father said. "Until they are defeated, no celebration of any kind can be completely joyful. I know that you are proud that your country stands among those which are dedicated to the achievement of this purpose. I know that you will agree with the thought of your mother and myself, who have decided that it would be a most fitting commemoration of this great day in your life for us to donate in your name a contribution to the Red Cross to bring back to health those who have been wounded in battle."

For a year or so, there were English evacuees at the Bronfmans' home — Doris Sassoon and her two children, Cynthia and Hugh, members of an exceedingly wealthy, aristocratic Jewish family who, on their way to Victoria, discovered that their assets had been frozen in the United Kingdom and that they were without a place to live. Spontaneously, although he had just met the Sassoons, Sam invited them to move in — sensing the embarrassment of such a family being in financial difficulties. For months there were six children in the Bronfman home, and a transplanted, angular English lady "in a state" over the inconveniences of her life as a refugee. Separated from her husband, Mrs Sassoon was "very difficult," as Saidye diplomatically put it — "a bitch on wheels," as Edgar remembered. Everyone except Sam seems to have discerned a condescending attitude on the part of the Sassoons, forced to camp among the colonials; Sam himself, however, refused to criticize his imperious guests, and advanced them whatever funds they needed. After some months the Sassoons' financial problems were settled, and the family moved out.[50]

Jewish refugees from Nazism posed the greatest challenge for

Sam and the Canadian Jewish Congress, and their problems, unfortunately, could not be addressed as easily as those of the Sassoon family. Beginning with the German attack on Poland, the Congress refugee committee, the UJRA, heard pathetic appeals for assistance from Jews, desperate to escape the clutches of Nazism by emigrating to Canada. Organized by Saul Hayes, the UJRA responded immediately in the most familiar way—raising money. By those standards, Congress's efforts were remarkable. After only a few months of campaigning, and despite competition from war bonds and local federation appeals, pledges were close to the original $310,000 target.[51] A year later, with money still pouring in, Sam reported on the refugee work of Congress as "another glorious chapter" in its history. And so it was by all the traditional standards of Jewish community mobilization. While the need was immense, the response was impressive. Within a year, Congress was managing fund-raising efficiently, on a national basis. Extending into the postwar period, the organization eventually raised some $20,000,000 for refugees.[52] Some of these funds were allocated to the Joint Distribution Committee and by various circuitous means reached Jews in Nazi-occupied Europe; some were spent in Canada to assist Jewish internees sent to Canada from England; and some helped support the tiny number of European Jews who actually managed to enter the country, despite all the obstacles that Canadian officials put in their path.

Congress faced an awkward challenge in the summer of 1940, when about 2,500 uprooted Central European Jews, sent to Canada and interned under the Enemy Aliens Act, landed on the doorstep of the UJRA. Strange as it appears to us now, Canadians had a genuine fear of these forlorn, mostly German-speaking young men, who were herded behind barbed wire in camps in Ontario and Quebec. Among them, it was assumed, could easily be some of the "Nazi fifth columnists" much discussed in war propaganda; according to Paula Draper, UJRA officials themselves had "strong suspicions" about the internees at the beginning.[53] Wary of adverse popular reaction, Congress proceeded with great care, avoiding too close an identification with the internees. Leaders even worried about appearing too prompt in calling for the relief of the harsh circumstances of their internment. In a confidential report to the Congress Executive in January 1941 Sam explained the fears that "the non-Jewish world might look with quizzical eyes upon our plans of spending thousands of dollars for internees even though they were wrongly interned. It is a question of public relations and a sense of values," he added, "and for this reason not everything that possibly could be done should be done on the treatment of internees."[54] Only as time passed did Congress feel able to assume more responsibility for the internees' welfare—providing them with some necessities, taking up their cause with the government, and also attempting to speed them on their way to the United States.

Despite Ottawa's stonewalling on Jewish refugees, Sam was consistently upbeat, refusing to chastise Canadian government policy. He never referred publicly to the rebuffs Saul Hayes and he received on the question of admitting Jews to Canada and he always accented the positive achievements of the UJRA. "The Refugee Committee has taken care of over two hundred families that had come to Canada prior to the outbreak of the war," Sam reported to a meeting of the Congress Central Region in January 1940. "It would do your hearts good, ladies and gentlemen, if you read the reports from the refugee committees in the various sections of our country." Sam was genuinely proud of the fact that the handful of Polish and Czech Jews who came to Canada in 1938 had been settled on the land—in refutation of the charges that Jews were incapable of becoming agriculturalists. With the help of Congress funds they were able to begin farming, and were already standing on their own feet, he suggested.[55] A year later, in a comprehensive report to the Congress's executive on the work of the UJRA, Sam talked mainly about the assistance Congress had provided to refugees who had already reached Canada. The closest he came to acknowledging the obstacles he and his colleagues met in Ottawa was a brief reference to the need for "propaganda and dissemination of literature . . . acquainting the Canadian people with the advisability of allowing refugees to come into the country."[56]

"This is the Empire which brought the banner of freedom to the farthest corners of the earth until the word 'British' itself became synonymous with 'fair play'," Sam told the delegates to the plenary meeting of the Canadian Jewish Congress in January

1942. "As for Jewry, this is the Empire which understood us first and understood us best."[57] Later that year, when news of the brutal deportations of Jews from France and other countries reached the western press, some Jewish activists protested the lack of an appropriate Canadian response and called for protest meetings like those being organized in the United States. Among Congress leaders, however, Sam was one of those most wary of activism; he feared that a demonstration would be a "disservice to the British Commonwealth," and he was suspicious of radical Jewish groups that might upset Congress's quiet diplomacy.[58]

In the summer of 1942 the collaborationist government of Vichy France lent its hand to the rounding up of thousands of Jews for the Nazis' deportation convoys — "to the east," as it was said. At first, only adults were taken on the terrible journey; amidst heartrending scenes of separation, the children were left behind. Unlike most other deportations, these occurred in the full glare of publicity, and as a result churches, international aid organizations and eventually governments raised their voices in protest.

Responding to urgent appeals from the Joint, Sam and Saul Hayes pleaded publicly with Prime Minister Mackenzie King to protest the deportations from France in 1942 and tried, behind the scenes, to get Thomas Crerar, the minister in charge of immigration, to allow several hundred of the abandoned children to enter Canada. King responded with a gracious letter, hoping "that these reports may prove to be exaggerated," but relaying the "grave concern of the Canadian Government over these reports." From Crerar, however, the Congress got nothing. As Abella and Troper have noted, the Canadian authorities proved unrelenting in their opposition to Jewish refugees entering Canada.[59] With its policies enforced by the meticulous and mean-spirited Frederick Blair, the stubborn opponent of Jewish refugees in the government's Immigration Branch, Ottawa dithered, and dug in its heels. Hayes, for once, felt betrayed, and would have told the government so if Sam and Laz Phillips had not persuaded him to tone down his outrage.[60]

Somewhat reluctantly, Congress agreed to a mass demonstration of Jews at the Montreal Forum on Sunday afternoon, October 11. Attempting from the start to maintain the proper decorum, Congress leaders billed the gathering as one of "dedication and protest," to voice "faith in the coming victory of the United Nations." Speakers included J. Pierrepont Moffat, the United States ambassador to Canada, Canadian Secretary of State Norman McLarty, Rabbi Herman Abramowitz of the Shaar Hashomayim synagogue, and Laz Phillips—along with messages of support from Prime Minister Mackenzie King, Malcolm MacDonald, the British High Commissioner to Canada, plus representatives from the Polish, Czech, Yugoslav, Chinese, Dutch and other embassies.

Sam, who took the chair, delivered a major address that helped set the tone of the meeting. "I want . . . to pay tribute here to our Government, which, but a few weeks ago, expressed through our Prime Minister, the Honourable William Lyon Mackenzie King, its grave concern, and made its vigorous representation touching the fate of Nazi-pursued Jewish refugees on French soil." His theme, which he did not alter throughout the war, was Jewry's unrelenting commitment to the war effort, expressed with the unmistakable, eclectic erudition of A.M. Klein: "With the same pious devotion with which we uttered the prayers of our Holy Days, we renew the sacred vow we took three fateful years ago. It is a vow we have cherished with all our hearts, with all our souls, with all our might. Like our very *tfillin*, we have bound it for a sign upon our arms, and put it as a frontlet between our eyes. It is a vow—not to cease from sacred strife, nor let the sword sleep in the hand, until Hitlerism and all that it stands for, is destroyed completely and beyond resurrection!"[61]

Speaking to the Congress Eastern Division in February 1943, Sam highlighted the achievements of Canadian Jewry during more than three years of war. "The Jews of Canada," he said, "have acquitted themselves so well that they may derive a sense of satisfaction and accomplishment even though the attainment of our ends is so tragically distant." Sam's pride in the achievements of his fellow Jews, which to us seem so meagre beside the immense suffering of European Jewry, comes into focus when seen through the prism of wartime Canada. Under the direction of Sam and Saul Hayes, Canadian Jewry spoke for the first time with a national voice. The amount of help they provided to their European brethren was unprecedented, as was their effort, albeit with little success, to pry loose some favours from the mandarins in Ottawa. Neither Sam nor other leaders of

Congress expected to transform Canadian immigration policy, which is one reason why they consistently rejected protest and militant action: thinking practically, they understood how little leverage they had as Canadian Jews, representing a small and relatively unpopular minority. Beyond this, they also feared the consequences of an aggressive strategy, aware of the hostility towards Jews that remained widespread. Practical men for whom the demonstration of Jewish patriotism was a primary objective, they did not dispute the Allied leaders' regular reply to Jewish calls for help, that winning the war had to come first. When rescue propositions began to circulate in the spring of 1943, Sam repeated this argument himself in another of his speeches prepared by A.M. Klein:

> Even now the cry is heard again, heard wherever free men still enjoy the divine gift of speech: 'Let our people go!' The embattled democracies of the world are convinced that that cry will not be heeded until upon the foe are visited all the plagues of war, and that the first step towards the rescue of captive Jews and the liberation of the enslaved must be the complete and unquestioned triumph of our arms. The British Empire, ever the champion of the oppressed, advances in this spirit; in this spirit the might of the United States moves against the hosts of Pharoah. The Russian peoples too have already shown how great rivers can be converted into Red Seas for the invader. We are passing through the 'second phase' of the Passover Saga.[62]

This was more eloquently put than the statements of Allied leaders, but the message was not different: European Jews, or rather those who remained alive, would have to wait.

■

ON MARCH 4, 1941, to honour Sam on his fiftieth birthday (using his "Canadian" birthdate), Jewish community leaders organized a dinner at the Montefiore Club, a programmatic *tour de force* that was the first in the series of birthday and other tribute dinners that Sam enjoyed for the rest of his life.[63] More than forty prominent citizens constituted a Committee on Arrangements, lending their names to the event; leaders and friends from coast to coast received engraved invitations; and Jews from across the country assembled to participate in a lavish outpouring of praise.

An elaborately orchestrated affair, even by Jewish community standards in which the "tribute" dinner was becoming an established institution, the evening was itself a tribute to the professionalism that Sam had brought to communal affairs. And there could be no mistaking the focus of the dinner. In his capacity of Congress General Secretary H.M. Caiserman wrote to every Congress invitee from Halifax to Vancouver, advising them that if they could not attend, they might send "a congratulatory message so that it can be incorporated into the presentation book which will constitute a permanent record of this event and its significance."[64] Advance publicity appeared in the Jewish press, and for the dinner itself, accompanied by an appropriate press release, there was fulsome coverage, including a special issue of the *Canadian Jewish Chronicle* with a large picture of Sam on the front page, a congratulatory editorial and a glowing description of the evening.[65]

Each guest received a souvenir menu that included an unsigned acrostic poem, written by A.M. Klein and presented to Sam by Rabbi Abramowitz of the Shaar Hashomayim as part of an illuminated address:

Sincere, laborious for the common weal,
Able, of heart capacious, broad of mind,
Militant for his country, of great zeal
Unto the human of earth's humankind,
Excellent in most wise philanthropy,
Leader well-chosen for his people's need,

Bringing where union was not, unity.
Resolving acts to implement the creed —
Out with it, Sonneteer, reveal his fame,
Name him, that all may know this kingly man,
Fervent of purpose, lofty in his aim!
Merit reveals him! His achievements scan
And thus acknowledge him by deed and name,
Name that does honour both to chief and clan![66]

After the meal, a parade of dignitaries offered their praise of the honouree — Moshe Dickstein, who in a witty and eloquent speech told of Sam's quest for unity in Canadian Jewish life; Mark Shinbane, who spoke of Sam's Jewish roots in the west; Marcus Sperber, who recounted Sam's work with the Federation of Jewish Philanthropies; Michael Garber, who saluted Sam as leader of the Canadian Jewish Congress; Horace Cohen, who bore greetings from Sam's Shaar Hashomayim synagogue; Harry Batshaw, who relayed congratulations from the Zionists; Archie Bennett, who represented the Congress refugee committee; Ernest Vaz, who represented Jewish community workers; and Laz Phillips who talked about Sam's role in Canadian business. More speeches followed, including gracious words from Allan, praising Sam as a family man. Finally Sam himself rose to speak, reading a lengthy address that touched on many of his favourite themes — his parents, commitment to philanthropy and unity within the Jewish community, praise for the British Empire (quoting the *Book of Ruth*: "Whither thou goest I shall go, and where thou lodgest I will lodge. Thy people shall be my people; where thou diest I will die . . ."), reference to a Jewish homeland in Palestine ("towards the fulfilment of which the British Empire has made so notable a contribution"), and Jewish participation in "the Canadian mosaic" ("in order to build for the future a unity and a mutual respect not only among ourselves as Jews, but . . . to gain the respect of other groups in this country of ours"). Sam's speech, published as a booklet in English and Yiddish, was distributed to the guests.

All that month Abe Klein worked overtime writing speeches for Sam — not only for the Jewish community tribute but for a Seagram birthday dinner that followed a few days later, plus Sam's Passover "message" to the Jewish community and other public statements. Discussing some of this material with Klein in his office as he liked to do, Sam discreetly slipped the poet a cheque, with his thanks. Klein wrote to his boss on March 24 expressing his sincere gratitude while acknowledging his financial dependency as well: "I want . . . to thank you again for what you did for me last week, and how you did it. I may say now that I was so overwhelmed when I took a peek at that folded cheque as you were on the telephone, that my usual fluency of speech abandoned me, and I was all heart and no tongue. Your very candid letter — which you saw should reach me early in the afternoon, made me very happy indeed, and was reward enough; at the subsequent conversation, I said, 'My cup runneth over'. I was even then sorely tempted to persist in my arrogant gesture of refusal, but your charming separating of the letter from the cheque completely unarmed me. Moreover, I shuddered to reflect what would have happened to me had I come home that evening and told my wife that I was such a 'knacker' — her vocabulary would have been very picturesque, indeed. And so my wife thanks you, and my son thanks you, and most certainly I do too."[67]

Personalizing his leadership and encouraging lavish tribute, Sam knew at the same time how to gratify the self esteem of a diverse range of Jewish constituents. "He had a genuine sense of identification with the people," Ben Lappin said, "and he tried very hard to show his solidarity with them."[68] In marked contrast with the uptown Jews of Montreal, Sam had a real affection for the Yiddishists, for example — donating substantial sums to their school, the *Volk Schule*, against the advice of his own rabbi, Herman Abramowitz, who opposed their leftist, secularist commitments. Sam personally kept Yiddish newspapers afloat in Montreal, Winnipeg and Toronto, when these would otherwise have sunk beneath the weight of financial difficulties. And although he would not brook his authority being diminished, Sam did not impress Congress activists as dictatorial. To the contrary, many contemporaries recall him consulting widely, seeking consensus, and quietly moving disparate elements under the Congress umbrella. Behind the scenes, to be sure, Sam almost always got his way. "The only fault that I have found with Mr Bronfman is that he is a little too democratic for my taste," Michael Garber once said, describing how Sam used to run meetings of the Congress. "He believes in letting them talk, but I sometimes wonder whether he is not always thinking of that famous line of Gilbert and Sullivan,

Let them exercise their brains
And their cerebellums too,
In the end they will vote
As I tell them to.[69]

Cultivating a populist image, Sam also commanded authority in part by the sheer strength of his personality. To poorer Jews of Montreal, the Westmount Jewish élite had always been distant and unapproachable. Many of the most wealthy among them were known to be anti-labour or were unpopular as landlords; Sam, by contrast, "was seen as a giver, not a taker"; he projected a "caringness" for the Jewish community as a whole, in the sense of being "a good Jew," as Ben Lappin put it. There was also an element of fear. "People who would cross anybody else would never cross him," Saul Hayes contended.[70] H.M. Caiserman trembled at his sight, and on one occasion even pulled up a chair for him at a meeting — a gesture that Sam abhorred. Apart from the few, like Hayes, who dealt with him as near-equals, Jewish community associates feared his occasional explosions. Ben Lappin recalled Sam borrowing a dime for a telephone call on one occasion. When Sam later returned the coin, Lappin said he thought of joking, "Never mind, Mr Bronfman, I always wanted to be able to say that the Bronfmans owed me money." But Lappin thought better of it, fearing one of Sam's terrible detonations. "What if he didn't take it right and the ceiling fell down on me? You never knew what his fancy would dictate."[71] Those who felt at all vulnerable avoided a test.

Populist or *Volksmensch* though he was, Sam and his family presided over their people much as did the aristocratic Rothschilds in some European Jewish communities, and they were often treated as a kind of Jewish royalty. Like a royal family, they were always on display. As a young girl, Phyllis remembers the family being "closely inspected as we entered and left the synagogue." When she, her sister and brothers had parties at 15 Belvedere, the non-presence of other Jewish children was a matter of community gossip.[72] Petitioners quite naturally approached the family about one thing or another. Sam and Saidye regularly opened their home to community meetings of all sorts, and the Bronfman imprimatur, as well as their donation, was constantly sought for fund-raising campaigns and any number of community causes.

In communal affairs, Sam's practical bent made him increasingly dependent upon Saul Hayes, whom he had brought into Congress via refugee activity, but whose diplomatic and managerial skills proved increasingly important to the Congress as the organization grew in stature. Intuitive and impulsive in his approach to Jewish leadership, Sam relied on Hayes's ability to manipulate the machinery of the Jewish community and communicate with people in authority. Together with Michael Garber and Moshe Dickstein, from whom Sam also took advice, Hayes provided him with a compass for his public deportment and community action. "Clear it with Saul," he would say, encouraging Hayes to build a screen protecting him from the constant press of business and the burden of correspondence, which Sam detested.[73]

Sam's concerns about efficiency and his dependence on Saul Hayes put him on a collision course with H.M. Caiserman, nominally the top civil servant of the Congress. Caiserman, whom Sam and virtually everyone else respected as a person and a literary critic, proved to be an utterly hopeless administrator. Effusive and emotional, he had a relatively poor command of English, lacked political sensitivity and kept his office in a shambles. In 1942, Sam had Hayes named to a new post, "executive director" of Congress, promoting his own lieutenant to run the organization and effectively easing Caiserman aside. According to David Rome, a junior official in the Congress at the time, Sam managed to accomplish this while sparing the older man pain or embarrassment. Caiserman remained the honoured "General Secretary" — a title that had a special resonance among his fellow East European Jewish immigrants — and maintained excellent relations with Hayes. "I have a policy [with] people who work for me," Rome remembers Sam as saying. "Whatever changes I make I respect them for the services they have rendered, and I do not get rid of people, that's just not my way of doing things."[74]

As this incident suggests, Sam managed a gradual transition away from traditional structures in the Jewish community — "from the old-world type of community leadership with its strong reliance on voluntary execution of decisions, to a growing cadre of full-time professionals," as community veteran J.B. Salsberg observed.[75] He wanted to bring a higher tone to Jewish public life, seeking a measure of sophistication and efficiency previously unknown in Congress circles — or any other Canadian

Jewish organization, for that matter. Sam's business experience guided him, providing a model for Congress in the middle-echelon executives who worked for Seagram on Peel Street or in the Chrysler Building in New York. Setting an example among other Jewish organizations in Montreal and in other places as well, Sam's transition brought forward a younger, more educated group of Jewish professionals—men like David Rome in Montreal and Ben Lappin in Toronto—who changed the tone of community affairs.

Practical concerns also prompted Sam to bring the major fund-raising efforts of the Montreal Jewish community under one roof, creating the Combined Jewish Appeal (CJA) in August 1941. Launched in the "sweatship" in Oaklands, and with Allan the first chairman, the CJA brought together three major campaigns — the Federation of Jewish Philanthropies, the Jewish General Hospital, and Congress's refugee organization, the UJRA. In October, the results of the first campaign were in — $498,700, a prodigious achievement, exceeding the original target by several thousand dollars.[76]

Sam's fund-raising strategy, which he pursued aggressively for the next three decades, was to make a substantial donation himself at the beginning, and then draw other major donors in his wake. "If you want to raise money," he once said, "plunk down money." Sam carefully assessed the fund-raising prospects at the start of each campaign before deciding on his own donation. "For years the goals of the campaign were determined in conjunction with Sam Bronfman who, together with his family, contributed 15% of the total," observes one student of the community.[77] Sam reserved his most fervent invectives for those who failed to live up to his idea of an appropriate donation — something that hardly endeared him to some of the wealthiest Jews in the city. "He considered them phonies," Max Melamet recollected, "and if there was anything he hated more than an ordinary phony, it was a rich phony."[78]

Sam made a point of not limiting his philanthropy to Jewish causes, and even in wartime, when Jewish needs overseas seemed limitless, he was a conspicuous supporter of institutions in the general community. One of the most important of these was McGill University—an interesting choice for Sam, because of the sense so many Jews had of the school's antisemitism. During the 1920s Montreal Jews figured importantly among the students at McGill, which was always considered a bastion of the city's anglophone, Protestant élite. In the Faculty of Arts of the mid-1920s there were more than five times as many Jews as Catholics, and Jews made up more than one-third of the total student body. Near the end of the decade, however, McGill's administrators identified a "Jewish problem," and began a policy of anti-Jewish quotas. As a result, the percentage of Jewish students fell steeply, with only the most brilliant among them being admitted. Strikingly, there were no public protests from the Jewish quarter during the 1930s, a sign of how the community viewed such unfair treatment as utterly beyond its capacity to change. At least one writer has noted a shift at the end of the decade, pointing towards an eventual removal of anti-Jewish restrictions. Principal Arthur Morgan appeared on Jewish platforms, and in 1938 McGill awarded an honorary degree to Harry Stern, a Reform rabbi involved in various liberal causes. A climate of antisemitism remained, however; there was no change in admissions policy, and Jewish bitterness over it persisted.[79]

Sam supported McGill as early as 1940, when he and his brothers assisted a branch of the university's medical school. In November 1941 he became involved with McGill's School of Commerce—strengthened substantially that year when Montreal publisher and financier J.W. McConnell donated a spacious Pine Avenue mansion as the school's new home. Responding to McConnell's appeal, Sam then presented McGill with two Bronfman professorships in commerce, promising the university $20,000 a year for five years. He participated in a committee of "outstanding businessmen" to aid in the establishment of the Commerce programme, and was doubtless gratified by the recognition this brought him in the editorial pages of the Montreal *Gazette*. In a characteristic gesture, Sam singled out for support a prestige institution that had poor relations with Jews, anticipating that his largesse would win favour with the university administration and the general community.[80] Anti-semitism remained at McGill, however, despite Sam's efforts, and quotas, whether official or unofficial, remained in place until the 1950s. As late as the early 1960s, Jewish students attending McGill believed that despite the Bronfmans' continued financial support the university would never name a building after them. And while Sam was finally made a governor of McGill, a post he had long coveted, this was not until 1964; he was blocked until then, according to one account, because of McConnell's strong personal opposition.[81]

■

SOME OF THE happiest times the Bronfman family spent together during the war years were at a country residence, in Ste Marguerite ("Saint Margaret," as anglophone Quebeckers called it), a village in the Laurentians not far from Montreal. With gasoline rationed and travel restricted, Sam decided to rent a country home close to the city, where he, Saidye and the children could spend weekends and holidays together. Several family members recall antisemitic incidents involving local inns in the vicinity that blacklisted Jews and property that could not be rented to them, but if Sam suffered from these indignities he left no record of it. Eventually he rented an estate belonging to Sir Arthur Purvis — a liberal-minded British businessman who came to Canada in 1924 to run Canada Industries Limited.

The principal building was a huge fieldstone house with enormous rooms, panelled in pine and with hand-hewn beams. Its living room was particularly capacious and went up two stories; at one end was a great fireplace, imported from Italy, practically large enough to stand in.[82] The property included stables with several horses, maintained by a grounds-keeper with eleven children, and a private lake for swimming and boating. During the winter, as Saidye recalled, "we would take the Friday evening train up north. The caretaker picked us up at the station in a horse-drawn sleigh." Unwinding, Sam loved the ride to the house, a distance of about two miles through the dark, bundled up in furs, with the children sometimes following behind on skis. Charles remembers his father's high spirits along the way, singing, "The tree was cold, the tree was bare, and Jack Frost said, 'I'll make the tree a gown myself' . . . 'Make the tree a gown myself.' "[83]

Far from the troubles of Seagram or the Congress, Sam relaxed at Ste Marguerite. As on Belvedere Road, one sign of relaxation was his curious concession to casual dress: Sam almost never discarded his business suits, and it was extremely rare that he would don a sports jacket; when fully at ease, however, he might appear in pyjamas—but with a suit worn on top. Saidye remembered him sitting on a sofa in front of the huge fireplace, sometimes in this odd garb, one imagines, "reading or playing cards with the children at a small table. Often, he sat at that table alone, playing his favourite card game, solitaire, nattering and scolding himself if he played the wrong card." Beyond this, and occasional singing, Sam was not an active vacationer in the Laurentians. Skiing was out of the question as we have already seen; the one time he tried it Sam took immediately to a hot bath and spent the night moaning and groaning in discomfort.[84] He never learned to swim, although the children tried to teach him during the summer. "They put life preservers and ropes around him and then lowered him into the water," Saidye remembered. "But it was hopeless—he was too frightened." Now and then Sam paddled about in a rowboat: "He rowed it backward to let off steam, but never went very far from the shore." From time to time there were visitors at Ste Marguerite—the Wachtels, who came up from New York, acquaintances and associates from Montreal, and friends of the children. On Sundays airmen from the base at nearby St Adele would come for a meal, and during the Christmas and New Year's vacation in 1942, Saidye recollected, there were as many as twenty-three guests, not including the servants. But much of the time the family were on their own—"a place of very warm memories," Saidye said, "a place where we were all together as a family."[85]

Sam may have found the relative isolation of the Laurentians particularly inviting because, to a far greater degree than before, the war years had him in the near-constant strain of being in the public eye—mainly as leader of the Canadian Jewish Congress, head of an important "home front" organization, but also leader of a business empire that was constantly assessed to see if it was "doing its bit." Sam made a determined effort to see that it was. At the start, with many employees joining the military, Sam organized a generous policy for all who enlisted. As one of his accountants, Max Henderson, described it, "Mr Sam simply told each employee that his salary or wages would continue to go to his family while he was away, that his job would be there when the war was over, and then wished him good luck. He said that the company would simply 'adjust the finances', as he put it, when the employee returned. It was a measure of their respect for him that they went off to war with easy minds on this basis."[86]

At the same time, Sam opened the doors of his plants to European Jews who somehow managed to find sanctuary in Canada. When Mel Griffin first came to the LaSalle distillery in 1945, he found many of these former refugees working as operators or labourers, looking upon "Mr Sam" as their saviour. Sam "knew them all by name," Griffin remembered, and "put them all on 'Cloud Nine'" by greeting them personally when he strolled through the plant.[87]

Shortly after the outbreak of war the Canadian government mobilized distillers, ordering them to convert to the production of alcohol used in the manufacture of smokeless powder and other military goods. Sam needed no coaxing. After one year of war, he told shareholders at the Mount Royal Hotel, Seagram, together with its Canadian competitors, had become "an essential war industry." Canadian distilling, he went on, "has taken its place shoulder to shoulder with major industries like steel, automobile, radio, transportation, communications and others in the ranks of those who are doing their war tasks quickly, quietly and efficiently." Seagram scientists were among the first to adapt whisky distilleries for war production, he indicated, working closely with the government and freely offering plans and suggestions. Seagram pioneered techniques for producing high-proof alcohol used in making synthetic rubber. "It was a Seagram scientist," Sam proudly announced, "who focused the attention of the State Department in the United States on the Russian dandelion-like plant, Kok-sagzy, as a possible source of natural rubber and Seagram has growing now, as a test, ten thousand of these magical plants."[88]

Working with a very small staff, and drawing upon Rex Vickers and his Vickers and Benson advertising agency in Montreal, Sam tirelessly spun off ideas to assist the war effort.

Seagram advertisements boosted war bonds and stamps, and the company produced and distributed posters to raise morale, and "counteract dangerous rumours" — a common concern of the day. Seagram fellowships sent employees to universities and scientific institutes for courses of study, and professors were brought to plants for the same purpose. The purpose of these programmes was not merely to improve productivity, as Sam put it, but to create "a sense of responsibility as citizens in a world which needs now, more than ever before, well-informed citizenship and leadership."[89] And Seagram's famous "Moderation" campaign, still going strong, developed a new twist — the theme that parents who had instilled the principles of moderation at home over the years had no need to worry about the behaviour of their sons overseas.[90]

Carstairs, one of Sam's U.S. subsidiaries, strayed slightly over the line in its enthusiasm in 1944, when invasion fever swept the United States, waiting anxiously for the Allied landings in France. In anticipation, Carstairs had Rand McNally mapmakers print a "Carstairs Invasion Map" of northern France, showing where the future landings and battles might occur. Distributed to Carstairs dealers and trade personnel in March, three months before the actual invasion, the maps were released to the public just as the first Allied soldiers struggled ashore in Normandy. The "Carstairs Invasion Map" proved to be a sensation — bringing down a swarm of FBI and Secret Service agents to the head office, who assumed a major breach of military security. "This was the kind of promotion that made Carstairs leaders in the trade," wrote one of its salesmen, Philip Kelly. "We were always several steps ahead of our competitors."[91]

Sam himself put a great deal of effort into the publication of an upbeat, patriotic history, *Canada: The Foundations of Its Future*, written by the Canadian humorist and McGill University political scientist, Stephen Leacock. When Sam conceived the book as a morale-booster in 1940, Leacock seemed the ideal choice to write it. A highly acclaimed author and champion of the Empire, he was best known in the company's Peel Street headquarters as a militant opponent of prohibition. It was Leacock who had pointed out the absurdities of much of the temperance propaganda in the period immediately after the First

World War, and his campaign against the "organized hypocrisy" of the anti-drink crusaders must have been enough to endear him permanently to anyone in Sam's position. What Sam and his advisers overlooked, however, were some less attractive qualities for a morale-raising author: Leacock's white-supremacism, his crotchety anti-immigrant bias and his ill-tempered dislike of the rich.

Approached by a literary agent in Montreal, Leacock agreed to see the man at his Orillia home on Lake Couchiching. "Please tell him to bring fishing rod," the humorist cabled. Being short of cash at the time, Leacock agreed to do the job for a hefty five thousand dollars, and promised to complete the work in four months—a considerable but not vast underestimation, as it turned out.[92] All went smoothly with the project until Leacock submitted the manuscript to Seagram for scrutiny as he had promised to do. Hoping to find an uplifting contribution to the national cause, the Seagram readers were horrified to find Leacock taking swipes at immigrants, French Canadians, Catholic priests, wealthy merchants, Americans and Irish. He had omitted to pay tribute to Central Europeans who helped colonize the west—an obvious sore point with Sam—slurred Count Frontenac, a French-Canadian icon, and at one point urged that after the war Canada not welcome "all the mongrels of unredeemed Europe" as immigrants.[93]

Wisely, Sam did not deal directly with Leacock but communicated instead through a Seagram committee, headed by A.M. Klein. Arduous negotiations ensued, and while the author yielded on most points he grumped about the loss of "some of the virility of the book." Sam kept a close watch on the project, as Saul Hayes remembered. "He spent so many hours on seeing the book through from several drafts on to distribution that had he been paid the going hourly rate he would have been a millionaire."[94] Sam had Klein draft a short preface in his name, and then submitted this to Hayes for criticism. He selected the paper, the printer, and oversaw the book's design. At last the work appeared, to general acclaim—illustrated by thirty-one original paintings by famous Canadian artists and released in two handsome editions, with ordinary volumes bound in blue and deluxe bound in red. Then, from Sam's point of view, the real work began.

Sam had 160,000 copies printed and distributed free of charge to schools, libraries and prominent persons in Britain and North America. Copies went to such diverse personalities as "George VI Rex Imperator," the Duke of Windsor, Haile Selassie, Jack Benny and Harry Hatch. In Canada Seagram addressed volumes to 600 provincial and federal government officials, 2,000 "high-ranking educators and libraries," 5,000 "executives," and 400 newspapers, magazines and weeklies.[95] Seagram personnel raised questions about distribution: all bank managers in towns of 10,000 people or more? Rotary, Kiwanis and other service clubs? and so on. A.M. Klein's task was to compose scores of handwritten dedications, which Sam would sign. To J.W. McConnell, for example, who disliked Sam heartily, Klein addressed a few words for "the man of understanding heart":

in appreciation of his fine qualities of heart and mind;
and in admiration of his outstanding record of
commercial service — in peace and war, a guiding star.

The best by far went to the Kremlin, capturing wonderfully the post-Stalingrad enthusiasm for "Uncle Joe":

To Marshal Joseph Stalin,
mighty leader, of mighty peoples, in war
so vigorous as in peace far-seeing,
whose hammer pounds Fascism, and
whose scythe reaps freedom, this
history of his ally and neighbour is
respectfully inscribed.[96]

Pouring his energy into such war-related projects, Sam also maintained a keen eye for the postwar prospects of the whisky industry. For example, conforming to wartime regulations requiring him to produce high-proof alcohol for munitions, he carefully retained in barrels some of the normally discarded, unpotable by-products — known as heads and tails. After the war, when aged whisky was in short supply, Sam could legally redistil these spirits and quickly had on hand hundreds of thousands of gallons of six-year-old light whisky for his various blends. This sort of technical virtuosity won the constant admiration of his production men, like Mel Griffin, for whom Mr Sam's long-term vision was a constant source of wonder and admiration.[97]

In strategic terms, Sam's wartime problem was the severe restrictions on production imposed by government — beginning with limited grain allocations and culminating in Washington's halt in the distilling of all alcoholic beverages in October 1942. Demand remained high — remarkably so, in comparison with the alcoholically more abstemious First World War. As *Business Week* pointed out in 1943, "any distiller could easily sell twice, three times, and perhaps ten times his present volume, if he had the stocks — and bottles — or if he cared to gamble on early peace." In order to conserve inventory Sam issued strict orders to ration the company's products, cutting back particularly on low-price blends, and watched his sales dip accordingly. Having climbed remarkably in the first three years of the war, to nearly a million cases a month, Seagram sales fell in 1943 and 1944, while his competitors, particularly Schenley, did better.[98] But Sam always maintained that one of his most important achievements during the war years was to resist the temptation to cut corners. Sam felt that his arch-enemy Lew Rosenstiel had done precisely this, substituting potato and cane spirits for grain in his Schenley blends. "As a company policy, we did not compromise with the quality," he later said. "We used no substitutes. We maintained first, last and always the prewar quality of our products."[99]

Going further, as *Fortune* later observed, Sam "used the wartime period to upgrade his customer's taste." Because of the company's internal rationing, several of Seagram's cheaper blends disappeared from the shelves, and medium-priced whiskies, such as Seven Crown and Calvert Reserve, became well-established popular products. "Since whiskey prices bear little relationship to production costs," *Fortune* went on, "this proved to be a tidy piece of long-range strategy. As Sam once explained candidly, 'Lower-price blends pay a little overhead. Deluxe products are where you make the money.' "[100]

For the long term, Sam accumulated stocks of aged whiskies through expansion — a daring strategy in wartime, particularly when profits fell off markedly in 1943. Sam began buying up American distilling companies even before the U.S. entered the war, beginning with Browne-Vintners for $15 million in 1940. This purchase brought Joe Reinfeld, one of Sam's customers during U.S. Prohibition and to whom he was always loyal, into the Seagram family. DC-SL acquired British Columbia Distillery in 1941, giving Sam a major plant on the Canadian west coast, and several more American firms the next year — Bedford Distilling, Blair Distilling, Old Colonel Distillery, William Jameson, Dant and Dant, Majestic Distilling and Kasko Distillers. Wartime prompted Sam to move in another direction as well — the production of rum in the West Indies. To make up for the shortage of whisky early in the war, Seagram imported large quantities of rum from Puerto Rico into the U.S. and from Jamaica for Canadian consumption. Looking to the future, Sam purchased Long Pond Estates in Jamaica, on the north side of the Island just east of Montego Bay, giving Seagram a sugar plantation and distillery where rum could be produced and aged for eventual sale in North America and elsewhere.

In 1942 Sam took his first steps in the California wine industry — prompted by his eagerness to help out a friend, Franz Sichel, whom he had met in Europe ten years before. A Jewish refugee from Nazism, Sichel came to Montreal from Mainz, where his family had been wine merchants for several generations. Eager to re-establish himself, Sichel first took a job with Seagram as a wine and brandy consultant. Sam then helped him set up a company in California with another refugee wine merchant, Alfred Fromm, with Seagram as the major share-holder. Through Fromm and Sichel, Seagram became the sales agency for Christian Brothers, a remarkable religious order with extensive wineries and vineyards throughout California — in what proved to be a major breakthrough in the state. Sam also backed Fromm and Sichel in the purchase of the small Mount Tivey winery. While designing a label for a Mount Tivey wine, Sam was crestfallen to learn that there was, in fact, no mountain: the winery was in a valley. Looking Fromm in the eye, Sam was categorical: "Alfred, find me a mountain!" Fromm finally came across the Paul Masson Vineyard, appropriately situated in the Santa Cruz chain, high above the town of Saratoga, California.

Sam bought Paul Masson in 1943, expanded it considerably, and watched the venerable, previously moderate-sized winery, founded in 1852, grow into a $100 million-a-year operation by the mid-1960s.[101]

To maintain sales, under wartime restrictions, Sam constantly needed inventory, which accounts for his purchase of Frankfort Distilleries of Louisville, Kentucky, and its huge stock of 20 million gallons of whisky in 1943. This was Sam's major move on the marketing chessboard, and one that secured his primacy after the war. With Frankfort came the well-known Four Roses and Paul Jones brands, and also one of the most famous names in U.S. distilling. Most important, as the fifth largest liquor enterprise in North America, Frankfort had one of the most important supplies of aging bourbon in the United States. Sam paid $41,831,000 for the company, bought in what *Business Week* called the biggest whisky deal since the end of prohibition. To carry the vastly expanded inventory, Seagram arranged for a $35 million line of credit from the Bankers Trust Company and the Manufacturers Trust Company, under a revolving credit arrangement. A few months later, Seagram obtained additional, long-term credit to finance its purchase and to provide working capital — a total of $75 million, drawing on a group of twenty-three U.S. banks nationwide. With the new stocks of whisky, it was estimated at the time, Seagram could maintain sales for three more years of wartime restrictions — more than enough, as it turned out, to see the company comfortably through the war.[102]

Impressive as these acquisitions were, they looked more to the future than the present; Sam's extended inventory was intended to compensate for the years when he was not producing whisky and storing it in barrels to age for the eventual postwar years. In the short run, Schenley's decision to meet demand by adopting substitutes for grain spirits paid off, enabling Rosenstiel to sell more whisky and expand his market share. Climbing to 20 percent of case sales, Schenley recaptured the leadership it had lost to Seagram in 1938; despite his impressive success with Four Roses, Sam's share dipped to 17 percent, where it remained until 1947. "I let him go for a few years," Sam later said. "Yes, it was bad whisky. I sat and let him take it." After the war, as *Fortune* pointed out, the public grew suspicious of substitutes for grain spirits, and Seagram recovered its lead—another vindication, Sam always thought, of his decision to maintain quality.[103]

■

THROUGHOUT THE WAR, Sam worked in a public environment charged with both anti-Jewish feeling and an aggressive neo-temperance campaign that targeted the Bronfman family and certainly threatened their interests. In Montreal, as wartime prosperity pumped money into the hands of new social groups, members of the old English and Scottish families that had once dominated society felt increasingly on the defensive. "For the first time, money began really to count," reported an unhappy member of the old élite. "You couldn't keep up the old style of life without it. Servants were very hard to get and demanded high wages. The *nouveaux riches* didn't know or care about who had been important before they came to town."[104] There was no appreciable change in the prewar anti-Jewish climate, the smug and sometimes vicious nativism that stigmatized Jews as unpatriotic, un-British or war profiteers. Anti-Jewish assumptions lay undisturbed in common speech, anti-Jewish bias kept jobs closed to Jewish applicants, and anti-Jewish stereotypes remained unchallenged in ordinary views of the world. With the outbreak of war, a good deal of anti-Jewish propaganda went underground or disappeared because it appeared transparently pro-fascist; in Quebec, however, where nationalist sentiment remained powerful and capable of challenging federal authorities, antisemitism had its place in the rhetoric of the right.

Numbering about 160,000 or around one percent of the population, many of them post-First World War immigrants, Canadian Jews took their vulnerability for granted, just as they had in the prewar period. Jews had no doubt that they were marginal in Canadian society, not mainstream; they scarcely questioned their exclusion from government and the civil service, and knew they were without influence and relatively alone. Sam Bronfman accurately reflected this community when he took such care, in his own public activity, to appear in the best public light, to reduce anxieties about Jews, and to drape himself in the flag. On both the Quebec and the national scenes, Sam said nothing publicly to cause offence. He kept his head down when antisemitic accusations flew, as they occasionally did, in the press. He made sure there was no Seagram advertising in the Jean-Charles Harvey's anti-nationalist, liberal newspaper *Le Jour*, lest he give credence to the periodic charges that the paper was being backed by the Jews.[105] He avoided public controversy, shunned the militant segments of the Jewish community, and generally left it to his subordinates, like Saul Hayes, to complain to government about Jewish internees or excluded refugees.

A good illustration of Sam's approach is what happened beginning in November 1943, when Quebec Opposition Leader and former premier Maurice Duplessis let fly with a preposterous allegation that an "international Zionist brotherhood" was seeking to settle one hundred thousand Jewish refugees in Quebec. However exceptional such rhetoric may have been in his career, Duplessis's charges "struck a responsive chord in the prevailing anti-refugee, or anti-Jewish, spirit in Quebec," as Abella and Troper note. In the controversy that followed, it was considered unthinkable to expose Sam to a counter-attack, and it was H.M. Caiserman, not Bronfman, who published "An Open Letter to the Hon. Mr Maurice Duplessis," and a Jewish parliamentarian, Maurice Hart, not the head of the Canadian Jewish Congress, who forced the issue into the public consciousness. Sam did speak as the controversy over Duplessis's charges raged, but his words communicated the genuine vulnerability many Jews felt during the 1940s, not an outraged rejection of antisemitism. "SAMUEL BRONFMAN FINDS JEWS HATE PAROCHIALISM; ARE NOT STIFF-NECKED," declared a carefully worded headline in the *Canadian Jewish Chronicle*, accurately reporting Sam's address to the Dominion Council of the Congress in December. In his highly apologetic speech Sam prudently avoided any reference to the Duplessis controversy or to antisemitism generally, pleading rather for the recognition of Jewish patriotism and commitment to the war effort.[106]

Sam's vulnerability as a Jew was compounded, especially in English Canada, by his unpopularity in some circles as a nefarious whisky man — an old charge, but one that was not quite dead and buried owing to the revival of wartime temperance sentiment. Cultivating this theme in 1941, Sam's former antagonist Rabbi Eisendrath fired away at whisky, decrying the "two hundred millions of dollars spent for 'booze' in the midst of a war to save civilization." From a less friendly quarter, the *United Church Observer* blasted liquor advertising and sales, denouncing Sam Bronfman in particular — "whom many in Saskatchewan will remember in another connection," it said. Predictably, the *Observer* was not impressed by Leacock's book on Canada. "It is a bid to the respectable elements in society for recognition on the part of a business which more than any other is unworthy of such recognition," the paper went on. "Westerners into whose hands this book comes, with its religious references and high idealism, will be thinking back a few years — and wondering." Nastiest of all was the *Moose Jaw Times Herald*: "When it comes to controlling the liquor traffic, or even wartime restrictions on consumption," the paper editorialized, "we are caught between the Bronfman interests, on the one hand, and the Bootlegger menace on the other hand. These two are allies and form a pincer movement. It but remains for action at Ottawa to show whether or not the Bronfman-Brewery-Bootlegger axis has a free people licked in regard to national liquor control for total war effort."[107]

Although most Canadians opposed a ban on the sale of alcohol, the wet majority eroded dramatically during 1942. Gallup found that while 72 percent of those surveyed rejected prohibition in February of that year, only 57 percent did so by December.[108] Politicians knew they had an important anti-liquor constituency, and there were regular delegations to Ottawa to remind them that temperance was alive and well. United Church lobbyists visited Mackenzie King regularly to ask for restrictions on alcohol, and were surprisingly well received by the prime minister, whose diary suggests that he was much more concerned with the beer and liquor questions than he was with the appeals on behalf of European Jewish refugees. King's confidential entries show him strongly opposed to alcohol advertising and consumption, even if unwilling to steamroller cabinet supporters of "the liquor interests," as he quaintly described them. "What was important," a pugnacious prime minister told the Liberal caucus on March

24, 1943, "was that the people should know whether we were a Government controlled by these interests or not."[109]

The Reverend Dr James R. Mutchmor, Secretary of the Board of Evangelism and Social Service of the United Church and its most visible official, was one of Sam's most vocal opponents during the war, hounding him constantly as an ex-bootlegger with undue influence in the federal government. In 1944, Mutchmor and a colleague, Dr John Coburn, publicly denounced Agriculture Minister Jimmy Gardiner, himself a former United Church official, for surrendering to the beer and liquor industries and for his associations with the Bronfmans. Gardiner, a teetotaller and a man of high principle, defended himself ably in a letter to the Board's Secretary, alluding to Allan's role in the meeting featuring Eleanor Roosevelt:

> I must say that it did not strike me as being anything to boast about that one of the Bronfmans, whom I do not know, was chairman at Mrs Roosevelt's meeting at Montreal. On the other hand, I noticed in the paper two or three days ago that he was also chairman at another meeting which had to do with the running of a hospital in Montreal which apparently is doing one of the best works being done in that city. Apparently some people in Montreal think he has good qualities, and I must say from reading his speech which was reported in the Gazette that he made a speech which would sound much better from some of the pulpits than some preachers make.[110]

"I take people as I find them," the minister continued evenly. But not everyone was impressed by Gardiner's low-keyed approach to the liquor question and the Bronfmans. Later that year the socialist premier of Saskatchewan, T.C. Douglas, heard a sermon denouncing Sam in Regina and immediately telephoned the minister, the Reverend J.S. Leith, to offer congratulations.[111] Towards the end of the war Douglas also repeated a United Church allegation that Sam was reaping huge profits by monopolizing the production of penicillin—charges that were thoroughly refuted by Health Minister Brooke Claxton who denied that any distiller was making the drug. Evidently, when it came to the Bronfmans, some people were prepared to shoot from the hip.[112]

Shrill and dogmatic, even by the standards of the 1940s, such accusations were nevertheless heard in Ottawa, where the astute saw Sam Bronfman as a political liability. Thus it was to Saidye, and not Sam, that the government turned in awarding an Order of the British Empire for war service in May 1943. Sam's long-time friend Deputy Minister of Revenue David Sim sat on the awards committee and later commented to Terence Robertson: "I don't remember anybody actually saying that Sam should not be honored. In fact, it was generally accepted that both he and his wife should be recognized for the contributions they were making to the war effort. But it did seem fairly safe to assume that any recommendation that Sam should be in some way rewarded or decorated by the Crown on the government's recommendation would receive considerable political opposition."[113] Sim slipped word to Sam about his wife's OBE on a rainy Sunday in May 1943, and he immediately called Saidye at Ste Marguerite: "I want you and the girls to take the train into town," he told her. "I'll meet you at home at five o'clock." As soon as Saidye opened the door, Sam appeared in the hallway, mysteriously knelt down before her and declared, "The King thinks as much of you as I do."[114]

Sam gave every sign of enthusiasm at Saidye's honour, and if he was disappointed at being passed over himself he left no indication whatever. "The children were jumping with excitement," Saidye wrote, recalling the festivity, "and the first thing I did was to phone my dear parents in Winnipeg, to tell them of the great honour. Then I paraded around singing patriotic songs, and the two girls followed me." Later, the children dubbed the award "The Order of the Boiled Egg." Sam and Phyllis accompanied Saidye to the awards ceremony in Ottawa later that autumn. Minda, at Smith College and unable to attend, congratulated "the most beautiful, gracious OBE that Canada has ever had." "Please write me a *detailed* account of the proceedings," she continued. "Was terribly sorry that I couldn't be with you on such a joyous and unique occasion, but such is life — but when Pops is knighted I'll be around to give Sir Samuel a big smack!"[115]

Sensing that little was to be won from the government on the subject of Jewish refugees during the last three years of war, Sam left to Saul Hayes most of the task of appealing to officials in Ottawa, trying to see the prime minister or seeking advice from well-disposed gentiles like Senator Cairine Wilson. Together with Toronto leader Ben Sadowski, Laz Phillips and others, Sam counselled caution, censoring Hayes's tone of bitter disappointment in his letters to the government over refugees, for example.[116] Sam did lead a group of Congress officials to see Mines and Resources Minister Crerar and his immigration director Blair on June 4, 1943, but Hayes spoke for the delegation and no change in government policy ensued. Never one to waste effort in a hopeless cause, Sam seems to have withdrawn, in large measure, from the frustrating efforts to open the doors of immigration to Canada.

As in his business, however, Sam turned his attention to the long term — on which only a small group of Jewish visionaries spent much time in the nightmare years of the Second World War. During 1940, Sam first met Nahum Goldmann, the handsome, worldly leader of the World Jewish Congress, who became one of his most important mentors in Jewish life. Goldmann was an international statesman of weight and experience; he was the kind of man, moreover, to whom Sam had always been attracted — one of the "top people" in Jewish politics, as even his enemies conceded. Goldmann was also one of the very few to look, quite early in the war, to the challenge of saving a remnant of European Jewry and securing their existence after the conflict was over. Sam heard him at the first Pan-American Jewish Conference in Baltimore in November 1941, at the Inter-American Jewish Council of which he was elected vice-chairman in February 1942, and again at the War Emergency Conference in Atlantic City in November 1944. Based in the United States for much of the war, Goldmann appeared regularly in Canada — speaking at least once at a Congress plenary, addressing Zionist meetings, and, in the spring of 1944, making an appeal on behalf of Zionism to Prime Minister Mackenzie King. Sam became friendly with the World Jewish Congress leader, who was one of the few people who viewed Sam Bronfman as modest and self-effacing. During the war, Sam offered cautious support to Goldmann's ideas, but no more; Goldmann, who acknowledged no equal as a maker of Jewish grand strategy, treated Sam politely in this period, but was hardly his intimate. "Samuel Bronfman," Goldmann commented in his memoirs with characteristic hauteur, "knew the limitations of his competence. In Jewish-political affairs I was the decisive authority for him, and he did nothing before first consulting with me."[117]

Goldmann's influence may have been responsible for Sam's somewhat more assertive Jewish posture on international affairs at the very end of the war, particularly looking towards a postwar Jewish state in Palestine. Until the conflict was over, however, Sam's Jewish politics, marked by restraint, caution and circumspection in dealing with public authorities, were those of the community he led and reflected the forbidding climate that so many of them felt.

CHAPTER VII

Postwar Visions

BRIGHT AND VIVACIOUS, Minda was Sam's eldest child, nearly twenty-one at the end of the war. Minda remembered Sam approaching her one day at Ste Marguerite in the Laurentians, with a serious message. "He used *the voice*," she recalled, "the voice parents used when they have to tell children something." Any number of possibilities immediately occurred to Minda, all of them embarrassing. What Sam had in mind, however, was more awkward than anything she feared; to her surprise, her father wanted to talk about money. "You are of age, my girl," Sam said, "and it is time you knew just how much money you have." "For the first time," a *Fortune* writer later noted, "she understood the scope of the Bronfman fortune: in 1950 her share of Seagrams' dividends alone would be some $200,000." "You are an heiress and don't ever forget it," Sam told his daughter sternly. "A lot of men may seem to be interested in you but in fact will be more interested in your money. If you fall in love make sure the man is sincere and not just another fortune hunter."[1] As usual Sam was thinking about the future. "I was absolutely horrified," Minda later reported, shuddering at the responsibility.

In 1946, Sam was fifty-seven and his other children, Phyllis, Edgar and Charles, were in their teens. When he spoke to Minda, he had been ruminating for some time about his Seagram empire, his children and himself. He had also been working furiously, and his entire family worried about him. "You are for the most part tired and distraught," Saidye wrote to Sam in June, when he was on the *Queen Mary*, sailing for London: "My patience is being tried. So let us find a solution where we can have each other to enjoy and cherish with our precious four. I feel that it is paramount now and I know you agree with me wholeheartedly."[2] "I pray that in your discussions and dealings that you can in some way resolve your personal problems," Saidye added a few weeks later. Sam's children joined in the chorus, telling him to slow down. "I trust that you are having a wonderful time," Phyllis wrote to him from Vassar, "for heaven's sake take it easy."[3] Minda spoke in a similar vein: "Remember Charles' and our frequent admonitions and don't take on too much responsibility. You have often mentioned the story whose punch line is 'Relax and enjoy it!' — Go thou and do likewise. . . ."[4] From Trinity College School in Port Hope, Ontario, seventeen-year-old Edgar mimicked his father: "Today I am taking a rest for myself, because I realize that one must be in good physical health to be able to write good exams, and I cannot afford to let myself be run down. The same goes double for you. You must now above all other things take care of your physical health, because we would all much rather live in poverty with a healthy Pappy than live in luxury with a man that continually worries himself into all kinds of ills. I know that everyone has to do a certain amount of worrying as you yourself said, but don't you think you have done much more than your share?"[5]

Sam's worries concerned the postwar direction of his Seagram empire, and as one of his options he had been toying with the idea of moving to London and taking control of what he suspected was the crumbling assets of the once-powerful British DCL. "Little Samuelie could go to town," his wife mused to him at the prospect. "If you want my reaction — it would be O.K. with me, if we can all be together and live like we have been accustomed to in the past." Still, there is no doubt that leaving Montreal would have meant an enormous sacrifice. Perhaps to communicate this, Saidye told her husband how much she appreciated their home on Belvedere Road, after just returning from New York. "I am writing this out of doors. What a wonderful feeling to be home, so much more security and how glorious everything looks and how deeply I appreciate this glorious house. The grounds, the peonies in full bloom, the roses, the trees are truly a heavenly sight. So serene, peaceful and quiet."[6]

While Sam plotted his next move, his twenty-fourth wedding anniversary found him still in England. "I am grateful to the Almighty for my good fortune in having you my darling for my husband," Saidye wrote to him. "You have been a wonderful life partner — and have made my twenty-four years seem but only yesterday. And at the same time, I cannot think of my life having been spent without you. . . . My heart is full — and also my eyes. I love you my darling with a love that is deep, strong and eternal. God bless you. Saidye."[7] Moved by her words, Sam replied immediately: "God bless you my sweet one — you are wonderful. The letter you wrote me on our anniversary is a masterpiece I shall keep it and cherish it forever. You have certainly developed greatly in your expressions and I love it. I love the thoughts and the heart that prompts them, [the] hand that pens them and I love you altogether."[8]

As in 1933, when he took the plunge into the huge U.S. market, Sam was prepared after the war for a major shift in the scale of his business operations. But again as in 1933, he brooded on how this would affect his family and their future. Sam reassured Saidye that she and the children remained his priority. "First and foremost my darling it is not good at all without you," he wrote from the Savoy Hotel. "I never did like being away from you ever since 'God made you mine' but thank God our love grows and flows so fiercely. I find it harder now being away from you than in the earlier days. On top of that being farther away than usual from our Magnificent Four adds a bit to distance and time. I keep taking stock of ourselves daily and hourly. Balance sheet results wonderful love account a million percent dividends above a million percent. . . . The important thing is to be together wherever it is and enjoy each other and our babes, God bless them."[9]

Saidye shared this with her daughters, as Minda told her father on June 15, reminding him of how he was the centre of their universe. "Your letter came tonight as your three loved and loving women were seated at dinner . . . it was the nicest part of the day and I am so glad that we were together and alone — thus able to enjoy it to the hilt. We loved every line and realized what a romantic guy you really are. Hope to heaven my hubby writes me love letters after 24 years of hitching!"[10]

Two days later, Saidye wrote to Sam on Father's Day, which she had spent with Phyllis and Minda. Once again, the message was full of love and devotion: "We spoke of you a great deal and your ears certainly should have been burning. Minda feels so much closer to you than she did and understands — and therefore has a great admiration for you. Phyllis says she would like to know you better and hopes that opportunity will be given her soon."[11]

■

SAM REPORTED AN excellent crossing on the *Queen Mary* in June 1946 — noteworthy, as were all of the earliest postwar sailings, because they signalled, for a small élite at least, the renewal of international mobility after six grim years of war. There were 825 civilians among the 1,450 people on board — all in the single class then used for transatlantic crossings — including former British War Minister Leslie Hore-Belisha, U.S. Admiral Harold Stark, and the British Labour leader Sir Walter Citrine. "A good crowd," Sam commented, mentioning also a group of scientists from all over the Empire travelling to England to consult with British colleagues and noting proudly to Saidye that the group included twelve from Canada.[12]

Together with his Montreal general manager, John MacLean, Sam reached London just in time for spectacular victory celebrations held that summer — including a two-hour military parade that he watched from an office window on Park Lane, as thrilled as a small boy. "First came the royal carriage," he told his wife. "We were quite close to it as we went across the street so we were right on the road where they passed. Then we saw all the high officers, generals etc. of all the allied nations (except Russia). . . . It was a great sight seeing all these representing so many nations coming all these great distances to take part. Then came the mechanized parade consisting of all the various planes, trucks, mine sweepers and many weapons we never heard of, all mounted on great trucks."

Sam was captivated by London. With MacLean, he reported
to Saidye, he set out at midnight, walking for hours together with
hundreds of thousands of celebrants — "down the Strand by
Charing Cross Road to Trafalgar Square, thence past our old
Carlton to St James, then to Piccadilly and down Piccadilly to
here. . . . It is not the same kind of crowd as we knew, and many
people were not even in dinner dress. . . . There are a lot of
buildings that show where the blitz hit and there are a lot of
vacant spaces where buildings were. But I am told that the
biggest damage is in the city across the river — have not been
there yet but will go first chance I get."[13] Sam and MacLean
stood in awe of the devastation around St Paul's Cathedral, heard
an intense parliamentary debate on the Finance Bill, and tried to
get a feel for the year-old Labour government of Clement Attlee.
"In spite of the many socialistic schemes and ideas presently
under consideration by the government," MacLean reported on
his first impression, "the feeling in high financial circles is that
they possess a lot of experience and good sense and that they will
yet guide the country back to a better world in the future."[14]

Looking over the field after several years' absence, Sam saw
firsthand how severely weakened was the whisky industry in the
U.K. as it faced its North American competitors. Although
Britain badly needed exports because of her heavy load of debt
and her dependence on imports, things were slow to improve.
The Labour government, some felt, were not doing all they
might to assist the whisky industry. Manufacturers continued to
operate under severe wartime restrictions: first, limitations on
shipping, and second, the rationing of barley, despite the urgings
of Winston Churchill who feared mightily for the future of
Scotch whisky — "this characteristic British element of ascendancy," as he put it, doubtless speaking from the heart, given his
own prodigious consumption.[15]

Sam had hoped to get control of Highland Distillers, an
important group of Scottish whisky makers, and he likely had his
eye on an even bigger fish as well — the giant DCL itself. Sniffing
out the terrain, he met with several of his former associates in the
British conglomerate and was not impressed with the prospects
for his one-time mentors. Several of his British colleagues had
aged considerably. Sir James Wilkinson and Peter Dewar had

already retired, "and it looks like the DCL is not going to be what she used to be," he told Saidye. "The new fellows that are coming in their place don't belong on the same street with the old set," he concluded.[16]

Sam spent more than a month abroad, eventually joined by Allan, Laz Phillips and several DC-SL executives. He returned to Montreal empty-handed later that summer, without any major deals in Britain and, having decided rather to clear the way for Canadian exports to the U.K., Sam felt that the British whisky industry was too weak and the governmental climate too restrictive for him to enter via any new partnership arrangement. Instead, he set his course upon expansion elsewhere, while maintaining his home base in Montreal.

With the war over, Sam found himself in a remarkably strong position. For one thing, blends, always his strong suit, had become extremely popular. Wartime restrictions, eventually shutting off entirely the production of new whisky in the United States, had forced all producers to stretch their stocks to keep up with demand. Stretching meant blends — even for those distillers formerly committed to straights — as every producer felt obliged to cut aged whiskies with neutral spirits. Constituting 30 percent of the U.S. output in 1941, blends reached 87 percent in 1946, shifting the consuming habits of Americans significantly in Sam's direction.[17]

Industrial concentration in the United States, however, had intensified competition by reducing the whisky stocks available to fill shortfalls. Concentration had been under way since the 1930s, and at the end of the war four major distillers shared about 75 percent of sales, as opposed to less than 50 percent before the conflict began. These distillers, known as the Big Four, "met each other warily in the cage of relatively fixed consumption," as *Fortune* put it. Having expanded considerably during the war, the market size remained stable, while the major producers battled over their respective shares.[18] Through the latter part of the war Rosenstiel's Schenley brands did better than Sam's whiskies, but Seagram nosed ahead in 1947 giving evidence, as *Business Week* put it, that "quality came back to its own."[19] In 1948 Seagram was in the lead with 25 percent, Schenley had 23 percent, National Distillers 16 percent and Hiram Walker 10 percent. Sam's explanation of his success was that while Rosenstiel had enjoyed a temporary advantage by using cane or potato spirits in a time of shortage, the postwar public preferred the labels that had consistently maintained standards by using grains.

This success, however, created problems. Sam was unable to maintain his inventory, despite substantial wartime accumulation. Having pushed his sales to over $400 million after the war, using 18 million gallons of whisky yearly, he was in an extremely vulnerable position. Schenley's stocks were more than twice as large, although its annual production required only 15 million gallons. Distributors of Three Feathers, one of Rosenstiel's brands, began an advertising campaign boosting the quality of the aged whisky making up its blends; the implication was that Seagram, reportedly cutting down on the proportion of aged whiskies in some of its blends as a conservation measure, was short-changing its customers.

Without realizing it, Sam suffered other problems that derived from the extraordinary growth of his company. While very much in command, he had never given much thought to organization, and the complex, sprawling structure that emerged from the war did not lend itself easily to efficient management and control. Headquartered on Peel Street in Montreal, Distillers Corporation-Seagrams Limited was his holding company, of which Sam and his family owned 53 percent of the shares, with the rest trading on Wall Street. DC-SL was the sole owner of several Canadian companies and the American branch, Joseph E. Seagram & Sons, based in the Chrysler Building in New York. As well as being a holding company in its own right, Seagram in the U.S. was both involved in production and owned three main sales subsidiaries that competed actively with one another: Seagram-Distillers Corp. (Seven Crown, Gallagher & Burton, Ancient Bottle Gin and the imported Canadian V.O.); Frankfort Distillers Corp. (Four Roses, Hunter, Paul Jones and Wilson); and Calvert Distillers Corp. (Lord Calvert, Carstairs and Calvert Reserve).[20] At the end of the war, as a result of a remarkable growth in liquor sales and Sam's significant expansion, these companies formed an industrial colossus — with sales of over $475 million in 1946 and profits, after taxes, of nearly $25 million. Sam presided over this enormous enterprise—"the president of presidents," as he liked to term himself—a job that even Sam Bronfman had difficulty carrying out.

To do so, Sam relied upon several highly talented barons of the realm—key retainers who believed in his philosophy of the whisky business and his religion of quality. Among his closest associates in the Chrysler Building were the heads of Seagram's three giant sales companies: William Wachtel of Calvert, who, as we have seen, was an intimate of Sam; Ellis D. Slater, of Frankfort Distillers Corp.; and Vic Fischel, a red-haired Montrealer who became president of Seagram-Distillers Corp. in 1947. General Frank Schwengel, Sam's prewar sales veteran, took over corporate public relations, shoring up the company's position in the halls of Congress and in the various state bureaucracies; the General also headed the American holding and operating company, Joseph E. Seagram & Sons. The financial boss of the empire was Jim Friel, a quiet-spoken Irishman who had been with Sam since repeal and who had a major hand in company administration as well. On Peel Street, Sam's closest associates included tall and craggy-faced Jim McAvity, a former Ridley College football star, war hero and his top Canadian salesman; Merle "Schneck" Schneckenburger, his advertising manager and a fervent loyalist; Alex Goldberg, who joined the company as a salesman in 1938 and later took over the rum operations, particularly in Jamaica; and the urbane Quintin Gwyn, in charge of international sales then operating out of the Montreal office.

But none of these personalities could set any independent course without Sam, who was the only real CEO of the entire group.[21] Seagram's sales companies, one should note, had no say about the whisky that went into the bottles they sold, or about the credit that might be extended to their wholesalers, or sometimes even what advertising they used. To newcomers it seemed that Sam controlled virtually everything and that he operated almost entirely on impulse.

Generally speaking, Sam remained far more at home with the world of whisky—both production and sales—than with the financing of his business, to which he devoted far less time and attention, and in which his main concern seems to have been to avoid long-term debt. When it came to finances, he relied heavily on his lieutenants, particularly Jim Friel, whose competence he deeply respected, and who was one of the only people in New York who called the boss "Sam." "You know, Jim Friel really has a way with the banks," Sam told Edgar one day. "Father, let me tell you something," Edgar replied, "with a balance sheet like yours anybody can have their way with the banks."[22]

Future Canadian auditor-general Maxwell Henderson, who joined Seagram's Canadian headquarters at the end of the war, believed the organization was a complete shambles. Henderson remembered being ushered into Sam's office on Peel Street: "Sam Bronfman, a cherubic figure of about fifty-five, sitting behind an enormous desk in the most ornate office I had ever seen, talked to me at length not about the duties I would have to perform but about the politics and people of the day. He was sounding me out as to the people I knew and the extent to which they could be valuable to him." A few days later, dining with John MacLean at the Chateau Laurier Hotel, Henderson learned what all Sam's lieutenants already knew: "everything was decided on the basis of emotions and family interests." "There was no such thing as an organizational chart or any definition of lines of authority," Henderson learned. "You got approval for what you wanted to do directly from Mr Sam or you went to his brother, Mr Allan, who appeared to possess authority in certain understood areas. Otherwise you acted at your own risk. Everyone from the switchboard operators up had their own individual mandates directly from Mr Sam or Mr Allan. Mr Sam, whether in his office in Montreal or at the one in the Chrysler Building in New York, was like a juggler keeping a number of balls constantly in the air. Mr. Allan probably made the greatest use of the long-distance telephone of anybody in North America. Unfortunately neither he nor Mr Sam ever made notes of what was said in their far-flung conversations, so that the bases for decisions and the intercompany lines of communication were always in a state of confusion."[23]

The real head office, as insurance specialist Robert Ruppel testifies, was wherever Sam was at any given time. And whenever he appeared, lines of responsibility could become extraordinarily fluid. "Mr Sam could beckon to you in the hallway," he recalls, "and charge you with some responsibility or another." Often totally unexpected, such commissions sent people down paths for which they felt totally unprepared, yet at the same time uniquely challenged. This meant plenty of room for initiative and sometimes an atmosphere of high excitement; it could also produce disasters, particularly when people overestimated their authority or the familiarity that Sam seemed to have shown them.[24] Different judgements about this system, or lack of system, are possible, but it is hard to believe that it derived from any carefully planned scheme. Seagram, says Edgar about those days, was "a company that was absolutely the worst managed in the business."[25]

Sam's personal loyalties, interests and commitments interfered constantly with his executives' decision-making. One of his beliefs, for example, was that his three sales companies should compete actively with each other as if they were completely unrelated. Calvert's successes, he told William Wachtel once, would get Seagram off its fanny. He didn't care which of his three companies were numbers one, two and three in the industry, he used to say — just so long as the top three were his companies. But in practice, Sam's Seagram brands were closest to his heart, as Wachtel learned one day, when the boss came charging into his office. Calvert had just outdistanced Seagram in sales and had run full-page ads across the United States in celebration:

CALVERT IS THE LARGEST SELLING WHISKEY IN NEW YORK —
CALVERT IS THE LARGEST SELLING WHISKEY IN AMERICA —
CALVERT IS THE LARGEST SELLING WHISKEY IN THE WORLD

Howls of pain rose from the Seagram offices in the Chrysler Building. Brandishing a copy of the ad, Sam told his Calvert chief, "Bill, the name of the company is Seagram, and they are wild!" Standing firm, Wachtel reminded Sam that the sales companies were supposed to compete with one another. Was Sam changing his mind? "No," he replied, "but I am making you

director of our parent company, and now you have to work with
me on company policy." "I looked at him in amazement,"
Wachtel later reported, "realizing then how he had outfoxed
me."[26]

"As long as the Seagram divisions had autonomy and were
headed up by strong individuals, the companies prospered and
we all went ahead," observed Philip Kelly, a leading light in the
Carstairs organization, which was part of the Calvert company.[27]
Sam's own dynamism and sixth sense for the future of the
industry drove the machine forward as well, but as the size of the
operation grew and the lines of authority became more confused
difficulties began to emerge. Kelly left the Seagram organization
after a time, and while he missed the genial chaos of the Chrysler
Building he was plainly worn out by the constant, low-grade
crisis he faced on a daily basis.

Seagram's postwar standing made Sam a prominent figure in the
U.S. business world, profiled flatteringly in 1948 in *Fortune* as
"the whiskey king of America." One would hardly guess from
seeing him, said the caption beneath a photograph of a
particularly benign and cheerful-looking Sam, that he was "one
of the last great tycoons, a vestigial reminder of the gone days
when a Vanderbilt or a Rockefeller could actually start from
scratch and create a family fortune of more than a hundred
million dollars." "There is something of the bright boy grown up
about him," *Fortune* continued, "as if he had got what he wanted
and yet is still on his way, as if he had swallowed the canary and
knows where there is another one."[28] Sam had obviously been on
his best behaviour for the *Fortune* interviewers, who described
him as suave and casual, with impeccable manners — although
they did take note of occasional "indelicate language."

Sam's personal wealth evoked some interest, but in an age of
less intrusive journalism there was no discussion of his private
finances beyond *Fortune's* vague allusion to a family fortune of a
hundred million dollars. Most of this was still in company shares,
divided within the family, as we have seen, some ten years before.
At the end of the war, Sam and his seven brothers and sisters
owned just over half the shares of DC-SL, the net assets of which
amounted to $108 million in 1945.[29] A Canadian publication in

1949 noted that Sam "denies being the second wealthiest man in America, and he doesn't even think he's among the top ten. He has no hankering to be," *New Liberty* continued. "He doesn't know how he ranks in Canada, but is probably among the top three."[30] Sam himself remained noncommittal.

In his private life, Sam was an unlikely model of the rich tycoon, and his behaviour hardly fit the conventional image of an exceptionally wealthy person. "He was of a generation . . . who kept pinching themselves in case this was all a dream," says Edgar, "and 'they' were going to take it all away." ("They" were usually the "goyim," the non-Jews who figured importantly in Sam's mind as a menacing force that might some day turn on him.)[31] Although much preoccupied with how the family's fortune was to be divided, as we shall see, Sam remained ill at ease with money. "He hates being rich," Minda observed in the mid-1960s, doubtless recalling her father's disapproval of her own palatial Parisian house. "I live a hell of a lot better than he does," Edgar commented at the same time.[32]

Within the company, Sam's economy-minded idiosyncrasies were famous. Employees remember Sam turning out the lights in offices, irritated at the waste of electricity. This may have been a throwback to his impoverished childhood in Brandon, when he and his siblings were castigated for wasting oil, a precious commodity. Over drinks in his office one day, a visitor commented that the Schweppes soda water Sam used with his whisky probably cost more than the whisky itself. Outraged, he told his secretary: no more Schweppes. "It's expensive. Thirty-five cents a bottle!"[33] Others remember Sam insisting on carrying his own suitcase in hotels, and clipping newspaper coupons for money-saving bargains. He was notoriously uncomfortable in stores, and loathed spending money in them. Saidye recalled shopping on Fifth Avenue in New York once with Sam and his sister Rose. Rather than buying the hat she wanted, which cost $45, Sam took the saleslady's card and bought the hat afterwards by telephone, having it sent to his hotel. "I don't want my sister to know I'd let you spend that much money on a hat," was his explanation.[34]

Sam had a horror of poverty, as we have seen. On rare occasions he recalled with extreme discomfort the penury he had known as a child and youth in the west—to the point that this seemed too painful even to mention. On the other hand, although he abhorred ostentatious spending, Sam insisted on the best for his wife, his children and his home—much like his obsession with quality in his business and his striving to be the top of the line in whisky—"the silken gown of the industry," as he used to say. Phyllis recalls her father's exhaustive research into furs at Holt Renfrew's in Montreal when buying Saidye a fur coat. Here too, he wanted "the best," and was not prepared to accept anyone else's certification of quality, at least not without careful inquiry on his own.[35]

Sam dressed extremely well—Arthur Gelber, an acquaintance, vividly remembers his tailor-made shirts—and enjoyed the quality that money could provide. But wealth had its obligations, as he lectured Charles on the occasion of his *bar mitzvah*: "To you who have been born to many comforts, your lot entails corresponding responsibilities. I cannot impress upon you to emphatically the ideal of service to the less fortunate than yourself." Wealth could never be taken for granted. "Do you have any idea what your sister spent for her house?" Sam once asked Edgar pointedly, referring to Minda's lavish accommodations. Edgar, then married with two children, was not impressed by the amount, claiming to have spent a comparable sum on his own house. "Yes," Sam told him, "but you're an earner."[36]

In Sam's mind, wealth stirred up deep feelings of insecurity, his sense of the fragility of his achievements that had been the product of so much toil and struggle. "Shirtsleeves to shirtsleeves in three generations," his children remember him saying. "I'm worried about the third generation. Empires have come and gone."[37] His fear, as Edgar points out now, was that he had no control over that third generation and the future they would fashion for the Seagram empire. "Blood counts," he repeated from time to time; his children would be fine, he felt, but beyond them he could never by sure. Here was one more worry for "the whiskey king of America."[38]

"FOR CANADIAN JEWRY," writes Irving Abella, "a new period of its development was ushered in after the Second World War. The raucous dynamism that marked the earlier phase of Jewish life was abruptly stilled by the trauma of the Holocaust and by the fragility of the tiny new Jewish state in the Middle East. The world had become too dangerous a place for Jews to allow themselves the luxury of internal dissent and divisiveness. The old economic tensions within the community dissipated. The radicalism and feistiness of the twenties and thirties seemed sadly out of place in the changed world of the fifties, sixties and seventies."[39] Some historians have referred to the first two postwar decades as a time of *"sha shtil"* — an internal admonition for Jews to keep a low public profile, turn the other cheek in the face of hostility and concentrate upon the urgent tasks of postwar relief and the securing of a Jewish national home. Certainly individual Jews were self-absorbed during this period and many remained fearful, even traumatized by the antisemitism of the 1930s and the war years. Activists within the Jewish community and some leading Jewish professionals, however, followed a different path in political and legal challenges to the discrimination Jews had known — striking down restrictive covenants in the sale of properties and eventually enshrining equal treatment in federal and provincial laws.

In postwar Europe, about a million Jews outside the Soviet Union had survived the depredations of Nazism, and more than a year after the guns were silent, nearly 250,000 of them remained uprooted refugees. Gaunt and disoriented in 1945, the pathetic, skeletal victims of Nazism had not disappeared in 1946 and 1947; on the contrary, many remained at the scene of the ghastly crimes against them, a standing affront to the world that was unable or unwilling to bring their trials to an end. Anti-Jewish outbreaks in Eastern Europe, notably the pogrom in the Polish town of Kielce in July 1946, horrified Jewish communities everywhere and seemed a portent of even more serious threats to come. Across Europe, Jewish refugees were on the move. Organized by Zionist emissaries, tens of thousands fled from east to west, many flocking into France and Italy from Eastern Europe, seeking to sail for Palestine. While there was widespread international sympathy for the Jewish remnant, Jews still in camps as well as those outside ran into a familiar obstacle: everywhere, even in Palestine to which many of them now wanted to go, the doors of immigration were closed.

Although he shared most Jews' reluctance to voice Jewish dissatisfactions publicly, Sam nevertheless expressed the frustrations within the community at the continuance of massive Jewish suffering in Europe after the defeat of Hitler. "The end of the war has not meant freedom to the Jewish people," Sam told a national meeting of the Canadian Jewish Congress in November 1945.[40] A year later, nothing had changed. "The hope for a postwar era of social and international justice, a hope which sustained the spirits of men during the darkest days of the ordeal, is still far from realization," Sam declared on the Jewish New Year, 1946. "That warm friendship which one naturally expected to ensue after a glorious comradeship-in-arms, has, singularly enough, not yet come to pass." Unusually for his New Year message, which normally avoided disputatious themes in favour of exhortations to national and Jewish unity, Sam alluded harshly to the maltreatment of Jews: "The statement that insofar as European Jewry is concerned, Hitler won his war, is not entirely without its foundation in fact. The 'displaced person' — the cold epithet by which the human wreckage of the war is designated in contemporary documents — is today, seventeen months after V-Day, more displaced and misplaced than ever. One gets the impression, indeed, that a fate even worse than that of a 'forgotten people' has overtaken European Jewry — the fate of a people misremembered, daily mistaken for enemy when it is ally, and for foe when it is friend."[41]

Fearing a postwar economic slump, worried about the demobilization of hundreds of thousands of servicemen, and wary of any new influx of foreigners, Canadian leaders clung rigidly to the administrative status quo: the gates of the country remained shut to virtually all refugees — all except the tiny handful who could claim to be "agriculturalists having sufficient means to farm in Canada." Canadian policy, contended A.L. Jolliffe, the new director of immigration, quite properly reflected "class and race discrimination." "Some form of discrimination cannot be avoided," the official continued, "if immigration is to be effectively controlled in order to prevent the creation in

Canada of expanding non-assimilable racial groups. . . ."[42]
Political leaders accepted this advice, and in Ottawa the cabinet
endorsed the continuance of prewar restrictions.

Saul Hayes did what he could, trying to protect from expulsion
the small number of Jewish refugees already in Canada on
temporary visas, seeking to pry loose new visas in particular
cases, and attempting to persuade the government to be more
receptive to refugees. Within the Jewish community dissatisfaction mounted, and some even challenged the Congress's top civil
servant, suggesting that Hayes had not been forceful enough in
dealing with Ottawa. But Hayes knew better than anyone how
difficult it was to liberalize immigration policy immediately after
the war. Prime Minister Mackenzie King wanted to steer clear of
the issue, and directed complaints to the ministerial level.
Although cracks appeared in Canadian policy, notably with
pressures for liberalization coming from the Department of
External Affairs, the Canadian public preferred restrictions for at
least two years after the war. Gallup polls taken in 1946 showed
Canadians hostile to a renewed immigration from Europe and
strikingly hostile to prospective Jewish immigrants. Canadians
felt that first the Japanese, then the Jews were the most
undesirable groups for entry into Canada.[43]

By the beginning of 1947, however, there were signs the
cabinet was beginning to relent. At a discussion of immigration
policy in January, the prime minister reported in his diary, "all
were agreed that in the long range view Canada would certainly
need to have a large population." "A good deal of confusion in
the minds of all of us as to where to draw the line and how to draw
it in the matter of discrimination between different races and
peoples who wish to come to Canada," King added a few days
later. "There should be no exclusion of any particular race. That
I think has really been wiped out against the Chinese but a
country should surely have the right to determine what strains of
blood it wishes to have in its population and how its people
coming from outside have to be selected."[44]

With a new wind beginning to blow, Sam actually got to see
the prime minister on February 7, 1947, by heading a Congress
delegation with Saul Hayes and several other Jewish dignitaries.
Typically, politics played a key role in King's decision to listen.

As David Bercuson points out, several of King's top advisers had urged him to receive the representatives from Congress to undercut the Zionists, whose call for a Canadian break with British policy on Palestine was even more unpleasant for the government than the call to admit more Jews to Canada. Louis St Laurent and Brooke Claxton told the prime minister that the Congress spokesmen were "real leaders" of the Jewish community, who had "rendered a valuable service in preventing the Jewish community in Canada from taking any embarrassing attitude with respect to the Palestine difficulties."[45] North America's top distiller was ushered into the prime minister's office immediately after a delegation of temperance activists, there to praise the prime minister for his anti-alcohol moves during the war. King may have missed the connection, and claimed not to be feeling well that morning—possibly attributable to too long a sleep the previous night, he wrote in his diary. But despite distractions, political and otherwise, King was moved by what he heard from Sam's group. "I was deeply impressed by stories of distress this delegation of able leading Jewish citizens brought out," he wrote. "There was real sorrow in the faces of some of these men."[46]

Canada's doors slowly began to open in 1947, although as Sam reported to the delegates at a Congress plenary meeting in June "the situation still remains grim and tragic."[47] The Canadian government decided to receive 1,000 Jewish war orphans and also permitted entry to selected workers in the needle and fur trades, along with close relatives of Canadian citizens. But bureaucratic restrictions remained in place and Congress had to negotiate the admission of Jewish displaced persons while fighting a rearguard action against continuing discriminatory policies against Jews. Leading officials of Congress, some trade unionists and some prominent Jewish businessmen worked behind the scenes, and Sam's own role receded.

It had been an uphill struggle. Sam had never spoken more clearly about shabby treatment of Jews by his own country than he had on the refugee issue after the war. Notably, however, neither he nor the other Congress leaders voiced any bitterness about their experience afterwards, or publicly indicated any regrets about their own diplomatic approach. In retrospect, indeed, they played down the political side of the refugee issue, and referred to their activity, as Sam did when addressing Jewish leasers in Winnipeg in March 1948, as a charitable exercise. Ashamed, perhaps, that their country had let them down, and convinced that they could have done nothing more at the time, they seldom spoke of their wartime ordeals with officialdom.[48]

When survivors of the Holocaust began to arrive in Canada, Congress and allied Jewish community agencies had much to do — finding homes for children orphaned in the war, assisting newcomers when they landed, and building up the community's welfare institutions. Sam concentrated on the fund-raising that kept the entire process going, but he also oversaw the significantly expanding community apparatus. People recalled him in those days as like a king with his entourage, seeing a constant stream of visitors and intervening on behalf of this or that petitioner — often dealing with people attempting to go over the heads of the community's social services.

David Weiss came to Montreal about this time to work with displaced persons as executive director of the Baron de Hirsch Institute and the Jewish Child Welfare Bureau. He noted that Sam's practical bent put him more often than not on the side of Jewish community workers — the "Jewish civil service" as he called it — rather than prominent lay leaders. "A street-wise man who had brilliant perception in interpersonal relations," was Weiss's assessment, "the kind of attitude I was most familiar with, having come from the east side of New York." Dealing with Sam, nevertheless, was not for the faint of heart. Although committed to consensus on matters of community high politics, he could be brutally assertive on matters of detail and from time to time his anger blew like a gale through the corridors of the Congress. Weiss recalled Sam's clash one day with a leading member of the community who differed with an agency professional over the placement of an adolescent refugee. Breathing fire, as so often in his business, Sam sided with the professional: "If you don't watch out, you son of a bitch, you're gonna be on your head. This kid's right. No argument about it."[49]

Although he was by now a senior statesman and the universally acknowledged leader of Canadian Jewry, Sam lost none of his craving for public recognition and acclaim. David Rome remembers Sam's acute disappointment when the community neglected to honour him in his tenth year of service to Canadian Jewry. Sam personalized the slight, as he often did, making Saul Hayes the butt of his anger. Hayes, of course, had long since lost his taste for organizing tributes to Sam; if he held any grudge over such indignities, however, he kept it to himself. Into their second decade together, the two formed a harmonious team, and continued to complement each other remarkably.

Outside Seagram and the Jewish community, Sam still struggled for acceptance in the postwar decade, and there is no doubt that he resented his exclusion from much of gentile society. Sam liked to see his senior executives move in such circles, however, and gave freely to charities associated with them. He liked his close business associates to be well connected, and indeed chose them, in part, on the basis of whether they would help him "be somebody," as he put it. Max Henderson recalled his own case: "I was a member of the Mount Stephen Club and the St James' Club of Montreal, along with Jim McAvity and some of my other colleagues." The Bronfmans were barred from entering such clubs and could not even be the guests of their own employees. Henderson wondered why Sam continued to make donations when their members approached him. "My gentile friends were quick enough to come after him for his money," Henderson observed, "but giving him thanks in the form of the public recognition he so ardently longed for came slow indeed. He would explode with anger to me privately after some of their visits. I would be left to apologize for the behaviour of many people who certainly should have known better."[50]

One break in this pattern came in 1948, with the award of an honorary degree from the Université de Montréal. Given the university's association in times past with an ultra-nationalist, even antisemitic student milieu, this was particularly noteworthy, and it was properly signalled by the Congress's public-relations staff. This was the first time, it was pointed out, that an important French-language institution paid tribute to a Jewish leader. In bestowing the degree, Msgr Olivier Maurault singled out the "civilizing role" of "the people of the Bible," their commitment to "mutual aid," and their "genius for business." "The devotion of Mr Bronfman extends far beyond his ethnic family," the distinguished cleric told the university audience, relating Sam's extensive support for community institutions, including the Federation of Catholic Charities and the Université de Montréal. And then, at the appropriate moment, The Most Reverend Joseph Charbonneau, the University's chancellor and archbishop of Montreal, a towering figure clothed in a brilliant, ermine-trimmed gown, bent to bestow the degree upon Sam Bronfman. A photograph shows them looking into each other's eyes, each with a broad grin on his face.[51]

■

LOOKING BACK FROM our vantage point, one must keep in mind how reluctant were North American Jews before 1948 to accept the Zionist vision — the idea of a Jewish national revival with the object of reconstituting a Jewish state in Palestine. In Canada, Zionism was dominated by the Yiddishist downtown working class; an important current, it was by no means dominant in Canadian Jewry, and was certainly not the leading force in the Canadian Jewish Congress. In the United States, Zionism was also a minority movement, although it began to make serious headway in established Jewish circles during the second half of the 1930s. In both countries, the turning point came with the war against Nazism, and the catastrophe that in the end destroyed two-thirds of European Jewry, one-third of the Jewish people worldwide. The extent of this horror became widely known only in 1944 and 1945, especially with the grisly discoveries in camps liberated from the Germans. Even at the end of the war, however, while larger numbers than ever before leaned towards Zionist goals, deep hesitations remained. Did Jews really need an independent state of their own? Would Jewish support for Zionism in Canada or the United States reflect badly upon Jews' patriotism at home?

Although he had participated prominently in the United Palestine Appeal in the 1930s, Sam was certainly not known before the war as a Zionist. His commitment to the Palestine

Appeal, as his other early involvement in Jewish affairs, was essentially philanthropic; he collected money for Palestine as a charitable exercise, not as a contribution to the Jewish national endeavour. In Canada, Zionism with a national focus was the lifeblood of several organizations. The largest, the centrist Zionist Organization of Canada, came together with the religious-oriented Mizrachi and the Labour Zionists in 1940 to form the United Zionist Council of Canada to lobby on behalf of the cause. Associated with the long-time activist A.J. Freiman of Ottawa, Allan's brother-in-law, financier Samuel Zacks of Toronto, Montreal lawyer Harry Batshaw and others, the Zionist movement in Canada linked with the Zionists internationally and campaigned, throughout the war, for an eventual recognition of a Jewish national home in Palestine.

While the Canadian Jewish Congress lacked a Zionist focus, Sam himself, as national president, became drawn into the wider sphere of Jewish politics during the war years and thus came increasingly into contact with prominent Zionist spokesmen. Foremost among these was Nahum Goldmann, head of the World Jewish Congress, whom Sam had met in 1940. Sam's first high-level exposure to Zionist politics probably came through Goldmann, who was then the Washington representative of the Jewish Agency. The two struck up a friendship about this time, and saw each other at various meetings in the United States and when Goldmann came to Canada as a spokesman for the Zionist cause. Exuding charm and *bonhomie*, and very much in need of allies, Goldmann had a keen eye for people who could be useful to him, and he undoubtedly grasped the importance of Sam Bronfman's role in Canada. And Sam, while he did not necessarily embrace his friend's political views, respected the brilliant, multilingual Goldmann as the most senior Jewish statesman he knew. Sam was proud to be associated with such a distinguished and imposing figure and his sense of this reverberated through his household. "When Nahum Goldmann would . . . come to the house for dinner," Edgar recalled, "that was an occasion. That was somebody important coming to the house." Irreverently, however, the children called him "the Fox" — because of his streak of white hair.[52]

Towards the end of the war, Sam became more deeply

involved in Jewish politics on the international level. In September 1944 he attended an important organizational conference of the United Nations Relief and Rehabilitation Agency (UNRRA) in Montreal.[53]

A few months later Sam had extensive conversations with key American Jewish leaders, attempting to mediate among rival Jewish groups in the United States. This flowed from the wartime attempt of the dynamic young B'nai B'rith leader Henry Monsky, Goldmann and others, to build a common approach for American Jewry to postwar problems — including a common commitment to a Jewish national home in Palestine. Monsky's appeal led to the calling of the American Jewish Conference at the Waldorf Astoria Hotel in New York in August 1943, at which Goldmann and prominent American Zionists were present. Unfortunately for the organizers, however, the conference broke up on the question of Palestine, with some representatives refusing to accept a nationalist goal. The rift remained open, and despite his conversations in 1945 Sam had no impact on the quarrelling factions.[54]

Monsky must have considered Sam a useful mediator precisely because he was not known to have a strong position on the demand for a Jewish state. Indeed, until the last year of the war, Sam and the Congress managed for the most part to avoid the Palestine question entirely. Although frequently in New York, Sam did not attend the conference of Zionist groups at the Biltmore Hotel in May 1942, a watershed meeting that mobilized a significant part of American Jewish opinion behind the goal of "a Jewish commonwealth integrated in the structure of the new democratic world." Thereafter, however, information about the horrors of the Nazi Holocaust and the energetic lobbying of Canadian Zionists seem to have had an effect.

For the first time, in his New Year's message in September 1944, Sam took the plunge — a carefully worded hope that "responsible authority will rectify the age-old wrong done to our people, and at last accord to dispossessed Jewry its just rights in a Jewish Homeland in Palestine."[55] More concretely, at a Congress meeting in January 1945, Sam made a careful public appeal on behalf of "a free and democratic Jewish commonwealth in Palestine." "Surely this is a demand upon which we have a right to insist," he said. "Our contribution to the great effort for the world's freedom — 1,500,000 Jewish soldiers in the armies of the United Nations . . . the tragic ordeal of an entire generation, 25 percent of our population murdered . . . cries out for it."[56] By the end of the war Sam was a nominal supporter of Zionist goals which had their place, if not a prominent place, in the platform of the Canadian Jewish Congress.

While Zionism was not a central question for the Canadian Jewish Congress in 1945, Sam knew that it was a troubling issue in the United States and that it was appearing inescapably on the world Jewish agenda. This prompted him, that spring, to attend the conference on the United Nations charter in San Francisco, his first important venture in Zionist politics. For the Jewish world, the San Francisco meeting was of central interest, not for details of the charter, but for one crucial issue: the future of the British mandate for Palestine. Zionists worried that, in the legal and administrative transition from the prewar League of Nations to the U.N., Britain might abandon her responsibilities in Palestine, and the Jews might lose, thereby, the commitment of one of the great powers to support the establishment of a Jewish national home. "The Zionists were among the welter of delegations that converged on San Francisco to plead their special causes and to press their — often fragile claims to national recognition," writes Howard Sachar. "No people had a more anguished vested interest in winning international support than the Jews."[57]

Quite apart from its political salience, Sam undoubtedly found the glitter of the San Franciso conference irresistible. All of the important American Jewish leaders were there, men of extraordinary talent and prominence — Rabbi Stephen Wise, "the mighty tribune," head of the American Jewish Congress; Rabbi Abba Hillel Silver, the leading American Zionist, "whose political maximalism and oratorical skills were transcended by an amour propre uncommonly engorged even for the rabbinate of that generation," as Sachar puts it; Louis Lipsky, chairman of the executive committee of the American Jewish Conference; Henry Monsky and others. Goldmann was present, of course, very much in his element, together with a sprinkling of Jews from abroad — Argentinians, representatives of the Board of Deputies of British Jews, and the highly regarded Jewish emissary from Palestine, Eliahu Elath.[58] Sam had come to San Francisco with Saidye, together with Saul Hayes, Archie Bennett and Samuel Zacks.

With the others, Sam attended daily strategy sessions of the united Jewish group, presided over by Henry Monsky. In the corridors of the St Francis Hotel as well, there was action. Sam and Saidye had a small sitting room off their bedroom, and received guests regularly for drinks. Saidye was "washing glasses almost continuously," as she remembers now.[59] At first, the Jewish representatives suffered from a lack of information — the various delegations having agreed not to brief the non-governmental representatives about the proceedings. But there was a breakthrough of sorts when Sam and the Canadians found one of the first direct Jewish conduits to the deliberations, in the Chinese delegation of all places. His name was Morris "Two-Gun" Cohen.

A few months younger than Sam, Morris Abraham Cohen was born in the East End of London in 1889, and had emigrated to Canada in 1908 after a period of time in a reform school for wayward Jewish boys. Oddly enough, Cohen's father first sent him to an acquaintance in Wapells, the tiny Jewish agricultural colony where Ekiel Bronfman first settled after emigrating from Czarist Russia. Cohen's father hoped that a bracing, pioneering experience in the Canadian west might turn his son into an upright, respectable citizen. Unfortunately, he was wrong.

After a rough education in the west, Cohen became a gambler, real-estate speculator, municipal politician and small-time gangster, living first in Saskatoon and then in Edmonton. His fortunes changed dramatically one day, however, when he befriended a Chinese restaurant owner threatened with robbery. Warmly accepted into the local Chinese community as a result of this incident, the tough, streetwise Cohen became a friend of the Chinese Nationalist cause, and was invited to become a bodyguard of the Chinese leader Sun Yat-sen when he visited North America. In 1922, Cohen joined Sun Yat-sen as an aide in China, and served his successor Chiang Kai-shek as well, furnishing weapons to the Nationalists and, remarkably, becoming a general in the Chinese army. Taken prisoner by the

Japanese after the fall of Hong Kong in 1941, he was repatriated to Canada. He moved to Montreal, and ended up, in the spring of 1945, with the Chinese representatives to the United Nations Conference.

Cohen contacted Saul Hayes at San Francisco, and indicated his willingness to help the Jewish cause in Palestine. He met Sam as well, who quite early in the conference helped introduce the romantic, well-connected delegate to the pro-Zionist lobby. "Samuel Bronfman suggested that I meet Maurice [sic] Abraham Cohen," wrote Eliahu Elath in his memoir of the conference.

Although he was hardly an old hand at international diplomacy, Sam pitched in with enthusiasm. Along with Cohen, Sam met with the Canadian delegates, the influential Wellington Koo, the Chinese ambassador to London and number two man in the Chinese delegation, and the young, stone-faced Andrei Gromyko, a rising star in the Soviet diplomatic corps, then ambassador to the United States.[60] On holiday from the more mundane routines of the Canadian Jewish Congress, Sam must have found this intrigue and its cast of characters completely absorbing; Sam and Saidye spent a few weeks at the conference, when a few hours would normally be all he could spare for such gatherings.

Although the results of the conference were relatively inconsequential for the Jewish lobbyists, Sam returned home from San Francisco in triumph — like a small-town boy who had played briefly in the major leagues. Significantly, however, the Congress tribute did not emphasize Zionism. In Winnipeg, where the Western Division of the Congress honoured him with a luncheon in July, the principal speaker alluded to Sam's striving for the "unity of world Jewry." In reply, Sam talked about the efforts at San Francisco to promote human rights. Speaking briefly of Palestine, the report in the *Congress Bulletin* was circumspect. The concern of Jewish lobbyists, it said, was "that ... the Jewish rights to that country will not diminish." "Mr Bronfman emphasized," the report concluded, "that all the nations represented at San Francisco are seriously desirous of building a permanent Security Organization and to grant to all mankind the benefit of the Four Freedoms."[61]

Despite these bursts of Zionist activity in 1944 and 1945, Sam

and the other Congress leaders were hardly among the most
zealous campaigners for a Jewish state in the immediate postwar
period. For the most part, the Congress left the question of
Palestine to the organized Zionist movement while it pursued
other issues of Jewish concern. For many patriotic Canadian
Jews, indeed, events in the Middle East were a source of
deepening embarrassment, as in Palestine itself Jewish fighters
clashed repeatedly, and violently, with the British mandatory
authorities. Canadians were notably outraged in July 1946 when
right-wing Irgun commandos set off a bomb in the King David
Hotel, the British headquarters in Jerusalem, killing ninety-one
people. "Great Britain . . . will be only too gratified to implement
a solution," Sam told the Canadian Jewish Congress in 1947;
understandably, he abhorred the idea of Jewish and British
interest being at odds.[62] But by 1947, as one historian notes,
"Palestine was the major trouble spot in the British Empire,
requiring some 100,000 troops and a huge budget to maintain";
and while Canadian opinion divided on the issue, support for the
British cause was very strong, discomfitting many Canadian
Jews.[63]

Reluctant to appear in an anti-British guise, fearing aspersions
that might be cast upon the loyalties of Canadian Jews if they
appeared strongly Zionist, and aware of the significant
opposition to Zionism that persisted among its constituents,
Congress kept its profile low. When Sam and a Congress
delegation met with Prime Minister King in January 1947, as we
have seen, they did not even mention Palestine, and concentrated
on seeking the entry of displaced persons into Canada.

In the autumn of 1947, as fighting flared throughout the Holy
Land and a U.N. report called for partition, Congress had no
choice but to support this solution, but did so against
considerable public feeling in Canada that backed the British.
The entire question was still considered extremely delicate,
however, with many Canadians outraged over the King David
Hotel bombings, the killing of British military personnel and
other activities of "Jewish terrorists." Reflecting the defensiveness of the Congress leadership, which he certainly shared,
Sam no longer called for a Jewish commonwealth, and in his

New Year's statement he cloaked his official remarks in ambiguity.[64]

Events moved quickly from the U.N. partition resolution to the Israeli declaration of independence, and war. In June 1948, during a short-lived truce in the fighting between the Jews and the Arabs, Sam did speak up, striking a conciliatory note. "At this very moment, the situation is so tense that I content myself with saying that an age old dream may soon see reality, that the scars and wounds of the present conflict may heal and that the Arab world will see that to live in cultural and economic harmony with a Jewish state in Palestine, is not a fate worse than death but on the contrary will improve their own destiny."[65] Sam headed a delegation to External Affairs Minister St Laurent in August, asking him to recognize the State of Israel and support its admission to the U.N.; he also raised funds prodigiously and personally assisted Canadian volunteers to help fight off the Arab invasion of Israel by underwriting life insurance policies — including that of RCAF flying ace "Buzz" Beurling, who crashed in Italy while en route to the fighting. Sam later denied helping to funnel arms and ammunition to the equipment-starved Haganah in 1947–8, and almost certainly his native caution precluded any smuggling of weapons. Doubtless such activity would have been a too-painful reminder of the whisky-smuggling 1920s — quite apart from putting himself unacceptably at risk. In keeping with his self-image of senior stateman and scrupulous public figure, Sam said and did little publicly about the Jewish state until after the Arab-Israeli armistice of 1949.[66]

Although genuinely supportive of the new Jewish state, as were virtually all Canadian Jews, Sam did not share the Zionists' enthusiasm at the time of its foundation. Israel's declaration of independence found Sam and Saidye on holiday in Saratoga, and he did not return home for the jubilant celebration rally at the Montreal Forum — sponsored by the United Zionist Council, not the Congress. Reflecting on Congress's secondary role to the Zionists during the Israeli War of Independence about this time, Saul Hayes coolly reiterated that "the Canadian Jewish Congress is not, by its constitution, a Zionist organization." Sam spoke similarly when referring to the Jewish state. His accent was on

Israel's role in rescuing "the homeless of our people," implying that it was not for those who already had a home, and while he proclaimed pride in the establishment of a Jewish state he made it quite clear that the future of Canadian Jewry lay in Canada. "This is our country," he pointedly told delegates to the plenary meeting of Congress in October 1949, "and here, with the resources of our Judaic tradition, and through the channel of our country's progress, we mean to make our contribution to civilization."[67]

In international affairs, Sam was not preoccupied with Israel. Grateful for the role of Canada in the establishment of the Jewish state, a role that he and Saul Hayes vastly inflated, Sam saw that task as completed, and declared the hope for a troubled world to lie in the strengthening of the United Nations. It was time, Sam made it clear, for Jews to concentrate on the home front. "Jewish life cannot always be run at a fever: after the crises and the emergencies, there are the day-to-day normalities of communal organization, communal culture, and communal life." While there was no question of abandoning Jews' commitment to their brethren overseas, Sam nevertheless insisted on a new focus — "our Canadian Jewish destiny," which "must now engage our efforts more than ever before."[68]

■

SAM'S TESTINESS OVER Zionist priorities likely had another reason than his defensiveness about his and his fellow Jews' Canadian loyalties. Just at the time of the birth of Israel, as it happened, Montreal newspapers were breaking a story that Sam had been living uneasily with for several years. BRONFMANS FACING $22 MILLION SUIT, was the headline in the Montreal *Gazette* on July 2, 1948. The defendants were Sam, Allan, Abe and Harry, along with one of their best customers from the days of prohibition, Joseph Reinfeld. The plaintiff was James "Niggy" Rutkin, a New Jersey racketeer with a criminal record, who had spent part of the war in Leavenworth Prison, convicted of operating an unlicensed still.

Rutkin's complaint went back to prohibition and the rum-running days of the early 1930s, and suggested that there

had been continuing skulduggery right through the 1940s. His
original quarrel concerned his former associate Reinfeld, one of
the major partners in a huge bootlegging operation that had
operated on the eastern seaboard—a syndicate that included
Abner "Longy" Zwillman and several other gangsters who had
"muscled in," Reinfeld claimed, on a previously modest liquor
smuggling operation. In 1931, according to Rutkin, he and
Reinfeld were on the verge of buying a controlling interest in a
Canadian whisky producer, L.L. & B. Distilleries Limited, of
Montreal, for $500,000, including two mortgages on the plant.
Then the deal fell through. Fearing competition, the Bronfmans
conspired with Reinfeld to break an agreement to purchase the
distillery, thereby cheating Rutkin out of his share and future
profits from the deal. Part of the payoff to Reinfeld, Rutkin
further alleged, ended up in a post-repeal whisky importing
company called Browne-Vintners, which in turn was purchased
by DC-SL from some members of the Reinfeld group in 1940.
Having feuded with Reinfeld for many years, Rutkin now
claimed to understand why he had been regularly shortchanged:
the Bronfmans had been behind it all.

To the general public, the details of transactions nearly two
decades old were less interesting than the personalities involved,
and the prospect of sleaze coming to the surface. As news of
the lawsuit broke in July, Walter Winchell gave the story a
particularly lurid colouring in his syndicated column, "Coast to
Coast":

Jimmy Rutkin, former New Jersey big shot bootlegger, who
backed several New York night clubs, will uncork a sensation
in his suit against a former partner and a Canadian distillery
... He will claim he was cheated out of $33,000,000 in a rigged
post-Repeal sale of a whiskey outfit with a world-famous
name, in line with a fabulous tie-in between mobsters and
liquor interests ... He will attempt to establish that the
international syndicate of gangsters now in control of chains of
hotels, priceless realty, big restaurants and trucking enterprises has tried to buy in or muscle in on the booze business,
with no little success.[69]

Drew Pearson, in one of his regular radio broadcasts, excoriated
Joe Reinfeld, whom he called, with some exaggeration, "one of
the biggest ex-bootleggers in the world." "Reinfeld once
controlled the rum boats off New Jersey, now works hand in
glove with Seagram's and has the exclusive distribution of Haig
& Haig, King William Scotch, and Martini Rossi Vermouth,"
Pearson said.[70] The columnist linked Reinfeld to a scheme to bilk
war veterans and line his own pockets, letting his partners go to
jail when they were caught. But the tantalizing connection, as
Pearson knew, was the Canadian whisky company — even if no
additional details were ready at hand.

Niggy Rutkin began threatening much worse publicity in early
1949, while at the same time fishing for a settlement. On
February 16 he telephoned Laz Phillips from New York, saying
that he had no personal animosity against Sam and wanted to talk.
Shocked at the call, Laz told Rutkin that the Bronfmans "had
decided the matter would have to go through the Courts . . . and
that we would not settle this case anywhere along the legal path
until it reached the Supreme Court of the United States . . . that
not one cent would be paid unless the highest Court in the land
would state that the Bronfmans were liable, a possibility which I
stated I could hardly conceive."[71] But Rutkin was persistent.
"There are many ways of skinning a cat," Laz remembered him
saying.

A few weeks later, Rutkin telephoned once again, this time
from Miami. Rutkin expressed his disappointment that Laz
would not set up a meeting with Sam, and told the lawyer this was
a "grave error." Then he got to the heart of the matter. Rutkin's
secret weapon was a Pulitzer Prize-winning right-wing columnist, Westbrook Pegler, known for his well-crafted but
venomous attacks on Roosevelt and the New Deal. "Mr Pegler,"
said Rutkin,

was arranging a series of articles which would go back into
the history of the Bronfman family since its inception, including the trial in Western Canada involving Harry's alleged attempt to bribe customs officials. That the trouble with the
Bronfmans in recent years was that they are so busy selling
whisky they don't appreciate the fact that other people are

interested in having their rights obtained from them, and their investigations do not go to whisky, but rather to the history of the Bronfman family.[72]

Rutkin "was the one who held the strings," Laz remembered him saying, but things might get out of hand. "He could not understand why Sam Bronfman and I were so stubborn in this matter," Laz reported. "Although Sam was a very able man, and even a genius in his field, nevertheless people who are stubborn sometimes can get themselves into very severe difficulties." Pegler's series would be sensational, he warned.

Rutkin's next telephone call to Laz was from a pay phone in Newark. Still fishing for a settlement, he now raised a new threat. "He said he had before him thousands of pages of evidence with respect to the Bronfman trial of 1935," Laz noted. "He again repeated that all he wants is arbitration; that he figures he has a claim against my clients. I told him he has chosen his forum before the courts," Laz continued, "and that I would not see him without his attorneys, nor could I recommend settlement, as I saw no merit to his claim." At that point the operator intervened, and the conversation ended.[73]

Rutkin, it turned out, had badly miscalculated. For although highly allergic to adverse publicity, particularly on his business dealings in the 1920s and 1930s, Sam's very insecurities could make him a tough, determined antagonist and a fierce defender of his own name. The main thing, as he explained to his own lawyers, was that Rutkin's charges were without substance.[74] And so as with Meyer Chechik many years before, Sam refused to be blackmailed, insisting as a matter of principle that his version of what happened prevail. "It had nothing to do with money," Edgar observes. "It had to do with being somebody."[75] Sam determined to see the suit through to the bitter end.

At least one newspaperman, David Charney, agreed with Sam that there was nothing much to Rutkin's sensational allegations and testified about it at the Kefauver Crime Commission hearings three years later. Rutkin originally approached Charney, an acquaintance and investigative reporter at the *New York Daily News*, hoping to interest him in the affair. "Rutkin told me that he was bringing a fantastic suit for about

$20,000,000," Charney remembered, "and that there was fraud involved, and everything else, which involved Seagram and the entire liquor industry, and it would bring in most every big name in the liquor industry. It sounded on the surface like a good, exclusive story for me." Upon further inquiry, however, Charney found that there was little substance to Rutkin's allegations. "It just didn't have much merit," Charney claimed. "I think my paper used about three paragraphs on the fact that such a suit had been filed."[76]

In the first round of the contest, Rutkin lost badly. Not only were his threats of newspaper stories an empty bluff, but his legal tactic backfired. During the pre-trial hearings, it came out that in 1943 Rutkin had pulled a gun on Reinfeld and extorted $250,000. Seizing the chance to put a notorious criminal behind bars, federal prosecutors charged Rutkin with evading taxes on the $250,000, and saw him convicted and sentenced to four years in prison in 1950. Eventually, Rutkin lost an appeal to the Supreme Court on this charge, making legal history: federal taxes, the Court ruled in a landmark five-to-four decision, had to be paid on money obtained by extortion, even at gunpoint.[77] Embittered, Rutkin remained more determined than ever to pursue his case against the Bronfmans, whom he now claimed had conspired with Reinfeld to silence him with the tax evasion charge.

While these preliminary skirmishes were taking place in his contest with Niggy Rutkin, Sam learned of other worrisome threats. In the U.S. government, the liquor industry was not as popular as he would have liked. Throughout 1948 and 1949 the Antitrust Division of the Department of Justice looked into the liquor industry, attempting to determine whether the four largest distillers were violating U.S. antitrust laws. Investigators combed through the offices of Seagram, Hiram Walker, National Distillers and Schenley — the so-called "Big Four." And while the Justice Department lawyers eventually decided against a full-scale probe, questions remained in Congress about the adequacy of the investigation and the possibility of political payoffs of Justice Department officials by all the major distillers. Congress, by 1950, was in an angry mood on the subject of "organized crime" and some legislators, remembering the days of prohibition, were particularly suspicious of the liquor industry.[78]

During the late 1940s, historian William Moore points out, Americans "discovered" crime. Nationwide probes into criminal activity promoted a postwar crime scare, and whether for its entertainment value or its insight into the national character, lawbreaking became a major American preoccupation. Newspapers reported extensively on the national threat posed by Al Capone and his "syndicate," New York's Frank Costello, called the "Prime Minister of the Underworld," and an enforcement agency known as "Murder, Inc." Gambling in particular was a focus of attention, and there were heated debates over the question of its legalization. "Talk of nationwide crime syndicates and of the rediscovered Mafia served the functions of scapegoating for the antilegalization forces and of titillating an increasing number of newspaper readers," Moore concludes. "The search for criminal conspiracies, moreover, paralleled the effort to ferret out communism and Communist sympathizers at home as the nation experienced frustration and disappointment abroad. Political forces, it became evident, would be forced to react to the vocal anticrime movement of the late 1940s."[79]

Responding to these concerns, Senator Estes Kefauver of Tennessee headed a widely publicized Congressional investigation of "organized crime" in the United States beginning in the spring of 1950, holding months of hearings, travelling to fourteen major cities and questioning over eight hundred witnesses. And among these, to Sam's embarrassment, was James Niggy Rutkin.

Kefauver's committee directed most of its attention to gambling, seen as the most important activity of a presumed "national crime syndicate." But liquor came up repeatedly in the criminal pasts of some of the shady characters who appeared as witnesses, and the investigators expressed continuing concerns about wholesale distributorships. "Some of the most widely sold brands of liquor," Kefauver said, "were in the hands of objectionable individuals in many profitable areas." Kefauver complained that many of these wholesalers had been bootleggers during the prohibition era — something that was widely known and accepted in the trade, and had never before been the object of

Congressional concern.[80] Together with other distillers' representatives, Victor Fischel attended a meeting in Washington about this matter, but no one from Seagram was called to testify about it. Something, the public demanded, had to be done.

Sam's name first came up when Niggy Rutkin took the stand. Happily for Sam, Rutkin's testimony was taken before the Committee reached New York, and hence before the hearings were televised—a startling novelty in 1951—and brought the proceedings to tens of millions of Americans from coast to coast. Questioning the witness, Chief Counsel Rudolph Halley linked Rutkin to Longy Zwillman, Joe Adonis and Frank Costello. Rutkin's gambling operations in Newark, he insinuated, at one time took in close to a million dollars a month in profits.

An uncommunicative witness, Rutkin was forthcoming on only one matter—the Bronfmans. Rutkin's version of the 1931 deal, for example, now focused on Sam: "Joe Reinfeld had told me that Sam Bronfman, chairman of Seagram's, got him drunk, and he turned the distillery to him for nothing, and dollar for dollar, I said, 'Sam is my friend, and I am going up and get it back dollar for dollar.' "[81] "Tell us more about the Bronfmans," Kefauver ordered, a few minutes later. "I have been very much interested in them." Rutkin now had his chance, but given his threats to Laz Phillips the blows he struck were hardly impressive:

> Rutkin: Well, the Bronfmans are four brothers from Montreal, Canada. They own little hotels up there. Now, if you want to find out more about the hotels, you can ask the Canadian Mounted Police, and they will tell you about the little hotels, and you can use your imagination.

> Kefauver: Is it like certain types of tourist camps down South? Is that the kind of hotels they are?

> Rutkin: Well, I don't know how they are there, but only from what I read of hotels, that people sleep very fast, they rent them quite a few times during the night.

> Kefauver: I want to explain that I did not mean to disparage

all of the tourist camps, but there are some very few that are alleged to do that sort of thing.

Rutkin: I don't know.

Kefauver: Tell us about the Bronfmans.

Rutkin: They have even got a lot of bad publicity in Canada. They have been accused of bribing Canadian officials or a Canadian official, and they have had big headlines in 1935 for defrauding the Canadian government of, I think it was 5 or 10 million dollars, or something like that, by sending whisky barrels of water back to St Pierre, because whisky is higher in tax there than it is in this country. They sure did a very good job up there with the distillery.[82]

Kefauver came back again to the Bronfmans after Halley took Rutkin through an ill-informed discussion of the whisky business.

Kefauver: How many of the Bronfmans are in Seagrams now?

Rutkin: Just the four brothers.

Kefauver: Two of them are farmers and two are business-men?

Rutkin: No: two were never farmers, they are probably retired.

Kefauver: I thought you said that two that were farmers would not speak to the other two.

Rutkin: The two were the original farmers of the company, Abe and Harry, and the younger two are Al and Sam. Sam is chairman of the board, and he really is a brainy man.[83]

After hearing Rutkin, Kefauver Committee staff contacted Sam, Abe, Allan and Harry through their New York attorneys,

White & Case, in early March 1951. Sam was the one they were interested in, however, and one investigator, Mr Shivitz, actually interviewed him, probably in order to see if he should be called to testify. "Nothing for us" was the conclusion scrawled on a memorandum, and the file was closed. The papers carried none of this, and Sam was in fact before the New York public at that very moment for quite different reasons. On the day Sam's lawyer was speaking with Mr Shivitz, Seagram threw a spectacular sixtieth birthday party for him at the Waldorf, attended by 2,000 people. New York newspapers covered the event, and noted particularly Seagram's creation of a million-dollar Samuel Bronfman Foundation in his honour, originally focused on Columbia University — "to promote understanding of the principles of democracy and freedom of opportunity in our free enterprise system," as the announcement put it. That day, someone in the Senate investigating committee clipped the account in the *Daily Mirror* and included it in the Bronfman file.[84]

A few days later, in the glare of nationwide publicity, the notorious New York racketeer Frank Costello faced the Committee in what turned out to be the climax of the entire investigation. As we have seen, Sam's name came up in questions put to him about liquor purchases during prohibition, but a nervous Costello denied having bought liquor directly from him. "I want to make it specifically on the record," he said, "that I bought in New York, whether it was Bronfman or anyone else, and if Bronfman shipped it to anyone else I bought it from someone else."[85] Beyond this, Costello had nothing to say about Sam. Longy Zwillman was similarly noncommittal — and a far cooler, more self-assured witness than the somewhat rattled Costello. He too had bought whisky from Canada, but he did not say from whom. He admitted that he knew Joe Reinfeld, but would not say if they had been partners.[86]

Finally, the Committee came uncomfortably close to Sam in the testimony of a former Treasury Department agent, Edwin Baldwin, who told how "the Zwillman-Reinfeld syndicate" bought vast quantities of liquor in Canada during prohibition and distributed it throughout the United States. Waxey Gordon, Dutch Schultz and other major bootleggers "were pikers compared with this mob," he said, claiming they had done

$50,000,000 worth of business—an echo of Henry Morgenthau, Jr.'s charges of 1935, taking the same inflated figures that the Secretary of the Treasury had used in his opening round of bargaining with all the Canadian distillers. Baldwin claimed that the post-repeal Browne-Vintners Corporation was a "front" for Reinfeld and Zwillman, loosely implying that the two had continued their criminal activity, and he mentioned that they eventually sold out to Seagram's.[87] These were not the most welcome comments to appear in the *New York Times*, but they were certainly not damaging in any legal sense.

Although Sam had come through the hearings unscathed, he was mortified at having even been mentioned, as his daughter Phyllis recalls.[88] Sam rose determinedly to the challenge, however, and just as with Rutkin's attempt at blackmail, he responded to the implied slight upon his company and his name with new resolve. His first shot was aimed at his own sales staff, but was also intended to influence the public at large. In San Francisco, as Baldwin took the stand, the company announced the "Seagram Family Achievement Association," a cross between a national sales meeting and a sustained pep rally for distributors and their families. Assembled for its first convention, at New York's Biltmore Hotel in November 1951, the Association received wide publicity. LIQUOR MEN START DRIVE FOR RESPECT, declared the *New York Times*, accurately capturing an important theme of the project. Victor Fischel characterized the programme "as a long-term effort to show the members of the trade how they could make it as respected as it was in Great Britain and other countries abroad." His ambition, Fischel told the more than fifty distributors, was that his young daughter would be proud to say that her father was in the liquor business. "You fellows here must pick it up," he urged. "You . . . have to do your job in your local communities. You have to help, whether it be through charity drives or whatnot, to build up respect for our industry so that it will be looked up to as it is in England, where the liquor industry is something to be respected." Wherever a bad liquor situation developed in their communities, he told the *Times* reporter, the distributors should lead the fight against it themselves.[89]

In addition to improving the image of the liquor trade, Sam

and his top executives felt it was time to strengthen their relations with their distributors, hitherto one of Seagram's strongest assets on the American market. With a heavy representation of former bootleggers from the prohibition era, the corps of distributors was now moving into a second generation — literally so in many cases, as fathers passed the highly profitable distributorships on to their sons. Sam had always been concerned about *esprit de corps* within his sales staff, and he now had serious questions about the future. Would the loyalty to the company remain as strong as it had been? Would the next generation of distributors have the same kind of close relationship as before with those in top management positions? "If we are to sit back and relax," said Vic Fischel, echoing one of Sam's favourite themes, "we will lose everything for which we have worked since repeal, and a long time ago I came to the conclusion that we older men, we men who have held the reins in our hands these many years, didn't build something as great as the Seagram Family merely for ourselves alone. We were thinking ahead. We were thinking of those who were to come after us."[90]

Sam himself was in excellent form, delivering a rambling, enthusiastic address on the virtues of family, honesty in business, the history of distilling, blends and salesmanship. Everything was there — his own father's admonition not to take excessive advantage in a business deal, his commitment to quality, his respect for consumers, his determination to succeed. The real focus of his talk, it became clear as his enthusiasm built, was himself: "I brought with me the courage to say that I think more people like uniform, light, tasty, blended whiskey than any other. I think I am proud enough, and yet humble enough, to say to you that I have not only proved it to our organization, I have not only proved it to our distributors, I have not only proved it to the retailers, but I have proved it to the consumer, and I think that even our competitors would be willing to say by now that they think so too."[91]

By all indications, Sam's enthusiam was infectious. At her father's office often during the construction of the Seagram Building on Park Avenue, Phyllis thought it laughable to see "grown men in business suits earnestly singing 'On Lord Calvert' to the tune of the football song 'On Wisconsin' " — a hallmark, as we have seen, of the company's sales meetings and social gatherings. But sing they did, in praise of their product and sometimes their boss—and not unusually so, as one sees with other successful family-built corporations of the day, such as Thomas J. Watson's IBM, for example.[92] Sam's charismatic message seems to have moved the writers who wrote the lines, and the executives and salesmen who sang them lustily. There was genuine feeling in those songs, and this came from Sam himself as much as anyone present.

Niggy Rutkin, meanwhile, went to prison on the tax evasion charge. By the time his civil suit actually came to trial, in New York in October 1953, he was even more bitter about the past, and ached for revenge. After jury members received mysterious telegrams denouncing Reinfeld the judge declared a mistrial, and when proceedings resumed the following year Rutkin's aggressive attorney, Maurice Edelbaum, pulled out all the stops. "You must understand that the Seagrams organization is a very large organization," Edelbaum told the jury. "You must understand that in Canada Mr Samuel Bronfman is a great man. You must understand that Mr Samuel Bronfman is trying to live down that he was a bootlegger, a plain, ordinary bootlegger."[93] Sam remained tough as ever, testifying briefly, mainly on technical matters. For the public at large, there was not much interest in the intense legal battles taking place, and Rutkin himself, brought into the courtroom in handcuffs each day, seemed too unsavoury a character to win much sympathy.

Still, he managed to salvage something from the jury. In March 1954, after a five-week trial, the court awarded Rutkin $77,200 in damages—a far cry from the $22,000,000 he had been asking.[94] Sam's lawyers immediately appealed. The matter dragged on for two more years, until a U.S. Court of Appeals finally overturned the verdict in January 1956.[95] For Rutkin, it was the end of the line. A few months later a federal judge refused to grant him a new trial on the tax evasion charge, and he was taken away to serve the balance of his sentence on April 19. That very day, he killed himself. "Underworld kingpin James (Niggy) Rutkin, big-time prohibition era rum-runner, gambling czar and convicted tax dodger," as the *Daily Mirror* called him, ended his life by slashing his throat with a borrowed razor.[96]

CHAPTER VIII

Consolidation

"I DON'T GET ulcers, I give ulcers," Sam once said. Of all the memories Sam's associates have of him today, none is more vivid than his explosions of temper, which seemed utterly out of proportion to whatever might have caused offence. So shocking were these detonations, especially to the uninitiated, that it is not surprising that sharp differences remain over how they should be understood, and what they might reveal about his deeply guarded inner feelings.

Several have suggested that Sam knew exactly what he was doing during his terrible outbursts of rage, which came on like a cyclone, violent and practically without warning, only to pass quickly after doing their worst. In their view, Sam's tantrums were calculated exercises, a way of dramatizing himself and imposing his will. He had an obsessive need to dominate, and anger was simply one weapon in his armoury to remind everyone who was boss. But others downplay Sam's explosions, seeing them as the product of his frustrations when things did not go right, a result of his intense concentration on the matter at hand. They remember his better side — his genial and courtly manners, and his warmth and generosity to those whom he respected. As they point out, while his fury was legendary, so also was his occasional magnanimity, his concern for his employees and his forbearance when he thought a slight not worth challenging. Both sides have testified to his emotional, highly volatile temper, underscoring how unpredictable Sam could be, and how intensely he felt whatever preoccupied him at the moment. Unquestionably, he was a complex, turbulent, many-sided person—a chameleon, as a close friend described him, whose mood transformed constantly, depending on whom he was with at any particular time.[1]

■

"HE WAS AT times gentle, soft, and deeply sentimental," said William Wachtel, "and then unexpectedly came the storm: the flashing blue eyes with electric pinpoints . . . the sarcasm and vitriol . . . the violent waving of his hands . . . the striding up and down the conference room like a caged tiger . . . all subsiding to a quiet demeanor just as suddenly and surprisingly as his passion had erupted a few minutes earlier."[2] "Every time he opened his mouth you shrank four inches," one employee testified. "When he was through, you felt like a midget under the table."[3] Another associate, then working for one of Seagram's advertising agencies, remembered Sam's face as the tempest swept over it—from "a little pink face, smiling and funny," to a visage "absolutely purple with rage"—"a terrifying sight," John Pringle recalled.[4]

Even the strongest personalities could wilt under the force of Sam's wrath. To many, Sam's profanity was so shocking that they were disarmed practically from the start. "I was in the South African army for five years," Max Melamet says, "but Sam taught me some words I had never heard before." In the Jewish world, where Sam's outbursts were less frequent than in his business, he could stun colleagues who were simply unused to hearing such foul language. Ben Lappin recalled the cascade of invectives Sam poured over the heads of Edward Gelber, Michael Garber and Ben Sadowski, proud barons of the Jewish community in the 1950s. These rather puritan community leaders were "paralyzed by the bad taste," Lappin concluded. "They could not join him in this kind of exchange," and ended up cowed.[5]

Seemingly anything could detonate Sam's anger. "If for some reason he was upset with his brother Allan, he could take it out on you," an Israeli associate, Jack Brin, remembered.[6] Long after Frederick Willkie had left the company, Sam could work himself into a fury over "that son of a bitch Willkie" as if he were savouring ancient wrongs. The mere mention of Lew Rosenstiel, Sam's arch-enemy in the liquor business, could set him off; criticism of any of his policies could also trigger a blast; so could the memory of some earlier outburst of anger; and so too could the most petty matters of protocol, in which Sam felt slighted or passed by. So especially could shoddy workmanship or the discovery that someone had not done his homework properly and was trying to skin by. Utterly self-centred, Sam was a perfectionist in his business, and found it difficult to understand why everyone did not have the same disposition. What seemed to be an utterly arbitrary outburst, therefore, was often the product of his genuine inability to understand the shortcomings of others.

Sam needed little time to find weak spots in someone's argument and when he did he might pounce — pinning his victim helplessly. Quite often, these attacks had spectators; indeed, on occasion, Sam sought them out — giving some credence to the view that the episode was sometimes staged for effect. Sol Kanee remembers hearing a tremendous commotion coming from inside Sam's office on Peel Street one day, and he hesitated to enter the room. Sam's secretary, Robina Shanks, who knew Sam's habits well, insisted on ushering him in nevertheless. Standing before Sam's desk, almost at attention, was a hapless Max Henderson, the butt of Sam's withering rage and extravagant profanity. "How nice to see you, Sol," said Sam, his face immediately brightened and transformed. Without further ado, however, the harangue against Henderson resumed, as if no one else were present.[7]

The story has it that Sam kept a repairman steadily employed replacing sheets of desk-top glass shattered when he banged the telephone in disgust. Pounding the table with all his might was certainly part of the routine. Sam's abuse of his brother Allan, which became part of the culture of the Peel Street offices, was just as violent as his ill-treatment of employees, and as with other famous flare-ups it even threatened life and limb on occasion. Working late one night in his office, Max Henderson heard a tremendous outburst of swearing from Sam's office. "I crossed the mezzanine floor to see what was wrong," he recalled. "I had no sooner looked around the corner into Mr Sam's office when a telephone, torn out of its wall socket, went sailing by my head to crash on the floor. I thought that Mr Sam had gone raving mad. His language was unbelievable. The issue this time was about invitations for a dinner being given at the Waldorf Astoria for the Queen Mother. Apparently Mr Allan and his wife had been invited to the head table instead of Mr Sam and his wife."[8]

Another time Sam let fly with a glass of icewater (with the ice still in it) at a DC-SL board members' luncheon, when a French-Canadian lawyer, J. Alexandre Prud'homme, questioned him closely about the company's dividend policy. ("He was a lousy shot, thank God," Edgar comments.) Prud'homme's inquiry involved some unflattering comparison with Hiram Walker, but there was much more to it than that. As Edgar remembers, "Father was in a filthy mood that day, and started breakfast with a gin and tonic, a sign of terrible things to come. His rage had to do with Allan, and some trusts that his father had set up, of which Allan was one of the trustees. What the real rage was about (since Allan was never a threat) I still don't know." But the anger, in this case, was real enough. After the glass was thrown, Edgar and Charles quickly escorted Sam from the room so he could calm down.[9]

"You know, Sam, you treat your mouth like a sewer," Mark Shinbane told him one day. Whenever similarly reproached, Sam told those closest to him that his explosions were really a way of letting off steam, typically ignoring the effect that they had on those around him. Virtually everyone who witnessed one of Sam's tantrums also saw how quickly the storm could pass, suggesting that at least part of his purpose was simply to draw attention to himself. "I bruises easy, but I heals quick," was one of his expressions. "He could swear in the most filthy way, but you know, as soon as he had to meet somebody, his face would relax and . . . he could have the most winning smile," Shinbane observed.[10] So terrifying was his display of anger, however, that even intimates were never sure it was feigned, and William Wachtel, at least, thought that sometimes it was not: "In many ways, Sam Bronfman was a consummate actor, but every now and then, given the proper provocation, his temper could really flare, and then it was wise to get out of his way."[11]

For Sam's executives, the unpredictability of his explosions was a source of continual unease. "You never knew what he was going to do or say," one of those who sat in on meetings with Sam recalled. "If he was in a funny mood or there was some reason that he didn't like what you were doing he could be unbelievably vicious."[12] "They were all afraid of him," Robert Sabloff felt.[13] At company conferences, whether small groups sitting around a table or massive sales meetings with hundreds of distributors and their associates present, everyone rose when Mr Sam walked into the room. "Whatever the hell you were doing, you stood up when he came in and you never took your eyes off him as long as he was there," says Mel Griffin. Throughout the proceedings, Sam remained the centre of attention — as he no doubt intended. "It was just amazing," Griffin continues. "I don't know whether people stood up because they were getting ready to run or what. Some of them undoubtedly were."[14]

Sam sometimes ensured that he was the centre of attention by falling asleep. Particularly in later years he would appear to doze during meetings — to the general annoyance and discomfort of everyone present — only to snap back to consciousness, revealing a complete grasp of everything that had been said.[15] Mel Griffin remembers riding once with Sam in a limousine to New York's Kennedy airport and briefing him on some subject or other. After about fifteen seconds, Griffin heard a buzzing noise. "I looked over, his eyes were closed, and he was asleep, slightly snoring . . . So I stopped talking." "Go on, go on," Sam burst out immediately, "I'm listening!" "Tell me something, Mel," Sam then mused. "How come you know so much about the whisky business?" "Gee, Mr Sam," was Griffin's reply, "I don't know, I guess I must have had a good teacher." Sam smiled, Griffin remembers, and a moment of friendship passed between them.[16]

Aware that his outbursts were of short duration, those who worked with Sam learned how to shelter during the storm, knowing that it would soon blow over and the skies would clear. Moreover, even if carried along by impulse, Sam saw clearly enough after his explosions to pull back from the brink, to apologize gruffly or even sweetly to those he had abused and to spare certain individuals, such as Abe Klein, for example, his terrifying wrath. And paradoxically, while feared for his bullying, Sam was also deeply admired as someone who cared about individuals, and who lacked all pretension, despite his wealth and power.

People came away impressed after meeting Sam because of his directness, and the clarity with which he communicated his views. "He had this straightforward way of speaking to you," Mark Shinbane said. Israeli leader Shimon Peres, who met Sam in the early 1950s, says that Sam's unadorned speech reminded him of a Chinese saying: If you want to learn to paint a tree, you do so in the winter when the tree has no leaves and you can see all its branches. "Sam was suspicious of the leaves," Peres observes.[17] Normally soft-spoken and polite, Sam received visitors cordially, and many thought of him as the very model of good manners and consideration. When Max Melamet was director of the World Jewish Congress in New York, he was struck by how Sam accompanied him to the elevator of the Seagram Building when their meeting was over. Sam had always been impressed, he told Melamet, when he had been shown this courtesy many years before by his Winnipeg lawyer, Alfred Andrews.[18]

Quite as extraordinary as his anger and his bluster was Sam's graciousness as an employer, a side of him that seemed in complete contrast to his temper tantrums. To this day, former employees brighten at the mention of "Mr Sam," recalling acts of solicitude — referring to them by name, to their surprise, or sending flowers to their wives, or showing unusual concern for their well-being. Abe Mayman, Sam's physician who also worked for the company at Ville LaSalle, testifies to Sam's concerns about the health of his executives, even as he was pushing them to the limit. On hearing they were ill, he would make searching inquiries about their condition — even to the point of researching an illness himself — sometimes making special company provision for them on his own initiative.[19]

Paternalism was built into Sam's work routine. Along with the businessmen visiting him regularly at his offices on Peel Street there were frequent delegations from the Jewish community and others who were seeking Sam's aid. Appeals for help would also come through the mail, with all sorts of people asking for money. Noah Torno remembers Sam's close attention to many of these requests, which he sometimes asked him to follow up: "Very often he would call me about somebody [who] had written a letter to say that they needed money. . . . He would come and say, 'I have a letter here from a woman, she says her son has a particular problem, and their doctors say that they can cure him and they can do this and that, and she doesn't have the money.' He gave me the name of the doctor. I would telephone the doctor, I would confirm that it was so, and he'd say, 'Fine, pay it.' "[20]

Enjoying this role, Sam revelled in the ritualistic praise and admiration he received at the staff parties and tributes that were part of the rhythm of life at Seagrams. In March 1941, in celebration of Sam's fiftieth birthday, the company staged one of the earliest and most elaborate of these tributes, without concession to wartime austerity. Across the Seagram empire, more than 4,000 employees attended birthday banquets in fifteen cities. Three days after attending Canadian dinners at the Waterloo and Ville LaSalle plants, Sam sat at the head table of another gala affair, at the Starlight Room of the Waldorf, and addressed the thousands across the United States using a "revolutionary telephone hookup."[21] "All of you I consider part of one big business family," Sam told his employees that evening with genuine feeling, using one of his favourite metaphors for the company.

Staff Christmas parties highlighted praise for "Mr Sam" and "Mr Allan" — a useful opening provided by the fact that Allan's birthday fell on December 21. On Peel Street, Robert Sabloff used to write a spoof of the Seagram annual report, read to the assembled employees by Jack Clifford, a talented raconteur who acted as master of ceremonies. As Clifford delivered his lines, Sabloff recalled, "everybody would look at Mr Sam to see if he laughed, and then if he laughed, everyone laughed."[22] In New York a Four Roses employee, Marvin Steinhardt, wrote odes in praise of Mr Sam for such occasions, some of which found their way into the company archives. "Out Front," for example, pictured Sam standing before one of his plants:

He stood right out front
   that cold fall day.
Just stopped in his tracks,
   and a short moment did stay.
An elegant picture was he,
   homburg and all
I can tell this now,
   he was having a ball.

"You can achieve two ways," Sam told a meeting of his top
distributors in 1951. "You can achieve in business, and you can
achieve in family life. If you can achieve in both ways—if you
can have a family spirit in business and see your family happy,
then you have really attained true happiness."[23] Head of his
"corporate family," Sam had an aversion to dismissing people—
despite his violent tirades against individuals whom he accused of
ruining the company or showing insufficient loyalty. "Sam ran
Seagrams like a little duchy where the lord of the manor took care
of the serfs," one former employee said. "Nobody was fired and
as long as you avoided trouble, nothing happened."[24] This is not
to say that Sam did not tell people they *were* fired; he did so
periodically in the heat of his explosions. But once he calmed
down, he would immediately make amends. One top executive
claimed to have been fired out of hand on no less than three
separate occasions.[25]

So preoccupied was he with how others perceived him, Sam
even hesitated to issue direct orders. "I like to make suggestions,"
he said. "If you suggest something, a man feels that he is doing it
himself. You don't make him feel like a robot."[26] Employees who
stood up to Sam often found that the boss's bark was worse than
his bite. The key, as several discovered, was to appeal to Sam's
self-esteem. When he was a very junior person in the advertising
department on Peel Street, Robert Sabloff showed him a new
series of ads one day, aimed at blue-collar workers in the
Toronto-Hamilton area. "I don't like them," Sam said curtly.
"Well, Mr Sam," Sabloff replied, "they weren't designed to be
liked by multi-millionaires." At that point, Sabloff saw Sam's
face flush with anger. "You think you're pretty goddamn smart,
don't you," he growled. "Mr Sam," Sabloff replied, "if I wasn't

smart, I wouldn't be working for you." Sam looked at his young employee, smiled, and said: "O.K., run them." "I was there for thirteen years after that," Sabloff recalled, "and I never had a minute's problem with that man."[27]

Sam had an uncanny ability to size up a situation or an individual quickly, often with a series of well-placed questions. He had a hunger for facts that could turn a brief encounter into a seminar. More than thirty years later, a former plant manager remembers how intensively Sam grilled him when he came on a visit: "He was always asking, you know, 'What's this, and what's this, and how does that work, and what do you think about that?' ... And he'd ask the same questions over and over."[28] "What amazed me," says Phyllis, "was that he had no fear of seeming ridiculous, let alone ignorant, by asking questions, many of which my sophisticated self considered incredibly stupid ..."[29] He was ceaselessly learning, and approached people high and low, seeking constantly to find out whether they could teach him something.

One day Sam piled into a taxicab on Sherbrooke Street in Montreal with his son Charles and one of his executives, Mike McCormick. According to McCormick, when the cab passed a billboard advertising tires, the whisky magnate began to ask the driver his views. "Men like you and I, observed Mr Sam, should always use only the best tires on our cars; tires are too important to compromise on quality. Don't you agree? The cab driver agreed. Mr Bronfman asked the cabbie more questions about tires — seeking his advice on type and servicing when, as the taxi was about to turn on Peel Street, there was a loud bang. One of the tires had blown out. The car bucked and heaved as the driver ground around the corner. He had just made it onto Peel and was edging to the curb when 'bang', a second tire blew. Mr Sam heaved himself out of the cab, disgusted. 'Imagine that damn fool giving me advice about tires.' "[30]

"Sam had the capacity to plough your mind," was how Mark Shinbane put it. He cut easily beneath the surface and sensed intuitively whether he was being told the truth on the most diverse range of subjects. William Wachtel told of the "steely blue eyes that penetrated right into your very soul" during these inquisitions; Max Melamet gave a prudent warning as a survival technique: "Don't ever try to bluff him. Don't try to pull the wool over his eyes. He is much too shrewd for you to succeed, and he hates anything insincere or phony."[31] When they strayed over that line, survivors testify, Sam responded as if he had just received a personal injury. "You can't imagine," says Abe Mayman, "he took it as though you had insulted him. It was literally like an insult."[32] "The best way of dealing with him," Alan Rose of the Canadian Jewish Congress claimed, "was to give him a short and exact reply. If not, you might be in trouble."[33]

Throughout the trade, Sam was renowned for his mastery of the technical side of whisky making—a grasp that astonished veteran Scottish distillers when he visited them. And until his far-flung empire got too large, he could comment on local details in a way that awed his top lieutenants. "He not only knew all about current operations but the names of his personnel as well. . . . He would astound his associates with facts and figures. . . . He was truly a walking encyclopedia," was William Wachtel's conclusion.[34] And even when out of his depth Sam displayed, in his business at least, the sort of sixth sense that enabled him to grasp the essentials. Although he pestered them endlessly, for example, Sam's advertising men swore that he was unsurpassed in his mastery of their trade. He would spend hours with the professionals, convincing them of the soundness of his instincts about how to appeal to popular tastes. Unschooled in accounting, to take another example, Sam had "a natural instinct for balancing," as Edgar put it. "He would look at the balance sheet and know whether it was sound."[35]

Sam not only could see quickly to the heart of a business problem, he had a prodigious memory, as everyone close to him has testified. Like many businessmen of the pre-computer age, Sam relied heavily on his capacity to recall facts and figures; his abilities, however, surpassed what most people could imagine. "He could recall with ease and accuracy the details of transactions not mentioned for decades," wrote Mike McCormick, who worked for him in the last years. Typically, Sam had no sense of just how remarkable his memory was, and had little patience for those who could not keep up with him in this regard.[36] Charles remembered sitting in his office on Peel Street with Jack Duffy, one of the top men in the Canadian business, musing about the boss, who was then in his seventies. "Jack," Charles asked, "if Mr Sam walks through the door, how long do you think it would take him to tie us up in knots by asking a question we don't know?" "Not longer than two minutes," was Duffy's reply, "and if he really worked at it maybe thirty seconds." Charles was astounded at Sam's grasp of numbers in a variety of fields. He was particularly struck, one day, watching Sam go through his paces with his chief of international sales. "I couldn't believe it," Charles recalled. "Dad . . . knew the numbers better than this guy did. And I looked on his desk to see if there were any pieces of paper, whether he had read up on it before the guy came in." There was nothing, however. "I asked him afterwards, 'How do you know all that stuff?' "[37]

For many years Sam owned half of a Winnipeg company, Globe Bedding, having once assisted a friend on the verge of bankruptcy. Every year during the 1950s Mark Shinbane, a director of the company, came to Montreal to show him a balance sheet — an exercise, Shinbane said, in "why the hell this and why the hell that." What so astonished Shinbane was that, despite a few drinks, despite a hard day's work, and despite the fact that Globe Bedding was hardly a major part of his empire, Sam remembered everything about the company's accounts. "He would sit up and say to me, 'Jesus Christ, I thought you told me last year that the balance was one hundred and seventy-seven thousand and two dollars, and now it's one hundred and fifty-four thousand. . . . What the hell happened?' He had it all in his head!"[38]

Working with this dynamic, sometimes genial, sometimes brutal "human encyclopedia" could not only be a trial, it could sometimes guarantee inefficiency. Sam constantly jangled the nerves of those who wanted to preserve lines of authority, maintain neat divisions and prepare blueprints for the future. Oblivious to the preoccupations of those around him, he thought nothing of calling Sol Kanee in Winnipeg, for example, telling him to drop everything immediately and fly to Montreal to take charge of a problem.[39] His restless urge to become involved in practically everything could produce intolerable bottlenecks when simply too much had to pass through him. "He didn't really order his priorities," says Edgar. "Whatever came to mind . . . even if it was an unimportant thing, it was on his mind so it had to be solved."[40] Moreover, Sam worried endlessly over details, and was sometimes paralyzed by his own procrastination—particularly over unimportant details. Sam's standing reservation on the Montreal–New York train was a case in point. Sam used to ask everyone around him, including his children, whether he should stay in Montreal or go to New York. "Dear, dear Daddy, was there ever a man so capable of taking enormous decisions and so hesitant in making small ones?" Minda wrote to Saidye in the mid-1950s.[41]

Ruminating endlessly over packaging, Sam would delay for weeks before giving his final approval—driving his staff to distraction. "He would weigh the basic facts of the situation and then ask as many people as were available for their views on the pros and cons before making up his mind," Max Henderson remembered. "If a reply made sense to him, Mr Sam would then charge the unfortunate individual who made it with pursuing it further, whether it was his corporate responsibility or not. Consequently, the company executives proceeded most of the time in a state of immense confusion. This, in turn, led to a host of misunderstandings, jealousies, indeed outright fights as everyone protected himself as best he could."[42] At any point along this chain of procrastination, Henderson noted, a deal might fall through or an opportunity might be lost. And whenever that happened Sam's temper could flare and the nearest person at hand could find himself the scapegoat.

Sam's work routine in this highly charged atmosphere reflected his complete preoccupation with himself. "The maestro," as Abe Klein liked to call Sam, not only led several orchestras, he also composed the music, repaired the instruments and planned the concert seasons as well; in addition he gave much thought to how musical tastes might evolve in the future. "A dynamo at the office," a journalist observed colourfully in 1949, "he has been known to conduct six separate meetings at one time, in two different rooms; and to carry on a 22-minute conversation with Vancouver and a 15-minute one with New York simultaneously, and then pick up the threads of a discussion with a visitor exactly where they had fallen." In Montreal, Robina Shanks guarded the entrance to his office, working beside Allan's secretary, Doreen Williams. Somewhat old-fashioned, prim and proper, in striking contrast to her younger, jollier partner, Shanks helped keep things on an even keel and seemed unimpressed by the roar of profanity coming from Sam's office. "Never make a lot of money," she told one journalist. "It's a damn nuisance!"[43] All day long Sam saw a stream of people, high and low in station, ranging from those who were seeking charitable donations to those who were planning major moves on the corporate chessboard. "His door was open to everybody and anybody," says Henderson. "After all, he would say, you learn something from everyone while everyone is a potential customer for your products."[44] Sam hardly ever wrote or answered letters. "Mail answers itself," was one of his dicta.

Petulant on occasion, Sam seems to have resented the work of Calvert's advertising agency in the early 1960s, Doyle Dane Bernbach, largely because Edgar, and not he, had hired them. D.D.B., as they were known, came up with a phenomenally successful ad in 1961 announcing "soft whisky" — a gentle whisky that would not burn your throat or be harsh on the tongue. John Pringle, one of Bill Bernbach's associates at the time, was struck by how reluctant Sam was to acknowledge the ad's success. "I don't think Sam ever said to Bernbach, 'Thank you, it's a great ad.' Never, never. The better the ad the more he'd criticize. 'You think your ad did that. Let me tell you, it never did, I'm telling you. . . .' "[45]

In fact, Sam may have felt threatened by his advertising agent, who pioneered a humorous, lighthearted approach to publicity that clashed with Sam's more traditional emphasis on luxury and high status. Remarkably, even while working himself into a rage against Bernbach, Sam saw wisdom in the latter's ideas, and on occasion realized that his advertising man was right. Sam told him once he wanted a series of ads showing bottles of Chivas Regal atop every important Grecian column — the ultimate putting of his prized whisky on a pedestal. Bernbach thought this a terrible idea, and told Sam so. "That was the beginning of hate," Pringle claimed, perhaps missing the real point, which was Sam's discomfort with the new ways of advertising. Yet the astonishing thing to Pringle and to others was that Sam seems to have *agreed* with the criticism; he accepted that he was wrong, even while burning with resentment that his idea had been rejected. Once again, Sam seemed to observers to have a divided self — one with the clearest sense of reality and the keenest appreciation of the forces at play, and the other insecure, petulant, sentimental and utterly self-centered.

With his efficiency limited by these sometimes bizarre work habits, Sam rushed about as if the very survival of his empire depended on his every decision. "Throughout the twelve years I worked for him," Henderson noted, describing the period from 1945, "Mr Sam directed practically every facet of the business." He personally scrutinized the blending process, determining the taste of each of his brands. "He also dictated the design of all labels, supervised the marketing of the products, handled relations with provincial and federal governments, and oversaw all major company matters."[46] All this was in Montreal. Then there was New York. And also, by the 1950s, new markets worldwide.

■

SPEAKING TO FOUR hundred distributors at a company conference called "Horizons Unlimited" in San Francisco in July 1951, Sam struck a triumphant note. "Do you know what happens when you really build a brand that everybody needs and wants and appreciates? Gentlemen, you've got a public utility." Swelling with pride, Sam was speaking like someone who had realized his life ambition. "When you build up a brand to a point where you've got consumers demanding it — walking into the store and saying, 'give me that brand' — the time inevitably comes when you begin to deliver bigger and bigger loads of goods. You are receiving that much more pay for your efforts. And when that happens, you really have built up a business with a long-lasting, sound foundation."

Sam's was not an idle boast. One of the best merchandisers in the industry, known for its "aggressive salesmanship," as the *Financial Post* reminded its readers, Seagram did 90 percent of its distribution outside Canada, mostly in the United States. The company had carved out one-fifth of the American market by the early 1950s, and although the popularity of blends had begun to dip, it was clearly the leader in the field. Its annual sales were running around $700 million or better — with its chief competitor, Schenley, standing at $425 million. Its inventories of whiskies, severely depleted during the Second World War, had more than doubled since 1946, and were valued at over $250 million in 1952.[47]

Sam remained ambitious as ever, reminding his distributors of the brazen, visionary projections he had made immediately after repeal and of the difficult conquests he had made thereafter. As always, his message was highly personal. "Seagram's will go much higher," he told the Horizons Unlimited conference. "Will you please have the confidence in me today, that you had in me eighteen years ago? . . . When I say Seagram's will go much higher, I know what I am talking about. I know what I put into those bottles. And I say to you, gentlemen, even the label, every letter, every line, every space on that label has taken time and sweat and blood." As his speech concluded, Sam spoke fervently about his company, and his message, as always when he got down to fundamentals, was just as plainly about himself: "I'll promise you the continuance of the great, important policies of our company, something we have drilled into all our people time and time again—that is, our integrity and self respect; for all our people are taught to walk with respect and with dignity, because that is the priceless ingredient of our company."

Seagram's supremacy was not undisputed, however, and despite Sam's words it was unclear, in the early 1950s, whether the company would be able to maintain its hard-won position. One problem was that Sam's own, intense commitments were not always consistent with consumer trends. Seagram's success had rested heavily on blends—blended Canadian whiskies, American blends, and later Chivas Regal. Blends accounted for nearly 90 percent of the market at the end of the war, and had done particularly well because the wartime ban on production required producers to stretch existing stocks with neutral spirits. Beginning in 1947, however, with all the liquor companies replenishing their supplies of aged whiskies, consumers began to turn away from blends—possibly, it was suggested, because of the poor reputation of neutral spirits, which had been distilled from potatoes or cane in war conditions.

Before long, people in the trade were referring to a "blend debacle"—a growing preference for straights, in which Seagram had no frontline contender to match those of its competitors.[48] Brash and critical, Edgar suggested that Seagram was partly at fault. "We had all the business," he said, "so we stopped selling *blends.* We just sold brands. We were fat and lazy." Sam, however, would not budge on his essential beliefs. In the late 1950s Edgar and some other executives tried to get him to introduce a Four Roses brand of straight bourbon, because the slippage in blends particularly hurt Four Roses. But Sam would have none of it. "Let no one say that Sam Bronfman is giving up on blends and supporting bourbon!" Edgar remembers him saying.[49] Sam eventually did enter some straights in the field, but his heart was never with them and he remained committed to blends whatever market trends indicated. "His entire quality control and blending staffs, which were vital to the success of the Company, were trained to admire the taste of blends, but not straights," Charles observes.[50] He feared mightily that straights, if brought under the Seagram banner, would simply undermine his beloved and highly profitable blended whisky.

Another mark of fallibility was Sam's disdain for what was known as "white goods" — gin and vodka — claiming that "anybody could make it." Vodka had no flavour, and like gin was not aged, qualities that were quite at odds with his fundamental beliefs about whisky. Sam hoped that the public would feel similarly, and would spurn these challengers as the inferior products he believed them to be. But to his chagrin, the white goods' share of the market grew prodigiously from the mid-1950s. Sam's antennae did not pick up the vodka threat at the start of the decade, and the advantages went largely to the Heublein company's remarkably successful Smirnoff brand. Seagram did acquire Wolfschmidt Vodka in 1956, but it did not begin to do well until the early 1960s. The experience with gin was somewhat better, although not without difficulties. When he finally did introduce his own brand he decided it would be aged in wood — not a standard practice in the trade — and the result was a slight coloration that customers rejected. Sam eventually overcame this problem by specially treating the barrels, and the resulting product is now the largest selling gin in the United States. He remained unhappy with "white spirits" even with success, however. Gin and vodka, he noted sadly towards the end of his life, can be found on good tables, are consumed by good families, and are stocked in first-class hotels. What, he seemed to be saying, was the world coming to?

Sam's mind was full of thoughts of expansion in the postwar decade, casting his eye across many fields at once — Canada, the West Indies, South America and Europe. "Sam simply had to buy whatever he saw," was the view of one acquaintance. Whenever possible, he financed these ventures out of profits, maintaining a relatively low level of debt.[51] Arguing that he wanted to keep funds available to build inventories and for acquisition purposes, he believed in paying low dividends to shareholders, defending himself against occasional criticism by pointing to Seagram's excellent long-term performance. "If people want to stay with me," Noah Torno remembers him saying, "they will be better off in the long run. I'll build something."[52] Cautious and far-sighted enough to champion diversification in this period, Sam steered Seagram into many new product areas, enabling it later to overcome the vicissitudes of the market. Some of these ventures did not do well — as his overly ambitious project to make whisky at an ultra-modern Seagram plant at Ixtapaluca, high in the mountains east of Mexico City, and a project of Edgar's, bottled cocktails. But others were more promising, including his purchase of the Leroux Liqueur Company in Philadelphia, the manufacturing of rum in Venezuela, and his substantial acquisitions of wine firms in France and Italy.

Straining for the long-term view, as always, Sam undertook to develop manufacturing facilities far afield — in Europe, in Central and South America, and, at the very end, in Japan. His rationale, which he repeated often to his sons and others in his entourage, was that plants in each of these countries would manufacture for their own domestic market, and would be advantageously placed to export to the others as well. Also, marketing strategies in these countries would include Seagram's Canadian, American and Scotch whiskies. In this way, Sam argued, Seagram could take maximum advantage of overseas sales forces wherever Seagram had manufacturing facilities. Through the Seagram Overseas Corporation that he formed in 1956 and the Seagram Overseas Sales Company that was launched in 1965, Sam looked increasingly to a global organization, rather than contracting his vision as he grew older.[53]

In investments too, his postwar path was one of diversification—another sign of his prescience and capacity to prepare for the future. By far the most important of his moves was into energy, which interested Sam in the early 1950s when he and Allan invested in the Alberta oil company, Royalite. After a run of what was assumed to be beginner's luck, Sam steered the giant DC-SL into similar activity; this was slow to show profits, however, and after three years experts assumed that he was better off sticking with whisky, which he knew best. But Sam remained confident. "When we went into this thing we didn't expect our earnings to shoot through the roof overnight," he told *Forbes* in 1957. "Our first success gave some stockholders a false idea; we were just fortunate. Oil is just a tiny trickle in our business. It's a long-range program."[54]

Convinced he was on the right track, Sam continued to expand, organizing a new acquisition, the Frankfort Oil Company, to manage production, and hiring a top Texas oil man, Carrol Bennett, to take charge. In retrospect, Sam might seem to have had an uncanny sense about the future of oil, and Edgar recalls him associating it with the Rockefeller family and obviously admiring their standing in American industry. But Sam's enthusiasm at the time waxed and waned, and he knew that with oil he lacked the sure hand he had with the whisky business. Speaking to Noah Torno one day, Sam said that he was unhappy with the oil business "because he couldn't have the contact with the people, because he didn't understand oil the way he understood things which crossed your tongue." "Father enjoyed the oil busness," Edgar concludes, "but it was never a consuming passion with him."[55]

In 1963, when production was about 10,000 barrels a day, Sam made his biggest plunge with the purchase of Texas Pacific, a major producer—"the venerable Texas Pacific Coal and Oil Company, founded in 1888 and possessing one of the oldest of Texas charters," said Sam about the pedigree, speaking as if it were a famous distillery.[56] While it is doubtful that Sam foresaw the energy crisis of subsequent decades as he later claimed, there is no question that his acquisition was a remarkable financial coup—at a time when "leveraged buyouts" were a concept of the future. With a Seagram working capital of $382 million and earnings of $34 million a year, Sam borrowed $75 million from institutional investors, in 25-year promissory notes. He put $50 million of that as a downpayment on the Texas Pacific purchase price of $266 million, and undertook to pay the balance out of future revenues — a strategy then facilitated by U.S. tax laws. The key player in these arrangements was Mark Millard, a partner in Loeb, Rhoades and Co. and the man who had recommended the appointment of Carrol Bennett. Millard convinced Sam of the wisdom of the oil payment scheme and nudged him to make the Seagram bid.

By 1975, Texas Pacific had paid off its debt, while in the process its oil and gas reserves expanded phenomenally. A handsome legacy to Seagram, the company proved to be one of Sam's shrewdest moves; bought with only $50 million in borrowed cash, it was sold in 1980 to the Sun Oil Company for a grand total of $2.3 billion. Here too, Mark Millard played a major role. A decade after Sam's death, Seagram used this capital to acquire a 20 percent interest in Dupont, taking the company that Sam had built from being a large wine and spirits company to a major diversified corporation.[57]

In the postwar period Sam still had fields to conquer in the whisky business, and his keenest interest remained in Scotland. For many years Sam had been working in the Scottish whisky market, buying "parcels" of Scotch when they became available, and patiently putting them aside for some unspecified use in the future. In a market crying for Scotch, Sam once again held back — allowing the casks to accumulate, and paying the mounting carrying charges on all that he put away. And then suddenly, in 1949, with bonded warehouses in Glasgow and elsewhere brimming with Sam's whisky, he saw his chance.

His principal broker was a legendary character named Jimmy Barclay — "one of the greatest whisky entrepreneurs ever to graduate into the respectable era from the bootlegging days," as Max Henderson says — a Scotsman who was literally raised in a distillery and who knew the history of the distilleries of Scotland like the back of his hand.[58] About this time, Barclay came to Sam with a remarkable prospect — Chivas Brothers Ltd., an old and successful firm of grocers and whisky merchants of Aberdeen, with a distinguished name going back to the nineteenth century.

The story of Chivas brothers began in 1836, an article in *The Scotsman* noted, "when James and his brother John Chivas, sons of a frugal farming family, set out on foot to walk the 20 miles from their home, Overtown of Dudwick, to the city of Aberdeen."[59] Entering the grocery business, the story had it, James came to supply whisky and groceries to the royal household, which vacationed at nearby Balmoral Castle. Eventually Chivas and his brother became leading provisioners of shooting parties nearby, and well-to-do Londoners when they returned home after a season in the Highlands. Respected for its service and quality, Chivas's company remained within the family, and became known for its fine wines and whiskies. Although only of modest size, it remained intact more than a century after it was founded, with its whisky appreciated by a small and discerning group of connoisseurs. Sam had his eye on the Chivas name for some time, having long sought to obtain its trade marks and coveted royal warrant. In 1950, thanks to Barclay, Sam finally purchased Chivas Brothers — essentially two grocery shops, their trade marks, plus a small inventory of high-class, well-aged Scotch — for a mere 85,000 pounds, and with these raw materials he set out to build what those in the trade came to see as his masterpiece, Chivas Regal.

His first need was a distillery. The grocers, in the past, had not made their own whisky; operating on a modest scale, as was the custom in Scotland, they purchased whisky from brokers on the open market and produced their own blends. Breaking through the "tartan curtain," as one former broker put it, Sam scoured the Scottish Highlands for a base of operations, intending to integrate production on the North American model. What he found was a perfect match for the venerable Chivas Brothers in tradition and reputation, the Strathisla-Glenlivet Malt Distillery at Keith in Banffshire, said to be the oldest in Scotland, with a pedigree extending to 1786. Run-down and neglected when Sam's agents first arrived on the scene, the old distillery had to be pried loose from the hands of an opera impresario and habitual gambler, Jay Pomeroy. Once again Jimmy Barclay's negotiating experience was put to use, and the plum fell into Sam's lap.[60]

Sam lavished attention on his new brand — "an artist producing his chef d'oeuvre," as one admirer put it. Holding back from the market, he expanded further, buying land for new distilleries and warehouses at Keith and at Paisley, west of Glasgow, and at Dalmuir on the Clyde. Sam's own account of the Chivas saga, ghostwritten by his assistant Mike McCormick, authentically communicates his romantic enthusiasm: "Each of our Scottish distilleries has its own springs of clear, cold water of purest quality which bubbles up from the cool depths of the mountain sides, trickles through rock and filters down through banks of peat which impart an almost miraculous softening effect. The breezes which come from these mountains are delightfully fresh and invigorating: excellent for maturing whiskies. Indeed, I'm so enchanted with the area that I call it the land of wind and stream and poetry."[61]

Never tempted to begin sales before he had accumulated enough inventory, Sam waited patiently until 1952 before introducing Chivas Regal. Philip Kelly remembered being summoned to Sam's office in New York some time before and being asked to start the company to market the new brand. "What do you think of that package?" Sam asked, producing an aged-looking bottle and carton. Kelly was appalled: "that is so bad it's good. You must have done it on purpose. It looks like it's a hundred and fifty years old." That was, of course, exactly what Sam had in mind—an evocation of the antiquity and tradition that to him assured quality. Seagram made what was at the time a huge initial promotional investment—$250,000—creating a product that wonderfully communicated Sam's own enthusiasms. Chivas was high-priced and aristocratic, "aimed at the educated palate," as *The Scotsman* noted. "We used the figure of Sir Robert Bruce as our trade mark," Kelly recounted. "Our first ad, announcing Chivas Regal twelve-year-old-Scotch whisky was produced in a beautiful tapestry-like effect that literally breathed Scotland and all its tradition and glory." Kelly did not neglect snob appeal. One of the most successful promotional ventures, he recalled, was a letter he wrote over the signature of Jimmy Barclay, on Chivas Brothers stationery, mailed from Aberdeen to some 200,000 officers of U.S. corporations rated over $100,000, including 50,000 in New York City. "The recipient was urged to visit his pub or his spirit shop and to ask for a bottle of Chivas, which would continue to be very limited in quantity and was to be sold only to those who appreciated the best in Scotch whisky. The recipient was reminded, of course,that he was a connoisseur in this class and therefore should insist upon getting his share—and that he should act quickly."[62]

The Chivas that came on the market in New York in 1952 was the product of distillations during 1939, and since there had been practically no distilling in Scotland during the war, twelve-year-old Scotch continued to be in short supply during the early and mid-1950s. Sam carefully targeted the upper end of the market, seeking to place Chivas in exclusive clubs and expensive restaurants. Sales rose only slowly, therefore, with Sam refusing pressures to follow up his successes by adding younger whiskies to his blend. "This is a temptation rarely resisted by many manufacturers," Kelly observed. Sam remained unfazed as well by the movement towards "lighter" Scotches, which began about this time. "With the backing of the management, Chivas remained firm. We did not compromise with the age or the quality. We sold our quota, maintained our price, and controlled our distribution."[63] Meanwhile, Sam concentrated on building up production for the future. In a Scotland where no malt distilleries had been built since the Victorian era, he took personal charge of design and construction of the company's new Glen Keith plant, close to Strathisla—"his pride and joy," as a company history put it. "In every man's heart there is a secret place he loves to go," declared the caption on a photograph of the woods and rushing waters of the site. "For Samuel Bronfman it was on the banks of the Isla—one of the most beautiful of Scottish rivers—where it flows between our two distilleries, Strathisla and Glen Keith."[64]

By the early 1960s Chivas had more than half the premium Scotch market in America—doing "for Seagrams what the Cadillac does for General Motors," as *Forbes* put it. By then American sales were a solid 148,000 cases a year, and were climbing steadily. In 1964 Sam himself opened a huge Paisley bottling plant, with its principal building looking like an eighteenth-century baronial chateau, against the background of an otherwise undistinguished industrial belt. Output climbed. By the time of Sam's death in 1971, Chivas sold 700,000 cases annually in the United States, and another 500,000 worldwide.

Sales are now in the neighbourhood of 3 million cases a year, all of it still bottled in the Paisley plant.[65]

On another front, Sam wanted to be "the rum king of the world," as he told his colleagues on Peel Street, building on wartime success with rum sales. Together with Bacardi, their chief competitor, Seagram became well established in the Caribbean, taking advantage of extensive tax-free havens and promoting rum internationally. Consistent with Sam's preferences, Seagram began as blenders, taking spirits from various distillers and using the company's vast resources and organization to market internationally. Immediately after the war the company started production, setting up Captain Morgan Distillers in Jamaica and buying a 51 percent interest in the Puerto Rico Distillers Group. In 1953, with the acquisition of the Long Pond sugar estate and rum distillery, Seagram began to distill. More expansion followed. With the help of Noah Torno, the company purchased the Nassau-based Myer's Rum, makers of the leading dark rum in the world, snatching the deal from under the noses of Hiram Walker. Then came the Puerto Rico Rum Company, producers of white rum, followed by the acquisition of other companies on that island. And then, moving beyond the Caribbean, Seagram became the first modern company to produce rum in Canada; by the 1960s rum was the second most popular distilled spirit in the country, second only to Canadian whisky and ahead of gin and vodka.[66]

As resort-manager and future advertising executive John Pringle remembered Sam in those days, he was restlessly on the lookout for companies to buy, even on holidays. "His mind never stopped working for a single second," Pringle recalls, having accompanied Sam on shopping expeditions all over the island.[67] But once the enterprise he looked at was safely within the Seagram fold, Sam took much less interest, as if convinced that the real payoff would come only in the future. "Except for watching the bottom line," Max Henderson claimed, "Mr Sam paid little attention to a company after it had been purchased, but his appetite for more acquisitions in the wine and spirit trade continued to grow. He was forever weighing up this deal or that from among the many that accumulated on his desk."[68]

Laying down the foundations of a giant international

enterprise, Sam made a particular point of buying a majority interest in local companies in South America and Europe, entering into partnerships with the former owners who would continue to run the business while maintaining the confidence of "Mr Sam" — the very strategy, indeed, that the Edinburgh-based DCL tried to employ with the Bronfmans in the mid-1920s. This was, for example, what drew Seagram heavily into Venezuela, after Sam struck up a friendship with Benjamin Chumaceiro, an importer and distributor in Caracas. Similarly, Sam began a major distilling operation in Argentina in 1963 in partnership with the Ibarzabal family, from whom he bought a large distillery in the northern part of the country.

Sam also moved heavily into wines in the postwar era. In 1948 DC-SL obtained control of the Jordan Wine Company of Ontario, putting it together with Noah Torno's family firm, Danforth Wines, which entered the Seagram empire at that point. Torno became managing director of the new enterprise, and eventually joined Sam's tiny circle of personal friends as well. "By far the ablest negotiator in the Seagram organization," in Max Henderson's view, Torno was deeply involved in Sam's rum operations, while extending Seagram's wine production to small-scale facilities in both British Columbia and Manitoba. At the same time, Seagram bought a major interest in one of the most famous Champagne companies of France, G.H. Mumm and Co., with its headquarters in Rheims, and in 1954 the company secured a substantial chunk of Barton & Guestier, one of the great French wine *négociants*, acquiring majority control some time later.

Growth continued in North America as well. With the unexpectedly high demand for V.O. on the American market, Sam expanded his inventory of Canadian whiskies in the early 1950s, acquiring facilities at Beaupré, Quebec, and United Distillers in Vancouver. Starting with the latter's production facilities he formed Thomas Adams Company to produce an entirely new line of Canadian whisky, putting Charles, then in his mid-twenties, in complete charge of its development. A few years later, with Edgar head of Joseph E. Seagram & Sons in New York, Sam had Charles, who was in charge of marketing for the Canadian companies, appointed president of

The House of Seagram Ltd., heading all Canadian operations. Sam, "the president of presidents," still roamed regularly between Montreal and New York, interfering constantly in everyone's sphere, energetically cooking up deals and increasingly turning to international sales and production as his particular interest.

Sam's foresight was very much in evidence during the Korean War, when distillers had to decide whether the conflict would expand and whether they would consequently face government restrictions such as had been imposed during the Second World War. Seagram gambled that there would be no diversion of production, while Sam's rival Schenley did the reverse. Unwisely as it turned out, Rosenstiel produced massive amounts of "hedge" whisky, laid away much more stock than he could afford and found himself at a severe disadvantage at the end of the war. Then, in an effort to ease his position, Rosenstiel began a major campaign to extend the tax-free warehousing period from the existing eight to twenty years — thus making it possible for him to carry his swollen inventory. Sam fought back in a political battle against his old rival, continuing their near twenty-year feud. "It was an all-out fight for the market," as the *Financial Post* later noted, with the old competitors now going head to head.[69] Rosenstiel ultimately triumphed with the passage of the Forand Bill in September 1958, although this was not enough for his company to close the gap with its Seagram rival. Schenley could not capitalize on its success, Edgar now implies, "because people were buying brands, not ages." "The whisky that Rosenstiel had made was close to undrinkable, and presented no real threat."[70]

Sam kept tabs on his international operations mainly from Montreal, working with two executives, Frank Marshall, in charge of Mexico, Central and South America, and Quintin Gwyn, whose responsibility was Europe and who spent much of his time in London. Sam formed the Seagram Overseas Corporation to pull it all together in 1956, overseeing international sales as well as the development of manufacturing facilities abroad. The company, by this point, was not only Canada's but "the world's biggest distiller," according to *Forbes*.[71] While 90 percent of its business was done in the United States, Seagram sold its whisky to 114 countries throughout the world, from Aden to Zanzibar; its sales amounted to $746 million, and its net profit was more than $25 million. Lew Rosenstiel's Schenley Corporation, once neck and neck with DC-SL, had a far more modest $470 million in sales and $11 million in profits.

Even when he had slowed down considerably at the end of the 1950s, when he was no longer so willing to cross the ocean for a quick chat with Jimmy Barclay, Sam's mind restlessly scanned the horizon for ideas and for possible deals. "I asked Miss Shanks the other day to tell you that I am hungry for news," Sam wrote plaintively to Quintin Gwyn in London. "Please satisfy my hunger . . ."[72] Taking brand names very seriously, Sam ransacked National Trust brochures looking for castles, manor houses or gardens with names he could use. He regularly asked Gwyn and Barclay to send him the history of his distilleries and those he wanted to buy. "An amazing person," recalled John Pringle, who knew Sam's terrible side, "querying and questioning everybody in a very, very gentle way."

■

IN 1957, SUFFERING from the obscure nervous illness that led him to withdraw entirely from public activity, Abe Klein worked on what must have been one of his least appealing assignments — Sam's personal coat of arms.[73] Sam obviously took great care with the project, and having toiled over labels and packaging for so many years he was familiar with the problems of communicating ideas in this particular form. He made it clear to Klein what he wanted; then, to instruct the heraldry expert, Klein prepared a memorandum, rewritten several times in his agitated, cramped handwriting.

"The point that is of paramount importance to Mr Bronfman," Klein told the expert, "is that out of the contemplation of the symbols of the coat of arms there should emerge a clear concept of the ideals which prompt him, and that these should be in harmony with the significances which in heraldry attach to these same symbols." Sam wanted an oak, "to convey the notion that with effort and perseverance, growth and strength may be achieved." He needed a ship, which "exemplifies the idea of scope of interest, of continuous pioneering, of increasing search for new horizons. It is also an allusion to Canada, the dominion which extends from sea unto sea." And he called for a globe, surmounted by clasped hands, "a symbol of faith and human brotherhood." "The ideal that is cherished," Klein observed, "is that of mankind throughout the world held together by pacts of friendship and loyalty." The motto, Sam instructed, was "Forward—the universal slogan of progress." It was probably A.M. Klein, hired as a wordsmith, who told Sam this should be "March Forth"—a reference to his birthday, March 4th.

Sam took the project seriously, and although he abandoned it in the end, after the design was produced, his interest sprang from an important part of his character. Sam hungered after the gentility that coats of arms suggested; he wanted to be respected for his moral authority, not just for his wealth; and he understood each of these, gentility and moral authority, as different sides of the same coin. Particularly later in life, when he insisted on the Jews' devotion to Canada, when he spoke of the "best people" who drank his whisky, when he was furious over not getting a seat in the Canadian Senate, he craved the sort of respect accorded to rank and titles, antiquity and tradition. Even when at leisure, as Mark Shinbane once observed, he wanted to be seen with "the horsey people"—at the Kentucky Derby, for example; but more profoundly, he wanted to enter the charmed circle of those to whom society declared itself grateful.[74] "There are two ways a man must live," Sam told a meeting of his distributors in Houston in April 1953, "two ways that a man must set up his examples in life, and that is, does he travel with one side of society or the other? Does he go with the good people or does he go with the people that are lackadaisical and not concerned very much about how their neighbours think of them?" Sam, for himself, had no doubts.

Like so many of his generation, Sam's attraction to rank and tradition drew him powerfully to the monarchy, of which he was a fervent admirer. A lifelong monarchist, whose meagre formal education in Brandon and Winnipeg at the turn of the century must have drummed into him reverence for the British crown, Sam loved association with kings and aristocracy. He showed this obviously with the names of his products: Crown Royal, Chivas

Regal, Royal Salute, Lord Calvert, King Arthur Dry Gin—to say nothing of the numerous coats of arms, crowns and other paraphernalia of nobility that adorned his bottles. One of the first times his photograph appeared in a newspaper, in April 1937, was when he personally paid for hundreds of special dinners for the Montreal Jewish poor on the occasion of the coronation of King George VI.[75]

The closest Sam got to monarchy was sixteen years later, when he attended the coronation of Queen Elizabeth II as the leading Canadian Jewish personality, or "king of the Jews," as Max Henderson remembers him saying.[76] Accompanied by Saidye, he rose at 4:00 A.M. to dress and go to Westminster Abbey for the ceremony. Sam "wore a white tie, tails and a top hat," Saidye recalled, "and I wore a white satin dress with a diamond tiara. The procession into the Abbey was splendid. First came the lords and ladies and their retinue, and then the heads of the states of the Dominions in their robes." Sam was enthralled, although he managed to retain his sense of humour, saying that the whole thing was "a great *simcha*"—an ironic contrast, by implication, with the boisterous, familial informality of Jewish festivities.[77] In fact, as Henderson attests, the Bronfmans' seats were originally behind one of the Abbey's giant pillars and they almost had no view of the ceremony at all. The problem fell into Max Henderson's lap, and he managed to trade tickets with Canadian industrialist D.P. Cruikshank and his wife, who were hardly interested enough to navigate the crowds in order to attend. "Mr Sam accepted the Cruikshanks' kindness almost as a matter of right," recalled Henderson, who was obviously resentful over the affair. "This so shocked me that I went to thank 'D.P.' myself and, unknown to Mr Sam, dispatched some of our finest products to his home in Rockcliffe." "After the ceremony," Saidye continued her description, "lunch was served in the Parliament Buildings. As we were crossing the square, I spotted the Queen's carriage and said to my Sam, 'I have never seen anything so beautiful. I'm going to touch it.' He replied, 'Don't be a farmer!' "

For much the same reasons as his attraction to the crown, Sam admired the rootedness, the self-assurance and the mastery seemingly embodied in the WASP social milieu he knew in

Montreal. In his dress, his speech, in many of the routines of his household, Sam adopted many of the motifs of the very society from which he and other Jews remained excluded. One of the best examples is the schooling provided for his children — although this was to some degree a pattern he authorized rather than consciously designed. With Sam away much of the time when the children were growing up, spending weekdays in New York and only weekends at home, it was Saidye who took charge of their care and education. The children went to private schools in Montreal: the boys to Selwyn House; and the girls to "The Study" — "a thoroughly WASP school specializing in teachers from England," Phyllis recalls, where she was one of only four Jewish girls (including her sister). Later, Edgar and Charles went as boarders to the élite Trinity College School in Port Hope, Ontario, about two hundred miles from home, where they were the first Jews ever to attend. Upon graduation, Minda went to Smith College and to Columbia for a master's degree under Jacques Barzun, Phyllis to Cornell and then Vassar. Edgar attended Williams College in Massachusetts where he lived a riotous life, and Charles went to McGill where he had difficulty adjusting to university and became increasingly miserable.

In the convention of the day, Sam envisioned no independent role for his daughters, and he criticized them heavily when they showed signs of assuming one. From time to time he would harangue Phyllis and Minda for being too smart, saying that too much education was not a good thing for young women, that they should not have left home, and should not have gone to college. In Sam's view, they would end up being dissatisfied, would want too much out of life, and so on. Quite likely, he also felt that their independence would injure their prospects of a good marriage.

Nevertheless, they did marry. Phyllis, chafing at the familial constraints she continued to feel after graduating from Vassar, wedded the self-described "economic consultant" Jean Lambert in 1949 — "a dark, tall, egocentric Middle European with the suave good looks of a French matinee idol and the throaty speech inflections of a first-rate Las Vegas impressionist pretending to be Charles Boyer pretending to be a Resistance leader about to die for the glory of France," in Peter Newman's exuberant description — wrong on only one point: Lambert was an Alsatian, not quite "Middle European."[78] Sam was undoubtedly more pleased with Minda's match four years later — the banker, Alain de Gunzburg, scion of an aristocratic Jewish banking family whose noble lineage extended to the Czarist Empire and who was a partner in the Banque Louis-Dreyfus in Paris.

Minda's wedding took place in Paris and was a relatively small affair since the groom's father, the aged Baron Jean de Gunzburg, was an invalid and unable to travel; about two hundred guests watched the religious ceremony from the drawing room of the bridegroom's grandmother, Madame Louis Hirsch, who lived in an adjoining apartment. The Bronfman party stayed at the Hotel Ritz on Place Vendôme where the wedding dinner afterwards was held, and on its stationery Minda wrote a sincerely felt tribute to her parents just before the ceremony: "I want to say how much I love you and how very much I appreciate everything you have done for me these past twenty-eight years. We've had our ups and downs, our ins and outs, but I've always known that when the chips were down you two were always ready to back me up. And if my children love me as much as I love you, then I will consider that I've done well and have been a good parent."[79] "Dear Puppums," she addressed Sam affectionately, "we shall try to carry on the splendid traditions of both our families and, above all, to create a home where love, respect and joy reign supreme."

Minda, who dubbed her new family as "the Ginsboigs" in letters home, thereby became a baroness, to her father's obvious delight: "my daughter, the baroness," as he proudly referred to her in an interview some years later — perhaps not without tongue in cheek, for Sam also felt ill at ease with his European aristocratic in-laws whose social and cultural sophistication he could not match, and he never entirely approved of his daughter's baronial style. Looking back, Phyllis comments on how unfair this was. "Minda really did everything he wanted and felt that he expected of her; wore furs, was elegant, married a title (i.e. good family) if not wealth, yet he continuously criticized her as extravagant."[80]

Edgar's marriage to Ann Loeb, also in 1953, linked Sam to an important New York family of German-Jewish origins, but according to Edgar, the social contacts with these in-laws left his father with similar, gnawing feelings of inferiority. Sam could not have asked for more in terms of social standing. Ann's mother was a Lehman, her maternal grandmother a Lewisohn, and her paternal grandmother, as Stephen Birmingham notes, "a Sephardic Moses, whose family had been plantation owners in the Old South." Ann's father, John Loeb, came from a patrician banking family that looked back to several generations of financiers; the family firm, Loeb, Rhoades, was itself related by marriage to the prestigious Bache & Co., and was second only to Merrill Lynch in the brokerage business. This was more than enough to make Sam insecure, and at the wedding the Loebs seem to have done their best to make him feel it. John Loeb claimed not even to have heard of the Bronfmans until his daughter was going out with Edgar, and at the reception the patriarch Carl Loeb, listening to one of the guests gushing about the young couple, suddenly replied, "That is true, Madame, but at my age I am not sure I can adjust to the idea of being the poor relation." Meanwhile, Mrs Arthur Lehman sniffily expressed the disdain of German-Jewish aristocracy for the Canadian parvenus: "But those Bronfmans," she reportedly said, "have just come down out of the *trees*."[81]

In the early 1950s, when Minda was still single and when Phyllis's marriage to Jean Lambert was on the rocks, Sam decided that his family needed "a place to go," as he put it, some sort of family retreat (he had his daughters particularly in mind) that would provide them with "the right background." As with so many of his decisions, Sam put great store in doing the "right" thing, establishing the "right" sort of environment, and to him, perhaps tired of the social networks of Montreal, this suggested a country estate in a wealthy suburb outside New York. He eventually settled upon a magnificent mansion near Tarrytown in the rolling hills of Westchester County, less than an hour from Manhattan. "The estate was magnificent," Saidye remembered, "22 acres planted with superb trees and lovely gardens. There was a small lake on the property and a large, heated swimming pool made of Italian tile. The house was modelled on a Spanish villa, a charming place with 25 enormous rooms and fireplaces everywhere with mantels of marble or Dutch tile. The master bedroom was magnificent, its windows offering a sweeping view of the Hudson River."[82]

Named "Belvedere," after their street in Montreal, the Bronfmans' Tarrytown estate was the family's principal summer residence for several years, and the place where Sam and Saidye would entertain American guests. It was close enough to New York so that Sam would often come there from the office with Edgar, for evenings and weekends. The other children would come as well — Charles spent summers in Tarrytown in the early 1950s, as did Minda and her husband and, less often, Phyllis. The couple's close friends, Dr Edgar Mayer, a distinguished physician, and his wife Cecile were close neighbours. As his sons recalled, Sam particularly liked the billiard room in a two-storey recreation house that overlooked the swimming pool, his prowess at the billiard table being one of his lasting achievements from his time as a hotel keeper on the prairies. "Ah, the relics of a misspent youth!" he would muse. (According to Charles, whom he beat regularly, Sam "played a great strategic game.")[83]

Apart from a few lapses, and in keeping with Sam's sense of propriety and decorum, the rhythm of life at Tarrytown was remarkably formal. The house had a staff of five or six and "was like a self-contained city," as one who once worked there said.[84] Meals were in the grand style. "I used to prepare two different menus for the weekends when a host of people visited us," Saidye recalled.[85] Luncheon was served on the terrace by the pool, under the shade of umbrellas, but even here there was ceremony: "there was never anything as informal as that you would get your own food," Phyllis noted.[86] Formal meals, in particular, were what struck Stanley Lewis, a sculptor who spent some time at Tarrytown doing a bust of Sam some years later. The chef in his white hat, Lewis remembered, put a roast lamb and little scissors before Sam at the table: "and he cut it, and there was a crown on each bone, and all the chops fell over. Every meal was a banquet. I had to dress up, a tie, a suit, you know."

Sam seems to have preferred the domestic formality of Tarrytown, surrounded by his family, to any other kind of holiday. Unused to relaxation, he experienced vacations simply as a way of doing business in an unfamiliar, and generally inconvenient, locale. Whether at Old Orchard, Maine, or Neponsit, Long Island, where Sam and Saidye spent some summers before the war, or at winter spots in Boca Raton or Palm Beach, Florida, or at Cuernavaca, Mexico, Sam was a restless vacationer, prowling about looking at real estate, checking the prices of this or that, and seeking information on the local economy. Wherever he was, he received a constant stream of messages from Montreal and New York, and conferred sometimes hourly with his associates at home. Detesting the cold winters of Montreal, he determinedly went south during the winters, particularly in his later years, but gave the impression almost of being there against his will. From Mexico in 1964, for example, he wrote grumpily to Abe Klein, sealed in his house in Montreal at this point, telling his friend how he could not stand the cold, "and besides I am building a plant in Mexico."[87]

For a few years at the end of the 1950s Sam and Saidye were attracted to the lush, trend-setting Roundhill resort in Jamaica, not far from Seagram's Long Pond Estates and close to Montego Bay. A deluxe hotel and luxury cottage complex originally organized by entrepreneur John Pringle, the Roundhill community was all the rage in the mid-1950s, as one of its most famous cottage owners, Noel Coward, recalled. "Since Roundhill opened everybody is coming to Jamaica," he wrote in 1957, when the Bronfmans were there. It was all too distracting, Coward felt, "packed with all the *soi-disant gratin* [so-called upper crust] of New York."[88] Sam and Saidye, in their mid-sixties, found their way in the rarefied community Noel Coward described. Renting a highly desirable cottage owned by William Paley, head of CBS, they made friends with several English guests with whom they socialized around their swimming pool. Sam also struck up a friendship with the tall, patrician Pringle, who had been an equerry to the Duke of Windsor during the war, and pestered him endlessly about the possibility of getting a royal warrant for some of his whisky.[89]

The Bronfmans' time in Roundhill ended suddenly at the beginning of the 1960s. Sam heard the cottage he had been renting was coming on the market and instructed Pringle to buy it. Unfortunately, he was too late, and the cottage was sold to someone else. Ever after, Sam felt he had been blackballed by the other members of the community because he was a Jew. Pringle (whose mother was Jewish) insists to this day that there was nothing to it, and that someone else simply made a deal first. Unconvinced, Sam never went to Roundhill again.[90]

■

"THE BEST PRESENT you can give me," Minda told her father shortly before her wedding in December 1953, "is to promise Mummy that you will not worry about Phyllis, that you will trust her and believe that all will turn out for the best. Think how much closer you are to her now. Notice what good friends Phyllis and I have become and realize that there are silver linings in all clouds, and that the present cloud will disappear very soon."[91] Sam was indeed worried. Phyllis left her marriage to Jean Lambert after a short time, and in early 1954 she moved to Paris and settled on her own in an artist's studio adjacent to the Montparnasse cemetery, committed to "making something of myself," as she explained. "Just have confidence in your strange daughter who must go about things in her own way and who is very determined about what she shall and must do," she told her parents.[92] Sam saw nothing worthwhile in Phyllis's artistic aspirations, and indeed found it difficult to take his daughters seriously at all. It never occurred to him that they would have such a thing as a career. "When I said I was going to get a divorce," Phyllis recalls, Sam's astonished reply was: "What? My pretty little daughter?" Sam had little understanding, therefore, when the twenty-seven-year-old Phyllis wrote from Paris of the need to find her own way, to develop her potential, and to make "something positive, worthwhile, meaningful and wonderful of the short time between birth and death." In his view, she should have come back to Montreal. Sam also felt guilty, Edgar guessed much later, that he had allowed the ill-starred marriage to Lambert to go forward in the first place. Phyllis would never have brooked his interference at the time, it was true, but Sam, who disliked his son-in-law from the start, might have prevented the marriage by cutting off any money to the new couple.[93] Guilty or not, however, Sam was unhappy.

In the spring of 1954, Sam and Saidye visited their daughter and mentioned an idea that had been percolating in Sam's mind for many years. Ever since the 1940s he had been thinking about the construction of a Seagram building in mid-Manhattan — "one so beautiful as to be a monument to the company and his personal efforts," William Wachtel remembered Sam saying. Only the lack of a site had prevented him from acting. Ever with an eye to "the silken gown," Sam would hear of nothing other than the gracious expanse of Park Avenue for his project, and nothing was possible, therefore, until 1951, when he was finally able to purchase the block between 52nd and 53rd Streets, along with most of the land between Park and Lexington Avenues. The price, according to Wachtel, was four million dollars.[94]

With his personal tastes running to the Tudor fortifications on Peel Street, Sam did not impose any design ideas, and to help drum up enthusiasm among the Seagram sales staff, Vic Fischel ordered provisional plans prepared by Charles Luckman, former president of Lever Brothers and the head of a well-known architectural firm. Announced in the *New York Times* and *Newsweek* in mid-July, Luckman's proposal for 375 Park Avenue, to be named the "House of Seagram," was for a rather conventional structure with the first four storeys of marble and bronze, topped by a thirty-storey steel and glass tower with the usual recesses to accommodate the city's building code. The design also had the sort of symbolism that Sam might have appreciated: it emphasized the four corners, to represent the major Seagram brands, and it had paving stones inscribed with the names of salesmen who sold the most whisky.[95] Phyllis had known of her father's project for years, but the July publication, with its detailed description, set her off. Revolted by the plan, which replicated some of the mechanically minded stereotypes of the day, she decided to act.

"I was boiling with fury," she recalled. "I wrote him that he wanted a really fine building, and he was lucky to be living in a period when there were great architects."[96] Mainly involved in painting and sculpture, she had developed an interest in architecture when at Vassar, and after graduation she studied architectural history with former Vassar professor Richard Krautheimer at the Institute of Fine Arts of New York University. Knowing of her artistic interests, Sam had sent his daughter some material on the Luckman proposal, but had probably not anticipated a strong reaction.

If so, he was wrong. In response to what she had seen, Phyllis closeted herself for several days and prepared a long critique of Luckman's plan. "If the thing is to be done it should be done properly," she told her mother with characteristic bluntness — certainly the kind of argument that appealed to Sam. Quite likely with an eye to getting her daughter back from Paris, Saidye proposed that Phyllis come to New York and take charge of the search for an appropriate design — a suggestion that Phyllis seized eagerly. But she had no intention of taking a back seat. "Now . . . what does Daddy have to say about it IN PRECISE TERMS," she asked her mother, "and enough of this tapping his little daughter on the head like a good dog. And when I come to the U.S. it will be to do a job and not to sit around in the St Regis making sweet talk . . . I should like the chance of doing a serious job that is all. I started off in this thing in a dilettantish way but the more I go in to it, the more it is what I would like to do, but I can only do it on the terms of someone employed to do a job and not dear little Fido Fifi."[97]

Impressed, as he often was by strongly held, well-articulated views, Sam agreed to give Phyllis a hearing. She flew to New York in August 1954, and lectured her father on the importance of her challenge to his plans: "the moment business organizations and institutions decide to build," she later wrote, "they claim responsibility and take a moral position; and upon the choice of architect depends the quality of the statement." She also appealed to her father's professional pride: "I pointedly told him that rather than copy others, he should set the standards for what should be copied, feeling at the time that he would understand that argument." To the amateur of old English and Scottish castles, Phyllis urged consideration of avant garde Central European designs — "the new architectural thinking that started to mature in the twenties," as she later put it.[98] On the advice of Lou Crandall, a friend and building contractor, Sam put the task of interviewing specialists and selecting the architect in the hands of his strong-willed daughter. "Don't talk to me until you've done it, until you've made your decision," Phyllis remembers Sam saying.[99]

"Now I really have a job," she wrote a friend. "Crandall . . . told my father that I could do a job that no one else could have done, going to these people and talking to them. Certainly no one in Seagram could (by virtue of being employed), and a daughter who is interested in seeing that her father puts up a fine building seems to have everyone's sympathy. And now I must say my prayers every day to be able to do the job as it should be done. What a unique chance I have!"[100]

Phyllis set about the task with energy and determination. "I must really go into it and get in touch with the best people," she told Saidye, sounding very much like her father. For the next two and a half months, with the help of Lou Crandall and Philip Johnson, then the Chairman of the Department of Architecture at the Museum of Modern Art, she identified the architects who were building the most significant buildings. From New York, she travelled to Philadelphia, New Haven, Detroit, Denver, Chicago and elsewhere to see them and their buildings. She interviewed young and old, academics and critics, leading designers and architectural historians. Very much like Sam, Phyllis had a keen eye for the future: "While looking at the buildings and talking to those concerned with architecture," she wrote, "the question to be asked was obviously not who should be the architect, but who was now going to make the greatest contribution to architecture?"

By the end of October, as Phyllis wrote to a friend, she had her answer — the celebrated German-emigré director of architecture at the Illinois Institute of Technology, Ludwig Mies van der Rohe. Mies, she felt, was at the very centre of the contemporary discourse on architecture: "Mies forces you in. . . . You might think this austere strength, this ugly beauty, is terribly severe. It is, and yet all the more beauty in it. . . . The younger men, the second generation, are talking in terms of Mies or denying him."[101] After a few weeks of the most intense consultation and study, she was commenting authoritatively on the course of modern architecture. Above all, she sounded a note of supreme confidence. She even lectured Sam on how her choice should be made public. "Daddy, the announcement must be made PROPERLY," Phyllis told him, "and no balling up by the Seagram public relations staff."[102]

Crucial, from Sam's point of view, was the matter of trust. Moved by his daughter's argument, he decided to rely on her capacity to make the vital choice. And similarly with Lou Crandall. Counting on his own instincts, Sam chose him to be the contractor of the building without bothering to invite others to bid on the project, as was common practice. Believing that Crandall would build the building "as if it were his own," and that he would keep an eye on costs, Sam was prepared to turn the gigantic project over to him. In Phyllis's mind, this is typical of how her father operated. "He picked certain people as partners and felt that his trust in them would be repaid. Not many trust others in this way."[103]

Convinced that he was getting "the best," Sam was prepared to back his daughter whenever it came to issues of importance. Early in the project, for example, Phyllis learned something of Philip Johnson's fascist sympathies of the 1930s, and his involvement with Father Coughlin and other pro-Nazi groups of the time. For the head of the Canadian Jewish Congress, this ought to have been a serious matter. But to his daughter's amazement, Sam offered no objection to Johnson's involvement, being convinced that those whom he trusted should be given a free hand, and keen to focus on the present rather than the past.[104] The imposing Mies van der Rohe, who exuded authority, seems to have brushed aside any of Sam's lingering doubts about the design. One thing he insisted on, the industrialist told the world-renowned architect: the building could not be "on stilts." "*Ja*," replied Mies in his heavy German accent, bending over a model of the structure so that his head was at street level: "but come down here and see how nice it looks." Sam knew when to yield, and did so, making only one stipulation: the building should be the "crowning glory" of both his and Mies's careers.[105]

Having invested so much energy in the project to this point, Phyllis was not prepared to sit back and let the men build the building. With Sam's agreement, she had herself named director of planning for the project at $20,000 a year — another victory wrested from her father. "He never gave me the job," Phyllis later explained. "I took it."[106] Completely without experience, Phyllis's task thereafter was to work closely with Mies as a faithful guardian of the master's vision. "On leaving Paris I had not expected to do more than to help choose the architect and then return," she wrote, "but it became increasingly clear to me that the person who had chosen the architect must stay with the job to fight for the concept."[107]

"The concept," as Mies envisioned it, was quite spectacular: a spare, thirty-eight-storey tinted glass and steel office tower, entirely sheathed in bronze, set back some ninety feet on a twin-fountained granite and marble plaza. A stunning success, the Seagram Building was considered by many at the time to be the city's finest postwar structure and a masterpiece of urban design. Lewis Mumford was enthralled, even though he was a sharp critic of much of modern architecture for its lack of human scale: "Out of this stalled, rush-hour clutter of new structures, brightly sordid, meretriciously up-to-date, the Seagram building has emerged like a Rolls-Royce accompanied by a motorcycle escort that gives it space and speed. . . . In their willingness to accept van der Rohe's judgment, rather than that of their realty experts, the Seagram executives deserve, in the cause of art, a special salute."[108]

Occasionally, Sam attempted to interfere in relatively small matters. On one occasion, at a meeting of a high-level building committee, he actually blew up at his daughter over a proposal for the plaza in front of the building. "You don't yell at me!" she retorted, and Sam eventually calmed down. But for the most part, Sam left Phyllis and Mies to do their work, preoccupied as he was at the time with the introduction of his Chivas brand.

Like her father in her obsession with quality, Phyllis fought fiercely over matters large and small. From some vantage points, she appeared on the job as tough an authoritarian as Sam, and as fearsome too. "As far as my input was concerned," remembers Robert Ruppel, an insurance specialist worried about costs, "Phyllis said 'Do it!' and it was done."[109] But in fact, getting her way was the result of constant struggle, on behalf of artistic integrity. To have nine-foot ceilings, for example, as opposed to the standard eight, she battled bitterly for ten, "until we graciously accepted nine"; she and Mies laboured over countless design problems — fire alarms, lettering standards, door handles, mail chutes, and so on — determined to get each one just right.

"From the framing of the windows to the total building, love has gone into it," Phyllis commented, "love for every detail."[110]

Partly as a result, the building cost a whopping $40 million — "no mortgage; right out of the cash box," as William Wachtel noted, glumly making calculations about rentals. "Prominent real estate brokers told me that we would never be able to rent space at seven dollars a square foot, as the price at that time for a good building was four dollars."[111] Sam also worried whether people would want to rent a building that carried the name of a whisky company. At one point, the rental agents proposed a solution — to put a bank on the ground floor. "That's ridiculous," was Phyllis' response, "I won't hear of it." Unwilling to give in so easily, Sam made some enquiries, but in the end Mies went out to Tarrytown and dissuaded him. "If I were you, Mr Bronfman," Mies said, "I would not do that."[112] Sam, once again, deferred to the master.

When 375 Park Avenue actually opened in December 1957, Sam's concerns proved to have been groundless. The building itself was showered with praise. Some years later, the *New York Times* called it "the most admired skyscraper in Manhattan — the one with which all new buildings have to be compared and which none so far has quite measured up." And this judgement has stood the test of time. "Twenty-five years after its completion," the American Institute of Architects commented on the Seagram Building in 1984, "it fully retains its enduring vitality and quiet beauty, and still holds a special place in the hearts and imaginations of all who see it, work in it, and admire its brilliant solution to the still vexing problems of urban design."[113] Soon after it opened there was a waiting list for tenants. Sam featured his new building on the cover of the company's annual report, and swelled with pride over the outcome: "an architectural masterpiece," as he himself later put it, ". . . regarded by many authorities as the most beautiful feature in the impressive New York skyline." In its commentary, *Fortune* referred to the tenacity and ambition Sam had managed to instil in his children. The building was, it said, "an almost defiant gift of filial love."[114]

■

ALTHOUGH SURROUNDED BY people, courted constantly in the business and the Jewish spheres, and at the centre of a vast industrial empire, Sam was something of a loner—seldom putting his trust in individuals for very long, and with few if any close friends. "You know, he'd go to a party and he'd always wind up in the corner in a serious conversation with somebody," says Charles. "He could not do small talk. He just wasn't equipped to do it."[115] Misreading social signals, Sam was prone to bouts of jealousy or vindictiveness, and could strike inexplicably at those around him, especially if they got too close. Charles knew that this was one of the dangerous aspects of relations with his father, and remembers warning one of his associates to "back off" at a certain point, precisely because of the danger of Sam lashing out.[116]

Like many egotists, Sam viewed the world as a hostile place, full of hazards and pitfalls. He saw his only shelter, ultimately, in his immediate family—and hence his constant admonition to his children: that they should stick together, that only as a unit were they a force to achieve good, that if they went their separate ways they would never amount to anything. Charles recalled one evening when his father received a phone call reporting one of Edgar's disastrous exploits at Williams College. Roaring down a highway on his motorcycle late one night on the way back from Bennington, Edgar went off the road and landed head first in a chicken coop. The college authorities wanted to throw him out, and there was a question of whether he would be arrested for drunk driving. "Dad was trying to do what a father would do in those cases," Charles remembered, "and I told him I thought it was terrible, [but] that if Edgar was guilty he should suffer like anybody else." Sam was furious at Edgar, but he blew up at Charles too: "When your brother's in trouble you don't talk that way," Sam roared, "you help him."[117]

By the early 1950s, Sam's dynastic concerns focused principally on his huge whisky empire. Everything he had built was vulnerable, he insisted. "Shirtsleeves to shirtsleeves in three generations," he repeated—and sometimes with the addendum: "And it's not going to happen in this family, goddamn it!"[118] Sam took his family responsibilities very seriously, and although given to violent, profanity-spitting diatribes against his brothers he was fiercely loyal to them at the same time. When Abe, for example, was about to be thrown out of the Montefiore Club for cheating at gin rummy, Sam went immediately to the board, insisting that his brother be reinstated.[119] "He might call his brothers any name in the book," Sam Cohen remembered, "but nobody else dared say it, because he had a fierce pride and, of course, a great love for his family."[120] Despite the strained relations, Sam's brothers and sisters assembled occasionally on Jewish holidays such as the breaking of the fast at the end of Yom Kippur, and Sam's and Allan's families attended each other's homes for Friday-night dinners. Sam was attentive to his brothers-in-law, both his own and Saidye's sisters' husbands, assisting them financially and setting up several with distributorships or other posts in the business. One of them, Moe Levine, married Saidye's widowed sister Freda in 1951, and when the couple moved to Montreal they became particularly close with Sam and Saidye. With his brothers, Levine took over the Workman Uniform Company in Montreal and became the suppliers of the famous Crown Royal purple bags.

But for all Sam's concerns with the wider family circle he seems to have had no doubt that his own sons would take over the business, and without saying so in so many words he communicated this to them from the time they were very young. Charles and Edgar were destined to become "merchant princes," Sam told Sol Kanee.[121] And to Edgar, the elder of his two sons, he seems consistently to have accorded pre-eminence. "I felt my father loved me more," Edgar once told an interviewer. "No, love is not the word — expected more from me as the No. 1 son. At first, I resented hell out of it. But when I was about twenty or twenty-one, I began to enjoy it." As early as 1946, when he had just turned sixteen, Edgar referred to himself as "the future President of Distillers Corporation-Seagrams" in a letter to his father.[122]

A few years later the two brothers, then in their early twenties, talked about their future together one summer evening at their home in Montreal: Edgar staked out his claim to move to New York and run the giant American branch, which accounted for

90 percent of the company's business. Charles had no objection: "I don't like New York and the throat cutting, the tremendous competitive drive that goes on. I said to Edgar that as far as I was concerned, he is No. 2 and I am No. 3. I don't particularly want to run this empire."[123]

What was awkward in all of this was the undisputed claim of Sam's own brothers, particularly Allan, to a share in the business. For Sam, this could not have been an easy problem. Certainly he had worked hard over the years to distinguish himself from his brothers in his effort to live down the past. Whereas Harry, for example, had a weakness for doing things on the cheap, Sam set his mark on the company by moving in precisely the opposite direction, with his constant emphasis on quality. In the lore of Sam's family, it was always Sam's brothers who were responsible for the family's brushes with the law during the 1920s and early 1930s — a view probably shared by Sam himself. At the same time, three of the brothers enjoyed a place of honour at the Seagram company for many years. Mel Griffin, who began to work at the LaSalle plant in 1945, remembers how this was symbolized in the family laundry, done at the plant's facilities and neatly bundled with the appropriate labels — "Mr Sam," "Mr Allan" and "Mr Harry."[124]

In 1951, Sam felt ready to broach with his brothers and sisters the long-delayed issue of how to apportion the family's enterprise. Sam was in a feisty mood. "My brothers had complicated matters," he told Terence Robertson, "by giving their families the impression that each one of them was the real brains behind our business, and none wanted to lose face by having to admit to his children that he wasn't really entitled to a lion's share. Harry and Allan seemed confident that their sons would inherit part of Seagram's on a more or less equal basis with my own sons. I could never allow this, mainly because I don't believe that anybody should clutter up his business with relatives. We have enough of that in government."[125]

The entire fortune, at this point, amounted to some $20 million in cash, property and investments, plus the family's 53-percent share of DC-SL. Calling his brothers and sisters together, Sam insisted that "it would have been the wish of our parents to have all the family benefit." He then unfolded his plan, which went something like this: of the assets, Sam would receive $8 million, Allan $3 million, Abe and Harry $2 million each, and each of Sam's four sisters $1 million; as to the family's 53-percent share of the company, Sam would retain 37.5 percent, with the balance shared by the rest. In Sam's version at least, he made it clear that from this point on, Seagram belonged to him. "The business is mine," he told Allan, taking him aside. "You must understand that the words 'we' and 'us' no longer apply." Sam remembered Abe and Harry protesting, and his sister Rose ending up on his own side. "Sam is being modest about his own share, and generous to all of us," was her view. "I for one am very proud of him." Long since having retired from the business, Sam's older brothers grudgingly accepted his scheme.[126]

The real problem, which did not come to the surface immediately, was Allan. Sam claimed to have cared deeply about his younger brother, with whom he had worked since Allan graduated from law school just after the First World War. "We were like father and son," Sam said. But Sam's feelings changed over time, and as his business grew in scope after the war his paternal affection mingled with a measure of contempt. Allan, as Sam saw him, was an increasingly dependent figure, deferring to Sam's superior business sense while sitting atop a gigantic industrial empire. With his unerring eye for weakness, Sam punished Allan for not living up to his own standards. Allan, for his part, slipped deeper and deeper into dependency. This was the time when Sam had a standing overnight reservation on the train to New York and fretted constantly, as we have seen, whether to take it or not. On those trips, Sam always took Allan. The younger brother, never sure until the last moment whether "they" were departing that night for New York, humiliatingly attended upon Sam.

Max Henderson pictured Allan as "a person of considerable dignity, well educated, suave and urbane ... patient and tolerant," and for many years people were struck by how he and Sam complemented each other in so many ways.[127] But once things began to go wrong, the relationship deteriorated progressively. Mild-mannered and courteous, Allan deferred gently to his fiery brother, and this very deference seems to have irritated Sam, confirming his sense of his brother's weakness and timidity. The man who feared that his empire might easily crumble, who cultivated a proud public presence, did not take easily to a prominent Bronfman who seemed weak, insecure and uncertain. The more Allan wilted under Sam's wrath, the more Sam seethed — as if this side of his younger brother evoked some deeply repressed, and deeply feared, part of his own complex character.

Allan could do nothing right. Sam resented Allan's education, regretting that he himself had never had the opportunity, and claiming, probably unfairly, that he had sacrificed in order to pay Allan's tuition. When Allan received the Legion of Honour from the French government in 1949, having donated tons of wheat to the hungry town of Troyes after the war, Sam burned with jealousy. Proximity also was a source of tension: living in adjacent houses on Belvedere Road, the brothers saw more of each other than they probably wished. Saidye, energetic and outgoing, did not get along with her other-worldly, frequently ailing sister-in-law Lucy — another source of irritation. By the 1950s, Sam's verbal abuse of his brother was legendary. "He would call him all the filthy names under the sun," said Mark Shinbane. On Peel Street, office workers became used to the sound of Sam's outbursts against Allan, his harangues and the crashing of telephones.[128]

Very much on Sam's mind, in the course of these tirades, was the problem of succession. He was absolutely determined that Allan's sons, Edward and Peter, who were just finishing their education at the beginning of the 1950s, would not assume a place in the family business. "When we were smaller," Minda told an interviewer, "we thought our cousins would also go into the business. Later we knew how things stood." As Sam had it, he was almost doing Allan's sons a favour. "I don't think it's good in a family, one leader and the rest sheep getting dividends," he said.[129]

Throughout these battles, things were made worse by the fact that Sam and Allan were yoked together in an unusual financial arrangement that technically controlled the Seagram company. Set up in 1942 by Laz Phillips and his junior partner, Philip Vineberg, it consisted of a series of interrelated trusts, to enable the two brothers to pass along their fortunes, and their stake in

Seagram, to their children. According to this mechanism, Sam's and most of Allan's share of Seagram ended up as the sole assets of Seco Ltd., whose stock was in turn completely owned by two groups of trust funds, named after the offspring of each brother — Edper, with trusts for each of Allan's children, Edward, Peter and Mona (who died in 1950); and Cemp, with funds for Charles, Edgar, Minda and Phyllis. The beneficiaries, however, were not the children of Sam and Allan, but the grandchildren. The trustees were identical except that Sam served as one of the trustees for each of the Edper funds, and Allan did the same thing for Cemp; and in a further complication, at age twenty-five each of the children served as trustees on their siblings' trust funds. With the Cemp funds owning a majority interest in Seco, amounting to almost 70 percent of the company, Sam's seniority was assured — or at least so it seemed to him.

By the mid-1950s Sam's sons were growing restive under what *Fortune* called the "skein of tangled connections between the two brothers and seven cousins."[130] For one thing, Charles and Edgar were unimpressed with the lacklustre management of the Cemp funds. Edgar persuaded Sam, who was rather conservative when it came to both personal and company finances, to hire Charles's friend, the twenty-eight-year-old Leo Kolber, to take charge of the Cemp investments. An acquaintance of Charles from his days at McGill, the intense, slightly built Kolber was the son of a Montreal dentist who had long since died, and seemed to Sam the very model of youthful self-assurance and determination — precisely the kind of influence he and Saidye decided was desirable at the time for their sons. While Edgar and Charles had lived in luxury, Kolber came from a modest home, had struggled through law school, and was fiercely ambitious. Sam encouraged the relationship. "I felt that it could do no harm for Charles to experience at first hand how less fortunate boys of his own age had to work that much harder to educate themselves for the future," he told Terence Robertson. "A touch of poverty around the place wouldn't do the children any harm at all," he added. Kolber, who saw a great future in commercial real estate — and who had some quite spectacular if small-scale success in previous investments with Edgar and Charles to his credit — became general manager of Cemp in 1957, with a salary of $18,500 a year, plus 10 percent of the profits on any deal he made. "It's a good idea," Sam commented. Kolber, he said, was "a little Jewish boy on the make. That's the best kind to have handle our money."[131]

Once again, Sam was right. After a stumbling start, during which Kolber miscalculated on two shopping centres, his policies began to bear fruit. Operating with some $10 million in borrowed funds and a few million of its own, Cemp soon controlled highly profitable shopping centres and office buildings across Canada, and launched several important construction projects — the Fairview Centre at Pointe Claire, the Ville d'Anjou in Montreal, the Toronto-Dominion Centre in Toronto, and the Pacific Centre in Vancouver. Through Fairview Corporation Limited, its real-estate arm (which Kolber later put together with Cadillac Development Corporation and the Canadian Equity and Development Corporation to form the gigantic Cadillac Fairview Corporation Limited), Cemp became the largest developer in Canada in about ten years, controlling an estimated $300 million in Canadian real estate by the time of Sam's death, in 1971.[132]

Careful and deliberate, Sam became an even more conservative investor in his later years — although with a canny business sense that veteran investors admired. As well, he showed a strong commitment to Canadian development, arguing that Canada lacked capital accumulation. "Sam Bronfman has the feeling that if a man has amassed a fortune," Kolber told a *Fortune* reporter, "he has a duty to keep it rolling in the economy." Almost to the end of his life, Sam kept his hands on the deals, having lunch with Kolber once a week and speaking to him constantly on the telephone. Sometimes it was a struggle to convince Sam, and not all were able to manage it. Everyone who wanted to get on his good side had to "technique" Sam, Edgar observes — a flattering process of diplomacy, as his son described it, which might invoke one of the patriarch's supposed earlier injunctions, as, for example: "Gee, Dad, I remember some years ago your saying . . ." "When you come up against some ideas father has," Edgar commented in 1966, "you have to move delicately."[133]

With Charles and Edgar taking over the management of the Canadian and American branches of the business respectively,

Sam felt it increasingly awkward to contend with Allan and his continuing financial involvement in the company, together with that of his sons Edward and Peter through the Edper trusts. Through the 1950s, Sam waged what must have been a debilitating psychological war against his younger brother. The two spoke little to each other, stopped going to each other's homes, and maintained only the thinnest veneer of cordiality for public consumption. By the end of the decade Allan was more or less pushed out of the business and occupied himself increasingly with Jewish communal affairs, particularly the Canadian Friends of the Hebrew University.

Alex Mogolon, who worked for Allan on Jewish matters, described part of his routine on Peel Street. "By 10:00 or 10:30 he'd call me into his office. Allan would serve coffee and dictate a few letters. Around 11:00 he'd say, 'Do you think we should have a drink now?' and by 11:30 we'd be having a drink." Even then, Allan had Sam to contend with. "Sam would come storming in, and when Sam came into the office you really knew it. 'You sit there, Alex, you're one of the family,' " Sam would say, working up one of his tirades. "Allan would sit there, listening to every word and say thoughtfully, softly, 'You're quite right, Sam, you're quite right, Sam, I'll look after it.' Allan, embarrassed, would explain Sam's behaviour. 'Sam is the kind of man who won't let anything eat his gut. He has to say it. He means well. There's no one who loves the Jewish people more than Sam. If something irritates him, he has to tell me about it.' "[134]

In the early 1960s, in a final spasm of family conflict, Sam forced a clean break between the company and the Edper trusts. For some $16 million, Cemp bought out Edper's 32.2 percent of the Seco company, delivering almost all of Allan's Seagram shares into the hands of Sam's children. Relations between Sam and Allan were officially restored, although the feuding between them continued at a low-grade level. Relations among the cousins were "polite," Edgar claimed, suggesting that by 1966 the quarrel was dead and buried. But resentment obviously smouldered and persisted long after the break.[135]

Sam never expressed regrets, and seems to have considered the break with Allan as necessary to secure the continuation of his life's work. In his last decade, with his sons in undisputed control of the company, he surveyed the scene with satisfaction. "I've set it up much better than the Rothschilds," he liked to say. "They spread the children. I've kept them together."

CHAPTER IX

Elder Statesman

IN 1966, WHEN Sam was seventy-seven, *Fortune* published the most lavish portrait of him ever, in a highly complimentary, richly illustrated two-part article on the Bronfman family, which touched on many themes of his career that Sam thought important.[1] The article began with a full-page photograph showing Sam with a quizzical smile, peering over his glasses, looking up from his favourite card game — solitaire — with a glass of V.O. on the rocks at his right hand. He was at the centre of the piece. His family, the author made clear, had amassed one of North America's great fortunes — estimated at $400 million — and his company was the dominant force in the industry, with annual sales that had just topped $1 billion. Drawing on extensive interviews with his wife and children, colleagues and competitors, the article paid due respects to Sam's immigrant father, Yechiel, and described the Bronfmans' humble beginnings as homesteading pioneers in the west. There was a tasteful section on Saidye, "the girl from Plum Coulee." Without any falsification, *Fortune* gave a sympathetic account on the family's exports to the United States during the bootlegging era of the 1920s, cursorily referred to Sam's quarrel with Henry Morgenthau, Jr., briefly mentioned the RCMP prosecution of 1934 and his troubles with Niggy Rutkin two decades later. The article dwelt upon Sam's dynamism, his commitment to blends, his "belligerent stubbornness," his "instinct for dynasty" and especially his remarkable success.

"I thought it was a great article," Edgar says, having read it on an airplane shortly after it appeared. Edgar remembers calling his father with the news, right after the plane landed: "Great article, you are going to love it." But Sam, who had already read the piece, was furious. "You know what?" he told Edgar, "I think I am going to sue." "You are going to sue them for *what?*" Edgar asked, incredulously. "For $10 million," Sam replied, "don't sneer at money." "Come on, Father," Edgar responded. "I never sneer at money, I like money. I am sneering at the idea that you are going to sue them. What did they *do?*"[2]

Sam never made it clear to his son just why he was so upset, and as so often during his explosions people hearing him fume had difficulty figuring out the true source of his anger. "It didn't make him out to be God Almighty or Jesus Christ or something," is the best that Edgar can think of now. Sam may not have been entirely clear in his own mind just why he found the article distasteful, and indeed he was deeply ambivalent about publicity of all sorts. On the one hand, he was exceedingly nervous about being portrayed in public — a trait the *Fortune* piece attributed to "memories of prohibition." While giving vast sums to charity, Sam did not like to put his family name on hospital wings, buildings and so on, at least until the mid-1960s, almost always preferring to see the Seagram company, rather than the Bronfmans, in the public eye. But on the other hand, Sam's appetite for praise and recognition was simply insatiable. "Nobody . . . said enough nice things about Father," Edgar recalls. "He was loved and adored, but never could be loved and adored enough." To those who heard him rant and rave about one slight or another, this trait could be passed off as incorrigible pettiness. At its source, however, was something much more serious — Sam's deeply felt need for the validation of his own primacy. Sam suffered constantly in his effort to prove to the world that he was number one, and he drove himself mercilessly to pile success upon success. "I don't think he could ever look back on himself and say, 'You made it, pretty good,' " Edgar muses. "I remember him saying to the kids so many times, to all of us, 'All you kids want is good times.' As if enjoying life was something that was evil or bad or something that we shouldn't do. And the great sadness is that he never really enjoyed his own life as much as he might have."

■

CANADIAN BUSINESSMEN OF the 1950s, noted the young journalist Peter C. Newman in *Maclean's* in October 1957, were far less visible and well-known than the Sir Henry Pellatts, Sir Herbert Holts or Sir William Van Hornes of yesteryear.[3] "Postwar Canadian prosperity," he continued, "has spawned a new hierarchy of big businessmen whose decisions help shape the economic existence and influence the working life of nearly all Canadians." Eager to dispel the vagueness about the men at the top, Newman's article focused on the "hundred busiest directors" of Canada's top corporations. And who, Newman asked, was the richest of them all? There were two possibilities, he speculated, with plenty of vagueness of his own. One was John David Eaton, president of T. Eaton Company, and the other was Samuel Bronfman, who earned "what may be Canada's highest salary" — cited as $351,042 (U.S.) in 1956, and whose family, Newman noted, "owns stock worth hundreds of millions." (Sam did not, the article noted without commentary, sit on the board of any Canadian banks or major industrial corporations.) Hardly a detailed exposé, *Maclean's* nevertheless underscored one of the facts of Sam's life by the mid-1950s, in Canada at least: like it or not, he was famous.

Regularly exposed to the chill winds of public scrutiny, Sam suffered from the political and social consequences, as everyone around him knew. He craved the accolades that non-Jewish society still doled out sparingly to Jews, and he experienced each setback as a personal slight which had to be overcome by other rewards and distinctions. Thus he found himself on a treadmill of honours, draining his emotional energy even at the peak of his career.

Sam's greatest setback was his failure to secure an appointment to the Canadian Senate — the prize patronage plum of the federal government — notwithstanding his intensive lobbying for the job. He was, of course, neither the first Canadian nor the last to lust after a seat in the upper house, for plenty of public figures have shamelessly ingratiated themselves with those in power in order to receive the call to the Red Chamber. Sam Jacobs and Archie Freiman each wanted to be the first Jewish senator, and while the two old friends believed they both came close they may in fact have cancelled each other out in the uphill battle for what was inevitably viewed as a "Jewish appointment." Jacobs had the longest and most faithful service to the Liberal Party, and Freiman had the closest ties with Mackenzie King, the Liberal prime minister during the 1920s and the second half of the 1930s. Jacobs even wrote to King about Freiman's political opportunism in 1930, noting that the latter had backed Arthur Meighen's Conservatives in 1926 in exchange for a seat. In the event, this and a variety of other political considerations ruined both of their candidacies.[4] Tired and discouraged in 1940, Freiman wrote to Mackenzie King reminding him of a "promise" the then-opposition leader had made to him seven years before, when he and his wife had been invited to dinner at King's Kingsmere residence. His case, Freiman ventured, was "on behalf of my people and myself":

if my appointment in 1933 was envisioned as a liberal gesture to the Jews of Canada, how much more significant it would be at this time when democractic opinion throughout the English-speaking world is imbued with a spirit of enlightenment in its great fight for the preservation of human liberties and equalities.[5]

Alas for Freiman, conditions were no more ripe for him in 1940 than they were in 1933 and he died disappointed, four years later.

From the early 1940s Sam had his eye on the Senate and it seems likely that his leadership of the Jewish community, where Sam Jacobs and Archie Freiman had wielded so much weight, only whetted his appetite. His unspoken sense of rivalry with Jacobs and Freiman also helped push the idea: Sam hoped to succeed where his two great predecessors had failed. His interest was also kindled by his American connections. Later, through his acquaintance with U.S. Senator Herbert Lehman, Sam noted

the prestige and authority the title commanded south of the
Canadian border; to be "Senator Bronfman," he hoped, would
virtually assure for him similar respect in the United States,
where he spent so much of his time.

As part of his quest, Sam donated generously to the Liberals
and cultivated his image as a faithful party supporter. In a
memorandum prepared to advance the cause, Abe Klein claimed
that Sam had been "a consistent and loyal supporter of the
Liberal Party and its ideals, and counts today among his personal
friends a host of personalities who in all parts of the country have
held aloft the banner of Liberalism." As one would expect, Klein
set Sam's loyalties in a Jewish context. "It is not entirely
irrelevant to Sam Bronfman's leadership of Canadian Jewry," he
said, "that the 180,000 Jews throughout Canada are largely of the
Liberal allegiance."[6] Max Henderson recalled that Sam took a
deep interest in political donations and conferred at length with
Liberal fund-raisers on political matters. "He would often call
for large sums for purposes of his own," Henderson notes,
"giving me only the barest detail to record in my books." Among
others, Sam cultivated Henderson's Ottawa friend, Duncan
MacTavish, the lawyer for the Association of Canadian Distillers
who became president of the National Liberal Federation. But as
MacTavish told Henderson, the candidacy never really had a
chance. "He said that despite Sam's generous contributions to the
Liberal Party, the Bronfman reputation from the old days would
render any consideration of his name out of the question."[7]

Sam saw his first chance for a Senate seat in 1943, when he
financed Laz Phillips's by-election campaign for the House of
Commons in Montreal's Cartier riding — the seat once held by
Sam Jacobs, who had been succeeded by another Jewish member,
Peter Bercovitch. The idea, apparently, was that Laz would
become the first Jewish cabinet member and Sam the first Jewish
senator.[8] Unexpectedly, however, the Liberals went down to
defeat in Cartier, with the Jewish Communist Fred Rose
emerging victorious. That night Mackenzie King is supposed to
have telephoned Phillips, asking him, "What do you regard as the
basic cause of your defeat?" "The basic cause of my defeat," Laz
replied, "was that Mr Rose got more votes than I did."[9]

Thereafter, the relationship between Sam and Laz soured, as

Laz began to lobby himself for the patronage post. Believing that his work for Seagram and the Bronfmans had lifted Phillips into public prominence, Sam felt betrayed. Laz had shown himself to be faithless, Sam fumed; he had lined his pockets at the company's expense and had used Sam's money to advance his own political ambitions. For years Sam would not speak to his old friend, generating endless complications since much of the company's legal work continued to be done by Phillips' partner and nephew, Philip Vineberg.

Oblivious to the harm his Senate campaign did to his dignity, Sam made no effort to keep his longings confidential. "We all knew about it," recalls Ben Lappin, a Canadian Jewish Congress official in Toronto. "I don't know how I knew it, but we talked about it a lot, everybody knew," says Robert Sabloff, hardly one of Sam's senior employees. Sam even asked Michael Comay, the Israeli ambassador in Ottawa, to intervene on his behalf. Comay did make some soundings, and when the reply was negative he told Sam so.[10] More than once when he heard such news, however, Sam continued to believe he had a good chance. The effort, moreover, was soon mired in intrigues. According to close friends, Sam was actually promised a seat, with the hint probably being dropped by Philippe Brais, a well-connected Montreal lawyer and Liberal fund-raiser. As time passed without a call from Ottawa, however, Sam began to suspect that something was wrong. Word reached him eventually that the problem was Jimmy Gardiner, the western dealer in the Cabinet and long-time minister of agriculture who had even been accused, during the war, of being part of the Bronfmans' "liquor interests." Gardiner, the story went, had a long memory of Harry's troubles in Saskatchewan in 1929, and believed a Bronfman appointment would be a major political liability.

Sam was predictably bitter when he heard this bit of gossip, since he had contributed to Gardiner's political war chest at the latter's request in the past.[11] Seeking help to break the log-jam, Sam called on his old Winnipeg friend Sol Kanee, who originally hailed from Melville, Saskatchewan, Gardiner's home riding. When he reached Montreal, Kanee found Sam furious: "It was Gardiner any more who was responsible, it was me, because a friend of Gardiner." In Ottawa Kanee saw Gardiner.

him he had no objections to Sam. Gardiner's name nevertheless, Kanee said, was being used as an excuse for not giving Sam a senatorship. Kanee asked Gardiner to telephone C.D. Howe, still a major power broker in the Liberal caucus, to tell him that he had no objections. Despite this intervention, however, the cause proved hopeless. Kanee saw Howe afterwards, and complained vigorously. "You know there's no way that Sam Bronfman's going to get appointed. So why do you permit a situation in which your fund-raisers in Montreal are taking a lot of money out of him with a promise that you know cannot be fulfilled?"[12]

Defeat finally came in 1955 when David Croll, the former mayor of Windsor who had been minister of labour in Premier Mitch Hepburn's Ontario Cabinet in 1934, and who had a distinguished war record, became the country's first Jewish senator. As was well known at the time, Croll really wanted a cabinet seat, and according to Kanee this avenue was blocked by Liberal insider C.D. Howe, who thought Croll "too left wing." Given Croll's stature among Liberals this put him in line for the Senate — at which point Sam finally realized his prospects had sunk. "He was almost inarticulate with anger over Croll's appointment," Henderson recalled, "declaring that no one had ever heard of Croll, and repeating his assertion that he, Sam Bronfman, and nobody else, was the 'king of the Jews' in Canada."[13] "There are things that even God can't do," Michael Garber is supposed to have commented, in the end, on Sam's senatorial candidacy.

Understandably, Sam remained tender on the subject of the Senate and his anger flared years later in February 1968 when, after years of service to the Liberals, Laz finally got a Senate appointment — only two years before his compulsory retirement at age seventy-five, in 1970. But Sam had mellowed by this point, and while deeply hurt he did not explode as he might have done some years before. "Well, at least one of us got it," Noah Torno remembers him saying the day he heard the news. Sam telephoned his congratulations, and by outward appearances the quarrel was settled. But close associates knew otherwise. "I think nothing healed it," Torno concludes, "it was just a bandage."[14]

From Laz's point of view, it was all extremely unfair. Sol

Kanee showed up one day for a reception at the Phillips household and heard his complaint from Laz's wife Rosalie. Laz, she said, was really entitled to the appointment because of his work for the party, and so on; the only reason it had been so long delayed was that the Liberals did not want to offend Sam. Kanee, she hoped, would get Sam to see reason.

A few weeks later Kanee happened to be in New York with Laz and Sam. The three of them had a few drinks together and then repaired to Sam's apartment at the St Regis for dinner. Seeking the right opening, Kanee hoped to get Sam to put the matter into perspective. Instead, he found, Sam still smouldered. "Laz," Kanee remembers Sam as saying, "I've made you rich beyond the dreams of avarice" — one of his favourite claims against close associates when things went wrong.[15]

Lester Pearson, who had known Sam for many years and knew also of his long-standing senatorial ambitions, persuaded Sam shortly after the Croll appointment that he would soon receive a post even "more prestigious" than the Senate. Sam, whose naiveté on the subject was boundless, may even have believed for a time that he would become "Canadian Ambassador to the Court of St James's," as he once put it.[16] Reality was much more prosaic. In 1957 Pearson's hint materialized in the shape of the newly born Canada Council, set up by the government that year with $100 million, to be spent in support of the humanities. Sam joined the first regulatory committee and served for four years — one of the "philanthropoids," as Council director David Trueman irreverently called prominent donors — but he took little pleasure in the position. He remained disappointed, Saul Hayes remembered Sam telling him, realizing that the Council was a poor substitute for the Senate. After a while Sam lost interest, and while he kept in touch with the Council's investments he stopped attending meetings regularly.[17]

The Senate was not Sam's only major disappointment in his quest for honours and recognition from the non-Jewish world. For years he wanted to sit on the board of governors of McGill University, a bastion of Montreal's WASP society, and for years he was blocked — probably by J.W. McConnell, the wealthy publisher of the *Montreal Star*. Sam did receive the appointment in the end — but not until 1964, when he was seventy-five.

Antisemitism may well have played a role here, for despite Sam's acquaintance with Principal Cyril James, and despite his substantial gifts to the university over the years, McGill only gradually made itself more hospitable to Jews after a period of institutionalized antisemitism in the 1930s and 1940s. Facing a similar milieu, albeit one that a few Jews had penetrated, Sam also sought long and in vain to join the boards of Canadian banks, of which he was such an important customer. Laz Phillips became a director of the Royal Bank in 1954, and Sam would dearly liked to have been asked as well; in the end he waited until 1962, when he finally became a director of the Bank of Montreal.

It would be wrong to assume that these setbacks prompted sorrow or self-pity on Sam's part. "He wasn't sad . . . he was very angry about it," was how Mark Shinbane described Sam's reaction.[18] Sam appeared often cutting ribbons, turning sod, making presentations, and he shared the widespread acclaim the Seagram company received for extensive public service. He put a great deal of personal effort into producing expensive, well-crafted supplements to the company's annual reports, surveying major themes of public interest: "Canada and the United States — Partners in World Affairs," "The St Lawrence Seaway," "The Story of the United Nations," "The Awakening North," "Canada and the United States — Partners in Democracy" and "The Pioneer Settlers of Canada." Sam laboured long and hard over a travelling art exhibit, "Cities of Canada," for which he commissioned twenty-three artists who were members of the Royal Canadian Academy (presumably "the best") to execute paintings of twenty-six Canadian cities.

Sam was not so driven as to fail to enjoy acclaim when it came his way for these and other philanthropic activities. One such occasion was the opening of the "Cities of Canada" exhibit at the Mount Royal Hotel in Montreal in 1954. "We had the whole of the ninth floor," he wrote in telegraphic style to Saidye, who was then in Paris:

> received with the Pilots and Lucy and Allan in the Normandy Room—paintings were in the Ball Room—the affair was lovely—it is agreed that never before in the history of

Montreal were so many top-ranking people of the English, French and Jews all together at a social affair — too bad you missed it but then we can't be everywhere so enjoying yourself in and with the happiness of our children must compensate — anyhow a lot of people missed you and I had to continuously explain your presence in Paris — there were between 1,200 and 1,400 guests — Joe Asselin spoke in behalf of the city and Paul Martin, acting Minister of External Affairs because Pearson was away, spoke in behalf of the gov't — I introduced them and then spoke myself — all speeches were excellent.[19]

Vickers and Benson, Sam's Canadian advertising agency, worked on the annual reports and put together this exhibit and many other service projects. For their time, these were extraordinarily ambitious undertakings. Seagram's "Cities of Canada," for example, travelled some 30,000 miles and appeared in fifteen countries in Europe and Central and South America; it was viewed by nearly a quarter of a million people abroad before going to a score of cities across Canada. And as the success of these ventures became more evident, so did Sam's personal involvement as introducer, presenter and chief impresario. The company reports in particular came to feature a full-page picture of Sam, followed by some background material on him that accented his role.

In New York, Seagram sponsored a series of high-level symposia with themes carefully chosen by Sam, reflecting his broadening concern with issues of global importance — "The Next Hundred Years," "The Future of Man" and so on. "The Future of Man," which took place in September 1959 with Sam as host, was one of the most successful; participants included Robert Frost, Sir Julian Huxley, Bertrand Russell, Ashley Montagu, and Milton Eisenhower, then president of Johns Hopkins University. Some 1,500 leaders of science, industry and education assembled at the Waldorf Astoria to ponder the future — and at the same time to attend the dedication of the nearby Seagram Building.[20]

Canadian themes remained prominent in many of these public-relations efforts, and Sam would tick off Americans at meetings if they condescended to their northern neighbours.[21]

Celebrating Canada's centennial in 1967 Seagram sponsored a widely distributed booklet on Canadian Confederation entitled "Henceforth We Shall Rank Among the Nations," and commissioned Juliette de Lavoye, a well-known artist, to carve miniature images of the Fathers of Confederation on ivory for presentation to the government. Sam and Seagram were also deeply involved in Montreal's Expo '67, for which the company sponsored twenty-two major statues, later donated to universities across the country. And in recognition of his service, Sam was one of fifteen Canadians named Companions of the new Order of Canada by Governor General Roland Michener in 1967.

In the Jewish world, Sam was revered and honoured as no other leader in Canadian history. There was no award he did not receive, no constituency, except the Jewish Communists, that did not at one point or another join the chorus of praise. As early as 1950, when he stepped down as head of the Federation of Jewish Philanthropies, he was referred to as "Canada's leading Jew" in a special issue of the *Canadian Jewish Chronicle*.[22] "If Sam Bronfman would consent to have his name on corner stones of Jewish institutions," wrote the Yiddish journalist M. Ginsburg, "it would soon be seen all over Montreal. Here he breaks ground, there he places a cornerstone, elsewhere he helps complete construction of another building, which waits for him as upon a Messiah."[23] In 1961, the Canadian Jewish Congress announced that its new headquarters would be named Samuel Bronfman House. When the building was finally dedicated, ten years later, Nahum Goldmann described Sam as "one of the grand dukes of world Jewry," renowned for his loyalty to the Jewish people. "Under the deluge of tributes Mr Bronfman's innate modesty took a rather severe beating," wrote Archie Bennett of Toronto about the occasion, with tongue in cheek. "But a debt must be paid sooner or later."[24]

Sam actively sought these plaudits, feeding his hunger for acclaim as a man of honour and distinction — "to be somebody in this world," as Edgar remembers him saying fervently. And the more prestigious these honours in the light of the non-Jewish world the better, in Sam's view, which is why he prized one in particular — membership in the Knights of Malta, formally known as "the Sovereign and Military Order of the Hospitallers of St John of Jerusalem." Founded as a Christian lay order in the Holy Land in the eleventh century, this was about as exclusive and venerable a club as one could imagine. An international philanthropic society by the time that Sam got around to it in the mid-twentieth century, the Knights of Malta were headed by the British monarch, had their headquarters in Rome, enjoyed diplomatic standing in twenty-seven countries and were active in African leprosaria and homes for the aged and retarded. Sam came to the order through one of his top executives, Quintin Gwyn, who was one of its high-ranking officers. Aided by at least one donation of $50,000, Sam himself rose through the ranks—from an Associate Officer Brother in 1954, to Commander in 1956, to the high rank of Knight of Grace in 1969—each step sanctioned by the Crown and conferred by the governor general at Government House in Ottawa. (Allan too joined the order, a notch or two behind Sam—Commander Brother Associate in 1963, for example, when Sam had been a full Commander for seven years.)[25]

Organized with considerable flair, Sam's publicly celebrated birthday parties were soaked in the filiopietism that both Seagram and the Jewish community had cultivated over the course of his long career. Through these events, both his company and his community praised Sam's achievements, but also spoke in some sense about themselves—two remarkable entitites that had grown and come of age under Sam's direction. In 1951 when he turned sixty (using his "official" birthdate), for example, festivities began on February 27 with a Seagram dinner at the Windsor Hotel in Montreal during which Sam received an illuminated address:

> Today, head of this great and growing industrial family whose ramifications now spread to all corners of the globe, you stand in the eyes of the world—a titan of commerce. And yet, as much claim as the world has upon you, its demands can never usurp your place in our hearts—for, as ever, your actions, your friendliness, your great and generous nature give ample evidence that above all else you are still our warm, loveable Mr Sam.

Four days later, in the midst of the Kefauver Commission hearings, 2,000 celebrants assembled at the Waldorf for another Seagram birthday banquet, when the company announced a million-dollar research programme at Columbia University in Sam's honour, "to promote understanding of the United States system of free enterprise."[26] Three weeks later, at a major conference in Montreal, Israeli ambassador to the United States Abba Eban presented him with a special medal in appreciation of his services to the community, Jews overseas and Israel. Speaking on behalf of the community, Edward Gelber referred to the unity of Canadian Jewry, its "glorious" wartime efforts and its vigorous representations to the Canadian government. "In all of these undertakings," he continued, "Canadian Jewry has had the devoted leadership of Sam Bronfman who brought to bear . . . a warm and understanding Jewish heart."[27]

Sam's seventieth birthday celebrations were particularly elaborate. Proceedings began with a lengthy birthday interview in the *Canadian Jewish News*, and a company symposium in New York on "Life in Other Worlds." In his honour, Saidye's sisters and their husbands ordered a bust of Sam sculpted by Alan Jarvis, which now sits in the Canadian Jewish Congress headquarters in Montreal. Then, on March 4, there was a Canadian Jewish Congress dinner at Montreal's Queen Elizabeth Hotel, announcing the construction of a Samuel Bronfman House for the Canadian Jewish Congress and, as a gift from his children, the building of a million-dollar archaeological and biblical museum in Jerusalem. Another million dollars, it was announced at the same time, was given by the Samuel Bronfman Foundation for studies to advance business and industrial development in Canada.[28] At the dinner itself no praise was too extravagant: "A pillar of man's humanity to man stands in our midst," said a commemorative leaflet introducing the chronological outline of his career. "We share the pride that he must feel, and look to the continuing attainment of his goals for the betterment of man everywhere, and the ascendancy of human values in the cause of man's everlasting well-being."

Two days later there was a more earthy party for Sam's Canadian employees at the Ritz—a heartwarming affair, with the diners singing in honour of Mr Sam from specially prepared songsheets. To the tune of "MacNamara's Band," for example, the hundreds of guests wished him well:

O my name is Samuel Bronfman, I'm the leader of the band,
Although we're few in number, we're the finest in the land;
We play it down the middle, we play it hard and straight,
And when we play together our music is just great—

With apologies to Gilbert and Sullivan, the banqueteers gave a spirited rendition of "When I Was a Lad" from *H.M.S. Pinafore*:

When he was a lad he served a spell
As office boy in his dad's hotel.
He cleaned up the windows and he swept the floor
And he polished up the handle on the big front door
    He polished up the handle on the big front door.
He polished up the handle so careful-lee
That now he is the Captain of the Industry
    He polished up the handle so careful-lee
That now he is the Captain of the Industry.

And in a final verse:

Now salesmen all whoever you may be
If you want to rise to the top of the tree
If your rear isn't glued to an office stool
Be careful to be guided by this golden rule
    Be careful to be guided by this golden rule:
Stay 'way from your desk—and sell like he
And you can be the Captain of the Industry
    Stay 'way from your desk—and sell like he
And you can be the Captain of the Industry...

A FIERY ICONOCLAST, poet Irving Layton complained bitterly about the Jewish community in 1959 in a letter to a friend, Desmond Pacey: "The besetting sin of my people is respectability; add to this, sanctimoniousness and hypocrisy. It isn't their soulless money-grubbing that makes my stomach turn sick; it's their stinking moralism." And from this vantage point, as the alienated Jeremiah of Montreal Jews, Layton could not resist a pot-shot at Sam: "In this city, Mr Bronfman, ex-smuggler of spiritous liquors, has every community effort sewn up from the Jewish General Hospital to the Public Library, and all the lesser plutocrats try to get as close to his behind as possible with their tongues out-stretched. The stink of money and moralism is everywhere."[29]

Had he talked to the "ex-smuggler," Layton might have been surprised to learn that Sam's leadership involved a creative spark — not to mention toil, worry, insecurity, and probably a measure of nostalgia as well, for a Jewish world that was rapidly disappearing. Still, for all his vituperation, the poet made no mistake about Sam's pre-eminence: in Montreal, the most important community of Canadian Jews, nothing important happened without Sam Bronfman's blessing.

Fund-raising, of course, was a major part of Sam's leadership, and in response to the substantial growth in the scale of community institutions in the postwar period he led Canadian Jews to new levels of financial support for Jewish social, educational, cultural and religious services. Sam worked closely with the Combined Jewish Appeal in Montreal, the annual collection of funds both for local needs and for Israel. Each year he hosted a "Samuel Bronfman Dinner" to honour major donors, an event that became the traditional end to pre-campaign events and the start of the public appeal. As we have already noted, Sam and his family contributed about 15 percent of the annual total. His influence counted particularly in the highest echelon of donors, whose gifts were decisive for the success of the campaigns. For as one student of the community has noted, a handful of givers at the top contributed almost a third of the entire collection. In 1968, according to Harold Waller, there were eighteen donations of $25,000 or more. "It is estimated that those eighteen gifts, including Sam Bronfman's, may have represented over $2.5 million, about 30 percent of the total."[30] In the name of his family, Sam's annual contribution to the Combined Jewish Appeal in the mid-1960s was close to $500,000.

Sam's fund-raising style was aggressive and unsparing, peppered with what Max Melamet delicately called "immensely vigorous language." Melamet remembered being shown into Sam's office one morning to find him smoking with rage. "His fists were clenched, and he was letting fly with uncomplimentary adjectives. I asked him what had upset him, and he told me. He had written to a powerful Wall Street stockbroker who, so Sam said, headed a firm that had made not less than sixty million dollars in the past two years, and asked this gentleman to call on him. This the stockbroker did, and after the usual greetings and pleasantries had been exchanged Sam said to him, 'I suppose you wonder why I asked you to come.' 'Yes,' the stockbroker said, 'I was a little surprised.' 'It's about money for Jews,' said Sam. 'I thought it might be something like that,' the stockbroker said. 'Well,' said Sam, 'what are you going to do about it? *Men shlogt Yidden. Men hargget Yidden* [They're beating Jews. They're killing Jews.]' The amount the stockbroker offered was far, far less than what Sam thought he had a right to expect from him, and apparently he had barely been able to prevent himself from being unpleasant to the caller."[31]

There were at least some who thought that Sam's fury against the insufficiently generous was part of a shrewd fund-raiser's charade—that the anger could be turned on and off like a tap. Mel Griffin recalls beginning a business meeting with Sam one day when his secretary announced that Montreal grocery-store owner Sam Steinberg was on the telephone. Sam took the call, which had to do with Steinberg's donation to a Jewish cause. "Mr Sam called Sam Steinberg everything you could think of for ten minutes," Griffin remembers. "His face was red and he was banging the table with his fist.... It was all because Sam Steinberg and his family gave only a half a million dollars to the latest appeal and Mr Sam thought it should have been at least a million. That was the gist of it. If I was Sam Steinberg I would have hung up long before, because the language was so terrible. At the end of it, he puts the phone down and he puts his glasses back on his nose and says, 'O.K., Mel, where were we?' ... And I guess Sam Steinberg finally coughed up the other $500,000, because the next time I heard him speak of him he was in good odour again."[32]

From the early 1950s, fund-raising in the Canadian Jewish community was closely intertwined with financial support for Israel — unexpectedly for community leaders such as Sam, who had anticipated that Israel would be able to take care of itself. After only a few years of independence, however, it became clear that the Jewish state might flounder on its own, and that the cost of defending the tiny country and of settling vast numbers of immigrants, particularly from Arab lands, required continuous infusions of capital from Jewish communities overseas. Responding to appeals to the Diaspora made by Israeli prime minister David Ben-Gurion, and also to initiatives taken by American Jews, Sam launched a vast project in March 1951, under the cover of a National Conference for Israel and Jewish Rehabilitation.

Meeting in Montreal, the Conference was a grand gathering of the leading agencies of Canadian Jewry — the Congress, the Zionists, the fund-raising agencies, and the B'nai B'rith — bodies that Sam had been attempting to bring together under his own authority ever since he became head of the Congress in 1939. The immediate challenge was Israel, together with the significant number of Jewish refugees from the Holocaust who still languished, unsettled, in Europe. As chairman of the conference, Sam delivered a keynote address that painted an impressive picture of need. He called for massive support for the Jewish state, on a scale that had never been contemplated before — a minimum national quota of $5,250,000 for 1951 for the United Israel Appeal and the United Jewish Relief Agencies; substantial private investment in Israel; and the formation of a Canada-Israel Foundation, to be initiated by the Congress and the Zionist Organization of Canada to channel development aid; and a new fund-raising scheme — Israel government bonds.[33]

Behind the scenes, the Conference signalled a success in Sam's efforts, begun in 1948, to bring the Zionists and the Congress under one roof. As president of the Congress, Sam had never been part of the pre-Independence Zionist movement, and he remained impatient with the ideological and political lesions for which it was famous in the Jewish world. Like many Diaspora Jews, he became convinced of the importance and significance of a Jewish state only with the dramatic achievements of 1947 – 8.

And even then his involvement was somewhat restrained by the standards of today. Sam rose to the occasion, however, when it came to philanthropy — the kind of Jewish involvement in which he could shine and where he felt comfortable. His leadership was vigorous and unstinting — and focused continually on his ambitions to bring all of Canadian Jewry into a common cause. In Montreal as Israel's first consul general in Canada, Avraham Harman learned that Sam's role in fund-raising was simply indispensible. "You had to enlist Sam Bronfman's support for any new venture," he recalls. "It just would not work without him."[34] Spearheading the Montreal campaign, he saw its quota of $1,837,500 almost immediately over-subscribed; a year later, although Sam was unhappy with the failure of some Conference initiatives, he remained the leading force behind Jewish fund-raising in Canada.[35]

In 1953, Sam took particular interest in the campaign to sell Israel bonds — a campaign that might well have divided the Canadian community, as it certainly did that of the United States. Sam had played no part in the Jerusalem Economic Conference in September 1950, when Ben-Gurion persuaded senior Diaspora leaders to use bonds as a way of raising money for Israeli development, and he never joined the inner circle of American Jewish leaders who plotted fund-raising strategy on a global level. But having committed himself to financial aid to Israel, he followed through energetically with the bond project — despite the apprehensions of other fund-raising agencies in the Jewish community. Sam's vigorous backing for the campaign, Harman believes, prevented a rift with the United Jewish Appeal fund-raisers, so great was his personal prestige and importance as an individual donor. And to the surprise of some, the UJA did not suffer and the bonds idea took hold. By 1955 Canadian Jewish support for Israel bonds impressed even hardened community activists, and close observers acknowledged that Sam was one of the major forces behind the drive.[36]

Sam became the president of Canada-Israel Securities Ltd., the company through which bonds were sold. He conceived the idea of a "Guardian Dinner," which became a personal project and which he personally paid for, down to the postage stamps. In

order to attend this event, donors had to buy a thousand-dollar
bond; they were then known as "Guardians" (Sam himself
thought up the name), received a letter from Israel telling them as
much, and earned their tickets to the dinner—for that year. A
unique idea at the time, this event stimulated the morale of
wealthy givers, and provided momentum for the sale of bonds
from year to year. It also certified Sam's personal standing as the
chief Jewish fund-raiser. Sam controlled the event—even to the
point of addressing the delinquent donors. Those who failed to
honour their pledge received letters on Sam's own stationery
saying "Please be good enough to send your cheque to me,"
together with a reply card: "Dear Mr Bronfman, Please find
enclosed my cheque for _____."

When he arrived in Canada from South Africa in 1958, Max
Melamet believed for a short time that Sam's superior position in
communal affairs derived exclusively from his wealth. But
experience soon showed him otherwise. "I saw how wrong such a
view was when not long after my arrival, I formed part of a small
delegation to a Cabinet Minister in Ottawa to present a
submission regarding an issue of critical importance to Israel,"
Melamet recalled. "Saul Hayes, Sam Bronfman and I travelled
on the same train, and Saul, than whom where is no better
draftsman, showed Sam a copy of the memorandum that had
been prepared and was to be left with the Minister. Sam began to
read this. Before long his pencil was out and he was querying
certain statements and commenting on the omission of certain
statistics mentioned some months earlier by [Israeli] Ambassador
Michael Comay. The changes he made were extensive enough
for Saul to have to call in a stenographer when we arrived in
Ottawa, and have the document retyped."[37] Sam was at his best in
this role—with his pencil in hand, his memory for statistics
sharpened by his years in business, his critical faculties in top
form, his keen sense of what could and what could not be had in
Ottawa, and with all of this backed up by the estimable, polished
diplomat, Saul Hayes. "He struck me as a community leader who
paid attention to minute details of anything that he handled,"
Harman recalled. "That was part of the impression he made upon
me and I was very, very impressed about it."[38]

Even with these advantages, however, Sam's effectiveness in

communal politics slipped from time to time during the 1950s and 1960s. It was evident by then that Canadian Jewry faced problems unknown in the late 1930s, the war and the immediate postwar years: during this period assimilation and intermarriage began to loom as serious, important issues, much closer to the concerns of ordinary Jews than Israel and fortunes of Jewish communities elsewhere. Jews began to worry about the quality of Jewish life, and whether Judaism adequately addressed the challenges of modern society. Faced with these seemingly new and quite different kinds of problems than they had ever dealt with before, many of the old guard with whom Sam had worked were simply baffled. The morale of Jewish community meetings notably declined as a result, Ben Lappin recalls.[39]

As opposed to his prodigious efforts in fund-raising, Sam had no particular contribution to make on such matters, nor did he have a grip on the important contest that was increasingly being waged between the Congress and the fund-raising apparatuses in local communities across the country. As with many leaders of his generation, Sam felt increasingly attracted to the folklore of Jewish identity as he knew it. In the latter part of his career as a Jewish leader Sam was often seen as the spokesman for East European Jewish folk culture, or *Yiddishkeit*, which he had once shunned and found personally distasteful. He became closely associated with the Peretz School in Montreal, an institution devoted to Yiddish culture and language — and which was chronically in debt.[40] When he retired as president of the Canadian Jewish Congress in 1962 (only to take up a new post as chairman of its board of governors), Sam struck what was for him a new and unfamiliar note. "We must recognize that there is no Canadian Jewish life in its virile and meaningful sense without authenticity," he said in his last presidential address. But would Jews keep their Jewishness when antisemitism was so much diminished and where they enjoyed such brilliant opportunities? The issue now, Sam claimed, was nothing less than survival — once threatened by persecution, Jewish existence was threatened by its opposite, emancipation and freedom.[41] Unfortunately, like most of his generation of Jewish leaders, Sam had little concrete to suggest.

Making his way in the Jewish world, Sam never completely

threw in his lot with *Yiddishkeit,* however, and even felt uncomfortable, without saying why, when interviewers from the non-Jewish press concentrated too much on the Jewish side of his public life. Undoubtedly, Sam's ambitions extended beyond the Canadian Jewish community, and he seems to have tired of the squabbling, the trials and the tribulations of what remained a relatively small Jewish world. He had no serious challengers to his position in the postwar period, and there were few occasions when anyone dared to cross him in argument. He continued to depend heavily on Saul Hayes, and apart from the occasional crisis, usually caused by events in the Middle East, communal affairs followed their own path, without Sam's strategic direction. Sam presided over meetings as he always did, committed very little to paper, as Congress historian David Rome has observed, and got what enjoyment he could from his remarkable pre-eminence.

Sam found some break from humdrum communal matters in conversations with Abe Klein, who continued in the postwar years to work for him as a speech-writer, secretary and adviser on Jewish affairs. A proud and complex character, Klein did not adjust easily to the patron-client relationship, although, as his biographer Usher Caplan notes, the question was much too delicate for the poet to raise directly with his powerful employer.[42] Sam considered Klein a friend, but as often in his relationships he had a keen eye for his own interests and did not hesitate to assert them. In the spring of 1944 when Klein sought and obtained the CCF nomination in the federal riding of Cartier (where the Communist member Fred Rose had defeated Laz Phillips the year before), Sam let Klein know how unhappy he was. His candidacy, the poet realized, might well injure Sam Bronfman's Liberal connections; rather than sitting in the House of Commons, Sam had told him, Klein would doubtless prefer a professorship at McGill. Sam's intervention may help explain why Klein suddenly withdrew from the race, with another explanation being his fears that the Bronfman connection might have been used against him.

Sam did use his connections with Cyril James at McGill to obtain for Klein a visiting lectureship in poetry for three years, paying his salary out of his own pocket.[43] Klein, who was already embarked on an ambitious study of James Joyce, threw himself into teaching with verve and considerable talent. He continued to edit the *Canadian Jewish Chronicle*, however, kept up his work for Sam, and remained vaguely dissatisfied. Possibly put off by the antisemitism that still existed at McGill, Klein left the university after his three-year term and in 1949 ran again for parliament in the Cartier riding, and lost.

Thereafter Klein burned his bridges both to politics and the academic life, and seems to have resigned himself to continuing his subordinate, employee relationship with Sam. He chose not to move to New York to become editor of *Commentary*, when the magazine was being launched by the American Jewish Committee. Later, he turned down the CCF when they approached him to run once again for parliament. And as he explained to Saul Hayes, he did not think of asking Sam to support his researches on Joyce, despite Hayes's suggestion that he do so. Klein, his biographer concludes, "would not dream of letting Bronfman risk embarrassment in Catholic Quebec by being connected in even the remotest way with the writings of the anti-Catholic Joyce."[44] Shortly after Klein's electoral defeat, Saul Hayes, undoubtedly with Sam's blessing, proposed that he go to Israel, North Africa and Europe on a fact-finding mission for the Canadian Jewish Congress. The trip was exceedingly important in Klein's artistic career, giving rise not only to remarkable articles on his voyage but also his celebrated novel, *The Second Scroll*. Klein departed on his tour, likely paid for by Sam, armed with letters of recommendation from Seagram, and a vague commission to develop "possible activity for our Seagram lines in Israel."[45]

"In the early fifties," Usher Caplan notes, "the last productive years of his life, Klein suffered a gradual mental breakdown from which he never fully recovered. By the end of the decade he had lapsed into almost total silence, which remained unbroken until his death in 1972."[46] Klein's illness, which remains mysterious, may have been exacerbated by any number of factors — overwork, his frustrations as a writer, and his unhappiness with the practice of law, which he still continued along with his investigations of Joyce, his poetry, his editorship of the

Canadian Jewish Chronicle and his work for Sam. But along with these factors Klein's relationship with his patron, which undoubtedly appealed to something deep in his character, was a source of tension. For while the friendship between the poet and the tycoon was genuine, it was also imbalanced, probably without either of them fully realizing it.

Klein served his patron without flinching, despite the loathing he sometimes had for the task. As early as 1942 he confided that his publicity for a banquet in Sam's honour was "a humiliation only a philanthropic world makes possible."[47] Seven years later, on Sam's tenth anniversary as head of the Canadian Jewish Congress, when Sam was furious that the date threatened to pass without notice, Hayes approached Klein to write a history of the Congress that would highlight the Bronfman years and, it was assumed, would glorify Sam's own role. Aided by David Rome who furnished documentation, Klein sputtered along with his text. But his heart was not in the project. Caplan describes the sad sequel: "On the publication of *The Second Scroll* in the fall of 1951, expectations were raised that this next work of his would be just as moving and eloquent. Klein did in fact try his best to dramatize what was really no more than a humdrum institutional history, but the results were somehow doomed to be disappointing. Hayes and Rome read each of his successive drafts and plied him with instructions on how to correct and improve the work. Worn down by this process, Klein finally submitted his last draft late in 1952, around the time that he was convalescing at home. Hayes and Rome decided not to push the matter any further and subsequently reported to Bronfman that the manuscript was unacceptable for publication. Klein was paid for his services but the history of the Congress was shelved."[48]

Klein also worked for the Seagram company in this period. As he had done with the wartime book by Stephen Leacock, the poet served as in-house editor to receive a manuscript on the history of whisky distilling by Argus Tresidder, a Seagram executive from Louisville, Kentucky. When it was decided that Tresidder's book would do the company no good in public-relations terms, it fell to Klein to convey the bad news to the disappointed author.[49] Klein prepared company brochures and material for the Seagram annual reports and even, at the end of the 1950s, wrote advertising copy for Cushman and Wakefield, New York rental agents for the Seagram Building on Park Avenue.[50]

Along with his fulsome praise of Sam in unsigned editorials in the *Canadian Jewish Chronicle*, Klein wrote scathingly of the mercenary poet who served a master. The following passage comes from his "Portrait of the Poet as Landscape" and was omitted from the published version in his book, *The Rocking Chair*:

> However, for bread and the occasional show,
> he finds him, kindler of copy, daily at desk.
>
> For mongers and martment he swings it, writing
> their war whoops, hailing their heroes, thrust
> to his task: *Pirouette, pica: triumph, O twelve point!*
> *Throw the sword to the scales, proud asterisk!*
>
> Skop of the sales-force, bard of their booty, he offers
>   to shoddy his shrilling, his gusto for gussets, to zippers
>   his zest.
> With housewives he's homey, and pally with paters, a
>   kinsman
> A con man, he butters his bosses, he jumps at their jests.
> A fighter with fables he is, and a queller with questions,
>   chapman of chattels, hawker at hest.[51]

Something in Klein revolted against the writing of "war whoops," just as he disdained, in the poem just quoted, his own role as one of those who,

> Upon the knees of ventriloquists, they own
> of their dandied brightness, only the paint and board.

Nevertheless, another part of Klein was unquestionably drawn to Sam, saw him as a real friend, and admired him deeply, as the epigrammatic notes he took on their conversations suggest. Klein enjoyed being a guest in Sam's home, did not protest when asked to write birthday poems for members of the family and other such tasks.

Each year Klein sent greetings to Sam on his birthday—not reciprocated, at least if the collection of Klein's carefully preserved private papers is any indication. Sam regularly responded to Klein's messages, however, with his thanks. "Am lonesome for my good friend," Sam wrote to the increasingly reclusive Klein in 1956, affectionately signing the note "Z"—referring to his Yiddish nickname, Zundal. "When do I see you?" he wrote beneath another letter of thanks for birthday greetings. "Call me and let me know."[52]

David Rome, reflecting on the relationship of the two, sensed "an almost brotherly affection. It was an intimate and yet, after all, rather unequal relationship which can be hard on both sides and can create peculiar tensions. I remember Klein speaking to me once about Sam Bronfman as a great and creative person. As he spoke I felt there was a confusion of identities, and I wasn't always sure when I was listening to Klein on Bronfman and when I was listening to Klein on Klein."[53]

Sam genuinely admired his poet friend, and would probably have been astonished to learn that the relationship at times caused Klein pain. Astute judge of character as he was, Sam sensed Klein's fragility and treated him with courtesy and respect—quite unlike his intolerant reaction to weaknesses he discerned among family members. But of the poet's deeply troubled and divided self he had little understanding, and indeed Klein himself probably never adequately sorted out his feelings on the matter. In any event, by 1960 or so, there was nothing more to be done. Sol Kanee, who knew Klein for many years, remembers running into him in a bookstore about this time, and was shocked to see that the poet no longer recognized him. Seriously ill, isolated and no longer answering his mail, Klein nevertheless took care each year, on Sam's birthday, to send the industrialist a letter or a telegram with his good wishes.[54]

■

ISRAELI OFFICIALS WHO met Sam in the early 1950s, notably two young emissaries to the United States, Shimon Peres and Teddy Kollek, were impressed by his blunt, practical approach to problems—a style that fit well with their own. "Very clear, very concise, very matter-of-fact," Kollek remembers today. "No monkey business," is how Peres presents it.[55] Sent to North America to mobilize support for the fledgling Jewish state, these Israelis had little patience with the tribulations or ambitions of Diaspora Zionists, and saw no role for themselves in the inner life of North American Jewry. Rather, they had concrete assignments that urgently needed attention.

Shimon Peres's task in 1950 was to purchase arms for the Israeli ministry of defence. Twenty-seven years old when he arrived in New York, he came as head of a supply mission, knowing practically no English—but hoping to study the language in the evenings at the New School for Social Research. Artillery was very high on his shopping list. At the time, Peres recalls, Israel had hardly any such equipment at all—only four elderly howitzers, in fact—and through an agent in Paris, a Polish count, the Israelis learned that the Canadians were prepared to sell the very guns they were seeking. In 1951, after receiving approval of the purchase from Ottawa, Peres showed up in Canada to close a deal on several batteries of twenty-five-pounders. The price, Peres recalls, was $2 million.[56]

Passing through Montreal, Peres dropped in to see the wealthy head of the Canadian Jewish Congress, Sam Bronfman, in his office on Peel Street—a meeting apparently arranged by Senator David Croll.[57] Alerted to Peres's mission, Sam had mobilized his friend Sol Kanee, who had spent four and a half years with artillery during the war and knew something about twenty-five-pounders. They began immediately to talk about the deal. "How much do they want?" Sam asked, getting quickly to the point. "Two million," Peres replied. "Too much," Kanee said. Kanee then made an appointment with C.D. Howe, the minister in charge, and twenty-four hours later the three of them bundled into Sam's Cadillac (it was an icy winter's day, Peres remembers, and they had blankets on their laps) and they set off for Ottawa. Along the way, Peres recalls, Sam proposed that they warm up with a V.O. —much to the Israeli's discomfort. "I came from a kibbutz," he says now. "What did I know about 'drinks,' and all that?"

In Ottawa, Peres was amazed as the Canadians got down to

business. Kanee immediately engaged in a scrimmage with Howe, with a somewhat bashful Sam, utterly at sea on the technical details, backing up his friend from the sidelines. After arduous discussions, according to Kanee, Howe agreed to cut the price in half; the guns would be sold for only one million. Shortly after, they got back into Sam's car for the long drive back to Montreal. "Even one million was a staggering sum for us at the time," says Peres, and along the way, Sam suddenly asked if the Israelis actually had the money. Peres had to admit that they did not. "Where are you going to get it?" Sam asked. "From you," the Israeli replied. "Sam liked the *chutzpah*," Peres recalls today, but he nevertheless blurted out: "Why didn't you tell me before?" "Because then, you wouldn't have gone with me," was Peres's reply.

At that point, Sam told his driver to pull off the road so that he could make a telephone call. He immediately contacted Saidye and told her to arrange a dinner party for fifty wealthy Montreal Jews the very next evening, so that he could raise the money. He dictated names, the menu and other details. Resuming the drive, Sam looked the Israeli over from head to foot, wondering if the young kibbutznik would be presentable at the evening. "Your socks are too light," Peres remembers Sam saying, and pulled over to the nearest men's clothing store to buy him a darker pair.

In the end Sam raised the money and the Israelis got their artillery free of charge. Pinhas Sapir, then director-general of Israel's defence ministry, was astonished to hear of Peres's coup; and this may have been the first time the Israelis took notice of Sam Bronfman, of whom they previously knew next to nothing. And as Kanee insists, Sam got all the credit: Peres sent him a silver-encrusted Bible from Jerusalem, while the Winnipeg lawyer received an inferior, cloth-bound collection of stamps. More important to the Israelis, as Peres notes now, the Canadian guns were the first real artillery pieces the Israeli army ever had.

Sam's work for Israel in the postwar period, as we have seen, eschewed ideology and concerned itself almost exclusively with the practical problems of furnishing aid. Having never joined the Zionist campaigns for a Jewish state before Israeli independence, he knew little of the disputes that had set sections of Diaspora

Jewry against each other, and he had no time for those still animated by such concerns. His views were probably not far from his daughter Minda, who wrote to her mother about "Jew business," shortly after assuming a high position in Youth Aliyah, one of the major Zionist organizations in Paris. "Since the state exists," she said grandly, "it is better to work for its success than to let it be a failure."[58]

During these years, the Canadian Jewish Congress worked hard to convince Canadians that Jewish support for Israel was compatible with Canadian patriotism. For Sam and his associates it was all the more important to emphasize that all Jews were united on this question. Unity remained their watchword, with the leadership emphasizing again and again that Jews were "Canadians first." As a result, Congress reacted sharply when, in June 1952, the Zionist Revisionists invited Menachem Begin, the leader of the Israeli opposition Herut Party, to speak in Montreal. Begin, at the time, was hardly a popular figure. He was the sworn enemy of Ben-Gurion, the Israeli prime minister, and was widely detested by the ruling Labour Party. Anglo-Canadians associated Begin with the militantly anti-British Irgun Zvai Leumi, which he led in the last stages of its fight against the mandatory authority, and felt him responsible for the terroristic assaults on British personnel at that time. The very mention of the Irgun brought a violent response from the general community and, it must be said, from many Canadian Jews as well.

Begin's appearance in Montreal, therefore, provoked a crisis. Sam and the leaders of the Congress, together with the mainstream Zionist leaders in Canada, were aghast. Not long before his arrival, Sam sent a telegram together with Edward Gelber, leader of the mainstream Canadian Zionists, demanding that Jewish organizations boycott the Begin visit. "The Canadian Jewish Congress and the United Zionist Council of Canada," they said, "are greatly disturbed that an extremist, Menachem Begin, has been invited by certain individual sponsors to express views concerning issues in Israel which are not consonant with those of the Canadian Jewish community in its effort to help in the upbuilding of a Jewish homeland and a bastion of democracy." Begin's views, they went on, were "destructive of the unity of Canadian Jewry and contrary to our loyalty and

patriotism as Canadian Jews and to our devotion to the true
interest of Israel."[59]

In what turned out to be a rare flouting of Sam's prestige and
the authority of the Congress, the meeting went ahead as
planned — albeit with the conspicuous absence of mainstream
leaders. Marcus Sperber, a Montreal lawyer and leader of the
right-wing Zionist Revisionists confronted the boycott and
mobilized a counter-demonstration in the form of a dinner in
Begin's honour at the Mount Royal. Sperber enlisted the support
of the liberally minded Reform rabbi in Montreal, Harry Stern,
to preside over the dinner. Congress representatives did their
best to block this move — to the point of pressuring Hyman
Grover, president of Stern's Temple Emanu-El Congregation, to
get the rabbi to back down. Defying these demands, Stern
insisted on going forward with the event, which drew a huge
crowd of dissidents, much to the embarrassment of Congress
officials.[60]

While of minor importance in itself, this incident highlights
some of the concerns of Sam and the mainstream Canadian
Jewish leadership at the time. Highly cautious in the way Israel
was to be presented outside the Jewish fold, they took pains to
block the expression of dissident views that might reflect poorly
on the patriotism of their co-religionists. Moreover, while
important, Israel was not central to their Jewishness, and they
looked upon their support for it as almost exclusively
philanthropic. Politics were to be avoided at all costs — as was any
internal division among Canadian Jews. Israel's main task, as
Sam put it in 1951, was "to complete the Ingathering," to absorb
the hundreds of thousands of immigrants, mainly from the Arab
countries. The job of the Diaspora was to help. This involved
extensive monetary assistance, but would not require an
indefinite amount of time. Indeed, the work was nearly done.
"We as a people have come a long way during the last five years,"
he told the National Conference for Israel and Jewish
Rehabilitation. "We have been granted the fulfilment of a vision
which was withheld from sixty generations of our forefathers. As
a people we have risen from the valley of the shadow, not yet to
the mountain-top, but well up the mountain-side. The summit is
already in view."[61]

While Sam and other Jewish leaders may have preferred

different priorities, Israel inescapably entered their Canadian Jewish agenda. At the beginning of the 1950s Ben-Gurion presented Diaspora Jews with the challenge of Israel bonds, as we have seen, and Sam certainly followed up, working hard to introduce these bonds into the mainstream of Canadian Jewish philanthropy. His view was that whatever important Jewish projects occurred in Canada, they should come under his and Congress's authority, and theirs alone.

A good illustration of this was the arrival of the first Israeli ambassador to Canada, Michael Comay, in August 1953. For Canadian Jewry the event was momentous — a real-life "Envoy Extraordinary and Minister Plenipotentiary" from the Jewish state was coming to Ottawa, would be received by the governor general, the government and the diplomatic corps. Barely used to seeing a flag with the Star of David in public, or hearing "Hatikva," the unofficial Israeli anthem, in a non-Jewish setting, Canadian Jews were understandably moved and highly expectant. Sam himself immediately grasped the historic significance of the event. "This is the first time in 2,000 years that a Jewish nation is being recognized in world capitals and Ottawa is one of them," he told Saul Hayes.[62]

Comay, a well-spoken World War II veteran of South African origins, planned to travel by train with his family from New York to Ottawa, where he would receive his official welcome. What would be the role of the Canadian Jewish Congress? Sam himself was fast off the mark. He wanted desperately to be at the head of the official party when the new diplomat disembarked, in order to establish his and the Congress's primacy on this auspicious occasion. Sam decided, therefore, to accompany the Comays to Ottawa. To learn their exact schedule, he bombarded the Israeli officials with phone calls. After endless complications, he managed to meet the train when it passed through Montreal after an overnight journey from New York. Comay, his wife, Joan, and their two children were hanging out of the window when the train pulled into the Westmount Station knowing that Sam Bronfman was about to join them. "There was a brisk, shortish, extremely well dressed gentleman walking up and down," Joan Comay remembers. "So I said to Michael, 'I think that must be Mr Bronfman.' And Michael said, 'Could be.'" Sam then

clambered aboard to spend the last part of their journey to
Ottawa with the newly arrived Israelis.[63]

"I had this odd impression that he was a very difficult man,"
Joan Comay carefully puts it today. To her surprise, however,
Sam turned out to be quite agreeable—despite the fact that the
Comays' ill-tempered Scotch terrier almost immediately bit the
president of the Canadian Jewish Congress through the shoe.
Sam breakfasted with the family, played Scrabble with the
Comays' daughter Jill, got on exceedingly well with the new
ambassador, and by the time they reached Ottawa they were all
on the best of terms. Once there, however, Sam jumped out of the
train and was among the very first to shake hands, warmly
greeting the new Israeli ambassador to Canada before the
photographers and the assembled dignitaries.[64]

In Ottawa, Sam was appalled to learn that the Comays had no
official residence: they installed themselves in a suite at the
Chateau Laurier, with their home in the bedroom and the
embassy in the living room. "How can the Jews of Canada allow
this historic event to be so miserly!" Sam exclaimed to Saul
Hayes. This was a characteristic concern—not only that the
ambassador of the Jewish state be housed in appropriate dignity,
comparable to that of other diplomats, but also that Canadian
Jews, of whom Sam was the leader, should not appear as the poor
relatives at the Canadian table. Sam told Hayes to find a suitable
house for the ambassador and to borrow the money, on his
account, at the Bank of Montreal. "Now let's have a campaign so
that hundreds of Jews of Canada can participate in the historic
event on this historic occasion," he said, beginning with his own
donation of $25,000.[65] Canadian Jews, and not just Sam himself,
would have to rise to the occasion.

The presence of an Israeli ambassador in Ottawa was one more
step in the evolution of a postwar Canadian Jewish relationship
with Israel. Hitherto, Sam or the Zionist leaders dealt with
government officials on matters concerning the Jewish state;
now, with an accredited diplomat in place and with an
increasingly sophisticated government apparatus in Israel with
which officials in Ottawa could negotiate, Canadian Jewish
leaders had a much less active role. These leaders had some
difficulty in adjusting to the new set of circumstances, Joan

Comay recalls, and she remembers "quite a lot of resentment." Adjustment was inevitable, however, and by the end of 1955, when the Canadian sale of twenty-four Sabre jets to Israel ran into difficulties, the scale and the diplomatic ramifications of the transaction had carried matters far beyond the days when Sam Bronfman and C.D. Howe could work out the details together. Sam, along with the other Canadian Jewish leaders, reluctantly accepted their minority status — although they could hardly admit this in public.

The fact that throughout all this period Sam had never actually *visited* Israel was hardly worthy of comment in the early 1950s. For the most part a Spartan, ill-equipped, if bustling place in the postwar era, the country did not rank high as a tourist attraction for North American Jews, and in any event the Israeli reality, as opposed to its symbolic importance, aroused relatively little interest. Sam actually set foot in Israel for the first time in 1956 as part of a forty-day Mediterranean cruise he undertook with Saidye and their Tarrytown friends, the Mayers, on the SS *Constitution*, leaving New York at the beginning of February. The trip took them from the Canary Islands to Casablanca and Marrakech in Morocco, to Algiers and Naples, to Valletta in Malta and to Alexandria, Cairo and Luxor in Egypt. They travelled to Beirut and Damascus, Athens, Dubrovnik, Venice, Florence, Paris and Madrid, finishing finally in London.

Sam and Saidye left the cruise for a brief, five-day stay in Israel — returning nightly to their room at the King David Hotel in Jerusalem. They were treated like visiting royalty and travelled about in a special car laid on by the government. "Everywhere we went we were entertained madly," Saidye recalled. "We met David Ben-Gurion, Teddy Kollek and Golda Meir. Dov Joseph, Israel's first minister of justice [a former Montrealer], and his wife had a dinner party for us. They invited all the cabinet ministers." On one occasion, the Jewish press reported, Israeli finance minister Levi Eshkol referred to Sam as "Mr Canada."[66]

On his return, Sam fairly burst with enthusiasm — and for the next two years at least he addressed the audiences saying that he had "just returned" from Israel.[67] "I have seen for myself the present-day miracle," he told a press conference at the

Vice-Regal Suite in the Ritz Carlton in Montreal just after he arrived. Sam then recounted his "few weeks" in Israel and briefed reporters on a wide variety of political, diplomatic, social and economic matters. "The young democracy of Israel, which I have just had the pleasure of visiting for the first time, has in eight years witnessed the equivalent of a century or more of achievement," he told them. Sam focused particularly on the country's economic development — electrical power output, sugar refineries, the copper smelting plant at Timma, the automobile assembly plant at Haifa, tire factories, refrigerator assembly plants, cotton fields and so on. "One of my greatest thrills was to see the huge plant of the fertilizers and chemicals industry which uses raw materials from the Negev, and potash and other chemicals from the Dead Sea," he said. Sam commented as well on Israel's strategic situation: BRONFMAN CONFIDENT THERE WON'T BE WAR, ran a headline in the Montreal *Gazette* on April 18.[68] In reality, war was only a few months away.

Shortly after his return to Canada the community honoured Sam with a spectacularly successful testimonial dinner at the Windsor Hotel, featuring an address by Sam and by the veteran Zionist tribune Rabbi Abba Hillel Silver. Thereafter, Sam threw himself into the bond campaign once again. That summer, with tension rising in the Middle East as a result of Nasser's threats over the Suez Canal, Sam announced his own pledge of $250,000 for a special "Emergency United Israel Appeal." War came on October 29, when Israeli forces, acting in concert with the British and the French, began their attack on Egypt, and the very next day the conflict widened when London and Paris issued an ultimatum to Egyptian president Nasser. The Canadian government of Louis St Laurent, which had only just agreed to sell Sabre jets to Israel for "defensive purposes," was indignant at the British and French action, believing that Ottawa had been deliberately kept in the dark during the weeks of war planning. Unhappy that the British, French and Israelis had attacked Egypt, the Canadian government broke with its allies, regretting the recourse to force; and for the duration of the Sinai Campaign, until November 5, Canadian opinion was deeply divided.

Under these circumstances, and in view of the fact that Israel was not yet fundamental to the lives of most Canadian Jews, Sam and the Canadian Jewish Congress kept their profiles low. Sam continued to work hard for Israel bonds, however. The Canada-Israel Securities Ltd. of which he was president reported a grand total of $20 million sold by 1958.[69] Sam remained an enthusiastic supporter of Israel, but avoided controversial stands, praising all the while "Canada's role in helping to resolve the conflicts in the Middle East."[70]

Rabbi Arthur Hertzberg describes the process by which Israel gradually moved to the centre of the agenda of Jews in the United States during this period, and what he has to say has a bearing on Canada as well. "For many," he notes, "the labors for Israel provided the major content and the emotional highs of their immediate existence as Jews. It was ever more widely held in the 1950s and 1960s that the effort of Israel would somehow guarantee their immediate existence as Jews."[71] Canadian Jewry, of course, differed from its American counterpart: it had a greater proportion of Holocaust survivors, was perhaps a generation closer to its European roots, had a larger Yiddishist constituency, and, thanks in part to Sam's own work, had a single representative body, the Canadian Jewish Congress. But for all the internal resources of the Canadian community, it came more and more to concentrate its energies on Israel in the postwar decades, as political, cultural and religious sources of commitment began to weaken.

Sam was not a leader in this process. Intensely preoccupied with Jewish standing in his society, he did not immediately link his Jewish future to the fate of the tiny state, whose trials did not interest other Canadians greatly. For ten years after the war his involvement with Israel was balanced by his relationship with Nahum Goldmann and the World Jewish Congress. But after his visit to Israel in 1956 his support for the Jewish state became an essential element in his own Jewish existence — arising out of pride in Israel's achievements, a deep sense of loyalty to his brethren in difficulty, and also as a way of asserting his own standing as a Jewish leader of the very first rank.

When his adrenalin flowed, as it evidently did at an informal speech he gave for the United Jewish Appeal at the Ambassador

Hotel in May 1958, Sam spoke for Israel like a cheerleader rooting for the home team. "And if you would see the city of Tel Aviv, you would think we've got a boom town there," he told his audience. "They've got a boom town there. I tell you it is wonderful what you see over there." Claiming once again that he "just came from the Mediterranean" (he had been back for two years), Sam presented his appreciation of the strategic situation. Egyptian president Nasser, he claimed, was just a stalking horse for the Soviet Union. "I got a pretty good insight as to what Mr Nasser wants. And I don't need Mr Dulles to tell it to me," he insisted. At the time, Sam was very much concerned with the sale of fighter aircraft to Israel, a matter still under consideration by the Canadian authorities. "I don't mind telling you gentlemen," he told his audience, "I wrote a letter to our department in Ottawa, and I made it very damn plain that the Jews are entitled to feel that Canada should deliver planes to Israel, and I am going to tell you right now, they are going to deliver them too. And I made it very plain to our government in Canada that if they want to avert a third world war, I think the best thing to do is to see that Israel has some planes." Sam's intelligence, he let his listeners know, came right from the top — from the Israeli prime minister himself:

> Yes, and I sat and talked to the fellows of the government, and I spent the last Saturday afternoon before I left Israel — that whole afternoon my wife and I spent with Mr Ben-Gurion and his wife — and at a certain moment he took me upstairs and he said, Sam, they are going to attack us. I feel it. But we are going to win.[72]

In the folksy vernacular of Diaspora leaders, Sam personalized his ties with Israel, constantly reminding audiences how close he was to Israeli decision-makers and how well he was received when he visited the country. Thereby, he fit within a wider historical trend. During the 1950s Israelis and American Jewish leaders defined a new relationship of Diaspora communities to Israel — described by Ben-Gurion as "involvement without interference," in which Diaspora leaders by and large found themselves reduced to the level of minor-level fund-raisers.

"American Jews were entitled to be proud of Israel," Hertzberg observes, "but not to meddle in it." While some were unhappy with this change, most came to accept it as an inevitable consequence of Israeli sovereignty. By way of compensation, Israeli leaders went out of their way to flatter visiting dignitaries from Diaspora communities and feed their self-esteem, a process that became institutionalized during the 1950s, in what came to be called "missions" — briefing tours, mainly for fund-raisers, which were organized by Israelis to boost the enthusiasm of donors and celebrate the achievements of the new state. Through these visits, Diaspora leaders received a vicarious sense of participation in Israeli affairs, reinforcing their own prestige and authority within the communities to which they inevitably returned — rather than, as Ben-Gurion wished, actually emigrating to Israel.

Sam played a major role in the "First National Canadian Leadership Mission" to Israel in 1960, which he "led" jointly with Lawrence Freiman, son of A.J. Freiman and head of the Zionist Organization of Canada. The plan was, as Sam and Freiman explained in telegrams of invitation that went out across Canada, to send a "select group" of Jewish community leaders in answer to an "invitation" sent by "the Prime Minister of Israel." As Freiman elaborated, the leaders were to travel "in an official capacity," would "get to know members of the government," would "receive an intimate briefing from those in charge of the social and economic planning of this young state," and would "see the inside story of the operation of Israel as a going concern, in a way not possible otherwise."[73] Sam, Freiman remembered, replied immediately when the idea was first broached. "Lawrence, I think this is a splended idea. When do we go?" Freiman was impressed, seeing Sam ready to drop everything and take off almost at the drop of a hat. (He was then seventy-one.) Famous for his procrastination on details, Sam could jump at an opportunity, and in this case he had no hesitation.[74]

Together with their wives (there were no women among the "select group," a point that went unnoticed in 1960), forty-eight "outstanding leaders," as the *Canadian Jewish Chronicle* described them, set off for ten days in Israel on January 6. In a

busy ten days they saw virtually all the important government
personalities of the day—President Yitzhak Ben Zvi, Prime
Minister Ben-Gurion, Minister of Finance Levi Eshkol,
Minister of Commerce and Industry Pinhas Sapir, Minister of
Social Welfare Joseph Burg, World Zionist Organization
President Nahum Goldmann, high-ranking military officers and
others. They were received in the private homes of Israeli
officials, were wined and dined in banquets and receptions,
visited schools and factories, archaeological sites, the port of
Haifa, Israel's atomic reactor, the Weizmann Institute of Science
and more. Widely mentioned in the Canadian press, the trip
was presented as a "comprehensive investigation of Israel's
social, spiritual and economic conditions," as a Reuters dispatch
put it.[75]

Sam travelled with Saidye and Minda, and was given priority
as the co-chairman of the mission in the press release written by
Saul Hayes, who accompanied the group. Hayes reported that
Sam "was interviewed over the Israeli radio and press which
carried several articles on the Mission" and went on to note that
Sam and Freiman "had further discussions with the Israeli Prime
Minister," over and above those that were held by the group as a
whole—all of which made the point, as officials from Teddy
Kollek to Pinhas Sapir were at pains to emphasize, that the
Canadians were a distinguished, highly respected group whose
views Israelis took very seriously indeed. Summing up the trip
before they left Israel the Canadians announced an ambitious
new departure that Sam was to head—a $5 million Canada-Israel
Development Corporation to direct private Canadian investment
in Israel.

As with his 1956 visit, Sam returned to Canada brimming
with enthusiasm. Taking charge as president of the Canada-
Israel Development Corporation, his involvement with Israel
deepened. "Sam Bronfman is truly concerned with the new
investment corporation," the Canadian Zionist Organization's
national treasurer Joe Frank confided to Eddie Gelber, then
living in Israel. "I have never known him so enthusiastic. We met
within a week to work out final details. This will not be an easy
operation, and everything depends on him."[76] The difficulty,
Frank saw, was raising the $5 million—which proved, given the

competing priorities of Israel bonds, the United Israel Appeal and the United Jewish Appeal, to be an overly ambitious target even for the extremely generous Canadian Jewish community.

In this effort, Sam worked with an experienced Israeli businessman and former civil servant, Jack Brin, dispatched by Finance Minister Levi Eshkol to help him raise the funds. Brin flew to New York and met Sam in the offices of the World Jewish Congress on Park Avenue. "A kind of roly-poly man," Brin recalls, Sam had only the vaguest of ideas about how the money was to be raised or spent. "Mr Bronfman," Brin said, "I've known you now for about half an hour or so, but I have heard a lot about you and read about you, and do you really mean to say that I have to come to Canada to help *you* raise money?" But Sam's professional instincts, it seems, made him nervous about garnering investment dollars for projects about which he had no real knowledge. His reply was succinct: "I'll open the doors, all you have to do is walk through." "Walking through," however, was not quite so easy as Sam had hoped. Brin began what he later described as "the most frustrating year and a half that I [ever] had." Together the two men travelled across the country making their pitch. Brin's job, thereafter, was to follow up—a process that could sometimes be painful:

> I remember one winter getting into Winnipeg, the plane couldn't land because there was fog. And then you had to go back, and you went the following week. The following week you got there and you managed to get fourteen people together and they pledged, say, $20,000. Then came the thing of collecting the pledges, and so you had to go back. Of course, they didn't know you could pay by way of . . . Israel bonds. Then they didn't have them, they had them in the safe. And then they had to go, they couldn't find the key, and it was a real to-do.[77]

Sam agreed to put up 10 percent of whatever he and Brin managed to raise—but even so the money just trickled in. Apparently when it came to investment, as opposed to the well-established bond drive or charitable donations, wealthy Jews were far more reluctant than Sam had hoped. At the end of

1961, the two had managed to raise only $2.3 of the expected $5 million, and Brin had had enough. "It seems like we're trying to flog a dead horse," he told Sam, "Let me start with $2.5 million and see where it gets us and then we'll take it from there." Sam agreed, and the first Israeli investments of the Canada-Israel Development Corporation actually began.

In 1959, the Englishman Israel Sieff, son of an immigrant from Lithuania and co-founder of Marks and Spencer, had his eye on Sam as a good ally for the strengthening of the World Jewish Congress. A close associate of Nahum Goldmann, Sieff approached Sol Kanee at a plenary meeting of the Congress in Stockholm that year, hoping that the Winnipeg lawyer could entice the prominent Canadian industrialist and head of the Canadian Jewish Congress to add yet another string to his bow of Jewish commitments. What Sieff and Goldmann had in mind was getting Sam to chair the "Western Hemisphere Section" of the World Jewish Congress. Kanee remembers telephoning Sam to persuade him to agree. "The phone call cost me about eighty dollars," he recalls. "I put the thing to Sam, and at first he demurred. I said something about the even closer relationship he would have with Israel and with Nahum. And he said to me, 'Do you really think I should take it?' 'Sam,' I said, 'if I've ever given you any good advice before, I urge you to take it.' So he took it. When I got back to Canada, several members of the family took issue with me, figuring Sam had already done enough. But I can tell you that that relationship was the best, the most enjoyable involvement on his part in Jewish affairs."[78]

The principal attraction was the co-founder and moving force of the Congress, Nahum Goldmann. "One of the great orators of the world," as Lawrence Freiman described him, "his shock of grey hair heightening the sparkle and deep intelligence of his grey eyes."[79] Goldmann had a broad intellect, great personal charm and a wide circle of acquaintances. Needing allies, he had enlisted Sam's aid before — both during the war on behalf of the Jewish cause in Palestine as we have seen, and with the Conference of Material Claims Against Germany in the early 1950s, on which Sam sat on the executive committee for a relatively short time, mainly represented by Saul Hayes. Over the years, Sam had detailed discussions with Goldmann on many issues. He corresponded with him before the Sinai Campaign in 1956 about a peace overture to Egypt that he hoped the Israelis would initiate.[80] A year later Goldmann persuaded Sam to provide some financial support for the Israeli newspaper *Haaretz* — "the best and leading paper in the country," Goldmann assured Sam. "It is fighting for a very sensible and moderate policy, both in foreign and internal affairs."[81]

With Goldmann, Sam realized, he could operate on a global stage, unencumbered by the Canadian Jewish environment, in whose workings he was less and less interested. Within a short time he became chairman of the North American branch of the World Jewish Congress, which included Canada, Mexico and the United States, and then a vice-president of the Congress itself. He also headed the ambitious Beth Hatfuzoth project, envisioned in 1960 as a major Israeli-based institute for the study of Diaspora communities—a project that fit closely into Goldmann's global Jewish vision. As a result of this work Sam met Jewish leaders periodically in Geneva, Amsterdam and London, and when he visited Israel he did so not just as a Canadian Jewish leader but as a statesman of note within the Jewish world. On behalf of the World Jewish Congress he entered the mainstream of the American Jewish community, seeking to drum up support within the local Jewish federations and organizing a one-hundred-member "Division Board" that included many of the prominent Jewish leaders in the United States. In addition to providing material help to Goldmann, Sam served as his Canadian contact for speaking engagements and related projects. He also, as we shall see, offered some support in one of the great struggles of Goldmann's life, his effort to enshrine an independent political existence for Jewish life in the Diaspora.

Goldmann's ideas on this subject provoked a long and sometimes bitter controversy with Ben-Gurion, a dispute that rumbled intermittently through the 1950s and 1960s. Believing that Jews everywhere had a duty to "make *aliya*" — actually to move to Israel — Ben-Gurion insisted on the absolute primacy of the Jewish state in virtually all aspects of Israeli-Diaspora relations. Ultimately, Ben-Gurion believed, the Jewish Diaspora had no future whatever. Goldmann, on the other hand, argued that Diaspora life for Jews would not disappear. Between Israel and the Diaspora, he felt, interaction should be based upon what he called "a sense of partnership and shared responsibility in Israel's future and destiny." "Israel," Goldmann wrote in his autobiography,

> is in great danger of becoming a small nation in the cultural sense, of falling victim to provincialism and relinquishing everything the country stands for to Jews all over the world and to mankind as a whole. Only through psychological and spiritual closeness to world Jewry, only through the mutual enrichment of the Diaspora by Israel and of Israel by the Diaspora, which has a share in many of the cultures of the world, can Israel become what might be called a 'great small nation.'[82]

The contest between the two men was highly unequal, as it turned out, since whatever the intellectual appeal of Goldmann's argument outside Israel, Diaspora leaders regularly deferred to Ben-Gurion on practical matters like bonds, economic invest-ment, political lobbying and the security needs of the Jewish state. Such practical considerations moved most Diaspora leaders, and certainly moved Sam, to support the Israeli political leadership in any important confrontation.

Sam skirted all direct reference to the debate by rehearsing a theme that had served him so well with Canadian Jewry — Jewish unity. But as it happened this was precisely the note Goldmann himself was attempting to strike in the early 1960s. President of the World Zionist Organization in 1959, Goldmann sought to enlarge the organization by bringing under its authority Jewish organizations from every point of the Jewish compass — including those that had refused to identify themselves with Zionism at all. At the twenty-fifth Zionist Congress, which opened in Jerusalem at the end of 1960, Goldmann assembled an unprecedentedly diverse gathering of Jewish organizations, attempting thereby to reconstitute the World Zionist Organiza-tion as a genuine global forum for Jewish opinion and a counterpoint to the Israeli government. Sam was there, as a representative of the World Jewish Congress, and he served

Goldmann well. Addressing the 3,000 delegates from all over the world on the meeting's theme, "On the Road to Jewish Unity," he reminded his listeners that the Congress was "not a Zionist body." "The World Jewish Congress seeks to give expression to the principle of organized unity of the Jewish people. Our concept of that unity is based upon our belief in its common destiny. We believe in the survival of the Jewish people both physically and spiritually."[83]

Although lacking Goldmann's subtlety or vision, Sam nevertheless championed one of his major themes: Diaspora Jews had an autonomous existence, he insisted, and while they "have the greatest admiration for the accomplishments of the Jews in Israel" they were also "citizens in each of their respective countries and they are all loyal sons of the Jewish people." Like Goldmann, Sam argued for a partnership between Israeli and Diaspora Jews, and like the head of the World Jewish Congress he maintained that there were "mutual obligations and duties" — another way of saying that each had to respect the autonomy of the other. "The Diaspora is as necessary to the well-being of Israel as Israel is to the spiritual and moral welfare of Jews everywhere," Sam told a World Jewish Congress meeting in Los Angeles in 1965, in a speech that could easily have been written by Goldmann himself.[84]

Sam contributed to Goldmann's enterprise in the early 1960s, just as he deferred respectfully to Ben-Gurion when he came to Canada with a message that local Jews were not always keen to hear. But it could not always have been easy for Sam, as Jack Brin observes, to play in the same league with two of the greatest statesmen of modern Jewish history, each of whom, in his own way, was known for his sometimes overpowering vanity. Indeed, there are indications that Sam was never fully at ease with these mighty Jewish personalities and reacted badly, on occasion, when he felt he was being exploited because of his wealth.

Sol Kanee recalls an incident in New York when Goldmann "made the mistake of saying that if he had Sam's resources he could do a great deal more for the Jewish people than he was doing." Sam resented the remark, Kanee notes, and was unwilling to treat it lightly, as Goldmann probably intended.[85] Sam similarly smouldered in 1962, when Ben-Gurion dedicated the cornerstone of the Jerusalem bibical and archaeological museum donated in Sam's name by his children. To the accompaniment of an orchestra that played "O Canada," Israel's redoubtable prime minister made his dedication speech in Hebrew and then broke into English with a message hardly tailored to please the guest of honour: "I want to tell Mr Bronfman," he said, "that with all his money — I don't know how much he has but it's certainly more than I have — he cannot get a real personal share in Israel unless and until one of his children or grandchildren lives permanently in this country."[86] Sam, one may assume, was not amused.

Max Melamet told a similar story — about Ben-Gurion's meeting with Sam and other Canadian Jewish leaders in Israel on a fund-raising visit. When the delegation was received by the great man in his office, a member asked him about the Diaspora fund-raisers' classic dilemma. How could they send every available dollar to Israel when there were crying needs at home, particularly Jewish education? "Ben-Gurion's reply," recounted Melamet, "was to the effect that he was sure that Canadian Jewry was rich enough to find money for both purposes, and he kept on referring to 'rich people like Sam Bronfman.' Sam said nothing, but after the third or fourth such reference, Ben-Gurion realized that this might not be in the best of taste, so he turned to Sam and said with a smile: 'I hope, Mr Bronfman, you do not mind my talking about you this way.' " Sam's reply, Melamet recalled, was instantaneous: " 'I am your guest.' Ben-Gurion did a double take and hurriedly changed the subject."[87]

However painful such encounters, Sam preferred them to the alternative, retreat from Jewish affairs. Into his eighth decade, he risked involvement in Jewish politics, as he once did in his business, committed to fundamental principles — in this case a deeply felt loyalty to the Jewish people. Yet he also suffered, again as in his business, the discomfort of vulnerability, plus the related sense that much of what he had accomplished could easily be undone by missteps. One particularly painful moment arose in 1964, when a large Israeli supermarket company, Supersol, of which his son Charles, then thirty-three, was chairman of the board of directors, found itself embroiled in one of the greatest business scandals in Israeli history. That summer, it emerged that

Supersol's manager in Israel, together with its Canadian president, Ottawa businessman and community leader Bertram Loeb, were involved in serious wrongdoing in the management of the company, leading to its near-collapse and to criminal prosecutions in Israel.

After the story burst, Jack Brin was called in to help deal with the shareholders and resuscitate the enterprise. Arriving in Montreal, Brin found Sam apprehensive that the scandal would wash up on his family—even though he had himself not been directly involved in Supersol. "I came in, he didn't say hello, have a drink, have a good trip or whatever," Brin recalls. Visibly upset, Sam uttered only one sentence: "Jack, save my Charles!" "I'll never forget it," Brin says today. Eventually, Brin got the company under control, Sam guaranteed a $450,000 loan for the ailing enterprise, and it was finally refloated. But Sam must have come away with a sense that in Jewish affairs, as in the business he had nurtured for so many decades, one could never rest. Certainly he did not.[88]

As with Jews the world over, Sam's fears intensified traumatically in the spring of 1967, when war erupted in the Middle East and it appeared as if Israel was in mortal danger. In late May, as tension mounted following Nasser's closing of the vital Gulf of Aqaba waterway to Israeli vessels, it was clear to the entire international community, including Egypt's Soviet ally, that war was a real possibility. Arab capitals proclaimed a *jihad* against the Jewish state, while a massive Egyptian army, nearly 120,000 regular troops, packed into the Sinai desert, ready to strike. Although he had virtually retired from involvement in the direction of the Canadian Jewish Congress, Sam leaped into action. On May 26, three days after the Israeli mobilization, he assembled an emergency meeting of top Jewish leaders at the Congress's Sherbrooke Street headquarters to plot the community's strategy. With a Jewish delegation, he went to Ottawa to meet Minister of External Affairs Paul Martin, to enquire about Canada's position. And then, on Sunday, June 4, the day before war broke out, Sam assembled a meeting of wealthy Jewish leaders from across the country at the Montefiore Club to launch a massive fund-raising effort.

Summoned by telephone calls from Sam's brother Allan,

about a hundred prominent Jews trooped into the wood-panelled club that morning to hear Sam say that he was tripling his own regular contribution to Israel, that those present should make a similar personal pledge, and should also make commitments on behalf of their communities. "We have to do something to help them," Congress official Alan Rose remembers Sam saying.[89] "I forget what he committed himself to," Rose continues, "but what happened was that it became a tidal wave, with each community vying [against the others]. At the end there was a slight scepticism that all this money would be raised—about six to seven times what we raise normally—but it was." Throughout the morning, Sam set the pace. According to one widely reported account, one of the donors wrote a cheque for $250,000; Sam eyed it with disdain, and quickly tore it up. "Get serious," was all he said.[90] Those present quickly got the message. The organizers expected about $2.5 million from the gathering—a prodigious sum in itself. But instead, Sam collected $13 million from the leaders on the spot, and organizers raised the national target from $10 million to $25 million—more than triple what Canadian Jews had raised in 1956. Sam's personal impact was overwhelming.[91]

The following Tuesday, seeking Canadian support for Israel at the U.N., Sam flew to Ottawa in his company plane with Sol Kanee to see Prime Minister Lester Pearson. Sam was looking rather ill when they arrived, Kanee recalls, and then suddenly, in a cab on the way to lunch with Liberal cabinet member Mitchell Sharp, he collapsed—having simply fainted from overwork, his doctor, Abe Mayman, assumes now. "So I'm patting his cheeks and so on," Kanee recalls, "and—nothing. I said to the taxi driver, 'There's a police car, pull over!' So we went over and . . . I said, 'Please get an ambulance!' And I'm sitting in the back with him and I'm patting his hand and I think, 'You can't do this to me!' Ambulance comes over, and all of a sudden, who's sitting up, but my friend Bronfman. He said, 'Where are we?' I said, 'We're in Ottawa!' And he said, 'We're going to the lunch.' I said, 'The hell we are, you're going to a hospital.' So he remonstrates with me, and I said, 'Look, after what you did you're going to the hospital!' So he wouldn't lie down on the stretcher, he sat in the front with the driver, and I stretched out on this thing at the back, and we get to this hospital, which he immediately takes over. And he sent an intern out for a bottle of V.O. and a bottle of Chivas."[92]

After a few hours Sam was released from the hospital and went with Kanee to Lawrence Freiman's house. "And then Sam really became nasty," Kanee remembers. "Every time I opened by mouth he tried to put both my feet in it, not only one. Because when he looked at me, he remembered that I had witnessed a moment of weakness on his part." The next day, Sam saw the prime minister, heading a delegation consisting of Kanee, Freiman, Sam Chait and Michael Garber. And after their presentation, Pearson promised support.

Flying home to Montreal Sam and Kanee fumed separately, and neither would speak to the other. It was all especially awkward, Kanee recalls, because he was staying overnight at Sam's house before flying off to Moscow. The next morning Kanee had breakfast with Saidye and Abe Mayman, Sam's physician, who was in attendance. Sam was upstairs in bed. As he kissed Saidye goodbye, getting ready to leave, she exclaimed: "Aren't you going to say goodbye to Sam?" "To hell with him," Kanee grumped. "Oh, come on," Saidye said, "you're such good friends, you must go." "No I won't," Kanee answered. "She said, 'Do it for me.' 'Well,' I said, 'for you I'll do it.' So I went up, and stood at the door of the bedroom, and he was up in bed, watching TV, and I just stood there. He looked at me and said, 'Sol, we've been friends a long time, haven't we.' I said, 'Yes.' He said, 'We're still friends.' "

While obviously strained by the exertion and excitement, Sam remained very active during the next months. As the senior statesman of Canadian Jewry, he addressed a public rally in Montreal in support of Israel, speaking briefly but with considerable vigour. Historian Richard Cohen, a McGill student at the time, was in attendance and remembers the awe with which Sam was received and the hush that greeted him when he rose to address the crowd.[93] In the wake of the war, Sam extended his fund-raising to the United States, beginning a campaign in the distilling industry, where there were large numbers of Jews. In July, working with Edgar, he brought the major Jewish distillers to a meeting at the Seagram Building in New York and he later

made an appeal to importers, distributors and even retailers. He
personally visited his old enemy Lew Rosenstiel, from whom he
extracted a cheque for $250,000, drawn on the Dorothy and
Lewis S. Rosenstiel Foundation. Rosenstiel sent his contribution
to Sam in a gracious letter, noting that he had to borrow the
money, and that "this is the first time in the history of our
Foundation that we deemed any cause so worthy of support as to
warrant extending ourselves in this way." Sam undoubtedly saw
this as a special coup, and the Seagram company immediately
issued the letter with a few background paragraphs as a press
release.[94]

ONE OF THE family rituals Sam's children recall to this day was
his solemn intoning, mainly for the boys, of what were called
"Lessons in Life" — or "L in L," as the youngsters flippantly
came to call them. These were paternal homilies on such matters
as the pleasures of self-discipline, the need for hard work, respect
for others, and so forth, all richly accompanied by directives from
Sam's parents and examples from his own career. For Sam, who
found it difficult to get close to his children, particularly when
they were young, these were often substitutes for intimacy, a way
of commanding attention and transmitting what he thought was
important. For the children, the "lessons" were difficult to relate
to at the time, but they may have had more effect than they knew.
"As Pappy and many other people realize, 'there is no substitute
for experience,' " fifteen-year-old Charles wrote to his mother
from boarding school, playing what was the family's trump card
in any argument.[95] Many years later, Edgar recalled a letter his
father wrote to him on his *bar mitzvah* — twelve pages or more
of Lessons in Life, sprinkled with quotations from Rudyard
Kipling and the like. "It had nothing in it about me," Edgar said,
"it had more to do with the course of my life and what I would do
as I grow up, etc. I don't think it had to do with how I felt, I don't
think Father knew how I felt about anything, that was not one of
his strong points."[96]

Toward the end of his life, Sam extended both the audience
and the subject matter of the Lessons in Life, but he com-

municated with the same paternal earnestness out of his own rich experience a series of directives to those he cared about and respected. Intensely curious, as we have seen, Sam's mind roamed across an enormous range of subjects, and those who discussed these with him found him endlessly probing and testing ideas. His intellectual tools, however, were those that had served him so well in industry; he thought instinctively in terms of mergers and enterprise, assembling capital and resources, mobilizing "the best," and emphasizing quality and innovation. With his enormous ego, as Leo Kolber notes, Sam had the idea that he could attack virtually any problem—and there were a good many that were far beyond his capacities to which he devoted considerable care and attention.[97] Sam moved to corner some of his top executives in New York and try out some of his ideas. At least some of them felt exasperated at being pinned down, as Sam's children once were, and decided that the better part of wisdom was simply to reformulate the boss's notions and feed them back to him.

Seagram provided Sam with a periodic platform to address his employees and others in the liquor business, giving him a forum for his advice and ideas about life and the world. But he sought a much broader audience with wide-ranging themes. He lectured his fellow industrialists, for example, about the civilizing force of industry throughout the ages. Human progress, he felt certain, was largely the result of the vision and energy of men of business. He discoursed on the importance of entrepreneurship in society, arguing that "the purpose of industry is to create and establish the practical media of human contentment."[98] He spoke to the Canadian Club in Toronto about poverty in the Third World, suggesting that the "have" nations should pool their human resources and capital into a huge organization that would then raise the standards of the "have-not" nations of the world.[99]

One of those Sam enjoyed talking to in New York in the 1950s was the president of his Frankfort sales subsidiary from 1943 until 1955, Ellis "Slats" Slater. "A man of presence," Charles recalls, Slater was a polished, well-dressed member of the WASP establishment, with very high standing in the Republican Party—the kind of personality whom Sam relied upon to compensate for his own insufficiencies in this area. Slater was a

long-standing admirer of Dwight Eisenhower and was one of
those who encouraged the general to run for president in 1952;
this later gave him some entrée to the White House, assisted by
the fact that Slater's wife, Priscilla, became Mamie Eisenhower's
closest friend. During the election campaign that year, Sam
pointedly told Slats, "If Ike is elected, I want to talk to him about
world peace." Sam was serious, and reminded him about this
after Eisenhower's victory. Eisenhower drank Chivas, rumour
had it — something that further commended the new president to
the head of the Seagram empire.[100]

Ike knew about Sam mainly because of the programme in free
enterprise that had been established in his name at Columbia
University, and when Slater mentioned Sam's eagerness to see
him, the president agreed. Sam and Slater showed up at the
White House on July 9, 1953. "Mr President," Slats began, "Sam
Bronfman, because he is who he is (Jews because of being pushed
around the world sometimes have a keener sense of what should
be done to avoid more conflicts that always end in harm to the
Jewish people), has some thoughts on how to attain permanent
peace, and because he considers you the most powerful,
influential person in the world today he naturally thinks you are
the only one who can do much about it."

"I presume you get a dozen crackpot ideas a week, so just stop
me if that's the way this idea begins to look to you," Sam told the
president. He then explained to Eisenhower that governments
should be run much like large industrial enterprises. In the world,
as in big business, there would be much less conflict if 51 percent
of the ownership remained in one hand, or one friendly group of
hands. Smaller companies, indeed, were bothersome; it was
extremely difficult to run an industry, Sam opined, if one
constantly had to be worrying about little fellows on the margins.
Then, as Slater described the conversation in his diary the next
day, Sam got to the point:

> the United States as the leading world power, headed by an
> individual who is universally respected, should put together
> control of the free countries of the world. The British Empire,
> the United States, and France, to begin with, and Germany if
> interested, should form an alliance which would be so strong

that no one would ever dare attack it — or start a conflict for fear of reprisals from the alliance or cartel — actually it was hoped a real union would result.

Eisenhower, Slater thought, was favourably impressed, but raised two difficulties — timing and the man. With all his experience and prestige, Eisenhower himself was the person to lead this enterprise, the three of them agreed. How and when to implement the scheme, however, posed something of a problem. "I'm sympathetic to the idea and think something should be done about it," Eisenhower said — suggesting that Slats follow the matter up with further study. And after an hour of pleasant discussion, the luncheon was over.

"Sam Bronfman was much impressed with the President," Slats observed, "commented on how itelligent, quick to grasp, etc., and thought better of his own idea since the President himself had given thought to the idea — and understood the problems and hurdles that had to be gotten over." "By no means did I consider Sam Bronfman's ideas the product of a crackpot," Eisenhower wrote to Slater a few days later. "It is difficult to foresee any truly effective method of preventing struggles among nations, with resulting waste and destruction, except through some eventual amalgamation of groups of those now existing. . . . I enjoyed the luncheon, and the presence of the two of you was the exact opposite of an imposition."[101]

Sam also had advice for the Jews. Shortly after the war, he speculated for a time on bringing together the various streams of Jewish religion — Orthodox, Conservative and Reform. Impatient with doctrinal differences himself, and hardly devout in any conventional sense, Sam supposed that it should be possible to modernize the Jewish religion and bring its laws up to date. He realized that the Orthodox would be unwilling to budge — at least at first — but Conservatives and Reform might well come together. So he hired an American rabbi to work on this scheme, and at Lake Placid, in New York, he spent part of one summer shortly after the war in deep discussions with him on the idea. Unfortunately, the rabbi died soon after, and Sam abandoned the project.[102]

In the mid-1960s, Sam had long discussions with Saul Hayes

about how Jewish history was taught and presented in Jewish textbooks — with Hayes, one senses from his own memoir, a rather uncomfortable, captive audience. Conventional historical accounts, Sam felt, spent far too much time on what the Columbia University historian Salo Baron once called "the lachrymose view of Jewish history" — with its accent on the persecution, suffering and victimization of Jews. "Mr Bronfman," Saul Hayes recounted, "felt that this had a bad effect on the Jewish mind and children should be taught of the great advances that the Jews made to civilization and the heroic aspects of their martyrdom."[103] Sam, Hayes continued, "felt that a pocket book edition of a history of Jewry, playing up its heroism, its deeds of valour, its other contributions, would be of more value to Jewish psyche than the constant recitation of its trials and tribulations." He had in mind hiring "the best historians" to write this work, and setting up an institution to publish, distribute and promote it. Sam even consulted public-relations experts on the problem — despite Saul Hayes' disapproval. After a time, Hayes concluded, "Mr Bronfman felt that he was not getting anywhere on it and the whole idea was shelved."

Other ideas that ran into the sand included peace proposals for Israeli governments, several of which he advanced with considerable earnestness. In the spring of 1956, for example, before the Sinai Campaign but when there was considerable tension between Egypt and Israel, Sam had an idea that Israel should develop "some heroic and imaginative plan . . . to remove the present incidence of the non-recognition of Israel and to terminate the large scale anti-Israel activity."[104] Israel, Sam thought, should settle massive numbers of Arab refugees in exchange for peace treaties with Egypt and the other Arab countries, and international loans to assist settlement. He thought the Israelis should offer to incorporate the Gaza Strip (a magnanimous gesture, he reasonably enough assumed, given its lack of resources), taking responsibility for its refugee population. "I pray that somehow we can bring peace and opportunity to our people in Israel," he scrawled on the bottom of a letter to Nahum Goldmann presenting the proposal, adding as well that, if the Israelis liked the idea, he would see Eisenhower about it.

Goldmann, who had his own troubles getting the Israelis to see things his way, answered Sam after a few days, claiming that he had taken the idea up with the moderate Israeli foreign minister Moshe Sharett. The time, Goldmann told Sam, was not ripe. Certainly, he added, "it is no use discussing it at this moment with B.G. [Ben-Gurion] who thinks only in terms of security and arms. Therefore, I would suggest that we keep your plan in storage waiting for the appropriate moment to come forward with it."[105]

As late as 1970 Sam pursued the idea of Israeli initiatives for a peace settlement, sending a confidential letter to Prime Minister Golda Meir, carried by Max Melamet — the substance of which has never been discovered. Then as now, giving advice to Israelis was a somewhat sensitive activity for North American Jewish leaders, and Melamet took some care in relaying what happened. "I tell this story now," he wrote in an obituary article, "to illustrate his deep concern for Israel, his eagerness to help, and his desire to avoid any publicity that might embarrass the leaders of Israel."[106] Sam, in all likelihood, would have agreed with the way this was put, even while regretting that this suggestion too, like so many others he earnestly offered about how the world should be run and life should be lived, did not seem to be taken up.

CHAPTER X

Epilogue

IN THE MID- to late-sixties Sam occasionally found himself at sea in the vast Seagram enterprise, the huge dimensions of which posed problems entirely foreign to his own experience. "Mr Sam ... was and is a volatile, shrewd, and highly individualistic leader," *Business Week* commented in 1962. "His technical knowledge of the industry and his financial acumen remain unchallenged. But his personal style of intuitive management is already becoming more and more a thing of the past."[1] Still, Sam had not made the mistake of keeping all the reins in his hands, and in fact he had been preparing a succession for more than a decade, easing his sons into positions of authority within the empire. This was the root of his quarrel with Allan, which erupted in the early 1950s. At that time, at Saidye's suggestion, Sam set Edgar up with a small desk in the corner of his own office — not without trepidation, as he told his wife. "What if I get annoyed and swear?" she remembered him asking — with a somewhat uncharacteristic concern on this score, to say the least. A few years later, when he was only twenty-two, Charles was placed in charge of the Thomas Adams subsidiary, just as Edgar went to New York for a senior posting in the United States company. "Why do you give this boy so much responsibility?" Saidye once asked when she thought that Edgar had more than he could handle. "Then he can make mistakes that I can correct when I'm alive," was Sam's succinct reply.[2]

456

By Edgar's account, his taking over Seagram's U.S. holding company followed an extraordinary exchange with his father. At dinner in Tarrytown one day, when they were discussing compulsory retirement, his twenty-eight-year-old son pointed out to Sam that Frank Schwengel, then the nominal president of Joseph E. Seagram & Sons, Inc., the U.S. parent company, was in his late seventies. (Schwengel, Edgar says pointedly now, was president in name only. "There was only one real president, and that was Sam Bronfman.") "Who do you suggest take his place?" Sam asked. "I should like to be president," Edgar replied. Sam then dug in his heels. "I don't want you to have to deal with all those ex-bootleggers all the time," Edgar remembers him saying. Whereupon, Edgar produced his trump: "If you had told me that I was too young and too inexperienced to be president," he told his father, "I would have to agree. But if you're telling me that the company is not good enough for me to head, then it isn't good enough for me to work for." At which point Sam capitulated.[3]

Meanwhile, in Canada, Charles's rise was also meteoric. Still under thirty, he became head of the Canadian House of Seagram in 1958, taking over marketing for the entire country. By the end of the 1950s, with the course of succession set, Sam concentrated on Seagram's overseas operation, a relatively small part of the company's overall sales and production. With these moves began the inevitable shift to a younger generation. James Friel, vice-president and treasurer of the American company and one of Sam's old cronies, died a few months after Edgar's arrival in New York. Max Henderson quit, realizing that a new Bronfman generation would increasingly call the shots in both the Canadian and American organizations. Edgar feuded for several years with Victor Fischel, another of Sam's long-standing lieutenants, until he too was eased out of central authority. Sorrowfully in the case of Fischel, with whom he had been particularly close, Sam insisted that everything be done to save the man's dignity. But he freely accepted that Edgar was now in a position to do what he liked. None of this could have been easy for the aging founder, but Sam knew well enough when to begin to let go.

Yet even while relaxing his hold over the huge Seagram enterprise, Sam remained a force to be reckoned with—

exploding in rage from time to time, bursting into offices with ideas, and dazzling executives with his grasp of details. Sam still fussed endlessly over packaging, something that struck Max Melamet in the late 1960s when he witnessed the boss interrogate a group of employees who had been working on such a problem. "Have you looked at the bottle with whisky in it?" Sam asked them one day. "Of course, Mr Sam," they replied. "Ah, but have you looked at it *half*-full of whisky?" he then asked. "Don't forget to do that as well."[4]

"I have much work to do so that I shall be able to report, in future years, that we have continued to make progress," he told the *Financial Post* in February 1971.[5] He still worked out of his wood-panelled office in the castle on Peel Street, although, as one journalist noted, the old suit of armour and the oaken galleries—marks of Sam's personal style—had disappeared. Another floor had sprouted behind the battlements, and the new offices were full of people who worked for Charles, now running his own show. In New York, at the same time, Sam occupied an office adjoining Edgar's and was on his son's payroll as a consultant at $100,000 a year. And as a journalist noted, when not on the scene Sam bombarded Edgar with almost daily telephone calls on all sorts of details. "The company belongs to Father," Charles respectfully told an interviewer as late as 1965. "Edgar and I only administer our parts of it."[6]

Until the early 1960s Sam still maintained his curious peripatetic style, travelling back and forth between New York and Montreal and keeping everyone guessing until the last moment as to his plans. Edgar prevailed upon his father to end this habit in 1962 when Charles, then thirty-one, married Barbara Baerwald, the granddaughter of a prominent Wall Street banker, and moved out of the family's home in Westmount. "Listen, Father, you have to live your life differently," Edgar told Sam. "Mother is going to be all alone, and you can't do that to her any more," he insisted. "You're really going to have to make up your mind when you're leaving Montreal and when you're coming back." "He screamed and ranted and raved," Edgar recalled, but in the end he finally agreed. Sam's old habits, he realized, simply would not do any longer.[7]

During summers the couple spent most of their time at their

Tarrytown estate until a frightening incident in 1964. One night, towards the end of August, two armed robbers broke into their house, tied Sam and Saidye to the bathroom sink with women's stockings, and made off with nearly $250,000 in jewellery. Sam, whom the thieves referred to as "Mr Belvedere," kept his temper throughout, Saidye later reported, but he was obviously shaken by the affair, and sold the estate a few years later.[8]

Around the office Sam showed signs of moodiness and irritability—which Max Henderson associated in part with Sam's disappointment over the lost Senate appointment, and which has also been attributed to his rather heavy drinking, beginning in the 1950s. "I guess he drank a lot," Mel Griffin recalls. "I remember we would have staff meetings sometimes, we'd have a meeting going at 9:00 A.M., and he would walk in, and Jack Duffy's secretary would be there, and he'd say, 'Dear, bring me the usual.' A gin and tonic was his morning eye-opener." Later, when he was under a doctor's care, Saidye would call Sam's secretary, instructing her not to give him a drink in the morning. In those cases, Griffin went on, Sam would sneak into Mike McCormick's office for a V.O. on the rocks, which he would then sip all morning.[9]

In 1962 Sam stepped down as head of the Canadian Jewish Congress, yielding to Michael Garber after almost a quarter of a century in the job. As with Seagram, he remained a forceful presence in the background thereafter, collecting honours, energizing specific projects and enlisting the support of others in a variety of ventures. As we have seen, Sam helped raise unprecedented sums of money during the Six-Day War in the Middle East, and saw both External Affairs Minister Paul Martin and Prime Minister Pearson in 1967 seeking Canadian government support for the beleaguered Isaelis.

Those closest to him saw Sam mellow appreciably in the few years before he died in mid-1971. To some he seemed more reflective, with his mind perhaps more at ease. Through Edgar's intervention, he buried the hatchet with Laz Phillips, with whom he had fought so irrationally, off and on, for nearly twenty years. Rather often, he talked about family — and was made particularly conscious of this when his brother Harry died in 1963, and Abe followed him in 1968. Mark Shinbane, who had known Sam since his days in Winnipeg, and who had seen both Sam's darker and his brighter sides, believed that his friend "had grown a great deal." "No question about it," Shinbane went on,". . . he had become a little more human."[10]

At the Seagram offices, Sam mused often about the past. "On one occasion," Mike McCormick observed, "an associate asked Mr Sam to name his most serious errors of judgement. 'Well,' he replied, 'much as I hate to admit it, I was wrong in not starting up our own distilling operations in Scotland not long before 1936. I underestimated the appeal of vodka years ago, and I didn't pay enough attention when it began to catch on. Also, I was not thinking properly when I didn't go straight into the bourbon business in the U.S.A. much sooner than I did. And,' he concluded, rising and reaching for his coat, 'that's three serious mistakes and it will damned well do for tonight!'"[11]

Much as ever, Sam loved to talk, particularly when he was at the centre of attention, and he seems to have relished one project his family pressed on him—the preparation of the full-length, popular biography, to be paid for in part by Cemp, the family trust. After extensive negotiations between Leo Kolber and the publisher Jack McClelland, a seasoned author, Terence Robertson, was hired, and a contract was signed with McClelland and Stewart. Work began at the end of 1967, with Robertson interviewing Sam extensively in December and January of the following year. Unfortunately, the project collapsed in 1969 when Robertson became wildly erratic, running up an enormous expense account and even disappearing, for a time, in an alcoholic haze. Robertson ultimately produced a rambling, highly laudatory, and completely unpublishable draft before committing suicide at the beginning of 1970.[12]

Sam undoubtedly found another historical project much more satisfying—a short, attractive company history, entitled *From Little Acorns*, which Sam wrote with the help of Mike McCormick, and which Seagram published along with its annual report in 1970. Prefaced by a tribute to Sam on his eightieth birthday from the company directors, the book took its title from David Everett's poem which closed with the words, "Large streams from little fountains flow/Tall oaks from little acorns grow." Sam liked the thought, and towards the end he reflected publicly on his humble origins from time to time, as he never would have done before, when he was on his way up. In his still firm hand, Sam wrote a dedication of the volume for his son Charles, explaining the additional symbolism that he saw in the picture of an oak tree opposite its frontispiece:

> This story of the building of our company is also partly the story of my life, but with one of the lessons of my dear parents of blessed memory — to be *steadfast* and *true* and build my life *brick* on *brick*. The symbol to the left [is] of the tree firmly planted with strong roots in the ground and growing ever upwards. The branches denote our children and grandchildren also the people of our organization spread around the world. The trunk is your mother and I pray it also represents you and Barbara and the branches of your children and some day please God your grandchildren. With all my love, Pappa. November 3, 1970.

Sam was as dependent upon Saidye as ever, particularly as illness weakened him in the last year or so of his life. And a couple they remained, sending little notes to one another as they had half a century before — and with much of the same language too. "Yes dear you're my baby," he wrote to her on her birthday, in 1968:

> For now at seventy-two
> We still can love and bill and coo
> And even on the way to seventy-three
> You're so fair and young to me
> So let us continue on the way
> To more and more good
> Loving every day
> As always your young Sam.

"The good old housewife and family life are still the best," he told the *Winnipeg Tribune* that year, untroubled with his traditional patriarchal role, like almost all men of his generation.[13] Sam continued to shower Saidye with flowers and poems on her birthday, his own birthday, St Valentine's Day and

Mother's Day, as had been his habit for so many years, signing "Sam," "Doody," "Pappa," or, as his French grandchildren dubbed him, "Poopa." "To you my darling," he wrote in a note accompanying flowers in 1970:

Love of my life
Companion of my every thought
Mother of our children fine
And splendid grandchildren fine
I sent these pretty posies
That they tell you of our love
And that it be undiminished, yea
Forever and ever as it is today
And that my darling
You shall be
Always fair and young to me.

Sam and Saidye were in Barbados for a two-week holiday for his seventy-ninth birthday in March 1970—in truth his eight-first—and when they returned to Montreal it was discovered that he was seriously ill. His disease, cancer of the prostate, was far advanced, and doctors in Montreal and New York declared there was nothing to be done. Saidye managed to keep the truth from her husband, and although in increasing discomfort, he remained active and in the public eye. That spring, he attended the season's opening game of the Montreal Expos—the team that Charles had bought two years before—seated between Prime Minister Pearson and Governor General Roland Michener, and bundled up against a spring chill. In May, the Montreal Jewish community organized a mass rally for Israel bonds on Israel Independence day, which was also, as one of the organizers made clear, a spectacular celebration of Sam's achievements as a Jewish leader. The event began with an early dinner at the Shaar Hashomayim, followed by an evening of speeches in the Montreal Forum, packed with over 18,000 people. The special guest was Abba Eban, then Israeli foreign minister. Describing Sam as "our leading spirit and our right hand," his friend William Gittes conveyed birthday greetings to Sam from the capacity crowd, wishing him well with the traditional *"bis hundert und zwanzig"* — until a hundred and twenty. Sam then addressed the multitude, held to be the largest assembly of Montreal Jewry ever, and probably of Canadian Jewry as well, speaking briefly, but with a clear, strong voice.[14]

A few days later Sam was present at the opening of the Samuel Bronfman House at the corner of McGregor Avenue and Côte des Neiges, the new headquarters of the Canadian Jewish Congress. He spoke again, in particular praise of the Congress with which he had been associated since 1939. "I think that there are not enough young people here," Mike McCormick remembers Sam telling him at the ceremony. "We need them to take over, and the sooner the better."[15]

Sam last appeared in public at a series of events to honour his eightieth birthday in 1971, beginning with a Seagram luncheon at the Americana Hotel in New York, at which he delivered a lengthy speech. Two days later it was the turn of the Canadian company, at the Château Champlain in Montreal. And three days after that, in the midst of a mammoth snowfall, the Canadian Jewish Congress organized a "Gay Nineties" evening for him at the Shaar Hashomayim, chaired by Sol Kanee. Praise and appreciation rained down, including telegrams from Jewish notables around the world, along with a special commemorative medal, honouring his career. In what could not have been an easy task, Sam's brother Allan added his own lavish words of congratulation, and then announced a substantial gift in Sam's name to the Canadian Jewish Museum. Later, in the midst of the festivities, the 250 people present hushed to hear Saidye, who rose to sing what Sam had crooned to her so many years before, and which the couple still considered "our song":

Baby face,
You've got the cutest little baby face.
There's not another one could take your place.

Baby face,
My poor heart is jumpin',
You sure have started somethin'.

Baby face,
I'm up in heaven when I'm in your fond embrace.
I didn't need a shove,
'Cause I just fell in love
With your pretty baby face.

Of his four children, Minda communicated most easily with her
father, with the least inhibition, and in a birthday letter to him she
spoke for her sister and brothers as well: "You have given us far
more than material advantages. You have given us a philosophy
of life that is central to our existence. You have set for us
guidelines and goals. You have taught us, by your example, that
excellence is the only standard and that hard work and singleness
of purpose are the only means of achievement." She then went on
to describe her father as she saw him that day. "More than anyone
I know, *you live what you believe* and that is perhaps what I love
most about you. For there is no pretense, no sham, no verbosity
about you, Father. You always state your position succinctly and
clearly. Your words and your actions are one. This is the sturdy
fibre of your inner core—this, your heart of oak. Your courage,
your vitality, your consistency, your plain thinking and plain
living—these are the qualities that make you such a whole
man."[16]

The last of Sam's eightieth birthday parties, the fourth such
event in just over a week, was hosted by the Canadian Association
of Distillers at the Château Laurier in Ottawa. One hundred and
fifty guests from across Canada, the United States and Britain
attended, including eight Liberal cabinet ministers, and
miscellaneous company presidents and top executives, many of
them Sam's competitors. Chairing the evening was Clifford
Hatch, president of Hiram Walker-Gooderham and Worts and
son of Sam's old rival from prohibition days. And the most
distinguished guest for those in the trade, whose presence
touched Sam deeply, was the elderly Sir Ronald Cumming, the
retired chairman of Distillers Company Limited and a leading
personality of the Scottish whisky trade. "Ronnie" Cumming,
who had been a junior associate in DCL when Sam first did
business with it in the 1920s, bantered with his friend Sam
throughout the evening—two old campaigners remembering

their exploits of yesteryear. The guest of honour was in excellent form, as Max Henderson recalled, trading jibes with the Ottawa mandarins and showing plenty of his old spark.[17]

In Sam's last months, then, his cup overflowed, as those around him mounted an almost continuous series of tributes. Yet as throughout his life, Sam was ambivalent about the steady diet of praise. "They're buttering me up," he told Noah Torno, although he went along with the process just the same, even enjoying it somewhat. "He loved to make a little speech and he liked to have speeches made about himself," Torno notes. "A nice word made him feel better."[18]

Drained by disease, he sat at home on Belvedere Road, playing solitaire and occasionally receiving a few old friends, mainly from the Jewish community. Along with his family, William Gittes saw him from time to time, as did Sol Kanee, and Jack Brin. "He had severe pains up his back," Saidye recalled. "When the pain became too great to bear, we called the doctor and he was given an injection so that he could function normally. I don't think he ever suspected the nature of his illness."[19] "The last days of his life were very painful," recalls Sol Kanee, who played gin rummy with him when he dropped in from Winnipeg. Never a conventionally religious person, Sam did not believe in afterlife. "He told me that we made our own heaven and hell," Phyllis recalls. Like many with a lust for life, he was terrified of dying. For years, when he travelled to New York he refused to sleep in a compartment with the upper birth lowered, because he had a nightmare once that he was in his coffin.[20] "As long as he had the will to live, he lived," Kanee observes. "And Sam had a lot of will."[21]

The end came just after the beginning of July, when he suffered a heart attack. He died at home on July 10, late in the evening. That afternoon, Saidye wrote, "I lay down beside him on the bed and he gripped my hand. Two nurses were on duty all the time. I called one over and asked, 'Where does he get the strength to cling so tightly?' I guess he was trying to retain his life." His last words, according to his doctor, Abe Mayman, were, "I'm afraid to die, but it pains too much to live."[22]

Unusual in Jewish practice, the funeral was delayed for several days while the body lay in state in the new Sam Bronfman House.

Hundreds paid their last respects, as leading members of the Congress's executive committee and regional committees stood watch over the casket. Telescoped, the tribute of the previous year or so was repeated, for one last time. Messages of condolence poured in to the family from all walks of life. Fifteen hundred attended the Shaar Hashomayim for the funeral itself — the largest such ceremony Montreal Jewry had ever seen. Four cabinet ministers attended — Labour Minister Bryce Mackasey, Treasury Board Chariman C.M. Drury, representing the prime minister, Solicitor-General Jean-Pierre Goyer, and Manpower and Immigration Minister Jean Marchand. Claude Simard and Victor Goldbloom represented the province of Quebec, and among the honorary pallbearers and others in attendance were U.S. Senator Jacob Javits (representing the United States government), Dean George James of Columbia University, Montreal mayor Jean Drapeau, former Ontario premier Leslie Frost, Canadian Jewish Congress president Monroe Abbey, CPR board chairman N.R. Crump, Royal Bank chairman Earle McLaughlin, Principal Robert Bell of McGill, former Manitoba premier Duff Roblin, and Israeli Ambassador to Canada Ephraim Evron. In his eulogy, Rabbi William Shuchat presented Sam as "almost a legend in his lifetime," and in a poignant salute, speaking of his former friend and antagonist, Laz Phillips described Sam somewhat oddly as a man with "a deep ingrained sense of democracy," adding that he "was courageous, resourceful and highly instructive. He walked humbly with the average man."[23]

With his funeral, it has been said, "Sam Bronfman had joined the Establishment at last." Sam himself would have found reason to disagree, one can be sure, for a constant striving to do even better, to the discomfort of both himself and everyone around him, was one of the driving forces of his life. Sam might easily have been uncertain whether the turnout was good enough.

Few of Sam's contemporaries got the full measure of the man, in part because his activity was so diverse and his personality so many-sided. He was a complex person, capable of abiding loyalties, deep antipathies, great generosity and consideration, and an awesome rage that scorched those around him. Depending on the circumstances, his speech could be gentle and courtly, or crude and earthy, even violent. He could be kind and generous, but also coarse and cruel — sometimes particularly so to those close to him. "He was a strange mixture of toughness and softness," Charles concludes.[24] Despite his craving for recognition, Sam felt ill at ease with publicity, likely a hangover from the days when the Bronfman brothers, especially Harry, appeared almost daily in Saskatchewan newspapers, blamed for many of the country's ills. His legal troubles of the mid-1930s had a similarly traumatic effect. In fact, Sam felt much more vulnerable than most people credited. Blessed with a happy marriage, and fortified by the family ties that he himself had forged, he faced the world boldly, however uncertain he may have felt inside. His family meant much to him, and he felt most comfortable in his paternal role. Otherwise, signs of insecurity remained — in his innate conservatism and caution in areas where he was not familiar, in his circumspection, for the most part, in dealing with authority, and in his reluctance, outside the business sphere, to assault convention.

It was as an industrialist that Sam achieved the most and revealed the greatest creative flair. Although out of touch with much of his industry by the late 1960s, he showed a stunning ability, during the heyday of Seagram's growth and development, to see far down the road and to pursue his course with a single-minded determination that left others far behind. "He had what the Scots used to call a far-seeing eye," says Noah Torno. "He was always looking way beyond."[25] For twenty years, *Forbes* noted after his death, Sam judged the U.S. market correctly — as virtually no one else in his industry did.[26]

"I once asked him the secret of his success in business," Nahum Goldmann recalled. "His answer was, 'My nose. I can detect good deals and bad deals.' "[27] Much of Sam's feeling for business was instinctive, as those closest to him realized to their dismay when they had to persuade him to adopt scientific marketing methods. But Sam also knew his industry inside out, and set the highest standards both for his products and himself. He learned his trade from the bottom, and indeed always thought of himself as a blender of whiskies, remembering the lore he learned from his Scottish masters in the early 1920s. Sam was also an extraordinarily talented imitator — sensing instinctively at various points in his career what he could adapt from the pre-World War I mail-order houses, from the whisky blenders of the Old Country, from scientific advances in other fields, and from Madison Avenue advertising. And finally, perhaps most importantly, he had a remarkable knack for discerning what the public wanted. In a way that sometimes astounded his employees, Sam sniffed out popular tastes, took what seemed to them extraordinary risks, and more often than not turned out to be right.

Can Sam's flair for marketing whisky be linked to the Jewish environment in which he lived so much of his life? A comparison suggests itself with the Jews of Hollywood, particularly Samuel Goldwyn, Louis Mayer, Adolph Zukor, Harry Cohn, Jack and Harry Warner, men whose career and personality profiles as newcomers to the United States and as brilliant, self-made and single-minded pioneers of their industry matched Sam's in many ways. Writing about these movie moguls, Neal Gabler has noted how they had "a peculiar sensitivity to the dreams and aspirations of other immigrants and working-class families." The Hollywood Jews, "proscribed from entering the real corridors of gentility and status in America," created a dazzling alternative on film — "an empire of their own," propagating an image of a prosperous, successful, good America, an image millions of people hungered for.[28] In a similar way Sam Bronfman, on the margins of Canadian society, at least as he felt it, may have been prompted by his background to sense something that others missed — that whisky could be sold to masses of people as a part of the good life, and that through his products people of all cultures and classes could have access to a world of quality, craftsmanship and tradition from which the desperately poor Jews of his generation had been excluded, and to which so many, like Sam himself, so fervently aspired.

As a Jewish leader, Sam riveted on a few fundamentals — Jewish responsibility for other Jews, for which he set the highest personal standards with his own philanthropy; a simplified notion of Jewish unity, for which he appealed in innumerable contexts; and a dignified Jewish standing in the non-Jewish world, for which he posed an example as an active contributor to his own, Canadian society. Sam was, as Nahum Goldmann liked to say about himself, a wholesaler and not a retailer in Jewish affairs. Unlearned in Judaism, he nevertheless felt the value of his Jewishness deeply, and he did his best to communicate this — whether in his lifelong commitment to the Canadian Jewish Congress, or in his visceral support of Israel, which grew powerfully after his visit to that country in 1956. In Jewish affairs, in which he was less confident and creative than in his business, Sam relied on a few friends and advisers — particularly Goldmann, Saul Hayes and Abe Klein — three brilliant personalities, who gave him ideas and oriented him to the wider Jewish world with which he was sometimes unfamiliar. In choosing these remarkable mentors, Sam showed another talent richly displayed in his Seagram company; he had a special capacity for sizing up individuals, sensing their strengths and weaknesses, and enlisting them in his own cause.

Canadian Jewry, with which Sam was so closely identified, came of age under his leadership and became a full participant in Canadian society. In 1939, when he assumed the presidency of the Canadian Jewish Congress, the numbers of native-born for the first time surpassed the foreign-born. Thereafter, the barriers that Sam and others had known began to crumble or were pushed aside. A new wave of immigration began in 1948, bringing Jews to a country no longer held in the tight grip of British cultural dominance. And as society opened, so the Jewish outlook began to change, abandoning much of traditional Judaism, luxuriating in social and professional success, and finding a new pole of Jewish identity in the State of Israel.

Like so many who had come from the Old Country, whose background was one of destitution and exclusion, Sam had difficulty grasping this transformation, and in many respects he was never fully at ease in gentile society. "The image of the Jew was always of concern to him in a defensive way," says Phyllis. "My impression is that Sam Bronfman's defensiveness was consuming — I don't think there was a minute that he was not conscious of it."[29] Preparing always for the worst, Sam and other Jewish leaders of his generation took their ideals from the past, and were suspicious of new directions in Jewish thought and politics. Their Jewish models were idealized visions of traditional Jewish society or, as in Sam's case, their own parents — to the exclusion, for example, of new Jewish possibilities or of new Jewish realities such as were being created in Israel. The Holocaust seems to have strengthened these trends, which have not yet been overcome, with the result that Jewish communal life in the Diaspora lacks much of the creativity it had before the Second World War.

These were not Sam's preoccupations, however. As befit someone who came to leadership from the world of business, his focus was intensely practical. And in this respect his achievements, and those of Canadian Jewry, were quite remarkable. To immigrant Jews who hungered for material success he provided a model of how Jews could succeed in Canadian society while remaining intensely Jewish. To a Jewish community with an only rudimentary national existence in 1939, he brought a flair for public relations, a sense of the importance of administration, and an ambitious programme of fund-raising. As in the liquor industry, he was deeply concerned with status — and he managed to give Canadian Jewry, in its public face at least, a position of authority and respect on the national plane. Needless to say, this was important to him on a personal level as well. "Jewish leadership brought Sam out," is how one close friend put it. Jewish involvement gave him stature and some inner satisfaction — particularly gratifying, in the light of his past and in view of the many disappointments he experienced, through much of his life, trying to obtain recognition from the non-Jewish world.

His life was not without its frustrations and failures, some of which were due to his own shortcomings, but it was a life of remarkable accomplishment — more than enough, as Sam would have insisted, for a seat at the head table.

Notes

ACJC Archives of the Canadian Jewish Congress
BESS Archives of the United Church of Canada, Board of
        Evangelism and Social Service
DC-SL Distillers Corporation-Seagrams Limited
NA   United States National Archives
PAC   Public Archives of Canada
PAS   Public Archives of Saskatchewan
RCCE Royal Commission on Customs and Excise, 1926–8
SA   Distillers Corporation-Seagrams Limited Archives
SBFP Samuel Bronfman Family Papers

PREFACE

[1]Introduction to Maxwell Henderson, *Plain Talk! Memoirs of an Auditor General* (Toronto: McClelland and Stewart, 1984), 8.

CHAPTER ONE

[1]Harry Bronfman, "The Story of the Bronfman Family," unpub. memoir [1937], SBFP, 3.

[2]Interview with Mark Shinbane, 20 October 1983, SBFP.

[3]Interview with Ben Kayfetz, 7 January 1991.

[4]Jacob Lestchinsky, "Bessarabia," in *The Universal Jewish Encyclopedia*

(10 vols., New York: KTAV Publishing House, 1940), II, 244–48; Eliahu Feldman, "Jews of Bessarabia from the Beginning of their Settlement until the End of the 19th Century" [Hebrew], in *Toledot ha-Yehudim be-Bessarabyah* (Jerusalem: Yad Vashem, 1969), II, 279–99; Michael Bruchis, *Nations — Nationalities — People: A Study of the Nationalities Policy of the Communist Party in Soviet Moldavia* (Boulder, Colorado: East European Monographs, 1984), 141.

[5]S.M. Dubnow, *History of the Jews in Russia and Poland from the Earliest Times Until the Present Day*, trans. I. Friedlaender (3 vols., Philadelphia: Jewish Publication Society of America, 1920), II, 385.

[6]A. Afanasiev-Chuzhbinksii, *Poezdka v Iuzhnuiu Rossiiu* (2 vols., St. Petersburg: n.p., 1863), II, 334–46; El. F., "Soroki," *Encyclopedia Judaica*, XV, 166; I. Hillels, "City of Soroki and Its Community (Second Half of the Nineteenth Century)" [Hebrew], in L. Kuperstain and Yitzhak Konen, eds., *Pirkei Bessarabyah* (Tel Aviv: n.p., 1952), 94–120.

[7]Prince Serge Dmitrivevich Urussov, *Memoirs of a Russian Governor*, trans. and ed. Herman Rosenthal (London: Harper and Brothers, 1908), 116.

[8]S.W. Dubnow, *History of the Jews*, Vol. 5, *From the Congress of Vienna to the Emergence of Hitler*, trans. Moshe Spiegel (London: Thomas Yoseloff, 1973), 539–40; Louis Greenberg, *The Jews in Russia: The Struggle for Emancipation* (2 vols., New York: Schocken, 1976), II, 68.

[9]Urussov, *Memoirs*, 147.

[10]Ibid, 170.

[11]Central State Archive of the Moldavian SSR, fond 134, folio 2, p. 757; ibid, fond 1437, folio 109, no. 6.

[12]Philip Siekman, "The Bronfmans: An Instinct for Dynasty," *Fortune*, November 1966, 146.

[13]Orest Subtelney, *Ukraine: A History* (Toronto: University of Toronto Press, 1988), 124.

[14]Dubnow, *History of the Jews in Russia and Poland*, II, 22, 124–5; Nikolai S. Leskov, *The Jews in Russia: Some Notes on the Jewish Question*, ed. and trans. Harold Klassel Schefski (Princeton, N.J.: Kingston Press, 1986), 27, 29, 37; Urussov, *Memoirs*, 142–3.

[15]Cyril Edel Leonoff, "Wapella Farm Settlement," Supplement to *Transactions, Manitoba Historical and Scientific Society*, Series III, no. 27 (1970–1971), 1–35; Louis Rosenberg, "Wapella, the Oldest Existing Jewish Farm Colony in Canada," *Jewish Post*, 14 September 1928.

[16]Abraham J. Arnold, "Jewish Pioneer Settlements," *The Beaver*, Autumn,

1975, 20; Benjamin G. Sack, *History of the Jews in Canada: From the Earliest Beginnings to the Present Day* (2 vols., Montreal: Canadian Jewish Congress, 1945), I, 184–7.

[17]Vladimir Grossmann, *The Soil's Calling* ([Montreal]: Eagle Publishing Co., 1938), 28.

[18]Tony Cashman, *Abraham Cristall: The Story of a Simple Man* (n.p.: n.p. [1963]), 10.

[19]Ronald Sanders, *Shores of Refuge: A Hundred Years of Jewish Emigration* (New York: Henry Holt & Co., 1988), 66–7.

[20]Gerald Tulchinsky, "Immigrants and Charity in the Montreal Jewish Community before 1890," *Histoire Sociale – Social History*, XVI (1983), 359–80; Benjamin G. Sack, *History of the Jews in Canada: From the Earliest Beginnings to the Present Day* (2 vols., Montreal: Canadian Jewish Congress, 1945), I, 183–7.

[21]Abraham J. Arnold, "The Earliest Jews of Winnipeg," *The Beaver*, Autumn 1974, 4–11.

[22]Idem, "Jewish Pioneer Settlements," *The Beaver*, Autumn 1975, 20–6.

[23]Ibid, 21–3.

[24]Cyril Edel Leonoff, "Pioneers, Ploughs and Prayers: The Jewish Farmers of Western Canada," reprinted from *The Jewish Western Bulletin*, September 1982, 3–5; idem, "Wapella Farm Settlement"; Harry Gutkin, *Journey into Our Heritage: The Story of the Jewish People in the Canadian West* (Toronto: Lester & Orpen Dennys, 1980), 57–9.

[25]Abraham J. Arnold, "The Contribution of the Jews to the Opening and Development of the West," *Transactions of the Historical and Scientific Society of Manitoba*, Series III (1968–1969), 23–37.

[26]Charles Drage, *Two-Gun Cohen* (London: Jonathan Cape, 1954), 22.

[27]Solomon Hirsch Jacobson, "Reminiscences of My Pioneer Days," *Jewish Post*, 30 November 1937.

[28]Idem, "Wapella Farm Settlement," 7–11.

[29]Cyril Edel Leonoff, *The Architecture of Jewish Settlements on the Prairies: A Pictoral History* (n.p.: n.p., 1975), 40–1.

[30]Margaret Prang, *N. W. Rowell: Ontario Nationalist* (Toronto: University of Toronto Press, 1975), 12–13.

[31]Arthur S. Morton, *History of Prairie Settlement* (Toronto: Macmillan, 1938), 68–71.

[32]Beecham Trotter, *A Horseman and the West* (Toronto: Macmillan, 1925), 94.

[33] Pierre Berton, *The Last Spike: The Great Railway 1881 – 1885* (Toronto: Penguin Books, 1989), 37.

[34] *Lovell's Directory of Manitoba and Northwest Territories for 1900 – 1901* (Winnipeg: John Lovell & Son, 1900); G.F. Barker, *Brandon: A City 1881 – 1961* (Altona, Man.: n.p., 1977); Fred McGuinness, *The Wheat City: A Pictorial History of Brandon* (Saskatoon, Sask.: Western Producer Prairie Books, 1988); W. Leland Clark, *Brandon's Politics and Politicians* (Brandon: Brandon Sun, 1981).

[35] Philip Siekman, "The Bronfmans: An Instinct for Dynasty," *Fortune*, November 1966, 146.

[36] Saidye Rosner Bronfman, *My Sam: A Memoir by his Wife* (Toronto: n.p., 1982), 9; James H. Gray, *Booze: The Impact of Whisky on the Prairie West* (Toronto: Macmillan, 1972), 112.

[37] Barker, *Brandon*, 61.

[38] Gerald Friesen, *The Canadian Prairies: A History* (Toronto: University of Toronto Press, 1987), 346.

[39] Louis Rosenberg, *Canada's Jews: A Social and Economic Study of the Jews in Canada* (Montreal: Canadian Jewish Congress, 1939), 308; *Manitoba Free Press*, 26 April 1887; *Herald* (Calgary), 1 February 1899.

[40] Arthur A. Chiel, *Jewish Experiences in Early Manitoba*, 74.

[41] Barker, *Brandon*, 58, 79; Arthur D. Hart, *The Jew in Canada* (Toronto: Toronto Jewish Publications, 1926), 169.

[42] Grant MacEwan, *Heavy Horses: Highlights of Their History* (Saskatoon: Western Producer Prairie Books, 1986), 5.

[43] Trotter, *Horseman*, 239.

[44] Terence Robertson, "Bronfman: The Life and Times of Samuel Bronfman, Esq." (unpub. manuscript, [1969]), 10 – 11.

[45] Gray, *Booze*, 112.

[46] Harry Bronfman, untitled, unpub. memoir, [1939], Harry Bronfman Papers.

[47] Bronfman, "Story of the Bronfman Family," 15.

[48] Laurie Hluchaniuk et al, *Yorkton: York Colony to Treasure Chest City* (Saskatoon: Modern Press, [1983]), 34.

[49] *Letters from America* (Toronto, 1916), 103 – 5, quoted in W.L. Morton, *Manitoba: A History* (Toronto: University of Toronto Press, 1961), 323.

[50] Reuben Bellan, *Winnipeg First Century: An Economic History* (Winnipeg: Queenston House, 1978), 49 – 50, 52, 71; Alan F.J. Artibise, *Winnipeg: A Social History of Urban Growth 1874 – 1914* (Montreal: McGill-Queen's University Press, 1975), 152.

[51]Friesen, *Canadian Prairies*, 243.

[52]Harvey H. Herstein, "The Growth of the Winnipeg Jewish Community and the Evolution of its Educational Institutions," *Transactions of the Historical and Scientific Society of Manitoba*, Series III (1965 – 1966), 27 – 66: Henry Manuel Trachtenberg, " 'The Old Clo' Move.' Anti-Semitism, Politics, and the Jews of Winnipeg," unpub. Ph.D. thesis, York University, 1984.

[53]Interview with Claire Taylor, 2 August 1990.

[54]Gray, *Booze*, 112 – 15.

[55]Phyllis Lambert memorandum, 7 May 1990.

[56]*Henderson's Manitoba and Northwest Territories Gazetteer and Directory for 1905* (Winnipeg: Henderson's Directories, 1905), 1087.

[57]Bronfman, "Story of the Bronfman Family," 21.

[58]Robertson, "Bronfman," 19.

CHAPTER TWO

[1]James H. Gray, *Booze: The Impact of Whisky on the Prairie West* (Toronto: Macmillan, 1972), 116 – 18.

[2]Terence Robertson, "Bronfman: The Life and Times of Samuel Bronfman, Esq." (unpub. manuscript, [1969]), 19; *Winnipeg Tribune*, 28 May 1952.

[3]Robertson, "Bronfman," 17 – 18; *Henderson's Winnipeg City Directory for 1913* (Winnipeg: Henderson's Directories, 1913), 725; *Henderson's Winnipeg City Directory for 1914* (Winnipeg: Henderson's Directories, 1914), 756; Harry Bronfman, "The Story of the Bronfman Family," unpub. memoir [1937], SBFP, 19 – 21; Gray, *Booze*, 115 – 16; interview with Mark Shinbane, 16 January 1984.

[4]Peter C. Newman, *Bronfman Dynasty: The Rothschilds of the New World* (Toronto: McClelland and Stewart, 1978), 72.

[5]Harry Bronfman, "The Story of the Bronfman Family," unpub. memoir [1937], SBFP, 21; interview with Charles Bronfman, 2 April 1979.

[6]See *Royal Commission on the Liquor Traffic in Canada*, Minutes of Evidence, 1894, questions 33949 – 54, 34226 – 30.

[7]PAS: Sessional Paper No. 57, 1908.

[8]Interview with Mark Shinbane, 16 January 1984.

[9]J.S. Woodsworth, *My Neighbour: A Study of Social Conditions. A Plea for Social Service* (Toronto: University of Toronto Press, 1972), 91.

[10]Robertson, "Bronfman," 18.

[11]Ramsay Cook, *The Regenerators: Social Criticism in Late Victorian English Canada* (Toronto: University of Toronto Press, 1985), 178.

[12]Gerald A. Hallowell, *Prohibition in Ontario, 1919–1923* (Ottawa: Ontario Historical Society, 1972), 15.

[13]*Manitoba Free Press*, 1 July 1914; ibid, 2 July 1914; ibid, 3 July 1914.

[14]Quoted in Erhard Pinno, "Temperance and Prohibition in Saskatchewan," unpub. M.A. thesis, University of Saskatchewan, Regina, 1971, 52–6; John H. Thompson, *The Harvests of War: The Prairie West, 1914–1918* (Toronto: McClelland and Stewart, 1978), 70–1.

[15]Interview with Mark Shinbane, 17 January 1984.

[16]Robertson, "Bronfman," 21.

[17]Thompson, *The Harvests of War*, 57.

[18]William L. Downard, *Dictionary of the History of the American Brewing and Distilling Industries* (Westport, Conn.: Greenwood Press, 1980), 113.

[19]Robertson, "Bronfman," 26–7.

[20]Philip Siekman, "The Bronfmans: An Instinct for Dynasty," *Fortune*, November 1966, 148.

[21]Robertson, "Bronfman," 41.

[22]Hallowell, *Prohibition in Ontario*, 108; W.H. Smith, *The Liquor Traffic in British Columbia* (Vancouver: Board of Home Missions and Social Service, 1922), 20.

[23]Gray, *Booze*, 107.

[24]Robertson, "Bronfman," 65.

[25]Royal Commission on Customs and Excise, 1927. Evidence, PAC: RG33/88, vol. 21, 23,041.

[26]Gerald Bronfman to Sam Bronfman, 2 November 1970, Gerald Bronfman Papers; James H. Gray, *The Roar of the Twenties* (Toronto: Macmillan, 1975), 160.

[27]N.W. Rowell to W.L.M. King, 5 March 1927, PAC: MG 26 JI, 125,678–88.

[28]Canada. Parliament, *Royal Commission on Customs and Excise. Interim Report No. 10* (1928), 52.

[29]Robertson, "Bronfman," 135; Bronfman, "Story of the Bronfman Family," 26; memorandum from Charles Bronfman, 19 June 1990; Pinno, "Temperance and Prohibition in Saskatchewan," 127; R.B. Weir, "Canada—Scotch Type Whiskey," unpub. manuscript, 1989, 2.

[30]Daniel J. Boorstin, *The Americans: The Democratic Experience* (New York: Random House, 1973), 77.

[31]Charles Merz, *The Dry Decade* (Garden City, N.Y.: Doubleday, 1931), 131. Cf. John C. Burnham, "New Perspectives on the Prohibition 'Experiment' of the 1920s," *Journal of Social History*, 2 (1968), 51 – 68; Norman H. Clark, *Deliver Us From Evil: An Interpretation of American Prohibition* (New York: W.W. Norton, 1976).

[32]R.J. Keyes to R.E.A. Leach, 30 November 1920. PAS: R-1064 ATG 3 A-41, Saskatchewan Liquor Commission, Export Houses 1920 – 1925.

[33]William J. McNulty, "Canada Reaping a Harvest from Liquor Business," *Current History*, June 1925, 374.

[34]Pinno, "Temperance and Prohibition in Saskatchewan," 168; N.W. Rowell to W.L.M. King, 5 March 1927, PAC: MG 26 JI, 125,678 – 88; PAS: R-1064 ATG 3 A-41, Saskatchewan Liquor Commission, Export Houses 1920 – 1925; *Winnipeg Evening Tribune*, 22 October 1922.

[35]Pinno, "Temperance and Prohibition in Saskatchewan," 205 – 7.

[36]*Presbyterian Witness*, 3 March 1921.

[37]Boorstin, *The Americans*, 82.

[38]Pinno, "Temperance and Prohibition in Saskatchewan," 200.

[39]PAS: R-1064 ATG 3 F-3, Saskatchewan Liquor Commission, Export Houses — Bienfait. Cf. Newman, *Bronfman Dynasty*, 99.

[40]Robertson, "Bronfman," 80 – 2; Jim Coleman, *A Hoofprint on My Heart* (Toronto: McClelland and Stewart, 1971), 80 – 2.

[41]*Winnipeg Evening Tribune*, 27 October 1922.

[42]Royal Commission on Customs and Excise, 1927. Evidence, PAC: RG33/88, 23,044.

[43]William F. Rannie, *Canadian Whisky: The Product and the Industry* (Lincoln, Ontario: W.F. Rannie, 1976), 109 – 10.

[44]Mel Griffin memorandum, 6 June 1990.

[45]*Winnipeg Tribune*, 27 October 1922.

[46]Gray, *Booze*, 121.

[47]Ibid, 126.

[48]"Memorandum re Partnership dealings of Meyer Chechik and Harry Rabinovitch," SA, 7 April 1934, SA.

[49]Robertson, "Bronfman," 110.

[50]King's Bench, Judicial District of Regina. Examination of Meyer

Chechik, 9 October 1923, SA; Pinno, "Temperance and Prohibition in Saskatchewan," 204.

[51] Harry Bronfman, "Statement of Facts" [1923], SA.

[52] Interview with Mark Shinbane, 16 January 1984.

[53] Gray, *Booze*, 178.

[54] Royal Commission on Customs and Excise, 1927. Evidence, PAC: RG33/88, 11798–816.

[55] Gray, *Booze*, 176; Newman, *Bronfman Dynasty*, 90.

[56] Harry Bronfman, "Statement of Facts" [1923], SA.

[57] Newman, *Bronfman Dynasty*, 94.

[58] Rose to Sam, 22 December 1918, SBFP.

[59] Philip Siekman, "The Bronfmans: An Instinct for Dynasty," *Fortune*, November 1966, 148.

[60] Sam Bronfman speech of 6 March 1948, SA; Sam and Allan's telegram to Weizmann, 20 February 1949, Weizmann Archives.

[61] Interview with Pearl Siver [1976].

[62] Saidye Rosner Bronfman, *Recollections of My Life* (Montreal: n.p., 1986), 36.

[63] Interviews with Saidye Bronfman, 30 October 1976, 12 February 1979, 13 February 1979, 18 June 1980.

[64] Saidye Rosner Bronfman, *My Sam: A Memoir by his Wife* (Toronto: n.p., 1982), 4.

[65] Ibid, 4–6.

[66] Sam to Saidye, 10 March 1922, SBFP; Norman H. Clark, *The Dry Years: Prohibition and Social Change in Washington* (Seattle: University of Washington Press, 1988), 153.

[67] Bronfman, *My Sam*, 23–4.

[68] Bernard Figler, *Lillian and Archie Freiman: Biographies* (Montreal, n.p., 1961), 212.

[69] Robertson, "Bronfman," 123–4.

[70] Gray, *Booze*, 159.

[71] *Winnipeg Evening Tribune*, 4, 5, 6, 7, 19, October 1922.

[72] Ibid, 16 October 1922.

[73] Bronfman, "Story of the Bronfman Family," 30, SBFP.

[74] Harry Bronfman, Gerald Bronfman papers, unpub. memoir, [1939].

[75] Interview with Saidye Bronfman, 7 November 1990.

[76] Bronfman, *My Sam*, 24–6.

CHAPTER THREE

[1]Terence Robertson, "Bronfman: The Life and Times of Samuel Bronfman, Esq." (unpub. manuscript, [1969]), 218.

[2]Phyllis Lambert memorandum, 6 August 1990.

[3]Saidye Rosner Bronfman, *My Sam: A Memoir by his Wife* (Toronto: n.p., 1982), 24 – 5.

[4]Carleton Stanley, "The Canadian Liquor System: II — Success of System Due to Commonsense View of Drinking," *Current History*, XXXI (October 1929), 74.

[5]Antonin Dupont, "Louis-Alexandre Taschereau et la législation sociale au Québec, 1920 – 1936," *Revue d'histoire de l'Amérique française*, 26 (1972), 400.

[6]John H. Thompson, *The Harvests of War: The Prairie West, 1914 – 1918* (Toronto: McClelland and Stewart, 1978), 103.

[7]Gerald Tulchinsky, "The Third Solitude: A.M. Klein's Jewish Montreal, 1910 – 1950," *Journal of Canadian Studies*, 19 (1984), 96; Louis Rosenberg, "The Jewish Population of Canada: A Statistical Summary From 1850 to 1943," *American Jewish Year Book*, 48 (1946 – 47), 19 – 50.

[8]Louis Rosenberg, *Canada's Jews: A Social and Economic Study of the Jews in Canada* (Montreal: Canadian Jewish Congress, 1939), 402; Pierre Anctil, *Le rendez-vous manqué: Les Juifs de Montréal face au Québec de l'entre-deux-guerres* (Québec: Institut québécois de recherche sur la culture, 1988), Ch. 1.

[9]Betty Sigler, "Montreal: The Bonds of Community," *Commentary*, April 1950, 345.

[10]*Congregation Shaar Hashomayim 1846 – 1946* [1946], 17.

[11]Michael Brown, *Jew or Juif?: Jews, French-Canadians, and Anglo-Canadians, 1759 – 1914* (Philadelphia: The Jewish Publication Society, 1987), 186.

[12]Bronfman, *My Sam*, 26 – 7.

[13]Deed of Sale, 29 September 1924, SA.

[14]David Daiches, *Scotch Whisky: Its Past and Present* (London: Fontana, 1976), 81: R.B. Weir, "Distilling and Agriculture 1870 – 1939," *Agricultural History Review*, 32 (1984), 50 – 1.

[15]Ross Wilson, *Scotch: Its History and Romance* (Newton Abbot, England: David & Charles, 1973), 283, 295; R.B. Weir, "Alcohol Controls and Scotch Whisky Exports (1870 – 1939)," *British Journal of Addiction*, (1988), no. 83, 1291; idem, "Rationalization and Diversification in the

Scotch Whisky Industry, 1900 – 1939: Another Look at 'Old' and 'New' Industries," *Economic History Review*, 2nd ser., XLII (1989), 380.

[16]Interview with Mark Shinbane, 4 January 1984.

[17]William L. Downard, *Dictionary of the History of the American Brewing and Distilling Industries* (Westport, Conn.: Greenwood Press, 1980), 207; Martin Mayer, "The Volatile Business," *Esquire*, August 1959, 106.

[18]William H. Ross and Thomas Herd, Distillers Company Limited report of 10 November 1926, 11. I want to record my gratitude to Dr R.B. Weir of the University of York who kindly sent me this report, which comes from the archives of the United Distillers of London. My thanks to them as well for permission to quote from this document; Charles Bronfman memorandum, 20 July 1990.

[19]Gerald Bronfman to Sam Bronfman, 2 November 1970, Gerald Bronfman Papers.

[20]Samuel Bronfman, *From Little Acorns: The Story of Distillers Corporation-Seagrams Limited* ([Montreal: DC-SL], 1970), 19.

[21]R.B. Weir, "Canada — Scotch Type Whisky," unpub. paper, 1989, a chapter in the forthcoming book on the Distillers Company by Dr R.B. Weir. My thanks to him for letting me see this paper.

[22]Robertson, "Bronfman," 319 – 21.

[23]Wilson, *Scotch*, 335 – 6.

[24]Sir Robert Bruce Lockhart, *Scotch: The Whisky of Scotland in Fact and Story* (London: Putnam, 1951), 137; R.B. Weir, "William Henry Ross," *Dictionary of Scottish Business Biography*, forthcoming.

[25]Interview with Roy Martin, 4 January 1984; Robertson, "Bronfman," 322.

[26]Ross and Herd, report of 10 November 1926.

[27]Robertson, "Bronfman," 323.

[28]Ibid, 327.

[29]Weir, "Canada — Scotch Type Whisky," 10 – 11.

[30]Ibid, 12; Robertson, "Bronfman," 328.

[31]Wilson, *Scotch*, 339 – 40.

[32]Harry Bronfman, "The Story of the Bronfman Family," unpub. memoir [1937], SBFP, 33.

[33]William F. Rannie, *Canadian Whisky: The Product and the Industry* (Lincoln, Ontario: W.F. Rannie, 1976), 112 – 13.

[34]See Gerald A. Hallowell, *Prohibition in Ontario, 1919–1923* (Ottawa: Ontario Historical Society, 1972), passim.

[35]Peter Oliver, *Public and Private Persons: The Ontario Political Culture 1914–1934* (Toronto: Clarke, Irwin, 1975), 78.

[36]Michael Bliss, *A Canadian Millionaire: The Life and Business Times of Sir Joseph Flavelle, Bart. 1858–1939* (Toronto: Macmillan, 1978), 429; Peter Oliver, *G. Howard Ferguson: Ontario Tory* (Toronto: University of Toronto Press, 1977), 273.

[37]Margaret Prang, *N.W. Rowell: Ontario Nationalist* (Toronto: University of Toronto Press, 1975), 435.

[38]C.W. Hunt, *Booze, Boats and Billions: Smuggling Liquid Gold!* (Toronto: McClelland and Stewart, 1988), 85.

[39]*Financial Post*, 31 December 1926.

[40]*Financial Post*, 23 March 1928; interview with Roy Martin, 4 January 1984.

[41]DC-SL Minutes, 11 September 1928.

[42]DC-SL Minutes, 18 October 1929; *Financial Post*, 3 February 1928; 14 September 1928; 15 March 1929; 10 October 1929; 3 April 1930; 17 April 1930.

[43]Ibid, 24 October 1929; 31 October 1929.

[44]William J. McNulty, "Canada Reaping a Harvest from Liquor Business," *Current History*, June 1925, 375.

[45]"Departmental Regulations Respecting Exportation of Duty Paid. Intoxicating Liquors," No. 689c, 15 May 1929, SA.

[46]McNulty, "Canada Reaping a Harvest from Liquor Business," 375.

[47]Robertson, "Bronfman," 245–6.

[48]Norman H. Clark, *Deliver Us From Evil: An Interpretation of American Prohibition* (New York: W.W. Norton, 1976), 165; John C. Burnham, "New Perspectives on the Prohibition 'Experiment' of the 1920s," *Journal of Social History*, 2 (1968), 51–68.

[49]*Ottawa Journal*, 3 January 1929; Richard N. Kottman, "Volstead Violated: Prohibited as a Factor in Canadian-American Relations," *Canadian Historical Review*, 43 (1962), 106–26.

[50]McNulty, "Canada Reaping a Harvest from Liquor Business," 374–5.

[51]Alfred Edward Cooke, "The Canadian Liquor System: I — Evils of Government Control," *Current History*, XXXI (October 1929), 72.

[52]Montreal *Gazette*, 28 February 1930.

[53]Wilson, *Scotch*, 302, 305 – 6.

[54]*Time*, 26 July 1971.

[55]Sam to Harry Hatch, 16 November 1932, SA.

[56]RCMP: 1934 Prosecution of Abraham Bronfman et al, 1933-HQ-768-Q-1.

[57]Royal Commission on Customs and Excise, 1927. PAC: RG 33/88, Vol. 19, 22,010 – 16.

[58]Hunt, *Booze, Boats and Billions*, 144.

[59]Maxwell Henderson, *Plain Talk! Memoirs of an Auditor General* (Toronto: McClelland and Stewart, 1984), 44.

[60]Interview with Roy Martin, 4 January 1984.

[61]Robertson, "Bronfman," 239 – 40.

[62]J.P. Andrieux, *Prohibition and St Pierre* (Lincoln, Ontario: W.F. Rannie, 1983), 25 and passim.

[63]Hunt, *Booze, Boats and Billions*, 252.

[64]"Summary of Evidence," RCMP: 1934 Prosecution of Abraham Bronfman et al, 1933-HQ-768-Q-1, 1080.

[65]Memorandum, 23 October 1935, RCMP: 1934 Prosecution of Abraham Bronfman et al, 1933-HQ-768-Q-1, 1128; NA: Memorandum of 22 December 1931. 811.114.

[66]Andrieux, *Prohibition*, 77.

[67]Memorandum, 16 August 1934, 23 August 1934, RCMP: 1933-HQ-768-Q-1, v.1, 86.

[68]Memorandum, 20 October 1934, F.W. Zaneth memorandum, 10 February 1935, RCMP: 1933-HQ-768-Q-1, v.1, 229, 780; Montreal *Gazette*, 9 April 1935.

[69]Sam to Harry Hatch, 16 November 1932, SA.

[70]Alfred Edward Cooke, "The Canadian Liquor System: I — Evils of Government Control," *Current History*, XXXI (October 1929), 64 – 73.

[71]"Whiskey," *Fortune*, November 1933, 33, 38.

[72]Henderson, *Plain Talk*, 110.

[73]Dennis Eisenberg, Uri Dan and Eli Landau, *Meyer Lansky: Mogul of the Mob* (New York: Paddington Press, 1979), 79; Stephen Birmingham, *"The Rest of Us": The Rise of America's Eastern European Jews* (Boston:

Little, Brown, 1984), 153, 374, Cf. Hank Messick, *Lansky* (New York: G.P. Putnam's Sons, 1971), 68–70; Martin A. Gosch and Richard Hammer, *The Last Testament of Lucky Luciano* (Boston: Little, Brown, 1974), 41.

[74]See Nora Ephron, "Seagrams with Moxie," *New York Times Book Review*, 11 March 1979, 13.

[75]United States Congress. Senate. Special Committee to Investigate Organized Crime in Interstate Commerce Pursuant to S. Res. 202 (81st Congress). (1951), 902–3.

[76]E.T. Burns memorandum, 2 March 1951; E.T. Burns to P.C. Murray, 3 March 1951; Agnes Wolfe to Rudolph Halley, 3 March 1951, NA: Records of the U.S. Senate, Record Group 46.

[77]Trial memorandum on behalf of defendants Joseph Reinfeld, Reinfeld Importers, Ltd., and Harold C. Reinfeld, n.d. [October 1953], SA.

[78]*New York Times*, 17 August 1951.

[79]Robertson, "Bronfman," 352–3.

[80]Hank Messick, *Secret File* (New York: G.P. Putnam's Sons, 1969), 279.

[81]Mark A. Stuart, *Gangster #2: Longy Zwillman, the Man Who Invented Organized Crime* (Secaucus, N.J.: Lyle Stuart, 1985), 44.

[82]Arthur Hertzberg, *The Jews in America. Four Centuries of an Uneasy Encounter: A History* (New York: Simon and Schuster, 1989), 206.

[83]Chaim Bermant, *The Jews* (London: Weidenfeld and Nicolson, 1977), 66.

[84]Albert Fried, *The Rise and Fall of the Jewish Gangster in America* (New York: Holt, Rinehart and Winston, 1980), 102–3.

[85]James H. Gray, *Booze: The Impact of Whisky on the Prairie West* (Toronto: Macmillan, 1972), 158.

[86]Peter C. Newman, *Bronfman Dynasty: The Rothschilds of the New World* (Toronto: McClelland and Stewart, 1978), 23 n.

[87]Royal Commission on Customs and Excise, 1927. PAC: RG 33/88, vol. 21, 21,998, 23,102.

[88]Prang, *Rowell*, 33, 139; Oliver, *Public and Private Persons*, 69.

[89]Oliver, *Ferguson*, 56.

[90]Interview with Mark Shinbane, 20 October 1983; interview with Roy Martin, 4 January 1984.

[91]Rowell to King, 5 March 1927, PAC: MG 26, Jl, Vol. 148.

[92]Royal Commission on Customs and Excise, 1927. PAC: RG 33/88, vol. 21, 22,098.

[93]Ibid, 23,041 – 2.

[94]Ibid, 23,064.

[95]Interview with Mark Shinbane, 20 October 1983.

[96]Canada. Parliament, *Royal Commission on Customs and Excise. Interim Reports* (No. 10) (1928), 105 – 16.

[97]Norman Ward and David Smith, *Jimmy Gardiner: Relentless Liberal* (Toronto: University of Toronto Press, 1990), 89 – 93.

[98]Gray, *Booze*, 185.

[99]*Regina Star*, 15 May 1929; Ernest Watkins, *R.B. Bennett: A Biography* (Toronto: Kingswood House, 1963), 77; William Calderwood, "Pulpit, Press and Political Reactions to the Ku Klux Klan in Saskatchewan," in S.M. Trofimenkoff, ed., *The Twenties in Western Canada (Papers of the Western Canadian Studies Conference, March 1972)* (Ottawa: National Museum of Man, 1972), 206; Patrick Kyba, "Ballots and Burning Crosses — The Election of 1929," in Norman Ward and Duff Spafford, eds., *Politics in Saskatchewan* (Toronto: Longmans Canada Limited, 1968), 105 – 23.

[100]David Ricardo Williams, *Duff: A Life in the Law* (Vancouver: University of British Columbia Press, 1984), 138 – 9.

[101]*Regina Leader*, 9 March 1930; *Manitoba Free Press*, 10 March 1930.

[102]Interview with Mark Shinbane, 17 January 1984.

[103]Gray, *Booze*, 187.

[104]Harry Bronfman, unpub. memoir [1939], Gerald Bronfman Papers.

[105]DC-SL Minutes, 30 October 1930.

[106]*Documents on Canadian External Relations, Vol. 4, 1926 – 1930*, ed. Alex I. Inglis (Ottawa: Information Canada, 1971), 531 – 3.

[107]Sam to Harry Hatch, 16 November 1932, SA.

[108]DC-SL Minutes, 30 November 1931.

[109]Minutes of Meetings Held in London 18th August 1931 to 1st September 1931 in Connection with the Proposed Canadian Merger, SA.

[110]*Financial Post*, 1 July 1933.

CHAPTER FOUR

[1]H.G. Norman to F.J. Mead, 22 November 1934, SA.

[2]*Financial Post*, 16 January 1930.

[3]Sam to Harry Hatch, 16 November 1932, SA; "Whiskey," *Fortune*, November 1933, 30, 126.

[4]Interview with Edgar Bronfman, 5 September 1979.

[5]Max Melamet, "Samuel Bronfman. A Personal Tribute," *Chronicle Review*, August 1971.

[6]Neal Gabler, *An Empire of Their Own: How the Jews Invented Hollywood* (New York: Doubleday, 1988), 39; Phyllis Lambert to Michael Marrus, 10 September 1989.

[7]Saidye Rosner Bronfman, *My Sam: A Memoir by his Wife* (Toronto: n.p., 1982), 29.

[8]Charles Bronfman memorandum, 20 July 1990.

[9]Interviews with Saidye Bronfman, 20 March 1979, 14 August 1979.

[10]Bronfman, *My Sam*, 33–4.

[11]Ibid, 35–8.

[12]Saidye Rosner Bronfman, *Recollections of My Life* (Montreal: n.p., 1986), 119–20.

[13]*Canadian Jewish News*, 24 February 1961; Max Bookman, "The End of an Era," *Chronicle Review*, August 1971; Bronfman, *Recollections*, 118–19; interview with Saidye Bronfman, 7 June 1978.

[14]Interview with Lilianne Lagadec, n.d.

[15]Phyllis Lambert to "Joey and Jensen," 11 March 1953.

[16]Interview with Phyllis Lambert, 8 January 1980.

[17]Phyllis Lambert memorandum, 6 August 1990.

[18]Interview with Edgar Bronfman, 5 September 1979.

[19]Phyllis Lambert memorandum, 6 August 1990.

[20]Montreal *Gazette*, 29 August 1935.

[21]Ross Wilson, *Scotch: Its History and Romance* (Newton Abbot, England: David & Charles, 1973), 336.

[22]Peter C. Newman, *Bronfman Dynasty: The Rothschilds of the New World* (Toronto: McClelland and Stewart, 1978), 26. Cf. *Les Rues de Montréal: façades et fantaisies* (Montreal, 1977), 73.

[23]*Montreal Star*, 14 August 1930.

[24]*Le Petit Journal,* 23 June 1935.

[25]Norman H. Clark, *Deliver Us From Evil: An Interpretation of American Prohibition* (New York: W.W. Norton, 1976), 199.

[26]Andrew Sinclair, *Prohibition: The Era of Excess* (London: Faber and Faber, 1962), 383, 405.

[27]"Industry Leaders I — Seagram," *Monopoly State Review,* August 1946, 9.

[28]Allan to Sam, 29 June 1932, SA.

[29]"Whiskey," 126.

[30]R.B. Weir, "Canada — Scotch Type Whisky," unpub. paper, 1989, 21.

[31]Terence Robertson, "Bronfman: The Life and Times of Samuel Bronfman, Esq." (unpub. manuscript, [1969]), 430.

[32]R.B. Weir, "Canada — Scotch Type Whisky," unpub. paper, 1989, 17 – 22.

[33]DC-SL Minutes, 6 January 1934.

[34]Theodore H. White, *The View from the Fortieth Floor* (New York: William Sloan Associates, 1960), 209.

[35]Stephen Birmingham, *"The Rest of Us": The Rise of America's Eastern European Jews* (Boston: Little, Brown, 1984), 234.

[36]Philip J. Kelly, *The Making of a Salesman* (New York: Abelard Schuman, 1965), 150.

[37]"Name, Schenley; Age, Three," *Fortune,* May 1936, 150.

[38]Hank Messick, "The Schenley Chapter," *The Nation,* April 5, 1971, 429 – 30. Cf. J. Robert Nash, *Citizen Hoover: A Critical Study of the Life and Times of J. Edgar Hoover and His FBI* (Chicago: Nelson-Hall 1972), 109 – 12; Kenneth O'Reilly, *Hoover and the Un-Americans: The FBI, HUAC, and the Red Menace* (Philadelphia: Temple University Press, 1983), 78 – 9; Richard G. Powers, *Secrecy and Power: The Life of J. Edgar Hoover* (New York: The Free Press, 1987), 221.

[39]Robertson, "Bronfman," 437 – 8.

[40]Philip Siekman, "The Bronfmans: An Instinct for Dynasty," *Fortune,* November 1966, 202.

[41]Bronfman, *My Sam,* 45 – 6.

[42]United States Congress. Hearings before the Temporary National Economic Committee Pursuant to Res. 113 (75th Congress). Part 6, Liquor Industry (1939), 2512.

[43]Bronfman, *My Sam,* 46 – 7.

44Ibid, 46 – 50; interviews with Saidye Bronfman, 14 September 1978, 18 July 1979.

45Interview with Abe Mayman, 7 November 1990.

46"Liquor in America: An Interim Report," *Fortune*, October 1934, 104, 107; W.J. Rorabaugh, *The Alcoholic Republic: An American Tradition* (New York: Oxford University Press, 1979), 225 – 33; Mark Edward Lender, and James Kirby Martin, *Drinking in America: A History* (New York: The Free Press, 1982), 173.

47Bronfman, *My Sam*, 49.

48Kelly, *Making of a Salesman*, 168.

49Address by Mr Samuel Bronfman, Seagram Distillers Corporation Annual Sales Meeting, 15 July 1954, SA.

50"Industry Leaders I — Seagram," *Monopoly State Review*, August 1946, 10.

51"Seagram in the Chips," *Fortune*, September 1948, 100.

52"Whiskey," 30; Morris V. Rosenbloom, *The Liquor Industry: A Survey of Its History, Manufacture, Problems of Control and Importance* (Braddock, Pennsylvania: Ruffsdale, 1937), 46.

53"Hiram Walker Digs In," *Fortune*, March 1939, 71.

54Interview with Melvin Griffin, 7 February 1990.

55DC-SL Minutes, 6 January 1934; *New York Times*, 6 December 1933; *Financial Post*, 16 December 1933; L.A. Keidel to H.I. Peffer, 12 April 1934, SA.

56DC-SL Minutes, 29 December 1934; "Seagram in the Chips," 158.

57"Seagram in the Chips," 158.

58Samuel Bronfman, *From Little Acorns: The Story of Distillers Corporation-Seagrams Limited* ([Montreal: DC-SL], 1970), 34.

59Ibid, 53.

60Ibid, 54 – 5.

61"Seagrams' Late Awakening," *Forbes*, 1 February 1973, 28.

62DC-SL Minutes, 29 December 1934, 9 January 1935.

63Bronfman, *Little Acorns*, 56.

64"Name, Schenley; Age, Three," *Fortune*, May 1936, 164.

65William Wendell Wachtel, *The Anatomy of a Hidden Persuader* (New York: Vantage Press, 1975), 150 – 1.

66Birmingham, *"The Rest of Us"*, 237.

[67]Kelly, *Making of a Salesman*, 149.

[68]Clark, *Deliver Us From Evil*, 211.

[69]Siekman, "The Bronfmans," 206.

[70]Ibid, 210.

[71]DC-SL Minutes, 4 November 1938.

[72]DC-SL Minutes, 30 November 1935; "Whiskey," 114 n; *New York Times*, 16 October 1934; *The Advertiser*, August 1952, 68; Paul Gardner, "Bronfman of Seagrams," *New Liberty*, July 1949, 13; Martin Mayer, "The Volatile Business," *Esquire*, August 1959, 103; interview with Saidye Bronfman, 8 August 1978.

[73]*Distillations*, September 1976.

[74]*New York Times*, 12 June 1960.

[75]Interview with Robert Sabloff, 23 January 1990; DC-SL Minutes, 9 January 1935.

[76]Paul Gardner, "Bronfman of Seagrams," *New Liberty*, July 1949, 15.

[77]Birmingham, *"The Rest of Us"*, 277.

[78]Martin Mayer, "The Volatile Business," *Esquire*, August 1959, 115.

[79]Remarks at the Economic Conference in Jerusalem, 31 March 1968, SA.

[80]"Remarks of Mr Samuel Bronfman on the Occasion of his Fiftieth Birthday," 8 March 1941, SA; Phyllis Lambert memorandum, 4 September 1990; Edgar Bronfman memorandum, 17 September 1990.

[81]David Daiches, *Scotch Whisky: Its Past and Present* (London: Fontana, 1976), 92; Robert Bruce Lockhart, *Scotch: The Whisky of Scotland in Fact and Story* (London: Putnam, 1951), 94, 114, 117, 119; R.B. Weir, "Obsessed with Moderation: The Drink Trades and the Drink Question (1870–1930)," *British Journal of Addiction*, 79 (1984), 93, 104–5.

[82]Kelly, *Making of a Salesman*, 149.

[83][Unsigned] to C.N. Cahan, 26 October 1934, SA; J.W. Tyson to H.F. Glass, 9 November 1934, SA.

[84]Interview with Mark Shinbane, 16 January 1984.

[85]Aimé Geoffrion to R.B. Bennett, 8 December 1934, SA; A. Jackson Dodds to R.B. Bennett, 11 December 1934, SA; Lillian Freiman to R.B. Bennett, 11 November [11 December] 1934, SA; F.J. Mead to Aimé Geoffrion, 10 December 1934, RCMP: 1933–HQ-768-Q-1, 375.

[86]Beaverbrook (William Maxwell Aitken), *Friends: Sixty Years of Intimate Personal Relations with Richard Bedford Bennett* (London: Heinemann, 1959), 12, 44 n.

87Peter White to Sam, 22 November 1934, SA; F.J. Mead to Commanding Officer, "H" Division, 11 December 1933. RCMP: 1933–HQ-768-Q-1, 14.

88Nora Kelley and William Kelley, *The Royal Canadian Mounted Police: A Century of History 1873–1973* (Edmonton: Hurtig, 1973), 172.

89F.J. Mead to Mark Vernon, 1 February 1934. RCMP: 1933–HQ-768-Q-1, 19.

90Montreal *Gazette*, 12 December 1934.

91Ibid, 18 December 1934.

92News Service Bureau memorandum, 11 January 1935.

93Interview with Sol Kanee, 13 September 1989.

94*Montreal Star*, 11, 12 January 1935.

95Ibid, 15 January 1935; Montreal *Gazette*, 16 January 1935.

96News Service Bureau memorandum, 4 February 1934, SA; *Montreal Star*, 4 February 1934.

97Interview with Mark Shinbane, 16 January 1984.

98Montreal *Gazette*, 9 April 1935.

99Mr Justice Desmarais, Notes. RCMP: 1933–HQ-768-Q-1, 1004 ff.

100Robertson, "Bronfman," 482.

101Wesley Frost memoranda, 25 April 1934 and 2 November 1934. United States National Archives: Record Group 59, Decimal file 1930–39; U.S. Consul General to J.H. MacBrien, 11 December 1934, RCMP: 1933–HQ-768-Q-1, 401.

102Aaron Sapiro to Laz Phillips, 26 April 1932; 20 June 1932; 2 July 1932, SA.

103Aaron Sapiro to Laz Phillips, 16 March 1933; 13 June 1933; 31 August 1933, SA.

104W.D. Herridge to Secretary of State for External Affairs, 2 December 1933, *Documents on Canadian External Relations, Vol. 5, 1931–1935*, ed. Alex I. Inglis (Ottawa: Information Canada, 1973), 133; *Financial Post*, 23 December 1933.

105Mayer, "The Volatile Business," 110.

106Wachtel, *The Anatomy of a Hidden Persuader*, 135–7.

107Frederick Willkie and Harrison C. Blankmeyer, *An Outline for Industry* (Springfield, Illinois: Charles C. Thomas, 1944), 137.

108John M. Blum, *From the Morgenthau Diaries: Years of Crisis, 1928–1938* (Boston: Houghton Mifflin, 1959), 105–6.

CHAPTER FIVE

[1]Interview with Mark Shinbane, 20 October 1983.

[2]Interview with Leo Kolber, 20 April 1990.

[3]Terence Robertson, "Bronfman: The Life and Times of Samuel Bronfman, Esq." (unpub. manuscript, [1969]), 464; interview with Edgar Bronfman, 21 July 1966.

[4]Interview with Phyllis Lambert, 12 June 1989.

[5]Interview with Charles Bronfman, 12 June 1989.

[6]Phyllis Lambert memorandum, 4 September 1990.

[7]Interview with Saidye Bronfman, 5 September 1979.

[8]Interview with Melvin Griffin, 7 February 1990.

[9]Interview with Saidye Bronfman, 7 November 1990; interview with Charles Bronfman, 3 December 1990.

[10]William Rodgers, *Think: A Biography of the Watsons and IBM* (New York: Stein and Day, 1969), 113–15; Charles Bronfman memorandum, 20 July 1990; interview with Charles Bronfman, 3 December 1990.

[11]W.D. Cleland to Sam, 21 January 1936, SA.

[12]Morgenthau Diaries, Book 9, 118A-D.

[13]*Financial Post*, 23 November 1935.

[14]H. Blair Neatby, *William Lyon Mackenzie King, Vol. 3, 1932–1939* (Toronto: University of Toronto Press, 1976), 147.

[15]H.H. Wrong telegram, 18 November 1935, *Documents on Canadian External Relations, Vol. 5, 1931–1935*, ed. Alex I. Inglis (Ottawa: Information Canada, 1973), 161.

[16]Neatby, *Mackenzie King, Vol. 3, 1932–1939*, 148.

[17]Cordell Hull, *The Memoirs of Cordell Hull* (2 vols., New York: Macmillan, 1948), I, 206.

[18]"Memorandum of a Conference in Cordell Hull's Office at 11 a.m.," April 6, 1936, Morgenthau Diaries, Book 20.

[19]Max Henderson, *Plain Talk! Memoirs of an Auditor General* (Toronto: McClelland and Stewart, 1984), 52.

[20]Hull, *Memoirs*, I, 206–7. Cf. John M. Blum, *From the Morgenthau Diaries: Years of Crisis, 1928–1938* (Boston: Houghton Mifflin, 1959), 118.

[21]DC-SL Minutes, 30 November 1935, 16 May 1936; William Wendell Wachtel, *The Anatomy of a Hidden Persuader* (New York: Vantage Press, 1975), 135–7.

[22]Interview with Robert Sabloff, 23 January 1990.

[23]Melvin Griffin memorandum, November 1989.

[24]William F. Rannie, *Canadian Whisky: The Product and the Industry* (Lincoln, Ontario: W.F. Rannie, 1976), 46.

[25]Special News Service Bulletin, 27 November 1937, SA.

[26]Interview with Charles Bronfman, 2 April 1979.

[27]Interview with Roy Martin, 4 January 1984.

[28]Interview with Noah Torno, 6 November 1990.

[29]Ibid; interview with Mel Griffin, 7 February 1990.

[30]Interview with Roy Martin, 4 January 1984; interview with Walter Goelkel, 13 January 1991.

[31]DC-SL Minutes, 9 January 1935.

[32]Wachtel, *Anatomy of a Hidden Persuader*, 126.

[33]Interview with Charles Bronfman, 3 December 1990; Samuel Bronfman, *From Little Acorns* ([Montreal: DC-SL], 1970), 20.

[34]Melvin Griffin memorandum, November 1989.

[35]Interview with Walter Goelkel, 13 January 1991.

[36]DC-SL Minutes, 4 November 1938.

[37]*Financial Post*, 13 April 1935.

[38]Interview with Robert Sabloff, 23 January 1990.

[39]Wachtel, *Anatomy of a Hidden Persuader*, 70.

[40]Ibid, 85.

[41]Ibid, 77; United States Congress. Hearings before the Temporary National Economic Committee Pursuant to Res. 113 (75th Congress). Part 6, Liquor Industry (1939), 2550.

[42]Philip J. Kelly, *The Making of a Salesman* (New York: Abelard Schuman, 1965), 155.

[43]Interview with Sol Kanee, 13 September 1989; interview with Robert Ruppel, 14 September 1990.

[44]Wachtel, *Anatomy of a Hidden Persuader*, 91.

[45]Robertson, "Bronfman," 491 – 2.

[46]Interview with Walter Goelkel, 13 January 1991.

[47]Harry Bronfman, unpub. memoir, [1939], Gerald Bronfman Papers.

[48]Interview with Marjorie Bronfman, 7 November 1990.

[49]Bronfman, *Little Acorns*, 58.

[50]Frederick Willkie and Harrison C. Blankmeyer, *An Outline for Industry* (Springfield, Illinois: Charles C. Thomas, 1944), 28.

[51]Interview with Walter Goelkel, 13 January 1991.

[52]Ibid, 29–30; DC-SL Minutes, 4 November 1938; Phyllis Lambert memorandum, 4 September 1990.

[53]"Seagram in the Chips," *Fortune*, 166.

[54]Willkie and Blankmeyer, *An Outline for Industry*, 95.

[55]Charles Bronfman memorandum, 13 August 1990; interview with Walter Goelkel, 13 January 1991.

[56]Max Melamet, "Sam Bronfman: A Personal Tribute," *Chronical Review*, August 1971, 4–5; interview with Max Melamet, 23 January 1991.

[57]Louis Rosenberg, *Canada's Jews: A Social and Economic Study of the Jews in Canada* (Montreal: Bureau of Social and Economic Research, Canadian Jewish Congress, 1939), 398 and passim.

[58]Gwethalyn Graham, *Earth and High Heaven* (Toronto: McClelland and Stewart, 1969), 13.

[59]Pierre Anctil, *Le rendez-vous manqué: les Juifs de Montréal face au Québec de l'entre-deux-guerres* (Québec: Institut québécois de recherche sur la culture, 1988), 214.

[60]Arthur D. Hart, *The Jew in Canada* (Toronto: Toronto Jewish Publications, 1926), 453.

[61]Ibid, 198.

[62]Betty Sigler, "Montreal: The Bonds of Community," *Commentary*, April 1950, 353.

[63]Interview with Mark Shinbane, 20 October 1983.

[64]Peter C. Newman, *Bronfman Dynasty: The Rothschilds of the New World* (Toronto: McClelland and Stewart, 1978), 56.

[65]Erna Paris, *Jews: An Account of their Experience in Canada* (Toronto: Macmillan, 1980), 39.

[66]Phyllis Lambert memorandum, 6 August 1990.

[67]Ibid.

[68]Ibid.

[69]Interviews with Saidye Bronfman, 4 July 1979; 9 July 1980.

[70]Interview with Charles Bronfman, 2 April 1979.

[71]Bronfman, *My Sam*, 76.

[72]*Canadian Jewish Review*, 9 November 1934.

[73]Ibid, 16 November 1934.

[74]H.M. Caiserman to M.N. Eisendrath, 20 October 1938. ACJC: Eisendrath Papers.

[75]Ibid.

[76]*Canadian Jewish Chronicle*, 11 October 1929.

[77]Irving Abella, *A Coat of Many Colours: Two Centuries of Jewish Life in Canada* (Toronto: Lester & Orpen Dennys, 1990), 168.

[78]*Canadian Jewish Chronicle*, 16 December 1932.

[79]Interview with Ben Kayfetz, 7 January 1991.

[80]*Canadian Jewish Chronicle*, 8 April 1938.

[81]Allan Bronfman to Chaim Weizmann, 18 March 1927; Chaim Weizmann to Allan Bronfman, 20 March 1927. Weizmann Archives.

[82]Interview with Saul Hayes, quoted in Irving Abella and Harold Troper, *None Is Too Many: Canada and the Jews of Europe 1933–1948* (Toronto: Lester & Orpen Dennys, 1982), 57.

[83]Samuel Lewin, "Canadian Jewish Congress in Introspect," *Viewpoints*, III, 3 (1967), 21.

[84]Abella, *Coat of Many Colours*, 190–1.

[85]*Canadian Jewish Chronicle*, 22 December 1950.

[86]Ibid, 23 August 1935.

[87]Bernard Figler and David Rome, *Hannaniah Meir Caiserman: A Biography* (Montreal: Northern Printing and Lithographing Co., 1962), 225.

[88]Egmont Frankel to S.W. Jacobs, 18 January 1936; Morris Waldman to S.W. Jacobs, 28 September 1936; S.W. Jacobs to Morris Waldman, 5 October 1936; Morris Waldman to S.W. Jacobs, 16 October 1936. PAC: MG III C3, vols. 9–10.

[89]*Canadian Jewish Chronicle*, 26 August 1938.

[90]David Rome, *Clouds in the Thirties: On Anti-Semitism in Canada 1929–1939* (13 vols., Montreal: National Archives, Canadian Jewish Congres, 1977–81), X, 471.

[91]H.M. Caiserman to M.N. Eisendrath, 20 October 1938. ACJC: Eisendrath Papers.

[92]Rome, *Clouds in the Thrities*, XII, 636, 655–60; C.M. Hanane, "The Canadian Jewish Congress," *Canadian Jewish Year Book*, 1939–1940, 122–3.

[93]Interview with David Rome, 4 July 1989.

[94]Ibid.

[95]Interview with Sol Kanee, 13 September 1989.

[96]*Montreal Daily Star*, 26 January 1939.

[97]*Canadian Jewish Chronicle*, 27 January 1939.

CHAPTER SIX

[1]Quoted in Tom MacDonnell, *Daylight Upon Magic: The Royal Tour of Canada — 1939* (Toronto: Macmillan, 1989), 114 – 15. Cf. Larry Zolf, *Scorpions for Sale* (Toronto: Stoddart, 1989), passim.

[2]*Canadian Jewish Chronicle*, 2 June 1939.

[3]Samuel Bronfman, *From Little Acorns: The Story of Distillers Corporation-Seagrams Limited* (Montreal: n.p., 1970), 23; "Story of Crown Royal," promotional film, n.d.; interview with Saidye Bronfman, 8 August 1978; interview with Charles Bronfman, 3 December 1990.

[4]Ibid, 24 March 1938.

[5]Irving Abella and Harold Troper, *None Is Too Many: Canada and the Jews of Europe 1933 – 1948* (Toronto: Lester & Orpen Dennys, 1982), 55, 58.

[6]Ibid, 60.

[7]Ibid, 62.

[8]Sam to R.B. Bennett, 25 January 1939 and 4 July 1939. PAC, Bennett Papers, M3169.

[9]Charlotte Whitton to Sam, 6 April 1939, SA; Ernest Vaz to Sam, 16 January 1940, SA; Sam to Ernest Vaz, 16 January 1940, SA; Richard Allen, *The Social Passion: Religion and Social Reform in Canada 1914 – 28* (Toronto: University of Toronto Press, 1973), 11, 66 and passim; P.T. Rooke and R.L. Schnell, *No Bleeding Heart: Charlotte Whitton, A Feminist on the Right* (Vancouver: University of British Columbia Press, 1987), 85 – 7.

[10]*Montreal Star*, 7 August 1939; Montreal *Gazette*, 8 August 1939; *The Albertan*, 7 August 1939.

[11]*The Albertan*, 9 August 1939.

[12]Montreal *Gazette*, 7, 8 August 1939; *Montreal Star*, 7 August 1939.

[13]David Rome, *Clouds in the Thirties: On Anti-Semitism in Canada 1929 – 1939* (13 vols., Montreal: National Archives, Canadian Jewish Congress, 1977 – 81), XIII, 644.

[14]*Canadian Jewish Chronicle*, 11 August 1939.

[15]Interview with David Rome, 5 July 1989.

[16]Adam G. Fuerstenberg, "The Poet and the Tycoon: The Relationship Between A.M. Klein and Samuel Bronfman," *Canadian Jewish Historical Society Journal*, 5 (1981), 50.

[17]Usher Caplan, *Like One That Dreamed: A Portrait of A.M. Klein* (Toronto: McGraw-Hill Ryerson, 1982), 54.

[18]*Canadian Jewish Chronicle*, 18 November 1938; Caplan, *Portrait of A.M. Klein*, 82.

[19]David Rome, *Jews in Canadian Literature: A Bibliography* (Montreal: Canadian Jewish Congress, 1962), 44.

[20]Caplan, *Portrait of A.M. Klein*, 81.

[21]Miscellaneous financial accounts, 1948, 28 March 1951 and n.d., PAC, Klein Papers, MG 30, M3622, v.15.

[22]Caplan, *Portrail of A.M. Klein*, 191. I am grateful for the assistance of Miriam Waddington on this point.

[23]Fuerstenberg, "The Poet and the Tycoon," 50.

[24]Interview with Mark Shinbane, 17 January 1984.

[25]Saidye Rosner Bronfman, *My Sam: A Memoir by his Wife* (Toronto: n.p., 1982), 128; interview with Saidye Bronfman, 31 August 1978.

[26]Sam to Klein, 18 March 1941, PAC, Klein Papers, MG 30, M3619, v. 1.

[27]Fuerstenberg, "The Poet and the Tycoon," 56.

[28]Saul Hayes, "Sam Bronfman — Quest for Unity," unpub. paper [1980].

[29]Rome, *Clouds in the Thirties*, XII, 648.

[30]Interview with Ben Lappin, 28 November 1989.

[31]Interview with Alan Rose, 12 June 1989; Harold M. Waller, *The Governance of the Jewish Community of Montreal*, Centre for Jewish Community Studies, Study Report No. 5, 1974, 92.

[32]*Canadian Jewish Review*, 14 September 1939.

[33]Saul Hayes, "Sam Bronfman — Quest for Unity."

[34]Address to the Annual Regional Conference, Canadian Jewish Congress (Central Division), 7 January 1940, SA.

[35]Rome, *Clouds in the Thirties*, XIII, 782 – 6.

[36]*Hebrew Journal*, 11 September 1939; *Canadian Jewish Chronicle*, 19 January 1940; *Hebrew Journal*, 7 January 1940; *Globe and Mail*, 7 January 1940; *Toronto Daily Star*, 7 January 1940; Montreal *Gazette*, 6 May 1940; Montreal *Gazette*, 8 July 1940; *Montreal Star*, 8 July 1940.

[37]Interview with Ben Lappin, 28 November 1989.

[38]"Samuel Bronfman" [1941].

[39]Saul Hayes, "Samuel Bronfman," unpub. memoir [1980].

[40]Sam to Archie Bennett, 17 July 1941, SA.

[41]*Winnipeg Free Press*, 6 September 1940.

[42]Interview with Saidye Bronfman, 12 September 1978; interview with Ben Lappin, 28 November 1989; Abella and Troper, *None Is Too Many*, 69.

[43]*Toronto Daily Star*, 15 January 1945; interview with Ben Lappin, 28 November 1989; *Official Opening. Samuel Bronfman House. Commemorating Fifty Years of Service by the Canadian Jewish Congress. Montreal, May 24, 1970* (Montreal: Canadian Jewish Congress, 1970), 32; David Rome, ed., *Canadian Jews in World War II* (2 vols., Montreal: Canadian Jewish Congress, 1947).

[44]*Canadian Jewish Chronicle*, 19 January 1940.

[45]Montreal *Gazette*, 27 September 1940; John Bryden, *Deadly Allies: Canada's Secret War, 1937–1947* (Toronto: McClelland and Stewart, 1989), 41–2; "Memorandum Re. War Technical and Scientific Development Committee" [26 July 1943], SA.

[46]*Le Devoir*, 21 July 1942; *La Patrie*, 21 July 1942; *Montreal Herald*, 21 July 1942; *Canadian Jewish Magazine*, August 1942.

[47]Joseph E. Davies to Allan Bronfman, 27 December 1942, SA.

[48]Montreal *Gazette*, 19, 20 January 1943; *Canadian Jewish Chronicle*, 22 January 1943; Eleanor Roosevelt to Allan Bronfman, 21 January 1943, Canadian Aid to Russia Fund—Quebec Branch, "List of Donations That Should Receive Special Attention," 18 February 1943, SA.

[49]*Canadian Jewish Chronicle*, 12 January 1940; 6 March 1942; 29 September 1943; Saidye Rosner Bronfman, *Recollections of My Life* (Montreal: n.p., 1986), 89, 135.

[50]Bronfman, *My Sam*, 82–3; interview with Saidye Bronfman, 13 April 1978; interview with Edgar Bronfman, 5 September 1979.

[51]*Canadian Jewish Chronicle*, 12 April 1940.

[52]"The War's First Victims—The Refugees," *Canadian Jewish Year Book*, 1941–2, 77; Ben Lappin, *The Redeemed Children: The Story of the Rescue of War Orphans by the Jewish Community of Canada* (Toronto: University of Toronto Press, 1963), 7.

[53]Donald Avery, "Canada's Response to European Refugees, 1939–1945: The Security Dimension," in Norman Hillmer, Bohdan Kordan and Lubomyr Luciuk, eds., *On Guard For Thee: War, Ethnicity and the Canadian State, 1939–1945* (Ottawa: Canadian Committee for the

History of the Second World War, 1988), 204 – 5; Paula Jean Draper, "The Accidental Immigrants: Canada and the Interned Refugees," unpublished Ph.D. dissertation, University of Toronto, 1983, 98.

[54]"President's Report," January 1941.

[55]Address to the Annual Regional Conference, Canadian Jewish Congress (Central Division), 7 January 1940, SA.

[56]"President's Report," January 1941.

[57]Canadian Jewish Congress, *Constitution, Resolutions and Presidential Address*, 10, 11, 12 January 1942, 8 – 9.

[58]Ben Sheps to Sam, 6 July 1942. CJC: CA 2447 – 8, ZA 1942, Box 12/120A UJR & WRA misc.; Abella and Troper, *None Is Too Many*, 98.

[59]Sam to Mackenzie King, 10 September 1942. CJC: 2342, 1942, Box 2. 25; Abella and Troper, *None Is Too Many*, 101 – 21.

[60]Saul Hayes to Michael Garber, 17 May 1942. CJC: CA, Box 25, 231, CNCR, 1943 – 44, 833; *Canadian Jewish Chronicle*, 25 September 1942.

[61]*Canadian Jewish Chronicle*, 9 October 1942; 16 October 1942; *Montreal Daily Star*, 12 October 1942.

[62]*Canadian Jewish Chronicle*, 16 April 1943.

[63]ACJC, Bronfman Collection, 3.

[64]H.M. Caiserman form letter, 25 February 1941, SA.

[65]*Canadian Jewish Chronicle*, 7 March 1941; *Winnipeg Jewish Bulletin*, 6 March 1941; *Daily Hebrew Journal*, 1 January 1941, 4 March 1941; *Canadian Zionist*, 14 March 1941.

[66]M.W. Steinberg and Usher Caplan, eds., *Beyond Sambation: Selected Essays and Editorials 1928 – 1955* (Toronto: University of Toronto Press, 1982), 92.

[67]Klein to Sam, 24 March 1941, PAC, Klein Papers, MG 30, M 3619, v. 1.

[68]Interview with Ben Lappin, 28 November 1989; interview with Ben Kayfetz, 7 January 1991.

[69]*Congress Bulletin*, January-February 1950.

[70]Saul Hayes, "Samuel Bronfman" [1980].

[71]Interview with Ben Lappin, 28 November 1989.

[72]Phyllis Lambert memorandum, 6 August 1990.

[73]Interview with Ben Lappin, 28 November 1989.

[74]Interview with David Rome, 5 July 1989; Sam to H.M. Caiserman, 20 January 1942. CJC: 2343, 1942, Box 2, 27.

[75]J.B. Salsberg, "How Sam Bronfman Brought Hayes into Congress," *Canadian Jewish News*, 7 February 1980.

[76]*Canadian Jewish Chronicle*, 29 August 1941; Canadian Jewish Year Book, 1941–2, 84; *Montreal Star*, 27 October 1941.

[77]Waller, *Governance of the Jewish Community of Montreal*, 37.

[78]Max Melamet, "Sam Bronfman: A Personal Tribute," *Chronicle Review*, August 1971, 5.

[79]Pierre Anctil, *Le rendez-vous manqué: Les Juifs de Montréal face au Québec de l'entre-deux-guerres* (Québec: Institut québécois de recherche sur la culture, 1988), 63–102; *Canadian Jewish Chronicle*, 13 November 1936.

[80]*Montreal Star*, 8 November 1940; Jewish Telegraphic Agency report, 26 November 1941; Montreal *Gazette*, 20 November 1941, 21 November 1941; 3 July 1942; *Montreal Herald*, 3 July 1942.

[81]Interview with Richard Cohen, 13 March 1989; *McGill Daily*, 2 December 1964; Peter C. Newman, *Bronfman Dynasty: The Rothschilds of the New World* (Toronto: McClelland and Stewart, 1978), 44–5.

[82]Interviews with Charles Bronfman, 2 April 1979; Phyllis Lambert, 8 January 1980; Bronfman, *My Sam*, 83–4.

[83]Interview with Charles Bronfman, 12 June 1989.

[84]Bronfman, *My Sam*, 84–5.

[85]Ibid, 83; Bronfman, *Recollections*, 114.

[86]Maxwell Henderson, *Plain Talk! Memoirs of an Auditor General* (Toronto: McClelland and Stewart, 1984), 110; "Industry Leaders I—Seagram," *Monopoly State Review*, August 1946, 12, 42.

[87]Mel Griffin memorandum, November 1989.

[88]DC-SL Minutes, 18 November 1941; *Montreal Herald*, 25 November 1940; *Montreal Star*, 25 November 1940.

[89]Montreal *Gazette*, 1 December 1943.

[90]*Montreal Herald*, 25 November 1940; Montreal *Gazette*, 1 December 1943; *New York Times*, 12 January 1960.

[91]Philip J. Kelly, *The Making of a Salesman* (New York: Abelard Schuman, 1965), 176–7.

[92]Albert Moritz and Theresa Moritz, *Leacock: A Biography* (Toronto: Stoddart Publishing, 1985), 200–5, 221, 311–12.

[93]Memorandum of conference with Dr Leacock, September 27, 1941, PAC, Klein Papers, MG 30, M 5467, v. 22.

[94]Saul Hayes, " 'The Bronfman Dynasty': A Friend's Reminiscence," *Viewpoints*, X (Spring 1979), 47.

[95]Klein Papers, PAC, MG 30, M 5467, v. 21.

[96]Ibid.

[97]Mel Griffin memorandum, November 1989.

[98]James E. Friel to Sam, 10 July 1945; *Business Week*, 30 October 1943; Montreal *Gazette*, 1 December 1943; R.H. Christian to Department of National Revenue, 12 March 1945, SA; "Seagram in the Chips," *Fortune*, September 1948, 156.

[99]*The Advertiser*, August 1952, 68.

[100]Philip Siekman, "The Bronfmans: An Instinct for Dynasty," *Fortune*, November 1966, 204.

[101]Sichel to Laz Phillips, 19 December 1944; *New York Times*, 24 October 1967; Doris Muscatine, "Note: The Wine Museum of San Francisco," in Doris Muscatine, Maynard Amerine, and Bob Thompson, eds., *The University of California/Sotheby Book of California Wine* (Berkeley, Calif.: University of California Press, 1984), 318–19; Bronfman, *Little Acorns*, 60–1; Philip Siekman, "The Bronfmans: An Instinct for Dynasty," *Fortune*, November 1966, 210; Charles Bronfman memorandum, 8 March 1991.

[102]*New York Times*, 22, 27 October 1943, 2 February 1944; *Business Week*, 30 October 1943; Montreal *Gazette*, 2 February 1944; Paul Gardner, "Bronfman of Seagrams," *New Liberty*, July 1949, 12.

[103]"Seagram in the Chips," *Fortune*, September 1948, 101; "The Seagram Saga: I—The Man with the Golden Shovel," *BEV/Executive*, 1 February 1966, 8–12.

[104]Margaret W. Westley, *Remembrance of Grandeur: The Anglo-Protestant Elite of Montreal 1990–1950* (Montreal: Editions Libre Expression, 1990), 274.

[105]Marcel-Aimé Gagnon, *Jean-Charles Harvey, Précurseur de la Révolution tranquille* (Montreal: Beauchemin, 1970), 91.

[106]*Canadian Jewish Chronicle*, 17 December 1943.

[107]*Globe and Mail*, 15 November 1941; *Toronto Daily Star*, 13 March 1942; *United Church Observer*, 1 November 1941, 7 February 1943; *Moose Jaw Times Herald*, 12 December 1942.

[108]*Montreal Star*, 23 December 1942.

[109]*Mackenzie King Diaries, Vol. II, 1932–1949* (Toronto: University of Toronto Press, 1980), entries for 12 November 1942, 10 December

1942, 15 January 1943, 28 January 1943, 23 February 1943, 2 March 1943, 12 March 1943, 18 March 1943, 24 March 1943, 14 March 1944.

[110]James Gardiner to James Mutchmor, 11 May 1944, BESS, Box 18, File 232.

[111]J.S. Leith to James Mutchmor, 1 November 1944, BESS, Box 18, File 233.

[112]Montreal *Gazette*, 4 June 1945.

[113]Terence Robertson, "Bronfman: The Life and Times of Samuel Bronfman, Esq." (unpub. manuscript, [1969]), 516.

[114]Bronfman, *My Sam*, 66 – 7.

[115]Minda to Sam and Saidye, 25 November 1943, SBFP.

[116]Abella and Troper, *None Is Too Many*, 146 and passim.

[117]Nahum Goldmann, *Mein Leben als deutscher Jude* (Munich: Langen Muller, 1980), 355.

CHAPTER SEVEN

[1]Philip Siekman, "The Bronfmans: An Instinct for Dynasty," *Fortune*, December 1966, 177; Terence Robertson, "Bronfman: The Life and Times of Samuel Bronfman, Esq." (unpub. manuscript, [1969]), 550 – 1.

[2]Saidye to Sam, 3 June 1946, SBFP.

[3]Phyllis to Sam, 1 June 1946, SBFP.

[4]Minda to Sam, 15 June 1946, SBFP.

[5]Edgar to Sam, 9 June 1946, SBFP.

[6]Saidye to Sam, 23 June 1946, SBFP.

[7]Saidye to Sam, 19 June 1946, SBFP.

[8]Sam to Saidye, n.d. [June 1946], SBFP.

[9]Ibid.

[10]Minda to Sam, 15 June 1946, SBFP.

[11]Saidye to Sam, 17 June 1946, SBFP.

[12]Sam to Saidye, n.d. [June 1946], SBFP; *New York Times*, 2 June 1946.

[13]Sam to Saidye, n.d. [June 1946], SBFP.

[14]John MacLean to [Philip] Vineberg, 21 June 1946, SA.

[15]Ross Wilson, *Scotch: Its History and Romance* (Newton Abbot, England: David & Charles, 1973), 92 – 3; Michael S. Moss and John R. Hume, *The Making of Scotch Whisky: A History of the Scotch Whisky Distilling Industry* (Edinburgh: James and James, 1981), 166 – 7.

[16]Sam to Saidye, n.d. [June 1946], SBFP.

[17]*Business Week*, 24 January 1948; *Financial Post*, 24 January 1953; "Seagram in the Chips," *Fortune*, September 1948, 100.

[18]Ibid, 97.

[19]*Business Week*, 25 September 1948.

[20]"Seagram in the Chips," *Fortune*, September 1948, 98; *Financial Post*, 20 November 1976.

[21]Edgar Bronfman memorandum, 10 September 1990.

[22]Interview with Edgar Bronfman, 13 December 1990.

[23]Maxwell Henderson, *Plain Talk! Memoirs of an Auditor General* (Toronto: McClelland and Stewart, 1984), 102 – 5.

[24]Interview with Robert Ruppel, 14 September 1990.

[25]Interview with Edgar Bronfman, 8 March 1990.

[26]William Wendell Wachtel, *The Anatomy of a Hidden Persuader* (New York: Vantage Press, 1975), 81.

[27]Philip J. Kelly, *The Making of a Salesman* (New York: Abelard Schuman, 1965), 170 – 1.

[28]"Seagram in the Chips," *Fortune*, September 1948, 96.

[29]James Friel to Sam Bronfman, 10 July 1945, SA.

[30]*New Liberty*, July 1949, 12.

[31]Edgar Bronfman memorandum, 10 September 1990.

[32]Philip Siekman, "The Bronfmans: An Instinct for Dynasty," *Fortune*, December 1966, 208.

[33]Stephen Birmingham, *"The Rest of Us": The Rise of America's Eastern European Jews* (Boston: Little, Brown, 1984), 212.

[34]Saidye Rosner Bronfman, *My Sam: A Memoir by his Wife* (Toronto: n.p., 1982), 25.

[35]Interview with Phyllis Lambert, 22 November 1990.

[36]Edgar Bronfman memorandum, 10 September 1990.

[37]Philip Siekman, "The Bronfmans: An Instinct for Dynasty," *Fortune*, December 1966, 208; interview with Saidye Bronfman, 18 October 1979.

[38]Edgar Bronfman memorandum, 10 September 1990.

[39]Irving Abella, "Jews in Canada: A Look at the Past," *Viewpoints*, January 1990, 1.

[40]*Montreal Star*, 26 November 1945.

[41]*Canadian Jewish Chronicle*, 25 September 1946.

[42]Irving Abella and Harold Troper, *None Is Too Many: Canada and the Jews of Europe 1933–1948* (Toronto: Lester & Orpen Dennys, 1982), 199.

[43]Ibid, 231–2.

[44]*Mackenzie King Diaries, Vol. II, 1932–1949* (Toronto: University of Toronto Press, 1980), entries for 23 January 1947 and 13 February 1947.

[45]David J. Bercuson, *Canada and the Birth of Israel: A Study in Canadian Foreign Policy* (Toronto: University of Toronto Press, 1985), 52.

[46]*Mackenzie King Diaries*, II, entry of 7 February 1947.

[47]"Presidential Address by Samuel Bronfman before the Seventh Plenary Session, Canadian Jewish Congress, Montreal, June 1, 1947," ACJS; "Resolutions Adopted by the Plenary Session of the Canadian Jewish Congress held in Montreal, May 31st, June 1st, June 2nd, 1947," ACJC.

[48]Samuel Bronfman, "Address at Winnipeg Meeting of Dominion Council and National Executive, March 6, 1948," SA; interview with Ben Lappin, 28 November 1989.

[49]Ibid; interview with David Weiss, n.d. [1979].

[50]Henderson, *Plain Talk*, 126.

[51]David Rome to Father S. Valiquette, S.J., 14 September 1948; "Samuel Bronfman, LL.D., University of Montreal — September 1st, 1948", SA; Distillers Corporation-Seagrams Ltd., *Annual Report, Supplement*, 1971, 59.

[52]Interview with Edgar Bronfman, 8 March 1990; interview with Saidye Bronfman, 28 June 1983.

[53]*Canadian Jewish Chronicle*, 22 September 1944, 29 September 1944, 6 October 1944.

[54]Sam Bronfman, "Introductory Remarks by National Chairman," National Dominion Council, Montreal, 25 November 1945; Nahum Goldmann, *Sixty Years of Jewish Life: The Autobiography of Nahum Goldmann*, trans. Helen Sebba (New York: Holt, Rinehart and Winston, 1969), 222.

[55]*Canadian Jewish Chronicle*, 15 September 1944.

[56]Montreal *Gazette*, 15 January 1945.

[57]Howard M. Sachar, foreword to Eliahu Elath, *Zionism at the UN: A Diary of the First Days*, trans. Michael Ben-Yitzhak (Philadelphia: Jewish Publication Society of America, 1976), ix – x.

[58]Ibid, xiv.

[59]Interview with Saidye Bronfman, 7 November 1990; Bronfman, *My Sam*, 86.

[60]Elath, *Zionism at the UN*, 110 – 11, 152, 251; Bercuson, *Canada and the Birth of Israel*, 30 – 1.

[61]*Congress Bulletin*, July 1945.

[62]"Presidential Address by Samuel Bronfman before the Seventh Plenary Session, Canadian Jewish Congress, Montreal, June 1, 1947," ACJC.

[63]Michael J. Cohen, *The Origins and Evolution of the Arab-Zionist Conflict* (Berkeley, Calif.: University of California Press, 1987), 122; Zachariah Kay, *Canada and Palestine: The Politics of Non-Commitment* (Jerusalem: Israel Universities Press, 1978), ch. 9 and passim.

[64]*Canadian Jewish Chronicle*, 12 September 1947; Bercuson, *Canada and the Birth of Israel*, 107.

[65]Address at the National Dominion Council, 20 June 1948, SA.

[66]Peter C. Newman, *Bronfman Dynasty: The Rothschilds of the New World* (Toronto: McClelland and Stewart, 1978), 46 n.; *Canadian Jewish Chronicle*, 13 April 1949.

[67]Interview with Saidye Bronfman, 28 June 1983; *Canadian Jewish Chronicle*, 23 September 1949, 21 October 1949; *Canadian Jewish Review*, 28 October 1949.

[68]*Montreal Star*, 24 October 1949; *Le Canada*, 29 October 1949; *Winnipeg Free Press*, 24 October 1949; *Canadian Jewish Review*, 28 October 1949; *Jewish Affairs*, December 1949; *Congress Bulletin*, January-February 1950.

[69]*Montreal Herald*, 22 July 1948.

[70]Transcript of broadcast of 23 January 1949, SA.

[71]Laz Phillips memorandum re: Messrs Bronfman, Rutkin and Reinfeld, 16 February 1949, SA.

[72]Laz Phillips memorandum, 14 March 1949, SA.

[73]Memorandum by Laz Phillips, 4 April 1949, SA.

[74]Memorandum re: Rutkin v. Reinfeld, 8 July 1948, SA; memorandum for Mr Samuel Bronfman re: his proposed examination for discovery in New York, 16 February 1949, SA.

[75]Interview with Edgar Bronfman, 8 March 1990.

[76]United States Congress. Senate. Special Committee to Investigate Organized Crime in Interstate Commerce Pursuant to S. Res. 202 (81st Congress). (1951), Part 7, 706–8.

[77]*New York Times*, 25 March 1952.

[78]United States Congress. House. Committee on the Judiciary. Report to the Committee on the Judiciary by the Subcommittee to Investigate the Department of Justice Pursuant to H. Res. 50 (83rd Congress, 1st Session). No. 1079 (1953), 33–5; *New York Times*, 27 June 1952.

[79]William Howard Moore, *The Kefauver Committee and the Politics of Crime 1950–1952* (Columbia, Missouri: University of Missouri Press, 1974), 41.

[80]*New York Times*, 9 November 1950.

[81]United States Congress. Senate. Special Committee to Investigate Organized Crime in Interstate Commerce Pursuant to S. Res. 202 (81st Congress). (1951), Part 7, 541.

[82]Ibid, 544.

[83]Ibid, 558.

[84]Special Committee to Investigate Organized Crime in Interstate Commerce. Investigative Files: Name Files — Bronfman, Sam. NA. Records of the U.S. Senate, Record Group 46; *New York Mirror*, 4 March 1951; *New York Times*, 4 March 1951.

[85]United States Congress. Senate. Special Committee to Investigate Organized Crime in Interstate Commerce Pursuant to S. Res. 202 (81st Congress). (1951), 902–3.

[86]Mark A. Stuart, *Gangster #2: Longy Zwillman, the Man Who Invented Organized Crime* (Secaucus, N.J.: Lyle Stuart, 1985), 178.

[87]*New York Times*, 17 August 1951.

[88]Phyllis Lambert memorandum, 6 August 1990.

[89]*New York Times*, 10 November 1951, 14 November 1951; The Seagram Family Association, First Convention, New York, 1951, 171, SA.

[90]Ibid, 8.

[91]Ibid, 40.

[92]Phyllis Lambert memorandum, 4 September 1990; interview with Charles Bronfman, 2 April 1990; William Rodgers, *Think: A Biography of the Watsons and IBM* (New York: Stein and Day, 1969), 113–17.

[93]United States District Court (Southern District of New York). James

Rutkin v. Joseph Reinfeld et al. Civ. 46 – 509. Mr Edelbaum's Summation. March 4, 1954, 2930.

[94]*New York Times*, 6 March 1954.

[95]Ibid, 26 January 1956.

[96]*New York Daily Mirror*, 20 April 1956.

CHAPTER EIGHT

[1]Interview with Sol Kanee, 13 September 1989.

[2]William Wendell Wachtel, *The Anatomy of a Hidden Persuader* (New York: Vantage Press, 1975), 125.

[3]"Seagrams' Late Awakening," *Forbes*, 1 February 1973, 24.

[4]Interview with John Pringle, 9 May 1990.

[5]Interview with Max Melamet, 20 December 1990; interview with Ben Lappin, 28 November 1989.

[6]Interview with Jack Brin, 11 March 1990.

[7]Interview with Sol Kanee, 13 September 1989.

[8]Maxwell Henderson, *Plain Talk! Memoirs of an Auditor General* (Toronto: McClelland and Stewart, 1984), 132.

[9]Ibid, 121; Edgar Bronfman memorandum, 3 October 1990; Philip Siekman, "The Bronfmans: An Instinct for Dynasty," *Fortune*, November 1966, 206.

[10]Interview with Mark Shinbane, 16 January 1984; interview with Walter Goelkel, 13 January 1991.

[11]Wachtel, *Anatomy of a Hidden Persuader*, 128.

[12]Interview with John Pringle, 9 May 1990.

[13]Interview with Robert Sabloff, 23 January 1990.

[14]Interview with Mel Griffin, 7 February 1990.

[15]Interview with Phyllis Lambert, 8 January 1980.

[16]Interview with Mel Griffin, 7 February 1990.

[17]Interview with Shimon Peres, 27 November 1989.

[18]Interview with Saidye Bronfman, 7 September 1978; interviews with Max Melamet, 20 December 1990, 23 January 1991.

[19]Interview with Abe Mayman, 7 November 1990; interview with Robert Ruppel, 14 September 1990.

[20]Interview with Noah Torno, 6 November 1990.

[21]*Montreal Daily Star*, 6 March 1941; Montreal *Gazette*, 6 March 1941; *New York Times*, 9 March 1941.

[22]Interview with Robert Sabloff, 23 January 1990.

[23]Seagram Family Achievement Association, First Convention, New York, 1951, 34, SA.

[24]Philip Siekman, "The Bronfmans: An Instinct for Dynasty," *Fortune*, November 1966, 206.

[25]*Business Week*, 20 October 1962.

[26]Michael McCormick ms., n.d. [March 1971], SA.

[27]Interview with Robert Sabloff, 23 January 1990.

[28]Interview with Walter Goelkel, 13 January 1991.

[29]Phyllis Lambert memorandum, 10 October 1990.

[30]"Samuel Bronfman C.C., LL.D.," *Your Community News*, 31 August 1971, 3.

[31]Wachtel, *Anatomy of a Hidden Persuader*, 72; Max Melamet, "Sam Bronfman: A Personal Tribute," *Chronicle Review*, August 1971, 5.

[32]Interview with Abe Mayman, 7 November 1990.

[33]Interview with Alan Rose, 12 June 1989.

[34]Wachtel, *Anatomy of a Hidden Persuader*, 128–9.

[35]Interview with Edgar Bronfman, 5 September 1979.

[36]Michael McCormick paper, August 1971.

[37]Interview with Charles Bronfman, 12 June 1989.

[38]Interview with Mark Shinbane, 16 January 1984.

[39]Interview with Sol Kanee, 24 September 1990.

[40]Interview with Edgar Bronfman, 5 September 1979.

[41]Minda to Saidye, 16 May 1955, SBFP.

[42]Wachtel, *Anatomy of a Hidden Persuader*, 126; Henderson, *Plain Talk*, 109.

[43]Paul Gardner, "Bronfman of Seagrams," *New Liberty*, July 1949, 13, 16.

[44]Henderson, *Plain Talk*, 107.

[45]Interview with John Pringle, 9 May 1990.

[46]Henderson, *Plain Talk*, 106 – 7.

[47]*Financial Post*, 24 January 1953.

[48]*Business Week*, 7 February 1953; "The Seagram Saga: I — The Man with the Golden Shovel," *BEV/Executive*, February 1, 1966, 12.

[49]Martin Mayer, "The Volatile Business," *Esquire*, August 1959, 112; Edgar Bronfman memorandum, 10 September 1990.

[50]Charles Bronfman memorandum, 18 October 1990.

[51]*Financial Post*, 13, 20 November 1976.

[52]Interview with Noah Torno, 6 November 1990.

[53]Bronfman, *From Little Acorns*, 32 – 3.

[54]DC-SL Minutes, 15 November 1955; *Forbes*, 15 December 1957; *Financial Post*, 20 August 1957.

[55]Interview with Edgar Bronfman, 13 December 1990; interview with Noah Torno, 6 November 1990.

[56]Samuel Bronfman, *From Little Acorns: The Story of Distillers Corporation-Seagrams Limited* ([Montreal: DC-SL], 1970), 69.

[57]Directors' Report to the Shareholders, 31 October 1964, DC-SL Minutes, 16 November 1964; *Financial Post*, 13 November 1976; Paul Gibson, "The Battling Bronfmans," *Forbes*, February 2, 1981, 42 – 3.

[58]Henderson, *Plain Talk*, 58; Ross Wilson, *Scotch: The Formative Years* (London: Constable, 1970), 444.

[59]*The Scotsman*, 30 June 1964.

[60]Interview with Ivan Straker, 9 May 1990; interview with Walter Goelkel, 13 January 1991; Michael S. Moss and John R. Hume, *The Making of Scotch Whisky: A History of the Scotch Whisky Distilling Industry* (Edinburgh: James and James, 1981), 271.

[61]Bronfman, *Little Acorns*, 31, 34 – 5.

[62]Philip J. Kelly, *The Making of a Salesman* (New York: Abelard Schuman, 1965), 196, 199 – 200.

[63]Ibid, 209; interview with Robert Ruppel, 14 September 1990.

[64]DC-SL Annual Report, Supplement, 1971, 18, 44; Moss and Hume, *Making of Scotch Whisky*, 168.

[65]Directors' Report to the Shareholders, 31 October 1964, DC-SL Minutes, 16 November 1964; *Forbes*, 1 February 1973; *The Scotsman*, 30 June 1964; *Scottish Licensed Trade News*, 26 June 1964; "The Seagram Saga: IV — *BEV/Exeuctive*, Another Rose, a Bottle and a Fast

Dark Horse," March 15, 1966, 14; Edgar Bronfman memorandum, 10 September 1990; interview with Walter Goelkel, 13 January 1991.

[66]Hugh Barty-King and Anton Massel, *Rum: Yesterday and Today* (London: Heinemann, 1983), 91, 151; Bronfman, *From Little Acorns*, 26.

[67]Interview with John Pringle, 9 May 1990.

[68]Henderson, *Plain Talk*, 119.

[69]*New York Times*, 26 July 1955; *Forbes*, 15 August 1958; *Financial Post*, 13 November 1976.

[70]Edgar Bronfman memorandum, 3 October 1990.

[71]*Forbes*, 15 December 1957.

[72]Sam to Quintin Gwyn, 17 April 1961, SA.

[73]Klein Papers, PAC: MG 30, M-5466, v.22.

[74]Interview with Mark Shinbane, 17 January 1984.

[75]*The Standard*, 17 April 1937.

[76]Henderson, *Plain Talk*, 117–18.

[77]Saidye Rosner Bronfman, *My Sam: A Memoir by his Wife* (Toronto: n.p., 1982), 102–3.

[78]Peter C. Newman, *Bronfman Dynasty: The Rothschilds of the New World* (Toronto: McClelland and Steward, 1978), 163.

[79]Minda to Sam and Saidye [1 December 1953], SBFP.

[80]Phyllis Lambert memorandum, 10 October 1990; Philip Siekman, "The Bronfmans: An Instinct for Dynasty," *Fortune*, December 1966, 176.

[81]Stephen Birmingham, *"The Rest of Us": The Rise of America's Eastern European Jews* (Boston: Little, Brown, 1984), 318; Philip Siekman, "The Bronfmans: An Instinct for Dynasty," *Fortune*, December 1966, 204; *Financial Post*, 13 November 1976; interview with Edgar Bronfman, 5 September 1979.

[82]Bronfman, *My Sam*, 96.

[83]Interview with Charles Bronfman, 12 June 1989.

[84]Interview with Stanley Lewis, [July] 1983.

[85]Saidye Rosner Bronfman, *Recollections of My Life* (Montreal: n.p., 1986), 111.

[86]Interview with Phyllis Lambert, 8 January 1980.

[87]Sam to Abe Klein, 4 March 1964, Klein Papers, PAC: MG 30, M-3619, v. 1.

[88] *The Noel Coward Diaries* (London: Weidenfeld and Nicolson, 1982), 346–7.

[89] Interview with John Pringle, 9 May 1990; interview with Charles Bronfman, 3 December 1990.

[90] Interview with John Pringle, 9 May 1990.

[91] Minda to Sam and Saidye [1 December 1953], SBFP.

[92] Phyllis to Sam and Saidye, 23 February 1954, SBFP.

[93] Interview with Phyllis Lambert, 12 June 1989; interview with Edgar Bronfman, 5 September 1979.

[94] Wachtel, *Anatomy of a Hidden Persuader*, 139.

[95] *Newsweek*, 26 July 1954; *New York Times*, 13, 21 July 1954; Phyllis Lambert memoranda, 10 October 1990, 19 March 1991.

[96] *Time*, 3 March 1958.

[97] Phyllis to Saidye [7 July 1954], SBFP.

[98] Phyllis Bronfman Lambert, "How a Building Gets Built," *Vassar Alumnae Magazine*, XLIV (February 1959), 13; Phyllis Lambert memorandum, 10 October 1990.

[99] Interview with Phyllis Lambert, 12 July 1989.

[100] Lambert, "How a Building Gets Built," 14.

[101] Ibid, 16.

[102] Phyllis to Sam and Saidye [4 October 1954], SBFP.

[103] Phyllis Lambert memorandum, 10 October 1990.

[104] Phyllis Lambert memorandum, 4 September 1990.

[105] Philip Siekman, "The Bronfmans: An Instinct for Dynasty," *Fortune*, December 1966, 200.

[106] Ibid, 198; interview with Phyllis Lambert, 8 January 1980.

[107] Lambert, "How a Building Gets Built," 16.

[108] *New Yorker*, 13 September 1958, 126.

[109] Interview with Robert Ruppel, 14 September 1990.

[110] *Time*, 3 March 1958.

[111] Wachtel, *Anatomy of a Hidden Persuader*, 142.

[112] Phyllis Lambert memorandum, 10 October 1990.

[113] David Spaeth, *Mies van der Rohe* (New York: Rizzoli, 1985), 168.

[114]Bronfman, *From Little Acorns*, 65; Philip Siekman, "The Bronfmans: An Instinct for Dynasty," *Fortune*, November 1966, 145.

[115]Interview with Charles Bronfman, 3 December 1990.

[116]Interview with Charles Bronfman, 12 June 1989.

[117]Interview with Charles Bronfman, 2 April 1979.

[118]Interview with Edgar Bronfman, 5 September 1979.

[119]Interview with Edgar Bronfman, 13 December 1990.

[120]Interview with Sam Cohen, n.d.

[121]Interview with Sol Kanee, 24 September 1990.

[122]Edgar to Sam, 2 June 1946, SBFP.

[123]Philip Siekman, "The Bronfmans: An Instinct for Dynasty," *Fortune*, December 1966, 200.

[124]Interview with Mel Griffin, 7 February 1990.

[125]Terence Robertson, "Bronfman: The Life and Times of Samuel Bronfman, Esq." (unpub. manuscript, [1969]), 526–31.

[126]Ibid; Philip Siekman, "The Bronfmans: An Instinct for Dynasty," *Fortune*, December 1966, 178.

[127]Henderson, *Plain Talk*, 107.

[128]Ibid, 132; interview with Mark Shinbane, 17 January 1984; interview with Robert Sabloff, 23 January 1990; interview with Mel Griffin, 7 February 1990.

[129]Philip Siekman, "The Bronfmans: An Instinct for Dynasty," *Fortune*, December 1966, 178.

[130]Ibid, 198.

[131]Ibid, 202; Robertson, "Bronfman," 563, 574; interview with Saidye Bronfman, 28 June 1983; interview with Leo Kolber, 20 April 1990.

[132]*Financial Post*, 29 April 1961, 15 August 1964; *BEV/Executive*, 15 July 1971.

[133]Philip Siekman, "The Bronfmans: An Instinct for Dynasty," *Fortune*, December 1966, 202, 204; Edgar Bronfman memorandum, 3 October 1990.

[134]Interview with Alex Mogelon, n.d.

[135]Philip Siekman, "The Bronfmans: An Instinct for Dynasty," *Fortune*, December 1966, 198; *Forbes*, 2 February 1981.

CHAPTER NINE

[1]Philip Siekman, "The Bronfmans: An Instinct for Dynasty," *Fortune*, November 1966; December 1966.

[2]Interview with Edgar Bronfman, 8 March 1990.

[3]Peter C. Newman, "Canada's Biggest Big Businessmen," *Maclean's*, 12 October 1957, 13; Toronto *Telegram*, 23 May 1958.

[4]Erna Paris, *Jews: An Account of Their Experience in Canada* (Toronto: Macmillan, 1980), 74–6; Reginald Whitaker, *The Government Party: Organizing and Financing the Liberal Party of Canada 1930–1958* (Toronto: University of Toronto Press, 1977), 70–1.

[5]A.J. Freiman to William Lyon Mackenzie King, 14 February 1940, Freiman Papers, PAC: Personal Papers 1940–44, vol. 1.

[6]"Samuel Bronfman Liberal," n.d., Klein Papers, PAC: M 5466, v. 22.

[7]Maxwell Henderson, *Plain Talk! Memoirs of an Auditor General* (Toronto: McClelland and Stewart, 1984), 129–30.

[8]Interview with Leo Kolber, 20 April 1990.

[9]Peter C. Newman, *Bronfman Dynasty: The Rothschilds of the New World* (Toronto: McClelland and Stewart, 1978), 57.

[10]Interview with Ben Lappin, 28 November 1989; interview with Robert Sabloff, 23 January 1990; interview with Joan Comay, 11 March 1990.

[11]Interview with Mark Shinbane, 20 October 1983.

[12]Interview with Sol Kanee, 13 September 1989.

[13]Henderson, *Plain Talk*, 130.

[14]Interview with Noah Torno, 6 November 1990.

[15]Interview with Sol Kanee, 13 September 1989.

[16]Newman, *Bronfman Dynasty*, 25.

[17]Saul Hayes, "Samuel Bronfman" [1980], SA.

[18]Interview with Mark Shinbane, 17 January 1984.

[19]Sam to Saidye, [May 1954]; *Montreal Star*, 27 April 1954; Montreal *Gazette*, 30 April 1954.

[20]*New York Times*, 30 September 1959.

[21]Interview with Alan Rose, 12 June 1989.

[22]*Canadian Jewish Chronicle*, 22 December 1950.

[23]M. Ginsburg, "Samuel Bronfman: On His Seventieth Birthday," trans. Bernard Figler [1961], SA.

[24]*Jewish Standard*, 1 June 1970; *Chronicle Review*, 29 May 1970.

[25]William Molson and Bernard Bloomfield to Sam, 30 April 1968; *Chronicle Telegram*, 9 August 1969; Ruth Ryer to Lolly Golt, 7 September 1978.

[26]DC-SL Minutes, 15 November 1951; *New York Times*, 4 March 1951.

[27]*Congress Bulletin*, April-May 1951; Montreal *Gazette*, 26 March 1951.

[28]*New York Times*, 12 March 1961.

[29]Layton to Desmond Pacey, 19 November 1959, in Frances Mansbridge, ed., *Wild Gooseberries: The Selected Letters of Irving Layton* (Toronto: Macmillan, 1989), 115–16.

[30]Harold M. Waller, *The Governance of the Jewish Community of Montreal*, Centre for Jewish Community Studies, Study Report No. 5, 1974, 37; *Your Community*, 3 November 1958.

[31]Max Melamet, "Samuel Bronfman: A Personal Tribute," *Chronicle Review*, August 1971, 5.

[32]Interview with Mel Griffin, 7 February 1990.

[33]*President's Address and Resolutions Adopted at the National Conference for Israel and Jewish Rehabilitation*, Montreal, 24–26 March 1951; *Canadian Jewish Chronicle*, 30 March 1951; *Congress Bulletin*, April-May 1951.

[34]Interview with Avraham Harman, 13 March 1990.

[35]I. Medres, "Canadian Jewry to Intensify Aid to Israel," *Canadian Jewish Chronicle*, 16 May 1952.

[36]Joseph Frank to Eddie Gelber, 4 December 1955. Frank Papers, PAC, MG 31, H29, v.3.

[37]Melamet, "Samuel Bronfman," 3.

[38]Interview with Avraham Harman, 13 March 1990.

[39]Interview with Ben Lappin, 29 November 1989.

[40]Montreal *Gazette*, 4 April 1960.

[41]*Canadian Jewish Chronicle*, 29 June 1962.

[42]Usher Caplan, *Like One That Dreamed: A Portrait of A.M. Klein* (Toronto: McGraw-Hill Ryerson, 1982), 123.

[43]Ibid, 127; Adam G. Fuerstenberg, "The Poet and the Tycoon: The

Relationship Between A.M. Klein and Samuel Bronfman," *Canadian Jewish Historical Society Journal*, 5 (1981), 61.

⁴⁴Caplan, *A.M. Klein*, 157.

⁴⁵F.L. Marshall to Spinney's Ltd., Haifa, 25 July 1949. Klein Papers, PAC, MG 30, M3619, v.1.

⁴⁶Caplan, *A.M. Klein*, 157.

⁴⁷Fuerstenberg, "Poet and Tycoon," 64.

⁴⁸Caplan, *A.M. Klein*, 189.

⁴⁹Tresidder to Klein, 15 October 1947; Klein to Tresidder, 17 October 1947; Tresidder to Klein, 22 October 1947, 5 January 1948. Klein papers, PAC, MG 30, M3619, v.1.

⁵⁰Phyllis Lambert to Klein, n.d. [1955]. Klein Papers, PAC, MG 30, M5468, v. 28.

⁵¹Miriam Waddington, *Apartment Seven: Essays Selected and New* (Toronto: Oxford University Press, 1989), 147.

⁵²Sam to Klein, 27 March 1956, 28 March 1961, 6 March 1963, 4 March 1964, 11 March 1966, 14 March 1967. Klein Papers, PAC, MG 30, M3619, v.1.

⁵³Caplan, *A.M. Klein*, 193.

⁵⁴Ibid, 210; interview with Sol Kanee, 24 September 1990; Klein to Sam, 14 March 1967, n.d. [1969], n.d. [1970]. Klein Papers, PAC, MG 30, M3619, v.1.

⁵⁵Interview with Teddy Kollek, 26 November 1989; interview with Shimon Peres, 24 November 1989.

⁵⁶Interview with Shimon Peres, 24 November 1989; interview with Sol Kanee, 16 October 1990; Shimon Peres to Sol Kanee, 4 December 1951; Shimon Peres, *David's Sling* (New York: Random House, 1970), 40; Matti Golan, *Shimon Peres: A Biography* (London: Weidenfeld and Nicolson, 1982), 21 – 5.

⁵⁷R. Warren James, *People's Senator: The Life and Times of David Croll* (Vancouver: Douglas & McIntyre, 1990), 143.

⁵⁸Minda to Saidye, 8 July 1956, 14 December 1956, SBFP.

⁵⁹National Joint Public Relations Committee, "Public Relations Information Bulletin," 23 May 1952.

⁶⁰Rabbi Samuel Cass to Rabbi Stern, 20 May 1952, Stern papers, PAC: MG31, F12; Harry Joshua Stern, *A Rabbi's Journey* (New York: Bloch, 1981), 93 – 4.

⁶¹*Congress Bulletin*, April-May 1951.

[62]Saul Hayes, " 'The Bronfman Dynasty': A Friend's Reminiscence," *Viewpoints*, X (Spring 1979), 48.

[63]Interview with Joan Comay, 11 March 1990.

[64]Edward Gelber to Joseph Frank, 29 August 1953, Frank Papers, PAC, MG31, H69, v.3; *Canadian Jewish Chronicle*, 28 August 1953.

[65]Hayes, " 'Bronfman Dynasty,' " 48.

[66]Saidye Rosner Bronfman, *My Sam: A Memoir by his Wife* (Toronto: n.p., 1982), 105; "Itinerary Prepared for Mr and Mrs Samuel Bronfman," Frank Travel Service, 24 January 1956; *Canadian Jewish Chronicle*, 6 April 1956.

[67]"Remarks by Mr Samuel Bronfman at an Informal Dinner of U.J.A.", Ambassador Hotel [New York], 23 May 1958, SA.

[68]H.J. Halperin to David Rome, 13 April 1956; "Text of Samuel Bronfman's Statement Upon his Return from the State of Israel," [17 April 1956], ACJC; *Congress Bulletin*, April 1956; *Canadian Jewish Chronicle*, 6 April 1956, 13 April 1956, 20 April 1956, Montreal *Gazette*, 18 April 1956.

[69]*Canadian Jewish Chronicle*, 2 May 1958.

[70]Ibid, 6 November 1959.

[71]Arthur Hertzberg, *The Jews in America. Four Centuries of an Uneasy Encounter: A History* (New York: Simon and Schuster, 1989), 344.

[72]"Remarks by Mr Samuel Bronfman at an Informal Dinner of U.J.A", Ambassador Hotel [New York], 23 May 1958, SA.

[73]Sam and Lawrence Freiman telegram, 4 December 1959; Lawrence Freiman to Bernard Alexander, 2 December 1959, Freiman Papers, PAC, MG30, A 82, v.17.

[74]Lawrence Freiman, *Don't Fall off the Rocking Horse: An Autobiography* (Toronto: McClelland and Stewart, 1978), 179.

[75]*Ottawa Citizen*, 29 December 1959; Montreal *Gazette*, 30 December 1959; *Medicine Hat News*, 8 January 1960; *Toronto Daily Star*, 8 January 1960.

[76]Joseph Frank to Eddie Gelber, 23 May 1960, Frank Papers, PAC, MG 31, H29, v.3.

[77]Interview with Jack Brin, 11 March 1990.

[78]Interview with Sol Kanee, 13 September 1989.

[79]Freiman, *Autobiography*, 178.

[80]Sam to Goldmann, 3 May 1956; Goldmann to Sam, 14 May 1956, Goldmann Papers, Central Zionist Archives, Z6/1125.

[81]Goldmann to Sam, 10 April 1957.

[82]Nahum Goldmann, *Sixty Years of Jewish Life: The Autobiography of Nahum Goldmann*, trans. Helen Sebba (New York: Holt, Rinehart and Winston, 1969), 315.

[83]*On the Road to Jewish Unity: The Participation of Organizations and Communities in the 25th Zionist Congress* (Jerusalem: World Zionist Organization, 1962), 19–20.

[84]Sam Bronfman, "The Changing World and the Jewish Position in It," 10 January 1965, ACJC.

[85]Interview with Sol Kanee, 13 September 1990.

[86]*Time*, 2 November 1962.

[87]Melamet, "Samuel Bronfman," 6; interview with Max Melamet, 23 January 1991.

[88]Interview with Jack Brin, 11 March 1990; Jack Bin memorandum, 13 December 1990; interview with Charles Bronfman, 3 December 1990; Freiman papers, PAC, MG30 B4, v.20; Frank Papers, MG31 H69, v.4; *Financial Post*, 11 April 1959; *Time*, 21 August 1964; *Toronto Daily Star*, 19 January 1966.

[89]Interview with Alan Rose, 12 June 1989.

[90]Harold Troper and Morton Weinfeld, *Old Wounds: Jews, Ukrainians and the Hunt for Nazi War Criminals in Canada* (Markham, Ontario: Penguin Books, 1988), 58.

[91]*Canadian Jewish Chronicle Review*, 4 June 1967, 9 June 1967; *Your Community News*, 31 August 1971, 8; Harold M. Waller, *The Governance of the Jewish Community of Montreal*, Centre for Jewish Community Studies, Study Report No. 5, 1974, 80–1.

[92]Interview with Abe Mayman, 2 November 1990; interview with Sol Kanee, 13 September 1989.

[93]Interview with Richard Cohen, 13 March 1990.

[94]Gil Rabin memorandum, n.d. [July 1967], SA.

[95]Charles to Saidye, 11 June 1946, SBFP.

[96]Interview with Edgar Bronfman, 5 Setpember 1979.

[97]Interview with Leo Kolber, 20 March 1990.

[98]Speech given by Mr Samuel Bronfman at Murray Bay, 6 July 1950, SA.

[99]"A World Half Prosperous, Half Starved," address by Samuel Bronfman to the Canadian Club, Toronto, 30 April 1962, SA.

[100]Interview with Charles Bronfman, 3 December 1990; inteview with

Edgar Bronfman, 13 December 1990; Ellis D. Slater, *The Ike I Knew* (n.p.: Ellis D. Slater Trust, 1980), 47–9; Eisenhower Appointment Book, 9 July 1953, Eisenhower Papers, Dwight D. Eisenhower Library.

[101]Eisenhower to Slater, 13 July 1953, Eisenhower Papers, Dwight D. Eisenhower Library.

[102]Interview with Charles Bronfman, 2 April 1979; interview with Edgar Bronfman, 5 September 1979.

[103]Saul Hayes, "Samuel Bronfman" [1980].

[104]Sam to Goldmann, 3 May 1956, Goldmann Papers, Central Zionist Archives, Z6/1125.

[105]Goldman to Sam, 14 May 1956, Goldmann Papers, Central Zionist Archives, Z6/1125.

[106]Melamet, "Samuel Bronfman," 6.

CHAPTER TEN

[1]*Business Week*, 20 October 1962.

[2]Interview with Saidye Bronfman, 18 October 1979.

[3]Interview with Edgar Bronfman, 5 September 1979; Edgar Bronfman memorandum, 16 January 1991; Philip Siekman, "The Bronfmans: An Instinct for Dynasty," *Fortune* December 1966, 200.

[4]Interview with Max Melamet, 20 December 1990.

[5]*Financial Post*, 20 February 1971.

[6]*Business Week*, 20 October 1962; *Time*, 5 March 1965.

[7]Interview with Edgar Bronfman, 5 September 1979.

[8]*New York Times*, 27, 28 August 1964; Saidye Rosner Bronfman, *Recollections of My Life* (Montreal: n.p., 1986), 112; interview with Saidye Bronfman, 13 July 1978.

[9]Interview with Mel Griffin, 7 February 1990.

[10]Interview with Mark Shinbane, 17 January 1984; interview with Robert Sabloff, 23 January 1990.

[11]Michael McCormick, uppub. paper, August 1971, SA.

[12]Interview with Leo Kolber, 20 April 1990; Terence Robertson, "Bronfman: The Life and Times of Samuel Bronfman, Esq." (unpub. manuscript, [1969]).

[13]*Winnipeg Tribune*, 17 May 1968.

[14]Montreal *Gazette*, 18 May 1970; *Canadian Jewish News*, 22 May 1970; interview with Chaim Lewin, n.d.

[15]Michael McCormick, unpub. paper, August 1971; *Official Opening. Samuel Bronfman House. Commemorating Fifty Years of Service by the Canadian Jewish Congress, Montreal, May 24, 1970* [Montreal: Canadian Jewish Congress, 1970]; *Canadian Jewish News*, 22 May 1970; *Chronicle Review*, 29 May 1970.

[16]Minda to Sam, 4 March 1971, emphasis in original, SBFP.

[17]Maxwell Henderson, *Plain Talk! Memoirs of an Auditor General* (Toronto: McClelland and Stewart, 1984), 296 – 7; Distillers Corporation-Seagrams Limited, *Annual Report, Supplement*, 1971,66.

[18]Interview with Noah Torno, 6 November 1990.

[19]Saidye Rosner Bronfman, *My Sam: A Memoir by his Wife* (Toronto: n.p., 1982), 141.

[20]Phyllis Lambert memorandum, 6 August 1990.

[21]Interview with Sol Kanee, 13 September 1990.

[22]Ibid; Bronfman, *My Sam*, 142.

[23]Montreal *Gazette*, 13, 14 July 1971.

[24]Charles Bronfman memorandum, 19 June 1990.

[25]Interview with Noah Torno, 6 November 1990.

[26]*Forbes*, 1 February 1973.

[27]Nahum Goldmann, "Memorial Tribute to Sam Bronfman during the 16th Plenary Assembly," [Canadian Jewish Congress, 1971], SA.

[28]Neal Gabler, *An Empire of Their Own: How the Jews Invented Hollywood* (New York: Anchor Books, 1988), 5 – 7.

[29]Phyllis Lambert memorandum, 6 August 1990.

A Note on Sources

A MAN OF action, who preferred the telephone to the mail and a personal conversation to the telephone, Sam Bronfman did not leave behind a large mass of private, community or business papers. Alan Rose, who worked with him at the Canadian Jewish Congress, contends that Sam "threw everything away," and David Rome, whose knowledge of the Canadian Jewish Congress archives is unsurpassed, believes that people around the office constantly helped Sam discard what he had written — leaving precious little in the way of correspondence or other first-hand material from which Sam's inner thoughts and feelings can be ascertained.

Still, such material exists. I have drawn upon private papers in the possession of his family, material in the Archives of the Canadian Jewish Congress, and Distillers Corporation-Seagrams Limited business records, which are housed at Seagram's LaSalle Records Centre outside Montreal. The Seagram material includes extensive legal correspondence and other documents that originated in the offices of Sam's Winnipeg attorneys Andrews, Andrews, Burbidge & Bastedo, and his Montreal lawyers Phillips & Vineberg, Sam's counsel for over forty years. In addition to these company sources there is a collection of photographs and memorabilia at the Seagram Museum in Waterloo, Ontario. Useful as well was Saskatchewan Liquor Commission documentation in the Public Archives of

Saskatchewan and a mass of material on the 1935 prosecution of
the Bronfman brothers, obtained from RCMP Headquarters in
Ottawa. At the Public Archives of Canada I found particularly
valuable material in the Joseph N. Frank Papers, Freiman
Family Papers, S.W. Jacobs Papers, A.M. Klein Papers,
Alexander Mogelon Papers, Harry Joshua Stern Papers, and
testimony before the Royal Commission on Customs and Excise
in 1927. Other information came from the Morgenthau Diaries at
the Franklin Roosevelt Library, in Hyde Park, New York; the
Archives of the United Church of Canada, Board of Evangelism
and Social Service at the University of Toronto; the United
States National Archives; and the Archives of the World Jewish
Congress in New York.

The mainstream Jewish press in Canada, particularly the
Canadian Jewish Chronicle, edited by A.M. Klein during much
of Sam's career as head of the Canadian Jewish Congress, is a
mine of information, although a critical word is hardly to be
found, either of Sam or of other leaders of the day. On the
business side, discussion is both more open and diverse. Yearly
evaluations of the Seagram Company, from Sam's and the
company's own standpoint, are available in the Minute Books of
Distillers Corporation-Seagrams Limited, kept in the Seagram
offices in Montreal. I have relied heavily on the business press
for assessments and analyses of the whisky industry, particularly
the *Financial Post*, and several key articles in *Fortune*, cited often
in the notes to various chapters and listed in the bibliography
that follows.

Interviews have been an important source. I have drawn upon
lengthy transcripts of taped interviews with family members,
friends and associates made by Lolly Golt, Phyllis Lambert, John
Scott and others, conducted during the late 1970s and early
1980s. I have myself conducted all those interviews dated in
1989, 1990 and 1991.

Valuable material also exists in Saidye Bronfman's two
volumes of memoirs, *My Sam* (1982) and *Recollections of My Life*
(1986), in Harry Bronfman's unpublished memoirs of 1937 (in
the Samuel Bronfman family papers) and 1939 (in the possession
of his daughter-in-law Marjorie Bronfman), and Sam's own
company history, *From Little Acorns* (1970). The late Terence

Robertson's unfinished manuscript, "The Life and Times of
Samuel Bronfman, Esq." (1969) is also useful, being based upon
extensive interviews with Sam near the end of his life. Other
first-hand accounts include unpublished fragments by Saul
Hayes, and the published memoirs of Maxwell Henderson,
William Wachtel and Philip Kelly.

Selected Bibliography

Abella, Irving, *A Coat of Many Colours: Two Centuries of Jewish Life in Canada* (Toronto: Lester & Orpen Dennys, 1990).

Abella, Irving and Harold Troper, *None Is Too Many: Canada and the Jews of Europe 1933–1948* (Toronto: Lester & Orpen Dennys, 1982).

Afanasiev-Chuzhbinksii, A., *Poezdka v Iuzhnuiu Rossiiu* (2 vols., St. Petersburg: n.p., 1863).

Allen, Richard, *The Social Passion: Religion and Social Reform in Canada 1914–28* (Toronto: University of Toronto Press, 1973).

Allsop, Kenneth, *The Bootleggers: The Story of Chicago's Prohibition Era* (London: Hutchinson, 1961).

An Observer, "The Ku Klux Klan in Saskatchewan," *Queen's Quarterly*, Autumn 1928, 592–602.

Anctil, Pierre, "H.M. Caiserman or Yiddish as a Passion," unpub. paper, June 1989.

_____, *Le rendez-vous manqué: Les Juifs de Montréal face au Québec de l'entre-deux-guerres* (Québec: Institut québécois de recherche sur la culture, 1988).

Andrieux, J.P., *Prohibition and St. Pierre* (Lincoln, Ontario: W.F. Rannie, 1983).

Archer, John H., *Saskatchewan: A History* (Saskatoon, Sask.: Prairie Books, 1980).

Arnold, Abraham J., "Jewish Pioneer Settlements," *The Beaver*, Autumn 1975, 20–6.

_____, "The Contribution of the Jews to the Opening and Development of the West," *Transactions of the Historical and Scientific Society of Manitoba*, Series III (1968–1969), 23–37.

_____, "The Earliest Jews of Winnipeg," *The Beaver*, Autumn 1974, 4–11.

Artibise, Alan F.J., *Winnipeg: A Social History of Urban Growth 1874–1914* (Montreal: McGill-Queen's University Press, 1975).

Avery, Donald, "Canada's Response to European Refugees, 1939–1945: The Security Dimension," in Norman Hillmer, Bohdan Kordan and Lubomyr Luciuk, eds., *On Guard for Thee: War, Ethnicity and the Canadian State, 1939–1945* (Ottawa: Canadian Committee for the History of the Second World War, 1988), 179–216.

Barker, G.F., *Brandon: A City 1881–1961* (Altona, Man.: n.p., 1977).

Barty-King, Hugh and Anton Massel, *Rum: Yesterday and Today* (London: Heinemann, 1983).

Beaverbrook (William Maxwell Aitken), *Friends: Sixty Years of Intimate Personal Relations with Richard Bedford Bennett* (London: Heinemann, 1959).

Belkin, Simon, *Through Narrow Gates: A Review of Jewish Immigration, Colonization and Immigrant Aid Work in Canada (1840–1940)* (Montreal: Canadian Jewish Congress, 1966).

Bellan, Reuben, *Winnipeg First Century: An Economic History* (Winnipeg: Queenston House, 1978).

Bercuson, David J., *Canada and the Birth of Israel: A Study in Canadian Foreign Policy* (Toronto: University of Toronto Press, 1985).

_____, *The Secret Army* (Toronto: Lester & Orpen Dennys, 1983).

Berg, A. Scott, *Goldwyn: A Biography* (New York: Knopf, 1989).

Bermant, Chaim, *The Jews* (London: Weidenfeld and Nicolson, 1977).

Berton, Pierre, *The Great Depression, 1929–1939* (Toronto: McClelland & Stewart, 1990).

_____, *The Last Spike: The Great Railway 1881–1885* (Toronto: Penguin Books, 1989).

Betcherman, Lita-Rose, *The Swastika and the Maple Leaf: Fascist Movements in Canada in the Thirties* (Toronto: Fitzhenry & Whiteside, 1975).

Birmingham, Stephen, *"The Rest of Us": The Rise of America's Eastern European Jews* (Boston: Little, Brown, 1984).

Bissell, Claude, *The Young Vincent Massey* (Toronto: University of Toronto Press, 1981).

Black, Conrad, *Duplessis* (Toronto: McClelland and Stewart, 1977).

Blake, Peter, *The Master Builders* (London: Victor Gollancz, 1960).

Bliss, Michael, *A Canadian Millionaire: The Life and Business Times of Sir Joseph Flavelle, Bart. 1858 – 1939* (Toronto: Macmillan, 1978).

_____, "The Bronfmans Observed," *Canadian Business*, December 1978, 98 – 102.

Blum, John M., *From the Morgenthau Diaries: Years of Crisis, 1928 – 1938* (Boston: Houghton Mifflin, 1959).

Boorstin, Daniel J., *The Americans: The Democratic Experience* (New York: Random House, 1973).

Booth, Amy, "The Bronfmans," *Financial Post*, 13 November 1976; 20 November 1976.

Bowker, Alan, ed., *The Social Criticism of Stephen Leacock* (Toronto: University of Toronto Press, 1973).

Brennan, J.W., "A Political History of Saskatchewan, 1905 – 1929," unpub. Ph.D. thesis, University of Alberta, 1976.

Bronfman, Edgar M., "Name Your Brand – In Any Market of the World," *Columbia Journal of World Business*, IV (November – December 1969), 31 – 5.

Bronfman, Harry, "The Story of the Bronfman Family," unpub. memoir [1937], SBFP.

_____, unpub. memoir [1939], Gerald Bronfman Papers.

Bronfman, Saidye Rosner, *My Sam: A Memoir by his Wife* (Toronto: n.p., 1982).

_____, *Recollections of My Life* (Montreal: n.p., 1986).

Bronfman, Samuel, "A World Half Prosperous, Half Starved," speech to the Canadian Club, Toronto, 30 April 1962.

_____, *From Little Acorns: The Story of Distillers Corporation-Seagrams Limited* ([Montreal: DC-SL], 1970)

_____, preface to Bernard Figler, *Sam Jacobs: Member of Parliament (Samuel William Jacobs, K.C., M.P.) 1871 – 1938* (Ottawa: n.p., 1970).

_____, preface to *Cities of Canada: Reproductions from the Seagram Collection of Paintings*, with commentary by Bernard K. Sandwell (Toronto: House of Seagram, 1953).

_____, preface to Stephen Leacock, *Canada: The Foundations of Its Future* (Montreal, n.p., 1941).

_____, text of address delivered by Samuel Bronfman at the Montefiore Club, Montreal, 4 March 1941.

_____, "The Changing World and the Jewish Position in It," speech at the Beverly Wilshire Hotel, Los Angeles, 10 January 1965.

Brown, Michael, *Jew or Juif?: Jews, French-Canadians, and Anglo-Canadians, 1759–1914* (Philadelphia: The Jewish Publication Society, 1987).

Brown, Robert Craig and Ramsay Cook, *Canada 1896–1921* (Toronto: McClelland and Stewart, 1974).

Bryden, John, *Deadly Enemies: Canada's Secret War, 1937–1947* (Toronto: McClelland and Stewart, 1989).

Brym, Robert J., "The Rise and Decline of Canadian Jewry? A Socio-Demographic Profile," unpublished paper, 1989.

Burnham, John C., "New Perspectives on the Prohibition 'Experiment' of the 1920s," *Journal of Social History*, 2 (1968), 51–68.

Calderwood, William, "Pulpit, Press and Political Reactions to the Ku Klux Klan in Saskatchewan," in S.M. Trofimenkoff, ed., *The Twenties in Western Canada (Papers of the Western Canadian Studies Conference, March 1972)* (Ottawa: National Museum of Man, 1972), 191–219.

Canada. Parliament, *Royal Commission on Customs and Excise. Final Report* (1928).

Canada. Parliament, *Royal Commission on Customs and Excise. Interim Reports* (Nos. 1 to 10) (1928).

Canada. Parliament, *Royal Commission on the Liquor Traffic in Canada, Minutes of Evidence*, 1894.

Canada. Parliament, *Royal Commission on the Liquor Traffic in Canada, Report*, 1895.

Caplan, Usher, *Like One That Dreamed: A Portrait of A.M. Klein* (Toronto: McGraw-Hill Ryerson, 1982).

Cashman, Tony, *Abraham Cristall: The Story of a Simple Man* (n.p.: n.p. [1963]).

Chiel, Arthur A., *Jewish Experiences in Early Manitoba* (Winnipeg: n.p., 1955).

_____, *The Jews in Manitoba: A Social History* (Toronto: University of Toronto Press, 1961).

Cities of Canada: Reproductions from the Seagram Collection of Paintings, with commentary by Bernard K. Sandwell (Toronto: House of Seagram, 1953).

Clark, Norman H., *Deliver Us From Evil: An Interpretation of American Prohibition* (New York: W.W. Norton, 1976).

_____, *The Dry Years: Prohibition and Social Change in Washington* (Seattle: University of Washington Press, 1988).

Clark, W. Leland, *Brandon's Politics and Politicians* (Brandon: Brandon Sun, 1981).

Cleator, Kenneth I. and Harry J. Stern, *Harry Joshua Stern: A Rabbi's Journey* (New York: Bloch, 1981).

Coleman, Jim, *A Hoofprint on My Heart* (Toronto: McClelland and Stewart, 1971).

Commemorative Report on National Bicentenary of Canadian Jewry 1759–1959 (n.p.: n.p. [1960]).

Congregation Shaar Hashomayim 1846–1946 [Montreal: n.p., 1946].

Cook, Ramsay, *The Regenerators: Social Criticism in Late Victorian English Canada* (Toronto: University of Toronto Press, 1985).

Cooke, Alfred Edward, "The Canadian Liquor System: I—Evils of Government Control," *Current History*, XXXI (October 1929), 64–73.

Coward, Noel, *The Noel Coward Diaries*, ed. Graham Payne and Sheridan Morley (London: Weidenfeld and Nicolson, 1982).

Daiches, David, *Scotch Whisky: Its Past and Present* (London: Fontana, 1976).

Davis, C. Mark, "Rum and the Law: The Maritime Experience," in James H. Morrison and James Moreira, eds., *Tempered by Rum: Rum in the History of the Maritime Provinces* (Porters Lake, Nova Scotia: Pottersfield Press, 1988), 40–52.

Decarie, M.G., "Paved with Good Intentions: The Prohibitionists' Road to Racism in Ontario," *Ontario History*, LXVI (1974), 15–22.

Dennison, Merrill, *Canada's First Bank: A History of the Bank of Montreal* (2 vols., Toronto: McClelland and Steward, 1967).

Documents on Canadian External Relations, Vol. 3, 1919–1925, ed. Lovell C. Clark (Ottawa: Information Canada, 1970).

Documents on Canadian External Relations, Vol. 4, 1926–1930, ed. Alex I. Inglis (Ottawa: Information Canada, 1971).

Documents on Canadian External Relations, Vol. 5, 1931–1935, ed. Alex I. Inglis (Ottawa: Information Canada, 1973).

Downard, William L., *Dictionary of the History of the American Brewing and Distilling Industries* (Westport, Conn.: Greenwood Press, 1980).

Drage, Charles, *Two-Gun Cohen* (London: Jonathan Cape, 1954).

Draper, Paula Jean, "Fragmented Loyalties: Canadian Jewry, the King Government and the Refugee Dilemma," in Norman Hillmer, Bohdan Kordan and Lubomyr Luciuk, eds., *On Guard For Thee: War, Ethnicity and the Canadian State, 1939–1945* (Ottawa: Canadian Committee for the History of the Second World War, 1988), 151–77.

—————, "The Accidental Immigrants: Canada and the Interned Refugees," unpub. Ph.D. dissertation, University of Toronto, 1983.

—————, "The Accidental Immigrants: Canada and the Interned Refugees: part 1," *Canadian Jewish Historical Quarterly*, 2 (1978), 1–38.

Dubnow, S.M., *History of the Jews*, Vol. 5, *From the Congress of Vienna to the Emergence of Hitler*, trans. Moshe Spiegel (London: Thomas Yoseloff, 1973).

—————, *History of the Jews in Russia and Poland from the Earliest Times Until the Present Day*, trans. I. Friedlaender (3 vols., Philadelphia: Jewish Publication Society of America, 1920).

Dupont, Antonin, "Louis-Alexandre Taschereau et la législation sociale au Québec, 1920–1936" *Revue d'histoire de l'Amérique française*, 26 (1972), 397–426.

Eisenberg, Dennis, Uri Dan and Eli Landau, *Meyer Lansky: Mogul of the Mob* (New York: Paddington Press, 1979).

Eisendrath, Maurice, *Can Faith Survive? The Afterthoughts of an American Rabbi* (New York: McGraw-Hill, 1964).

—————, *The Never Failing Stream* (Toronto: Macmillan, 1939).

Elath, Eliahu, *Zionism at the UN: A Diary of the First Days*, trans. Michael Ben-Yitzhak (Philadelphia: Jewish Publication Society of America, 1976).

English, John, *Shadow of Heaven: The Life of Lester Pearson*, Vol. I, *1897–1948* (Toronto: Lester & Orpen Dennys, 1989).

Ephron, Nora, "Seagrams with Moxie," *New York Times Book Review*, 11 March 1979, 13.

Everest, Allan S., *Rum Across the Border: The Prohibition Era in Northern New York* (Syracuse, N.Y.: Syracuse University Press, 1978).

Fairbairn, Garry Lawrence, *From Prairie Roots: The Remarkable Story of the Saskatchewan Wheat Pool* (Saskatoon, Sask.: Western Producer Prairie Books, 1984).

Feldman, Eliahu, "Jews of Bessarabia from the Beginning of their Settlement until the End of the 19th Century" [Hebrew], in *Toledot ha-Yehudim be-Bessarabyah* (Jerusalem: Yad Vashem, 1969), Il, 279–99.

Figler, Bernard, *Lillian and Archie Freiman: Biographies* (Montreal: n.p., 1961).

_____, *Sam Jacobs: Member of Parliament (Samuel William Jacobs, K.C., M.P.) 1871 – 1938* (Ottawa: n.p., 1970).

Figler, Bernard and David Rome, *Hannaniah Meir Caiserman: A Biography* (Montreal: Northern Printing and Lithographing Co., 1962).

Fontenay, Charles L., *Estes Kefauver: A Biography* (Knoxville, Tennessee: University of Tennessee Press, 1980).

Forbes, Ernest, " 'Rum' in the Maritimes' Economy During the Prohibition Era," in James H. Morrison and James Moreira, eds., *Tempered by Rum: Rum in the History of the Maritime Provinces* (Porters Lake, Nova Scotia: Pottersfield Press, 1988), 103 – 9.

Foster, Peter, *Family Spirits: The Bacardi Saga* (Toronto: Macfarlane Walter & Ross, 1990).

Frank, Philip, "What's America Drinking?" *Advertising and Selling*, 30 August 1934.

Freiman, Lawrence, *Don't Fall off the Rocking Horse: An autobiography* (Toronto: McClelland and Stewart, 1978).

Fried, Albert, *The Rise and Fall of the Jewish Gangster in America* (New York: Holt, Rinehart and Winston, 1980).

Friesen, Gerald, *The Canadian Prairies: A History* (Toronto: University of Toronto Press, 1987).

Fuerstenberg, Adam G., "The Poet and the Tycoon: The Relationship Between A.M. Klein and Samuel Bronfman," *Canadian Jewish Historical Society Journal*, 5 (1981), 49 – 69.

Fulford, Robert, "Joan of Archictecture," *Imperial Oil Review*, Winter 1989, 8 – 12.

Gabler, Neal, *An Empire of Their Own: How the Jews Invented Hollywood* (New York: Anchor Books, 1988).

Gagnon, Marcel-Aimé, *Jean-Charles Harvey, Précurseur de la Révolution tranquille* (Montreal: Beauchemin, 1970).

Gardner, Paul, "Bronfman of Seagrams," *New Liberty*, July 1949, 12 – 17.

Gibbon, Ann and Peter Hadekel, *Steinberg: The Breakup of a Family Empire* (Toronto: Macmillan, 1990).

Gibson, Paul, "The Battling Bronfmans," *Forbes*, 2 February 1981, 42 – 3.

Ginsburg, M., "Samuel Bronfman: On his Seventieth Birthday," trans. Bernard Figler, unpub. manuscript [1961].

Golan, Matti, *Shimon Peres: A Biography* (London: Weidenfeld and Nicolson, 1982).

Goldmann, Nahum, *Mein Leben als deutscher Jude* (Munich: Langen Muller, 1980).

_____, *Mein Leben USA, Europa, Israel* (Munich: Langen Muller, 1981).

_____, *Sixty Years of Jewish Life: The Autobiography of Nahum Goldmann*, trans. Helen Sebba (New York: Holt, Rinehart and Winston, 1969).

Gorman, Joseph Bruce, *Kefauver: A Political Biography* (New York: Oxford University Press, 1971).

Gosch, Martin A., and Richard Hammer, *The Last Testament of Lucky Luciano* (Boston: Little, Brown, 1974).

Granatstein, J.L., *Canada 1957–1967: The Years of Uncertainty and Innovation* (Toronto: McClelland and Stewart, 1986.

Grant, John Webster, *A Profusion of Spires: Religion in Nineteenth-Century Ontario* (Toronto: University of Toronto Press, 1988).

Gray, James H., *Bacchanalia Revisited: Western Canada's Boozy Skid to Social Disaster* (Saskatoon, Sask.: Western Producer Prairie Books, 1982).

_____, *Boomtime: Peopling the Canadian Prairies* (Saskatoon, Sask.: Western Producer Prairie Books, 1979).

_____, *Booze: The Impact of Whisky on the Prairie West* (Toronto: Macmillan, 1972).

_____, *The Roar of the Twenties* (Toronto: Macmillan, 1975).

Greenberg, Louis, *The Jews in Russia: The Struggle for Emancipation* (2 vols., New York: Schocken, 1976).

Greene, B.M., ed., *Who's Who in Canada, 1932–33* (Toronto: International Press, 1933).

Grossmann, Vladimir, *The Soil's Calling* ([Montreal]: Eagle Publishing Co., 1938).

Gutkin, Harry, *Journey into Our Heritage: The Story of the Jewish People in the Canadian West* (Toronto: Lester & Orpen Dennys, 1980).

Hallowell, Gerald A., *Prohibition in Ontario, 1919–1923* (Ottawa: Ontario Historical Society, 1972).

Hart, Arthur D., *The Jew in Canada* (Toronto: Toronto Jewish Publications, 1926).

Harvison, C.W., *The Horseman* (Toronto: McClelland and Stewart, 1967).

Hayes, Saul, " 'The Bronfman Dynasty': A Friend's Reminiscence," *Viewpoints*, X (Spring 1979), 45 – 9.

_____, "Sam Bronfman – Quest for Unity," unpub. paper [1980].

_____, "Samuel Bronfman" (from eulogy given by Saul Hayes at his funeral) [1971].

_____, "Samuel Bronfman" [1980].

Henderson's Manitoba and Northwest Territories Gazetteer and Directory for 1905 (Winnipeg: Henderson's Directories, 1905).

Henderson's Winnipeg City Directory for 1913 (Winnipeg: Henderson's Directories, 1913).

Henderson's Winnipeg City Directory for 1914 (Winnipeg: Henderson's Directories, 1914).

Henderson's Yorkton Directory for 1913 (Winnipeg: Henderson's Directories, 1913).

Henderson, Maxwell, "My Bronfman Years," *Saturday Night*, September 1984.

_____, *Plain Talk! Memoirs of an Auditor General* (Toronto: McClelland and Stewart, 1984).

Herstein, Harvey H., "The Growth of the Winnipeg Jewish Community and the Evolution of its Educational Institutions," *Transactions of the Historical and Scientific Society of Manitoba*, Series III (1965 – 1966), 27 – 66.

Hertzberg, Arthur, *The Jews in America. Four Centuries of an Uneasy Encounter: A History* (New York: Simon and Schuster, 1989).

Hillels, I., "City of Soroki and Its Community (Second Half of the Nineteenth Century)" [Hebrew], in L. Kuperstain and Yitzhak Konen, eds., *Pirkei Bessarabyah* (Tel Aviv: n.p., 1952), 94 – 120.

"Hiram Walker Digs In," *Fortune*, March 1939.

Hluchaniuk, Laurie et at, *Yorkton: York Colony to Treasure Chest City* (Saskatoon, Sask.: Modern Press, [1983]).

Hochman, Elaine S., *Architects of Fortune: Mies van der Rohe and the Third Reich* (New York: Weidenfeld and Nicolson, 1989).

Hoffer, Israel, "Reminiscences," *Saskatchewan History*, 5 (1952), 28 – 32.

Horrall, S.W., *The Pictorial History of the Royal Canadian Mounted Police* (Toronto: McGraw-Hill Ryerson, 1973).

Howard, Esme, *Theatre of Life*, Vol. 2, *Life Seen from the Stalls 1903 – 1936* (Boston: Little, Brown, 1936).

Hull, Cordell, *The Memoirs of Cordell Hull* (2 vols., New York: Macmillan, 1948).

Hunt, C.W., *Booze, Boats and Billions: Smuggling Liquid Gold!* (Toronto: McClelland and Stewart, 1988).

"Industry Leaders I — Seagram," *Monopoly State Review*, August 1946.

Jackson, James A., *The Centennial History of Manitoba* (Toronto: McClelland and Stewart, 1970).

Jacobson, Solomon Hirsch, "Reminiscences of My Pioneer Days," *Jewish Post*, 30 November 1937.

James, R. Warren, *People's Senator: The Life and Times of David Croll* (Vancouver: Douglas & McIntyre, 1990).

Jenkins, Kathleen, *Montreal: Island City of the St. Lawrence* (Garden City, N.Y.: Doubleday, 1966).

Jones, R.L., "Canada's Cooperation in Prohibition Enforcement," *Current History*, 32 (1930), 712 – 16.

Kage, Joseph, *With Faith and Thanksgiving: The Story of Two Hundred Years of Jewish Immigration and Immigrant Aid Effort in Canada (1760 – 1960)* (Montreal: Eagle Publishing, 1962).

Kay, Zachariah, *Canada and Palestine: The Politics of Non-Commitment* (Jerusalem: Israel Universities Press, 1978).

Kayfetz, Ben G., "Rabbi Maurice Nathan Eisendrath (1902 – 1973)," *Canadian Jewish Archives*, N.S. No. 6 (1976), xv – xix.

Keenleyside, Hugh L., *Memoirs*, Vol. 1, *Hammer the Golden Day* (Toronto: McClelland and Stewart, 1981).

Kelley, Nora and William, *The Royal Canadian Mounted Police: A Century of History 1873 – 1973* (Edmonton: Hurtig, 1973).

Kelly, Philip J., *The Making of a Salesman* (New York: Abelard Schuman, 1965).

Kerr, K. Austin, *Organized for Prohibition: A New History of the Anti-Saloon League* (New Haven, Conn.: Yale University Press, 1985).

Knowles, Valerie, *First Person: A Biography of Cairine Wilson, Canada's First Woman Senator* (Toronto: Dundurn Press, 1988).

Koch, Erich, *Deemed Suspect: A Wartime Blunder* (Toronto: Methuen, 1980).

Kollek, Teddy, *For Jerusalem: A Life* (New York: Random House, 1978).

Koskoff, David E., *Joseph P. Kennedy: A Life and Times* (Englewood Cliffs, N.J.: Prentice-Hall, 1974).

Kottman, Richard N., "Volstead Violated: Prohibition as a Factor in Canadian-American Relations," *Canadian Historical Review*, 43 (1962), 106 – 26.

Kyba, Patrick, "Ballots and Burning Crosses — The Election of 1929," in Norman Ward and Duff Spafford, eds., *Politics in Saskatchewan* (Toronto: Longmans Canada Limited, 1968), 105 – 23.

Lambert, Phyllis Bronfman, "How a Building Gets Built," *Vassar Alumnae Magazine*, XLIV (February 1959), 13 – 19.

Langlais, Jacques and David Rome, *Juifs et Québécois français. 200 ans d'histoire commune* (Montreal: Fides, 1986).

Lappin, Ben, *The Redeemed Children: The Story of the Rescue of War Orphans by the Jewish Community of Canada* (Toronto: University of Toronto Press, 1963).

Larsen, Grace H. and Henry E. Erdman, "Aaron Sapiro: Genius of Farm Cooperative Promotion," *Mississippi Valley Historical Review*, 49 (1962/3), 242 – 68.

Leacock, Stephen, *Canada: The Foundations of Its Future* (Montreal: n.p., 1941).

Lender, Mark Edward and James Kirby Martin, *Drinking in America: A History* (New York: The Free Press, 1982).

Leonoff, Cyril Edel, "Pioneers, Ploughs and Prayers: The Jewish Farmers of Western Canada," reprinted from *The Jewish Western Bulletin*, September 1982.

——————————, *The Architecture of Jewish Settlements on the Prairies: A Pictorial History* (n.p.: n.p., 1975).

——————————, "Wapella Farm Settlement," Supplement to *Transactions*, *Manitoba Historical and Scientific Society*, Series III, no. 27 (1970 – 1971).

Leskov, Nikolai S., *The Jews in Russia: Some Notes on the Jewish Question*, ed. and trans. Harold Klassel Schefski (Princeton, N.J.: Kingston Press, 1986).

Lestchinsky, Jacob, "Bessarabia," in *The Universal Jewish Encyclopedia* (10 vols., New York: KTAV Publishing House, 1940), II, 244 – 8.

Levitt, Joseph, *Henri Bourassa and the Golden Calf: The Social Program of the Nationalists of Quebec (1900 – 1914)* (Ottawa: Editions de l'Université d'Ottawa, 1972).

Lewin, Samuel, "Canadian Jewish Congress in Introspect," *Veiwpoints*, III, 3 (1967).

Linteau, Paul-André, René Durocher and Jean-Claude Robert, *Quebec: A History 1867–1929* (Toronto: James Lorimer & Co., 1983).

"Liquor in America: An Interim Report," *Fortune*, October 1934.

Lockhart, Robert Bruce, *Scotch: The Whisky of Scotland in Fact and Story* (London: Putnam, 1951).

Lovell's Directory of Manitoba and Northwest Territories for 1990–1901 (Winnipeg: John Lovell & Son, 1990).

Lovell's Montreal Directory for 1900–1901 (Montreal: John Lovell & Son, 1901).

MacDonnell, Tom, *Daylight Upon Magic: The Royal Tour of Canada — 1939* (Toronto: Macmillan, 1989).

MacEwan, Grant, *Heavy Horses: Highlights of Their History* (Saskatoon: Western Producer Prairie Books, 1986).

McGuinness, Fred, *The Wheat City: A Pictorial History of Brandon* (Saskatoon, Sask.: Western Producer Prairie Books, 1988).

Mackinnon, Clarence, *The Life of Principal Oliver, Ph.D., D.D., LL.D., F.R.S.C.* (Toronto: Ryerson Press, 1936).

McLean, R.I., "A 'Most Effectual Remedy': Temperance and Prohibition in Alberta, 1875–1915," unpub. M.A. thesis, University of Calgary, 1969.

McNulty, William J., "Canada Reaping a Harvest from Liquor Business," *Current History*, June 1925, 374–7.

McWilliams, Carey, *A Mask for Privilege: Anti-Semitism in America* (Boston: Little, Brown and Company, 1948).

Mansbridge, Francis, ed., *Wild Gooseberries: The Selected Letters of Irving Layton* (Toronto: Macmillan, 1989).

Marlyn, John, *Under the Ribs of Death* (Toronto: McClelland and Stewart, 1971).

Massey, Vincent, *What's Past Is Prologue* (Toronto: Macmillan, 1963).

Mayer, Martin, "The Volatile Business," *Esquire*, August 1959, 102–18.

Merz, Charles, *The Dry Decade* (Garden City, N.Y.: Doubleday, 1931).

Messick, Hank, *Lansky* (New York: G.P. Putnam's Sons, 1971).

_____, *Secret File* (New York: G.P. Putnam's Sons, 1969).

_____, "The Schenley Chapter," *The Nation*, 5 April 1971.

_____, *The Silent Syndicate* (New York: Macmillan, 1967).

_____, with Joseph L. Nellis, *The Private Lives of Public Enemies* (New York: Peter H. Wyden, 1973).

Moore, William Howard, *The Kefauver Committee and the Politics of Crime 1950 – 1952* (Columbia, Missouri: University of Missouri Press, 1974).

Morgan, Henry James, ed., *The Canadian Men and Women of the Time: A Hand-Book of Canadian Biography of Living Characters* (2nd ed., Toronto: William Briggs, 1912).

Moritz, Albert and Theresa Moritz, *Leacock: A Biography* (Toronto: Stoddart Publishing, 1985).

Morton, Arthur S., *History of Prairie Settlement* (Toronto: Macmillan, 1938).

Morton, W.L., *Manitoba: A History* (Toronto: University of Toronto Press, 1961).

Moss, Michael S. and John R. Hume, *The Making of Scotch Whisky: A History of the Scotch Whisky Distilling Industry* (Edinburgh: James and James, 1981).

Mumford, Lewis, "The Sky Line: The Lesson of the Master," *The New Yorker*, September 1958, 128 – 36.

Muscatine, Doris, Maynard Amerine and Bob Thompson, eds., *The University of California/ Southeby Book of California Wine* (Berkeley, Calif.: University of California Press, 1984).

"Name, Schenley; Age, Three," *Fortune*, May 1936.

Neatby, H. Blair, *William Lyon Mackenzie King*, Vol. 2, *1924 – 1932* (Toronto: University of Toronto Press, 1963).

_____, *William Lyon Mackenzie King*, Vol. 3, *1932 – 1939* (Toronto: University of Toronto Press, 1976).

Newman, Peter C., *Bronfman Dynasty: The Rothschilds of the New World* (Toronto: McClelland and Stewart, 1978).

"Of Men, Money, and Marriage," *Fortune*, April 1963, 131 – 2.

Official Opening. Samuel Bronfman House. Commemorating Fifty Years of Service by the Canadian Jewish Congress. Montreal, May 24, 1970 [Montreal: Canadian Jewish Congress, 1970].

Oliver, Edmund H., *The Liquor Traffic in the Prairie Provinces* (Saskatoon: Board of Home Missions and Social Service, Presbyterian Church in Canada, 1923).

Oliver, Peter, G., *Howard Ferguson: Ontario Tory* (Toronto: University of Toronto Press, 1977).

_____, *Public and Private Persons: The Ontario Political Culture 1914–1934* (Toronto: Clarke, Irwin, 1975).

On the Road to Jewish Unity: The Participation of Organizations and Communities in the 25th Zionist Congress (Jerusalem: World Zionist Organization, 1962).

Palmer, Howard, *Patterns of Prejudice: A History of Nativism in Alberta* (Toronto: McClelland and Stewart, 1982).

Paris, Erna, *Jews: An Account of Their Experience in Canada* (Toronto: Macmillan, 1980).

Patton, Janice, *The Sinking of the* I'm Alone (Toronto: McClelland and Stewart, 1973).

Pearson, Lester B., *Mike: The Memoirs of the Right Honourable Lester B. Pearson*, Vol. I, *1897–1948* (Toronto: University of Toronto Press, 1972).

Peres, Shimon, *David's Sling* (New York: Random House, 1970).

Pickersgill, J.W., *The Mackenzie King Record*, Vol. 1, *1939–1944* (Toronto: University of Toronto Press, 1960).

Pinno, Erhard, "Temperance and Prohibition in Saskatchewan," unpub. M.A. thesis, University of Saskatchewan, Regina, 1971.

Popham, Robert E. and Wolfgang Schmidt, *Statistics of Alcohol Use and Alcoholism in Canada 1871–1956* (Toronto: University of Toronto Press, 1958).

Prang, Margaret, *N.W. Rowell: Ontario Nationalist* (Toronto: University of Toronto Press, 1975).

Rannie, William F., *Canadian Whisky: The Product and the Industry* (Lincoln, Ontario: W.F. Rannie, 1976).

Rasporich, Anthony W., "Early Twentieth-Century Jewish Farm Settlements in Saskatchewan: A Utopian Perspective," *Saskatchewan History*, XLII (1989), 28–40.

Richler, Mordecai, *Solomon Gursky Was Here* (Markham, Ont.: Viking, 1989).

Robertson, Terence, "Bronfman: The Life and Times of Samuel Bronfman, Esq," unpub. manuscript, [1969].

Rogger, Hans, *Jewish Policies and Right-Wing Politics in Imperial Russia* (London: Macmillan, 1986).

_____, "Russian Ministers and the Jewish Question 1881–1917," *California Slavic Studies*, VIII (1975), 15–76.

_____, "Tsarist Policy on Jewish Emigration," *Soviet Jewish Affairs*, 3 (1973), 26–35.

Rome, David, *Clouds in the Thirties: On Anti-Semitism in Canada 1929-1939* (13 vols., Montreal: National Archives, Canadian Jewish Congress, 1977-81).

_____, *Jews in Canadian Literature: A Bibliography* (Montreal: Canadian Jewish Congress, 1962).

_____, ed., *Canadian Jews in World War II* (2 vols., Montreal: Canadian Jewish Congress, 1947).

Rooke, P.T. and R.L. Schnell, *No Bleeding Heart: Charlotte Whitton, A Feminist on the Right* (Vancouver: University of British Columbia Press, 1987).

Rorabaugh, W.J., *The Alcoholic Republic: An American Tradition* (New York: Oxford University Press, 1979).

Rosenberg, Louis, *Canada's Jews: A Social and Economic Study of the Jews in Canada* (Montreal: Bureau of Social and Economic Research, Canadian Jewish Congress, 1939).

_____, "The Jewish Population of Canada: A Statistical Summary from 1850 to 1943," *American Jewish Year Book*, 48 (1946-47), 19-50.

_____, "Wapella, the Oldest Existing Jewish Farm Colony in Canada," *Jewish Post*, 14 September 1928.

_____, "Changes in the Geographical Distribution of the Jewish Population of Metropolitan Montreal in the Decennial Periods from 1901 to 1961 & the Estimated Possible Changes during the Period from 1961 to 1971: A Preliminary Study, Bureau of Social and Economic Research, Canadian Jewish Congress." *Research Papers*, Series A., No. 7, 1 December 1966.

Rosenbloom, Morris V., *The Liquor Industry: A Survey of Its History, Manufacture, Problems of Control and Importance* (Braddock, Pennsylvania: Ruffsdale, 1937).

Rudin, Ronald, *The Forgotten Quebecers: A History of English-Speaking Quebec 1759-1980* (Québec: Institut québécois de recherche sur la culture, 1985).

Sack, Benjamin G., *History of the Jews in Canada: From the Earliest Beginnings to the Present Day* (2 vols., Montreal: Canadian Jewish Congress, 1945).

Salsberg, J.G., "How Sam Bronfman Brought Hayes into Congress," *Canadian Jewish News*, 7 February 1980.

Samuel, Maurice, *Jews on Approval* (New York: Liveright, 1932).

Sanders, Ronald, *Shores of Refuge: A Hundred Years of Jewish Emigration* (New York: Henry Holt & Co., 1988).

Sarna, Jonathan, "Jewish Immigration to North America: The Canadian Experience," *Jewish Journal of Sociology*, 18 (1976), 31–41.

Schreter, Sheldon M., "French-Canadian Anti-Semitism," *Strobe*, 3 (1969), 73–110.

"Seagram in the Chips," *Fortune*, September 1948.

"Seagrams' Late Awakening," *Forbes*, 1 February 1973, 24–9.

Siekman, Philip, "The Bronfmans: An Instinct for Dynasty," *Fortune*, November 1966; December 1966.

Sigler, Betty, "Montreal: The Bonds of Community," *Commentary*, April 1950, 345–53.

Sinclair, Andrew, *Prohibition: The Era of Excess* (London: Faber and Faber, 1962).

Slater, Ellis D., *The Ike I Knew* (n.p.: Ellis D. Slater Trust, 1980).

Slater, Leonard, *The Pledge* (New York: Simon and Schuster, 1970).

Smith, David E., *Prairie Liberalism: The Liberal Party in Saskatchewan 1905–1971* (Toronto: University of Toronto Press, 1975).

Smith, W.H., *The Liquor Traffic in British Columbia* (Vancouver: Board of Home Missions and Social Service, 1922).

Spaeth, David, *Mies van der Rohe* (New York: Rizzoli, 1985).

Spence, F.S., *The Facts of the Case: A Summary of the Most Important Evidence and Argument Presented in the Report of the Royal Commission on the Liquor Traffic* (Toronto: Newton & Treloar, 1896).

Stanley, Carleton, "The Canadian Liquor System: II – Success of System Due to Commonsense View of Drinking," *Current History*, XXXI (October 1929), 74–7.

Steinberg, M.W. and Usher Caplan, eds., *Beyond Sambation: Selected Essays and Editorials 1928–1955* (Toronto: University of Toronto Press, 1982).

Stern, Harry Joshua, *A Rabbi's Journey* (New York: Bloch, 1981).

Strasser, Susan, *Satisfaction Guaranteed: The Making of the American Mass Market* (New York: Pantheon, 1989).

Stuart, Mark A., *Gangster #2: Longy Zwillman, the Man Who Invented Organized Crime* (Secaucus, N.J.: Lyle Stuart, 1985).

Tedlow, Richard S., *New and Improved: The Story of Mass Marketing in America* (New York: Basic Books, 1990).

"The Seagram Saga: I – The Man with the Golden Shovel," *BEV/ Executive*, 1 February 1966, 9–12.

"The Seagram Saga: II — Autonomy Comes Full Circle," *BEV/Executive*, 15 February 1966, 12–15, 23.

"The Seagram Saga: III — The Noble Experiment that Worked," *BEV/Executive*, 1 March 1966, 9–12.

"The Seagram Saga: IV — Another Rose, A Bottle and a Fast Dark Horse," *BEV/Executive*, 15 March 1966, 12–16.

"The Seagram Saga: V — The Straight Whiskey Dilemma," *BEV/Executive*, 1 April 1966, 9–11.

"The Seagram Saga: VI — Won't You Step into the Friendship Room," *BEV/Executive*, 15 April 1966, 9–11.

Thompson, John H., *The Harvests of War: The Prairie West, 1914–1918* (Toronto: McClelland and Stewart, 1978).

Thompson, John H., with Allen Seager, *Canada 1922–1939: Decades of Discord* (Toronto: McClelland and Stewart, 1985).

Thomson, Dale C., *Louis St. Laurent: Canadian* (Toronto: Macmillan, 1967).

Trachtenberg, Henry Manuel, " 'The Old Clo' Move': Anti-Semitism, Politics and the Jews of Winnipeg," unpub. Ph.D. thesis, York University, 1984.

Troper, Harold and Morton Weinfeld, *Old Wounds: Jews, Ukrainians and the Hunt for Nazi War Criminals in Canada* (Markham, Ont.: Penguin Books, 1988).

Trotter, Beecham, *A Horseman and the West* (Toronto: Macmillan, 1925).

Trueman, Albert W., *A Second View of Things: A Memoir* (Toronto: McClelland and Stewart, 1982).

Tulchinsky, Gerald, "Contours of Canadian Jewish History," *Journal of Canadian Studies*, 17 (1982–83), 46–56.

_____, "Immigrants and Charity in the Montreal Jewish Community before 1890," *Histoire Sociale — Social History*, XVI (1983), 359–80.

_____, "The Third Solitude: A.M. Klein's Jewish Montreal, 1910–1950," *Journal of Canadian Studies*, 19 (1984), 96–112.

United States Congress. Hearings before the Temporary National Economic Committee Pursuant to Res. 113 (75th Congress). Part 6, Liquor Industry (1939).

United States Congress. House. Committee on the Judiciary. Report to the Committee on the Judiciary by the Subcommittee to Investigate the Department of Justice Pursuant to H. Res. 50 (83rd Congress, 1st Session). No. 1079 (1953).

United States Congress. Senate. Special Committee to Investigate Organized Crime in Interstate Commerce Pursuant to S. Res. 202 (81st Congress) (1951).

Urussov, Prince Serge Dmitrivevich, *Memoirs of a Russian Governor*, trans, and ed. Herman Rosenthal (London: Harper and Brothers, 1908).

Vigod, Bernard L., *Quebec Before Duplessis: The Political Career of Louis-Alexandre Taschereau* (Kingston and Montreal: McGill-Queen's University Press, 1986).

Wachtel, William Wendell, *The Anatomy of a Hidden Persuader* (New York: Vantage Press, 1975).

Waddington, Miriam, *Apartment Seven: Essays Selected and New* (Toronto: Oxford University Press, 1989).

Walker, D.A., "Rum Running and Vessel Design," in James H. Morrison and James Moreira, eds., *Tempered by Rum: Rum in the History of the Maritime Provinces* (Portes Lake, Nova Scotia: Pottersfield Press, 1988), 143–51.

Waller, Harold M., *The Governance of the Jewish Community of Montreal*, Centre for Jewish Community Studies, Study Report No. 5, 1974.

Ward, Norman, "James Gardiner and Federal Appointments in the West," in R.C. Brown et al, eds., *Twentieth Century Canada: A Reader* (Toronto: McGraw-Hill Ryerson, 1986), 97–116.

Ward, Norman, and David Smith, *Jimmy Gardiner: Relentless Liberal* (Toronto: University of Toronto Press, 1990).

Watkins, Ernest, *R.B. Bennett: A Biography* (Toronto: Kingswood House, 1963).

Weinfeld, Morton, "A Note Comparing Canadian and American Jewry," *Journal of Ethnic Studies*, 5 (1971), 95–103.

Weir, R.B., "Alcohol Controls and Scotch Whisky Exports (1870–1939)," *British Journal of Addiction* (1988), 83, 1289–97.

_____, "Canada — Scotch Type Whiskey," unpub. manuscript, 1989.

_____, "Distilling and Agriculture 1870–1939," *Agricultural History Review*, 32 (1984), 49–62.

_____, "Obsessed with Moderation: The Drink Trades and the Drink Question (1870–1930)," *British Journal of Addiction*, 79 (1984), 93–107.

_____, "Rationalization and Diversification in the Scotch Whisky Industry, 1990–1939: Another Look at 'Old' and 'New' Industries," *Economic History Review*, 2nd ser., XLII (1989), 375–95.

Westley, Margaret W., *Rememberance of Grandeur: The Anglo-Protestant Elite of Montreal 1900–1950* (Montreal: Editors Libre Expression, 1990).

"Whiskey," *Fortune*, November 1933.

Whitaker, Reginald, *The Government Party: Organizing and Financing the Liberal Party of Canada 1930–1958* (Toronto: University of Toronto Press, 1977).

White, Theodore H., *The View from the Fortieth Floor* (New York: William Sloan Associates, 1960).

Williams, David Ricardo, *Duff: A Life in the Law* (Vancouver: University of British Columbia Press, 1984).

Willkie, Frederick and Harrison C. Blankmeyer, *An Outline for Industry* (Springfield, Illinois: Charles C. Thomas, 1944).

Wilson, Ross, *Scotch: Its History and Romance* (Newton Abbot, England: David & Charles, 1973).

_____, *Scotch: The Formative Years* (London: Constable, 1970).

Woodsworth, J.S., *My Neighbour: A Study of Social Conditions. A Plea for Social Service* (Toronto: University of Toronto Press, 1972).

Zolf, Larry, *Scorpions for Sale* (Toronto: Stoddart, 1989).

Index